McLAREN - THE CARS 1964-2008

THIS BOOK IS NUMBER

80/1000

OF THE BOXED LIMITED EDITION
SIGNED AND NUMBERED BY THE AUTHOR WILLIAM TAYLOR

William Taylor

MAY 2008
COTERIE PRESS · LONDON · ENGLAND

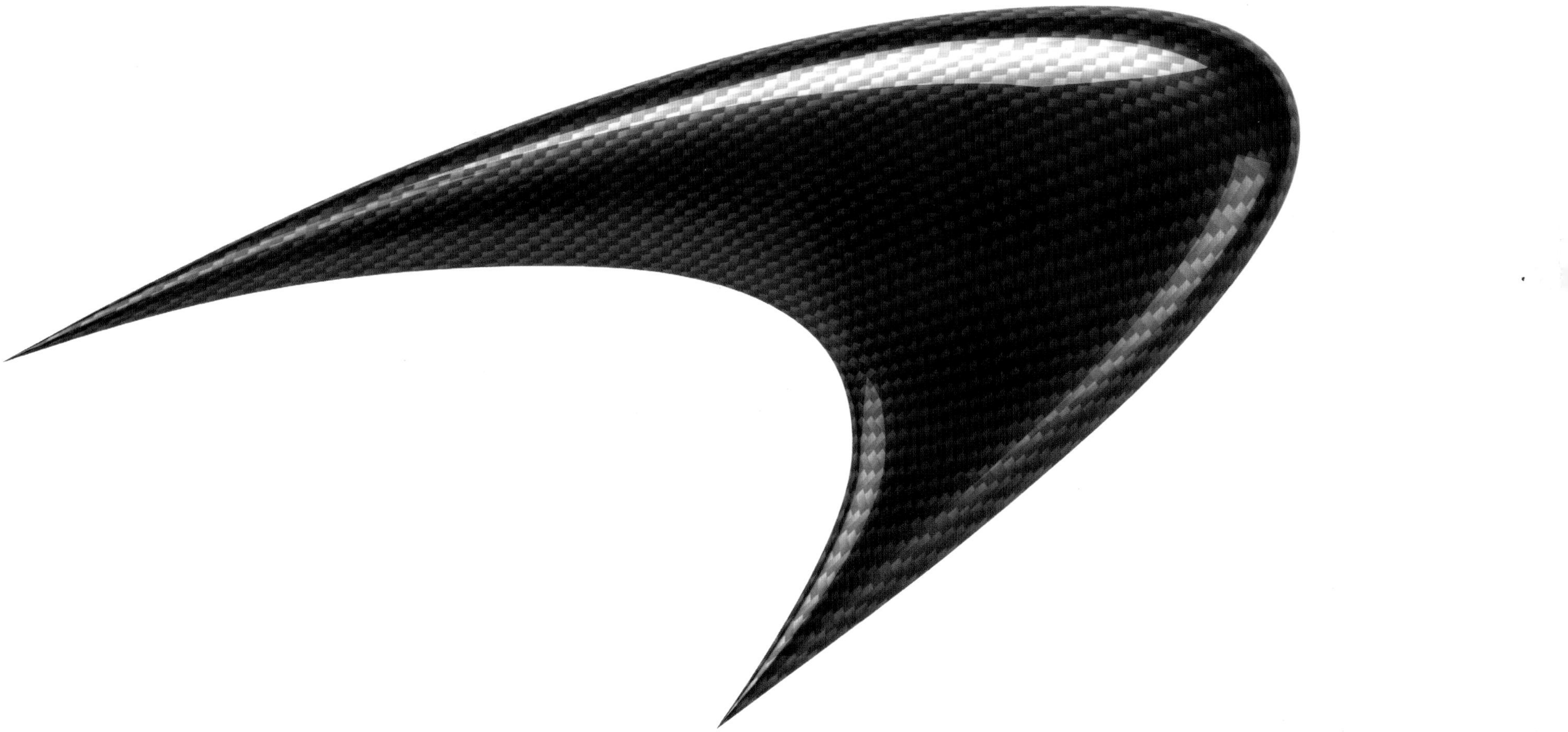

PUBLISHERS INFORMATION
McLAREN – THE CARS 1964-2008

A COTERIE PRESS BOOK

First British Edition May 2008
Published in the UK by Coterie Press Limited,
22-36 Hastings Street, Luton, Bedfordshire LU1 5BE
Tel: 001 303 933 2526 (Head office USA)
Fax: 001 303 904 9294 (Head office USA)
coterieltd@aol.com
www.coteriepress.com

Produced under licence from
McLaren Group Limited,
McLaren Technology Centre,
Chertsey Road,
Woking,
Surrey GU21 4YH
www.mclaren.com

ISBN: 978 1 902351 32 2 Standard Edition
ISBN: 978 1 902351 33 9 Limited Edition
ISBN: 978 1 902351 34 6 Special Edition
ISBN: 978 1 902351 35 3 Publishers Edition

A copy of this title is available from the British Library

AUTHOR: William Taylor
EDITOR: David Tremayne
ADDITIONAL TEXT: David Long
CREATIVE DIRECTOR: William Taylor
TECHNICAL EDITOR: Ian Gosling
PUBLISHING CONSULTANT: James Bennett
PRODUCTION MANAGEMENT: Jo Taylor
DESIGN & ARTWORK: Scott Wilson, McLaren Marketing, Andy Howell
IMAGE MANIPULATION: Dan Colberg, Susan Roushey
PRINTED & BOUND BY: Colorprint, Hong Kong
ORIGINATION BY: Coterie Press

The author & publisher extend their special thanks to: Ron Dennis, Martin Whitmarsh, Ian Gosling, Harry Mathews, Jan McLaren, David McLaughlin, Neil Oatley, Diana Kay, John Allert, Harold Dermott, Clare Robertson, Matt Bishop, Tom Wheatcroft.

We would also like to thank Emerson Fittipaldi, Niki Lauda, Alain Prost, Mika Häkkinen and Lewis Hamilton for taking time out of their busy schedules to offer their memories and thoughts on McLaren. In addition, thanks must of course go to the owners of all the cars listed on page 303. Without their cars a book such as this would not have been possible.

Thanks also to everyone who helped on this immense project:
Simon Diffey, John Storr at The Bruce McLaren Trust, Greg Mathews at The Mathews Collection, Stuart Leuthner, John Bolding, John Arnold, Ron Smith, Roy Lane, Zoe Schafer at LAT, Jon Day at MPL, Rick Hall at Hall & Hall, Kerry Adams & Jim Chisman at AM Engineering, David Davidson at IMS, The Design Museum, Bruce Weiner, Mark Childs, Rick Parent at Prisma Cars, Mike Longacre at bmc Racing, Jimmy Aretakis, Peter Reeve at Conrod Cars, Tony Nicholson & John Steenson at Robin Automotive, Patrick Hogan, Simon Hadfield, Gerry Kroninger, Pam Shatraw, Garry Rankin & Dave Williams at The Donington Collection, Thor Thorson & Tom Nuxoll at VRM, Bill Roushey, Tony Harrison, Steve Courts, Jeremy Morrison, Christopher Tate at The Masters.

BIBLIOGRAPHY:

Racing Line, Motor Sport, Autosport, Motoring News, Autocourse (Hazleton Publishing/CMG Publishing), Can-Am (Motorbooks), Driving Ambition (Virgin), McLaren Sports Racing Cars (Motorbooks), McLaren! (Bond Parkhurst), Marlboro McLaren (Aston), McLaren Honda Turbo (Haynes), McLaren The Epic Years (Haynes), McLaren, The Grand Prix, Can-Am & Indy Cars (Hazleton), Can-Am Racing Cars 1966-1974 (Brooklands Books), Indianapolis 500 Chronicle (Publications International Ltd), Grand Prix Guide (Charles Stewart & Company (Kirkaldy) Ltd), Le Mans 24 Hours Yearbook (IHM Publishing), the archives of the McLaren Heritage and Media Departments, Coterie Press, Harry Mathews, Jim Bennett, Jeff Allington, John Arnold.

CONTENTS
McLAREN – THE CARS 1964-2008

FOREWORD

RON DENNIS 06

INTRODUCTION

WILLIAM TAYLOR 08

THE 1960s

INTRODUCED BY EMERSON FITTIPALDI 12

McLaren M1A 14
McLaren-Elva M1A 16
McLaren M2A 18
McLaren M1B 20
McLaren-Elva M1B 22
McLaren M2B 24
McLaren M3A 26
McLaren-Elva M1C 28
McLaren M4A 30
McLaren-Trojan M4A/B 30
McLaren M4B 34
McLaren M5A 36
McLaren M6A 40
McLaren-Trojan M6B 44
McLaren M7A 48
McLaren M7B 50
McLaren M8A 52
McLaren M6GT 54
McLaren M7C 56
McLaren M7D 58
McLaren M8B 60
McLaren M9A 64
McLaren-Trojan M10A 66
McLaren-Trojan M10B 66
McLaren-Trojan M12 70

THE 1970s

INTRODUCED BY NIKI LAUDA 72

McLaren-Trojan M8C 74
McLaren M8D 76
McLaren M14A 80
McLaren M14D 82
McLaren M15 84
McLaren-Trojan M8E 86
McLaren M8F 88
McLaren-Trojan M8F/P 88
McLaren M16 92
McLaren M16B 94
McLaren-Trojan M18 96
McLaren M19A 98
McLaren M19C 100
McLaren M20 102
McLaren M21 106
McLaren-Trojan M22 110
McLaren M16C 112
McLaren M16D 112
McLaren M16E 112
McLaren M23 (1973) 116
McLaren M23 (1974) 118
McLaren M25 122
McLaren M23 (1975) 124
McLaren M23 (1976) 126
McLaren M23 (1977) 126
McLaren M26 130
McLaren M24 134
McLaren M24B 134
McLaren M28 136
McLaren M29 138
McLaren M29C 138

THE 1980s

INTRODUCED BY ALAIN PROST 140

McLaren M30 142
McLaren MP4/1 144
McLaren MP4/1B 148
McLaren MP4/1C 150
McLaren MP4/1D 150
McLaren MP4/1E 150
McLaren MP4/2 152
McLaren MP4/2B 156
McLaren MP4/2C 160
McLaren MP4/3 164
McLaren MP4/3B 166
McLaren MP4/4 168
McLaren MP4/4B 172
McLaren MP4/5 174

CHAPTER 01

CHAPTER 02

CHAPTER 03

THE 1990s

INTRODUCED BY MIKA HÄKKINEN 178

McLaren MP4/5B 180
McLaren MP4/5C 184
McLaren MP4/6 186
McLaren MP4/7 190
McLaren MP4/8 194
McLaren MP4/8B 198
McLaren F1 200
McLaren MP4/9 204
McLaren F1 GTR (1995) 206
McLaren MP4/10 208
McLaren F1 LM 212
McLaren MP4/11A 214
McLaren MP4/11C 216
McLaren F1 GTR (1996) 218
McLaren MP4-12 220
McLaren F1 GT 222
McLaren F1 GTR (1997) 224
McLaren MP4-98T 228
McLaren MP4-13 232
McLaren MP4-14 236

CHAPTER 04

THE 2000s

INTRODUCED BY LEWIS HAMILTON 238

McLaren MP4-15 240
McLaren MP4-16 242
McLaren MP4-17A 246
McLaren MP4-T5 248
McLaren MP4-18A 250
McLaren MP4-17D 252
Mercedes-Benz SLR McLaren 256
McLaren MP4-19A 260
McLaren MP4-19B 262
McLaren MP4-20A 264
McLaren MP4-21A 266
Mercedes-Benz SLR McLaren 722 270
McLaren MP4-22 272
Mercedes-Benz SLR McLaren Roadster 276
McLaren MP4-23 280

CHAPTER 05

POSTSCRIPT

MARTIN WHITMARSH 282

APPENDICES

THE CARS - SPECIFICATIONS 284
GRAND PRIX SEASON RESULTS 286
GRAND PRIX WINS BY DRIVER 286
GRAND PRIX WINS 288
FORMULA 1 RESULTS 290
INDIANAPOLIS RESULTS 298
LE MANS RESULTS 299
CAN-AM RESULTS 300
CAN-AM WINS BY DRIVER 301
CAN-AM CHAMPIONSHIPS 302
CARS PHOTOGRAPHED CREDITS 303

FOREWORD
RON DENNIS CBE

Although the subject of this book – the cars – is the product that we are best known for here at McLaren, it is only half the story. And the reason for that is that the other half of the story is the people who make the cars.

I am one of them, but only one of them. Indeed, I have often said that I am merely one of the chapters, not the book. Now, in writing only this foreword, but leaving others to write the book, I am proving exactly that.

I feel privileged to have worked alongside some truly brilliant people at McLaren these past 27 years, but it would be wrong to single out any of them. Currently, I have 1300 colleagues at McLaren, and each is as crucial as his or her colleague, however long or short his or her service with the company and however senior or junior his or her position within it.

From the outside, I am told that McLaren can appear austere, clinical, unfriendly. We who work here find that hard to believe, because from the inside McLaren people tend to form strong and resilient working relationships – kinships even – that weather storms incredibly impressively. So I can only surmise that we sometimes appear unfriendly or clinical or austere because in fact we are focused and efficient and confident. Because we are certainly all those things.

But, more than that, we are utterly passionate about what we do, totally committed to moving heaven and earth to do it better than our competitors, and immensely proud of not only our here-and-now but also our there-and-then. Our heritage, in other words. And although I have been at the helm of McLaren since 1980, the company was actually founded in 1963 by a 25-year-old New Zealander, Bruce McLaren, whose name it carries still.

Today, motorsport is a highly professional global business, and as such it is almost unrecognisable from the parochial sport practised largely by enthusiastic amateurs back then.

I say almost unrecognisable because, if you peel back the marketing razzmatazz that any global sport is necessarily sustained by in the 21st century, you still find brave drivers, driving fast cars, created by ingenious engineers.

By 1966 – incidentally the year in which I entered Formula One, as a 19-year-old mechanic working for the Cooper-Maserati team – McLaren had started its first Grand Prix, at Monaco. And just two years later, on June 9th, 1968, Bruce won the Belgian Grand Prix at Spa-Francorchamps. Second was Pedro Rodriguez in a BRM, third was Jacky Ickx in a Ferrari. *Plus ça change…*

Almost exactly two years after that, on June 2nd, 1970, disaster struck. Bruce had been testing the McLaren M8D Can-Am car at Goodwood, when its rear bodywork became detached at high speed, causing a fatal accident. He was just 32.

But the McLaren DNA had already taken root; and, under the stewardship of Teddy Mayer, who had taken command when Bruce died, over the next 10 years the team was impressively successful, winning Formula 1 World Championships in 1974 and 1976 courtesy of, respectively, Emerson Fittipaldi and James Hunt.

My chapter began in 1981, when I brokered the merger of my own Formula Two team, Project Four, with McLaren's Formula One team, to create McLaren International. I am glad to say that, in our case, thanks to the unstinting work of a large number of wonderfully talented people, the past quarter-century has proven that success really does breed success. At the time of writing – in the lead-up to the 2008 Formula 1 season – McLaren has recorded 156 Grand Prix wins, 11 Drivers' World Championships and eight Constructors' World Championships.

I have already mentioned Emerson and James, who tragically died of a heart attack at his Wimbledon home in 1993. Emerson, I am glad to say, is a hale and hearty 61 year-old, and I am delighted that he has contributed an introduction to the section of this book that deals with the 1970s. To date, four other men have won Drivers' World Championships for McLaren - Niki Lauda, Alain Prost, Ayrton Senna and Mika Häkkinen – and I would like to take this opportunity to thank Niki, Alain and Mika, too, for their contributions to this book.

Like James, Ayrton is no longer with us, of course. I have never spoken about what he meant to me, and now is not the time to do that. Suffice it to say that he was great friend and a great driver, and many motorsport fans around the world miss him still. When visitors walk through the reception area of our Lord Foster-designed headquarters in Woking, Surrey, they always appear to pay particular attention to the cars that Ayrton drove.

But, cliché though it may be, life must go on. I have written about McLaren's there-and-then as well as its here-and-now, but it is McLaren's future that is of paramount importance. Over the past 42 years, Bruce, Teddy and I have set firm foundations – foundations that others will take on into what I confidently predict will be a golden era of success for the team that we all gave so much to see succeed.

I have said it before and I will say it again: I am merely one of the chapters, not the book. So nothing would please me more than, at some point in the future, to be able to watch McLaren win Grands Prix, and go from strength to strength as a company, while I sit on a beach somewhere and reflect on a job well done by one and all.

Hopefully, this book will give you a flavour of how that job was, is, and always will be, done.

Ron Dennis CBE
Chairman and CEO, McLaren Group

vodafone
Mobil 1
BOSS
BRIDGESTONE
MUMM
G.H. MUMM

INTRODUCTION
WILLIAM TAYLOR

Bruce Leslie McLaren's earliest competitive driving experiences came at the wheel of a highly modified 1929 Austin Ulster, an open-topped version of Britain's cheap and ubiquitous Austin Seven. Spurred on by his father, Les, a skilled engineer and a keen motorsports enthusiast, Bruce's initiation into the relatively small community of New Zealand and Australian racing drivers took place at a hillclimb at Muriwai Beach in 1952. It was about 25 miles from the McLaren family home in Auckland, and happened to be part of their holiday home. He had just turned 15.

The Ulster had already been in the family for almost three years, having been acquired by Les, in many pieces, for $110. He planned to fix it up himself, and turn a quick profit. Bruce, however, though just 13 at the time, had other plans for the car and persuaded his father to let him keep it. Several years later, Bruce remembered his first sight of his father's new purchase thus: "*I eyed the dilapidated Ulster on the end of the rope with deep suspicion. Racing car indeed!*"

Soon he was embroiled in literally every stage of the car's painstaking restoration using secondhand Austin Seven parts. Though he could not have been aware of the importance of it at that time, the experience would be a crucial learning process for the future racecar designer and builder. And no sooner had he reassembled the car than Bruce set out to remodel the family garden into a miniature circuit. That was where he first learned to drive.

He passed his driving test shortly after his 15th birthday, albeit opting for a more conservative 1949 side-valve Morris Minor, then soon headed off in the now famous Seven for the gravel hill at Muriwai Beach. Les McLaren was hospitalised with a gallstone, but his son had his paternal warning still ringing in his ears: "*If you damage so much as a mudguard, the Ulster's gone for good.*" As a result, Bruce admitted many years later, "*I forgot to be nervous about my debut. I took things reasonably, with Pop's lecture in mind, as the tail of the little Ulster slid on the loose metal corners and reached the top in one piece. When all the runs were over, I learned with some amazement that I had set the fastest time in the 750cc class.*"

While he was learning how to compete at this level, the Ulster period was of crucial importance to Bruce when it came to gaining an understanding of the mechanical side of the sport. As a result, by the early 1950s he was already a highly capable and ingenious mechanic, something he ably demonstrated when the Ulster's cylinder head eventually cracked. Rescuing a suitable replacement from a humble 1936 Austin Ruby saloon, he filled the combustion chambers with bronze which he then expertly ground to the appropriate shape using a rotary file. Once the engine was reassembled the Ulster proved good for 87mph, a 20 per cent improvement on its official quoted maximum of 72mph.

Thereafter such detail improvements came one after another. Over a three-year period the somewhat skeletal but still highly effective little car gradually metamorphosed into a completely different machine from the one Les had handed over to his teenaged son. New, flatter rear springs dealt with the problem of oversteer, whilst the front set was turned upside down to set the car lower to the ground. 16in disc wheels were fitted up front, and with 17s at the rear in place of the original 19s. The short tail was extended, twin SU carburettors replaced the single standard Zenith, and were fitted to a bespoke manifold which Bruce designed and fabricated himself.

Throughout this period he and schoolfriend and fellow Austin pilot Phil Kerr – who had finished second to him at that hillclimb at Muriwai Beach and would go on to become joint Managing Director of Bruce's racing team in England – were fettling their cars in the McLaren family garage. This they did very much on their own terms, Les McLaren reasoning that his son would fare better and learn more if he was left to work out problems for himself. Shop foreman Harold Bardsley was generally on hand to offer advice if it was needed, but mostly the preferred route was to explain to the youngsters how a job was best done and then leave them to get on with it.

When Bruce left for England in 1958, and for many years afterwards, the tired and well-used Ulster languished in a small museum on New Zealand's South Island. In 1989, however, a deal was made with McLaren Group to buy the car for its collection and, with the help of a friend and close associate of Bruce's called Bruce Sutcliffe, and a lot of detective work, it was finally restored to its present condition. It now takes its rightful pride of place alongside its faster and more illustrious successors on the boulevard at the McLaren Technology Centre in Woking, UK.

Bruce spent his early teenage years building, modifying and racing the 1929 Austin Seven Ulster that his father had bought intending to restore. 'Pop' McLaren (standing) and Bruce proudly show off the contents of the rapidly expanding family trophy cabinet.

Working on the Austin's tiny 4-cylinder 750cc engine gave Bruce a wealth of engineering experience that would serve him well in the years to come.

The Muriwai Beach hillclimb was the start of a racing career that would take Bruce McLaren to a win in the Le Mans 24 Heures, four Grand Prix wins as well as both Can-Am and Tasman titles.

58

INTRODUCTION
WILLIAM TAYLOR
CONTINUED

Long before he moved to England, Bruce had replaced the Austin with his father's Healey 100-Four and worked hard on that throughout 1957. By then he had amassed some experience of single-seater racing courtesy of a supercharged 3-litre Maserati 8CLT on which he had been working on behalf of the owner. Frank Shuter planned to use this car for record-breaking attempts and was clearly delighted with the whole affair. Bruce was too, and soon after leapt at the opportunity to drive a 1750cc Formula 2 Cooper, which he used in his bid to secure the New Zealand International Grand Prix Association's prestigious 'Driver to Europe' scholarship.

From then on it would be in Coopers that the young Kiwi made his name. Guided by his fellow Antipodean Jack Brabham, who met the McLarens after staying with the family in 1954 during his first overseas trip to drive his famed RedeX Special in the New Zealand Grand Prix, Bruce made rapid progress and won the coveted scholarship for 1958.

In March that year Bruce's Cooper was loaded onto the Orantes for shipping to England. On the 15th he and mechanic Colin Beanland boarded a plane bound for the UK, where Bruce was scheduled to compete in his first European race, for Formula 2 cars, at Aintree near Liverpool on April 15th. He was, he admitted, *"20, and a young 20 at that."*

He finished only ninth in that race, but what really mattered was that he was in Europe and working on his own car. Later that season, in the German GP at the vaunted Nürburgring, he succeeded in making his mark even more emphatically by overhauling Phil Hill's Ferrari to win the F2 race-within-a-race whilst finishing fifth overall.

Father and son duo Charles and John Cooper assured him of a drive in their works team for 1959, and Bruce was now on his way. Success came quickly. Victory in the US GP at Sebring on December 12th made him, at 22, the youngest driver at the time ever to win a World Championship Grand Prix.

The following season began just as strongly, with victory for Cooper in Argentina, but then came a slump, and over the ensuing years of the 1.5-litre formula, he won only once more, at Monaco in 1962. It was not surprising that his mounting frustration at the lack of development at Cooper encouraged him to form his own team and race his own cars back home, where he took the Cooper as his starting point. Similarly it must by now have been obvious to many that, once Bruce McLaren Motor Racing Limited was up and running, that same Cooper base car would steadily metamorphose just the way the Austin Ulster had, until he created a machine that Bruce could call his own: the first pukka McLaren.

Inevitably his next step forward had its origins in another Cooper, Roger Penske's somewhat controversial Zerex Special which competed as a sportscar but was in essence a Cooper Grand Prix car with a 2.7-litre Climax engine.

Superseded by similar machines with larger American V8s, the Zerex had been forgotten until two of Bruce's trusted lieutenants – Tyler Alexander and Wally Wilmott – acquired it on his behalf from American magnate John Mecom's team in April 1964. They also acquired an aluminium 4-litre F85 Oldsmobile V8 with eight fairly crude stub exhausts, and this soon replaced the ageing Climax four. Bruce enjoyed success with his new car, but having conducted considerable testing for Ford on its GT Le Mans car he came to appreciate that the Zerex's primitive tubular chassis was flexing too much. It was replaced with a structure of his own design, and in June, on its debut at Mosport in Canada for the Player's 200, he took the flag first. Ironically, the Chaparral that he beat was driven by Penske. To rub it in, Bruce repeated the feat in the Guards Trophy at Brands Hatch two months later.

The Zerex Special was diplomatically referred to as a Cooper-Oldsmobile to avoid offending the Coopers, and was nicknamed the Jolly Green Giant after its emergency livery was forced upon the team because it was painted on a Sunday and that was the only tin of paint available in the workshop. Its performance was amazing for a two-year old car, especially one in the hands of a very young team, and it earned the outfit its first major wins. But at the new base in Feltham, into which another of Bruce's allies, Teddy Mayer, had moved the team in between the Players 200 and the Guards Trophy, the next chapter was already well underway.....

At Sebring in 1959, aged just 22 years and 104 days, Bruce McLaren took his first World Championship Grand Prix win. Driving a Cooper-Climax T51 he became the sport's youngest GP winner, a record not beaten until 2003.

In May 1966 Bruce competed in his first Grand Prix driving a car bearing his own name, the McLaren-Ford M2B. At the British Grand Prix that year the car finally started its first race using the Italian Serenissima V8 engine.

In 1968 the McLaren team moved to new premises in Colnbrook. Here Chief Designer Robin Herd (left) shows his latest designs to Bruce McLaren (centre) and Teddy Mayer.

To avoid offending the Cooper family, the heavily revised Zerex Special was officially referred to as a Cooper-Oldsmobile. Owing to the hasty paint job it received, it wasn't too long however before it was nicknamed 'Jolly Green Giant'.

CHAPTER
01

EMERSON FITTIPALDI

During the early days of my career in the late-1960s, if you had asked me to drive for McLaren, would I? Of course! It was one of the new teams in Formula 1 but it would have been my dream to race alongside drivers such as Bruce, Denny Hulme and Dan Gurney.

When I first saw the M23 when it appeared in 1973, it was obvious that there was an enormous leap in performance between it and the M19 which it replaced.

When I decided to leave Lotus at the end of 1973 I went to see Brabham, Tyrrell and McLaren. Immediately I liked Teddy Mayer's organisation, which was amongst the best in F1 with an almost American style of business. Marlboro said to me: "Choose whichever you want and we'll take our budget to them," so I tested the M23 at Paul Ricard late that year. It was incredible, very quick on the fast corners, which I liked.

It was more conventional than the Lotus 72, with which I had won my first Grand Prix in 1970 and the World Championship in 1972, without the difficult torsion bar suspension, and straight away I felt I had made a good decision. In Argentina in 1974, my first race, I felt I was in a position to take the lead but then accidentally activated the engine cut-out, so I finished only eighth as Denny won. I went on to win the next race, at home in Brazil, though. That was a wonderful feeling!

That year Teddy and the team were very focused, very committed to winning, and I think the New Zealand mechanics - from Bruce's day - were harder working than their counterparts in some of the other teams. McLaren was very fast to react to any problems, so for example constant improvements were made to the suspension and even a completely new geometry was devised which drastically improved the car throughout the season.

Even so, winning the World Championship with McLaren M23 was much harder than winning my first one in 1972. Clay Regazzoni and I were on equal points, and side by side on the grid, for the last race, in the USA. I think it was the only race where I didn't sleep well the night before. Clay too, probably. With so many good drivers around we needed a real team effort, but I always felt that McLaren was better prepared, and this was the day it really showed.

Emerson Fittipaldi
Drivers' World Champion 1974
McLaren M23

1964 GROUP 7
McLAREN M1A

Whilst Bruce the racing driver was busy on the track winning trophies, Bruce the astute businessman and hard-working executive was also guiding his small but dedicated crew at Feltham as they laboured flat-out on what was to be the first true McLaren racing car. Publicity photographs taken at the time show that the 4,000sq ft workshop boasted a variety of different machines, from a scale model of the new M1A and its half-finished spaceframe chassis, to the Cooper-Oldsmobile and a Tasman Cooper.

Built around a simple spaceframe of Bruce's own design, the new M1A employed round and square-section tubing with light magnesium alloy sheeting bonded and riveted in place to form a strong, stressed undertray. Power for the new, much stiffer car came from what was called the 'Strong Mother', the Traco-built Oldsmobile V8 from its predecessor, mated to a four-speed Hewland HD4 gearbox. Cooper wheels, uprights and steering arms were used. In testing at Goodwood in the summer of 1964, the finished design immediately knocked three whole seconds off the Zerex's best-ever lap time.

The new car was to make its debut that September at Mosport in Canada, in the forerunner to the celebrated Can-Am (Canadian-American Challenge Cup) series. Rather than green it was now painted in New Zealand's official racing colours of black with a silver stripe. The knee-high slingshot quickly proved to be the fastest car on the circuit by far and Bruce soon took the lead from Jim Hall's Chaparral 2. Unfortunately, failure of the throttle linkage sent him into the pits. After a long stop - and despite equalling the lap record four times and breaking it seven more - Bruce could only finish in third place, three laps behind.

At Riverside for the LA Times Grand Prix he qualified second behind Dan Gurney's Lotus 19, but by lap three had built a nine-second lead before a water hose blew off and forced him into the pits, where he lost four laps. He rejoined the race and climbed back into third place only for the same thing to happen again, this time prompting retirement.

Having qualified in fourth place, water-hose history repeated itself yet again at Laguna Seca. But in Nassau for the Speed Weeks six weeks later - by which time the car had been repainted a shocking orangey-red in what was to be the first step towards the team's eventual trademark colour - Bruce finished second behind Roger Penske's Chaparral in the Nassau Trophy race. He could only note (as Jack Brabham had previously had cause to) that winning could be a lot more difficult when racing on one's own account than on someone else's.

The immediate success of the M1A, not to mention its singular design and appearance, quickly created high demand for customer replicas. This was an attractive opportunity to Bruce that was simply too good to miss, but the hard fact was that the payroll at the Feltham factory still amounted to only seven people, just about sufficient to keep the team's own race cars running but certainly not enough for a limited run of production or to service privateers' cars. A partial answer to these financial and logistical difficulties arrived in the person of Frank Nichols of Elva Cars Ltd., a small specialist car maker based in Rye, Sussex. The name, derived from the French '*elle va*' - she goes - had first been applied to a cycle-winged sportscar in the late 1950s. Now, having the workforce, skills and equipment necessary to do the job, Nichols suggested to Bruce that their two companies co-operate to build customer cars with the McLaren team receiving a royalty on each car sold.

It made plenty of sense to the small, impecunious team and in November 1964 a deal was struck between McLaren and Peter Agg of the bubble-car maker Trojan, Elva's parent company. With the ink barely dry, the M1A went into production with the replica racing cars being branded officially as the McLaren-Elva Mark I. Work began immediately with the intention of having the first customer car ready to display at the 1965 London Racing Car Show in January. Elva met the exceptionally tight deadline, despite several not inconsiderable build problems.

The most obvious flaw was that the staff there had nothing to work from. No design drawings existed, the M1A having quite literally grown out of the Cooper-Oldsmobile project, driven to completion by some truly inspired guesswork as to how the end might be achieved. At the same time the only M1A which did exist was elsewhere - busy racing in America - leaving very little to go on. The main stumbling block was a pretty fundamental one: the bodyshell. The original intention was that the coachwork for the new cars would be formed by moulding glass-fibre copies from the hand-formed and beaten alloy body of the team car. Obviously this was not going to be possible now so, lacking any solid reference material, stylist Tony Hilder and the crew at Elva were instead forced to build the mould from the few photographs they had available.

After a brief test at Goodwood in early September 1964 the M1A (right) was painted black & silver. Here it sits outside the 3000-square foot McLaren factory in Belvedere Works, Feltham, waiting to be shipped to its first event at Mosport Park, Canada. Bruce led the first 55 laps (above) before pitting with a throttle problem.

The cockpit of the M1A could be described as 'spartan' with just a rev-counter, oil pressure and water temperature gauges alongside the manufacturer's chassis plate. The spare wheel and tyre still required by the regulations was carried under the large windscreen, above the driver's legs.

In early 1964, noted motorsport artist Michael Turner designed a badge for the newly formed 'Bruce McLaren Motor Racing Team'. This had the outline of the famous New Zealand kiwi bird as a central feature, on a chequered flag background with a racing car silhouette on top of the shield - *"A kiwi being run over by a Cooper!"* - as it was famously described.

M1A GROUP 7
SPECIFICATION

MODEL	McLaren M1A
TYPE/FORMULA	Group 7 Sportscar
YEAR OF PRODUCTION	1964/1965
DESIGNER	Bruce McLaren
EXAMPLES BUILT	2
ENGINE	Oldsmobile V8
CUBIC CAPACITY	3900cc
CARBURATION	Four twin-choke downdraught
POWER OUTPUT	340bhp

TRANSMISSION	Hewland LG400 4-speed or ZF
CHASSIS	Large diameter round & square tubular frame
BODY	Four section polyester resin moulded body
FRONT SUSPENSION	Single top link & radius arm, lower wishbone,
	outboard coil spring/damper, anti-roll bar
REAR SUSPENSION	Twin radius arms with single top link, reversed
	lower wishbone, anti-roll bar & coil spring/damper
BRAKES F/R	Dual circuit Girling discs
WHEELS DIAMETER x WIDTH F/R	15x8/15x10in

TYRES F/R	Firestone
LENGTH	164in - 4166mm
WIDTH	64in - 1625mm
HEIGHT OF BODYWORK	30in - 762mm
WHEELBASE	91in - 2311mm
TRACK F/R	51/51in - 1295/1295mm
WEIGHT	1828lb - 829kg
PRINCIPAL DRIVERS	McLaren
IDENTIFYING COLOURS	Black & Silver, Red

1964 GROUP 7 McLAREN-ELVA M1A [MkI]

CONTINUED

Not surprisingly the results were not all they might have been and, when he returned from the US, Bruce did not like what he saw. He quickly ordered numerous detail changes to be made, which can be seen in later iterations of the M1A. The cars themselves, however, achieved some success and certainly left their mark. After duly going on display at the Racing Car Show, the first car to be completed (of a production run of 24) was eventually sold to Surrey Jaguar dealer John Coombs. Equipped with a 4.5-litre Oldsmobile V8 it was readied for Graham Hill to drive at Silverstone in the forthcoming new season.

Not for the last time perseverance was to pay dividends for McLaren. While Bruce continued to drive for Cooper in Formula 1 – specifically while he was crossing the line in fifth place at Monaco in 1965 – fellow New Zealander Chris Amon took the new M1A sportscar to its first victory, at St Jovite in Quebec. Thereafter, with Bruce temporarily out of action with a mildly burned neck, it was Amon again who drove the M1A in the Martini International Trophy at Silverstone. Once he again he was victorious, despite having to start from the back.

Silverstone was also to be the venue for what was perhaps the M1A's most memorable outing. This time it was to be in the hands of its creator who went head-to-head with John Surtees' Lola T70, the two gladiators providing race-goers with a truly epic battle in which Bruce and the M1A emerged the victors. It was a narrow triumph, however, and before long the team was forced to accept that the ageing Oldsmobile V8 could not hold its own for ever against the Lola's larger-capacity Chevrolet V8. There was an interesting footnote that typified the level of attention to detail and professionalism which continues to characterise the team today: for the first time the M1A bore on its elegant nose a new Bruce McLaren Motor Racing Team badge designed by eminent motorsport artist Michael Turner.

McLaren's superb preparation and craftsmanship was now much in evidence, if not in the hastily hand-painted number '2' which adorned the car at Riverside, then certainly in the gleaming Hewland gearbox assembly and the handsome exhaust system which was a far cry from the crude stub exhausts of the Zerex. Rival and close friend Jim Hall was far from being the only one to admire Bruce's team, which he quickly identified as "*highly professional, and extremely competitive.*"

Bruce's ongoing quest for new technical solutions led to the M1A being fitted with a dual-speed Ferguson automatic transmission. In April 1965 at Oulton Park he led Jim Clark (Lotus 30) and Frank Gardner (Willment Cobra Coupe) in the first heat until a transmission leak forced him out of the running. In the second heat the engine blew, leaving the team to reflect that the cost of developing the auto 'box was too high in terms of both time and money. The project was shelved.

Unfortunately for the Coombs car its debut, planned for March 1965, saw the first race of the sportscar season take place in a torrential downpour. The conditions were so bad that after just 18 laps of the scheduled 25 proceedings were halted, which was as well for Hill; he had thus far been unable to coax the two cylinder banks of his exceptionally wet V8 to fire up at the same time. He tried again with the car in October, this time in the predictably drier environment of the LA Times Grand Prix at Riverside, USA, but this time a wheel stud broke whilst he was lying third and sent the car into a wall.

Nevertheless this same car, chassis 20-01, pictured here, proved to be an important marker in the company's illustrious history, not just as McLaren's first production car but also as the first, indeed the only McLaren, ever to have been driven by 'The King' himself. Selling the car to noted Californian racer Jerry Entin after the LA race, Coombs returned to Surrey but was soon to see it again, this time on the big screen after Hill's old car had landed a part in the movie 'Spinout' starring Elvis Presley.

At the same time several other customer cars were seeing action, sometimes with Bruce himself at the wheel. After some "*Five thousand miles of race testing,*" he reported himself delighted with the quality of the customer cars. As for M1A 20-01, it now forms part of The Mathews Collection in Colorado. Fitted with a 400bhp, 5.6-litre Chevrolet V8, and painted gold and white, it is one of just five or six survivors remaining and, as well as being the most significant historically, is almost certainly the most original one left.

ERY MOTORIST

At the 1965 Oulton Park Gold Cup (top) the 'Automatic' M1A (#9), now painted red, was in the middle of the front row, John Surtees' Lola (#1) is to his left and Jim Clark's Lotus (#4) between them. Bruce led before a transmission leak put him out. At the Player's 200 in the USA (above) the car was using a 5-litre version of the Traco.

The V8 Oldsmobile engine was fed by four enormous twin-choke downdraught Weber carburettors and in various capacities and states of tune gave anything between 300 and 400bhp.

M1A [MkI] GROUP 7
SPECIFICATION

MODEL	McLaren-Elva M1A [MkI]
TYPE/FORMULA	Group 7 Sportscar
YEAR OF PRODUCTION	1965
DESIGNER	Bruce McLaren
EXAMPLES BUILT	24
ENGINE	Oldsmobile/Ford V8
CUBIC CAPACITY	3900-5000cc
CARBURATION	Four twin-choke downdraught
POWER OUTPUT	300-400bhp

TRANSMISSION	Hewland LG400 4-speed
CHASSIS	Large diameter round & square tube frame
BODY	Four section polyester resin moulded body
FRONT SUSPENSION	Single top link & radius arm, lower wishbone,
	outboard coil spring/damper, anti-roll bar
REAR SUSPENSION	Twin radius arms with single top link, reversed
	lower wishbone, anti-roll bar & coil spring/damper
BRAKES F/R	Dual circuit Girling discs
WHEELS DIAMETER x WIDTH F/R	15x8/15x10in

TYRES F/R	Firestone
LENGTH	166in - 4216mm
WIDTH	64in - 1625mm
HEIGHT OF BODYWORK	30in - 762mm
WHEELBASE	91in - 2311mm
TRACK F/R	51/51in - 1295/1295mm
WEIGHT	1828lb - 829kg
PRINCIPAL DRIVERS	McLaren, Amon, G.Hill, etc.
IDENTIFYING COLOURS	n/a

1965 PROTOTYPE SINGLE SEATER
McLAREN M2A

An experimental prototype which was never raced, the Robin Herd designed McLaren M2A was completed in September 1965, just seven months after the first designs had been conceived. Construction on the first single-seater to bear the McLaren name didn't begin until June 1st and took exactly three months.

Showing a degree of inspired thinking which was to become something of a trademark, Herd opted to use an innovative material with which he had become familiar during his time at Farnborough working on various advanced aerospace applications. As senior scientific officer for the National Gas Turbine Establishment, he came upon a product called Mallite, which consisted of a sheet of endgrain balsa wood sandwiched between aluminium panels. According to Herd this was so strong that it could support the weight of a tank over rough territory.

Once working at McLaren he planned to use glued sheets of Mallite for the internal and external skins of an entirely new monocoque chassis, the corner joints being fluid-sealed and the space within the tub employed for fuel storage, thereby negating the need for separate internal rubber bags. Originally the car was designed to accept a de-stroked 4.2-litre Indianapolis Ford V8 engine and to compete in Formula 1, but in the event it was fitted with yet another version of the lightweight 4.5-litre Oldsmobile unit. This was another example of Bruce having to defer politically to the situation with the Coopers, for whom he was still driving in F1. Clearly he had his sights set on a different horizon, but when the M2A was conceived he was obliged to deny any possible F1 role for it.

After test sessions at both Goodwood and Silverstone, in October of 1965, Bruce was finally caught by the press testing the M2A at a windswept Zandvoort circuit in Holland. Once again strongly denying that Bruce would be driving his own car in next years Formula One World Championship, team members made every effort to keep details of the car from being released. Bruce's best lap time of 1m 28s compared favourably with Jim Clark's F1 lap record from that year's Grand Prix of 1m 30s. In the event though, after covering nearly 2000 miles of testing the car never went near a Grand Prix meeting and was instead employed as a high-speed test mule for Firestone.

By March 1967 the car had been fitted with an experimental strut-mounted rear wing which cut lap times by as much as three seconds at Zandvoort. In Doug Nye's seminal book, 'McLAREN The Grand Prix, Can-Am and Indy Cars', Herd cheerfully admitted to the fact that this device was all but forgotten about until 1968: *"Just put it down to incompetence and short memories… we were fully extended on other ideas."*

Eventually the chassis was sold to Briton John Ewer, a used car dealer and keen amateur racer. He fitted a 4.7-litre Ford V8 mated to a ZF transaxle in what would be the car's final configuration. With both Ewer and club racer Syd Fox behind the wheel, it made several appearances in British national races, most frequently at Brands Hatch and Snetterton, before being sold to Robert Ashcroft. He prepared it for upcoming racer Peter Gethin before it went on the move again, passing through the hands of talented racer Tony Dean (who won a minor Formula Libre race in it at Rufforth) to reach Welshman Dave McCloy in early 1968.

With only one or two exceptions, the car was now firmly relegated to the club circuit. McCloy crashed it heavily on his third outing, at Oulton Park in 1968, and it disappeared for a year to be rebuilt before resurfacing at Llandow and Castle Combe. An exception to the 'lower league' races was the F5000 International at Koksijde (also known as Coxyde) in Belgium for the Trophee International de la Mer Nord in August 1969. McCloy qualified 11th for the first heat, more than 18s behind poleman Andrea de Adamich's works Surtees TS5. He finished eighth, four laps behind the winning TS5 of Trevor Taylor. He was 10th in the second heat, but was again unclassified after having completed just 19 of the 22 laps by the time Taylor crossed the line. Thereafter a major bearing failure prevented the car making the following weekend's meeting, another round of the European F5000 Championship at Zandvoort; and in mid-September a gearbox malfunction prevented McCloy appearing for the Hockenheim round.

The car's next appearance was back at Brands Hatch two weeks later, when Peter Gethin qualified on pole with his 'semi-works' Church Farm Racing McLaren M10A. This time the M2A was almost 21 seconds slower, qualifying 13th for the first heat, in which a broken engine mounting put paid to it on the 15th of the 20 laps.

Undeterred, McCloy took the car back to Wales intending to develop it further for the 1970 season. However, fate intervened; in November chassis M2A-1 was completely destroyed in a garage fire. The likely culprits were a group of children throwing fireworks. There was, however, to be an important further development of the M2A concept, designated M2B.

After putting in some very fast laps in the M2A at Silverstone, Bruce contemplates the future for his first 'single seater' and the McLaren team's possible entry into Formula One.

Although the team went to great lengths to ensure that the press was kept away, its own photographer was on hand to record the M2A test session (top) at Silverstone. After the first test at Goodwood the team realised that the Hewland gearbox fitted to the car wasn't up to transmitting the 350 bhp given out by the V8 engine and fitted the stronger ZF unit (left).

The M2A was finally caught on camera by the press at Zandvoort in Holland. It put in some seriously quick lap times which compared favourably with the lap record held at that time by Jim Clark's Lotus.

M2A PROTOTYPE
SPECIFICATION

MODEL	McLaren M2A
TYPE/FORMULA	Single Seater prototype
YEAR OF PRODUCTION	1965
DESIGNER	Bruce McLaren/Robin Herd
EXAMPLES BUILT	1
ENGINE	Oldsmobile/Ford V8
CUBIC CAPACITY	4500/6000cc
CARBURATION	Four twin-choke downdraught
POWER OUTPUT	350bhp

TRANSMISSION	ZF 4-speed
CHASSIS	'Mallite' bathtub monocoque, steel bulkheads
BODY	Monocoque sides, GRP nose & cockpit surround
FRONT SUSPENSION	Welded cantilever top arm, lower wishbone, inboard coil spring/damper
REAR SUSPENSION	Reverse lower wishbone, top link, twin radius rods, coil spring/damper, anti-roll bar
BRAKES F/R	Outboard Girling discs
WHEELS DIAMETER x WIDTH F/R	13x8.5/13x12in

TYRES F/R	Firestone
LENGTH	156in - 3962mm
WIDTH OF MONOCOQUE	28.5in - 724mm
HEIGHT	35in - 998mm
WHEELBASE	96in - 2438mm
TRACK F/R	50/52in - 1270/1321mm
WEIGHT	1000lb - 450kg
PRINCIPAL DRIVERS	McLaren
IDENTIFYING COLOURS	Red

1965 GROUP 7 McLAREN M1B

The M1B was the official McLaren team car for 1965, and subsequently - as the McLaren-Elva M1B Mark II - the new customer car for the following season.

The purposeful design was based on the earlier car with Robin Herd taking the basic frame from a production chassis then extensively revising it to make it 20 per cent stiffer while keeping its weight the same. He achieved this by using a familiar mix of larger diameter round and square mild steel tubes with, once again, sheet alloy riveted and bonded to the frame to form the bulkheads and undertray.

The structure weighed 1300lbs with the twin 25-gallon rubber fuel cells drained, and the much more rigid machine sported the familiar Traco-built 4.5-litre Oldsmobile V8, four-speed Hewland LG gearbox, dual-circuit Girling brakes and a 40:60 rearward weight bias. The external appearance of the M1B, however, was quite different. Artist Michael Turner followed Bruce's strict guidelines with the bluff shape, drawing a blunter nose and more sharply truncated tail. Although it shared the same wheelbase as the M1A, the M1B was over a foot shorter.

McLaren benefited strongly in the genesis of the M1B from the presence of Massachusetts-born Tyler Alexander. Bruce had met Tyler via their mutual friendship with the Mayer brothers: Timmy, the racer, and Teddy, the lawyer who took time off to manage his brother's career until Timmy was killed at Longford, Australia, in 1963. Tyler was trained in aircraft engineering but could turn his hand to anything and had become the mechanic for the Rev-Em team run by upcoming American race driver Peter Revson. After working for John Mecom's team he graduated to a mechanic's role at McLaren when Bruce bought the Zerex Special from Mecom. He already knew Teddy Mayer from their time together on the American circuits, and would soon become McLaren's chief mechanic before moving on to special engineering projects. Today he remains one of the longest-serving McLaren employees, a true keeper of Bruce's flame.

Alexander's aerospace knowledge was to prove invaluable as he laid out the ducting inside the car's nose and formed the internal structure to secure the radiator. The body sections fitted to the first car were made entirely of aluminium but future Mk1Bs had glass-fibre bodywork.

Bruce took the first 'alloy' prototype, painted red, to Canada for its inaugural run at St Jovite. Eoin Young was another New Zealander who had come over from to England at Bruce's invitation, to act as his secretary and company publicist. He was the first McLaren employee, and would later establish himself as one of the great motorsport writers. When the crankshaft on the M1B broke, Young told the world that it destroyed the engine in "*a most comprehensive manner*". It took the transmission with it, too.

Happily things went better on the car's 'official' debut at Mosport. With a new engine Bruce took pole and, having led for 96 of the 100 laps, finished a close second to the well-sorted Chaparral 2 of designer/racer Jim Hall. For the next event, at Kent in Washington state, Phil Hill took over the M1B, but having again led for much of the race and set fastest lap he was forced to pit by a sticking throttle.

Bruce was back for the LA Times GP at Riverside, the car now equipped with a new front spoiler and a cockpit cooling duct. After winning his qualifying race and smashing the lap record, a tyre lost pressure in the main race. The resultant pit stop dropped him a lap down. In a superb display he unlapped himself and eventually finished third behind Hap Sharp's victorious Chaparral and Jim Clark's Lotus 40.

Three more M1Bs were built in 1966 before Elva took on the construction of the customer versions: a "*half production*" car for Dan Gurney, as Bruce described it, and two further revised team cars.

Bruce was becoming increasingly aware that the Oldsmobile engines were likely to suffer in the face of Chevrolet's heavier but significantly more powerful 6-litre V8s, and the inauguration of the new Can-Am series for 1966 served only to highlight this. The rules merely called for 'two seater unrestricted sportscars'. There was no upper limit on engine size. This 'big banger' formula was very popular with the race-going public and large crowds made for big purses. The total prize money for the six-race season was $385,000, and the winner at each race received more than $30,000.

The M1B was substantially reworked for 1966, primarily to accommodate the Chevrolet engine. This offered an additional 100bhp, albeit at a cost of around 200lbs. Bruce was confident that this could be offset to a greater degree by employing a lighter ZF transmission. The new cars were also now fitted with additional chassis tubes to take account of the heavier burden, wider wheels and a separate rear spoiler.

After being demoted to a role as tyre test car for Firestone and engine test chassis on the Indy V8 destined for Lotus for Ford's KarKraft development department in Detroit, the prototype M1B was rescued from the back lot at KarKraft by a local racer who set about restoring it. He decided to use it on the road and by 1972 it was fully street legal and to this day is still used once or twice a year for short trips to car shows and exhibitions.

Bruce debuted the all-alloy prototype M1B in the Canadian 'Grand Prix' at Mosport (left & above) in September 1965. In both heats he battled for the lead with Jim Hall but eventually had to give best to the well sorted Chaparral 2 and finished just a few feet behind.

The chassis plate attached to the dashboard of the prototype M1B is easily readable, and simply identifies the car as a BMMR (Bruce McLaren Motor Racing) 'Test' car.

The bare polished alloy body panels of the prototype M1B show just how hand built the early cars were. Despite being stripped of its original red paint back in 1970 there are still places where it can be seen. The round air vents at the front, currently used for turn indicators, were only seen on the prototype and one team car.

M1B GROUP 7
SPECIFICATION

MODEL	McLaren M1B
TYPE/FORMULA	Group 7 Sportscar
YEAR OF PRODUCTION	1965/1966
DESIGNER	Robin Herd/Bruce McLaren
EXAMPLES BUILT	4
ENGINE	Oldsmobile/Chevrolet V8
CUBIC CAPACITY	4700-5400cc
CARBURATION	Four twin-choke downdraught
POWER OUTPUT	340bhp

TRANSMISSION	Hewland LG400 4-speed, ZF
CHASSIS	Large diameter round & square tube frame
BODY	Four section hand made aluminium alloy
FRONT SUSPENSION	Single top link & radius arm, lower wishbone,
	outboard coil spring/damper, anti-roll bar
REAR SUSPENSION	Twin radius arms with single top link, reversed
	lower wishbone, anti-roll bar & coil spring/damper
BRAKES F/R	Dual circuit Girling discs, 12.5/11.5 in diameter
WHEELS DIAMETER x WIDTH F/R	15x8.5/15x11.5in

TYRES F/R	Firestone 5.50-15/6.50-15
LENGTH	145in - 3683mm
WIDTH	63in - 1600mm
HEIGHT	31in - 787mm
WHEELBASE	91in - 2311mm
TRACK F/R	52/52in - 1320/1320 mm
WEIGHT	1300lb - 589kg
PRINCIPAL DRIVERS	McLaren, P.Hill, Amon
IDENTIFYING COLOURS	Red

1966 CAN-AM McLAREN-ELVA M1B (MkII)

"*The fastest car we've ever tested,*" screamed Road & Track in July 1966. Putting racer Charlie Hayes' Chevrolet-engined McLaren-Elva M1B Mk II on the cover, and describing it in the opening pages as "*an example of the latest thinking in sports/racing cars*", the prestigious American magazine acknowledged the rare privilege of such early access to a state-of-the-art machine.

The chassis it took to California's Riverside Raceway was an authentic showstopper, having made its public debut at the Racing Car Show in London. It was chassis 30-01 of the 28 which were to be built at Rye, each to the same basic specification as Bruce's team car which he had campaigned to good effect the previous year. 'Basic', that is, because the $11,500 Elva-built cars were sold without an engine so that the customer could tailor the machine to their own personal requirements with a choice of Oldsmobile, Chevrolet or Ford powerplants.

Hayes had opted for a 5.4-litre Chevrolet V8 prepared by Traco Engineering, together with Airheart disc brakes in place of the standard Girlings. Perhaps mindful of Bruce's multiple water hose disasters with the M1A, Hayes and his chief mechanic, Ed Schafer, had the car equipped with aircraft-style Aeroquip hardware and Wiggins quick-release units at those points where regular maintenance would require their periodic removal.

Accordingly R&T's road test team put the price-as-tested closer to $25,000 but even this, it acknowledged, was more than respectable for a race-ready machine which, thanks to four side-draft, double-barrel 58mm Weber carburettors, put out 466bhp at 6,500rpm and developed 445lb ft of torque at 4,500. "*Dirt cheap*" was its chosen expression, which must have pleased the guys at Rye particularly when Hayes went on to win the first United States Road Racing Championship (USRRC) race at Laguna Seca. No less impressively, the M1B was still winning three seasons later. Expatriate Englishman John Cannon provided one of the biggest upsets in Can-Am history when wet-weather Firestones handed him a crucial advantage in the sodden 1968 race at Laguna Seca. Driving, as he put it, "*like a bloody demon,*" he lapped the entire field, which included Denny Hulme in the normally dominant works McLaren M8A.

Photographs give little impression of the compact dimensions of the M1B, which is perhaps why Road & Track was at pains to stress just how small it was. With a 91 inch wheelbase and an overall length of just 146, the Mark II in plan was comparable to an MGB or Lotus Elan, although considerably lower at just 31 inches from the track to the top of the minimal, swept-back screen. Its frontal area was some 30 per cent smaller than either roadcar.

The basic structure impressed the testers, who thought it combined "*some of the characteristics of the semi-monocoque chassis with the multi-tube spaceframe*". This they called an "*admirably practical form for a car that is going to be rigorously campaigned by a private entrant.*" Exceptionally rigid and durable, the construction also ensured that "*the almost inevitable collision damage of a minor nature can be repaired using hand tools and portable welding kit.*"

Besides Cannon, other privateers achieved many excellent results with the M1B, the most notable being Peter Revson, the Revlon cosmetics heir turned racer who would play a significant role in the ongoing McLaren story. He ran his car with a Ford engine at a support race for the 1966 British Grand Prix at Brands Hatch, as well as at the Nassau Speed Weeks where he led for most of the race before his brakes gave out. He also took part in the final race of the 1966 Can-Am series, starting ninth and finishing a creditable fourth, albeit two laps down on Bruce in the works M1B.

Other drivers to run a McLaren-Elva M1B with the Chevrolet engine that year included Chuck Parsons, Earl Jones, and Masten Gregory. Lothar Motschenbacher ran with an Oldsmobile, whilst Bud Morley, Sam Posey, Skip Scott and Dick Brown all used the less popular Ford unit.

The majority of customer cars run by such drivers used the Hewland LG500 four-speed gearbox fitted to Hayes' car. This unit, with its straight-cut, non-synchronised gears, must have seemed a little crude even in the mid-1960s, particularly when compared to the full-synchro units which were now making their presence felt. But more than occasionally, simplicity in motorsport scores highly. Just as the essentially straightforward structure of the Mark II made these customer cars easy to work on, owners found their LG500s durable, dependable and far less awkward than many of the more advanced transmissions of the time.

Road & Track magazine concluded that the M1B was: "*A fine machine, beautiful in the intelligent simplicity of what is necessarily a complicated mechanism.*" A wonderful resume indeed, for a successful and highly significant design in the McLaren story.

Bruce's first race (top) in the 'productionised' version of the M1B was in the Archie Scott-Brown Memorial Trophy race at Snetterton in April 1966. He retired on lap 18 of the second heat due to oil pressure problems. Chris Amon (above) in one of the earlier M1Bs, which still had the smaller round air vents, finished second to Denny Hulme in both heats.

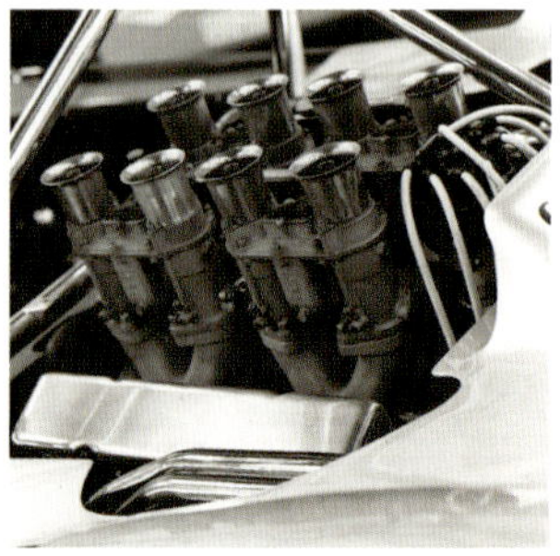

More often than not customers for the Elva-built cars fitted the M1B with a Chevrolet engine fed by four huge downdraught carburettors.

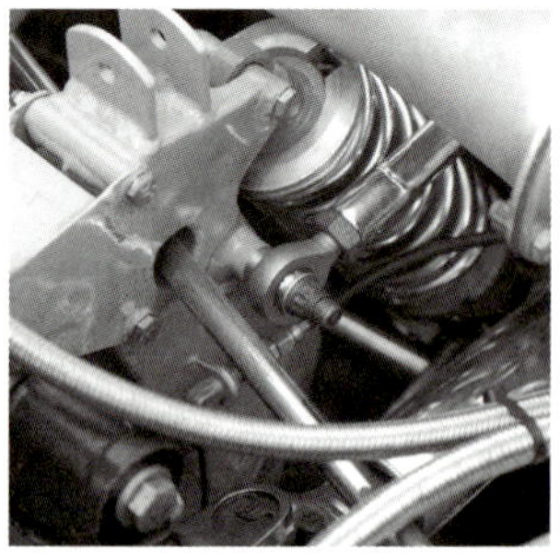

Rear suspension detail at the top of the coil/spring damper shows the gear selector rod passing through the rear chassis bulkhead.

M1B [MkII] CAN-AM
SPECIFICATION

MODEL	McLaren-Elva M1B [MkII]
TYPE/FORMULA	Group7/Can-Am
YEAR OF PRODUCTION	1966
DESIGNER	Bruce McLaren/Robin Herd
EXAMPLES BUILT	28
ENGINE	Oldsmobile V8 (optional Chevrolet or Ford)
CUBIC CAPACITY	4700-5400cc
CARBURATION	Four twin-choke downdraught
POWER OUTPUT	350bhp

TRANSMISSION	Hewland LG400 or LG500
CHASSIS	Large diameter round & square tube frame
BODY	Four section polyester resin moulded body
FRONT SUSPENSION	Single top link & radius arm, lower wishbone, outboard coil spring/damper, anti-roll bar
REAR SUSPENSION	Twin radius arms with single top link, reversed lower wishbone, anti-roll bar & coil spring/damper
BRAKES F/R	Dual circuit Girling discs, 12.5/11.5 in diameter
WHEELS DIAMETER x WIDTH F/R	15x8.5/15x11.5in

TYRES F/R	Firestone or Goodyear
LENGTH	146in - 3708mm
WIDTH	64in - 1625mm
HEIGHT TO TOP OF WINDSCREEN	31in - 787mm
WHEELBASE	91in - 2311mm
TRACK F/R	51/51in - 1295/1295mm
WEIGHT	1400lb - 635kg
PRINCIPAL DRIVERS	McLaren, Amon, Cannon, Revson
IDENTIFYING COLOURS	n/a

1966 FORMULA 1 McLAREN M2B

Bruce soon confirmed his intention to field a two-car McLaren Grand Prix team for the new 3-litre Formula 1 in 1966, a relief after all the cloak-and-dagger stuff which had been necessary to reassure his employers at Cooper that the M2A was not a Formula 1 car-in-waiting.

He would drive one car, with fellow Kiwi Chris Amon in the other. It seems probable that just the two cars were built, although contemporary evidence suggests the possible existence of a third tub. Power was to come from an Indianapolis Ford V8, a 4.2-litre, quad-cam unit sleeved down to the appropriate capacity.

It was the construction of the monocoque which attracted most attention, however. Herd described it at the time as *"an inverted top-hat section tub,"* formed from Mallite sheets with outer skins of conventional aluminium sheet providing additional stiffness and crash protection for the driver. Rubber fuel bags were fitted in the spaces between the inner Mallite tub and the outer skins.

Herd's monocoque was further stiffened by four fabricated steel bulkheads, the first and fourth supporting the front and rear suspension respectively, while the two centre units formed a mounting for the dashboard and instruments and the seatback support.

The suspension was conventional. At the front this meant upper rocker arms operating inboard coil spring and damper units, with bottom location courtesy of lower wishbones. Braking stresses were transferred to the tub via a short radius-rod running rearwards from the upper rocker arms' outer ends. At the rear the M2B sported lower wishbones, with a single top link and twin radius rods, and outboard coil springs and dampers.

Bruce took his new McLaren-Ford, and the only engine currently available, to Monaco for its race debut on May 22nd 1966. Little of the original Ford internals remained, just the original block together with the bottom end and head castings. The rest, including virtually all the moving parts, had been redesigned and remanufactured courtesy of Gary Knutson and Traco in Culver City, California. In theory, driving through a five-speed ZF transaxle, the Hilborn fuel-injected unit should have been good for 335bhp at 9,500rpm. But despite the quite phenomenal noise that the over-ported unit produced, the anticipated power never materialised and with only 303bhp at 8,750rpm Bruce qualified only 10th. He didn't last long in the race, either. An oil pipe union came undone, squirting lubricant into the cockpit, and after 10 laps he retired before the engine suffered damage.

Even in Monaco he had admitted the necessity to *"make some fairly drastic moves in the engine room"*, and by the Belgian Grand Prix at Spa-Francorchamps the Ford was out and a new unit took its place: the Italian Serenissima V8. This was at least a full 3-litre so didn't require sleeving down or de-stroking, and weighed significantly less than its American predecessor, but it suffered serious oil leaks during practice and soon ran its bearings. Now the team was engineless as there was no spare powerplant, so having qualified 16th with fellow rookie F1 constructor Dan Gurney, Bruce was obliged to miss the race.

He had to pass up the French Grand Prix too, but the Serenissima V8 was rebuilt in time for the British Grand Prix at Brands Hatch on July 16th. He qualified the underpowered and overweight car 13th, but brought it home sixth, two laps behind winner Jack Brabham in his eponymous Brabham Repco, to score the McLaren marque's first World Championship point. It was a fine effort by an F1 newcomer.

Zandvoort was less rewarding, with another non-start due to engine problems after qualifying 14th. McLaren missed both the German and Italian races, as Bruce preferred to concentrate the effort on the more lucrative Can-Am events.

An improved version of the Ford V8 was reinstalled in the M2B for the US and Mexican GPs which completed the F1 season. With power upped to a rumoured 325bhp, Bruce qualified 11th at Watkins Glen and finished fifth, three laps behind Jim Clark's winning Lotus BRM, but was forced into retirement in Mexico after qualifying 15th by yet another engine failure. It was to be the last works outing for the M2B. Bruce had lost interest in both the car and the largely abortive Indy Ford engine experiment, but not in Formula 1 itself. McLaren would be back.

The car's swansong came in 1968 as Hertfordshire-based Ken Sheppard Sports Cars reportedly acquired three M2B chassis, planning to fit them with Coventry Climax V8s. M2B-2 appeared at the Silverstone International Trophy meeting, where it struggled around the paddock before being trailered home. At Brands Hatch on Easter Monday, M2B-1 appeared for practice in an F5000 race, fitted with a 4.5-litre Oldsmobile V8.

As the first in the highly distinguished line of Formula 1 cars, the M2B holds a special place in the history of the McLaren. Chassis M2B-1 made its way back to the United States and has lain for many years awaiting restoration, while M2B-2 was acquired by Tom Wheatcroft's Donington Grand Prix Collection. After many years in restoration it is expected to take its place in the McLaren Hall there by the end of 2008.

A McLaren Formula 1 car first appeared on the grid at the Monaco Grand Prix (above) in May 1966. Bruce qualified 10th but retired on lap 10 of the race when the Ford V8 engine (left) lost all its oil pressure.

The sleeved-down Ford 'Indy' engine used Lucas fuel injection but despite the prodigious noise only produced somewhere around 300bhp.

By the next race, the Belgian Grand Prix at Spa in June, the M2B was fitted with the Italian Serenissima V8 engine. Bruce didn't even make the start after it expired in practice.

Driving the M2B fitted with the Serenissima engine, Bruce finished sixth in the 1966 British GP at Brands Hatch, scoring the first Formula 1 World Championship point for a McLaren car.

Reverting to the Ford 'Indy' V8 engine for the last two races of 1966, Bruce scored two points for fifth place in the US GP but retired from the Mexican Grand Prix with engine failure.

MZB FORMULA 1
SPECIFICATION

MODEL	McLaren M2B
TYPE/FORMULA	Formula 1
YEAR OF PRODUCTION	1966
DESIGNER	Bruce McLaren/Robin Herd
EXAMPLES BUILT	2
ENGINE	Ford 'Indy' V8/Serenissima V8
CUBIC CAPACITY	3000cc
CARBURATION	Lucas Fuel Injection/4 twin-choke downdraught
POWER OUTPUT	321/260bhp

TRANSMISSION	ZF 4 or 5-speed
CHASSIS	Aluminium 'Mallite' sheet monocoque
BODY	Monocoque sides, GRP nose & cockpit surround
FRONT SUSPENSION	Welded cantilever top arm, lower wishbone,
	inboard coil spring/damper
REAR SUSPENSION	Reverse lower wishbone, top link,
	twin radius rods, coil spring/damper, anti-roll bar
BRAKES F/R	Outboard Girling discs
WHEELS DIAMETER x WIDTH F/R	13x8.5/13x12in

TYRES F/R	Firestone
LENGTH	159in - 4039mm
WIDTH	74in - 1880mm
HEIGHT	36in - 914mm
WHEELBASE	96in - 2438mm
TRACK F/R	50/50in - 1270/1270mm
WEIGHT	1180lb - 535kg
PRINCIPAL DRIVERS	McLaren
IDENTIFYING COLOURS	White/Green

1966 FORMULA LIBRE McLAREN M3A

The M3A was another of McLaren's early screen stars, this time with the company providing the car driven by James Garner in the MGM movie Grand Prix. The fabled 'whooshbonk' car - of which just three were built - was another exceptionally neat Robin Herd/Bruce McLaren spaceframe design, this time an open-wheel single seater intended for Formula Libre racing as well as hillclimb and speed events.

With such a broad remit, the trio of cars enjoyed relatively long working lives, appearing first at the Belgian Grand Prix in 1966 - the year Bruce and Chris Amon won Le Mans in the 7-litre Ford Mark IIA - and still clearly highly competitive four years later when the late Patsy Burt was confirmed as the 1970 RAC British Sprint Champion after several memorable performances in her Traco Oldsmobile V8-powered 4.5-litre version.

That first Grand Prix outing in Belgium was not, of course, as a competitor, but rather as a camera car. Chassis M3A-3 was fitted with a 4.7-litre Ford V8 so that Phil Hill could track the action to provide some highly atmospheric footage - all of it obtained during just one lap of the circuit - for the aforementioned John Frankenheimer Hollywood blockbuster.

Following filming chassis M3A-3 was then sold to erstwhile M2A owner/driver John Ewer, who in turn passed it on to David Bridges who recruited Lancastrian upcomer Brian Redman to drive it for him in 1967. Driver and car performed admirably during a high-speed encounter in the BRSCC Mallory Park Easter Trophy race meeting, as Redman won and set a new outright fastest lap.

By the end of May the car had changed ownership again and in the hands of Robin Darlington was to score a trio of club victories at Llandow, Silverstone and Snetterton. Unfortunately a serious road crash prevented him rebuilding the car after it more or less fell apart whilst progressing at speed down the straight at Silverstone. Eventually it fell to David Prophet to gather the pieces together, shipping them off to South Africa where Bob Olthoff planned to join the 1968 South African F1 Championship once the rules were relaxed to allow Formula A cars to compete.

Unfortunately much less is known about chassis M3A-1. It was bought new by Swiss hillclimb driver Dr Harry Zweifel but disappeared after being raced regularly in Swiss and other European hillclimbs up to the early 1970s. By 1972 M3A-1 was reported as residing somewhere in France and sadly was probably modified beyond all recognition into some sort of hybrid special.

In 1970 Frenchman Pierre Soukry used his M3A to take part in several rounds of the well-supported European Formula 5000 Championship. At the 10th round at Silverstone in June he qualified last on the 18-car grid, 25s slower than Peter Gethin's semi-works M10B, and retired from the race on the warm-up lap with an oil leak.

Happily Burt's well-documented exploits in the second car mean no such mystery attends M3A-2. Now housed in the Donington Collection it is the sole known survivor of the three and thus a uniquely important part of the unfolding McLaren story.

The 1970 RAC British Sprint Championship comprised nine events, with each competitor's six best scores determining the overall winner. Burt won the first six events she entered, breaking the course record at no fewer than four of them, an achievement which will probably never be beaten.

She became the first woman to win a National Championship, something rightly hailed as "*a great personal achievement,*" in her 2001 obituary in the Bruce McLaren Trust newsletter, but it was just one of more than 600 awards she received during a career as a seriously versatile racer. During her four-year campaign with the M3A she took part in both domestic and international events, hitting the headlines several times, most notably when she completed a standing kilometre in just 19.84s. At the time that was the fastest time ever recorded in the UK.

Burt deserved the headlines she got, but sadly the car in which she scored so many great triumphs has been all but forgotten. Part of the reason the M3A was overshadowed was the other models McLaren was producing at the time: a glittering family of thundering sportscar racers that would lead to the company's domination of the much more mainstream Can-Am series.

Patsy Burt used the M3 to compete in hillclimb events (top: at Great Auclum in 1967) throughout the UK and Europe. In October 1968 her crew fitted a high 'streamliner' style screen and nosecone (above) and at RAF Elvington Patsy set several British speed records.

Chassis M3A/2 was ordered by and built specially for Patsy Burt. Fitted with a 4.4-litre 'Traco' Oldsmobile and 5-speed ZF gearbox, the car was hugely successful, winning speed championships and setting records everywhere it went.

M3A FORMULA LIBRE
SPECIFICATION

MODEL	McLaren M3A
TYPE/FORMULA	Formula Libre
YEAR OF PRODUCTION	1966
DESIGNER	Bruce McLaren/Robin Herd
EXAMPLES BUILT	3
ENGINE	Oldsmobile/Ford/Chevrolet V8
CUBIC CAPACITY	4500-5400cc
CARBURATION	Four twin-choke downdraught
POWER OUTPUT	340-380bhp

TRANSMISSION	Hewland LG500 or ZF 5-speed
CHASSIS	Large diameter tubular spaceframe
BODY	GRP nose, cockpit surround & panels to suit
FRONT SUSPENSION	Unequal length double wishbones,
	adjustable coil spring/damper, anti-roll bar
REAR SUSPENSION	Reverse lower wishbone, top link,
	twin radius rods, coil spring/damper, anti-roll bar
BRAKES F/R	Outboard Girling 10.5in discs
WHEELS DIAMETER x WIDTH F/R	13x8.5/15x12in

TYRES F/R	Firestone
LENGTH	148in - 3759mm
WIDTH	67in -1702mm
HEIGHT TO TOP OF WINDSCREEN	29in - 736mm
WHEELBASE	96in - 2438mm
TRACK F/R	51/52in - 1295/1321mm
WEIGHT	1080lb - 490kg
PRINCIPAL DRIVERS	P.Hill, Burt, Soukry
IDENTIFYING COLOURS	Blue

1967 CAN-AM McLAREN-ELVA M1C (MkIII)

The last tubular frame chassis car built by Elva to sell as a McLaren customer car, the M1C was also known as the McLaren-Elva MkIII, particularly in North America where many of the 25 examples built headed. Most of these, unsurprisingly, went on to race in the USRRC but the cars were also campaigned in the higher profile Can-Am championships where lessons learned with the earlier M1A and M1B soon reaped dividends for several privateers.

The M1C was very much the offspring of its two predecessors, a new car but one very closely based on the same spaceframe design. It thus represented the final evolution of the concept, something of a farewell tour for those early cars, since by this time the works McLaren team had moved on to develop the all-conquering monocoque M6A.

The M1C's chassis was constructed using a modified version of the familiar large-diameter round and square tubing, with the structure receiving important additional stiffness and strength from undertrays and bulkheads that were formed using riveted and bonded light-alloy sheets, as well as additional tubes in the front and rear bays. The suspension remained unchanged: an independent set-up at the front using unequal-length, wide-base wishbones designed to facilitate anti-dive and anti-roll, and rear trailing arms with lower wishbones, single top links and fully adjustable coil spring/damper units.

While the spaceframe was even stronger than before, the bodywork was largely similar. Formed from four reinforced polyester resin sections with the twin side sections each housing a 25-gallon rubber fuel cell, externally it gained a separate rear 'spoiler' wing. This distinguishing feature was fitted on the majority of the cars destined for the US and was made adjustable so that the aerodynamics could be tuned to suit the very different characteristics of the circuits there. Fifteen-inch diameter custom-made McLaren-Elva cast magnesium wheels were fitted front and rear.

Once again the car was engineered to accept a variety of different power units, most commonly Chevrolets, but customers could opt for Ford or Oldsmobile V8s. The Chevrolet V8 came with a choice of a four- or five-speed Hewland gearbox, though a ZF option was still offered.

The M1C pictured here was originally owned and run by Jerry Hansen of Minneapolis. He entered it in the 1967 Can-Am series and it made its debut in the first race of the season on September 3, at Road America in Wisconsin. That race naturally also marked the first outing for Team McLaren's two gleaming new M6As, and developed into the first episode of what rapidly became known as the 'Bruce and Denny Show'. A full field of 32 cars started the race, no fewer than 17 of them various different McLarens; the M1C drivers that year included luminaries such as Skip Scott, Peter Revson, Chuck Parsons and Bob Bondurant.

Unsurprisingly, Bruce and Denny's matched pair of M6As came home first and second but production M1Cs finished fifth, sixth, seventh and eighth with Hansen securing a respectable sixth after starting back on the seventh row of the grid. When the USRRC circus came to Riverside in April, Bondurant and Lothar Motschenbacher took their M1Cs to second and third place behind Mark Donohue's Penske Lola T70. The cars were still apparently competitive against the bigger-engined Lolas, and there was plenty more to come from the M1C. Chuck Parsons, for example, arguably the most successful M1C driver of the year, was the first representative of the model on every grid during 1967.

For 1968 it was a case of more of the same. Elkhart Lake saw four M1Cs on the startline, Canadian store magnate George Eaton's being the highest placed in position eight. Having already notched up a 10th place at Edmonton in a car which was certainly becoming outdated, he drove to an impressive third place at Laguna Seca, helped in no small part by torrential downpours. With a tenacious and determined driving style, he had kept going long after the big boys called it a day, to give the M1C its highest placing in a Can-Am fixture.

Incredibly, the M1C was still going strong in 1969, three of them appearing on the grid at Mosport, with John Cordts finishing fourth behind Bruce and Denny in their much more advanced works M8Bs. And then came 1970, when the M1C refused to go away. A trio of customer cars still raced confidently and competitively throughout that final season. The spaceframe era might finally have ended, but at McLaren it certainly enjoyed a long run.

As late as 1971 the M1C chassis was still highly competitive in British sportscar racing. John Jordan (above) in the ex-Ken Wilson, ex-Alistair Cowin, Ford V8-engined M1C heads for another victory at Snetterton.

The final concept of the M1 line, the M1C could be fitted with a variety of engines and featured air extraction vents on top of the front wheel arches, behind the wing mirrors. Rather than the fixed rear spoiler of the previous M1B model, the M1C featured an adjustable rear wing and proved highly successful in the hands of privateer drivers.

M1C [MkIII] CAN-AM
SPECIFICATION

MODEL	McLaren-Elva M1C [MkIII]
TYPE/FORMULA	Can-Am
YEAR OF PRODUCTION	1967
DESIGNER	Bruce McLaren/Robin Herd
EXAMPLES BUILT	25
ENGINE	Chevrolet, Oldsmobile, Ford V8
CUBIC CAPACITY	4500-6000cc
CARBURATION	Lucas fuel injection
POWER OUTPUT	400-540bhp

TRANSMISSION	Hewland LG400 or LG500, optional ZF
CHASSIS	Large diameter round & square tube frame
BODY	Four section polyester resin moulded body
FRONT SUSPENSION	Single top link & radius arm, lower wishbone, outboard coil spring/damper, anti-roll bar
REAR SUSPENSION	Trailing radius arms with single top link, reversed lower wishbone, anti-roll bar & coil spring/damper
BRAKES F/R	Dual circuit Girling discs, 12.5/11.5 in diameter
WHEELS DIAMETER x WIDTH F/R	15x8.5/15x11.5in

TYRES F/R	Firestone
LENGTH	146in - 3708mm
WIDTH	66in - 1676mm
HEIGHT TO TOP OF WINDSCREEN	31in - 787mm
WHEELBASE	90.5in - 2298mm
TRACK F/R	52/52in - 1321/1321mm
WEIGHT	1300lb - 590kg
PRINCIPAL DRIVERS	Hulme, Gethin, Revson
IDENTIFYING COLOURS	n/a

1967 FORMULA 2
McLAREN M4A & McLAREN-TROJAN M4A/B

Despite the fact that it could draw bigger crowds than either Formula 1 or Formula 2, big banger Group 7 sportscar racing went into decline in the UK in 1966. Looking forward, McLaren decided to build a new car to compete in the 1967 1600cc Formula 2 class, Formula 3 and even the US Formula B Series. The most recognised version of this pretty car was probably the slot-car version produced by Scalextric.

Relatively flush with money from the success of the M1 and its various derivatives, as well as useful experience and the invaluable technical know-how he had gained from helping the giant Ford Motor Company to develop its Le Mans-winning Mark II contender, Bruce settled down with Robin Herd to create the all-new single-seater which they type-numbered M4A.

Right from the start the plan called for a series of replicas, which would be called M4A/Bs. These would be built off-site at Purley in Surrey, by Lambretta-Trojan. An initial batch of 10 was soon being laid down at Peter Agg's premises and it was hoped they could be sold to new and existing McLaren customers, most probably in North America for Formula B.

The M4A was relatively straightforward, based on a constant-section bathtub monocoque. This time Herd ignored the chemically bonded Mallite sandwich which, though immensely strong, posed a number of problems as far as series production was concerned, and opted instead for more conventional aluminium panels. These were bonded and riveted to a quartet of strong steel bulkheads to make up the lower half of the car's structure, and were far easier than Mallite to repair after accident damage.

The nose and cockpit surround were in glass-fibre, and the suspension sprang no surprises: double wishbones located by long radius arms front and rear, with conventional outboard springs and dampers. Supplemented by a small, five-gallon seatback tank, the bulk of the fuel was held in a matched pair of 10-gallon tanks, one mounted either side of the cockpit. The wheels were cast-magnesium 13 inch diameter items unique to McLaren and Elva, with 7 inch width rims at the front and 10 inch at the rear. The complete car weighed in at 960lbs, just above the stipulated Formula 2 series minimum.

The Formula 2 version, which appeared in February 1967, was designed to accept the brand new Cosworth four-valve A series engine, the FVA. This light and compact four-cylinder unit, built with Ford backing, the design and manufacturing genius of Cosworth founders Keith Duckworth and Mike Costin, and some characteristically far-sighted encouragement from Colin Chapman at Lotus, would spawn the all-conquering Ford Cosworth DFV F1 powerplant that appeared so dramatically later that season.

The FVA developed around 230bhp, which was delivered to the rear wheels via a Hewland FT200 gearbox.

Early in the season Bruce found himself sidelined from the Grand Prix scene owing to the late delivery of the new V12 engine he had been promised by BRM for his new contender, the M5A. He thus took part in an M4A in several F2 Championship rounds. There were some potent driver/car combinations in the series that year, and second place at Rouen in July, his last race driving chassis M4A-1 as an F2 car, was the best he could manage. His other six races provided consistent if unspectacular results: two thirds, a fourth, two fifths and sixth.

A number of American drivers seemed pleased with the car though, and 25 M4A/Bs were sold in the States where Formula B was proving popular on the ever-expanding North American racing scene. In Europe the M4A/B also appeared in a handful of F3 races, albeit with little success.

The orange car pictured here is one of these exports, chassis number 200-27B which was built in 1967. With a Lotus Twin Cam engine, it was originally owned and raced by Chuck Dietrich and enjoyed a short but highly distinguished career. It won seven races in 1968, five in Formula B and two in the Sports Car Club of America (SCCA) GP Formula class. The very original red M4A photographed is one of the few chassis that stayed in Europe and is currently on display, complete with its original FVA engine, in the Donington Collection.

Having raced an M4A/B for John Coombs in Europe, with little in the way of results, Piers Courage bought the car from him and raced it in the Tasman series. A string of good finishes earned him some headlines and ultimately a drive with BRM.

The M4A/B was a beautifully clean, simple and elegant single seater design, formed around a relatively small Formula 2 size all-aluminium alloy 'bathtub' style monocoque.

The 1600cc Cosworth FVA which developed somewhere around 240bhp was the basis for the DFV engine which would dominate the Formula 1 scene for many years.

The Trojan production versions of the M4A/B featured a sleek fibre-glass body that was moulded from the aluminium version created for the first prototype car built at the McLaren works.

1967 FORMULA 2
McLAREN M4A & McLAREN-TROJAN M4A/B
CONTINUED

Other drivers who competed in these attractive little cars included New Zealander Graeme Lawrence, who campaigned his McLaren in Europe to great effect before taking it home. He continued driving it Down Under and was competitive for a number of years; more recently his car has been restored by Bruce McLaren Trust member Peter Herbert.

Old Etonian Piers Courage, one of Britain's rising stars of the late 1960s, used an M4A while racing in the European F2 series for veteran entrant John Coombs. It was a season dominated by the Brabhams and Matras, and despite taking part in virtually every round the brewery heir more often distinguished himself through his tendency to spin off or commit other embarrassing gaffes. His nickname, 'Porridge', was soon applied to anyone who spun or otherwise came a cropper after losing control of a racing car. This, and his lack of results with the McLaren, left him somewhat despondent by the end of 1967 but the M4A would yet prove crucial to his career. Overlooked by BRM for F1 duties in favour of his smoother and less impetuous fellow countryman Chris Irwin, Courage purchased the car from Coombs and took it Down Under to compete in the 1968 Tasman series as a privateer.

Here, at last, he and the car showed their true potential. Approaching the final race, in Longford, he had achieved a second place and three thirds, fighting the works Lotus-Fords of Jim Clark and Graham Hill, and the works Ferrari of Chris Amon, all of which had 2.5-litre engines. His newfound success would later prompt Colin Chapman to offer him a drive alongside Hill after Clark's death in April. Longford provided Courage with his greatest day thus far in a career that had been in danger of stalling, as he took the McLaren to victory in appalling conditions. It was a wholly apposite swansong for the model.

Driving the red works McLaren M4A-Cosworth, Bruce took part in several rounds of the 1967 European Formula 2 Championship. A second place at the French race held at Rouen-les-Essarts in July was his best result of the season.

The rear suspension of the M4A/B used the conventional single top link, reverse lower wishbone and twin radius arm set-up attached to the rear bulkhead.

The sides of the 20swg aluminium monocoque formed the lower half of the body. The coil spring/damper units were outboard at front and rear.

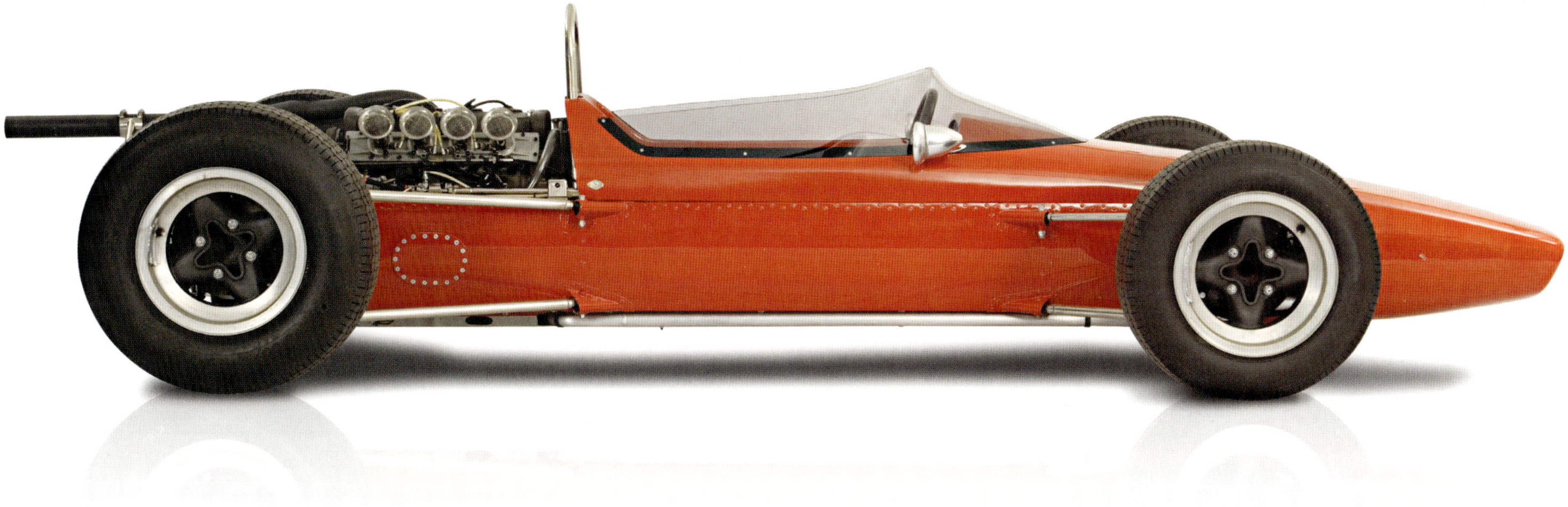

M4A FORMULA 2
SPECIFICATION

MODEL	McLaren M4A
TYPE/FORMULA	Formula 2
YEAR OF PRODUCTION	1967
DESIGNER	Robin Herd
EXAMPLES BUILT	2 + 25 M4A/B Trojan built customer cars
ENGINE	Ford Cosworth FVA
CUBIC CAPACITY	1598cc
CARBURATION	Lucas fuel injection
POWER OUTPUT	230bhp

TRANSMISSION	Hewland HD5 or FT200 5-speed
CHASSIS	20swg aluminium alloy monocoque, steel bulkheads
BODY	Monocoque sides, GRP nose & cockpit surround
FRONT SUSPENSION	Single top link & radius arm, lower wishbone, outboard coil spring/damper, anti-roll bar
REAR SUSPENSION	Reverse lower wishbone, top link, twin radius rods, outboard coil spring/damper, anti-roll bar
BRAKES F/R	Outboard 10.5in discs
WHEELS DIAMETER x WIDTH F/R	13x7/13x10in

TYRES F/R	Firestone 5.00-13/6.25-13
LENGTH	138in - 3505mm
WIDTH	70in - 1778mm
HEIGHT	30in - 762mm
WHEELBASE	90in - 2286mm
TRACK F/R	54/54in - 1372/1372mm
WEIGHT	960lb - 435kg
PRINCIPAL DRIVERS	McLaren, Courage
IDENTIFYING COLOURS	Red

1967 FORMULA 1 McLAREN M4B

Bruce was confident that the M4A concept had more to deliver than it had so far, and in the continued absence of the BRM V12 one of the factory F2 cars was sidelined for additional development by Herd and his team. It was revamped so that the boss could race it as an 'interim' Formula 1 car. In the way of these things, the resultant machine was somewhat confusingly type-numbered as a McLaren M4B.

Bruce planned to use it in the early races of 1967, until arrival of BRM's V12 would enable completion of the new M5A. It was made at the factory in Colnbrook rather than coming off the 'production line' at Purley, and Herd modified the rear end to accommodate an ex-Tasman Series 2070cc BRM V8 which was said to produce around 280bhp. That was less even than the Indy Ford or Serenissima V8s had managed in 1966, but the M4B was much lighter. It was fitting with long-range pannier tanks either side of the cockpit to provide sufficient fuel for a Grand Prix, but nevertheless had to be ballasted in order to meet the 500kg minimum weight.

The hybrid made its debut at the Race of Champions in March 1967, finished in brick red as Bruce and Teddy Mayer were still undecided on the precise colour the team's livery should be. After breaking a camshaft in practice, Bruce had to race with a borrowed 1,960cc BRM V8 but still did well. Only three 3-litre cars outqualified him: the Eagle Weslake V12s of Dan Gurney and Richie Ginther, and John Surtees' V12 Honda. With only two thirds of their engine capacity, Bruce was still able to finish fourth and sixth in the two heats. Unfortunately, in the ferociously competitive 40-lap final he missed a gear on the opening lap, over-revved the engine, and snapped another camshaft.

The next outing came at Oulton Park for the minor-league Spring Trophy race. With the 2.1-litre BRM engine reinstalled, Bruce qualified sixth. He finished fifth in both heats, and took the same place, a lap down, in the final. At the end of April, in the Daily Express International Trophy at Silverstone, he finished fifth once again on a track rendered slippery with oil.

In a bid to improve reliability for Monaco in May, where it was hoped that the tight street circuit would favour the smaller car, McLaren fitted a heavier-duty Hewland DG gearbox, as well as larger oil and water radiators. The nose was also cut back, as was the custom in those days, to avoid bumping in early-race traffic. Bruce qualified 9th and was running a strong third by the 71st lap when he was forced into the pits by a misfire, which he believed to be caused by lack of fuel. Jack Brabham, who had retired on the opening lap, ran into the McLaren pit as Bruce called for more fuel, shouting: "*It's your battery, it's your battery!*" *Bruce was quick to acknowledge the debt to a rival, later writing, "Good old Jack. It was the battery and we quickly whipped another one on.*"

The stop proved costly. Following Lorenzo Bandini's fiery crash McLaren could have finished second behind fellow Kiwi Denny Hulme, who scored his maiden win in Brabham's second car. As it was he slipped to fourth, separated from Hulme by Graham Hill's Lotus-BRM and Chris Amon who was making his debut for Ferrari. It was, nevertheless, a very respectable performance.

The M4B's final outing came at Zandvoort for a Dutch Grand Prix that saw the arrival of the new Lotus 49 and its Ford Cosworth DFV V8 engine. As the Lotus Fords dominated, Bruce struggled with his horsepower deficit and some electrical difficulties, and qualified only 14th. To compound that, he spun on oil on the second lap and crashed through a fence. Although the car was reportedly badly damaged the monocoque itself was, in Bruce's own words, "*completely unharmed*". The team nevertheless called it a day, elected not to travel to Spa where the power deficit would have been even more of a handicap, and Bruce thereafter accepted an offer from his old friend Dan Gurney to drive a second Eagle Weslake for the next three races.

The M4B was subsequently repaired, and in the late summer Bruce took it tyre testing at Goodwood. Unfortunately, it caught fire out on the circuit and was completely burnt out. Years later, looking back at the company's success in the 1960s and early 1970s, the respected British motoring writer Leonard Setright was to describe these early machines as having what he called, "*a nicety of construction and an honesty of purpose.*" And he noted that, "*much the same could be said about Bruce.*"

Just one year on from the team's maiden GP, Bruce took the V8-engined M4B-BRM to a superb fourth place in the 1967 Monaco Grand Prix. It was the best World Championship event finish yet for a McLaren.

The pannier tanks fitted to the Formula 2-based M4B were needed to carry the fuel necessary to complete the longer Formula 1 races. The truncated nose was a 'Monaco' speciality which most teams adopted for the race on the narrow streets of Monte Carlo.

Bruce heads up the hill at Monaco where the smaller F2-size car (with a specially fitted heavy-duty gearbox) was in its element. He ran in third place for much of the race, only dropping to fourth after a pit stop to change a faulty battery.

Opposite:
At the XIX International Trophy race for Formula 1 cars held at Silverstone in April 1967, Bruce made it to the finish in fifth place, a lap down on the Ferrari of winner Mike Parkes.

M4B FORMULA 1
SPECIFICATION

MODEL	McLaren M4B
TYPE/FORMULA	Formula 1
YEAR OF PRODUCTION	1967
DESIGNER	Robin Herd
EXAMPLES BUILT	1
ENGINE	BRM V8
CUBIC CAPACITY	2070cc
CARBURATION	Lucas fuel injection
POWER OUTPUT	280bhp

TRANSMISSION	Hewland FT200 5-speed
CHASSIS	20swg aluminium alloy monocoque, steel bulkheads
BODY	Monocoque sides, GRP nose & cockpit surround
FRONT SUSPENSION	Single top link & radius arm, lower wishbone, outboard coil spring/damper, anti-roll bar
REAR SUSPENSION	Reverse lower wishbone, top link, twin radius rods, outboard coil spring/damper, anti-roll bar
BRAKES F/R	Outboard 10.5in discs
WHEELS DIAMETER x WIDTH F/R	13x7/13x10in

TYRES F/R	Goodyear
LENGTH	124in - 3150mm
WIDTH	72in - 1828mm
HEIGHT	30in - 762mm
WHEELBASE	93in - 2362mm
TRACK F/R	54/54in - 1372/1372mm
WEIGHT	928lb - 420kg
PRINCIPAL DRIVERS	McLaren
IDENTIFYING COLOURS	Red

1967 FORMULA 1 McLAREN M5A

Bruce's outings as Dan Gurney's partner in the Eagle team, in the French, British and German Grands Prix, saw him run little slower than the fleet American, but each time he retired with engine or engine-related maladies. It had been a convenient arrangement that kept him fresh, but doubtless it was a relief finally to be able to climb into Robin Herd's extremely handsome new M5A for the remaining four races of the 1967 season.

The delays with BRM's customer version of its V12 engine effectively rendered the long-finished M5A something of a stop-gap model, not unlike the M4B, and seriously compromised McLaren's second F1 season. But at least the car was a pukka F1 machine. It was a step forward from the smaller car, with its main fuel supplies located within the chassis in tanks fitted both above and beneath the driver's legs, as well as in the extended booms that projected rearwards from the monocoque to support the relatively long engine.

The new combination was finally ready for a 30-lap shakedown at Goodwood in August before being sent out to Mosport for the Canadian Grand Prix. With a little more foresight, its debut could have been sensational.

There were reassuringly few teething troubles in practice, where Bruce qualified a promising sixth just over a second slower than Jim Clark's pole position Lotus. The race began in pouring rain, however, and Bruce spun down to 12th early on before tigering back to fifth place after 10 laps. On the 11th he went past Graham Hill, and by the 13th Jack Brabham had been forced to concede third. Seven laps later Bruce slipped past Clark to take second place, with only Denny Hulme now ahead. As the rain stopped around lap 27, and the track started to dry out, he moved in on the Monaco winner's Brabham Repco, but both were repassed by Clark. By lap 59, however, the downpour began again, but instead of Bruce storming after Clark and Hulme again, a bid to save weight started to backfire. As Eoin Young was later to put it: "*For want of a nail this particular McLaren horse lost the race.*"

The decision had been taken to run the car without an alternator, since the engine had a mechanical fuel pump and in any case made low demands on the electrical system. But the battery was losing charge and the engine was beginning to misfire. It may simply have been that the battery was affected by exhaust heat which boiled it dry, but whatever the cause, Bruce was forced to pit to change the unit. He lost three laps and eventually rejoined to finish a disappointed seventh, just out of the points.

Monza too was to end in disappointment. There, for the Italian Grand Prix, he qualified the M5A on the front of the grid, close to Clark and Brabham. Crucially, he was also ahead of Amon in the tifosi's beloved Ferrari, which led to a farcical scene which paints a delightful picture of the occasionally amateurish nature of even topline racing in the 1960s.

The M5A had the same brick red livery as the M4B because, according to chief mechanic Alastair Caldwell, that was all they had in the workshop at the time. The race organisers were displeased since red was Ferrari's colour, and several times ordered the team to paint its car green without delay since it was based in England and green was the British racing colour. It mattered little to them that the car had a vestigial green stripe on the nose. Miffed to be nagged repeatedly about what seemed to him to be a minor point, a busy Caldwell sent someone to buy aerosols containing the most offensive shade of green they could find.

"*We were going to paint the whole car bright lime green,*" Caldwell later told Vintage Racecar. "*Wheels, tyres, springs, everything.*" But then Bruce qualified on the front row, and the organisers suddenly realised that there wasn't a Ferrari alongside him and rushed back to the McLaren pit. "*They said, 'The car's still red? Good. Leave it red!',*" Caldwell remembered. "*Turns out it would have been the first instance, since the dawn of time [actually 1962], when there wasn't a red car on the front row of the Italian Grand Prix!*"

Unfortunately, the race story was less amusing. Bruce ran quite strongly after a terribly ragged start that was so typical of Monza at that time, but by the time John Surtees narrowly beat Jack Brabham to the finish line, the M5A had long been gone with a suspected shattered cylinder liner.

At the wheel of the M5A, Bruce could well have won the new car's first race, the Canadian GP at Mosport. A flat battery was all that stood between him and a historic first victory.

The front suspension featured single top links and radius arms, lower wishbones, an anti-roll bar mounted to the front bulkhead and Koni outboard coil spring/damper units.

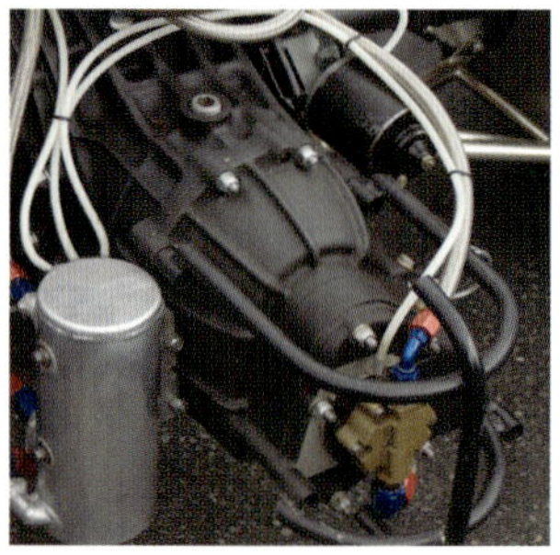

The very first BRM V12 engine built was supplied to McLaren for use in the M5A. Mated to a Hewland DG 5-speed transaxle it could, with a bit of good fortune, have won its first race.

The aluminium alloy panelled monocoque formed over steel bulkheads had long pontoon extensions at the rear to support the BRM V12 engine. The rear suspension was bolted to the bulkhead.

1967 FORMULA 1 McLAREN M5A

CONTINUED

In October at Watkins Glen a split coolant hose removed the car from the US GP after just 16 laps, after Bruce had qualified ninth. The season ended in Mexico three weeks later, and there Bruce felt that they never got the V12 running cleanly in the thin air at high altitude. He qualified eighth but, lacking the horsepower to be truly competitive, struggled in sixth place before the oil pressure began to droop. Keen to preserve his team's one and only F1 engine, he quit from 13th place after 45 laps and was able to watch Denny Hulme roar on to clinch the World Championship title.

Bruce had dramatic plans for 1968 which centred on a two-car team of Ford Cosworth-powered M7As for himself and new signing Hulme, but the M5A lived to fight another season, initially in the hands of the reigning World Champion. For the first time a single seater McLaren appeared in what had become the team's trademark papaya orange thanks to the successes the previous year of the Can-Am M6As. Running with very limited resources as Bruce stayed at home working on the M7As, Denny put the car ninth on the grid for the South African GP and raced it home to a solid fifth place, marking the only time it ever scored World Championship points in works' hands.

Thereafter it was sold to Swedish racer Joakim (Jo) Bonnier, who was in the twilight of his career. He painted it in his Joakim Bonnier Racing Team livery of yellow with white and red stripes and campaigned it as a privateer, with a best placing of sixth in a race of high attrition at Monza. M5A-1 was subsequently transformed into a unique work of art when JoBo famously hung it vertically on a wall in his Lausanne home. It remained there until, some time after his death at Le Mans in 1972, his widow Marianne sold it to fellow Swedish enthusiast Gunnar Elmgren. After undergoing a full restoration in the UK, it appeared at the Goodwood Revival race meeting in September of 1999, when unfortunately Sir Jack Brabham crashed it heavily backwards into a bank after a collision with Jackie Oliver's Lotus. It was restored for a second time and now resides in Seattle, Washington, as part of telephonics magnate Bruce McCaw's collection.

After being used by Hulme in the first race of 1968, the South African GP, the M5A was sold to Jo Bonnier. His first outing was the Race of Champions at Brands Hatch, he retired on lap 30.

Back at Brands for the British Grand Prix in July, Bonnier's race was even shorter. On lap seven he pulled into the pits with a suspected dropped valve on the BRM engine.

The first race for the M5A was the Canadian Grand Prix at Mosport at the end of August 1967. Bruce drove the M5A for the last time. Although he finished seventh, he could have won.

In the final race of 1967, the Mexican Grand Prix, Bruce drove the M5A for the last time. From seventh on the grid he ran sixth for much of the race but retired on lap 45 with failing oil pressure.

M5A FORMULA 1
SPECIFICATION

MODEL	McLaren M5A
TYPE/FORMULA	Formula 1
YEAR OF PRODUCTION	1967
DESIGNER	Robin Herd
EXAMPLES BUILT	1
ENGINE	BRM V12
CUBIC CAPACITY	2998cc
CARBURATION	Lucas fuel injection
POWER OUTPUT	370bhp

TRANSMISSION	Hewland DG500 5-speed
CHASSIS	20swg aluminium alloy monocoque, steel bulkheads
BODY	Monocoque sides, GRP nose & cockpit surround
FRONT SUSPENSION	Single top link & radius arm, lower wishbone,
	outboard coil spring/damper, anti-roll bar
REAR SUSPENSION	Reverse lower wishbone, top link, twin radius
	rods, outboard coil spring/damper, anti-roll bar
BRAKES F/R	Outboard Lockheed discs & calipers
WHEELS DIAMETER x WIDTH F/R	13x8.5/15x12in

TYRES F/R	Goodyear
LENGTH	162in - 4115mm
WIDTH	70.5in - 1791mm
HEIGHT	26.5in - 673mm
WHEELBASE	95in - 2413mm
TRACK F/R	58/58in - 1473/1473mm
WEIGHT	1180lb - 535kg
PRINCIPAL DRIVERS	McLaren, Hulme, Bonnier
IDENTIFYING COLOURS	Red, Orange

1967 CAN-AM McLAREN M6A

The McLaren M6A was the third major design that Robin Herd prepared for the team in 1967, and the most successful. Working with draughtsman Gordon Coppuck, a colleague from his days at Farnborough, Herd sat down early to work out the parameters of the company's first monocoque Can-Am racer. Using similar chassis technology to that applied earlier to the M5A, and after wind tunnel testing with a modified model of the M1B, the team built three examples of a new sportscar which clearly hit the spot straight out of the box. The M6A was a major turning point in McLaren's fortunes, and was more than to compensate for the late arrival of the BRM F1 engine and its lack of real success thus far in the ultra-lucrative Canadian-American Challenge Cup series.

The M6A also enjoyed the distinction of being the first example of the marque to be painted in the definitive hue that came to be called 'McLaren Orange,' a soft shade of that colour known as papaya. Teddy Mayer had long been unhappy with the team's choice of colour and, having seen a yellow Lola T70 run by British entrant Jackie Epstein, opted for a similar colour which, it was felt *"would show up like a beacon on TV."*

Based around a simple stressed-skin hull, the monocoque was formed via bonded and riveted magnesium and aluminium-alloy panel box structures welded to a square-section tube frame. Fuel was carried in three rubber tanks - one either side of the driver, a third beneath his knees - these being linked via a series of one-way valves to allow the fuel to run freely through the system even under heavy acceleration. The structure was clad in a simple but distinctive aerodynamic glass-fibre body which featured a sharply raked nose to enhance downforce.

Power came from a Bartz-modified, Lucas fuel-injected 6-litre Chevrolet V8 which McLaren built itself in Los Angeles under Gary Knutson's supervision, mated to a five-speed Hewland LG gearbox.

The front suspension comprised outboard coil spring/damper units with lateral links to the top and bottom located by trailing radius rods, and at the rear upper and lower wishbones were employed, with twin radius rods. Once again the car sported McLaren's own cast magnesium wheels, 15 inch diameter all round, and 8.5 inch wide at the front and 13.25 at the rear. Crucially, Bruce had also negotiated a lucrative tyre deal with Goodyear, so the Firestones of yesteryear made way for American-built rubber on the new Group 7 contender.

The M6A was to be Herd's last car for McLaren before he left to design a four-wheel-drive F1 car for Cosworth. It was uncomplicated, apparently straightforward to maintain and run and met Bruce's initial brief to the letter. Impressively it took just 11 weeks to progress from pen-and-paper to a running prototype, M6A-1 being ready for a test session at the Goodwood circuit on June 19th, a full two and a half months before the first race of the season.

With this unusual luxury, Bruce was keen to put 2000 test miles on the car before the season kicked off in order to identify and iron out any possible faults. With a 40:60 weight bias to the rear, the car handled well, and the steep nose seemed to work; to balance the downforce several attempts were made to modify the rear end with small aerodynamic attachments, although none seemed to do much for lap times apart from a small vestigial spoiler on the tail. In hindsight, the effort clearly paid off. After the team devoted so much time to fine-tuning an already impressive machine, the M6A was one of the finest handling machines of its era, as well as boasting one of the greatest success rate in the history of Can-Am racing.

Its first win came on its debut at Road America, Elkhart Lake, on September 3rd 1967. It also marked the beginning of the so-called 'Bruce and Denny Show'. The duo dominated proceedings completely in the first of five McLaren victories that year, and they lost only one of the six races as they crushed their opposition in the J-Wax Can-Am Championship.

At Elkhart Lake it was Denny's turn, Bruce qualifying on pole position but being forced to quit when his engine ran a bearing. Hulme qualified second but led the race from start to finish, setting the fastest lap time, and winning by a resounding 93s. Two weeks later in the Chevron GP at Bridgehampton he did it again, romping home ahead of the field despite a mid-race spin. Bruce finished right behind him to give the team its first 1-2. Significantly, the M6A had also sliced more than three seconds off Jim Hall's 1966 record, thereby signalling the end of Chaparral's dominance.

On September 23rd the cars were in action again, taking first and second places on the grid for the Players 200 at Mosport Park with polesitter Hulme a full 1.6s faster than Jim Clark had been in the F1 Lotus Ford in the recent Canadian Grand Prix. Denny was beginning to look unstoppable after scoring a third consecutive victory. Then Bruce bounced back in the Monterey GP at Laguna Seca on October 15th. He took pole as Denny qualified only third due to ignition and injector trouble. Dan Gurney provided some All American Racers meat in the M6A sandwich, but the 'orange elephants' resumed their habitual places at the front when the American's Lola T70 expired. They stayed that way until the 81st lap, when Hulme's engine blew. Setting the fastest lap, breaking the course record, and actually lapping Hall's Chaparral 2G, Bruce finished a comfortable first.

June 19th 1967 and Bruce takes the M6A for its first run at Goodwood. The team was able to put almost 2000 miles of testing on the car before the first race of the Can-Am season at Road America in September.

Lucas fuel injection gave the 6-litre Chevrolet engine around 630bhp, more than enough to help Bruce and Denny dominate the 1967 Can-Am season.

The M6A was the first McLaren to be painted in what would become the team's trademark colour, papaya orange or, as it familiarly became known, 'McLaren Orange'.

4

4
McLAREN CARS
Bruce McLaren
VALVOLINE
FRAM FILTERS
GOODYEAR
76
STP
CHAMPION
EAGLE
GOODYEAR

1967 CAN-AM McLAREN M6A

CONTINUED

Comfortable, that is, except for the scorching heat of the day - something rectified in part by a member of the pit crew who, acting on orders, threw a bucket of water over Bruce as he passed the pits at the halfway point.

At Riverside the Los Angeles Times GP was altogether tighter. Gurney took pole position, but in the race it was Hall in the Chaparral 2G who hounded Bruce to the flag. The American was only three seconds adrift at the finish. Denny was black-flagged after his M6A sustained bodywork damage thanks to a tyre marker thrown into his path by Parnelli Jones's Lola T70. Thus Bruce now had 30 points and Denny was three shy of him as they headed the final round, the Stardust GP in Las Vegas.

There a broken rocker left Denny on the third row of the grid. Bruce was on pole, but he started the race knowing his engine was mixing oil and water and was duly forced to retire by the eighth lap. Hulme, despite a bad start and a near-miss in traffic in the first turn, steadily began to fight his way through, knowing a fourth place would be sufficient to hand him the Can-Am Championship to go with the F1 World Championship. He had actually risen to third when his engine self-destructed in front of the grandstands. That left 1966 Can-Am champion John Surtees to salvage something from his season, once fellow T70 driver Mark Donohue had run out of fuel. Neither McLaren had finished the race, but Bruce was the new Can-Am champion, with Denny those three points behind in second place. It was a fabulous result for a team that, Bruce admitted, had been brought to its knees in the previous three seasons while "*learning how to go motor racing properly.*"

For 1968, the Championship-winning M6A-1 passed into the hands of the Penske Racing Team, to be driven by Donohue in the 1968 USRRC series. The team installed a 7-litre aluminium-block Chevrolet V8 and with the 'Sunoco Special' painted in Penske's familiar blue and yellow colours, Donohue became the only driver to win back-to-back USRRC titles, with victories in four of the championship rounds. At the end of this, the final year of the USRRC series, Penske sold the double championship-winning chassis to Jerry Hansen and bought a brand new M6B with which to contest the 1969 Can-Am Championship. Hansen also ran in the series, but with the great car now years old and somewhat outdated he didn't have much in the way of results. A seventh at Riverside was the best he could muster.

M6A-1 is possibly the most historically significant Can-Am car in existence, and has been fully restored to its original specification. It now forms a key part of the Mathews Collection in Denver, Colorado. Apart from appearing at the Goodwood Festival of Speed in 2000, it is run just once a year, at the US Can-Am reunion meeting at Road Atlanta.

On the car's debut at the opening round of the 1967 Can-Am season at Road America, Elkhart Lake, Bruce and Denny in their M6As were fully 10 seconds under the previous lap record.

The Penske team took over M6A-1 for 1968 and with the larger 427 block engine, Mark Donohue easily won his second USRRC title.

Opposite.
Bridgehampton 17th Sept 1967. Denny #5 and Bruce #4 line up on the front row alongside Dan Gurney in a Lola T70. Behind them is Jim Hall #66 in the 'Big Wing' Chaparral 2G.

M6A CAN-AM
SPECIFICATION

MODEL	McLaren M6A
TYPE/FORMULA	Can-Am
YEAR OF PRODUCTION	1967
DESIGNER	Robin Herd/Gordon Coppuck
EXAMPLES BUILT	3
ENGINE	Chevrolet V8
CUBIC CAPACITY	5900cc
CARBURATION	Lucas fuel injection
POWER OUTPUT	527bhp

TRANSMISSION	Hewland LG600 5-speed
CHASSIS	Aluminium alloy monocoque, steel bulkheads
BODY	Monocoque sides with 4 GRP body sections
FRONT SUSPENSION	Single top link & radius arm, lower wishbone, outboard coil spring/damper, anti-roll bar
REAR SUSPENSION	Single top link, reverse lower wishbone with twin radius arms, outboard coil spring/damper, anti-roll bar
BRAKES F/R	Outboard 12in Girling ventilated discs
WHEELS DIAMETER x WIDTH F/R	15x8.5/15x13.25in

TYRES F/R	Goodyear
LENGTH	153in - 3886mm
WIDTH	68in - 1727mm
HEIGHT TO TOP OF WINDSCREEN	31in - 787mm
WHEELBASE	91.5in - 2324mm
TRACK F/R	52/52in - 1321/1321mm
WEIGHT	1300lb - 590kg
PRINCIPAL DRIVERS	McLaren, Hulme, Donohue, Hansen
IDENTIFYING COLOURS	Papaya

1968 CAN-AM McLAREN-TROJAN M6B

Whatever the original intention had been, the sensational performance of Bruce and Denny's M6As in their first season in North America - and the factory's continuing dominance of Can-Am racing over the next four years - made the production of cash-generating replicas a certainty. The team's partner company was soon building the first of 26 McLaren-Trojan M6B customer cars that would seemingly form the bulk of the cars running in the Can-Am series for the next few seasons.

Demand for a car capable of consistently good performance - and of defeating not just the likes of Lola and Chaparral but also Ferrari - was naturally strong, with many privateers both in Europe and the US aspiring to replicate its success for themselves. Here the strength and simplicity of Herd and Coppuck's original design came into its own, the truth being that the majority of privateers had neither the resources of a professional works team, nor the technical know-how required to succeed with some of the doubtless brilliant but otherwise temperamental machines from some rival constructors. In the aerodynamically efficient M6B with its race-proven and relatively unstressed American V8, they found a car which, priced around a very competitive $36,000, was ready to race and, in the rights hands, to win.

Of all the privateers associated with McLaren at this time, the best known was Daniel Sexton Gurney, the New York-born son of an opera singer. A keen hot-rodder who was later drafted and served in Korea, Gurney made his name in F1 driving for Ferrari in the late 1950s and thereafter BRM, Porsche and Brabham in the early 1960s before, like Bruce, pursuing his goals as a constructor from 1966 onwards with his F1 and Indianapolis Eagles which raced respectively under the Anglo-American Racers and All-American Racers (AAR) auspices. In 1968, in search of a replacement for the Lola T70 that All-American Racers had fielded in 1967, he bought an M6B. He was impressed with the car, and his sound friendship with Bruce led him to drive a third works McLaren M7A in the Canadian, United States and Mexican GPs that year as Bruce reciprocated Dan's generosity in letting him drive the works Eagle the previous season when Bruce had been betwixt the M4B and the M5A.

Dan was always full of ideas for his cars, and the M6B was heavily modified with many parts manufactured in titanium to minimise weight, and revisions to the suspension geometry. The result was the so-called 'McLeagle', a machine that, though outwardly bearing close resemblance to the standard M6B, was nevertheless unique.

The McLeagle rarely appeared twice in the same guise, such was the pace of its development. Gurney tried different wing set-ups and tail sections, particularly as tyre sizes increased for 1969, and championed his own small-block Ford engines with Gurney Weslake cylinder heads. Eventually when a breakdown in supply caused the team to forfeit six races, a switch was made to a Chevrolet big-block for the final three races in 1969.

In performance, even mostly with the gifted Gurney behind the wheel, the car was never a match for the new McLaren M8A or the subsequent M8B; after a long run of non-finishes, however, Dan finished a respectable fourth at his beloved Riverside in 1969 after running second for much of the race.

At the conclusion of the season the car was purchased by Bob Brown who ran it into 1970 and early 1971 more or less unchanged but for the removal of the high suspension-mounted rear wing in accordance with new regulations. Perhaps because he did not drive the car as quickly, he enjoyed rather more success than Gurney had, with five top 10 finishes in 1970.

The man who won a Can-Am race in an M6B was Mark Donohue, who steered Roger Penske's pristine example to victory at Bridgehampton in September 1968. He fought hard with the M8As and Jim Hall's Chaparral, and when combustion gas blow-by in the M8As' engines pressurised the sump and blew all the oil out, causing them eventually to blow up, and Hall to slow with mechanical difficulties of his own, 'Captain Nice' scooped the spoils.

Since McLaren was always working on its own cars for 'The Bruce and Denny Show', customer cars were always based on the previous year's model. Bruce naturally liked to keep to himself any small detail improvements in terms of both hardware and application. But while they might not have been able to challenge the works car, many customer cars enjoyed a good long run of activity and were competitive with the best of rivals' products.

Privateer Dick Brown of Detroit drove his car competitively in both the 1968 and '69 Can-Am seasons, before selling it to fellow Detroiter Gordon Barrett who, after completing a rebuild, entered it for a further two years with Tom Dutton as the driver. Remarkably it was back for more punishment in 1972, now with a replacement 7-litre Ford engine. This was a not uncommon conversion, which was usually accompanied by the fitting of a four-speed gearbox, the larger engines having sufficient torque to do without an extra ratio.

Roger McCaig's M6B Chevrolet heads Jim Paul's M1C in the penultimate round of the 1968 Can-Am championship at Riverside in October. Both cars failed to finish.

The basic simplicity of the car combined with the strength of the unstressed American V8 used in the M6B made it an ideal customer car. In both 1968 and 1969 it made up a large percentage of the grids in the Can-Am series.

The Trojan-built M6B could be bought as a competitive race ready car for around $36,000 and helped turn around the financial situation at McLaren.

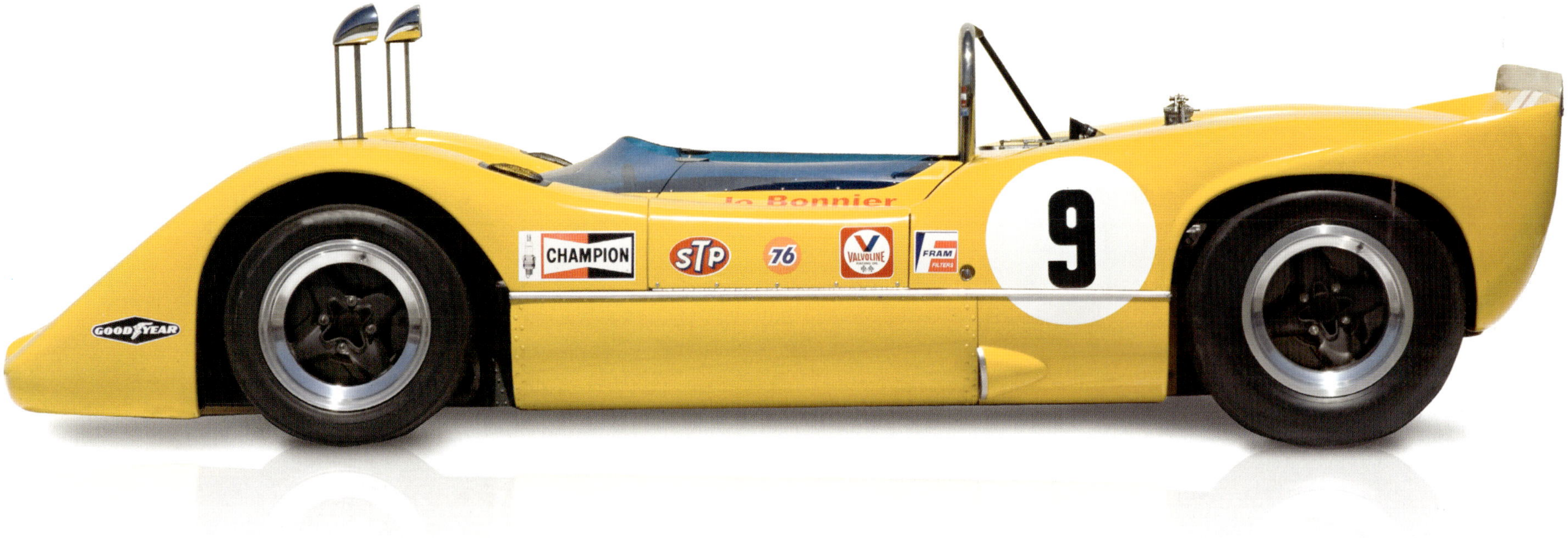
GOODYEAR
CHAMPION
STP
76
VALVOLINE
FRAM
9

1968 CAN-AM McLAREN-TROJAN M6B

CONTINUED

In the 1968 Riverside Can-Am race Jerry Titus (McLaren M6B-Chevrolet) qualified 10th but pulled into the pits to retire on the 50th of the 62 laps.

A fourth place finish in the Can-Am race at Riverside in 1969 gave Dan Gurney his best result in the revised 'McLeagle' McLaren M6B-Chevrolet.

M6B CAN-AM
SPECIFICATION

MODEL	McLaren-Trojan M6B
TYPE/FORMULA	Can-Am
YEAR OF PRODUCTION	1968
DESIGNER	Robin Herd/Gordon Coppuck
EXAMPLES BUILT	26
ENGINE	Chevrolet V8
CUBIC CAPACITY	5900cc
CARBURATION	Lucas fuel injection
POWER OUTPUT	527bhp

TRANSMISSION	Hewland LG600 5-speed
CHASSIS	Aluminium alloy monocoque, steel bulkheads
BODY	Monocoque sides with 4 GRP body sections
FRONT SUSPENSION	Single top link & radius arm, lower wishbone, outboard coil spring/damper, anti-roll bar
REAR SUSPENSION	Single top link, reverse lower wishbone with twin radius arms, outboard coil spring/damper, anti-roll bar
BRAKES F/R	Outboard 12in Girling ventilated discs
WHEELS DIAMETER x WIDTH F/R	15x8.5/15x13.25in

TYRES F/R	Goodyear
LENGTH	155in - 3937mm
WIDTH	68in - 1727mm
HEIGHT	31in - 787mm
WHEELBASE	93.5in - 2375mm
TRACK F/R	52/52in - 1321/1321mm
WEIGHT	1300lb - 590kg
PRINCIPAL DRIVERS	Donohue, Elford, Gurney
IDENTIFYING COLOURS	n/a

1968 & 1969 FORMULA 1
McLAREN M7A & M7B

The elegant M7A tends to be mistaken as the first single seater McLaren that was designed specifically for Formula 1, doubtless because it was the first to succeed. It was another product of the fruitful Robin Herd/Gordon Coppuck pairing.

Like the M6A, the new car proved a winner not just first time out, but on its first two outings. Bruce won the 1968 Daily Mail Race of Champions at Brands Hatch in March, and the following month Denny fought back from a problem when a stone smashed a lens in his goggles, to win the Daily Express International Trophy race at Silverstone. Both were non-championship events, but the M7A was to make the McLaren marque a Grand Prix winner that season, too.

Herd conceived McLaren's first Ford Cosworth DFV-powered contender around a simple, three-quarter length monocoque, following Lotus's lead in using the V8 as a structural element. Transmission was provided by a standard Hewland DG300 five-speed transaxle.

The 1968 Belgian Grand Prix at Spa-Francorchamps gave Bruce McLaren his maiden Grand Prix win as a driver/ constructor. Here M7A/1 leads Pedro Rodriguez in his works BRM P133. After leader Jackie Stewart's Matra stopped for fuel on the penultimate lap they finished first and second.

The chassis was of the so-called bathtub type, open to the top in the fashion of the Lotus 25, and was skinned mainly in 22-gauge L72 aluminium sheet or, in a few places, 20-gauge magnesium sheet, which was riveted and bonded to three internal 20-gauge steel bulkheads. 40 gallons of fuel were distributed between four rubber bag tanks, one each longitudinally on either side of the tub, another behind the driver's seat, and the fourth in the scuttle. Sleek glass-fibre bodywork completed the attractive package. Other notable points were the use of Lockheed brakes, at a time when every other British team opted for Girling.

The suspension was conventional and derived from the M6A's, via outboard coil spring/dampers units both ends and single lateral links and trailing arms at the front and single lateral top links, reversed lower wishbones and twin radius rods at the rear.

There was a story behind the suspension, for Herd had left McLaren to join Cosworth shortly after drawing the M7A's chassis. Bruce had schooled him in the rigours of applying his impressive aerospace knowledge to the practicalities of motor racing, and felt aggrieved when his design protégé upped and left. It was left to Coppuck to do the detail design on the suspension, after Bruce had largely been responsible for the geometry.

McLaren was now reasonably well funded via commercial deals with both Goodyear and Shell, and the two non-championship race successes provided a much-needed boost following Denny's fifth place with the M5A in the opening race in South Africa. Once the Grand Prix season resumed in Spain and Monaco in May, Graham Hill put Lotus back on top. But then came Spa and the Belgian Grand Prix on June 9th, which would prove to be a Red Letter Day for the marque. After early leaders John Surtees in the Honda and Chris Amon in a Ferrari had dropped out, Denny was embroiled in a battle for the lead with Jackie Stewart's Tyrrell-Matra-Ford. Then Denny retired after 18 laps with a driveshaft failure, leaving Bruce fighting the BRMs of Pedro Rodriguez and Piers Courage, and Jacky Ickx's Ferrari, for second place in Stewart's wake. Gradually Bruce dropped his three challengers and was convinced he had finished as the runner-up as he crossed the line. But Stewart had pitted for fuel on the penultimate lap, leaving Bruce to emulate Jack Brabham as only the second man ever to win a Grand Prix in a car bearing his own name. He discovered this from one of BRM's mechanics, who said: "*You've won, didn't you know?*" Bruce recalled later: "*It was about the nicest thing I'd ever been told.*"

As Matra and Ferrari, on Dunlop and Firestone tyres respectively, won subsequent races, and Graham Hill and his Firestone-shod Lotus set the pace aerodynamically after full-blown wings had appeared on the Ferraris and Brabhams at Spa, McLaren lost pace. Its wings were less effective, mounted in the middle of the car on the sprung mass rather than, in Lotus style, at the rear on the unsprung suspension uprights, and Goodyear suffered a dip in competitiveness. But its new G9 tyre came as a boost by Monza in September, where Denny scored a great victory in the Italian GP. He repeated the feat in the next race, at St Jovite in Canada, albeit after faster runners Amon, Jochen Rindt and Jo Siffert had all met trouble, and Bruce brought his M7A home behind him to record McLaren's first-ever 1-2 in a Grand Prix.

The M7A was the first McLaren to use the Ford Cosworth DFV, an engine that would go on to dominate Grand Prix racing for many years.

Denny Hulme won two Grand Prix races in 1968 (Italy and Canada) and finished the season third in the World Drivers' Championship, ahead of Bruce. For the Constructors' title, McLaren came an impressive second behind Lotus with the all conquering Type 49.

REYNOLDS
ALUMINUM
1
Denny Hulme
McLAREN CARS
GOODYEAR

1968 & 1969 FORMULA 1 McLAREN M7A & M7B

CONTINUED

Suddenly the outcome of the World Championship was a three-way fight between Denny, Hill and Stewart, McLaren, Lotus and Matra. The New Zealander and the Englishman had 33 points each, the Scot 27.

Stewart beat Hill in the US GP at Watkins Glen, but Denny unfortunately was forced into retirement while chasing the Lotus driver. First he damaged a rear brake pipe after sliding off course on oil, and lost ground having repairs effected; then he slid off the road again, badly damaging his car but not himself. Now he trailed Hill (39 points) and Stewart (36) with his 33. The only consolation was Dan Gurney's fourth place in the third M7A.

This time there was to be no New Zealand fairy tale in Mexico. Hill wrapped up the title with victory for Lotus, as a fuel feed problem left Stewart seventh and Denny crashed out after 11 laps with a suspected broken rear damper. He thus had to be content with third place in the World Championship for Drivers as Bruce finished fifth overall, having taken second place in Mexico. Despite the disappointment, their placings were an indication of the growing strength of the young marque. In its first full season with a pukka F1 car, McLaren had won three Grands Prix and two non-championship races, challenged for the title, and finished second (ahead of Matra) in the World Championship for Constructors, just 13 points shy of Lotus.

1969 was less successful, and saw Jackie Stewart's Dunlop-shod Matra Ford dominate. Bruce nevertheless repeated Denny's third place in the World Championship for Drivers, mainly through consistency, while Denny had to settle for sixth after a frustrating year of poor reliability. But 'The Bear' bounced back with a crushing victory in the Mexican Grand Prix as he ran away and hid even from the fleet Brabhams of Ickx and proprietor Jack Brabham which enjoyed the same new Goodyear G20 tyres as his McLaren.

Bruce's regular 1968 M7A was sold to South African Basil van Rooyen for 1969 and at that year's Grand Prix at Kyalami he was the fastest local qualifier before brake trouble put him out of the race. He would remain a leading light in South Africa's domestic F1 series with the car, and was leading overall after the first three races with 24 points to rival John Love's 15. But then M7A-1 was destroyed late in May in a spectacular accident during testing for the Republic Festival Trophy race at Kyalami when a rear tyre deflated at 160mph.

Despite the diversion with the four-wheel-drive M9A, development of the M7 concept continued. M7A-3, which Gurney had raced in 1968, is believed to have been reworked substantially to become the unique M7B, though even today the situation remains unclear.

Pursuing one of his pet themes concerning fuel placement to enhance rear tyre grip, Bruce had Coppuck redesign the chassis with wide pannier tanks skinned into the car's central structure.

Coppuck also did a lot of work on aerofoil-section front wings, after making do with just small trim tabs in 1968, and a succession of increasingly large rear wings located on tall struts on the rear suspension uprights.

On the M7B's South African debut, Bruce drove to a steady fifth place. Two weeks later, at Brands Hatch for the Race of Champions, the car had acquired a tall suspension-mounted front wing but it was removed after practice. Bruce ran fifth until a pit stop to replace the spark box, and having rejoined briefly before retiring, he cast the M7B aside and switched his focus to the forthcoming M7C, disappointed that his experimental car had not delivered the performance advantage expected of it.

Classic car enthusiast Colin Crabbe, of Antique Automobiles, had been so excited when his driver Vic Elford took an aged Cooper-Maserati to seventh place at Monaco that he bought the M7B. It was repainted in his maroon and white colours and Elford qualified it last for the Dutch GP in June before finishing 10th.

The car was subtly modified in time for its next appearance, for the French GP at Clermont-Ferrand early in July, with new anti-roll bars and a downforce generating tea tray-shaped cover over the engine. After a steady run and the retirement of more fancied runners, the former rally star brought the car home fifth, to Crabbe's undisguised delight. Later that month Elford took sixth place at Silverstone in the British GP.

The team headed for the German GP full of optimism, especially as Elford was widely recognised as a 'Ring expert and had an extra 300rpm from a revised exhaust system. He qualified a brilliant sixth, only two seconds off Denny in his M7A and nearly two faster than Bruce in the M7C.

Sadly, the race brought disaster. Elford made a poor start, and hit one of the wheels torn off Mario Andretti's four-wheel-drive Lotus 63 when that car bottomed out on the opening lap and crashed. The M7B was completely destroyed as it was launched over a fence and landed upside down. Elford suffered a seriously dislocated right arm. Crabbe's dream was over.

In 1970 Formula 5000 hotshoes Peter Gethin and Reine Wisell had outings in the non-championship races at Brands Hatch and Silverstone respectively in M7A-2, before it was sold to privateer Tony Dean who ran it in Formula 5000 in 1971 with a 5-litre Chevrolet.

At the 1968 Spanish Grand Prix chassis M7A/3 ran with a pair of Lancia D50-style pannier fuel tanks. Bruce dropped out of the race with a mechanical problem after 77 laps.

In Monte Carlo both team cars featured the customary 'Monaco' style short nose. Having run as high as third, Denny Hulme finished fifth, scoring points for the third race in a row.

The British Grand Prix at Brands Hatch in July 1968 saw the team experimenting with 'wings'. Here Bruce tries the small version mounted in a fairly low position above the engine,

After practising M7B-1 (the heavily revised M7A/3) at the 1969 Race of Champions with high wings both front and rear. Bruce chose to run the race with just the tall rear wing. He retired on lap 10.

Denny Hulme used M7A/2 with just the rear wing fitted all weekend and finished the race in third place, behind Stewart's Matra (which led from start to finish) and Hill in the Lotus 49.

M7A FORMULA 1

SPECIFICATION

MODEL	McLaren M7A
TYPE/FORMULA	Formula 1
YEAR OF PRODUCTION	1968/1969
DESIGNER	Robin Herd/Gordon Coppuck
EXAMPLES BUILT	3
ENGINE	Ford Cosworth DFV
CUBIC CAPACITY	2993cc
CARBURATION	Lucas fuel injection
POWER OUTPUT	410bhp

TRANSMISSION	Hewland DG300 5-speed
CHASSIS	Aluminium 'bathtub' monocoque, steel bulkheads
BODY	Monocoque sides, GRP nose & cockpit surround
FRONT SUSPENSION	Single top link & radius arm, lower wishbone, outboard coil spring/damper
REAR SUSPENSION	Reverse lower wishbone, top link, twin radius rods, outboard coil spring/damper, anti-roll bar
BRAKES F/R	Outboard 11.66in ventilated discs
WHEELS DIAMETER x WIDTH F/R	15x10/15x15in

TYRES F/R	Goodyear
LENGTH	158in - 4013mm
WIDTH AT COCKPIT	28in - 711mm
HEIGHT AT WING	35in - 889mm
WHEELBASE	94in - 2387mm
TRACK F/R	58/57in - 1473/1447mm
WEIGHT	1140lb - 517kg
PRINCIPAL DRIVERS	McLaren, Hulme
IDENTIFYING COLOURS	Papaya

1968 CAN-AM McLAREN M8A

"*McLaren's Mephistophelian M8*," Motor Sport once reported, "*fires up like the Battle of Jutland.*" It was certainly a monster, in more ways than one. Possessed of immense power and presence, the car that the magazine memorably described as "*the world's fastest slice of Double Gloucester*", soon built up a formidable reputation for winning, and doing so consistently.

Once again the design credit for the M8 series goes to Gordon Coppuck, who this time worked closely with new recruit Jo Marquart. Legend has it that since, at 33, neither was quite yet ready to design a complete car, one took the front end and the other the rear. While Marquart tidied up the nose - not dissimilar to the earlier M6A's, and with a huge, flat scoop to keep the brakes cool - and drew the new, wider bathtub monocoque, Coppuck was charged with the more complex task of mounting the engine and hanging the rear suspension on a Hewland LG500 transmission.

Whatever the truth, the results spoke themselves. In various forms - at one point the team was using mammoth liner-less 9.3-litre blocks for qualifying - from 1968 onwards the simple but immensely strong M8s were to enjoy a fabulous winning streak until the final victory came courtesy of French Tyrrell Formula 1 star François Cevert with an M8F at Donnybrooke in 1972.

Inevitably the M8A shared much with Robin Herd's M6A, but to save weight and enhance torsional stiffness the engine was now employed as a fully-stressed member rather than being located between twin pontoons. The concept of using the engine as a stressed chassis member had been pioneered on the Lancia D50 in 1954 and reintroduced on BRM's P83 H16 and the Lotus 43 in 1966 before being repeated on all Ford Cosworth DFV-powered F1 cars since the Lotus 49 in 1967.

It was unusual for a sportscar's engine to be installed thus, but everything on the M8 was done for a reason. The car was four inches wider, the extra width needed to accommodate the larger tyres available from Goodyear; 74-gallon fuel tanks also took up much of the extra space and were necessary to keep up with the thirst of the larger capacity engine – an aluminium-block 7-litre Chevrolet as usual developed in McLaren's Los Angeles facility by Gary Knutson and Bruce's former mechanic from New Zealand, Colin Beanland. These units were not especially lightweight, offering very little advantage in this regard over the previous season's iron-block 6-litre, but they produced some 100bhp more.

The cars also lost a gear as the Hewland gearbox used four rather than five ratios; this was predominantly because Can-Am's rolling starts meant a conventional first was unnecessary, but also because it saved 12lb over the LG600 gearbox and facilitated the use of shorter driveshafts that were less likely to suffer under the immense torque.

What the press referred to as "*the McLaren Magic*" was to earn the team four wins out of the six Can-Am races that season, but it took it until fairly late in the series to get to grips with the engines. Several problems manifested themselves in the new dry-sump lubrication system, which enabled the V8s to sit five inches lower than in the M6A.

The M8A was more conservative than radical, but as Coppuck later observed the plan wasn't to innovate but to win. "*We could have made it lighter, used a bigger engine, fitted a wing," he admitted, "but reliability was a prime function.*"

The M6A's flowing, sinuous shape gave way to a dramatic square-shouldered wedge which inspired Motor Sport's cheese reference. Alongside the likes of Jim Hall's 2G Chaparral, with its large overhead rear wing, the brutish M8As certainly looked the part: neat, trim and reassuringly threatening.

The Can-Am Championship had now become a major series and in 1968 massive crowds were on hand to see McLaren cars win all six of the races. Two of the victories went to privateers, Mark Donohue and John Cannon driving an M6B and an M1B respectively, but the other four were down to Bruce and Denny. Bruce won at Riverside and Denny took the honours at Road America, Edmonton and Las Vegas to clinch the championship as Bruce placed second overall. Throughout the year McLaren's performance consistency was reflected as the M8A took pole position for all six races.

At the end of the year the three M8As were rebuilt as M8Bs and used by the team for the 1969 season. In 1970 one of them, M8B-2, which had originally been M8A-2, passed nto the hands of privateer Lothar Motschenbacher. After being involved in a crash at Elkhart Lake it was put aside and later turned into an M8D showcar for Goodyear. In 1978 the car was returned to New Zealand to be restored and put on display at the Museum of Transport and Technology in Auckland.

After disappearing for several years and nearly being destroyed, the only surviving M8A is now in the hands of the Bruce McLaren Trust. With work having started in 2006, it is planned to have it restored (see photographs on right) to full running condition by the end of 2008.

The M8A design by Gordon Coppuck and Jo Marquart was a clean, simple and logical development of the M6A. Its wide, squat look was the epitome of sportscar design.

For 1968 McLaren finally went over to using the 'big-block' 7-litre Chevrolet engine that some other teams had been testing for nearly two seasons. The tall curved hand crafted 'stack-pipes' were highly distinctive.

More Goodwood testing. Once again Bruce put many miles on the new car in preparation for the forthcoming season. It paid off with the M8A dominating the 1968 Can-Am series.

In January of 1969 Denny Hulme's Can-Am Championship-winning M8A from the previous year was displayed at the Racing Car Show held at Earls Court in London.

M8A CAN-AM
SPECIFICATION

MODEL	McLaren M8A
TYPE/FORMULA	Can-Am
YEAR OF PRODUCTION	1968
DESIGNER	Gordon Coppuck/Jo Marquart
EXAMPLES BUILT	3
ENGINE	Chevrolet V8
CUBIC CAPACITY	6997cc
CARBURATION	Lucas fuel injection
POWER OUTPUT	620bhp

TRANSMISSION	Hewland LG500 4-speed
CHASSIS	Aluminium sheet monocoque with steel bulkheads
BODY	Monocoque sides, with 4 GRP body sections
FRONT SUSPENSION	Single top link & radius arm, lower wishbone, outboard coil spring/damper, anti-roll bar
REAR SUSPENSION	Reverse lower wishbone, single top link, twin radius rods, coil spring/damper, anti-roll bar
BRAKES F/R	Outboard 12in ventilated discs
WHEELS DIAMETER x WIDTH F/R	15x10/15x15in

TYRES F/R	Goodyear
LENGTH	154in - 3911mm
WIDTH	72in - 1829mm
HEIGHT	30in - 762mm
WHEELBASE	94in - 2387mm
TRACK F/R	58/56in - 1473/1422mm
WEIGHT	1450lb - 658kg
PRINCIPAL DRIVERS	McLaren, Hulme, Motschenbacher
IDENTIFYING COLOURS	Papaya

1969 ROADCAR McLAREN M6GT

An even more remarkable notion than the 26 Can-Am winner replica M6As built by Trojan - and perhaps the best possible expression of the original American 'Win on Sunday, sell on Monday' philosophy - was Bruce's decision to build a short run of roadgoing McLarens.

It was never that straightforward, however. Following the M6A's runaway success in Group 7, McLaren announced its intention to join the lucrative Group 4 GT series for 1969. It was a fast, exciting, and glamorous series with big names including Ferrari, Porsche and Alfa Romeo all fighting for glory, and the plan was to mate the existing M6 chassis to a new coupe body which would be more suitable for endurance racing.

Unfortunately for McLaren, after the initial 'official' paperwork had been completed, the FIA changed the rules governing homologation for the World Championship of Makes, requiring manufacturers to complete a minimum of 50 examples before a car could be considered. Faced with such a requirement McLaren - which had always intended to sell the cars without engines - shelved the project realising that it was simply too big to take on.

Nevertheless, a prototype was completed for Bruce's personal use while evaluating it as a possible McLaren-branded roadcar which might be licensed to an outside manufacturer such as Trojan. The Can-Am victories had brought funds into the company, and now Bruce - always more than just a driver - was keen to test his skills as an innovator, designer and entrepreneur.

The intention was to build the car, which Bruce designed himself, to the very highest specification possible - something echoed decades later in the awe-inspiring McLaren F1 project - with as many as 250 units being completed each year. It was a tall order, as were the performance parameters - it was to have the fastest top speed of any roadcar in the world, and be the fastest-accelerating - though McLaren hoped to enhance its chances by using an off-the-shelf 7-litre Ford engine. This would save both development time and costs, as well as reduce the need for sophisticated aftersales service and maintenance. As a 'McLaren' it would, needless to say, be based on the latest developments in race engineering, something Bruce recognised would be an immense draw when it came to sales in the large and lucrative US market.

Ultimately no more than three, possibly four, M6GTs were ever built, and only one was built at the McLaren Racing factory. Registered OBH 500H, this was the development car which Bruce used on the roads of South England until his death in June 1970; the other examples were contracted out to Trojan.

Something of a schizophrenic machine, destined always to be a racing car with a new body rather than a convincingly civilised roadcar, the M6GT was surprisingly light and at 1600lb weighed no more than a Mini. It was also phenomenally noisy. Even with the tyres set at the recommended pressures for what the factory referred to as 'quiet driving', the sound of the engine and tyre noise inside the cockpit was nothing less than deafening. At the same time the wider rear wheels made carrying a spare more than a little impractical, as did the need for the driver to get out and raise the headlights manually. Unlike the F1 roadcar of the 1990s, luggage space was virtually non-existent.

The M6GT was also so low at 41 inches that many other road users simply failed to notice it despite an appearance which could hardly be considered discrete, and the noise it generated. It was nevertheless an intoxicating concept: a genuinely street-legal roadcar based like its Can-Am cousins on an authentic monocoque chassis with aluminium panelling over steel bulkheads. The 370bhp Bartz-tuned Chevrolet 5.7-litre LT1 engine used in Bruce's car ensured sparkling performance, with a top speed estimated to be in excess of 165mph and a zero to 100mph time of eight seconds.

Bruce used the prototype as his daily transport for more than six months, travelling to and from the office as well as attending race meetings that were relatively close to home, as he was keen to discover exactly what it was like as a roadcar. He was intimately involved in the development of what was very much a pet project, and in the final analysis the M6GT is best viewed as a personal testament to his vision for the company.

Perhaps because of this, the project died with him. Denny Hulme bought OBH 500H, chassis BMR6GT-1, with its original engine (No.8932386) from the factory and shipped it home to New Zealand, where it went on display in Auckland at the Museum of Transportation and Technology. The car changed hands a couple of times thereafter, before joining the other McLarens in the Mathews Collection. It is still in remarkably original condition - even the fuel and brake lines are unchanged - and with just 1,918 miles on the odometer it still has the same tyres it had when Bruce used it back in 1970.

The official FIA homologation papers for the M6GT, submitted to the RAC in August 1967, show the M6GT as nothing more than an M6A fitted with lights, a rudimentary roof and crude luggage bags strapped to the tail section.

The headlights on the M6GT were manually operated and had to be raised and lowered by using the finger hole provided in the leading edge of the pod.

Bruce arrived in the paddock at Brands Hatch for the 1970 1000 km race in the M6GT. He was named on the entry list to drive the Ecurie Evergreen M8C and, having tested the car at Goodwood earlier in the week, agreed to drive the car in official practice. However, after suspension problems lost the team a lot of time, he never drove the car that weekend.

M6GT ROADCAR
SPECIFICATION

MODEL	McLaren M6GT
TYPE/FORMULA	Roadcar
YEAR OF PRODUCTION	1969
DESIGNER	Bruce McLaren/Gordon Coppuck
EXAMPLES BUILT	1 (+3 Trojan built)
ENGINE	Chevrolet LT1
CUBIC CAPACITY	5740cc
CARBURATION	Quad four-barrel Holley
POWER OUTPUT	370bhp

TRANSMISSION	ZF 5DS-26, 5-speed
CHASSIS	Aluminium alloy sheet monocoque, steel bulkheads
BODY	Reinforced polyester resin panelling
FRONT SUSPENSION	Single top link & radius arm, lower wishbone,
	outboard coil spring/damper, anti-roll bar
REAR SUSPENSION	Reverse lower wishbone, single top link,
	twin radius rods, coil spring/damper
BRAKES F/R	Outboard Girling 12in ventilated discs
WHEELS DIAMETER x WIDTH F/R	12x10/15x14in

TYRES F/R	Goodyear
LENGTH	166in - 4216mm
WIDTH	75in - 1905mm
HEIGHT	39in - 990mm
WHEELBASE	93.5in - 2375mm
TRACK F/R	53.5/56in - 1359/1422mm
WEIGHT	1600lb - 725kg
PRINCIPAL DRIVERS	McLaren
IDENTIFYING COLOURS	Red

1969 FORMULA 1
McLAREN M7C & M7D

Another one-off design creation, the M7C was another of Bruce's pet projects that used a monocoque similar to that employed in the recently launched McLaren M10A Formula 5000 car.

Created by Gordon Coppuck for the start of the European leg of the 1969 season, the M7C's chassis differed markedly from the open-topped bathtub-style chassis of the M7As. Now the aluminium skin extended all the way over the driver's legs as well as around the cockpit opening, creating a cigar tube shape more akin to the 1964 BRM P261. From start to finish it was clearly something of a hurried project, as Bruce was concerned that his other 1969 experiment, the wide-panniered M7B, lacked the torsional rigidity and straight-line speed it required to be fully competitive.

Accordingly, the sole M7C to be built was completed only the night before practice for the 1969 International Trophy non-championship F1 race at Silverstone. It was logical to use many M10A components in its construction, since that car was more recent than the now dated M7A and boasted better torsional rigidity and safety. The nose was straight from an M10A, while the monocoque was a clear derivative albeit with the pontoons that were used to support a heavy 5-litre Chevrolet or Ford V8 cut off so that the Ford Cosworth DFV engine could be used as a stressed chassis member. The suspension components, running gear and fuel tanks were still M7A specification, however.

On that non-championship debut the car was equipped with a strutted and endplated rear wing mounted on the suspension uprights and braced to the roll-over hoop. Bruce drove to a steady sixth in a race spoiled by rain, a lap down on winner Jack Brabham.

By the time the M7C arrived for the Spanish Grand Prix, it had been equipped with wider front wheels which lightened the steering by allowing reduced offset, and mounting points on the front suspension for another wing, as yet unfitted. Bruce was unhappy with the handling in practice, but this was a general complaint for Goodyear's runners. The race was better, as Bruce steadily worked his way up as both Jochen Rindt and Graham Hill crashed their Lotuses heavily due to wing failures, and Chris Amon's Ferrari blew its engine. From his uninspiring 13th on the grid he climbed to a survivor's second place by the finish, albeit two laps adrift of fortunate winner Jackie Stewart.

At Monaco in mid-May the bright orange M7C appeared in its most flamboyant form as it now sported high, strutted wings at both ends. McLaren had finally started to catch up with Lotus and Brabham in the aero department. But it was too late. Following the Lotus crashes at Montjuich Park during the Spanish GP, the CSI moved quickly and overnight banned such devices after first practice on the Thursday. That obliged everyone to think again, and the McLarens appeared subsequently with small ducktail lips over their engines. Neither the M7C nor Denny's conventional M7A performed well on the famous street circuit. Bruce finished fifth, one place ahead of his team-mate.

Revised aerodynamic tea tray 'wings' appeared on the cars in Holland, where Denny finished fourth but a stub axle problem sidelined Bruce, who subsequently took the M7C to fourth place in the French GP at Clermont-Ferrand after Denny was delayed by a broken anti-rollbar having started from the front row in his M7A. By the British GP interpretations of the CSI's rules had stabilised around low-mounted aerofoils, and the McLarens were thus equipped for the British GP at Silverstone in July. Denny again started from the front row but succumbed this time to a suspected broken camshaft as Bruce took the M7C to a distant third place. For the German Grand Prix in August Bruce had 13in diameter front wheels of 12in width on the M7C and again took third as Denny retired with transmission failure, and both cars sported extra strap-on fuel tanks for the Italian GP at Monza. Bruce finished fourth as a quartet of drivers lunged for the finish line. He was 0.19s away from the victorious Stewart, with Jochen Rindt and Jean-Pierre Beltoise somehow shoehorned between them.

Denny suffered yet again at Monza with fading brakes and clutch, while poised to fight for the victory, and fell victim to distributor failure in Canada where Bruce took fifth place well behind a Brabham 1-2. Denny started from the front row in the US GP at Watkins Glen but retired with gear selector problems. Bruce failed to start after qualifying sixth only 0.6s off Rindt's pole position, following engine failure on the warming up lap. Exactly the same thing happened to him in Mexico, where a piece of metal jammed the fuel pressure relief valve open, but at least Denny won going away in the M7A to end the season on a high note.

John Surtees had decided to follow the examples of Jack Brabham, Bruce and Dan Gurney and become an F1 constructor in 1970, but until his own Surtees TS7 was ready he purchased the unique M7C. It was repainted in Surtees red with the distinctive white arrow stripe down the nose, and he participated in the Race of Champions and four Grands Prix. He scored a point for sixth place with it in the Dutch GP, but none of the other outings was successful. He was sidelined by engine failure in South Africa and Monaco, the gearbox in Spain, and by a sticking throttle in the non-championship race at Brands Hatch.

The TS7 made its debut in the British GP at Brands Hatch in July and the M7C passed into the hands of Jo Bonnier to replace the aged M5A. Racing now as Ecurie Bonnier, he failed to qualify in Italy and burst a water pipe in the USGP at Watkins Glen.

In the paddock at the 1969 Dutch Grand Prix at Zandvoort, M7C/1 (#6) driven by Bruce and Hulme's car M7A/2, on the left, are fuelled up for the start of the race.

In a concept pioneered by Colin Chapman on the Lotus 49, the DFV engine used on the M7 series was bolted directly to the back of the monocoque and was a fully stressed part of the car on which the gearbox and rear suspension were hung.

The front 'high' wing was bolted on to the chassis bulkhead of the M7C where it picked up the front suspension. The rear wing was attached directly to the suspension uprights, applying a significant amount of downforce directly to the rear tyres.

M7C FORMULA 1
SPECIFICATION

MODEL	McLaren M7C
TYPE/FORMULA	Formula 1
YEAR OF PRODUCTION	1969
DESIGNER	Gordon Coppuck
EXAMPLES BUILT	1
ENGINE	Ford Cosworth DFV
CUBIC CAPACITY	2993cc
CARBURATION	Lucas fuel injection
POWER OUTPUT	420bhp

TRANSMISSION	Hewland DG300 5-speed
CHASSIS	360° aluminium monocoque, steel bulkheads
BODY	Monocoque sides, GRP nose & cockpit surround
FRONT SUSPENSION	Single top link & radius arm, lower wishbone,
	outboard coil spring/damper, anti-roll bar
REAR SUSPENSION	Reverse lower wishbone, top link, twin radius
	rods, outboard coil spring/damper, anti-roll bar
BRAKES F/R	Outboard 11.66in ventilated discs
WHEELS DIAMETER x WIDTH F/R	15x10/15x15in

TYRES F/R	Goodyear
LENGTH	158in - 4013mm
WIDTH OF MONOCOQUE	28in - 711mm
HEIGHT OF REAR WING	58in - 1473mm
WHEELBASE	94in - 2387mm
TRACK F/R	58/57in - 1473/1447mm
WEIGHT	1140lb - 517kg
PRINCIPAL DRIVERS	McLaren, Hulme, Bonnier, Surtees
IDENTIFYING COLOURS	Papaya, Red

1969 FORMULA 1 McLAREN M7C & M7D

CONTINUED

The M7C next appeared at the non-championship Gran Premio de la Republica Argentina in Buenos Aires in January 1971, under the auspices of Ecurie Bonnier YPF, repainted silver and driven by local upcoming Formula 2 racer Carlos Reutemann who was making his F1 debut. He did so in some style, his handling of the ageing car showcasing his innate talent. He qualified fifth for the first heat and finished it in sixth place, then came third in a second heat notable for attrition. That was sufficient for third overall, behind the victorious Chris Amon's Matra and Henri Pescarolo in Frank Williams' March Ford.

Bonnier's F1 swansong came later that season as he failed to qualify in Germany, non-started in Austria and ran without distinction in the South African, Italian and US GPs before switching to sportscar racing in 1972.

The M7C was hardly a seminal McLaren, any more than was the M7B which preceded it, but both one-off chassis were testament to Bruce's willingness to experiment, and his canniness in not committing to building more than one chassis until a concept was proven.

The final iteration of the M7 series was another one-off, the M7D, but this one was more than just an experiment. The McLaren Register refers to the construction of the car under 'exploratory use', but the company is believed to have been paid to build it by Alfa Romeo's technical director Carlo Chiti, who often had to resort to subterfuge to avoid the political pressures on his Autodelta racing offshoot that were a frequent corollary of working for a state-run manufacturer. The M7D would be powered by a modified version of Alfa Romeo's 3-litre V8 which had its roots in sportscar racing and would see duty that season in Autodelta's 33 racers in long distance events. Reportedly it was a brand new chassis numbered M7D/1-5 (to demonstrate it was the fifth car built in the M7 series), built on the old M7A jigs, but a question mark remains over whether the chassis was actually the original M7A-3 whose chassis number had been used on the M7B.

The car first appeared at Jarama for the 1970 Spanish Grand Prix in mid-April. The V8 was said to produce around 425bhp but its trump card, according to Alfa Romeo, would be its healthy torque which should have been perfect for the sinuous Spanish track. Unfortunately, McLaren would soon discover wide discrepancies in performance between individual engines. Autodelta works driver Andrea de Adamich was 14th of the 22 runners in first practice, with a respectable lap of 1m 25.8s compared to pacesetter Denny Hulme's 1m 24.1s. Curiously, they recorded exactly the same times and occupied exactly the positions in the second session, on Friday afternoon. As Jack Brabham improved the pole position time to 1m 23.9s in the final session, de Adamich cut his time to 1m 25.15s but dropped a place, and in any case the time was recorded in a special qualifying session for non-seeded drivers which did not count for grid positions. Overall, he missed the cut by 0.1s, and after talk of letting the non-qualifiers into the race faded in the face of CSI refusal, did not get to start.

By Monaco the Alfa engine was reportedly producing its 425bhp, and bearing in mind its torque, de Adamich was expected to qualify well. Again he started well, with 14th fastest time in the first practice session, but ultimately lost out in the non-qualifiers' shoot-out when his 1m 26.1s best left him seventh after he had brushed a kerb, and therefore just out of the picture. Ironically, had he been a seeded driver with that time, it would have been good enough to make the grid.

The M7D's next appearance was to have been at Spa in June but, together with the two works M14As and John Surtees' private M7C, it was withdrawn in the aftermath of Bruce's death at Goodwood on June 2nd.

De Adamich had a new M14D to try in Holland, but reverted to the M7D for the French GP at Clermont-Ferrand on July 5th. There he qualified 15th but finished an unclassified last after a pit stop on the third lap with the engine overheating madly. It was thought that a weak cylinder head seal was pressurising the engine, which was why a water hose had blown off. He continued, made three more pit stops for further attention to the same problem, on laps six, nine and 10, and was nine laps down by the finish.

In the quest for more horsepower Alfa Romeo came up with a half-inch deeper sump for the engine for the British GP at Brands in mid-July, the additional depth requiring the ride height to be set higher to avoid the car bottoming out on the notoriously bumpy track. Even so, the M7D duly did just that and the new sump was damaged. De Adamich was forced to run with the original pan and qualified 19th on 1m 27.1s, but a leaking bag tank was discovered as the car was fuelled just before the race, and since there was no time to change it, he was sidelined yet again.

Thereafter the saga of the M7D Alfa ended as de Adamich reverted to his M14D from the German GP onwards. The M7D never raced again as a works car, but was instead fitted with a Cosworth DFV engine and, together with the experimental M9A, sold to Tom Wheatcroft. In 1973 it went on public display in the Donington Collection, where it can still be seen in this form.

The M7C has been restored to the exact specification that the car was in for the first practice session at Monaco in 1969. The final moments of the 'high wing' era.

The oil tank was hung low down off the back of the gearbox. The engine oil cooler was placed much higher and on top of the gearbox where it protruded into the flow of cooler air coming over the car.

In his second race in M7C/1, the 1970 Race of Champions at Brands Hatch, John Surtees qualified a poor 10th out of the rather small field of just 12 cars. The race went even worse and on lap 10 he was the first to retire, after suffering throttle problems.

After John Surtees progressed to his own TS7 car, Jo Bonnier took on the M7C but couldn't get it round the Nürburgring quick enough to qualify for the 1971 German Grand Prix. He was almost a minute slower than polesitter Jackie Stewart's time of 7m 19s in his Tyrrell 003.

During practice for the Monaco Grand Prix in May 1969 the M7C was in its most flamboyant format. With a full complement of 'high wings' Bruce flashes through the tunnel at high speed.

Andrea de Adamich qualified the Alfa-Romeo engined M7D 18th for the 1970 British GP at Brands Hatch but was a non-starter after a fuel tank split during the pre-race warm up.

M7D FORMULA 1
SPECIFICATION

MODEL	McLaren M7D
TYPE/FORMULA	Formula 1
YEAR OF PRODUCTION	1970
DESIGNER	Gordon Coppuck
EXAMPLES BUILT	1
ENGINE	Alfa Romeo T33 V8
CUBIC CAPACITY	2995cc
CARBURATION	Lucas fuel injection
POWER OUTPUT	425bhp

TRANSMISSION	Hewland DG300 5-speed
CHASSIS	Aluminium 'bathtub' monocoque, steel bulkheads
BODY	Monocoque sides, GRP nose & cockpit surround
FRONT SUSPENSION	Single top link & radius arm, lower wishbone, outboard coil spring/damper, anti-roll bar
REAR SUSPENSION	Reverse lower wishbone, top link, twin radius rods, outboard coil spring/damper, anti-roll bar
BRAKES F/R	Outboard 11.66in ventilated discs
WHEELS DIAMETER x WIDTH F/R	15x10/15x15in

TYRES F/R	Goodyear
LENGTH	160in - 4064mm
WIDTH OF MONOCOQUE	28in - 711mm
HEIGHT OF MONOCOQUE	29in - 736mm
WHEELBASE	96in - 2438mm
TRACK F/R	58/57in - 1473/1447mm
WEIGHT	1140lb - 517kg
PRINCIPAL DRIVERS	de Adamich
IDENTIFYING COLOURS	Papaya

1969 CAN-AM McLAREN M8B

The competition in Can-Am during 1968 had been formidable, but the M8A had prevailed in stunning fashion and Bruce and his team were not about to rest on their laurels.

1969 saw this exciting class of unlimited sportscar racing peak, with 11 races and a $1 million purse. It was also to be a stunning triumph for McLaren, a perfect season in which it won all 11 races, scored an incredible eight 1-2 finishes, and at Michigan a unique Can-Am 1-2-3 as Dan Gurney joined Bruce and Denny. This was a period that saw McLaren under Bruce's management attain a peak of planning, preparation and performance.

The seminal M8B was a common sense evolution by Coppuck. The chassis was lightened and modified, with the aluminium 7.1-litre Chevrolet engine now producing 680bhp and once again acting as a structural member. The key change was the deletion of an unstressed chassis section behind the front wheels to create a cutaway area which appeared to be done to help brake cooling but actually avoided damage to the tub when the car ran over kerbs or grounded heavily. Elsewhere the 75-gallon fuel system was revised, and the suspension geometry was worked over to help maximise the amount of travel available.

Bruce, Denny and Teddy Mayer all believed the M8B was quite simply the best racing car the factory had ever produced. It had a clean, functional shape, was neat and efficient, and a joy to drive. Denny in particular revelled in the way he could throw the big machine into corners and steer it on the throttle.

More power, and wider front and rear tracks to cater for wider tyres were typical of the improvements which accompanied refinements to the car's basic aerodynamics. The most obvious visual change on the M8B was the adoption of the high, strut-mounted aerofoil that had already made the Chaparrals iconic. These devices were mounted on the rear suspension uprights and thus generated their high downforce loadings directly through the rear wheel hubs. Over the winter of 1968 the concept had famously been tested by the team on one of its Minivans on the roads around Colnbrook, although how it affected the handling of a little roadcar is best left to the imagination!

The problem with the M8B, if there was such a thing, was that others argued that its total dominance was actually scaring off rivals, and certainly other factory teams had promised cars and full support for the 1969 series but then cried off, apparently unwilling to waste time and money failing to beat the ratings of the 'Bruce and Denny Show'. But in hindsight, so many of their rivals' efforts seemed half-hearted. McLaren, at that period of its existence, was a totally professional racing team that had its act finely honed. It had, in Bruce's words, learned how to go motor racing properly, and it showed.

Dan Gurney believed that the high-winged machine was: "*Light years ahead of the rest of the cars running in Can-Am.*" Indeed when the Chevrolet in his M6B-based 'McLeagle' died in practice at Michigan – the first and only time the series visited that state – he literally jumped at the chance to drive Bruce's spare car. Not having qualified it (Jack Brabham did that) he had to start at the back of the grid, but in typical Gurney style he soon fought his way through the traffic until he was lying third behind Bruce and Denny's team cars and was the only other runner on the same lap. At the time he said: "*What a great car to drive!*" The result: that spectacular 1-2-3 for the M8B.

With Bruce winning the 1969 Canadian-American Challenge Series and Denny finishing second, both drivers scored twice as many points as their nearest challenger. The team had suffered only four non-finishes and the season's winnings totalled a staggering $305,000. This brought the Bruce McLaren Motor Racing Team's earnings in the Can-Am series to well over half a million very welcome US dollars.

Writing in that year's Autocourse annual Pete Lyons explained McLaren's success thus: "*It is not Bruce's budget that makes him win, but the manner in which he goes about the whole job. He has a very practical conception of what machines he needs to win. He starts to build and test on time. He hires the best brains and keeps them happy. He organises bases, transport and supply lines in a paramilitary manner. He keeps close tabs on the life of each component, and has a continuing programme of refinement that amounts to a restless search for perfection. He keeps himself liberally supplied with spares, even to a second driver and a third car. Perhaps most important of all, he never lets his men ease up. They are taught to think of themselves at all times as racers.*"

Lyons had captured the McLaren culture that remains to this day, while unwittingly outlining the blueprint for F1 teams of the future.

Over the course of the ensuing seasons, as had happened with the original M8A cars, the three team M8Bs were cannibalised in order to build cars for the new season and to keep the existing cars running. Eventually no complete example of the legendary M8B was known to exist so, a decade later, Chuck Haines and McLaren mechanic and fabricator Tom Frederick set about finding all the original parts to recreate a truly genuine replica. After almost 20 years of searching they managed to assemble all the components necessary to complete their mission and the car photographed here took to the track for the first time at the Goodwood Festival of Speed, forming part of a 'Tribute to Bruce McLaren' feature.

Underneath its dramatic exterior, the M8B was a lightened and modified version of the previous year's M8A. Regular drivers Bruce and Denny were joined by Dan Gurney for one memorable race at Michigan, where they finished first, second and third.

The M8B featured a heavily revised version of the 7-litre Chevrolet V8 that had first been used on the previous year's M8A. The new development engines were built up by George Bolthoff, an ex-Traco engineer who joined the team after Gary Knutson left.

With all Can-Am races getting underway from a rolling start, the M8B had the 4-speed version of the Hewland LG500 gearbox rather than 5-speed. This saved a few more vital pounds of weight.

In the words of Dan Gurney, the M8B was "*simply light years ahead of the rest of the cars in Can-Am*". It was a highly developed yet simple machine and the attention to detail in every aspect was incredible. Even the wheels were cast with the car type and part number.

Having won the 1968 Can-Am Championship, in 1969 despite winning five races in the M8B Denny Hulme had to concede his crown to Bruce.

At the third round of the 1969 Can-Am season at Watkins Glen, Bruce (seen here) and Denny scored their third consecutive 1-2 finish of the season.

1969 CAN-AM McLAREN M8B

CONTINUED

The first M8B chassis was tested by Bruce at Goodwood in the early part of 1969. As usual McLaren was well ahead of the other teams in developing its new car.

M8B CAN-AM
SPECIFICATION

MODEL	McLaren M8B
TYPE/FORMULA	Can-Am
YEAR OF PRODUCTION	1969
DESIGNER	Gordon Coppuck/Jo Marquart
EXAMPLES BUILT	3
ENGINE	Chevrolet V8
CUBIC CAPACITY	6997cc
CARBURATION	Lucas fuel injection
POWER OUTPUT	680bhp

TRANSMISSION	Hewland LG500 4-speed
CHASSIS	Aluminium sheet monocoque with steel bulkheads
BODY	Monocoque sides, GRP body sections, aluminium wing
FRONT SUSPENSION	Single top link & radius arm, lower wishbone, outboard coil spring/damper, anti-roll bar
REAR SUSPENSION	Reverse lower wishbone, single top link, twin radius rods, coil spring/damper, anti-roll bar
BRAKES F/R	Outboard 12in ventilated discs
WHEELS DIAMETER x WIDTH F/R	15x11/15x16in

TYRES F/R	Goodyear
LENGTH	154in - 3911mm
WIDTH	75in - 1905mm
HEIGHT OF BODY	32in - 812mm
WHEELBASE	94in - 2387mm
TRACK F/R	58/56in - 1473/1422mm
WEIGHT	1405lb - 637kg
PRINCIPAL DRIVERS	McLaren, Hulme, Gurney
IDENTIFYING COLOURS	Papaya

1969 FORMULA 1 McLAREN M9A

Clever, controversial, but destined to disappear rather than rewrite the rules of Formula 1, the McLaren M9A designed by Jo Marquart made its public debut at the British GP in 1969 with Derek Bell at the wheel.

There was nothing particularly new about four-wheel-drive (4WD) in F1. Tractor king Harry Ferguson and Le Mans winner Tony Rolt had first unveiled an all-wheel drive Formula 1 car called the Ferguson P99, driven in particular by Stirling Moss, as far back as 1961. BRM produced a similar sort of car in 1964. Towards the end of that decade, however, it was widely felt within the sport that all-wheel drive held the key to harnessing the considerable power of the latest generation of 3-litre engines, in particular the 405bhp Ford Cosworth DFV. Unfortunately, while such cars were still at the concept stage during 1968, the development of wings gathered so much pace that, ultimately, they would render 4WD an expensive blind alley.

Lotus, Matra, McLaren and Cosworth all produced such cars for the 1969 season. Lotus's 63 was an elegant wedge-shaped car that was a very serious effort on Colin Chapman's part to make the concept work. Matra's MS84 was slightly less so, since designer Derek Gardner opted for a spaceframe chassis for ease of manufacture, maintenance and modification of the experimental prototype. The slab-sided Cosworth was the work of Bruce's former designer Robin Herd, the man behind the M7A.

It was typical of Bruce that the M9A most closely rivalled the Lotus, for he did nothing by halves. While Gordon Coppuck worked on the M7A, B and C derivative cars in F1, Marquart looked after the M9A. Like the Lotus it was a monocoque design, but the McLaren differed in employing the engine as a fully stressed member. The DFV was turned back to front with the gearbox positioned ahead of it in the chassis, and the drive taken out to the left as in the Lotus via a two-shaft McLaren-designed, Ferguson-style gearbox with five Hewland ratios. Inboard brakes were used, with hollow discs for more efficient cooling, in conjunction with conventional suspension that featured inboard coil spring/damper units. The rear wheels were marginally wider than the fronts and power was fed to them via differentials fitted with Hewland-ZF spin locks as Marquart sought to avoid the need for limited-slip units. The central differential had been designed with quick-change torque-split ratios; these could be changed in less than 15 minutes. It is also interesting to note that despite all the additional equipment the finished car was said to weigh a little over 10lbs more than the conventional rear-wheel-drive M7A. This caused not inconsiderable dismay at Colnbrook at the time, but a 10lb weight penalty sounds pretty modest today.

Even before the car first ran in public, Bruce was having serious reservations about it. In his book McLAREN The Grand Prix, Can-Am and Indy Cars, Doug Nye outlines Teddy Mayer's recollections of a conversation that BRM's chief designer Tony Rudd had with Bruce. "*When Tony heard we were building a four-wheel-drive car he said to Bruce: 'Have you tried fitting a hundredweight of cement in your car?' No, Bruce hadn't. 'Well, have you tried setting up your brakes so that they bind all the time?' No, Bruce hadn't. 'Well have you tried de-tuning your engines to run only 300 horsepower?' No, we hadn't tried that either. And Tony said: 'Well you might just as well, 'cos that's what it's like with four-wheel-drive.*"

The press seemed optimistic and impressed with early test results, but by the time the team arrived at Silverstone for the British Grand Prix several key members were already uncomfortably aware that they had almost certainly been barking up the wrong technological tree. One that, at £70,000, had probably accounted for a sixth of the total 1969 budget, according to Mayer. As Bruce put it, piloting the M9A, "*was like trying to write your signature with somebody jogging your elbow.*" Why bother, was the question he put to workshop staff after the car had undergone its first test at Goodwood. Certainly, designing and building such a novel and technically complex machine took the team's eye off several other arguably more worthwhile exercises and progressing the project from first drawings to finished prototype took at least four months of very hard - and costly - work. It now seems incredible that McLaren was reportedly hoping to build half a dozen M9As. In reality, only that prototype was ever completed.

In its original guise (as seen here) with nothing more aerodynamic than a pair of small front wings during early practice at Silverstone, Bell described the car as, "*A right royal handful. Its handling characteristics were completely different to a conventional car. I found that the only way to get it round a corner was to back off the throttle momentarily, give a great wrench on the steering wheel and then go hard on the power again.*" Subsequently the team fitted a rear tea tray assembly from one of the M7s and Bell, taking part in only his third Grand Prix, qualified the recalcitrant machine 15th with a lap of 1m 26.1s. That compared with Jochen Rindt's pole time of 1m 20.8s and Denny's third fastest 1m 21.5s in the M7A. In contrast, John Miles lapped his better sorted Lotus 63 in 1m 25.1, Jo Bonnier the other 63 in 1m 28.2s, and Jean-Pierre Beltoise the Matra MS84 in a slightly unrepresentative 1m 31.2s. Bell ran 12th, ahead of the other 4WD cars, on the opening lap, but fell back quickly before retiring after five laps with a broken rear suspension carrier. It was the end of the road for the M9A.

Interest in 4WD evaporated soon after Bell's abortive run, and not just at McLaren. In theory it offered advantages that, in reality, failed to match those conferred instead by aerodynamic devices which added download to the tyres. But if the M9A was a flop, it yet again endorsed Bruce's belief in experimentation, and his commonsense ability to admit when something was wrong and cut his losses.

In the M9A's only race, Derek Bell qualified 21st but lasted only five laps of the British Grand Prix at Silverstone, before the suspension failed.

With the DFV turned 180° in the chassis, the gearbox and torque split unit was situated in the space between the engine and the driver's seat back.

This is how the new M9A first appeared in the paddock at Silverstone. Before practice was over it had gained a huge rear wing taken from the spare M7A.

M9A FORMULA 1
SPECIFICATION

MODEL	McLaren M9A
TYPE/FORMULA	Formula 1
YEAR OF PRODUCTION	1969
DESIGNER	Jo Marquart
EXAMPLES BUILT	1
ENGINE	Ford Cosworth DFV
CUBIC CAPACITY	2993cc
CARBURATION	Lucas fuel injection
POWER OUTPUT	420bhp

TRANSMISSION	McLaren 4-wheel drive 5-speed
CHASSIS	Aluminium monocoque, steel bulkheads, tubular subframe
BODY	Monocoque sides, GRP nose & cockpit surround
FRONT SUSPENSION	Upper wishbone/rocker arm, lower link & radius arm, inboard coil spring/damper, anti-roll bar
REAR SUSPENSION	Upper rocker arm, lower wishbone, twin radius rods, inboard coil spring/damper, anti-roll bar
BRAKES F/R	Outboard/Inboard Girling 12in ventilated discs
WHEELS DIAMETER x WIDTH F/R	13x12/13x14in

TYRES F/R	Goodyear
LENGTH	148in - 3759mm
WIDTH OF CHASSIS	36in - 914mm
HEIGHT OF ROLLBAR	37in - 940mm
WHEELBASE	95in - 2413mm
TRACK F/R	63/59in - 1600/1499mm
WEIGHT	1160lb - 526kg
PRINCIPAL DRIVERS	Derek Bell
IDENTIFYING COLOURS	Papaya

1969 & 1970 FORMULA 5000 McLAREN-TROJAN M10A & M10B

With the majority of the main test and evaluation work being carried out by Bruce himself, the handsome Chevrolet-powered McLaren-Trojan M10A was designed by Gordon Coppuck to be a production Formula A/Formula 5000 car for the works and for customers. 20 of them were built in 1969, along with an additional 21 M10B versions the following year for Formula 5000.

The M10A monocoque was based on the previous year's Formula 1 M7A but with full 'up-and-over' aluminium-alloy panelling bonded and riveted to the steel bulkheads to form a cigar tube rather than a bathtub. There were also pontoons that extended rearwards to support the 5-litre American V8 engines which, unlike the Ford Cosworth DFV, couldn't be used as fully stressed members.

Suspension was by the familiar single top link with radius arm, lower wishbone, anti-roll bar and outboard coil spring/damper at the front, and single top link, reversed lower wishbone, twin radius arms and with the spring/damper unit at the rear. Wheels were McLaren cast magnesium 15 inch diameter items, 11 inch wide at the front and 16 at the rear.

Since its inaugural race in the US in 1967 Formula A had been a category with classes for 3.0, 1.6 and 1.1-litre racing engines, but in the absence of sufficient numbers of serious contenders the governing authorities at the Sports Car Club of America (SCCA) took the decision for 1968 to extend the formula to include stock-block engines of up to 5-litres. Opening the floodgates for such production-based 302 cubic inch pushrod engines such as the Chevrolet and Ford V8s proved to be the major breakthrough for what came to be called Formula 5000 worldwide.

This change in rules caught the interest of several chassis manufacturers, and many of the sport's big names – including Eagle, Lola and McLaren – rushed to complete their own designs. The formula grew accordingly, with a similar class being announced in Britain for 1969, and South African, New Zealand and Australian national championships being launched.

The papaya orange M10A prototype was a star of the 1969 Racing Car Show in London and was to be run as a works-assisted entry under the banner of Church Farm Racing in the Guards European Championship in the UK. It was driven by 28-year-old Peter Gethin who took the car to early wins at Oulton Park, Brands Hatch and Mallory Park. He so dominated the early going that the team ventured abroad to race successfully in America. While it was absent, former F1 driver Trevor Taylor also amassed four victories in new constructor John Surtees' eponymous TS5 chassis, and it was only after Gethin returned to defend his title chances that he succeeded narrowly in the final round at Brands after both men were put off the road by a backmarker.

The M10A was one of the first monocoque Formula 5000 cars, and besides its performance its superior safety factors quickly obliged Lola to follow suit for 1970 as its new T190 superseded the spaceframe T140 and T142 models. The McLaren also came at a competitive price. Supplied as standard with a Bartz-tuned Chevy V8 it cost £7,055 ex-works at its launch in 1969, or £4480 as a rolling chassis. Drivers quickly sensed the way things were moving and switched to McLarens as soon as they could for the forthcoming season.

Typical of these was Canadian Eppie Wietzes of Formula Racing. He made the decision during the off-season to switch from his Chevrolet-engined Lola T142 to a McLaren M10B and never looked back. He won five out of the seven rounds of the Gulf Canada Series, to clinch the title.

The M10B cars built for 1970 differed from the M10A in several respects. Revising the engine bay and lowering the engine by almost two inches necessitated revisions to the rear suspension, and a DG300 Hewland gearbox replaced the previous LG600. The steering geometry was also slightly revised, as was the shape of the nose. Overall, the M10B was also slightly lighter.

Of all the M10A/B drivers, Gethin's record was the most outstanding. The new 5-litre cars were as powerful as their Formula 1 contemporaries, if not quite so agile, so he had ample opportunity to demonstrate that he could handle the extra power. His domination of the 1970 UK series, with eight victories, further prompted McLaren to give him the chance to drive in F1, and his successor in the Sid Taylor Racing car that year, Reine Wisell, simply took up where he left off. Both Wisell and New Zealander Howden Ganley also got their Formula 1 breaks on the strength of their F5000 performances.

In their day the M10A and M10B McLarens were the class of the field in Formula 5000. They made champions of Gethin, former M1C racer John Cannon, David Hobbs, Eppie Weitzes and Graham McRae, and besides them provided championship race wins for Niel Allen, Kevin Bartlett, Howden Ganley, Ron Grable, Frank Matich, Sam Posey, Brian Redman, Mike Walker and Reine Wisell.

The two cars were also a great favourite of club racers as well as sprint and hillclimb competitors throughout Europe. Driving an M10A Sir Nicholas Williamson won the RAC Hillclimb Championship in 1970, in 1972 Bob Rose used an M10B to win the British Sprint Championship and in both 1975 & '76 this title was won by Dave Harris also driving an M10B. It was the perfect customer car.

The M10A was revealed to the press at the McLaren works in January of 1969. In this rear view the 'high wing' had been removed and when seen from this angle, the Hewland 'LG' gearbox certainly was, as denoted, 'large.'

The M10A was derived from the previous season's M7A Formula 1 car. When it was launched in early 1969 the 'high wings' developed for Formula 1 were still legal, but not for long.

Bruce McLaren conducted the majority of the development work on the first F5000 car to come from Colnbrook. Early testing at Brands Hatch was conducted with the high wing still in place and the first few F5000 races of 1969 were run with most cars in this guise.

Opposite
This is Teddy Pilette in the 'Team VDS' M10B at Snetterton in August 1971. In the two-heat race he finished third overall behind Graham McRae in his heavily modified M10B and the Lola T192 of Mike Walker.

M10A FORMULA 5000
SPECIFICATION

MODEL	McLaren-Trojan M10A
TYPE/FORMULA	Formula 5000/Formula A
YEAR OF PRODUCTION	1969
DESIGNER	Gordon Coppuck
EXAMPLES BUILT	20
ENGINE	Chevrolet V8
CUBIC CAPACITY	5000cc
CARBURATION	Lucas fuel injection
POWER OUTPUT	500bhp

TRANSMISSION	Hewland LG600 5-speed
CHASSIS	360° aluminium monocoque, steel bulkheads
BODY	Monocoque sides, GRP nose & cockpit surround
FRONT SUSPENSION	Single top link & radius arm, lower wishbone, outboard coil spring/damper, anti-roll bar
REAR SUSPENSION	Reverse lower wishbone, top link, twin radius rods, outboard coil spring/damper, anti-roll bar
BRAKES F/R	Outboard Lockheed 12in ventilated discs
WHEELS DIAMETER x WIDTH F/R	15x11/15x16in

TYRES F/R	10.55x15/12.50x15
LENGTH	161in - 4089mm
WIDTH	75in - 1905mm
HEIGHT TO TOP OF SCREEN	26.5in - 673mm
WHEELBASE	97in - 2464mm
TRACK F/R	59.5/58.5in - 1511/1485mm
WEIGHT	1285lb - 583kg
PRINCIPAL DRIVERS	Gethin
IDENTIFYING COLOURS	n/a

1969 & 1970 FORMULA 5000 McLAREN-TROJAN M10A & M10B

CONTINUED

Roy Lane used his M10B chassis #400-03 to great effect in 1971. That year he won several rounds of the British RAC Sprint and Hillclimb Championships, setting a course record at Harewood.

Peter Gethin in the Sid Taylor M10B, chassis #400-06, at the Silverstone International Trophy F1/F5000 race in April 1970. Having finished seventh overall and first in the F5000 category in the first heat, he retired from the second with a broken rocker.

The front suspension on the F5000 M10B was essentially the same as it had been on the M10A and was based on the 1968 M7A Formula 1 car.

At the rear of the M10B the revised engine position meant that the suspension was extensively reworked, dropping the top beam and pick-up points by almost two inches.

M10B FORMULA 5000
SPECIFICATION

MODEL	McLaren-Trojan M10B
TYPE/FORMULA	Formula 5000/Formula A
YEAR OF PRODUCTION	1970
DESIGNER	Gordon Coppuck
EXAMPLES BUILT	21
ENGINE	Chevrolet V8
CUBIC CAPACITY	5000cc
CARBURATION	Lucas fuel injection
POWER OUTPUT	500bhp

TRANSMISSION	Hewland DG300 5-speed
CHASSIS	360° aluminium monocoque, steel bulkheads
BODY	Monocoque sides, GRP nose & cockpit surround
FRONT SUSPENSION	Single top link & radius arm, lower wishbone, outboard coil spring/damper, anti-roll bar
REAR SUSPENSION	Reverse lower wishbone, top link, twin radius rods, outboard coil spring/damper, anti-roll bar
BRAKES F/R	Outboard Lockheed 12in ventilated discs
WHEELS DIAMETER x WIDTH F/R	15x11/15x16in

TYRES F/R	10.55x15/12.50x15
LENGTH	157.5in - 4000mm
WIDTH	77in - 1956mm
HEIGHT TO TOP OF SCREEN	26.5in - 673mm
WHEELBASE	98in - 2489mm
TRACK F/R	59/60.5in - 1499/1536mm
WEIGHT	1251lb - 567kg
PRINCIPAL DRIVERS	Gethin, Pilette
IDENTIFYING COLOURS	n/a

1969 CAN-AM & GROUP 7
McLAREN-TROJAN M12

With the designation M11 left out in order to avoid confusion with the 1966 M1B Trojan-built McLaren MkII, the M12 was the McLaren production sportscar for the 1969 season. Trojan made 15 examples to compete in Can-Am and Group 7 racing.

Naturally it was based on the phenomenally successful works McLaren team's M8-series cars, bringing together an M8A-style body and a chassis not dissimilar to that of the M6. The latter was a straightforward version of the simple but successful stressed-skin hull, the structure once more being formed from bonded and riveted magnesium and aluminium alloy panel box structures. Again these were attached to a square-section tube frame. Power came from an aluminium-block 7-litre Chevrolet V8, the engine on which Can-Am continued to depend, which now developed a reliable 600bhp. A true M12 is easily identifiable by the fact that side sections of the chassis are curved under, like the M6's, rather than flat-sided as on the M8, and extend all the way to the front wheels, again like the M6, rather than tapering behind the front wheel arch.

The M12 was never going to topple the high-wing works-run M8Bs, but it was nevertheless to acquit itself adequately. In particular, 1966 Can-Am champion John Surtees made no bones about the fact that he far preferred the car Jim Hall purchased while finishing off his radical, and ultimately hugely unsuccessful, Chaparral 2H with its exceptionally narrow track and reduced frontal area.

Surtees qualified fourth and finished third in the season opener at Mosport, then collided with Bruce while disputing second place at St Jovite. He fought with Chris Amon's Ferrari for third at Watkins Glen prior to retirement, then returned to the M12 for the Bridgehampton race after unhappy outings in the Chaparral, and ran strongly until another failure to finish. Surtees' F5000 driver, Andrea de Adamich, took over the M12 to finish fifth at Michigan Raceway after the Englishman fell ill.

Two other stand-out M12 combinations finished ahead of ninth-placed Surtees in the final reckoning: Canadian George Eaton and American Lothar Motschenbacher in fifth and seventh respectively. Eaton's best results were a second, a third and a fourth, Motschenbacher's two fourths.

At least two M12s went east, where Toyota planned to rebody and re-engine them to take on Nissan's all conquering machines in the Japanese Group 7 series. According to reports at the time, the company had an impressive 5-litre quad-cam V8 unit it wanted to race, though Toyota's car only ran with it once.

Several years later one M12 resurfaced in Japan. Hiroshi Kazato's bright yellow machine spent 26 years in a shrine-like display in a local restaurant window after the young driver had been killed at Mount Fuji Raceway. The restaurant owner eventually sold the car to the Bruce McLaren Trust in New Zealand. After receiving minimal attention – the Trust believes it to be the most original Can-Am car in the world and wanted it to retain its patina – it fired up and took to the track at Whenuapai, more than 30 years after it had last turned a wheel in anger.

A one-off car designated M12C, with an older M6 style body and carburettors rather than the regular injection on the 7.2-litre Nicholson McLaren engine, was commissioned by UK hillclimb expert Phil Scragg. After crashing the car in his first event at Doune, he sold it to fellow competitor Tony Harrison who campaigned it for several years in the major British speed championships. The car was once loaned to Patsy Burt of M3 fame. She used it, equipped with fuel injection borrowed from the factory and streamlined bodywork, on another of her speed record breaking runs but the engine blew up in a big way.

M12-60-08 was sold to the Toyota Corporation in Japan and fitted with its 5-litre V8 engine. Seemingly, it raced only once, in a sportscar race at the Mt. Fuji circuit.

John Surtees drove Jim Hall's M12 in the first three races of the 1969 season. Here he passes Johnny Servoz-Gavin's Matra M650 during the round at Watkins Glen. Later in the season when the engine on his Chaparral expired in practice at Bridgehampton, he used the back-up M12 for one last race.

Commissioned by British hillclimb driver Phil Scragg, chassis M12C-60-11 was built at the factory with an M6B-style body and regular carburation. It was then sold to Tony Harrison who campaigned it on the hills for many years.

In 1969 Lothar Motschenbacher was the only driver to run an M12 in all the Can-Am races. His best results in his bright red car were a pair of fourth places at St.Jovite and Bridgehampton.

M12 CAN-AM
SPECIFICATION

MODEL	McLaren-Trojan M12
TYPE/FORMULA	Can-Am/Group 7
YEAR OF PRODUCTION	1969
DESIGNER	Gordon Coppuck
EXAMPLES BUILT	15
ENGINE	Chevrolet V8
CUBIC CAPACITY	6997cc
CARBURATION	Lucas fuel injection
POWER OUTPUT	590-615bhp

TRANSMISSION	Hewland LG 5-speed
CHASSIS	Aluminium alloy sheet monocoque, steel bulkheads
BODY	Formed by monocoque sides with GRP top panels
FRONT SUSPENSION	Wide based unequal length double wishbones anti-roll bar, coil spring/damper
REAR SUSPENSION	Reverse lower wishbone, single top link, twin radius arms, coil spring/damper, anti-roll bar
BRAKES F/R	Outboard 12in Girling ventilated discs
WHEELS DIAMETER x WIDTH F/R	15x10/15x15in

TYRES F/R	Goodyear
LENGTH	155in - 3937mm
WIDTH	75in - 1905mm
HEIGHT AT WINDSCREEN	31in - 787mm
WHEELBASE	93.5in - 2375mm
TRACK F/R	57/55in - 1448/1397mm
WEIGHT	1300lb - 590kg
PRINCIPAL DRIVERS	Surtees, Motschenbacher
IDENTIFYING COLOURS	n/a

THE 1970s

CHAPTER 02

When I quit racing at the end of 1979 I did so completely, I didn't even watch the races on TV but concentrated 100 per cent on my airline. Ron Dennis would call me though, every three or four months, and we'd chat and he started to break my resolve. Finally, in 1981, I went to a Grand Prix again, as a TV commentator in Austria. There was a huge startline crash during a support race and for the first time I thought: 'This is good stuff,' and could feel the old spirit coming back.

A month after that I accepted an invitation from Ron to go to Monza. I saw John Watson's huge crash at the exit of the second Lesmo corner when he went off going flat in fourth and hit the guardrail backwards so hard that the car broke in two parts. The engine and the gearbox came apart from the carbon-fibre monocoque but the latter survived remarkably well – John Barnard had clearly built an incredible car – so when Ron rang on the Monday and offered me a test, I said yes.

I'd had another approach, from Frank Williams, but when I went to Donington and saw the McLaren set-up and how they worked as a team it was clear to me that I would only ever go there. Eventually I decided I would do just that. 1982 was a good year and I won two races with the Cosworth-engined MP4/1B. That said, 1983 was a disaster, because we had no chance against the turbo guys at Ferrari, Renault and BMW, unless they crashed or retired. Because of this I went to Ron and said why don't we introduce the turbo car this year, do a couple of races and then we are much better prepared for the following year?

John Barnard, ever the perfectionist, said no way and Ron went with him, so I called the president of Philip Morris, told him my worries and asked him to ask the team to run the turbo engine earlier. Ron thought I was crazy, but we got to run the car from Zandvoort onwards and it was the right decision as it prepared us well for the 1984 season.

Of the eight races I won with McLaren, the best was probably Monza that year. It was the toughest of races and gave me the impetus to go on and win the '84 Championship. As ever we had very little emotion in the team but always very high quality cars. Other teams are driven by emotions and as long as you perform they love you, but if you don't perform you get sacked like anybody else. But McLaren is the opposite, being a high quality, high-tech team, making the best racing cars ever built, and run with Ron's British coolness.

Niki Lauda
Drivers' World Champion 1984
McLaren MP4/2

1970 CAN-AM
McLAREN-TROJAN M8C

One of the works M8Bs was retained as a development mule for the new M8D which appeared in 1970, leaving only two chassis available for purchase by non-works drivers eager to emulate Bruce and Denny's outstanding 1969 successes. It came as little surprise then, that the company announced the launch of a new M8B-based customer car for others, the McLaren-Trojan M8C. Given that the 1969 customer car had been the M12, the nomenclature was slightly confusing to those who didn't understand its origins.

The 15 examples of the M8C that were built differed in several details from the M8Bs, and in real terms were not based around it at all but more on the 1968 M8A. For example, instead of simply feeding the stresses directly through the slightly larger 7.4-litre Chevrolet V8 as the works cars did, the M8C used a supporting structure. As a consequence, however, customers could opt to fit the Ford V8 or other engines.

With the high wings which had sprouted on almost all of the front-running cars the previous year now significantly truncated by new regulations, the M8C sported a low wing on its tail. It was rather less prominent than its counterpart on the M8D. The side sections of the M8C chassis were very much the same as on the M8B, with the area behind the front wheel cut away in a long tapered section extending to a point below the front edge of the door.

The M8C made its first race appearance at the opening round of the 1970 Can-Am Championship held at Mosport Park in June. With ace privateer Lothar Motschenbacher and colourful Pole Oscar Kovaleski running the two ex-works M8Bs, it was left to Roger McCaig and John Cordts to debut the new customer car. With McCaig qualifying in fifth and Cordts back in 17th it wasn't exactly a dream start, but McCaig finished the race in a strong fifth place as the first of the non-works McLarens.

These two cars were the only M8Cs to run in that year's series. McCaig finished a creditable 10th, albeit with another pair of fifth places being the best results he could muster. For the final two races of the year Cordts passed his M8C over to Motschenbacher who had started the season campaigning his M8B before switching to an M12 after damaging the former. At the season finale at Riverside, 'Low Tar' too managed to bring the car home fifth and the points from the race lifted him to an excellent second place in the Can-Am standings for 1970. But on 65 points, he had less than half the score of championship winner Denny Hulme's total of 132.

Throughout 1971 four M8Cs raced in Can-Am, all of which had by now sprouted the large low rear wing that was also fitted to the 1971 customer car from Trojan, the M8E. Cordts, George Drolsom, Charlie Kemp and Bill Wonder were their drivers, though by the end of the season Cordts, who in 12th overall was the best placed M8C pilot in the series, had switched allegiance to Lola's T163.

A few M8Cs stayed in Europe. The Interserie sportscar championship was founded in 1970 as a European version of the Can-Am series and during the early seasons many original Can-Am cars – from McLaren, Lola, Porsche, March and BRM – raced against Group 5 and 6 cars from the World Championship of Makes.

One car was bought by British privateer team Ecurie Evergreen for F3 and saloon racing star Chris Craft to drive and was modified to run with 3-litre Cosworth DFV power. It proved very quick in several UK sportscar races, and at the British round of the Interserie championship at Croft in July Craft put chassis M8C-70-07 on pole position and set the fastest lap before retiring from the lead after a spin. At the Swedish Grand Prix (for sportscars) in August, Craft and co-driver Alain de Cadenet scored a superb win ahead of a strong field including several Porsche 917s and Lola T70s.

Ironically, McLaren's only other strong performance in the series that year came from Vic Elford, who took a 7-litre M6B/12 to victory in the Solituderennen at Hockenheim.

Another M8C was adapted to accept a Toyota engine, although according to Bill Meace, a manager at Trojan, this proved to be an *"exercise which unfortunately did not work out."* The engine started to misfire badly, and rather than tinker with the internal mechanisms of a unit that was on loan the crew decided to return it to its maker and the project was terminated abruptly.

The M8C of Chris Craft and Trevor Taylor arrives for the 1970 Brands Hatch 1000km. Craft retired with ignition problems on lap 25, before Taylor even got to drive. Bruce McLaren was on the entry list as a third driver but chose not to drive.

With a rather interesting triple layer rear spoiler, Tom Dutton dives down the Corkscrew at Laguna Seca in George Drolsom's M8C Chevrolet. He retired from this, the 8th round of the 1972 Can-Am series, with gearbox problems on lap 18.

Rather than being used as a stressed member, the engine on the M8C was supported by extensions to the chassis. This enabled different engines to be used without the need for changes to the rear suspension.

The front suspension on the M8C was essentially the same as it had been on all the M8 derivatives. The upright was supported at the top by a short adjustable top link and radius arm just visible going off to the left of picture, behind the antiroll-bar.

M8C CAN-AM
SPECIFICATION

MODEL	McLaren-Trojan M8C
TYPE/FORMULA	Can-Am
YEAR OF PRODUCTION	1970
DESIGNER	Gordon Coppuck/Jo Marquart
EXAMPLES BUILT	15
ENGINE	Chevrolet/Ford V8
CUBIC CAPACITY	7000-7500cc
CARBURATION	Lucas fuel injection
POWER OUTPUT	650-700bhp

TRANSMISSION	Hewland LG500 4-speed
CHASSIS	Aluminium sheet monocoque with steel bulkheads
BODY	Monocoque sides with 4 GRP body sections
FRONT SUSPENSION	Single top link & radius arm, lower wishbone,
	outboard coil spring/damper, anti-roll bar
REAR SUSPENSION	Reverse lower wishbone, single top link,
	twin radius rods, coil spring/damper, anti-roll bar
BRAKES F/R	Outboard 11.9in ventilated discs
WHEELS DIAMETER x WIDTH F/R	15x11/15x16in

TYRES F/R	Goodyear
LENGTH	153in - 3886mm
WIDTH	74in - 1880mm
HEIGHT	30in - 762mm
WHEELBASE	94in - 2387mm
TRACK F/R	58/55in - 1473/1397mm
WEIGHT	1425lb - 646kg
PRINCIPAL DRIVERS	McCaig, Cordts, Craft, De Cadenet
IDENTIFYING COLOURS	n/a

1970 CAN-AM McLAREN M8D

The McLaren M8D is inevitably remembered as the car in which Bruce died, but it gave his team one of its best years in Can-Am. Rallying superbly after the tragedy, McLaren took nine wins from 10 rounds, and Denny Hulme his second title despite driving with his hands still bandaged after the fire in the M15 at Indianapolis.

The M8D inspired confidence. Peter Gethin, brought on board after Bruce's death when a clash between the team's Gulf Oil sponsorship and Dan Gurney's Castrol associations eased the American out of the team, admitted that the first time he saw an M8D going past the pits with Denny driving: "*The ground literally shook, and I wondered what I had let myself in for.*" After taking the wheel himself he discovered: *"The car was fantastic… and of course by the end of the session you were asking for another 100bhp."*

The M8D differed visually from the M8B. With new rules banning the strut-mounted wings that had proliferated in 1969, the solution at McLaren comprised a pair of tail fins which acted as fences to channel airflow over a wide, low-mounted wing located eight inches above the rear bodywork. The distinctive appearance earned the car the nickname 'the Batmobile'. It was less efficient aerodynamically without the M8B's high wing, so to maintain performance the team sought even greater horsepower. A new deal with Reynolds Aluminium gave it access to that company's new silicon-aluminium Chevrolet blocks, 8-litre versions of which were said to be capable of producing 700bhp. In the interests of reliability a slightly smaller 7.6-litre was chosen, giving 670bhp.

Jo Marquart's new car was wider and longer than any previous Can-Am racer, with the additional girth being used to provide even greater fuel capacity. With both the V8 and the transmission now forming part of the rear chassis structure, the monocoque was constructed using aluminium sheets and a magnesium floor.

Bruce's death came during a test session on a Tuesday at Goodwood. New Zealand mechanic Cary Taylor warmed up the M8D, as Bruce lapped in an M14A that Gethin would race at Spa in place of the injured Denny. Bruce then switched to the M8D, popping in and out of the pits for adjustments to the rear wing to reduce oversteer. At 12.19 he left the pits for the last time. In a fast left-hand kink leading on to the main straight part of the tail section lifted at 170mph, causing the car to spin. It struck a marshals' protective embankment on the right-hand side of the track with enormous impact. Bruce was thrown from the wreckage, and killed instantly.

The team was told not to report to work the following day, but Bruce's men were racers to the core, and not one of them was missing that Wednesday. The F1 cars were withdrawn from the following weekend's Belgian GP, but two M8Ds were on the grid when the Can-Am series kicked off with the Labatt's Blue Trophy race at Mosport on June 14th, because that's how racers react to crises.

Dan Gurney was drafted in to replace Bruce, and qualified on pole despite never having driven the car before. And he won. Denny, who had been devastated by Bruce's death, demonstrated his towering inner strength. His hands were still healing after Indianapolis, and every time he grasped a steering wheel, let alone used one to fight a 670bhp race car through a corner, the tender skin cracked and the process had to start all over again. In Bruce's name he raced home third, after qualifying alongside Dan. It was one of many acts of genuine heroism from 'The Bear' that were so instrumental in helping the shattered team to regroup.

At St Jovite Dan led from start to finish, and Denny only quit when his engine overheated. He had a smaller 7.1-litre engine in his car at Watkins Glen, but led from start to finish. In his final race in the M8D, Gurney fell back to ninth with rising coolant temperatures. Like Denny, he had done what he set out to do, which was to support Bruce's team when it most needed it.

At Edmonton in late July Gethin made his debut, qualifying second behind Denny, and finishing second to his team-mate. Denny won at Mid-Ohio, where Gethin suffered engine problems.

At Elkhart Lake, Wisconsin, Gethin inherited victory after Denny had been disqualified for a push-start. Both were outqualified at Road Atlanta by Vic Elford in the Chaparral 2J 'sucker' car and damaged their cars in a chaotic race won by privateer Tony Dean's 3-litre Porsche 908. At Donnybrooke the team recovered its form with another Denny-led 1-2, and he won again at Laguna Seca. Once again Elford upstaged the M8Ds in qualifying at Riverside's finale, but Denny took an early lead and was never challenged. Gethin lost second in the Championship after his engine blew.

In the most trying circumstances, McLaren had pulled through. It had been shaken to the core, but it was a tribute to the philosophy with which Bruce had imbued every member that they were able not just to carry on, but to keep winning.

Having already clinched the Championship, Denny Hulme easily won the Can-Am race at Riverside, California, in November 1970 and finished the season with more than double the points total of second place finisher Lothar Motschenbacher's M12.

With the banning of the 'high wing' concept used on many of the cars in 1969, the M8D had a huge low-slung rear wing supported by tail fins on either side of the rear bodywork. These fins, along with smaller ones on the front end, helped channel airflow over the car and create huge amounts of downforce.

The familiar 'stack' of injection trumpets on the works cars fed the Chevrolet V8 engine which was now enlarged to over 7.5- litres in capacity. Benefiting from something approaching 700bhp the 'works' cars completely dominated the 1970 Can-Am series.

6

REYNOLDS ALUMINUM
5
McLAREN CARS
Denny Hulme
Gulf
GOODYEAR
BOSCH SPARK PLUGS
REYNOLDS ALUMINUM
Gulf

1970 CAN-AM McLAREN M8D

By 1971 the works M8Ds had passed into the hands of privateer drivers. Here at Road Atlanta the M8D of Motschenbacher leads Bondurant (M8E/D), Adamowicz (M8B) and Elford (M8E).

Peter Gethin's last race in the works M8D was in the final race of the 1970 Can-Am series at Riverside, California, in November. After suffering engine problems he retired on lap 21.

M8D CAN-AM
SPECIFICATION

MODEL	McLaren M8D
TYPE/FORMULA	Can-Am
YEAR OF PRODUCTION	1970
DESIGNER	Jo Marquart
EXAMPLES BUILT	4
ENGINE	Chevrolet V8
CUBIC CAPACITY	7100-7600cc
CARBURATION	Lucas fuel injection
POWER OUTPUT	680bhp

TRANSMISSION	Hewland LG500 4-speed
CHASSIS	Aluminium sheet monocoque with steel bulkheads
BODY	Monocoque sides, GRP body sections, integral wing
FRONT SUSPENSION	Single top link & radius arm, lower wishbone, outboard coil spring/damper, anti-roll bar
REAR SUSPENSION	Reverse lower wishbone, single top link, twin radius rods, coil spring/damper, anti-roll bar
BRAKES F/R	Outboard 12in ventilated discs
WHEELS DIAMETER x WIDTH F/R	15x11/15x16in

TYRES F/R	Goodyear
LENGTH	164in - 4166mm
WIDTH	76in - 1930mm
HEIGHT AT TAIL	45in - 1143mm
WHEELBASE	94in - 2387mm
TRACK F/R	62/58.5in - 1575/1486mm
WEIGHT	1398lb - 634kg
PRINCIPAL DRIVERS	Hulme, Gurney, Gethin
IDENTIFYING COLOURS	Papaya

1970 FORMULA 1
McLAREN M14A & M14D

Superstition ruled out any model under the designation M13 so the new Formula 1 design for 1970 – with Bruce's personal race car the first chassis to be completed – became the M14A.

It was another full monocoque design, Bruce making a contribution to the evolutionary concept as Gordon Coppuck and Jo Marquart handled the detailing. It bore evidence of the lessons learned from the Formula 5000 M10A as well as the derivative M7C, using fully-stressed sections fore and aft of the cockpit. 18 gauge aluminium skinned the tub, bonded and riveted over a series of internal bulkheads formed from mild steel.

Whereas on the M7s the front suspension had incorporated rearward trailing links those on the new car ran forward, thereby negating the need for an additional bulkhead to provide anchorage points. This saved weight and left more room for fuel in the pontoons running down either side. Additionally, the M14A now enjoyed an improved degree of steering lock.

Further weight was saved by using tubular Can-Am style anti-roll bars and new front uprights. At the rear Coppuck and Marquart followed popular practice by mounting the 10.9 inch brake discs inboard to reduce unsprung weight. The coil spring/damper unit were mounted inboard as before, and with larger McLaren-cast 15 inch diameter wheels it was possible to clean the airflow by concealing larger front discs within the wheels, together with the twin-pot Lockheed calipers.

Forward of the scuttle a simple detachable glass-fibre panel finished off the cigar tube section, while the M10B-style nose enclosed a larger but lighter radiator slung out front on a tubular frame. Power for the 1180lb car came from the trusty Ford Cosworth V8. McLaren owned four and ordered two more.

The team travelled to Kyalami in March for the M14A's debut in the South African GP. An ageing M7A went along as a spare car, as a third M14A would not be completed until later in the year. Bruce failed to finish after his engine expired on lap 40 when he was running fourth, but Denny came in second eight seconds adrift of the victorious Jack Brabham in his BT33.

Bruce crashed on oil at Clearways in the Race of Champions, requiring a rebuild for M14-1 around a new monocoque, but Denny was third. Both cars sported 13 inch front wheels in Jarama for the Spanish GP, where Denny retired when his distributor's rotor arm shaft sheared but Bruce finished second behind Jackie Stewart's March 701. His final race appearance, his 101st Grand Prix start, came on May 10th at Monaco. The M14As had been fitted with stronger driveshafts, new uprights and the larger front wheels, but he damaged the front suspension badly enough to be forced into retirement on lap 19 after misjudging the chicane while trying to overhaul Jo Siffert. Denny kept the team respectable with fourth place ahead of the Swiss pilot who was also driving a March 701.

McLaren withdrew from the Belgian GP at Spa early in June in the immediate aftermath of Bruce's death, and when it returned for the Dutch race later that month Dan Gurney had taken over Bruce's M14A-1 and Peter Gethin had replaced Denny, whose hands were still too raw after the Indianapolis fire, in M14A-2. The former's engine broke its timing gears after he had started from the back of the grid, while the latter crashed out on the 19th lap, necessitating a rebuild around a fresh tub.

Denny made a brave return at the French GP at Clermont-Ferrand to claim fourth place right behind Brabham in M14A-1, officially listed in the entry as M14D-1. He took that to third place in Britain after a very close battle with rookie Clay Regazzoni's Ferrari which was only four-tenths of a second adrift at the flag. In Germany he was third again in what was effectively a new car although the chassis plate concealed this having been swapped over in order to ease the company's progress through international customs. He drove M14A-3 which bore the chassis plate from M14A-2. He went on to finish fourth at Monza, where in practice he had seen the tragedy in which Jochen Rindt was killed, and third in Mexico.

The UK debut for the M14 was at the 1970 Brands Hatch 'Race of Champions' in March. Bruce crashed out on lap 21, while Denny finished third behind Stewart in Ken Tyrrell's March 701 and Rindt in the Gold Leaf Team Lotus Type 49.

The M14 was the last Formula 1 car to be driven by Bruce. His final appearance in the 1970 Monaco Grand Prix was 12 days short of four years since his first GP in a car bearing his own name at Monaco in May of 1966. In five seasons he competed in 34 GPs and scored a total of 60 World Championship points.

Following on from the M7C and M10A which both had the new full monocoque style chassis, the M14 had the same aluminium sheet panels bonded and riveted to three steel bulkheads with the main fuel tank situated in the space created behind the driver's seat.

Back at Brands Hatch for the British Grand Prix in July, Denny Hulme once again finished third. This time Rindt (now in the new Lotus Type 72) was the winner, passing Jack Brabham halfway round the last lap when the Australian ran out of fuel.

REYNOLDS
ALUMINUM
Autolite
BORG & BECK
LOCKHEED
11
Denny Hulme
McLAREN CARS
REYNOLDS
ALUMINUM
GOODYEAR
GOODYEAR

1970 FORMULA 1 McLAREN M14A & M14D

CONTINUED

Gurney scored the final point of his illustrious F1 career with sixth place in France, before electing to retire from the category after suffering engine failure in Britain. Thereafter Gethin had a patchy season as Hulme's team-mate, with only sixth place in Canada to celebrate.

McLaren ran the M19 in 1971, but for a while an M14A reappeared alongside it as Gethin's race car. The South African, Spanish and Monaco GPs yielded little, though he was generally competitive in the ageing car. His best result came at Oulton Park's Spring Cup, where he was able to show his true mettle as he beat Jackie Stewart's Tyrrell, challenged eventual winner Pedro Rodriguez's BRM and set a new lap record before dropping back to finish second just under five seconds adrift after inadvertently hitting the ignition switch on the 20th lap.

Jackie Oliver later raced this car as a third works entry in the British and Italian Grands Prix, without championship point-scoring success. Later the car was acquired by Tony Dean who converted it to Formula 5000 configuration with a Chevrolet V8, without notable success.

There was one other M14 built in 1970, the M14D, for Andrea de Adamich as part of the Autodelta agreement. It was similar to the M14A in all respects apart from modifications to the rear end to accept the Alfa Romeo V8. It first appeared in the Italian's hands at Zandvoort, but yielded no upturn in the fortunes he had encountered with the M7D. He reverted to the latter briefly before resuming with the M14D at Hockenheim. At Österreichring, Monza and St Jovite he was competitive with Denny's Cosworth-powered M14 in qualifying, but his only notable finish was eighth place in the Italian Grand Prix and after non-starting in Watkins Glen he did not make the trip to Mexico City.

The 1970 Spanish Grand Prix at Jarama would be Bruce's last Grand Prix finish. In a race of attrition, he finished an excellent second, albeit a full lap down on winner Jackie Stewart's March 701. The six points left him a posthumous 14th in the Drivers' World Championship at the end of the year.

Peter Gethin was the sole representative of Bruce McLaren Motor Racing at the Silverstone International Trophy meeting in May 1971, when he drove M14A-2 in the two-heat event. After finishing sixth in the first race and fourth in the second, he was classified second overall behind Graham Hill's Brabham BT34.

M14A FORMULA 1
SPECIFICATION

MODEL	McLaren M14A
TYPE/FORMULA	Formula 1
YEAR OF PRODUCTION	1970
DESIGNER	Gordon Coppuck/Jo Marquart
EXAMPLES BUILT	3 +1 (M14D)
ENGINE	Ford Cosworth DFV
CUBIC CAPACITY	2993cc
CARBURATION	Lucas fuel injection
POWER OUTPUT	430bhp

TRANSMISSION	Hewland DG300 5-speed
CHASSIS	18/16swg aluminium skins over mild steel bulkheads
BODY	Monocoque sides, GRP nose & cockpit surround
FRONT SUSPENSION	Single top link & radius arm, lower wishbone, outboard coil spring/damper, anti-roll bar
REAR SUSPENSION	Reverse lower wishbone, top link, twin radius rods, outboard coil spring/damper, anti-roll bar
BRAKES F/R	Outboard/inboard 10.9in discs
WHEELS DIAMETER x WIDTH F/R	15x11/15x16in

TYRES F/R	Goodyear
LENGTH	156in - 3962mm
WIDTH	27in - 686 mm
HEIGHT AT WING	36in - 914mm
WHEELBASE	95in - 2413mm
TRACK F/R	62.5/60in - 1585/1524mm
WEIGHT	1180lb - 535kg
PRINCIPAL DRIVERS	McLaren, Hulme, Gurney, Gethin, Oliver
IDENTIFYING COLOURS	Papaya

1970 INDYCAR
McLAREN M15

Bruce was pleased with certain aspects of the pannier-tanked M7B, which aimed to make the handling more consistent thanks to the weight distribution. This partly explains the genesis of the Gordon Coppuck-designed M15 built for Indianapolis, which was effectively a single-seat version of the outstanding M8.

The decision to tackle the lucrative 500-mile race was said to have been inspired by a radio broadcast detailing Denny Hulme's exploits there in Dan Gurney's Eagle in 1969, and team sponsor Goodyear's keenness to beat rival Firestone at the 'Brickyard'. Having conquered one series of American racing, Bruce characteristically decided: "*Let's have a go.*"

The M15's monocoque terminated immediately behind the driver, and the 2.6-litre turbocharged four-cylinder Offenhauser engine was bolted to two plates on the rear bulkhead. Twin A-frames extended back to the bellhousing which joined it to the Hewland LG500 four-speed transaxle.

The rear suspension comprised reversed lower wishbones and twin radius arms, while up front there were single top links with radius arms, lower wishbones, anti-roll bars and outboard coil spring/damper units. The wheels were McLaren cast magnesium units with knock-off hubs. Goodyear safety fuel cells in the sills held 68 US gallons, helping to give the 1,380lb car the enhanced weight distribution Bruce sought, and its distinctive bulbous profile.

After the first test session at Goodwood in November 1969, Denny accompanied Bruce and Chris Amon to Indianapolis to help them familiarise themselves with the car, the circuit and the unique characteristics of turbo-lag in a 650bhp engine running at 9,000 rpm on Hillborn fuel injection. Hamstrung by a testing regime which allowed only one car out at a time, they nevertheless posted impressive results, Denny lapping the circuit at 168mph and Bruce 162mph. Chris, a driver in Jim Clark's class on his day, simply didn't like the concrete walls that lined the circuit. Eoin Young joked that they should paint some trees on them to make him feel at home.

Once again, with a new car and in a previously unknown motor racing environment, McLaren was beginning to look highly competitive. Pre-race modifications included systems to jack the weight across the car to cater for the high fuel load burning down or to alter the ride heights, adding more than 100lbs to Coppuck's original design weight, but it was still the lightest car in the field. Bruce admitted how much it meant to the company: "*Two months ago we were saying 'Right, remember now, it's just another race...' but there's never been a single race that we've got this excited about.*"

On the first day of official practice in May 1970, the three McLarens really shook the establishment and everybody remarked upon their high standard of construction. But tragedy lay around the corner.

First, came misfortune for Denny. A vibration in the 'Offy' engine caused the springs that were meant to hold the fuel filler caps closed, to flip them open at speed. Mechanic Alan McCall had been forced by scrutineers from the United States Auto Club (USAC) to change the original snap-down design to incorporate an extra spring so that they flipped open faster during pit stops. The caps opened as Denny was out on a fast run, and methanol was sucked from the tanks. At first he thought it was raining, as liquid sprayed the shallow windscreen, but when he braked for the next corner the weight transfer threw more fuel out of the now open left-hand tank. This was blown back by the slipstream on to the hot engine, particularly the turbocharger, and suddenly the car was on fire at 180mph. Methanol, which had been mandated at Indianapolis following the fiery 1964 accident which claimed the lives of Dave Macdonald and Eddie Sachs, burns with an invisible flame but when Denny felt the pain in his leather-clad hands he realised he was in serious trouble. All he wanted was out of the cockpit. He talked of watching the leather disappearing from his gloves and seeing the plastic screen melting before his eyes as, fearing an explosion, he braked harder. That sent more fuel to the fire. Finally, after his first attempt to bale out was thwarted when he forgot to undo his seatbelt, he leapt overboard at 70mph. Rescuers were more concerned about the car, and initially few noticed that the hapless driver's overalls were on fire as he rolled on the grass trying to quell the invisible flames. Denny sustained serious burns to his hands, and would clearly be out of action for the race.

It was not Bruce's intention to race himself at Indianapolis, and with Denny out and Chris electing to give Indianapolis a miss, Peter Revson and USAC specialist Carl Williams were drafted into the cockpits at late notice, the team's plans now heavily compromised. Williams qualified 19th at 166.590mph and finished ninth, three laps down. Revvie qualified 16th at 167.942mph but was classified 22nd after the magneto broke on the 88th lap.

Three days after the race, which was run on Memorial Day, May 30th, came the second hammer blow when Bruce died at Goodwood. Sadly, he would never know how successful McLaren would go on to become at Indianapolis.

The M15s were also raced in the 500 milers at Ontario and Pocono. At the former Revson qualified strongly and was leading by his final pit stop but dropped to fifth after the coil needed changing. Gordon Johncock, another USAC star who had acquired one of the cars after Indianapolis, was fourth. He crashed that very same car at Indianapolis in 1971 after qualifying it 12th at 171.388mph. Other privateers raced M15s, with negligible success.

It is important not to underestimate the disruption caused to the M15 programme by Denny's burns at Indianapolis, then Bruce's death. It did a more than respectable job under traumatic circumstances.

After Hulme was injured and Amon just couldn't come to grips with driving on an oval circuit, Peter Revson and Carl Williams were brought in as the team's two drivers for the 1970 Indy 500. Williams finished a solid ninth but Revson (above) retired after 87 laps.

With fuel consumption of around 2mpg. and the Indy 500 lasting 200 laps of the 2.5-mile circuit, cars were required to refuel several times. An Avery Hardoll 'spill-proof' aircraft style filler unit was fitted to the left side of the car.

With fast fuel stops essential, quick release caps were fitted to both tanks allowing the air inside the each tank to escape and the 68 gallons of methanol fuel to enter faster. It was one of these caps that sprang open and triggered the fire in which Denny sustained the burns to his hands.

M15 INDYCAR
SPECIFICATION

MODEL	McLaren M15
TYPE/FORMULA	Indianapolis/USAC
YEAR OF PRODUCTION	1970
PRINCIPAL DESIGNER	Gordon Coppuck
EXAMPLES BUILT	3
ENGINE TYPE	Offenhauser 4-cylinder turbo
CUBIC CAPACITY	2600cc
CARBURATION	Garrett turbocharger
POWER OUTPUT	650bhp

TRANSMISSION	Hewland LG500 4-speed
CHASSIS	Broad aluminium alloy sheet monocoque, steel bulkheads
BODY	Monocoque sides, GRP nose & cockpit, engine cover
FRONT SUSPENSION	Single top link & radius arm, lower wishbone, outboard coil spring/damper, anti-roll bar
REAR SUSPENSION	Reverse lower wishbone, top link, twin radius rods, outboard coil spring/damper, anti-roll bar
BRAKES F/R	Outboard 11.97in Lockheed ventilated discs
WHEELS DIAMETER x WIDTH F/R	15x10/15x14in

TYRES F/R	Goodyear
LENGTH	156in - 3962mm
WIDTH AT COCKPIT	45in - 102mm
HEIGHT	36in - 914mm
WHEELBASE	99in - 2515mm
TRACK F/R	57.75/58in - 1467/1473mm
WEIGHT	1490lb - 676kg
PRINCIPAL DRIVERS	Revson, Williams, (Hulme, Amon)
IDENTIFYING COLOURS	Papaya

1971 CAN-AM McLAREN-TROJAN M8E

Given McLaren's superb track record in sportscar racing and the high level of support it enjoyed from Chevrolet, Goodyear, Reynolds and Gulf, it was only natural that its continuing domination of the Can-Am series should bring in not just much-needed revenue, but awards too.

Just before Bruce's death Britain's Royal Automobile Club was preparing to announce the presentation to him of the prestigious Segrave Trophy. At the same time, loyal customers were clamouring for something similar to the all-conquering M8D. The result was a new McLaren-Trojan replica for the 1971 season. It received the type number M8E as the team cars' designation was M8F.

The M8D was a sizeable car – pictures taken at the time show the jockey-sized Peter Gethin almost disappearing from view in the cockpit – but though the M8E was based on it, it inherited dimensions from the more compact M8B. It had a four inch narrower track and a low, strut-supported rear wing rather than the M8D's distinctive apparatus. The changes shaved a useful 22lb off the dry weight, making the total 1,425lb.

Construction was mostly of 16 and 20 gauge L72 aluminium alloy, using argon-welded steel bulkheads which were bonded and riveted into place. For the first time in a customer Can-Am McLaren the engine was employed as a stressed unit, although suspension pick-ups were taken from the welded steel bulkheads in order to impart maximum strength. Once again a low centre of gravity was ensured by carrying 56 gallons of fuel in foam-filled rubber Marston cells located within the outer sections of the tub.

The customer cars also generally had larger powerplants than the outgoing M8D, typically a dry-sump aluminium-alloy 8-litre Chevrolet such as the unit shown here. With a stated output of 700bhp with this larger engine, the M8E's transmission was via the familiar Hewland LG500 gearbox with Trojan/BRD splined driveshafts and a triple-plate Borg & Beck clutch.

The M8E pictured here was originally delivered to Roy Woods Racing, to be driven by Vic Elford. It made its debut at Road Atlanta, where Elford qualified six places ahead of another M8E driven by Roger McCaig, before retiring after 35 laps with a broken clutch.

Both were back again two weeks later, however, by which time the field at Watkins Glen was crowded out with a variety of Group 4 and 6 sportscars from the previous day's six hour endurance race. The M8Es qualified 14th and 21st, Elford eventually finishing a respectable eighth.

On August 22nd at Lexington four M8Es took part, but none finished. Neither of the works cars finished either, suffering driveshaft failures. As Hulme's car spun in the pack, causing much confusion, McCaig shot through from 14th to fourth but eventually retired on lap 64 when his engine expired. He was classified 13th, well ahead of the other McLarens.

As the M8Fs dominated, the M8E's best day came at Elkhart Lake. Elford made a strong start from the third row of the grid and finished a well-deserved third behind Peter Revson's team car and Jo Siffert in the fast-improving Porsche 917.

Donnybrooke marked Elford's last drive in the car; he qualified on the third row and finished fourth behind the works cars of Revson and Hulme, and Greg Young's M8E/D.

By 1972 several of the customer cars in the M8 series had become outclassed in a Can-Am series increasingly being dominated by Porsche, and began to find their way back to the UK for the Interserie championship. Appearing alongside the few M8Cs which had been delivered directly to European customers as well as an M12 and the occasional M6B which had run in the series since 1970, the M8E (and later the M8F) was the stalwart of the larger-engine class until it was overcome by the turbocharged Porsche 917s of Willi Kauhsen and Helmuth Kelleners.

At Silverstone for the third round of the 1973 'Interserie' championship, Rolf Gotz in his M8E was disappointed to retire on lap one of the 70-lap race with chronic fuel starvation.

In October 1972 Bill Cuddy finished 12th in the Cuddy Racing Inc. Chevrolet-powered M8E during a rather wet round of the Can-Am series at Laguna Seca. 1972 was the first year of Porsche domination and George Follmer's 917/10K won the championship with 130 points to Denny Hulme's 65.

Teddy Pilette in the Team VDS M8E (chassis 70-08) finished eighth in the 70-lap Super Sports 200 Interserie Championship race at Silverstone in May 1972. The European series was also dominated by Porsche, with Leo Kinnunen in his 917/10 taking the title.

M8E CAN-AM
SPECIFICATION

MODEL	McLaren-Trojan M8E
TYPE/FORMULA	Can-Am
YEAR OF PRODUCTION	1971
DESIGNER	Jo Marquart
EXAMPLES BUILT	15-18 (insufficient records)
ENGINE	Chevrolet/Ford V8
CUBIC CAPACITY	7000-8095cc
CARBURATION	Lucas fuel injection
POWER OUTPUT	650-700bhp

TRANSMISSION	Hewland LG500 4-speed
CHASSIS	Aluminium sheet monocoque with steel bulkheads
BODY	Monocoque sides, GRP body sections, aluminium wing
FRONT SUSPENSION	Single top link & radius arm, lower wishbone, outboard coil spring/damper, anti-roll bar
REAR SUSPENSION	Reverse lower wishbone, single top link, twin radius rods, coil spring/damper, anti-roll bar
BRAKES F/R	Outboard 11.9in ventilated discs
WHEELS DIAMETER x WIDTH F/R	15x11/15x16in

TYRES F/R	Goodyear
LENGTH	153in - 3886mm
WIDTH	74in - 1880mm
HEIGHT TO WINDSCREEN	30in - 762mm
WHEELBASE	94in - 2387mm
TRACK F/R	58/55in - 1473/1397mm
WEIGHT	1425lb - 647kg
PRINCIPAL DRIVERS	Elford, McCaig, Drolsom
IDENTIFYING COLOURS	n/a

1971 & 1972 CAN-AM
McLAREN M8F & McLAREN-TROJAN M8F/P

Somewhat belatedly, Peter Revson in 1971 became the first North American to win his 'home' Can-Am Championship. And though nobody knew it at the time, his success in the M8F would prove to be McLaren's last year of domination of the series. The baton would pass to Porsche and its turbocharged 917/10K, but not before M8s had chalked up 32 wins in 37 races, 19 of them in succession.

In a pattern which was becoming increasingly familiar, Gordon Coppuck created the strongest, longest, widest and heaviest Can-Am McLaren thus far. The chassis comprised another simple but effective monocoque with steel bulkheads, now employing Reynolds-sourced aluminium inner and outer skins of slightly heavier gauge than that used in previous M8s.

Two foam-filled rubber fuel cells on either side of the driver created a total capacity of 72 US gallons. Well-balanced as it undoubtedly already was, the additional size and ballast did much to improve the M8F's handling. The braking system was also improved, thanks to moving the rear discs and calipers inboard.

The track dimensions were reduced slightly to enable 17 inch rims to fit within the rear bodywork, but the uncompromisingly brutal body shape was otherwise very similar to the 'Batmobile' M8D albeit with aerodynamic fences now running the full length of the body atop the wing line. These helped to channel airflow more efficiently over the top of the bodyshell to the low-mounted rear wing and, allied to a revised nose shape, helped the M8F to generate 1.5 tonnes of downforce.

By the first race of the sixth season of Can-Am, Peter 'Revvie' Revson had been signed to partner Denny Hulme following his impressive showings the previous year in Carl Haas's Lola T220. In qualifying at Mosport in mid-June it was clear that the M8F drivers' strongest competition all season was likely to come from 1969 World Champion Jackie Stewart in a bespoke Lola T260. The Scot took pole, but within five laps Denny had put five seconds of clean air between himself and the rest of the field. The result was another 1-2, with second an excellent result for new boy Revson.

At St Jovite a fortnight later pole was Denny's and Revvie started in third place, having been busy in the meantime with his USAC McLaren commitments. Stewart's Lola was the filling in the McLaren sandwich, but in the race itself the Scot sprang a surprise by leading an unwell Denny and Revvie home.

Highly concerned, McLaren went directly to Road Atlanta to test prior to the next race, where Revvie used a new lineless Reynolds all-aluminium 7.9-litre Chevrolet V8. Stewart led again but retired, and Revvie led Denny home in another 1-2 though the New Zealand veteran was running out of brakes.

Stewart was on pole again at Watkins Glen on July 25th, and led until the Lola sustained a puncture. Thereafter it was Revvie all the way, using another new Reynolds-block engine enlarged this time to 8.4 litres thanks to a longer-throw crankshaft. Denny was second again.

Stewart won at Mid-Ohio, where both McLarens suffered universal joint failures, while Denny led and looked set to head another M8F 1-2 at Elkhart Lake until a broken crankshaft forced him out, leaving Revson to take the honours. Revvie led from start to finish at Donnybrooke, with Denny inheriting second place when Stewart's Lola retired.

Denny won at Edmonton and Revvie at Laguna Seca, where he ignored a black flag at the start of his last lap for dropping oil. Riverside marked the last outing for the works M8-series cars. The championship was already wrapped up, so both drivers ran the sleeveless 8.3-litre engines. Denny smashed the course record to take pole by a full second from Revvie, and won the race going away. Revvie was happy to keep Stewart at bay, aware that sixth place would be sufficient to clinch him the title, and duly finished runner-up. He took the title with 142 points to Denny's 132, five wins to three. Lola had won twice, its first successes since John Surtees won at Vegas in 1967, but for McLaren the season had virtually been business as usual.

While the works team was developing the radically different M20 to run in the 1972 Can-Am, Trojan was putting the M8F into limited production - just 10 were built - as a customer car. Designated M8FP, these models were virtually identical to the '71 team cars and as such were seemingly only ever referred to by the factory as M8Fs. With eight different drivers listed as driving M8Fs or M8FPs, the best result of the year and the only McLaren victory other than those taken by Denny in the works M20, came courtesy of Tyrrell F1 star François Cevert who pedalled Greg Young's M8F to a superb triumph at Donnybrooke in September after the works cars failed, and the dominant turbo Porsches ran out of luck.

The Mid Ohio Can-Am round in August 1971 was one of the two races won that year by Jackie Stewart. In a controversial weekend with concerns over the safety of the circuit, Hulme (seen here in practice) crashed out on the first lap and Revson retired on the last of the 72 laps.

Peter Revson won four races to Hulme's three (and Stewart's two in the Lola) and took the 1971 Can-Am title with a second place at the final race at Riverside and a total of 142 points to Denny's 132.

1971 saw the first appearance of drinks giant Coca-Cola as a sponsor of the McLaren team, and the company logo could be seen on both the rear tail fins as well as the lower bodywork.

M8F CAN-AM
SPECIFICATION

MODEL	McLaren M8F
TYPE/FORMULA	Can-Am
YEAR OF PRODUCTION	1971
DESIGNER	Gordon Coppuck
EXAMPLES BUILT	3
ENGINE	Chevrolet V8
CUBIC CAPACITY	7900-8400cc
CARBURATION	Lucas fuel injection
POWER OUTPUT	700-720bhp

TRANSMISSION	Hewland LG600 5-speed
CHASSIS	Aluminium sheet monocoque, with steel bulkheads
BODY	Monocoque sides, GRP body sections, integral wing
FRONT SUSPENSION	Single top link & radius arm, lower wishbone, outboard coil spring/damper, anti-roll bar
REAR SUSPENSION	Reverse lower wishbone, single top link, twin radius rods, coil spring/damper, anti-roll bar
BRAKES F/R	Outboard 12in ventilated discs
WHEELS DIAMETER x WIDTH F/R	15x11/15x17in

TYRES F/R	Goodyear
LENGTH	167in - 4242mm
WIDTH	76in - 1930mm
HEIGHT	32in - 812mm
WHEELBASE	98in - 2489mm
TRACK F/R	60/58.75in - 1524/1492mm
WEIGHT	1520lb - 689kg
PRINCIPAL DRIVERS	Hulme, Revson, Gethin
IDENTIFYING COLOURS	Papaya

1971 & 1972 CAN-AM
McLAREN M8F & McLAREN-TROJAN M8F/P
CONTINUED

At the third round of the 1972 'Interserie' Championship at Silverstone, the Helmut Felder-entered M8F/P was driven by Helmut Kelleners. After coming second in the first heat, he retired on the seventh lap of heat two with a broken cam follower.

M8F/P CAN-AM
SPECIFICATION

MODEL	McLaren-Trojan M8F/P
TYPE/FORMULA	Can-Am
YEAR OF PRODUCTION	1972
DESIGNER	Gordon Coppuck
EXAMPLES BUILT	10
ENGINE	Chevrolet V8
CUBIC CAPACITY	8093cc
CARBURATION	Lucas fuel injection
POWER OUTPUT	710bhp

TRANSMISSION	Hewland LG600 5-speed
CHASSIS	Aluminium sheet monocoque, with steel bulkheads
BODY	Monocoque sides, GRP body sections, integral wing
FRONT SUSPENSION	Single top link & radius arm, lower wishbone, outboard coil spring/damper, anti-roll bar
REAR SUSPENSION	Reverse lower wishbone, single top link, twin radius rods, coil spring/damper, anti-roll bar
BRAKES F/R	Outboard 12in ventilated discs
WHEELS DIAMETER x WIDTH F/R	15x11/15x17in

TYRES F/R	Goodyear
LENGTH	167in - 4242mm
WIDTH	76in - 1930mm
HEIGHT	32in - 812mm
WHEELBASE	98in - 2489mm
TRACK F/R	60/58.75in - 1524/1492mm
WEIGHT	1520lb - 689kg
PRINCIPAL DRIVERS	McCaig, Cevert, Agor
IDENTIFYING COLOURS	n/a

1971 & 1972 INDYCAR McLAREN M16 & M16B

The M15 performed more than adequately on its debut at Indianapolis in 1970, but having seen how effective Colin Chapman's wedge-shaped Lotus Type 72 was in the summer of that season, Gordon Coppuck was very taken with the idea of running a car of similar shape at the American oval.

He believed that McLaren had learned a lot about Indy from the M15, and while he wasn't convinced the 72 was the right shape for Grand Prix racing, he thought the basic concept would work well for an Indy car. He told Doug Nye in McLAREN The Grand Prix, Can-Am and Indy Cars: "*For Indy we thought it must be a dead cinch. Your aerodynamic forces are very constant at Indy, with only about a 60mph difference in running speed at each corner; you're doing about 210mph on the straights and 150mph through the corners.*" Work on a new design started immediately after the 1970 race and the result, when the papaya orange cars were shown to the press at Colnbrook in January 1971, was quite sensational.

Without building a prototype the team had gone straight into production with a really striking car based on another L72 aluminium-skinned monocoque with steel bulkheads, but this time with a more wedge-shaped cross-section. Once again sponsorship came from Goodyear, Gulf and of course Reynolds Aluminium.

As in the M15, the Offenhauser turbo engine was mounted in a triangulated supporting frame. The 2.6-litre, overhead cam unit might have been one of the oldest powerplants then in production, tracing its origins to a Miller design of 1931, but with tweaks from Gary Knutson it was still good for around 700bhp while pulling up to 9000rpm. Allied to the familiar Hewland LG500 transaxle – McLaren favoured a three-speed unit over the usual Indy two-speed – it was to prove a formidable combination, with the additional ratio offering especially rapid acceleration out of the pits and after any yellow-light period.

With the radiators moved to the cars' hips, where they were enclosed by glass-fibre ducts, the Specialised Mouldings nosecone now contained little more than fire-extinguishing equipment, thereby creating a smooth and especially penetrative shape. To smooth the airflow still further the front suspension was moved inboard as the tub width was kept to a minimum. Coppuck incorporated a degree of rising rate in the suspension which offered greater resistance the greater the deflection, to help keep the car stable at high speeds.

There was space within the chassis for 75 US gallons of methanol-based fuel, via Goodyear cells on either side. This was crucial in a series where three fuel stops were mandatory per race and cars did well to achieve two miles per gallon.

In all its various guises the M16 concept would go down in motorsport history as one of the most successful cars in the long and illustrious history of the Indianapolis 500. Competing in 11 races and taking three victories, four seconds and two third places, it laid the foundations for an astonishingly fruitful adventure for what was still a small team.

The radical, Lotus-inspired wedge shape, while familiar in F1, caused astonishment at Indianapolis, where just as Coppuck had suspected, it proved ideal for the continuous high-speed running which characterised the racing. It generated significant aerodynamic downforce, though initially it proved quite challenging to balance this correctly over the front and rear ends. There was a lot of downforce at the front, and this had to be balanced by the large rear wing which operated in conjunction with a smooth engine cover, and by improving airflow over the whole car. Small canard fins either side of the nose helped with this trimming, while the turbocharger was sited as low as possible on a bespoke manifold to keep it out of the airstream. In comparison with many other Indy cars of the time, which tended to metamorphose each year, the M16's engine installation was astonishingly tidy. Cleverly, Coppuck had also incorporated the rear wing into the bodywork, rightly suspecting that rivals would attempt to protest that wings were not allowed. The USAC scrutineers looked at the car, and said they were happy that its wings were bodywork and that it complied with the rules.

Within days of the 1,380lb racer being shown to the press, testing began in earnest with Denny Hulme and Peter Revson taking the controls at the new Ontario Motor Speedway in California. Subsequently M16-1 was taken over by Roger Penske, so that Mark Donohue could test further at Phoenix with engineer Don Cox. By March they had moved on to Indianapolis, where Donohue stunned rivals with a lap of 172mph. When official practice for the 500 started in May, he upped the Penske car's speed to 174.757mph against the previous best of 171.953 which dated back to 1968. Denny lapped in 172.944, and the old hands threw up their hands in horror. The following day Donohue hit 177.901mph, averaging 176.3 over four laps. And he wasn't finished. A week later he topped out at a staggering 180.900mph, while Revvie lapped at 174 for second fastest time.

In early March 1971, prior to its first run at Indy, Denny Hulme tested the new M16 at Ontario Motor Speedway in California. He turned in some very fast lap times of well over 190mph.

This aerodynamic 'engine cover' which some felt was nothing more than a rear wing, caused a great deal of controversy at the 1971 Indy 500. By 1972 the authorities had relented and allowed 'proper' wings.

Opposite.
Denny Hulme qualified fourth on the grid for the 1971 Indy 500 but retired from eighth position with engine problems on lap 138 of the race.

M16 INDYCAR
SPECIFICATION

MODEL	McLaren M16
TYPE/FORMULA	Indianapolis/USAC
YEAR OF PRODUCTION	1971
DESIGNER	Gordon Coppuck
EXAMPLES BUILT	3
ENGINE	Offenhauser 4-cylinder turbo
CUBIC CAPACITY	2600cc
CARBURATION	Hilborn injection, Garrett Airesearch turbocharger
POWER OUTPUT	700+bhp

TRANSMISSION	Hewland LG500 3-speed
CHASSIS	Full aluminium monocoque, steel bulkheads
BODY	Monocoque sides, GRP nose & cockpit, engine cover
FRONT SUSPENSION	Welded cantilever rocker arm operating
	inboard coil spring/damper, lower wishbone
REAR SUSPENSION	Reverse lower wishbone, top link, twin
	radius rods, coil spring/damper, anti-roll bar
BRAKES F/R	Drilled outboard 11.9in discs
WHEELS DIAMETER x WIDTH F/R	15x10/15x14in

TYRES F/R	Goodyear
LENGTH	155in - 3937mm
WIDTH AT RADIATORS	61in - 1550mm
HEIGHT OF ROLLHOOP	38in - 965mm
WHEELBASE	101in - 2565mm
TRACK F/R	58/58in - 1473/1473mm
WEIGHT	1380lb - 626kg
PRINCIPAL DRIVERS	Hulme, Revson, Donohue
IDENTIFYING COLOURS	Papaya

1971 & 1972 INDYCAR McLAREN M16 & M16B

CONTINUED

Immediately Donohue had seen McLaren's new M16, on a flying visit to the Colnbrook factory early in 1971 while he and Penske were shopping for a Can-Am car and were talking with Lola about a new Indy contender, he had said that he "*knew they had a much better overall package than we were discussing with Lola. They had obviously learned a lot about wings in Formula 1 and were applying that knowledge to Indy.*"

The McLarens dominated official qualifying later that week, as Revvie grabbed the pole at a towering 178.696mph, Donohue was right behind him on 177.087, their respective best laps in their mandatory four-lap qualifying averages being 179.354 and 178.60. Bobby Unser squeezed his Eagle into third place, but Denny was right behind him at 174.900mph to give the M16s three out of the top four grid slots for the race on May 29th. It was a quite remarkable performance, and as Donohue put it later: "*The new McLarens obsoleted every other car on the track.*"

Following the traditional rolling start, Donohue led the way with Revson taking second place and Hulme spinning at Turn Three, though he later recovered to eighth place before a broken valve forced him out on lap 138. Donohue was also to experience problems and slowed with transmission difficulties, eventually dropping out after 66 laps. Revvie, who had been suckered at the start by Donohue and Unser, had the last laugh, though the crew were disappointed that having lost confidence in his car's handling, he did not attack defending champion Al Unser Snr (Bobby's brother) in a Johnny Lightning Colt Ford in the closing stages as he headed for second place. He crossed the line 24s adrift.

One car finishing out of three was well short of what the team was aiming for, but its achievement was nevertheless considerable. Second place at an average speed of 183.378mph, and some record-breaking qualifying times, had enabled the distinctively designed McLarens to make their lasting mark on the home crowd at the Speedway. Pushing forward with a truly revolutionary design, the team hitherto best known to Americans for its Can-Am sportscars demonstrated in the clearest terms that it was one to watch out for in the future.

The Penske M16 had been written off at Indianapolis after its retirement when it was struck where it lay by the side of the track as Mike Mosley lost control of his Eagle on the exit of Turn Four. The chassis was rebuilt at Colnbrook, and in the inaugural Pocono 500 Donohue scored McLaren's first Indy racing victory. To prove it was no fluke, he backed it up by winning at Michigan. He could have won the California 500 at Ontario too, but for running out of fuel when unaccountably he missed pit signals.

Donohue, a highly respected and very well-liked figure on the US scene, was more than justified in his original view that by the time Penske had finished converting a Lola for Indy racing the result would be, in comparison with the McLaren, "*cobbled together*". His admiration for the totality of the M16 design, not to mention its storming performances in 1971, persuaded the factory of the wisdom of investing in further development of its existing car rather than designing a new one for 1972.

As Dan Gurney worked on a slippery new Eagle designed by Roman Slobodynskyj, the M16 morphed into the M16B. Together with deeper front and rear wings it gained revised steering geometry, a sleek new bullet-shaped fairing over the plenum chamber and 25 per cent larger radiators. The nose was shortened too, taking on a bluff shape rather than its pointed wedge, so that the rear wing could be moved even further back yet still stay within the stipulated 158 inch maximum car length.

Penske ordered two of the new cars immediately, one for Donohue and the other for Gary Bettenhausen, scion of one of Indy racing's most famous families. The works entered two cars at Indianapolis, for regular Peter Revson and private M15 owner Gordon Johncock, but it was for the Sunoco Penske team, rather than for McLaren itself, that the new M16B was to turn its most significant trick in the famed '500'.

The previous season the rest of the field had complained about what they saw as McLaren's unfair advantage; in particular there was a hue and cry about it having too much of the engine exposed and 'illegal' wings. Beaten rivals were quick to learn, however, and it was Bobby Unser in Gurney's new Eagle who took the top slot on the grid as speeds rocketed. The 1968 race winner averaged a staggering 195.940mph to take the pole for 1972 Indy 500. Revvie got the closest to him, at 192.885mph in the fastest of the M16Bs. Donohue was third at 191.408.

In the race itself, however, both Unser and Revson retired early, with a broken distributor rotor and gearbox respectively. Then Gurney's second driver, Jerry Grant, made a pit stop on lap 188 to investigate a tyre vibration, handing the lead to Donohue. In the interests of reliability, Penske had insisted on his driver running less turbo boost, and the ploy paid off handsomely. Donohue had a clear run to the flag and didn't squander the opportunity. The M16B averaged 162.962mph, and while it wasn't a works car which achieved it, a car inspired by Bruce McLaren had won the Indy 500 for the first time.

Prior to its departure for the 1972 Indy 500 Peter Revson and chief designer Gordon Coppuck pose with the sensational looking M16B. Having taken the pole in 1971, 33-year-old Revson was, to quote the Gulf-McLaren press release, "*hoping to take it all*" in that year's race.

This style of 'flat bottomed' steering wheel favoured by Denny Hulme was used on the M16. It featured a rather basic 'crash pad' in the centre and became common in oval racing. The Garrett Airesearch turbo gave the 30-year-old 'Offy' engine 700+ bhp. It would be 1977 before the Cosworth DFX would surpass its impressive level of horsepower.

The car featured here and on the right is the Sunoco-Penske winning car from 1972. Mark Donohue started third on the grid and set a steady pace waiting for the leaders to hit trouble. Sure enough they did, and he cruised home to win McLaren's first Indy 500 and the $218,763 prize money.

M16B INDYCAR
SPECIFICATION

MODEL	McLaren M16B
TYPE/FORMULA	Indianapolis/USAC
YEAR OF PRODUCTION	1972
DESIGNER	Gordon Coppuck
EXAMPLES BUILT	4
ENGINE	Offenhauser 4-cylinder turbo
CUBIC CAPACITY	2600cc
CARBURATION	Hilborn injection, Garrett Airesearch turbocharger
POWER OUTPUT	700-750bhp
TRANSMISSION	Hewland LG500 4-speed
CHASSIS	Full aluminium monocoque, steel bulkheads
BODY	Monocoque sides, GRP nose & cockpit, engine cover
FRONT SUSPENSION	Welded cantilever top arm operating inboard coil spring/damper, lower wishbone
REAR SUSPENSION	Reverse lower wishbone, top link, twin radius rods, coil spring/damper, anti-roll bar
BRAKES F/R	Drilled outboard 11.9in discs
WHEELS DIAMETER x WIDTH F/R	15x10/15x14in
TYRES F/R	Goodyear
LENGTH	158in - 4013mm
WIDTH	76in - 1930mm
HEIGHT	38in - 965mm
WHEELBASE	101in - 2565mm
TRACK F/R	58/58in - 1473/1473mm
WEIGHT	1380lb - 626kg
PRINCIPAL DRIVERS	Hulme, Revson, Donohue
IDENTIFYING COLOURS	Papaya/Blue

1971 FORMULA 5000 McLAREN-TROJAN M18

The M17 designation was intended for a 3-litre sports prototype design which was abandoned and the next McLaren in line, the M18, was a new Formula 5000 car for the 1971 season.

Once again it was built by Trojan and power came from the usual 5-litre Chevrolet V8. As such it had much in common with the earlier M10A/M10B even though it used the five-speed DG300 in place of the LG600, but it also owed something to the M16 in an attempt to adopt a wedge shape, and was substantially lighter than its class predecessors. As indicated by the Trojan suffix, it was always intended as a customer car although one owner, Irishman Sid Taylor, enjoyed some works support.

With most of the main test and evaluation work carried out by Bruce McLaren himself, the M10A was a successful machine that saw off the likes of Lola's T142 spaceframe contender and remained the class of the field against the monocoque offerings from that rival, Surtees and Leda. It followed that it would be a hard act to follow, and the Ralph Bellamy-designed M18 never really looked like the car to do it. Its performance was a disappointment both for the company and Trojan, although Brian Redman's talent at the wheel won the M18 early success in the UK until Surtees' TS8 and, later in the season, Lola's new T300, hit their stride. Altogether 10 cars were completed, eight with official chassis numbers and two more apparently built up from completed tubs at a later date. But many observers had the distinct impression that the older M10B was actually a quicker car than the £4,850 machine which replaced it.

Bellamy's penmanship ensured it was at least a handsome machine, its flatter nose redesigned with high-sited wings and a larger radiator, and the fuel tank had a central filler. With 45 gallons held in foam-filled Marston cells located in the side sections the top fuel bag was eliminated, thereby lowering the centre of gravity. At the same time all the pipework for delivery and return of water was mounted externally to optimise cooling.

In a form which was by 1971 wholly familiar, the bonded and riveted monocoque weighing just 80lb was constructed from panels of 16 gauge aluminium formed around steel bulkheads. The front suspension used a lower wishbone with a top link and radius arm, whilst at the rear reversed lower wishbones were mated to top links and radius rods. Formula 1 Lockheed ventilated discs were standard, with actuation via twin master cylinders. The driven wheels were 15x16 inch magnesium alloys with similar 13x11 inch rims up front. All-up weight was 1,350lb.

McLaren made more than 50 Formula 5000 cars, but the M18's record fell a long way short of impressive. Chassis M18 500-1, Redman's Sid Taylor Racing car which was actually built by McLaren rather than Trojan, won one of its first three races, posted two seconds and another late season victory at Brands Hatch, to come fifth in the European Championship. It was then taken over by the McLaren team itself, but Reine Wisell crashed it out of the final race of the season, the Rothmans World Champion Victory Race at Brands Hatch. This chassis was then developed into the prototype M22 that was raced in the 1972 Tasman Series by David Hobbs.

The next car, the Trojan Team 500-02, was raced by Graham McRae in 1971 but crashed and described in Britain's Autosport magazine as destroyed. In any case, he preferred his heavily modified M10B. The whereabouts of 500-03, the so-called Eppie Wietzes car, are currently unknown, but the fourth car in the series was raced by Tim Schenken, Howden Ganley (who crashed it) and Jean-Pierre Jaussaud in Barry Newman's dark green livery. It raced into 1974, without distinction, and in at least one libre race.

Chassis 500-05 was another Team Trojan car, driven by Ulf Norinder before being sold to Speed International Racing which campaigned it throughout 1972 with David Prophet, Ray Allen and Gijs van Lennep. In 1973 it was sold to Shell Oil for use in static displays and popped up in HSCC events for several years before a bad crash at Oulton Park.

The history of 500-06 is far less clear, this 1971 car being rebuilt with a new tub after being destroyed by Al Lader in an end-of-season US crash. It joined the 1972 New Zealand Tasman series and then went on to the US, scoring a second place in its Edmonton debut but was crashed at Watkins Glen before being rebuilt yet again. Since then a car known as chassis 500-06A has appeared in California, perhaps having been built up from one of the damaged tubs, while another, 500-06B, surfaced in New Zealand and is thought to have been rebuilt from a new tub - originally supplied after Lader's wreck - for the 1974 Tasman series. The car still exists in this form, and has been described as both a McLaren M18/22 and a McLaren M18C.

The existence of other M18 chassis has been suggested and the probable remains of 500-07 have also been traced, while parts thought to have come from 500-08 are believed to have been reused in the building of the rival Gardos F5000 machine.

Round 11 of the 17-round European F5000 championship was the Esso Uniflo Trophy at Silverstone on August 14th 1971. Brian Redman in the Sid Taylor M18 qualified seventh but ran out of fuel on lap 22 of the 25 lap race.

The McLaren-Trojan M18 was based on an M16 style chassis with Formula 1 style suspension and, after the M10 and M10B which had dominated F5000 in Europe, the USA and Australia, was a huge disappointment.

On the Saturday before the 1972 Brands Hatch Race of Champions there was a round of the European F5000 series. Teddy Pilette in the VDS Racing M18 finished fifth and qualified to take part in Sunday's RoC where he finished 11th overall and second in the Formula 5000 category.

The Chevrolet V8 engine bolted to the back of the tub was used as a fully stressed member and produced around 530bhp.

M18 FORMULA 5000

SPECIFICATION

MODEL	McLaren-Trojan M18
TYPE/FORMULA	Formula 5000/Formula A
YEAR OF PRODUCTION	1971
DESIGNER	Ralph Bellamy
EXAMPLES BUILT	8
ENGINE	Chevrolet V8
CUBIC CAPACITY	5000cc
CARBURATION	Lucas fuel injection
POWER OUTPUT	530bhp

TRANSMISSION	Hewland DG300 5-speed
CHASSIS	Full aluminium monocoque, steel bulkheads
BODY	Formed by monocoque, GRP nose & radiator shroud
FRONT SUSPENSION	Single top link & radius arm, lower wishbone, outboard coil spring/damper, anti-roll bar
REAR SUSPENSION	Reverse lower wishbone, single top link, twin radius rods, coil spring/damper, anti-roll bar
BRAKES F/R	Outboard/inboard 10.5in discs
WHEELS DIAMETER x WIDTH F/R	13x11/15x16in

TYRES F/R	Goodyear
LENGTH	166.5in - 4229mm
WIDTH OVERALL	77in - 1956mm
HEIGHT TO WINDSCREEN	26.5in - 673mm
WHEELBASE	100in - 2540mm
TRACK F/R	59.5/59.75in - 1511/1517mm
WEIGHT	1350lb - 612kg
PRINCIPAL DRIVERS	Redman, McRae, Pilette
IDENTIFYING COLOURS	n/a

1971 & 1972 FORMULA 1 McLAREN M19A & M19C

The M19 was Australian Ralph Bellamy's 1971 Formula 1 contender, with which McLaren hoped to make amends for the rather disappointing M14 design.

Wider and longer, the M19A's most distinctive feature was the way its belly swelled out in what Bellamy described as "*a Coke-bottle shape, like a Matra MS80,*" referring to Jackie Stewart's 1969 World Championship-winning car. Conceived by Jo Marquart around a longer wheelbase to accommodate the fuel as centrally as possible, the double curvature panelling was worked in 16 gauge NS4 aluminium by Don Beresford and Leo Wybrott.

Upon viewing the car Motor Sport magazine's technically minded writer, Denis Jenkinson, reported: "*As with all the McLaren racing cars the detail work is a joy to see, the standard of finish being very high indeed.*"

As on the M14A the brakes were mounted outboard at the front and inboard at the rear, but the suspension differed radically as Bellamy opted for a degree of rising rate in which the resistance to movement increased as wheel deflection increased. This was achieved by using conventional, inboard-mounted linear springs activated by a novel linkage system which worked to compress both spring and damper to a greater or lesser extent as the wheels rose and fell over bumps.

The system was chosen not least because in the early 1970s F1 cars were sprung relatively softly, which meant running quite generous ride heights. When carrying a full fuel load cars were liable to bottom out on undulating circuits. The Lotus 72 had to an extent demonstrated the previous year that rising rate suspension could be used to circumvent that problem with its complex torsion bar system; now McLaren believed it had discovered a simpler and less expensive alternative means.

The new system was more complicated to set-up but Denny liked the car on the smooth surface of Kyalami and, having qualified only fifth for the season opener, was already fourth at the end of the opening lap. Then he overtook Jacky Ickx's Ferrari, Emerson Fittipaldi's Lotus and the leading Ferrari of Clay Regazzoni and soon pulled away. Then on the 76th of the 79 laps Denny began to feel the M19A squirming beneath him. Fearful of a puncture he dropped back to a sixth place finish one lap down; later it transpired that the bolt securing the upper right radius arm in the rear suspension had sheared.

Thereafter Denny notched up fourths in Monaco and Canada and a fifth in Spain, and they would be his best results in a season that flattered only to deceive. McLaren had two M19As by the Dutch GP in June. Peter Gethin and Jackie Oliver both drove the second car, each taking a ninth, the former in France, the latter in Austria.

Ironically, the M19A's best performance was achieved by Grand Prix debutant Mark Donohue who drove a Penske-liveried version superbly to third place in the rain in Canada behind only Jackie Stewart and Ronnie Peterson. In his biography, The Unfair Advantage, Donohue described the result as a gift, thanks to the weather.

Problems in the M19A's inconsistent performance were put down to understeer induced by tyre vibration associated with the low-profile rubber that was becoming fashionable, continued difficulties setting up the rising rate suspension, and an imbalance in the aerodynamics. In the US GP at Watkins Glen late in the year, Denny ran his car with an experimental wide nose, without noticeable improvement in its performance.

With Gordon Coppuck tied up working on the Indy cars, and Jo Marquart leaving to co-found junior formula race car manufacturer Huron, Bellamy had complete responsibility for the M19A, and he summarised the 1971 season thus: "*The rising-rate suspension offered many clear theoretical advantages, but in practice it worked well enough at the front of the car and less well at the back. Trying to sort it out and find a set up that the driver felt happy with and could understand what was going on, proved rather tricky.*"

The answers were slow in coming even when Roger Penske agreed to put Donohue, a renowned car sorter, in an M19A for a prolonged test at Silverstone. He complained about the car oversteering, so more rear wing was added only for the car to oversteer even more. When the same thing happened again the team was even more confused until someone eventually suggested that the more downforce they were putting on the back of the car the more it tended to push the car into the stiffer part of the suspension's rate curve. Eventually the radical rear suspension was ditched in favour of a non-rising rate M14A rear end. Bellamy thought the improvement was dramatic, but his podium position first time out in Canada notwithstanding, Donohue was forever frustrated that even he couldn't figure out the rising rate front suspension properly. He finally concluded that half the problem was that the rear wing rarely worked efficiently.

The big change as the M19A went into 1972 was a change of colour scheme, a consequence of Yardley Cosmetics switching from BRM. The new white livery with the black, brown and gold Yardley 'Y' left a small space for some papaya orange flashes on the sides as a sop to tradition.

On Monday 15th February 1971 the curvy Ralph Bellamy-designed M19 was shown to the press for the first time. Seen here inside the tidy-looking McLaren workshops at Colnbrook (it was raining), the pronounced 'Coke-bottle' shape of the M19 is clearly visible.

The rear of the M19A was fairly conventional, with the Cosworth DFV mounted directly to the rear bulkhead of the chassis and carrying the rear suspension on a slender-looking bridge over the gearbox. As at the front, the rear dampers were mounted inboard and operated by a rocker arm and cantilever.

Peter Gethin's M19A is prepared for the 1971 German Grand Prix at the Nürburgring. Of the 22 starters he could only qualify 20th and spun out of the 12-lap race on lap five. Team mate Hulme faired even worse, retiring on lap three with a fuel leak.

Opposite.
In his first GP appearance, the 1971 Canadian race at Mosport Park, Mark Donohue qualified Roger Penske's M19 eighth on the grid and ahead of Denny Hulme. He finished the rain-soaked race on the podium in third place. Hulme was fourth.

M19A FORMULA 1
SPECIFICATION

MODEL	McLaren M19A
TYPE/FORMULA	Formula 1
YEAR OF PRODUCTION	1971/1972
DESIGNER	Ralph Bellamy
EXAMPLES BUILT	2
ENGINE	Ford Cosworth DFV
CUBIC CAPACITY	2993cc
CARBURATION	Lucas fuel injection
POWER OUTPUT	440bhp

TRANSMISSION	Hewland DG300 5-speed
CHASSIS	Full aluminium monocoque, steel bulkheads
BODY	Formed by monocoque, GRP nosecone
FRONT SUSPENSION	Double wishbone, with push rod and rocker operating inboard coil spring/damper, anti-roll bar
REAR SUSPENSION	Lower wishbone, top link, push rod acting on inboard coil spring/damper, twin radius rods, anti-roll bar
BRAKES F/R	Outboard/inboard 10.5in ventilated discs
WHEELS DIAMETER x WIDTH F/R	13x11/13 or 15x16in

TYRES F/R	Goodyear
LENGTH	160in - 4064mm
WIDTH OF CHASSIS AT COCKPIT	42in - 1066mm
HEIGHT OF REAR WING	34in - 864mm
WHEELBASE	100in - 2540mm
TRACK F/R	63/62in - 1600/1575mm
WEIGHT	1230lb - 558kg
PRINCIPAL DRIVERS	Hulme, Gethin, Oliver
IDENTIFYING COLOURS	Papaya, Blue

1971 & 1972 FORMULA 1 McLAREN M19A & M19C

CONTINUED

The other crucial change, initially made on the M19As but then carried over once the new M19Cs arrived later in the season, was the permanent adoption of conventional rear suspension. That, and other subtle changes which led to better understanding of the rising rate front suspension, transformed the M19A. Peter Revson had done so well for McLaren in USAC and Can-Am in 1971 that he was promoted to the F1 team, returning to the category after initial outings in the mid-1960s as a privateer.

Back at Kyalami for the South African GP, Denny in M19A-2 was able to expunge his 1971 disappointment by winning as former motorcycle champion Mike Hailwood's Surtees retired. Revson brought M19A-1 home third to complete a highly satisfying weekend for the revitalised team. Later, the duo completed a McLaren 2-3 at the Österreichring, finishing just a second behind Emerson Fittipaldi in the all-conquering Lotus 72 that took the Brazilian to that season's title.

By then Denny was driving a revised car designated M19C-1 with Revvie taking over M19A-2 which had received some updated modifications itself when it had to be rebuilt around one of the simpler and lighter new monocoques after being crashed by Brian Redman, who stood in at Monaco and Clermont-Ferrand when Revvie was racing in USAC events.

The M19C, which first appeared at the Race of Champions in March, took up where the revised M19A left off. Minor changes, such as the front bulkhead being fabricated rather than cast, together with lighter suspension wishbones, solid driveshafts of smaller diameter than the previous tubular components, and less complex mounts for the rear wing, all contributed to making the M19C lighter than its predecessor.

Denny scored points regularly: besides South Africa and Austria there were thirds in Belgium, Italy (which he inherited as Chris Amon's Matra lost its brakes and leader Jacky Ickx's Ferrari retired in the pits), Canada and America, plus a fifth in Britain. Revvie also kept his end up; besides that third in South Africa he repeated the result in Britain and Austria, took second in Canada and fourth in Italy. Denny started from the front row five times, Revson once, and Denny set one fastest lap. The M19 had proved itself at last.

M19A-1 was rebuilt with larger fuel tanks for Redman to drive in the unique Rothmans 50,000 Formula Libre race at Brands Hatch, where he earned well for the team by finishing second behind Fittipaldi's Lotus.

Gordon Coppuck's new M23 was ready for 1973, but the M19Cs continued into the new season until sufficient M23s had been constructed. Modifications were limited to minor tweaks such as new F2 upright castings for the rear suspension, a new fabricated rear bulkhead, and a revised profile for the roll-over hoop. The rear suspension was also revised again, the better to accommodate the requirements of Goodyear's massive new 26 inch wide rear tyres.

The Rothmans 50,000 race at Brands Hatch in August 1972 was officially a Super Formula Libre race with everything from Group 6 sportscars to works Formula 1 cars taking part. Brian Redman drove the heavily revised M19A-1 chassis and was the only serious challenge to winner Emerson Fittipaldi in his JPS Lotus 72.

The season kicked off this time in Argentina, where Denny avoided a big shunt when his throttle jammed open in qualifying. He finished a lapped fifth, Revvie eighth. In the Brazilian Grand Prix at Interlagos he was lying in third place when his clutch began to malfunction, obliging him to drive the rest of the race in top gear. He got away with it, retaining his podium place in the wake of another Fittipaldi victory. Revvie, fighting food poisoning, lasted only three laps before suffering gearbox failure.

Jody Scheckter took over Denny's car as a third works entry in his native South Africa, as the New Zealander got his hands on the new M23. The young South African started from the front row, took the lead when Denny sustained a puncture, but was overhauled by Jackie Stewart's victorious Tyrrell and was forced to retire with tyre problems and a broken engine. Revvie tigered his way home second, half a second ahead of an attacking Fittipaldi, and stayed there when a protest from McLaren that Stewart had passed Scheckter under a yellow flag was thrown out.

That was the end of the Grand Prix road for the M19, but an early car was acquired by club racer Brian Robinson, who had it fitted with a Chevrolet V8 for Formula 5000 racing. In 1973 his best results were a seventh, an eighth and a ninth, but 1974 yielded joint 12th overall in the European Formula 5000 Championship as he scored a fourth, a fifth, a seventh and two 10ths to add to second place in a race of attrition at Snetterton in October. In 1975, with the wide nose fitted, he finished ninth overall, netting a third, a fourth, two sixths, a seventh, an eighth and a ninth. There was also talk in the Press of upcoming Frenchman René Arnoux racing a Shell-backed M19A mid-season, but nothing came of it.

The revised M19, designated M19C, put McLaren back in the winner's circle after two years without a victory. Hulme won the South African GP and a string of excellent results left him second in the title race. Revson was second in Canada and ended the year fifth in the Championship.

New sponsor for 1972, the Yardley cosmetics company, brought a change of colours and a new driver to the team. Peter Revson joined Denny Hulme and scored his first World Championship points in only his second race for the team at Kyalami. At the Belgian Grand Prix (left) he could only finish seventh.

M19C FORMULA 1
SPECIFICATION

MODEL	McLaren M19C
TYPE/FORMULA	Formula 1
YEAR OF PRODUCTION	1972/1973
DESIGNER	Ralph Bellamy
EXAMPLES BUILT	2
ENGINE	Ford Cosworth DFV
CUBIC CAPACITY	2993cc
CARBURATION	Lucas fuel injection
POWER OUTPUT	450bhp

TRANSMISSION	Hewland DG400 5-speed
CHASSIS	Full aluminium monocoque, steel bulkheads
BODY	Formed by monocoque, GRP nosecone
FRONT SUSPENSION	Double wishbone, with push rod and rocker operating inboard coil spring/damper, anti-roll bar
REAR SUSPENSION	Lower wishbone, adjustable top link, twin radius rods, outboard coil spring/damper, anti-roll bar
BRAKES F/R	Outboard/inboard 10.5in ventilated discs
WHEELS DIAMETER x WIDTH F/R	13x11/13x16 or 17in

TYRES F/R	Goodyear
LENGTH	178in - 4521mm
WIDTH	84in - 2134mm
HEIGHT OF AIRBOX	45in - 1143mm
WHEELBASE	100in - 2540mm
TRACK F/R	63/63in - 1600/1600mm
WEIGHT	1257lb - 570kg
PRINCIPAL DRIVERS	Hulme, Gethin, Oliver
IDENTIFYING COLOURS	White/Papaya/Brown

1972 CAN-AM McLAREN M20

The M8 concept had finally reached its conclusion by the end of 1971, and the M20 became the staple for the 1972 Can-Am Championship. Underlining the intensity of the latest challenge, reigning World Champion Jackie Stewart joined Denny Hulme, to replace Peter Revson, who planned to concentrate solely on Formula 1.

In response to Porsche's turbocharged 917/10K, Gordon Coppuck planned a car quite different to the M8, with bigger brakes, the weight concentrated within the wheelbase, and the driver isolated from the radiators now located amidships.

McLaren had hoped to produce a turbo engine of its own using a Chevrolet block as the basis, but lack of development time ultimately obliged it to settle for another normally aspirated V8, Chevy's aluminium 8.1-litre. In addition to mounting this slightly forward, the new chassis also relocated the 79 US gallon fuel load in twin cells mounted in each of the side pontoons and linked them via an 18-gallon tank located behind and beneath the driver's seat across the full width of the structure.

The M20 also featured a wing across the front, working in conjunction with a strut-mounted rear wing slung between the usual M8D/M8F-style fins. Once again, the car also featured full-length fences atop the bodyshell to control airflow. It was hoped that the revised front end would fix a perennial understeer problem. The engine, still a stressed member, transaxle, suspension, brakes and wheels were all familiar. The chassis was constructed from 16 and 20 gauge L72 aluminium alloy with argon-welded steel bulkheads providing suspension pick-up points.

Only three M20s were built, but once pre-season testing began hopes for the new car were high. With happy memories of 19 consecutive wins between 1968 and '70, McLaren was confident it could retain its mastery of Can-Am despite Porsche's burgeoning challenge.

In testing at Silverstone Denny and Jackie clocked up record-breaking lap times, but before the start of the Can-Am season Stewart was forced to stand down on doctors' orders after being diagnosed with a stomach ulcer. Revvie was hastily called up. The other unsettling news was that Porsche's campaign would be run by Roger Penske, and that naturally meant that technically minded Mark Donohue would pilot the awesome 917/10K.

The first race of the season – the 50th in Can-Am history – was at Mosport on June 11th where, in a foretaste of what was to come, Donohue's Porsche took pole. Revvie was second on the grid and Denny third. Donohue lost the lead with induction issues and, despite jumping the start Revvie was able to take the advantage from Denny, whose engine was sick. Then Revvie's engine broke with two laps to go, handing the win to Denny, whom a recovering Donohue was catching hand over fist. Revson was classified third. Already the alarm bells were beginning to ring in Colnbrook thanks to Porsche's competitive pace.

McLaren improved the brakes, tyres and aerodynamics in time for practice at Road Atlanta, where Revvie blew another engine. Denny took the pole after running neck and neck with George Follmer in the Penske 917. Follmer had been drafted in to replace Donohue, who had been injured in a massive accident during a test there the previous week which had written off his original 917/10K. In a dramatic race, Follmer surged to victory first time out after Denny backflipped his M20 at 180mph while giving chase. Revvie had stopped at that very spot with an ignition problem, saw the whole incident, and helped to rescue Denny who was knocked out and briefly hospitalised but otherwise unhurt. The M20 was written off. Revson rejoined for long enough to break the lap record, before his engine failed.

At Watkins Glen a fortnight later tough old Denny was back at the wheel of the M20 prototype. Despite a lingering headache he qualified right behind Revvie, who took the pole. In the race that order was quickly reversed as Denny raced to his 22nd Can-Am win and he and Revvie secured McLaren's first 1-2 of the season. At Mid-Ohio, however, Denny finished only fourth after five tyre changes, and Peter retired. Follmer won. Road America saw Denny on pole and leading until ignition problems on the 12th lap; after Revvie retired, Follmer won again.

At Donnybrooke in September both McLaren drivers struggled in practice with their further modified M20s as a recovered Donohue joined Follmer to put the Porsches on the front row. None of them finished; François Cevert won in Greg Young's M8F after Denny's block split as he was challenging Donohue. Revvie took up the cudgels until a valve dropped. Donohue blew a tyre, and Follmer ran out of fuel on the last lap while leading. Edmonton saw another second place for Denny after he had led for the opening 31 laps, and sixth for Revson, but Donohue won with Follmer third after dropping back with a puncture. Porsche was steadily pulling ahead, and when both McLarens retired in the Monterey GP at Laguna Seca, and Donohue let Follmer by into the lead close to the finish to win, the American veteran took the title.

At the Riverside finale Denny took a front row slot as he, Revvie, Donohue and Follmer lapped at almost identical speeds. But 'The Bear's' final Can-Am race ended with another engine failure, leaving Revson to finish second after Follmer had returned the Laguna favour and let Donohue into the lead, only for Mark to drop back with a puncture. Revvie was 45s behind Follmer by the finish.

An era had ended, and with it McLaren's domination of the Canadian-American Challenge Cup series. With it's place in the record books assured, the works team never returned.

The M20 was the last car in which Denny Hulme would win a major Championship sportscar race, the Watkins Glen round of the Can-Am series in July 1972.

By 1972 the Chevrolet V8 engines used in the three M20 chassis built had grown to a massive 8369cc and were putting out more than 750bhp.

With the water radiators now side mounted and helping keep the driver a little cooler, a huge aerodynamic flap was mounted between the front wheel arches.

The first Can-Am race of 1972 saw the appearance of the works Penske Porsche team which fielded a single 917/10K for Mark Donohue. It was Denny Hulme, however, who took the victory after Donohue pitted with throttle linkage problems and leader Revson's engine expired with just two laps to go.

5
GULF McLAREN

McLAREN CARS
Gulf
BOYD JEFFERIES
Denny Hulme
GOODYEAR
5
CHAMPION
Gulf
EAGLE

When teams came to Laguna Seca in October 1972 the Can-Am title had already been decided in favour of George Follmer and Porsche. Hulme retired from the race with timing chain problems but still finished the season second in the Championship.

Despite the dominance of the works Porsches, McLaren was still highly competitive in Can-Am. Here Peter Revson's M20 leads Gary Wilson's M8E and Tom Dutton's M8C at Laguna Seca.

By 1973 M20-03 was being used by the Felder Racing Team in the Interserie Championship. At Silverstone Helmut Kelleners didn't even make the start when the engine blew during race warm up.

M20 CAN-AM
SPECIFICATION

MODEL	McLaren M20
TYPE/FORMULA	Can-Am
YEAR OF PRODUCTION	1972
DESIGNER	Gordon Coppuck
EXAMPLES BUILT	3
ENGINE	Chevrolet V8
CUBIC CAPACITY	8095cc
CARBURATION	Lucas fuel injection
POWER OUTPUT	750bhp

TRANSMISSION	Hewland LG MkII 4-speed
CHASSIS	Aluminium sheet monocoque, with steel bulkheads
BODY	Monocoque sides, GRP body sections, integral wing
FRONT SUSPENSION	Single top link & radius arm, lower wishbone, outboard coil spring/damper, anti-roll bar
REAR SUSPENSION	Twin parallel lower links, single top link, twin radius rods, coil spring/damper, anti-roll bar
BRAKES F/R	Outboard/inboard 11.8in discs
WHEELS DIAMETER x WIDTH F/R	15x11/15x17in

TYRES F/R	Goodyear
LENGTH	178in - 4521mm
WIDTH	81in - 2057mm
HEIGHT AT TAIL	46in - 1168mm
WHEELBASE	100in - 2540mm
TRACK F/R	61.8/60in - 1570/1524mm
WEIGHT	1520lb - 689kg
PRINCIPAL DRIVERS	Hulme, Revson
IDENTIFYING COLOURS	Papaya/Blue

1972 FORMULA 2 McLAREN M21

The key ingredient in McLaren's short-lived return to Formula 2, after an absence of four years, was the Impact-sponsored M21 that upcoming South African Jody Scheckter chauffeured to a classy victory over champion-elect Mike Hailwood at Crystal Palace. Another Ralph Bellamy design, and the best-looking car in its class at the time, the neat little machine boasted a low monocoque, distinctive large cockpit surround and a sharp nose with a pronounced and aggressive lower lip.

The M21 was designed to accept both the Broadspeed-developed 1.8-litre BDA engine or one of only four specially prepared 2-litre Cosworth BDGs. The simple monocoque used 16 gauge aluminium side panels, with 18 gauge material employed elsewhere. Lower wishbones were employed at both ends together with outboard spring/damper units; the front suspension incorporated a single top link and rearward radius rods with the wishbone reversed. At the rear transverse links and twin radius rods were used. The wheelbase was 92 inches, the front track 58 and the rear 60; at 150 inches long and 74 wide, it was just about the biggest car in that year's F2 championship, but in Scheckter's hands it proved highly effective.

After successful testing by team stalwarts Denny Hulme and Peter Gethin, the papaya orange car was first shown to the press with no visible sponsorship livery. Shortly afterwards the commercial building and property group, Impact BS Holdings Limited, came on board keen to raise its profile via motorsport after moving into vehicle rental and petrol retailing.

World Champion-to-be Scheckter was entered in all the European F2 and John Player F2 Championship rounds. Hopes went unrealised for a second car to be built for Barry Newman for Howden Ganley to drive.

Scheckter made his debut with the M21 at Mallory Park on March 12th for the opening round of the European Championship, which was also the opener for the John Player series. The car ran on Goodyear tyres and with the larger capacity Cosworth engine, the Broadspeed having blown a head gasket earlier in the week. Being a McLaren, reported Autosport four days later, the M21 "*was of course immaculately turned out*".

The results were an aggregate of two 50-lap heats, and underrated Briton David Morgan's Brabham took the flag ahead of Niki Lauda and Carlos Reutemann. Scheckter was fourth, 42.2s behind Morgan after a suffering a misfire and trouble selecting the right gears. With the McLaren finishing ahead of the works cars of Mike Hailwood (Surtees) and Ronnie Peterson (March) in a 20-car field, Autosport suggested that it was "*a very deserving fourth after a sensible first outing*".

Scheckter non-started at Hockenheim, then ran with the Broadspeed engine at Pau for the fourth round of the European Championship. Despite finishing a good sixth in his heat, he was denied a place in the final following some 'creative' rule bending to allow Frenchman Jean-Pierre Beltoise to participate.

The Whitsun weekend in May provided the highlight of the year for the M21 and for McLaren as its cars scored wins in three major categories worldwide. Mark Donohue in Roger Penske's M16B triumphed in the Indianapolis 500; Denny won the Oulton Park Gold Cup in an M19A, and Jody won the Euro round at Crystal Palace after a performance that stunned the more experienced graded drivers and rival F2 teams. He beat Hailwood by two seconds after a gripping wheel-to-wheel battle.

A month later at Rouen, Scheckter was quickest in a wet practice session on the Friday. Then, after leading his heat comfortably until he was forced into the pits, he fought hard in the final to overhaul Hailwood, Emerson Fittipaldi and Reutemann. He was scorchingly fast, matching the pace of the leaders as he ran 10s behind, and eventually neither Reutemann, François Cevert nor Beltoise could resist his challenge. He was safe in third place and was just about to challenge for second, after Hailwood had spun, when his engine failed due to a crack in the block caused earlier in the day when it had overheated. He was classified 11th.

Generally the luck ran against Scheckter and the Impact M21 that season, and they ended the year eighth overall in the European F2 standings with 15 points to Hailwood's total of 55. The result was not a genuine reflection of the combination's potential, and consideration was given to putting the car into limited production for 1973, but plans were eventually shelved.

The design lived on, however. After considering converting the M19A into a production Formula 5000 car, Trojan elected to take the simpler chassis from the M21 tub and the rear end from the M22 to create a contender for the 'big banger' single seater series which was initially codenamed M21X. Completed by a concave, full-width nose, the design eventually became the 1973 Trojan T101. It was not a pukka McLaren, but its antecedents were clear and it upheld McLaren honour in the formula by scoring five victories in the UK series that year. Coincidentally, Scheckter also used a T101 (in conjunction with a Lola T330) and scored three wins with it on his way to claiming the L&M Formula 5000 Championship in the US.

After three years away from Formula 2 McLaren returned with the sleek and purposeful looking Ford BDA-engined M21.

Despite it's low-line look, the Ralph Bellamy-designed M21 was modelled on his Formula 1 M19 design and was the biggest car on the Formula 2 grid in 1972.

Despite claims that it produced an impressive 270bhp, the Broadspeed-developed fuel injected version of the Ford BDA engine probably developed closer to 250bhp.

As the season progressed the engine gained various differing versions of an airbox on the right-hand side of the car. This is the earlier more bulbous iteration used at the Mallory Park round of the series.

McLAREN CARS
Jody Scheckter
GOODYEAR
GOODYEAR

1972 FORMULA 2 McLAREN M21

CONTINUED

At the first round of both the European and British Formula 2 Championships held at Mallory Park in March, Jody Scheckter and the M21 surprised the established runners with a strong fourth place.

The M21 waits on the grid for the start of the Rothmans 50,000 race at Brands Hatch in August. Jody was running in fourth place when the engine expired on lap 15.

The Euro F2 round at Crystal Palace in May of 1972 was the M21's finest hour. Jody won an exciting race from champion elect Mike Hailwood in his Matchbox-Surtees TS-15

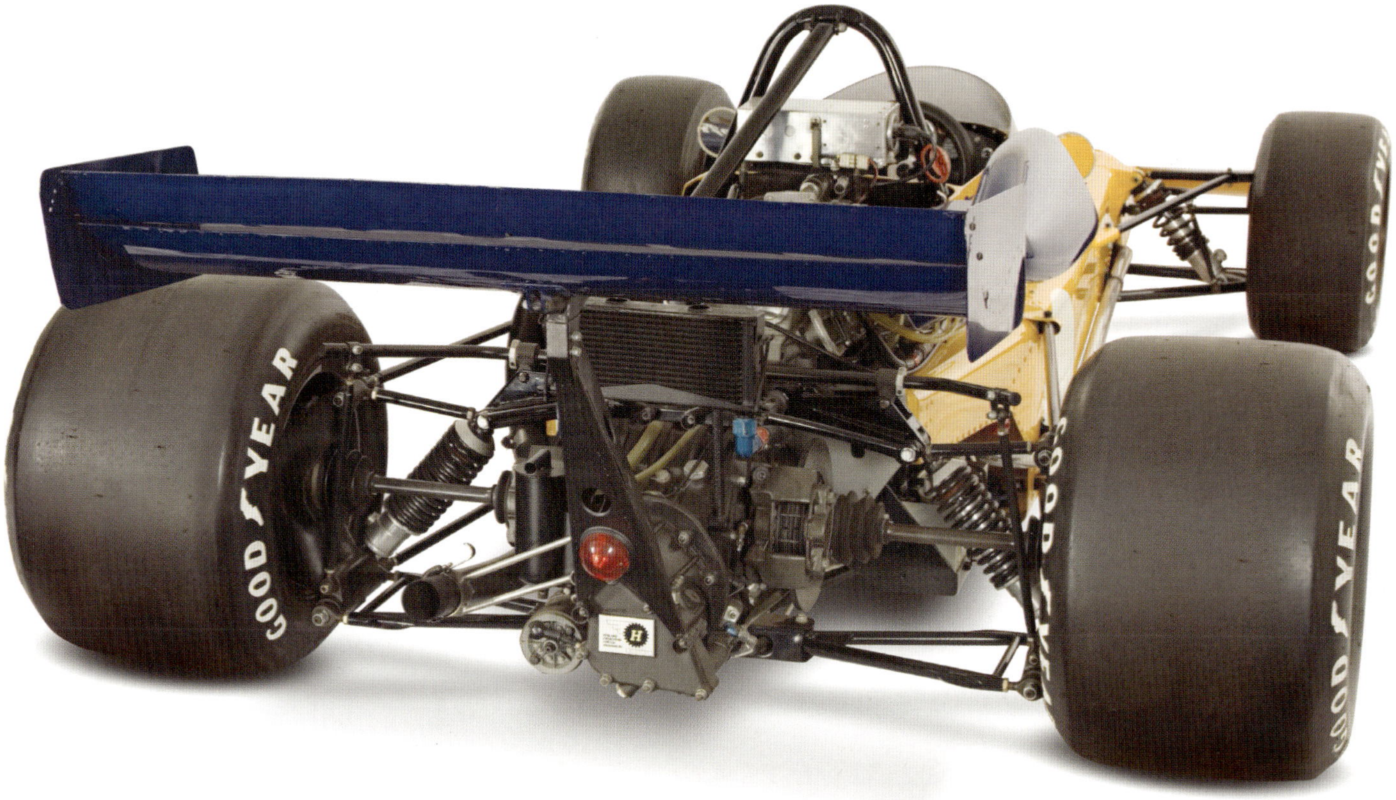

M21 FORMULA 2
SPECIFICATION

MODEL	McLaren M21
TYPE/FORMULA	Formula 2
YEAR OF PRODUCTION	1972
DESIGNER	Ralph Bellamy
EXAMPLES BUILT	1
ENGINE	Ford Cosworth BDA or BDF 4-cylinder
CUBIC CAPACITY	1899/1998cc
CARBURATION	Lucas fuel injection
POWER OUTPUT	250+bhp

TRANSMISSION	Hewland FG400 5-speed
CHASSIS	Full aluminium monocoque, steel bulkheads
BODY	Formed by monocoque, GRP nosecone
FRONT SUSPENSION	Single top link & radius arm, lower wishbone, outboard coil spring/damper, anti-roll bar
REAR SUSPENSION	Reverse lower wishbone, single top link, twin radius rods, coil spring/damper, anti-roll bar
BRAKES F/R	Outboard ventilated/inboard solid discs
WHEELS DIAMETER x WIDTH F/R	13x10/13x16in

TYRES F/R	Goodyear
LENGTH	160in - 4064mm
WIDTH	74in - 1880mm
HEIGHT AT WING	36in - 914mm
WHEELBASE	92in - 2337mm
TRACK F/R	58/60in - 1473/1524mm
WEIGHT	1036lb - 470kg
PRINCIPAL DRIVERS	Scheckter
IDENTIFYING COLOURS	Papaya

1972 FORMULA 5000 McLAREN-TROJAN M22

With McLaren devoting more of its time to the increasingly prestigious and more lucrative Formula 1, Indy and Can-Am championships, the Formula 5000 M22 became one of the least known of its single seaters.

The company's M10A and M10B models had been the class of Formula 5000 in 1969 and '70, in both the UK and America, and later in Australia and New Zealand. The replacement model, the stressed-engine M18, proved to be much less successful. It was hard to set up and its handling could be unpredictable, and even a driver of Brian Redman's talent could only muster two victories in the 1971 season. In a bid to improve the car another British F5000 star, David Hobbs, was brought into the fold in late 1971 to test a modified M18. Described as the M18/22, or sometimes even just M22, in contemporary reports it was intended to be the prototype for a totally new M22 which would race in 1972.

Hobbs and the car were sent to Pukekohe in New Zealand in January that year for the opening round of the Tasman Championship. Once a series for 2.5-litre Formula 1 cars, it had adopted Formula 5000 rules as well from 1970 onwards. Against the likes of former F1 driver Frank Gardner in a Lola T300, Mike Hailwood in a works Surtees TS8B and local hero Graham McRae in a Leda GM1, Hobbs took the M18/22 with its additional cooling courtesy of a pair of side-mounted radiators, to seventh on the grid. In the 101.5-mile race he reached third position by the 48th lap and eventually finished there, half a minute behind winner Gardner but a more respectable 4.1s shy of runner-up Hailwood. It was nevertheless clear that the M18/22, which was still running with the M18's squared nose rather than the M21-inspired scooped version that would follow, had inherited rather too much from the M18.

The car failed to score in Levin, Wigram, Teretonga and Warwick Farm, but after another third at Sandown Park and fourth at Surfers' Paradise, Hobbs struck gold in Adelaide when he won the final round from Hailwood and Teddy Pilette's M10B.

The Autosport story from Sandown had reported: "*David Hobbs, who has not been having a happy time recently in the Kirk F White-entered M22, seems to have got it sorted out.*" and suggested that the car "*was much improved.*" In Adelaide Hobbs was second only to local star Frank Matich in his eponymous Matich A50, qualifying ahead of McRae, Hailwood and Pilette. He got away third, fell to fourth behind Hailwood, survived a spin, and then inherited victory when McRae's engine failed, Matich broke his differential, and Hailwood lost time with a rear tyre failure on the main straight on the 48th of the 70 laps. The result lifted him to joint fifth overall with M10B-mounted Kevin Bartlett on 20 points, compared to the 39 of champion McRae.

Back at Colnbrook the works was completing the first production version of the M22 for the European F5000 series. This to all intents and purposes resembled the M18/22, but now had the shovel-shaped nose with protruding lower lip. At some point Trojan would have been expecting to productionise the new car for private customers, but by this time McLaren's interest had waned to such a degree that there was little point in continuing.

Pilette raced the M22 in Europe for Count Rudi van der Straaten's VDS Racing Team. Delivery of the car was delayed and he too had to resort to the old M18/22, but met with little success. He was the slowest to qualify for the Race of Champions at Brands Hatch in March, a full six seconds off Emerson Fittipaldi's pace and, in the race itself, finished three laps behind in 13th place overall but second in F5000 to Allan Rollinson's Lola T300.

The following month, at Silverstone for the International Trophy, he improved his overall finishing position by only two places and was fourth in F5000. The M22 was ready for the Oulton Park Gold Cup in May where, as Denny won in the M19A, Pilette finished ninth, and fifth F5000 home. Elsewhere, in the Rothmans European F5000 series, he picked up two seconds, a fourth and a fifth in the M18/22, then a third, a fourth, a fifth, and an eighth in the M22 to finish fifth overall on 25 points to Surtees-mounted champion Gijs van Lennep's 65. It had been an up and down season that provided a muted postscript to McLaren's otherwise illustrious time in Formula 5000.

The M22 was the last car to be built under the McLaren-Trojan partnership. McLaren was to concentrate its efforts on Formula 1 and Indianapolis, while Trojan went on to build its own Formula 5000 as well as Formula 1 cars.

Front suspension on the M22 was by the tried and tested single top link, radius arm and lower wishbone set-up, mounted on the front bulkhead.

The M22 was little more than a heavily revised version of the M18 with the Chevrolet V8 again being used as a fully-stressed part of the chassis.

M22 FORMULA 5000
SPECIFICATION

MODEL	McLaren-Trojan M22
TYPE/FORMULA	Formula 5000
YEAR OF PRODUCTION	1972
DESIGNER	Gordon Coppuck
EXAMPLES BUILT	3
ENGINE	Chevrolet V8
CUBIC CAPACITY	4950cc
CARBURATION	Lucas fuel injection
POWER OUTPUT	540bhp

TRANSMISSION	Hewland DG500 5-speed
CHASSIS	Full aluminium monocoque, steel bulkheads
BODY	Formed by monocoque, GRP nose & radiator shroud
FRONT SUSPENSION	Single top link & radius arm, lower wishbone, outboard coil spring/damper, anti-roll bar
REAR SUSPENSION	Reverse lower wishbone, single top link, twin radius rods, coil spring/damper, anti-roll bar
BRAKES F/R	Outboard/inboard 10.5in discs
WHEELS DIAMETER x WIDTH F/R	13x11/15x16in

TYRES F/R	Goodyear
LENGTH	176in - 4470mm
WIDTH	77in - 1956mm
HEIGHT OF AIRBOX	50in - 1270mm
WHEELBASE	100in - 2540mm
TRACK F/R	59.5/59.75in - 1511/1517mm
WEIGHT	1450lb - 657kg
PRINCIPAL DRIVERS	Hobbs
IDENTIFYING COLOURS	n/a

1973-1976 INDYCAR
McLAREN M16C, M16D & M16E

Throughout 1972 Indy racing speeds had soared. After qualifying at Indianapolis at 195.940mph, Bobby Unser had taken his Eagle round Michigan International Speedway at 199.889 and, after team-mate Jerry Grant did one lap at 201.414 at Ontario, Unser upped that the next day to 201.965s. The rulemakers at USAC, realising they had opened Pandora's Box when they relaxed wing regulations, attempted to reduce speeds for 1973.

McLaren built six new M16Cs, which sported a new full-length cowling to smooth airflow between the headrest and a new rear wing that was similar to that fitted to the Formula One M23. Airflow was further improved by adopting a more rounded cockpit surround, and the radiator ducts were also subtly reshaped.

Joining Peter Revson this time for the Indy 500 was the fleet but often unlucky Johnny Rutherford, 'Lone Star JR' from Texas. He quickly set the scene by qualifying on pole at 198.413mph and was the quickest driver/car combination of the whole weekend. Revvie qualified 10th at 192.606, but for the works team that was to be as good as it got. Rutherford was soon black-flagged after a fuel leak, then lost boost pressure and ultimately finished ninth. The race was initially rained off, restarted two days later and then spiralled into a nightmare involving Swede Savage's ultimately fatal accident and the death of STP mechanic Armando Teran. Revvie crashed after just three laps, in Turn Four. The best placed McLaren was the blue and white Lindsey Hopkins Buick-sponsored ex-works M16A of Roger McCluskey, which finished third. Later, McCluskey used the same car to win the Michigan 200.

Rutherford later won twice at Ontario and at Michigan, while Gary Bettenhausen won the Texas 200 in Penske's M16C. The fly in the works team's ointment was the withdrawal of Gulf Oil's sponsorship at the end of the season.

USAC sought to enhance safety for 1974, requiring smaller 40-gallon fuel tanks to be more safely accommodated within the centre section of the monocoque and on the left of the car, away from the more vulnerable right-hand side. Overall length was also reduced in order to restrict wing size and an 80in/Hg pop-off valve was mandated on all turbo-engined cars to restrict boost. Cars would now be required to stop at least six times during 500-mile races.

McLaren's response was the new M16C/D, which gained a more pronounced M23-style cockpit cowling, had its nose truncated again and was fitted with a new monocoque-pillar rear wing with a sharply curved-section aerofoil, taken from its Formula 1 cousin. The engine cowl was also modified to stop short of the wing.

After missing the first weekend of qualifying and the chance to be at the front of the field, Rutherford could only qualify a lowly 25th. But his speed of 190.446mph was impressive and would have put him second on the grid. David Hobbs, in the second, Carling Black Label-sponsored, M16C/D qualified ninth at 184.833 mph.

Rutherford still had a chance. By lap 65 he was fighting for the lead with 191.632mph polesitter A. J. Foyt's Coyote. Then Foyt's scavenge pump broke on lap 143 and Rutherford was left leading Bobby Unser's Eagle by a margin of 22s. Reeling off the remaining laps without incident, he handed McLaren a second Indy victory, and the first for the works team. The winner's purse was $245,032 from the total prize money pool of $1,015,686. To add to the euphoria, Hobbs brought his car home fifth.

Once again Rutherford triumphed in the Ontario 100, as well as in the Milwaukee 150 and another 500-miler, at Pocono.

In 1975 the now five-year old design morphed again, the new M16E being the work of Coppuck's new assistant, John Barnard, as he himself was flat-out on the F1 side. Indy veteran Lloyd Ruby joined Rutherford in the team, but the car's longer wheelbase and new parallel lower-link rear suspension failed to stem the bad luck which seemed to dog the career of the man whom a biography described as "*the greatest driver never to win the Indy 500*". Having qualified his white, red and blue Allied Polymer car sixth at 186.986mph, Ruby was out with a burned piston on lap seven. For the rest of the field a freak rain storm cut the race to just 174 laps, with Bobby Unser's Eagle taking the flag after a long battle with A.J. Foyt and a disappointed Rutherford who had to be content with another second place for McLaren after qualifying his white, green and orange Gatorade-sponsored car seventh at 185.998mph. The race was also notable for the horrific mid-race accident which destroyed Tom Sneva's Norton Spirit Penske M16C/D which he had qualified fourth at 190.094mph. Miraculously, he was unharmed.

The even years were good for McLaren at Indianapolis at this time, and JR won once again in 1976 in a slightly updated M16E sponsored by Hy-Gain, which he had planted on the pole at 188.957mph. That was not the fastest speed of qualifying, however. Mario Andretti in Penske's Cam 2 Motor Oil M16C/D achieved 189.404mph, albeit on the second weekend which thus obliged him to start 19th under Indy's rules. Rutherford struggled initially until the front wing angles were adjusted and the right-hand side tyres were changed. Then the M16E suddenly came to life and he established a comfortable lead by the time the race was flagged off because of rain after only 102 of the scheduled 200 laps. It was the shortest 500 on record, but that didn't bother JR who took McLaren's third, and final, victory in five years as the curtain came down on the M16's works career.

The M16C was visually quite different from the preceding 'B' spec car and featured a more rounded cockpit surround similar to the 1973 Formula 1 car, as well as a new full-length engine cowling to aid airflow to the rear wing.

McLaren's development of the M16C for 1974 was the M16C/D variant. Johnny Rutherford used the revised M16C-5 chassis to win the 1974 Indy 500 trophy and the $245,032 prize money.

For 1975 the M16E featured a completely new design around the sides of the chassis and radiator ducting. The pod type radiator surround cleaned airflow around the rear end and helped Rutherford in the works Gatorade car to finish second to Bobby Unser's Eagle.

Rutherford's win in the 1976 Indy 500 was the last year that the works team used the American turbocharged Offy engine. In 1977 it went over to the turbocharged Ford Cosworth DFX unit, developed in the UK.

Johnny Rutherford at speed in the Boyd Jeffries McLaren-Offy M16C, August 1973. This shot was taken during the second heat run prior to the following week's 500-mile race at Ontario Motor Speedway in California.

1973-1976 INDYCAR
McLAREN M16C, M16D & M16E
CONTINUED

M16C/D INDYCAR
SPECIFICATION

MODEL	McLaren M16C/D
NAME/FORMULA	Indianapolis/USAC
YEAR OF PRODUCTION	1974
DESIGNER	Gordon Coppuck
VOLUME	6
ENGINE	Offenhauser 4-cylinder turbo
CUBIC CAPACITY	2600cc
CARBURATION	Hilborn injection, Garrett Airesearch turbocharger
POWER OUTPUT	780bhp

TRANSMISSION	Hewland LG500 4-speed
CHASSIS	Full aluminium monocoque, steel bulkheads
BODY	Monocoque sides, GRP nose & cockpit, engine cover
FRONT SUSPENSION	Welded cantilever top arm operating
	inboard coil spring/damper, lower wishbone
REAR SUSPENSION	Reverse lower wishbone, top link, twin
	radius rods, coil spring/damper, anti-roll bar
BRAKES F/R	Outboard 11.9in discs
WHEELS DIAMETER x WIDTH F/R	15x10/15x14in

TYRES F/R	Goodyear
LENGTH	175in - 4445mm
WIDTH	76in - 1930mm
HEIGHT	39in - 991mm
WHEELBASE	104in - 2642mm
TRACK F/R	58/58in - 1473/1473mm
WEIGHT	1380lb - 626kg
PRINCIPAL DRIVERS	Rutherford, Hobbs, Hiss
IDENTIFYING COLOURS	Papaya

M16E INDYCAR
SPECIFICATION

MODEL	McLaren M16E
TYPE/FORMULA	Indianapolis/USAC
YEAR OF PRODUCTION	1975/1976
DESIGNER	John Barnard
EXAMPLES BUILT	2
ENGINE	Offenhauser 4-cylinder turbo
CUBIC CAPACITY	2600cc
CARBURATION	Hilborn injection, Garrett Airesearch turbocharger
POWER OUTPUT	780bhp
TRANSMISSION	Hewland LG500 4-speed
CHASSIS	Full aluminium monocoque, steel bulkheads
BODY	Monocoque sides, GRP nose & cockpit, engine cover
FRONT SUSPENSION	Welded cantilever top arm operating inboard coil spring/damper, lower wishbone
REAR SUSPENSION	Reverse lower wishbone, top link, twin radius rods, coil spring/damper, anti-roll bar
BRAKES F/R	Outboard 11.9in discs
WHEELS DIAMETER x WIDTH F/R	15x10/15x14in
TYRES F/R	Goodyear
LENGTH	177in - 4496mm
WIDTH	78in - 1981mm
HEIGHT	39in - 991mm
WHEELBASE	106in - 2692mm
TRACK F/R	58/58in - 1473/1473mm
WEIGHT	1380lb - 626kg
PRINCIPAL DRIVERS	Rutherford, Ruby
IDENTIFYING COLOURS	White/Green

1973 FORMULA 1 McLAREN M23

The McLaren M23 was one of the most outstanding designs of its era and was designed by Gordon Coppuck for new regulations which, from the Spanish GP on April 29th, required fuel tanks to be protected by new deformable structures. He opted for a wedge shape and integral sidepods to achieve that. A modified form of the M19's complex rising-rate suspension was used at the front, and a much simpler interpretation at the rear.

It was immediately obvious that McLaren's new car was a very serious contender. Denny Hulme liked it straight away and in testing at Kyalami, prior to its debut in the South African GP, it easily chalked up faster times than the M19A. "*It oversteers and stays out there in a nice comfortable slide,*" he said.

He revelled in it as he secured his first-ever Grand Prix pole position. And he led from the start, as Jody Scheckter pushed his M19C into second place ahead of Emerson Fittipaldi's Lotus and Revvie's M19C. Denny seemed capable of running away with the race, but there had been a fiery accident on the third lap and he picked up a puncture on debris and pitted for a replacement tyre on the fifth lap, then had to do the same thing again four laps later. As Jackie Stewart raced through to win from Revson, Denny recovered to fifth place after a strong run back from 19th place on lap 10.

It took a while to recapture the Kyalami form, however. Clutch trouble cost Denny his chances in the Brands Race of Champions and he was lucky to finish second only millimetres ahead of hungry debutant James Hunt, in a Surtees TS9B hired by Lord Hesketh. Revvie was fourth in the International Trophy race at Silverstone. Back on the Grand Prix trail, the American was fourth and Denny sixth in Spain, but a front-row start for Denny in Belgium resulted in only seventh place after he slid off on oil. In Monaco they were fifth and sixth, Revvie leading Denny home. And then came Sweden, and payback for Kyalami.

Denny qualified only sixth, behind Ronnie Peterson's Lotus, the Tyrrells of François Cevert and Jackie Stewart, Emerson Fittipaldi's Lotus and Carlos Reutemann's Brabham. Revvie was seventh. Early on he was happy to follow Peterson, Fittipaldi, Cevert, Stewart and Reutemann, before picking off the Argentinian. Then he was baulked by Jackie Oliver in a Shadow, who threw dirt into the M23's throttle slides. He resigned himself to the almost inevitable pit stop, but suddenly the slides freed up. By now he had lost 15s, and was angry. Switching off his rev limiter, he charged. He caught Cevert on lap 61, then Fittipaldi and Stewart hit brake problems. Suddenly the M23 was second and hauling in Peterson, the local hero. Maybe Denny could have done it without the intervention of Fate, but with two laps to run the Lotus picked up a puncture, and the race was McLaren's. It was the M23's first triumph, and richly deserved.

Another victory was on the cards in the French GP at Paul Ricard, as Jody Scheckter had his first outing in an M23. He qualified on the front row between polesitter Stewart and Fittipaldi, and grabbed the early lead. Neither Peterson nor Fittipaldi could dislodge him, but the stalemate ended when Fittipaldi's attempt to overtake Scheckter backfired on the 42nd lap and they collided. Jody got going in second place as Emerson retired on the spot, but a lap later McLaren number eight was in the pits with damaged suspension. Denny was a delayed eighth.

Revson made it three M23s when he returned at Silverstone, and prior to qualifying on the front row with a time equal to Denny's he bet £100 on himself to win at 14 to 1. It was a prescient move.

Peterson led the opening lap from pole position, but Stewart leapt up from the second row and suckered him for the lead at Becketts. As they approached the finish line at the end of the lap, Reutemann was chasing them and then came two McLarens, side by side as Jody squeaked past Denny. But the South African's car slid ever wider until it was on the grass on the exit to Woodcote corner and then spun a complete 360 degrees before crunching head-on into the pit wall and bouncing back into the path of the rest of the field. Mayhem ensued. By the time the dust settled, and the race was red flagged, nine cars were out of the running. When the race was restarted, Peterson soon established a lead from Fittipaldi, Revvie, Denny and James Hunt, now driving a March. Fittipaldi broke a driveshaft on the 37th lap, and Revson closed in on Peterson and passed him on the 39th before pulling away to score his maiden Grand Prix triumph. It was 'Champagne Peter's' greatest day. Denny just fended off Hunt for third.

Peter finished fourth in Holland as Denny's engine broke, then Ickx had a one-off ride deputising for USAC-occupied Revson in Germany to finish third. In Austria Revvie lost his clutch on the first lap and, having had handling trouble at the Nürburgring, Denny now ran into problems with a plug lead while fighting the Lotuses for the lead. Monza yielded third for Revson as Denny had brake trouble. Then came Canada, where Revvie was awarded a second victory after complications with deployment of the pace car for the first time in a Grand Prix threw lap charts into hopeless confusion. Denny was 13th as Scheckter blotted his copybook again by colliding with Cevert as they squabbled over fourth place. In the final race of the season, the USGP at Watkins Glen, Denny led Revson home in fourth place, as Jody retired with broken rear suspension.

Three victories, and the other good placings, left McLaren a strong third in the Constructors' World Championship, behind Lotus and Tyrrell.

In 1973 Peter Revson won two Grand Prix races, his first at Silverstone in July and a second in Canada at the end of the year. Here in Monte Carlo he finished fifth, one place ahead of team-mate Hulme.

The tubular top wishbone on the M23 operated the inboard spring/damper unit via a push-rod system. This gave a much cleaner airflow to the large, low, side-mounted radiators.

Denny Hulme qualified a strong third on the grid for the Monaco Grand Prix but made a terrible start and slipped down the order to ninth place. By lap 46 he had fought back to fourth but a spin dropped him down the order and he could only finish sixth, two laps down on winner Jackie Stewart.

M23 (1973) FORMULA 1

SPECIFICATION

MODEL	McLaren M23
TYPE/FORMULA	Formula 1
YEAR OF PRODUCTION	1973
DESIGNER	Gordon Coppuck
EXAMPLES BUILT	4
ENGINE	Ford Cosworth DFV
CUBIC CAPACITY	2993cc
CARBURATION	Lucas fuel injection
POWER OUTPUT	460bhp
TRANSMISSION	Hewland DG400 5-speed
CHASSIS	Deformable double skinned aluminium monocoque
BODY	Monocoque lower, GRP nose, cockpit & engine cover
FRONT SUSPENSION	Tubular upper rocker arm, operating inboard coil spring/damper, lower wishbone, anti-roll bar
REAR SUSPENSION	Adjustable top link, reverse lower wishbone, twin radius rods, coil spring/damper, anti-roll bar
BRAKES F/R	Outboard/inboard ventilated discs
WHEELS DIAMETER x WIDTH F/R	13x11/13x18in
TYRES F/R	Goodyear
LENGTH	170in - 4318mm
WIDTH	80in - 2032mm
HEIGHT OF AIRBOX	46in - 1169mm
WHEELBASE	101in - 2565mm
TRACK F/R	65.5/62.5in - 1664/1587mm
WEIGHT	1270lb - 576kg
PRINCIPAL DRIVERS	Hulme, Revson, Scheckter, Ickx
IDENTIFYING COLOURS	White/Papaya/Brown

1974 FORMULA 1
McLAREN M23

The M23 had plenty of development left in it for 1974, and the really significant change was the creation of the Texaco-Marlboro McLaren superteam, as 1972 World Champion Emerson Fittipaldi quit Lotus to join Denny in M23s that were now painted red and white. It was a major coup for McLaren that brought in the sponsorship dollars to stage a major title assault, but a high degree of juggling was needed to placate Yardley. In the end, agreement was reached to run a third works car in its livery. Teddy Mayer's initial plan was to run Peter Revson in it, but the American finally lost patience with the ongoing negotiations and left to join Shadow in a decision that would ultimately cost him his life when he was the victim of suspension failure during testing at Kyalami. In his place, Phil Kerr would run the M23 for Mike Hailwood.

Prolonged winter testing by the enthusiastic Fittipaldi at Paul Ricard led to changes to the car, such as a longer wheelbase and wider track, based on his considerable experience of the Lotus 72. Years later, historic racer Willie Green would call it "*easily the best*" of the many 1970s Formula 1 machines he had driven round Brands Hatch. Good aerodynamics, he contended, "*were one of its strong suits and the lack of buffeting in the cockpit at high speeds bears this out.*"

Gordon Coppuck described the car a decade and a half on as, "*The best F1 car for three years. Yes, it was a good design, but it also benefited from a lot of good development. The chassis changed very little, but we did a great deal of suspension work to keep it competitive. The chassis was much stiffer than those of our rivals' cars, but it was pretty flexible by modern standards.*"

Compared to the previous season the M23's weight distribution had been improved by fitting a new bellhousing spacer between the engine and gearbox, hence the three-inch longer wheelbase. With an additional two inches of track, traction was also improved out of slow corners, while the rear wing was brought forward by 10 inches in order to comply with a new set of regulations. During the season three different wheelbase variations were employed, together with a distinctive narrow 'winklepicker' nose which saw service at Brands Hatch, Jarama and Monaco where its wider wings generated more front-end downforce.

Fittipaldi loved testing. According to Coppuck, "*He enjoyed this side of his job more than the races.*" That was to prove a valuable factor as a tough season progressed. It began superbly for the new team, though it was Denny who won the opening race in Argentina after passing Reutemann's ailing Brabham with two laps to run. Emerson inadvertently delayed himself while in a position to challenge for the win by knocking off the ignition. He finished 10th. But the Brazilian did not have to wait long to make amends, as he won his home event from pole position, finishing 13s ahead of Regazzoni.

In a year characterised by the battle with a newly emergent Ferrari team and its drivers, Niki Lauda and Clay Regazzoni, and the threats from Reutemann, Tyrrell's Jody Scheckter and Lotus's Ronnie Peterson, all of whom enjoyed victories, Emerson won again in Belgium and Canada to head into the final race, at Watkins Glen, neck-and-neck with Regazzoni.

In the Yardley car, meanwhile, Hailwood had some strong races, most notably the Dutch GP where he matched Fittipaldi as he raced home fourth behind the Marlboro car to add to another fourth in Argentina and third in South Africa. But his F1 career ended when his M23 landed badly on a jump at the Nürburgring and crashed heavily, inflicting leg injuries. David Hobbs drove the car in Austria and Italy, before upcoming German Jochen Mass left Surtees to take over the car for the two final races.

The American shootout went Emerson's way as he brought the M23 home fourth to clinch his second world title, and the first-ever World Championship for the McLaren marque. That day was historic for two other reasons: it marked the end of McLaren's association with Yardley; and Denny's final Grand Prix appearance. His engine failed after four laps. Without The Bear's mountainous courage in the aftermath of Bruce's death, there might not have been a McLaren team for Fittipaldi to drive for.

The M23's outstanding combination of performance, predictable and controllable handling, superb preparation and reliability had left an indelible mark in the record books.

In 1974 Emerson Fittipaldi won three races for his new team, Brazil, Belgium and Canada. Here at the Spanish GP the team experimented with a narrow 'winklepicker' nose and bigger front wings (top) on Emerson's car, whilst Hulme stuck with the regular wide nose/shorter wing option.

With two new title sponsors coming onboard for 1974 the cars received a striking new red and white colour scheme. By the end of the season the team was rewarded with both the Drivers' and Constructors' titles.

Marlboro
5
TEXACO
Marlboro

Marlboro
GOODYEAR
TEXACO
EMERSON FITTIPALDI
TEXACO-Marlboro
5
HEUER
Lockheed
CHAMPION
GOODYEAR

Denny Hulme gets airborne on his way to seventh on the grid for the German Grand Prix at the Nürburgring. He crashed out of the race on the first lap.

MZ3 (1974) FORMULA 1

SPECIFICATION

MODEL	McLaren M23
TYPE/FORMULA	Formula 1
YEAR OF PRODUCTION	1974
DESIGNER	Gordon Coppuck
EXAMPLES BUILT	4
ENGINE	Ford Cosworth DFV
CUBIC CAPACITY	2993cc
CARBURATION	Lucas fuel injection
POWER OUTPUT	460bhp

TRANSMISSION	Hewland DG400 5-speed
CHASSIS	Deformable double skinned aluminium monocoque
BODY	Monocoque lower, GRP nose, cockpit & engine cover
FRONT SUSPENSION	Tubular upper rocker arm, operating inboard coil spring/damper, lower wishbone, anti-roll bar
REAR SUSPENSION	Adjustable top link, reverse lower wishbone, twin radius rods, coil spring/damper, anti-roll bar
BRAKES F/R	Outboard/inboard ventilated discs
WHEELS DIAMETER x WIDTH F/R	13x11/13x18in

TYRES F/R	Goodyear
LENGTH	165in - 4191mm
WIDTH	80in - 2030mm
HEIGHT OF AIRBOX	48in - 1219mm
WHEELBASE	104.2in - 2647mm
TRACK F/R	64.2/66in - 1631/1676mm
WEIGHT	1270lb - 576kg
PRINCIPAL DRIVERS	Fittipaldi, Hulme, Hailwood, Hobbs, Mass
IDENTIFYING COLOURS	Red/White

1974 FORMULA 5000 McLAREN M25

The M25, detailed by John Barnard, was another car derived from the World Championship-winning, Gordon Coppuck-designed, M23. The sole car to be built was McLaren's last official entry into the Formula 5000 arena. With just two races to its credit in F5000, and a further nine as a Ford Cosworth DFV-powered F1 car, its real claim to fame is that it was the last McLaren single seater to race from new in the company's trademark papaya orange.

Trojan had by this time moved on to build its own F5000 cars, so M25-1 was built in the Colnbrook factory around the customary Chevrolet V8 and uncharacteristically brought little that was new to the mix. It was tested by Howden Ganley and engine builder-cum-Formula Atlantic racer John Nicholson in 1973, and possibly later by Denny Hulme, but it was never a works racer and eventually the tub, in the words of motoring historian Doug Nye, "*lay unloved for long months on a rooftop at Colnbrook.*"

In February 1974 the car was sold to Brazilian Carlos Avallone, who some believe may have commissioned it. He wanted to race in European F5000 as a precursor to making it to F1. However, no sooner had he taken possession than the M25 was impounded over a dispute concerning a proposed sportscar series in Brazil that Avallone had been involved with, and sat out the rest of the 1974 season under lock and key. In early 1975 it found its way into the hands of Yorkshire hillclimber David Hepworth, only for another legal battle to ensue. When the dispute was finally resolved early in 1976, Hepworth decided to take the car racing.

Still in its ex-factory papaya hue, the Shell-backed car made its race debut carrying number one on its nose in the ninth round of the 1976 Shellsport G8 Championship at Brands Hatch on August 30th. Driving what Autosport confusingly described as a "*Brand new, three-year-old 5-litre McLaren M25,*" in the 35-lap race, Bob Evans came an excellent second behind David Purley's 3.4-litre Chevron B30. This result was extremely promising given that the team had done absolutely no testing and that a minor coming-together early in the race had bent the front left nose wing upwards at more than 30 degrees.

Two weeks later, at the Thruxton round of the series, the McKechnie Racing-run car again looked competitive before it retired with piston problems after just 19 laps. With no spare engine and very little money available, this sadly spelt the end of the season for the underfinanced team. Evans was later to comment that despite being so beautifully built, with its rising-rate suspension it was, "*The twitchiest car I've ever driven in seven years of racing.*"

Hepworth then advertised the car for sale stating that: "*I would love the car to go to an 'ace' since I still believe it could be a winner. It would mop up on both sides of the Atlantic.*" For a while there were rumours that American Can-Am star George Follmer was keen to buy the car so that he could race it in the high-profile US Formula 5000 series. Hepworth let it be known that McLaren would be consulted as to whom the car could be sold, and suggested that Mike Hailwood might be a contender.

In the end it was acquired by Giuseppe Risi's Iberia-backed team for Spanish bank manager Emilio de Villota, a true gentleman racer who was later to have some reasonable success in the Aurora AFX F1. Acquiring the M25 following some experience in the 1977 BRSCC Group 8 series with the ex-F1 Lyncar, Risi replaced the Chevy V8 with a Cosworth DFV to give M25-1 a new life as a second-string back-up car to M23-6 that de Villota had attempted to qualify for several GPs in 1977. To bring the car up to then current Formula 1 regulations, most of the M25's original features, such as its early M23 style wings and nose, along with its unusually shaped airbox, were to disappear. Much of its 1973 style suspension was also reworked to later M23 specification, and to all intents and purpose the M25 was transformed into an M23, complete with a front roll-hoop which had become mandatory in F1 midway through 1976.

In 1978 de Villota attempted to qualify what the press rather confusingly referred to as M25/23-1, or even mistakenly as M23-7, for the Spanish Grand Prix, only to fail after spinning spectacularly at the exit of the corner leading to the main straight. As he sat at the side of the circuit waiting for help from marshals, he let his foot slip off the brake and the car rolled backwards on to the track, causing a collision with fellow McLaren driver James Hunt. Having damaged his M26 race car quite severely Hunt was forced to use his back-up car, something which didn't go down too well with the works Marlboro-McLaren team.

Away from the Grand Prix circuit, de Villota nevertheless enjoyed better results with the M25, and in the Aurora AFX Championship that same year finished in third place overall behind champion Tony Trimmer's Melchester Racing M23.

After de Villota and his Iberia team had moved on to running a Lotus 78, the M25 was sold to David McLaughlin before becoming part of the John Foulston collection. Now in the hands of collector and historic racer Abba Kogan, the one-of-a-kind M25 has been restored to something approaching its original F5000 specification, complete with Chevrolet engine and resplendent in the papaya orange colour scheme in which it originally left the McLaren works.

Emilio de Villota drove the heavily modified ex-F5000 M25, now virtually a Grand Prix spec M23 to second in the 1978 Oulton Park Gold Cup. He finished the race just half a second behind Tony Trimmer in M23/14, the last Formula 1 car supplied to an outside team, Chesterfield Racing, in 1977.

Although the M25 has been restored to its original Formula 5000 specification it still retains the front cockpit roll-hoop that had become mandatory in Formula 1 halfway through the 1976 season.

When originally conceived the M25 had a 500+bhp Chevrolet V8 engine fitted to the M23-derived chassis. If the car had made it on to the circuits in 1974 as intended it would surely have proved highly competitive. Instead it languished on a roof-top at Colnbrook and first raced in 1976.

M25 FORMULA 5000
SPECIFICATION

MODEL	McLaren M25
TYPE/FORMULA	Formula 5000
YEAR OF PRODUCTION	1974
DESIGNER	John Barnard
EXAMPLES BUILT	1
ENGINE	Chevrolet V8
CUBIC CAPACITY	5000cc
CARBURATION	Lucas fuel injection
POWER OUTPUT	500bhp

TRANSMISSION	Hewland DG500 5-speed
CHASSIS	Deformable double skinned aluminium monocoque
BODY	Monocoque lower, GRP nose, cockpit & engine cover
FRONT SUSPENSION	Upper rocker arm, operating inboard coil
	spring/damper, lower wishbone, anti-roll bar
REAR SUSPENSION	Adjustable top link, parallel lower links,
	twin radius rods, coil spring/damper, anti-roll bar
BRAKES F/R	Outboard/inboard ventilated discs
WHEELS DIAMETER x WIDTH F/R	13x11/13x16in

TYRES F/R	Goodyear
LENGTH	166in - 4216mm
WIDTH	78in - 1981mm
HEIGHT OF AIRBOX	46in - 1168mm
WHEELBASE	104.2in - 2647mm
TRACK F/R	64.2/66in - 1631/1676mm
WEIGHT	1420lb - 644kg
PRINCIPAL DRIVERS	Bob Evans
IDENTIFYING COLOURS	Papaya

1975 FORMULA 1 McLAREN M23

Jochen Mass now joined new World Champion Emerson Fittipaldi in the two-car Marlboro team, as the M23 went into its third season largely unchanged. The most significant mechanical development, in the search for better front-end grip, was a new front suspension along Brabham lines for Fittipaldi to try. The original tubular links and rocker arms were replaced by a much sturdier and sweptback fabricated upper rocker with pull-rods actuating the coil spring and damper. After several iterations of the idea, the team finally settled on a non-rising rate set-up for the first time.

Gordon Coppuck still fondly recalls the Brazilian's "*fantastic testing mileages*", which enabled the team to generate small but crucial changes from race to race as the season progressed. And McLaren needed all it could find as Niki Lauda and the new Ferrari 312T proved the dominant combination. Fittipaldi's input was invaluable, Coppuck making no bones about it being "*crucial in our development of the car*".

There was also experimentation with the length of the wheelbase, and incorporation of a cockpit-adjustable front anti-roll bar. At the same time John Nicholson worked progressively to boost the Ford Cosworth DFV's 440bhp, adding some 20bhp during the season while also improving the torque curve. Attempts were also made to fit transparent skirts around the lower edge of the chassis to maintain an area of low pressure beneath the car to generate some ground effect. Coppuck had tried the idea the previous season without convincing himself that the skirts worked. This time around the experiment was not successful as the skirts ground away on the track surface as the suspension moved up and down. Some other aerodynamic innovations proved more worthwhile, with a variety of different bodywork styles being tested including revised nose profiles, kick-ups ahead of the rear wheels, and extended bodywork to accommodate the oil coolers. Many were adopted and also appeared on the car's eventual successor, the M26.

In Argentina Fittipaldi drove a brilliant tactical race. Sitting back initially while Carloses Reutemann and Pace in their Brabhams fought for the lead with Niki Lauda and James Hunt, he then began to force the pace as the Englishman found himself leading in the Hesketh Ford. Hunt spun under the pressure, leaving Emerson to claim his 12th Grand Prix victory by 5.9s. In Brazil, however, there was to be no repeat of his 1974 success. Pace won, with Emerson leading Mass home in a McLaren 2-3.

Scheckter won for Tyrrell in South Africa, where Fittipaldi failed to score thanks to a misfire and Mass finished sixth. In Spain Mass scored the only Grand Prix victory of his career in trying circumstances, only earning half points as the race was stopped before half distance following an horrific accident when Rolf Stommelen's leading Embassy Hill suffered rear wing failure and killed four spectators as it vaulted a guardrail. This had already developed into an acrimonious weekend for Formula 1 as bitter feelings were aroused in practice by the poor state of safety measures around the track. Many team personnel were obliged to pick up spanners to tighten loose securing bolts on the Armco barriers. Fittipaldi, in particular, an active member of the Grand Prix Drivers' Association, was outraged. He qualified on the back row after deliberately doing the bare legal minimum of running, and then withdrew after the race warm-up lap in protest.

There were times in the year when several observers questioned the Brazilian's commitment. When victory was possible, he went for it. But when it did not appear to be he seemed content merely to pick up points. This prompted speculation that he was considering retirement, but his performance in appalling conditions at Silverstone demonstrated that he could still exhibit his inherent class when he chose to. The M23 had been updated with a new rear wing which sported a vee-shaped leading edge not dissimilar to Mario Andretti's Parnelli, but once again he only qualified on the fourth row of the grid and was content to sit back in the early stages before moving up to challenge Pace for the lead as it began to rain after 20 laps. Several drivers pitted for wet tyres, but Fittipaldi did not. Driving beautifully on a track that was as slippery as a skating rink, he moved back into the lead by the 43rd lap as conditions changed again, prompting further stops for those who had changed to wet tyres. Then came a downpour of almost Biblical proportions, prompting him to pit for wet tyres on the 56th lap. He did one more lap before bemused officials called a halt to the farce after 16 drivers had crashed as a consequence of the cloudburst, and was declared victorious.

It was not until Monza in September that the real Emerson Fittipaldi reappeared, driving a feisty race. As Lauda won to secure his first World Championship, Fittipaldi split the Ferraris to head Clay Regazzoni home. At Watkins Glen he was only narrowly beaten by Lauda for the pole. In the race he was right on the Austrian's tail until they came up to lap Regazzoni, who shamelessly blocked the red and white car. That let to scenes in the pits as Ferrari team manager Luca di Montezemolo scuffled with the Clerk of the Course who had shown the Swiss driver the black flag. By the time Fittipaldi found a way by, Lauda was long gone. Mass supported him by taking a strong third.

In the end, Lauda's Championship triumph was well deserved and Fittipaldi had to be content with second place, nearly 20 points behind. In the final reckoning, Brabham pipped McLaren by a single point for the runner-up slot behind the red cars. It had been a curate's egg of a season, good and bad in parts, and there was to be a final sting in the tail. Far from retiring, Fittipaldi suddenly announced his intention to leave the team in order to join his older brother Wilson's fledgling Copersucar outfit. Suddenly, McLaren was in dire need of a new number one driver for 1976.

In April 1975 Jochen Mass driving M23/8 (top) won the shortened Spanish Grand Prix. This would be the only GP win of his career, in which he started 104 World Championship races. Emerson Fittipaldi in M23/9 refused to start the Spanish race over concerns about the safety of the guardrails.

Opposite.
After the race was halted by a torrential downpour, Emerson Fittipaldi was declared winner of the 1975 British Grand Prix held at Silverstone. His M23 sported a vee-shaped rear wing, first seen on the Parnelli Indy and Formula 1 cars.

M23 [1975] FORMULA 1
SPECIFICATION

MODEL	McLaren M23
TYPE/FORMULA	Formula 1
YEAR OF PRODUCTION	1975
DESIGNER	Gordon Coppuck
EXAMPLES BUILT	2
ENGINE	Ford Cosworth DFV
CUBIC CAPACITY	2993cc
CARBURATION	Lucas fuel injection
POWER OUTPUT	465bhp

TRANSMISSION	Hewland DG400 5-speed
CHASSIS	Deformable double skinned aluminium monocoque
BODY	Monocoque lower, GRP nose, cockpit & engine cover
FRONT SUSPENSION	Upper rocker arm, operating inboard coil
	spring/damper, lower wishbone, anti-roll bar
REAR SUSPENSION	Adjustable top link, parallel lower links,
	twin radius rods, coil spring/damper, anti-roll bar
BRAKES F/R	Outboard/inboard ventilated discs
WHEELS DIAMETER x WIDTH F/R	13x10/13x18in

TYRES F/R	Goodyear
LENGTH	167in - 4242mm
WIDTH	82in - 2083mm
HEIGHT OF AIRBOX	49in - 1245mm
WHEELBASE	105.75in - 2686mm
TRACK F/R	64.2/65in - 1631/1651mm
WEIGHT	1325lb - 601kg
PRINCIPAL DRIVERS	Fittipaldi, Mass
IDENTIFYING COLOURS	Red/White

1976-1977 FORMULA 1
McLAREN M23

After the shock of Emerson Fittipaldi's sudden decision to leave the team, the problem of selecting his replacement was quickly solved. The Brazilian's defection coincided with a plea for further funding from Lord Hesketh, who announced that without it he could not afford to keep his eponymous team running in the style to which the upcoming James Hunt had become accustomed for the past three years.

Teddy Mayer and John Hogan of Marlboro lost no time in snapping up the Englishman. They signed him within 36 hours of Fittipaldi informing them that he was heading to his brother's team, at what would subsequently look like an absolute bargain basement price for a World Champion.

Gordon Coppuck had a new M26 design in preparation, but the M23 was pressed into service now bearing a new dayglo shade of Marlboro red and McLaren's own six-speed development of the Hewland FGA transmission which Team Manager Alastair Caldwell had calculated would enable them to make better use of the trusty DFV's torque curve. With lighter body panels, lower wishbone rear suspension, an innovative compressed air start and, from the Spanish GP onwards, new low-line airboxes, regular driver Jochen Mass and his new partner would race cars that were also 30lb lighter.

The first race of 1976 was the Brazilian GP at Interlagos where Hunt made the best possible start to his time at McLaren by qualifying ahead of reigning World Champion Niki Lauda and his Ferrari. It was James's first-ever pole position for a Grand Prix. A confused, controversial, traumatic and ultimately magnificent year was about to kick off.

Both Lauda and team-mate Clay Regazzoni made much better getaways, but the second Ferrari subsequently slipped back with a puncture as Hunt pressured Lauda. But Niki went on to win as the M23 lapsed on to seven cylinders due to a dislodged fuel injection trumpet, which later jammed the throttle open and spun James into the fence.

Despite McLaren being forced to remove new underskirts after protests in South Africa, Hunt again took pole but, wary of burning his clutch, got away gently and ran fourth initially. Once he was able to stop worrying about a minor oil leak he got the hammer down and began to chase after Lauda, who was 10s ahead. Then the Austrian's left rear tyre slowly began to deflate, setting up a gripping conclusion in which he held on by 1.3s to lead the McLaren across the line. Mass had a strong race too, finishing third.

At Brands Hatch in March James's early promise was realised when, for the second time in front of his home crowd in a non-championship race, he won the Race of Champions after overhauling the Surtees TS19 of early leader Alan Jones.

Using 35 per cent larger Can-Am style brakes at Long Beach for the US GP West, James qualified alongside Lauda on row two behind Regazzoni and the Tyrrell 007 of Patrick Depailler. James beat Depailler away and stayed ahead despite a momentary vapour lock, but then a coming together with the Frenchman put him hard into the wall on lap three to his intense chagrin. He worked out his frustration by standing by the side of the track for several laps, shaking his fist at his rival.

Back home at Silverstone for the non-championship International Trophy, he thrilled the crowd to win that race for the second time, starting from pole and setting the fastest lap as well.

By the Spanish GP at Jarama in May it was increasingly apparent that James was becoming the team's big winner even though, for all his poles and fastest laps, he was still one place lower in the rankings than Jochen. Then he scored his first win for McLaren after catching and passing Lauda, who was suffering bruised ribs after a tractor accident the previous week. But then the win was taken away from him in parc fermé when post-race scrutineering showed that the M23, around which a new dimensional regulation had been specifically formed since it was the largest F1 car, was 1.8cm, five-eighths of an inch, too wide across the rear wheels. McLaren tried everything it could think of to rectify the problem, but the organisers disqualified James.

In a season in which the politics were already fast becoming unsavoury, Mayer lodged an immediate appeal only to have it thrown out by the Spanish organisers. He then appealed to the FISA, but for the time being Lauda was the winner.

Niki won in Belgium and Monaco, where engine and transmission problems respectively stymied James and left McLaren with only Mass's fifth and sixth places as consolation. Jody Scheckter won in the six-wheeled Tyrrell in Sweden, where Lauda was third and James fifth. Then James put a run of three superb races together, winning in France and Britain, where he vanquished Lauda fair and square, and Germany where Niki crashed.

The same weekend he won in France Hunt learned that the FISA had given him back his Spanish victory, but then his British win was taken away on a technicality after his car was deemed to have been worked on, in contravention of the rules, having sustained damage after the original start had to be abandoned. That news was not imparted on a day when the British crowd let its anger be known when officials initially sought not to let their hero take part in the restart. Ironically, Clay Regazzoni was the culprit who had triggered the accident on the first attempt to start the race, after crashing into team-mate Lauda.

Gilles Villeneuve's first Grand Prix was the 1977 British GP at Silverstone. Driving M23/8 he finished 11th, two laps down on James Hunt who took the first win for the M26.

By 1976 the M23 was in its fourth season in Formula 1 and had already won 10 Grands Prix. Even so, with some serious development it remained highly competitive and would give James Hunt six more victories.

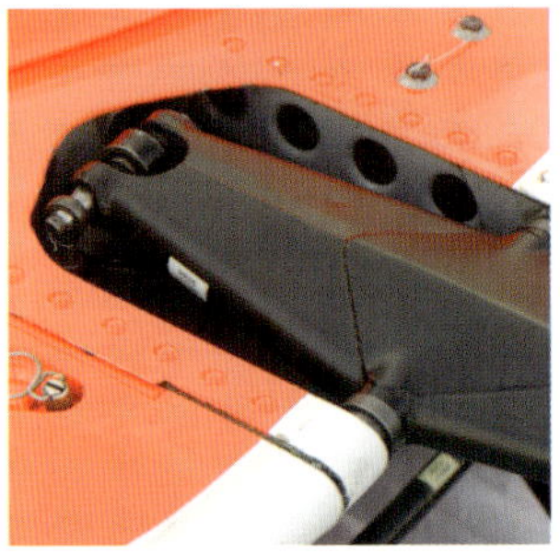

Modifications made in 1975 and carried over to 1976 included a fabricated top rocker arm on the front suspension, which operated directly on the damper unit.

In early 1976 a change in the regulations saw the end of the high airboxes that had grown taller and taller since their introduction back in 1971. Still with a 'high box' James Hunt won the Race of Champions at Brands Hatch by nearly 20 seconds over Alan Jones in the works Surtees.

Marlboro
11
GOODYEAR
TEXACO

Marlboro

GOODYEAR
Marlboro
GOODYEAR
Marlboro
11
CHAMPION
BORG & BECK
TEXACO

1976-1977 FORMULA 1 McLAREN M23

CONTINUED

Far worse was the news at Nürburgring. James won, but Lauda lay at death's door after his Ferrari crashed heavily at the Bergwerk corner following suspension failure and was engulfed in flames. He survived, having received the last rites, but his title challenge seemed precarious, especially as James went on another winning spree.

He had to be content with fourth in Austria after fighting with eventually victorious John Watson's Penske, then won in Holland, Canada and America. Between the European race and the north American rounds, however, there was yet more controversy when allegations about the McLaren's fuel octane, since disproved, saw Italian authorities place James and Jochen at the back of the grid. In his frustration, the former spun out early on. Lauda's come back at this race was truly heroic, finishing fourth to keep his title hopes alive.

Most famously, the 1976 World Championship came to its showdown at a wet Mt. Fuji for the Japanese GP. It was run in appalling conditions that saw Lauda, his burned eyelids still improperly healed, withdrawing after two laps in which visibility was minimal. James, perhaps more desperate to win his first title than Lauda was for a second, led for 61 of the 73 laps, then had to make a dramatic pit stop to have a deflating wet weather tyre replaced as the conditions improved. He was lucky to make it, as the tyre blew just before the pit lane entry. He was able to duck in to have it replaced, but the stop dropped him to fifth and for a moment the title was Lauda's. James drove the remaining laps in a red mist as he recovered to the third place he needed to beat the Austrian by a single point. No Hollywood scriptwriter could have dreamed that one up.

The Hunt/Lauda battle completely overshadowed Mass's contribution that year, and surely the most frustrating day of his career came at the Nürburgring. Braving slicks on a track surface initially dampened by pre-race rain, he had disappeared into the distance when Lauda's crash brought that part of the event to a halt. On the restart he had to be content with third place behind his team leader, and Jody Scheckter. Besides his third in South Africa, he took fourth in America, fifths in Long Beach, Monaco and Canada, and sixths in Brazil and Belgium.

The lighter and stiffer M26 was scheduled to appear in 1977, but initially McLaren played it safe and the mighty M23 soldiered on into its fifth season. James put M23-8 on pole position for the Argentine GP at Buenos Aires and easily led the first 32 laps before a suspension bolt sheared, sending him off the road and into the catchfencing. A couple of weeks later, at Interlagos in Brazil, he again led from pole but could only finish second to Reutemann's Ferrari. He led in South Africa too until a problematic front tyre slowed him enough for Lauda and Scheckter, now driving for Wolf, to overtake. Towards the end, Depailler also pushed his Tyrrell past the McLaren. Back home in the UK, James won the only non-championship race of the season, at Brands Hatch.

After a long, hard-fought and controversial season, James Hunt clinched the 1976 Drivers' title with third place at the wet Japanese Grand Prix held at the Mt. Fuji circuit.

Later, while still awaiting his M26, Jochen led very briefly in the wet in Belgium before spinning on lap 39 after he had switched to dry tyres, then scored a good second in the Swedish GP at Anderstorp before emergent Canadian Formula Atlantic racer Gilles Villeneuve made a stunning debut in an M23 at Silverstone. Qualifying ninth, ahead of Jochen's M26, the former skidoo racer was running a comfortable seventh when a faulty water temperature gauge tricked him into making a precautionary and unnecessary pit stop which dropped him to 11th. But for that he would have finished fourth in his first-ever Grand Prix.

Over its long working life the iconic M23 was piloted in its heyday by some of the greatest names in Formula One: Denny Hulme, Peter Revson, Jody Scheckter, Jacky Ickx, Emerson Fittipaldi, Jochen Mass, James Hunt and Gilles Villeneuve. Even after it was past its best, it provided a ride for the emergent Nelson Piquet courtesy of BS Fabrications in 1978, and was also driven by the likes of Bruno Giacomelli, Brett Lunger and Emilio de Villota.

More than any other car, even the M7A, it was the machine that truly put McLaren on the Formula 1 map.

M23 (1976) FORMULA 1

SPECIFICATION

MODEL	McLaren M23
TYPE/FORMULA	Formula 1
YEAR OF PRODUCTION	1976
DESIGNER	Gordon Coppuck
EXAMPLES BUILT	4 modified (No new chassis for 1976)
ENGINE	Ford Cosworth DFV
CUBIC CAPACITY	2993cc
CARBURATION	Lucas fuel injection
POWER OUTPUT	465bhp

TRANSMISSION	Hewland FG400 6-speed
CHASSIS	Deformable double skinned aluminium monocoque
BODY	Monocoque lower, GRP nose, cockpit & engine cover
FRONT SUSPENSION	Upper rocker arm, operating inboard coil spring/damper, lower wishbone, anti-roll bar
REAR SUSPENSION	Adjustable top link, parallel lower links, twin radius rods, coil spring/damper, anti-roll bar
BRAKES F/R	Outboard/inboard ventilated discs
WHEELS DIAMETER x WIDTH F/R	13x10/13x18in

TYRES F/R	Goodyear
LENGTH	165in - 4191mm
WIDTH	82in - 2083mm
HEIGHT	36in - 914mm
WHEELBASE	107in - 2718mm
TRACK F/R	64.2/65in - 1631/1651mm
WEIGHT	1295lb - 587kg
PRINCIPAL DRIVERS	Hunt, Mass, Villeneuve, Giacomelli
IDENTIFYING COLOURS	Red/White

1976-1978 FORMULA 1
McLAREN M26

Despite making a brief debut at the Dutch GP in 1976, the M26 was still under development at the start of 1977, and although Ferrari, Lotus and Wolf were all strong, teething problems with the M26 obliged reigning World Champion James Hunt to continue relying on the older M23 for the first four rounds, and team-mate Jochen Mass for the first nine.

In testing at Kyalami M26-1 had been seriously damaged when a bolt came loose from a front brake caliper, throwing James off the track. By the time the season reached Jarama for the Spanish GP in May, however, chassis M26-2 was ready for it's 'second' debut. James found its handling unbalanced and unpredictable, qualified only seventh and retired with a misfire on lap 10. He returned to the M23 for the next race, at Monaco, and it was not until Zolder for the Belgian GP in June that the M26 reappeared. The wings had been modified, and the oil cooler was now relocated in the nose. The car proved better balanced, but Mass nevertheless outqualified Hunt in the older M23. Choosing slicks for the race in the belief that the rainswept circuit would soon dry out, James was lapped as Mass led briefly. Hunt finished out of the points, in seventh.

At Dijon for the French GP James put the M26 on the front row alongside Mario Andretti's Lotus, and led the American away at the start until Ulsterman John Watson pushed his Brabham Alfa Romeo past both of them. As the McLaren's began to understeer Andretti overtook Hunt for second on lap 17 and took the win when the Brabham faltered on the final lap and stuttered home second. James was third.

The breakthrough came at Silverstone, where Mass had an M26 for the first time and Gilles Villeneuve joined the team in an M23. Hunt grabbed pole but failed to prevent Watson from thrusting the Brabham Alfa into the lead for the first 50 laps. Then further fuel delivery problems sent the red car into the pits, and James took the flag in front of the predictably partisan crowd. With Jochen finishing fourth it was a long overdue successful day.

Using the same car and engine at Hockenheim, James was running third before a broken exhaust pipe and a faulty fuel pump handed the position to Jochen, who soon lost it when his gearbox failed. The Austrian race was little better: Hunt led for 43 laps before his engine expired, but Mass took a point for sixth place.

Hopes were higher for Zandvoort, where Hunt had won the two previous races. From third on the grid he took an early lead from a challenging Andretti. Then they touched wheels on the exit to the Tarzan Hairpin on lap six as the American attempted to run round the outside. An angry Mario spun; James landed hard after momentarily becoming airborne and sustained damage to the M26's suspension and a water pipe. His day was over. Jochen, too, had a short run, getting turfed off by Alan Jones's Shadow at the start.

At Monza McLaren fielded its regular M26s and an M23 for Formula 2 star Bruno Giacomelli. James qualified on pole, Jochen ninth, and after brake problems accounted for the Englishman, the German took fourth place.

James was buoyant at Watkins Glen for the US GP East, despite spinning into a barrier on Friday. After taking his third pole position of the season, he found himself trailing German Hans Stuck's Brabham-Alfa in the early wet going. Inheriting the lead after Stuck went off after 14 laps, and with a comfortable lead over Andretti, he was nevertheless stalked by trouble. His engine was overheating, and as the field nursed their wet weather rubber on a rapidly drying track, he pressed on with a slowly deflating tyre. He pulled it off, winning his second GP of the season and his second consecutive one at the Glen, but it was a close call as Andretti was only two seconds behind at the finish.

Canada went less well, and was a tense weekend despite Hunt joking about Mosport being a great circuit to drive on, "*But not so nice to drive off.*" He and poleman Andretti had all but lapped the field by lap 59 and were about to overhaul Mass, in third place, when Mario lost ground and leader James was accidentally taken out by his own team-mate approaching the right-hander just after the pits. He hit the wall head-on, wrecking the M26's tub, and was briefly trapped in the car by his feet. Understandably furious, he punched a marshal who unwisely attempted to prevent him crossing the track to get back to the pits. Hunt left Canada with his reputation as a bad boy confirmed, and a $2,750 fine for his trouble. Jochen recovered to finish third.

The final race of the year at Mount Fuji saw Andretti pip Hunt for pole position. Having damaged M26-2 at Mosport and been dissatisfied with M26-1, James was now driving Jochen's chassis M26-3, and as the flag dropped he leapt into the lead as Andretti hit Jacques Laffite's Ligier and was forced out. When Jochen moved up to second place on lap six it seemed that the M26 really had come good, but the total McLaren domination ended when his engine broke on the 28th of the 73 laps. For Hunt, however, it was to be an easy run home as he led every lap to take what would be his last-ever Grand Prix victory. It left him fifth in the World Championship with 40 points, a long way adrift of Lauda on 72, and 15 ahead of sixth-placed Mass. The success would also be McLaren's last for three and a half years.

Despite the performance of the ground effect Lotus 78 in 1977, McLaren went into 1978 feeling very optimistic, which was understandable given the performance of James and the M26 in the final two races of the previous season. As he replaced Jochen Mass, popular Frenchman Patrick Tambay could be excused for thinking he had gone to the right place at just the right time. History would prove otherwise.

In the 1978 United States Grand Prix at Watkins Glen and the following Canadian race in Montreal, both the M26s appeared in the colours of Lowenbräu beer.

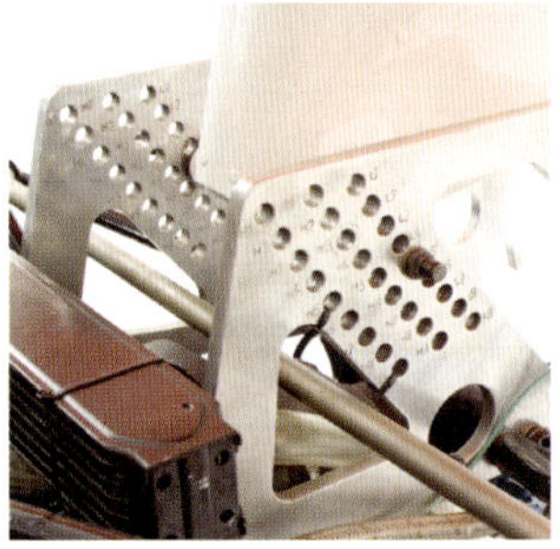

In an effort to find the optimum set-up for the broad range of circuits the team visited throughout the year, the M26 featured a multitude of different settings for the rear wing.

In an experiment that harked back to 1969 McLaren found a loophole in the regulations and tried this 'high' front wing on 26/3 in practice at the 1978 Spanish Grand Prix at Jarama.

The reigning World Champion James Hunt had a tough season in 1977. After he used the M23 in the first four races of the season the M26 finally made its debut in the Spanish Grand Prix at Jarama. In Belgium (above) the car scored its first race finish, out of the points in seventh.

1976-1978 FORMULA 1
McLAREN M26
CONTINUED

At the Brazilian GP at the new Jacarapagua circuit in Rio, that optimism did not seem misplaced as James qualified M26-4 on the front row alongside poleman Peterson's Lotus Type 78. At the start he chased eventual winner Carlos Reutemann, in his Michelin-shod Ferrari, then Andretti once the American had overtaken him, but the pace destroyed a front tyre and he pitted for a replacement on the ninth lap. Trying to make up time, he tangled with Riccardo Patrese's new Arrows and was out after 26 laps.

Kyalami went little better. After qualifying third James ran fourth until his engine quit on the fifth lap, and Patrick, who qualified alongside James on the second row, only managed an unclassified last place in M26-5 after clutch trouble cost him time at the start and he later slid off on oil.

Silverstone in March saw James do likewise in the sodden non-championship International Trophy meeting that was eventually won by the then unknown Finn Keke Rosberg in a Theodore. Back on the Grand Prix trail in Long Beach the McLarens were out of luck again, James crashing on the fifth lap and Patrick finishing 12th. An uneasy feeling began to pervade the team. James qualified sixth at Monaco, Patrick 11th, but the former's anti-roll bar broke as the latter finished seventh, out of the points. Not only had the new Lotus 79 rewritten the design parameters, but the Brabham Alfa Romeos had plentiful horsepower and the Michelins on the Ferraris endowed them with a significant advantage on some circuits. McLaren was beginning to struggle.

Hunt and old rival Niki Lauda collided on the grid in Belgium, where they had started fifth and fourth respectively. Bruno Giacomelli was elevated to second-car status after a leg injury sustained in the Pau F2 race the previous Monday kept Tambay out of action. The Italian finished eighth. In Spain Hunt tried a high (but just legal) front wing to try to cure the M26's inherent understeer problem, but though he qualified fourth it was not used in the race. He struggled home sixth after a tyre stop, as the returned Tambay dumped his car in the gravel after spinning on lap 17.

The Swedish Grand Prix was all about Lauda's controversial victory in the Brabham 'fan car', which detracted from the M26's poor performance. Neither qualified well, and Hunt finished out of the points as Tambay dragged his machine home fourth. The cars were better suited to the smoothness of Paul Ricard, where James qualified fourth and Patrick sixth, as 'Jack O'Malley' put the third car 22nd in the line-up. In a halfway decent car James drove one of his stronger races to place third, Patrick ninth; Giacomelli's engine broke.

In a desperate attempt to revive its flagging fortunes, McLaren took no fewer than six M26s of varying specification and two M23s to Brands Hatch for the British GP. The most interesting was M26-4, whose chassis had been rebuilt to incorporate large sidepods which, curiously, did not contain the crucial shaped underwings that were the secret of the Lotus's ground effect. The entire rear end was also boxed in. Teddy described it as being: "*Thirty per cent of the way to being a Lotus, but only twenty per cent of the way towards our new car.*" James raced his regular M26-3, which he crashed in very unusual circumstances along the Bottom Straight early in the race. Patrick was sixth. Bruno inadvertently helped Carlos Reutemann to win by blocking Niki Lauda to the point where the Argentinian was able to use superior momentum out of Clearways corner to overtake the Brabham driver; Giacomelli finished a chastened seventh only two seconds behind Tambay.

In Germany James sustained a punctured left front tyre and was disqualified for taking a short-cut to the pits; Patrick crashed after picking up a puncture of his own. Austria brought two more accidents, Holland ninth and 10th places and a retirement for Bruno.

It was crystal clear to Teddy Mayer and the McLaren management that the poor performance of their car was not inspiring their former World Champion driver, and tensions between the parties were high. Teddy was adamant that James was no longer "*really*" interested in driving, and found him little help in trying to resolve the ongoing technical problems. Soon, it became clear that when Hunt's contract expired at the end of the season, it would not be renewed. Instead, Mayer turned to Ronnie Peterson, the prodigal son at Lotus. Lured by the promise of an all-new ground effect McLaren M28 for 1979, 'Superswede' signed for the Marlboro-backed team and the news was announced shortly before the Italian Grand Prix at Monza. A week later, Ronnie was dead and Teddy admitted that, after the euphoria of signing the highly popular racer, his death was an even bigger blow than Bruce's. In the tragic circumstances, Patrick's fifth place went unnoticed.

After Monza Mayer tried to keep James, but his new contract with Walter Wolf was binding and in the end the little American opted for the fast but underrated and sensitive John Watson, who in Austria and Holland in 1976, and France and Britain in 1977, had shown himself capable of challenging James even when the latter had the fire of victory in his heart. Against this sad backdrop McLaren's 1978 season petered out with lowly placings at Watkins Glen after tyre troubles, and more disillusionment in Canada.

While the works team switched to the M28 in 1979, and American privateer Brett Lunger did not drive his M26 (chassis six) beyond 1978, an M26 was resurrected for Patrick Tambay to race in Brazil in 1979 before his M28 was ready to use in Argentina. A car that had won three races, it nevertheless flattered to deceive as it was left floundering by the development of ground effect.

Despite the support of the home crowd at Brands Hatch for the 1978 British GP, Hunt (top) could only qualify 14th. In the race he lasted just seven laps before spinning off in front of his fans on South Bank. Running three chassis had made for hard work but the team was at least rewarded by finishes from the other two drivers. Tambay (middle) made it home sixth and in the points whilst Giacomelli (lower) was right behind him in seventh.

M26 [1977] FORMULA 1

SPECIFICATION

MODEL	McLaren M26
TYPE/FORMULA	Formula 1
YEAR OF PRODUCTION	1976/1977
DESIGNER	Gordon Coppuck
EXAMPLES BUILT	7
ENGINE	Ford Cosworth DFV
CUBIC CAPACITY	2993cc
CARBURATION	Lucas fuel injection
POWER OUTPUT	465bhp

TRANSMISSION	McLaren/Hewland 6-speed
CHASSIS	Double skinned aluminium & Nomex monocoque
BODY	Monocoque lower, GRP nose, cockpit & engine cover
FRONT SUSPENSION	Upper rocker arm, operating inboard coil
	spring/damper, lower wishbone, anti-roll bar
REAR SUSPENSION	Adjustable top link, parallel lower links,
	twin radius rods, coil spring/damper, anti-roll bar
BRAKES F/R	Outboard/inboard ventilated discs
WHEELS DIAMETER x WIDTH F/R	13x10/13x18in

TYRES F/R	Goodyear
LENGTH	172in - 4368mm
WIDTH	83in - 2108mm
HEIGHT	34.5in - 876mm
WHEELBASE	108in - 2743mm
TRACK F/R	65/66in - 1651/1675mm
WEIGHT	1300lb - 589kg
PRINCIPAL DRIVERS	Hunt, Mass
IDENTIFYING COLOURS	Red/White

1977 & 1978 INDYCAR McLAREN M24 & M24B

Long since out of Can-Am and Formula 5000, McLaren's presence in the US during the mid- to late-1970s was nevertheless still significant, with the works continuing to make good showings at the Indianapolis 500.

While many privateers continued running ex-works or ex-Penske M16s of varying vintages into the 1980s, by 1976 it was clear that as far as frontline racing was concerned the M16E had come to the end of its competitive life. But the factory was ready with its replacement for 1977, in the shape of the new M24.

Five years earlier the back end of an M19, complete with the Ford Cosworth DFV, had been grafted onto an M16 Indy car front end as Gordon Coppuck sought solutions to the F1 design for 1973. He was pleased with the outcome, much of which was to find expression in the double World Championship-winning M23.

In 1976 Cosworth had unveiled its new Indy engine, a 2.65-litre turbocharged version of the famed DFV known as the DFX. Now, as the four-cylinder Offenhauser was finally coming to the end of the road it was time for that 1972 experiment to come full circle and Coppuck leapt at the chance to create an Indy version of the M23. The basic M23 chassis design was metamorphosed with a heavier gauge aluminium skin and heftier bulkheads to comply with USAC safety regulations, and fitted with M16E-style suspension. The result, while very obviously an oval racer, could not conceal its F1 ancestry.

The works team, now sponsored by First National Citibank Travellers' Checks, ran a car for Johnny Rutherford in 1977, while Penske Racing took one for Mario Andretti to race with Cam 2 Motor Oil backing. In such capable hands they made their mark immediately. In the first four races of the season Rutherford took a pole for the works, led two races and won one. Andretti became the first to lap Indianapolis over 200mph in his M24, running 200.311mph when practice began. In official qualifying that honour fell to Tom Sneva, driving Penske's second car under Norton Spirit sponsorship as he lapped the two-and-a-half-mile oval at 200.401mph. Sneva eventually took the pole at 198.884mph. Rutherford qualified third fastest behind Sneva but under Indy rules he was obliged to start 17th. It wasn't his year at the Brickyard, however, as he retired after 12 laps with gearbox failure. Sneva, though, brought his M24 home second.

1978 marked McLaren's ninth year at Indianapolis, and Rutherford's sixth as the team's number one driver. The new M24B was slightly lighter and had the oil cooler repositioned horizontally to the left of the transmission. A third win for JR soon began to look unlikely as engine trouble twice forced the M24B into the pits. On a day when Al Unser Snr won for Lola and JR was classified an unhappy 13th, the highest-placed McLaren was the quaintly named Sugaripe Prune M24 driven to fifth by Wally Dallenbach.

The 1979 season was riven with controversy as CART was founded in direct competition to USAC. The latter retained control of the prestigious Indy 500, and added to the controversy by reducing turbo boost from 80 to 50 inches of manifold pressure for qualifying and to 70 for racing. The plan was not just to reduce speeds, but also to give stock block engines a fresh lease of life. McLaren's development for the race embraced heavy revision of the M24B's monocoque, albeit not of sufficient magnitude to warrant a new type number, and an attractive slimmer nose profile similar to the M26's but without that car's oil cooler.

Rutherford found himself on the third row, eighth fastest at 188.137mph and in the works team's final outing at the Brickyard, JR lost 30 laps in the pits with gearbox problems and was classified 18th. Veteran Roger McCluskey was left to salvage McLaren's honour, with 13th place in Warner Hodgdon's National Engineering M24. By the end of the season Rutherford was still fourth in the new USAC/CART series, albeit courtesy of results such as thirds at Phoenix and Michigan and a fourth at Ontario. McLaren's real star that year was Sneva, who wrung great speed out of Jerry O'Connell's Sugaripe Prune M24; he was second at Atlanta and Michigan, and third at Trenton.

The writing was on the wall, however, written largely by the speed of the ground effect Chaparral 2K designed by former McLaren man John Barnard, who had further chapters yet to write in the marque's story. By the end of a tough season, Team McLaren faced 1980 with no sponsorship and a car that was no longer a match for Penske's own chassis, let alone the Chaparral, and growing trouble on the Formula 1 front. The only option was withdrawal.

That did not quite mark the end of the McLaren story in Indy racing, however, as Rutherford moved over to drive the Chaparral. For much of 1980 the indefatigable Sneva thrilled spectators with his now three year-old Jerry O'Connell-owned M24. Second at Ontario for the opening race of the season, he was forced to start at the back of the grid for the Indy 500 after cutting a tyre on his brand new Phoenix ground effect racer on debris in practice and crashing it heavily enough to warrant a switch to a back-up chassis. The only alternative was 'Ole Hound', as O'Connell's faithful M24 was nicknamed. In a superb drive fully worthy of McLaren's heritage on the oval, he climbed all the way into the lead from 33rd place by lap 72 until, ironically, Rutherford's Chaparral caught and passed him on lap 148.

Other private McLarens would continue to race in the USAC/CART National Championship until 1981. In that year's controversial 500, Australian former Formula 1 driver Vern Schuppan dragged his Theodore Racing M24B from 18th starting slot to a superb third behind disputed winner Bobby Unser and an angry Mario Andretti. That drive, and Sneva's before it, captured the spirit of McLaren's quest for success in Indy racing, leading to its three superb victories.

The 1977 Indy 500 saw the appearance of another car derived from the M23 Formula 1 car, the Cosworth DFX-engined M24. Mario Andretti in the CAM2/Penske-entered car (top) finished sixth. At the 1978 race Wally Dallenbach in the Sugaripe Prune M24 was the highest placed McLaren in fifth.

The revised First National City-sponsored works M24B of two-time Indy winner for McLaren Johnny Rutherford qualified fourth on the grid for the 1978 Indy 500. Engine trouble meant he was never in with a chance for a third win and after several pit stops he crossed the line 20 laps down in 13th place.

M24 INDYCAR
SPECIFICATION

MODEL	McLaren M24
TYPE/FORMULA	Indianapolis/USAC
YEAR OF PRODUCTION	1977
DESIGNER	Gordon Coppuck
EXAMPLES BUILT	6 (+3 M24B)
ENGINE	Ford Cosworth DFX
CUBIC CAPACITY	2650cc
CARBURATION	Hilborn injection, Garrett Airesearch turbocharger
POWER OUTPUT	820bhp

TRANSMISSION	Hewland LG500 4-speed
CHASSIS	Deformable double skinned aluminium monocoque
BODY	Monocoque lower, GRP nose, cockpit & engine cover
FRONT SUSPENSION	Upper rocker arm, operating inboard coil
	spring/damper, lower wishbone, anti-roll bar
REAR SUSPENSION	Adjustable top link, parallel lower links,
	twin radius rods, coil spring/damper, anti-roll bar
BRAKES F/R	Outboard/inboard ventilated discs
WHEELS DIAMETER x WIDTH F/R	15x10/15x14in

TYRES F/R	Goodyear
LENGTH	178in - 4521mm
WIDTH	78.5in - 1994mm
HEIGHT AT WING	36in - 914mm
WHEELBASE	107in - 2718mm
TRACK F/R	66.5/62.5in - 1689/1587mm
WEIGHT	1521lb - 690kg
PRINCIPAL DRIVERS	Rutherford, Sneva, Andretti
IDENTIFYING COLOURS	White/Red/Blue

1979 FORMULA 1 McLAREN M28

The M27 was intended to be a non-ground effects car but circumstance rendered it obsolete even before it had been built. Thus the design team moved on to the M28 in time for the 1979 season as Patrick Tambay was joined by John Watson, the replacement for James Hunt.

Gordon Coppuck quickly set to work on a second replacement for the M26, a ground effect machine dubbed the M28. Not surprisingly, it was the World Championship-winning Lotus Type 79 that most influenced his thinking. By harnessing airflow beneath the chassis to generate downforce, and going one better than he had with the revolutionary Lotus 78 in 1977, the fertile Colin Chapman had caught the opposition unawares.

In order to increase the downforce figures that McLaren calculated for the 79, the new DFV-powered M28 took its chassis and bodywork dimensions to the limit prescribed by the governing body. Accordingly the most obvious feature of the aluminium Nomex honeycomb monocoque was the two vast sidepods. Each accommodated not only a Marston radiator and an oil cooler but also a fuel cell (with a third one placed behind the driver to give a total capacity of 40 gallons) and the shaped underwings which were intended to optimise the undercar airflow.

To facilitate the latter the Koni-damped suspension was moved inboard, out of the airstream. At the front this meant top rocker arms, lower wishbones and inboard coil spring/ dampers, at the rear lower and upper wishbones together with lower rocker arms and inboard spring/ dampers. With a wheelbase of 113 inch wheelbase, a 70 inch front track and 64 inch rear track, the 1,378lb car looked somewhat slab-sided and bulky.

The prototype was running by the end of 1978 and with time for plenty of testing ahead of the Argentine opener, so by that race numerous detail changes had already been made which included a repositioned rear anti-roll bar and minor modifications to the bodywork.

The team was confident it had ironed out earlier problems with the bonding of various magnesium castings to the monocoque's honeycomb sections, but it soon became apparent that there were still technical issues to be ironed out even though some were effectively masked by some excellent Goodyear tyres. As Jacques Laffite dominated the race for Ligier, chased by Lotus's Carlos Reutemann, John Watson brought his M28 from sixth on the grid to what seemed a promising third place. He struggled in Brazil, however, finishing eighth.

By Kyalami the M28s had undergone further modifications following experiments with and without nose fins, and with a double-deck rear aerofoil and a low-mounted one. Unfortunately, Tambay's new M28-3 refused to run correctly and he was forced back into M28-1. He finished 10th, three laps down on the winning Ferraris, as Watson wrestled with M28-2 before retiring on lap 63 with ignition trouble.

When the series reached Spain the cars had morphed again with reduced front and rear tracks, a shorter wheelbase and heavily revised aerodynamics. But both were still well off the pace, running three seconds slower than Laffite's pole-winning Ligier. "*Little better than the old design*" was Autosport's post-race judgement on cars that were never in contention.

Such a large machine was no better suited to Monaco either, and by the time the McLaren team reached the Principality they had another new version ready, this one christened M28C. Though built up from the monocoque of M28-3 the changes were now more substantial - hence the C suffix. Again the inspiration had come from Lotus, this time Chapman's Type 80 'wingless wonder'. The M28C now had a longer, slimmer nose and the front suspension pick-ups were moved inboard with the suspension components themselves reprofiled to present a tidier appearance. The theoretical aerodynamic advantage allowed the air a clearer route through to the radiator intakes and beneath the sidepods.

Watson took this car, with Tambay taking over the B-variant which had been developed using M28-2 as a base. Wattie at least finished fourth out of six survivors, still on the lead lap, but Tambay didn't even qualify. In France Patrick was 10th, Wattie 11th. The unloved M28's final appearance was in Tambay's hands in the British GP, where he finished seventh. Watson by then was driving its replacement, the hastily conceived M29.

Teddy Mayer did not spare anyone in his criticism of the M28, which was overweight, slow on the straights, aerodynamically weak and had poor grip despite the plan-form size of its ground effect areas. It was, he said trenchantly, "*Ghastly, a disaster, quite diabolical.*" Querying Coppuck's track record, Mayer continued: "*We ignored all the crucial design precepts that a car should be as light, agile and as compact as possible.*" In creating a car designed to get as much air underneath it as possible, McLaren had gone too far in the wrong direction.

Throughout 1979 the M28 appeared in several different guises. Early in the season the car ran with a low sidepod set-up. At Long Beach where both works cars once again ran in Lowenbräu livery, Tambay (top) retired on lap one. At the Race of Champions Watson (middle) was out by lap 17. By the time of the British Grand Prix both cars had high side fences to help direct air over the rear wing. Tambay (bottom) was seventh.

M28 FORMULA 1
SPECIFICATION

MODEL	McLaren M28
TYPE/FORMULA	Formula 1
YEAR OF PRODUCTION	1979
DESIGNER	Gordon Coppuck
EXAMPLES BUILT	3
ENGINE	Ford Cosworth DFV
CUBIC CAPACITY	2993cc
CARBURATION	Lucas fuel injection
POWER OUTPUT	470bhp

TRANSMISSION	McLaren/Hewland 6-speed
CHASSIS	Double skinned aluminium & Nomex monocoque
BODY	GRP nose, side pods, cockpit & engine cover
FRONT SUSPENSION	Upper rocker arm, operating inboard coil
	spring/damper, lower wishbone, anti-roll bar
REAR SUSPENSION	Upper wishbone/rocker arm operating inboard
	coil spring/damper, lower wishbone & link
BRAKES F/R	Outboard/inboard ventilated discs
WHEELS DIAMETER x WIDTH F/R	13x11/13x18in

TYRES F/R	Goodyear
LENGTH	174in - 4420mm
WIDTH	84in - 2134mm
HEIGHT OF ROLLBAR	40in - 1016mm
WHEELBASE	113in - 2870mm
TRACK F/R	70/64in - 1778/1626mm
WEIGHT	1378lb - 625kg
PRINCIPAL DRIVERS	Watson, Tambay
IDENTIFYING COLOURS	Red/White

1979 & 1980 FORMULA 1
McLAREN M29 & M29C

Though they proved extremely resistant to all attempts to alleviate them, the McLaren M28's numerous shortcomings had not taken long to identify. Nor did it take long for the team to complete and commission its replacement once Teddy Mayer had stepped in at the start of May demanding that a brand new car be ready in time for the British Grand Prix in July 1979.

By Gordon Coppuck's own admission more of a Williams FW07 copy than a replica of the Lotus 79, the M29 was accordingly much more compact than its unloved predecessor. With some elements of Ligier thinking in its design and make-up, the car's cockpit was now situated well forward within the wheelbase, and the new monocoque was constructed in a more conventional manner using sheet aluminium in place of the M28's radical honeycomb.

Still powered by the evergreen Ford Cosworth DFV mated to a Hewland gearbox, and with a new Williams FW07-style secret heat exchanger hidden away within the left-hand sidepod, the car also incorporated a single fuel cell in place of the three which featured on the older car. The wheelbase was slightly shorter and the track narrower, and the M29 weighed in 58lb lighter than the M28. It was duly ready in time for the Silverstone race, as per Mayer's order, but once again the team took along M28-3C as a spare car just in case. Tambay was still using M28-2. He qualified that car 18th, while Watson was a promising seventh in the new car. He got caught out at the start and dropped down to 16th, fought back, but then had to pit to replace a tyre. Thereafter he fought back again, slicing past Scheckter's understeering Ferrari to claim fourth in front of his 100,000-strong home crowd. Nobody could have known it at the time, but it was to be the best performance of the M29's life.

By just missing out on a podium place, Wattie was able to demonstrate that his own spirit and drive had not been damaged by the disappointments with the M28. But no matter what the team did to the M29 after Silverstone, it became increasingly clear that it was not the answer to the inherent problems. Experiments continued with undercar aerodynamics and the rear suspension, but to little avail. Watson could only pick up minor placings. By the end of the season it was abundantly clear that Tambay's confidence had not survived the difficult couple of years he had spent with the team. He headed off to pastures new, and his place alongside Watson for 1980 was taken by fellow countryman Alain Prost, who had starred in Formula 3 that season.

The diminutive Frenchman had been introduced to Mayer by Marlboro's Paddy McNally and participated in a test at Paul Ricard that November. Wattie had lapped a modified M29C, with outboard rear suspension, 2.7s faster than the standard car, to everyone's delight. When Prost went faster than Wattie in 10 laps, Teddy went running to his car for a contract. The little Frenchman immediately became a McLaren team member.

His early promise was quickly borne out in 1980 with the lighter, M29C. 'The Professor,' as he quickly became known, finished sixth on his Grand Prix debut in Argentina and followed that with fifth in Brazil, outpacing the experienced Watson to establish himself as the team's number one.

Things went awry at Kyalami during the South African GP meeting. A suspension failure pitched Prost's M29C off the road in practice and left him with a broken wrist. That forced him to miss the race and the following Long Beach event. There, clutch problems prevented promising British F2 driver Stephen South from qualifying. Watson recovered form sufficiently to cross the line in fourth place, but that was something of a false dawn.

Eventually, after crashing in Spain and then again at Watkins Glen, having taken sixths in Britain and Holland, the injured Prost decided to quit to join Renault. Against this backdrop, pressure continued to mount for a merger between McLaren and Ron Dennis's Project Four Racing team.

The previous year, 1979, Dennis and Marlboro had suggested such a thing to Teddy Mayer, who rebuffed the idea. Having been angered not to get the credit he felt was his due for designing Jim Hall's revolutionary Indianapolis Chaparral 2K, John Barnard had turned down a previous offer from Mayer to head McLaren's design department fearing his input might be diluted by the presence of his former boss, Gordon Coppuck. Mayer refused to consider sacking Coppuck, so the situation reached stalemate. Barnard instead joined forces with Ron Dennis, and began designing a revolutionary Formula 1 car for Project Four. Now John Hogan of Marlboro was again pressing Mayer to reconsider a merger between the two parties. In the end it came down to a simple ultimatum: take the Project Four deal or face the loss of Marlboro's funding. Mayer knew how tough it was to find a major corporate sponsor at short notice and conceded. The merger went ahead in September, with Dennis and Mayer as joint-Managing Directors of a new entity called McLaren International. Towards the end of 1980 work began on the construction of Barnard's all-new car, the carbon fibre MP4 which would, the following year, turn F1 design on its head and play a significant role in restoring the team's fortunes.

In the meantime, the M29 soldiered on into 1981, with more detail changes, including a switch from Goodyear to Michelin tyres. Watson picked up two points for fifth place in the South African GP, which was promptly declared not to be of Championship status by the governing body, now known as the Fédération Internationale du Sport Automobile (FISA). The M29Fs were outclassed at Long Beach and Brazil, the MP4 could not come soon enough.

The M29's first race appearance was at the 1979 British Grand Prix at Silverstone. It proved much faster than the M28 and John Watson qualified the car seventh, finishing the race an encouraging eighth.

By 1980 the ground-effect M29 had evolved into a lighter M29C specification. It featured new front suspension, revised bodywork and a marginally greater rearward bias to the overall weight distribution. The cockpit was dominated by the high front roll-hoop demanded by the regulations.

The 1980 Monaco Grand Prix was a dismal weekend for the McLaren team. Watson failed to qualify and Prost (left) who at least made the race, was out by the first corner. Starting from a reasonable 10th on the grid he was caught up in a four-car pile up at Ste. Devote involving Jarier, Daly and Giacomelli.

M29 FORMULA 1
SPECIFICATION

MODEL	McLaren M29
TYPE/FORMULA	Formula 1
YEAR OF PRODUCTION	1979/1981
DESIGNER	Gordon Coppuck
EXAMPLES BUILT	3 (+2M29C)
ENGINE	Ford Cosworth DFV
CUBIC CAPACITY	2993cc
CARBURATION	Lucas fuel injection
POWER OUTPUT	470bhp

TRANSMISSION	McLaren/Hewland 6-speed
CHASSIS	Double skinned aluminium & Nomex monocoque
BODY	GRP nose, side pods, cockpit & engine cover
FRONT SUSPENSION	Upper rocker arm, operating inboard coil spring/damper, lower wishbone, anti-roll bar
REAR SUSPENSION	Upper wishbone/rocker arm operating inboard coil spring/damper, lower wishbone & link
BRAKES F/R	Outboard/inboard ventilated discs
WHEELS DIAMETER x WIDTH F/R	13x11/13x18in

TYRES F/R	Goodyear
LENGTH	173in - 4394mm
WIDTH	81in - 2057mm
HEIGHT	40in - 1016mm
WHEELBASE	106in - 2692mm
TRACK F/R	68/62in - 1727/1575mm
WEIGHT	1295lb - 587kg
PRINCIPAL DRIVERS	Watson, Tambay
IDENTIFYING COLOURS	Red/White

CHAPTER

03

ALAIN PROST

Before I started racing, McLaren was obviously one of the top names you heard about. With Bruce himself, the Formula One cars, the Can-Am cars, the Indy cars, and of course the orange livery - which I have very strong memories of as a boy - it was already so strong from a marketing point of view.

Even so, in 1979 I turned down the chance to take part in my first Grand Prix and drive for the team at Watkins Glen. It was almost my only opportunity at that time – I had started talks with Ligier, and with Bernie Ecclestone at Brabham – but when Marlboro's Paddy McNally contacted me and asked if I would drive, I knew it was too soon. I said that I would prefer to do some testing on a track I knew, he agreed and in January of 1980 I went to Paul Ricard with McLaren. To be honest, without that opportunity I wouldn't be writing this now.

After that I was very happy to be at McLaren, with a good team-mate in John Watson, good relations with Teddy Mayer and the guys, and everyone made me very welcome. That first year I had many accidents, some were bad ones, but otherwise it was a very good year for me.

In 1981 I moved to Renault at a time when the new technology was improving fast but the turbos were unreliable. I always remained on good terms with Ron Dennis and after three seasons at Renault I was really happy to go back to McLaren. Even though I am French I prefer to work with English people, the ambience at McLaren was more the way I like it and I felt comfortable. Everyone goes in the same direction at McLaren, it is well organised and has key people who are experienced. It's so much easier when you are professional and serious – much better!

In fact, looking back, of my four World Championships, the one with McLaren in 1986 was the toughest and the one I am most proud of. By then McLaren was my family. We had a difficult time in my last year with the team, fighting with Ayrton, but today, you know, I don't care too much about that. It's a shame how it worked out and why I left in 1990, because 'my team' really was McLaren.

After I stopped racing I worked with McLaren again and was involved on the technical side alongside Ron. It was a really good time for me but in 1997 I left again - but only to try and build my own team in France, you must realise. If I have one regret it is that I would have preferred to stay at McLaren, to have an involvement and to continue working with the team. To be part of the great team that it is today.

Alain Prost
Drivers' World Champion 1985, '86 & '89
McLaren MP4/2B, MP4/2C & MP4/5

1980 FORMULA 1 McLAREN M30

The M30 was Gordon Coppuck's last design for McLaren, and the last Formula 1 contender to be raced by the team prior to the arrival in September 1980 of Ron Dennis and new Technical Director John Barnard. It was also the machine that contributed to Alain Prost leaving the team, following successful overtures from Renault.

It was introduced mid-season at Zandvoort, and despite having a two-inch shorter wheelbase and inch-wider track both front and rear, it weighed the same as the M29C, 1,320lbs. The running gear such as engine, transmission, suspension, brakes, wheels, steering assembly and instruments, was largely a carry-over from the M29C but crucially the honeycomb aluminium chassis was 50 per cent stiffer and the aerodynamics were improved. This was after Teddy Mayer himself had taken an M29 to the Motor Industry Research Association's (MIRA) wind tunnel. A major effort went into improving downforce with the M30 in the hope of restoring McLaren's competitiveness, but the results were patchy.

Though Alain Prost thought the car was an improvement over the M29, he was overshadowed in Holland as Watson put the spare M29C on the fifth row despite a heavy crash in practice with his intended race car. The Frenchman qualified the M30 in 18th, half-a-second slower, after complaining of oversteer. While Watson raced strongly and was running seventh when his engine broke, Prost also chased hard and brought his new car home a reasonably encouraging sixth on its debut. That would, however, be its sole World Championship point.

Two weeks later the M30 was back in action as the Italian GP switched briefly from Monza to Imola. Again, Watson in the M29C was faster as Prost struggled on to the back row of the grid after problems with his brakes and clutch and the handling. After a smooth drive he brought it home seventh, just outside the points.

In Canada later that September Watson was again quicker in qualifying in the old car, and Alain retired after 41 laps. John Barnard's arrival as Technical Director generated more development on the car in the form of a revised engine cover and floor and revisions to the suspension, but on the opening lap Prost clashed with Arrows driver Riccardo Patrese, and subsequently suffered suspension failure. The story was no happier in the US GP East at Watkins Glen, where the M30 was still almost a second slower than the M29C before Prost had a nasty accident when the car went straight on in a fourth-gear left-hander in practice. Another suspension failure was suspected. The Frenchman was still feeling giddy on race morning, and having tried out the spare M29C wisely opted not to start.

At the time it was widely reported that the only M30 ever built had been destroyed in the incident, but in all honesty that was more because the team felt it would be better to stick with a revised version of the M29 for the start of the 1981 season. Thus the car, which had enjoyed a very limited topline racing career that encompassed just 172 competition laps and barely more than 485 miles, was left back in the stores in Colnbrook, slightly damaged and accompanied by a complete spare monocoque.

With hindsight it is easy to argue that using the M29 as a starting point, a car which was itself a stop-gap, meant the basic design of the M30 was always going to be compromised. But it came at a time when McLaren was struggling for its very survival as a competitive racing team and every avenue had to be explored. Subsequently the car was restored by Tony Dunne using the spare tub, and raced in the UK by Irishman Alo Lawler. He won two non-F1 championships with it in 1984 and '85. Then it was sold to a collector in the USA before passing into the hands of Sean Allen, who currently campaigns the one-off in US historic events.

The M30 made its first press appearance (top) at a mid-year Silverstone test day. At the Canadian Grand Prix in Montreal (above) Prost ran as high as fourth in the race before suffering suspension failure and spinning out on lap 42.

The squared-off front roll-hoop of the M30 is clearly visible in this high angle shot taken in the pit lane at the Italian Grand Prix. Alain Prost started last on the 24-car grid and made it to the finish just out of the points in seventh place.

M30 FORMULA 1
SPECIFICATION

MODEL	McLaren M30
TYPE/FORMULA	Formula 1
YEAR OF PRODUCTION	1980
DESIGNER	Gordon Coppuck
EXAMPLES BUILT	1
ENGINE	Ford Cosworth DFV
CUBIC CAPACITY	2993cc
CARBURATION	Lucas fuel injection
POWER OUTPUT	470bhp

TRANSMISSION	McLaren/Hewland 5-speed
CHASSIS	Double skinned aluminium & Nomex monocoque
BODY	GRP nose, side pods, cockpit & engine cover
FRONT SUSPENSION	Upper rocker arm, operating inboard coil
	spring/damper, lower wishbone, anti-roll bar
REAR SUSPENSION	Upper wishbone/rocker arm operating inboard
	coil spring/damper, lower wishbone & link
BRAKES F/R	Outboard/inboard ventilated discs
WHEELS DIAMETER x WIDTH F/R	13or15x11/13x16or18in

TYRES F/R	Goodyear
LENGTH	169in - 4293mm
WIDTH	82in - 2082mm
HEIGHT	38in - 965mm
WHEELBASE	104in - 2642mm
TRACK F/R	69/63in - 1752/1600mm
WEIGHT	1320lb - 598kg
PRINCIPAL DRIVERS	Prost
IDENTIFYING COLOURS	Red/White

1981 FORMULA 1 McLAREN MP4/1

"*It was a big step into the unknown….. like flying Concorde when you've only ever flown a Boeing 707*". If anything, John Watson's famous description of his first drive in John Barnard's completely new McLaren MP4/1 vastly undersold the concept. In reality what is arguably still the most significant car in McLaren's long history had more to do with space travel than commercial airline flying, even such a swift and elegant one such as Concorde.

The MP4/1 brought a change to McLaren's established nomenclature, standing for McLaren Project Four, and bore the distinction of being the first carbon composite Formula 1 design. The material had been used for small components since Graham Hill's eponymous Embassy-backed cars had used it for their rear wing supports in 1975, but not until the MP4/1 made its bow on March 5th 1981 had it been used for the entire chassis. Together with Lotus chief Colin Chapman whose controversial Lotus 88 would also use the material, Barnard had come to appreciate not just the lightness of carbon fibre but also its tremendous strength, and his new car would set a trend every bit as influential as Chapman's introduction of the monocoque chassis two decades earlier. It laid the groundwork for material innovation that has become such a hallmark of the McLaren Group's activities with cars such as the three-seater F1, the world's first fully composite road car, and the later Mercedes-Benz SLR McLaren as the world's first series production carbon composite car.

Born out of a singular vision, the MP4/1 remains as much as anything a testament to Barnard's character, drive and imagination. He had cut his teeth with Lola, and then McLaren in the early 1970s, before moving to Parnelli and Chaparral in the United States, yet it was his relative inexperience in F1 that paradoxically freed him to think outside the box. The focus in F1 at that time, he said, was very much on ground effects. "*The objective was to optimise it, and that meant using the biggest underwing I could get, which entailed a very small section chassis. I wanted to get my chassis down to not to much bigger than the driver's bum.*" To Barnard, the only way to reduce the chassis section while retaining the necessary torsional stiffness was to use an entirely new material rather than just a different gauge of aluminium.

Sometimes controversial but never anything less than a highly gifted and always adventurous designer, he had been thinking about this particular problem long before the merger between Marlboro McLaren and Project Four Racing. He had also been hearing good things about carbon fibre composites: given the correct application it was clearly light, stiff, and extremely strong – perfect, in theory, for Formula 1.

Very few people knew much about it, however. A contact at British Aerospace provided some clues at a time when the material was being used for engine cowls for the Rolls-Royce RB211 turbofan engine. At the same time, however, its mysterious properties were called into question, Barnard remembers, when someone easily snapped a piece of it in half (actually, a unidirectional piece which he bent the wrong way). Perhaps it was not, after all, the ideal material with which to build an entire Formula 1 car.

Others too, Barnard confirmed years later, "*thought we were mad,*" and even the man he describes as his design hero, Colin Chapman who was busy working on his technically brilliant but ultimately doomed Type 88 with its complex composite-mix 'twin chassis', went on record to say that a pure-carbon car of the sort McLaren was planning simply would not be safe enough.

Typically Ron Dennis showed a far more positive approach, or as Barnard characterised it, "*He was very gung-ho. It was a very simple deal between us. He said, 'You tell me what you want to do technically, and I'll get the money.' That's how it went, and it worked, too!*"

Around this time a contact from Barnard's Indycar days with Parnelli and Chaparral pointed him towards the Utah-based Hercules Corporation which had 'Skunk-Works' research and development section, and finally he was in business. Expressly conceived to think the unthinkable and play around with crazy ideas and odd one-offs, Hercules was the obvious place to start building his dream.

Barnard jumped on a flight to Salt Lake City with a quarter scale model of his proposed design in the cabin alongside him, and soon after the staff at Hercules set to work the MP4/1 began to take shape. As they lacked the technology and know-how to create curved pieces, the first monocoque was assembled using five major components, each one with flat faces. It had only a single major aluminium component, the internal front suspension bulkhead, compared to a conventional F1 car of the time which boasted around 50. Perhaps it looked a little rough and wrinkled in places, but it turned out even stronger than Barnard felt necessary, so for the next chassis plies were pulled out of the skin to make it lighter still.

History in the making - On March 5th 1981 the revolutionary new MP4/1 is prepared for it's first official test run at a rainswept Silverstone circuit.

Even though it didn't make its race debut until Argentina, the sleek carbon fibre car was already a winner. MP4/1 won the '*Concours d'Elegance*' award presented by the Californian organisers at the Long Beach Grand Prix.

The official name for the new car, MP4 was understood to stand for 'Marlboro Project 4' although everyone recognised the car as a McLaren. It wasn't until 1982 and the MP4/1B was announced that the original car became known as the MP4/1.

UNIPART
UNIPART
MICHELIN
MICHELIN
Valvoline

1981 FORMULA 1 McLAREN MP4/1

CONTINUED

Unfortunately the new car wasn't ready for the start of the 1981 season, so John Watson and his new team-mate Andrea de Cesaris found themselves campaigning the outdated M29C. But it was well worth the wait.

In its first two races the sole MP4/1 qualified 11th and seventh, making it to the line for its first race finish in San Marino in 10th. Watson qualified the MP4/1 a promising fifth on its debut at Zolder in the Belgian GP and ran a comfortable fourth until the late stages when gearbox problems dropped him back to seventh by the flag. He qualified 10th at Monaco and was heading for fourth place when the engine broke. Then came the start of what Wattie would later refer to as his 'Ted Rodgers' sweep, referring to the comedian's popular Three Two One game show. From fourth on the grid he finished third in Spain; in France a front-row starting position translated into a superb race drive and second place just over two seconds behind first-time winner Alain Prost. Suddenly, McLaren was back. And then came the 1981 Marlboro British Grand Prix at Silverstone.

Watson and de Cesaris qualified fifth and sixth respectively as the turbocharged Renaults headed the grid. Watson's performance that day, July 18th, would be a vindication of so many things: Marlboro's faith in the team; Ron Dennis's faith in his inspired designer; and of course John Barnard's faith in novel materials and a whole new way of doing things. It also represented a stunning return to form for the team Bruce McLaren had founded.

Alain Prost led initially for Renault, with team-mate René Arnoux riding shotgun. Watson was seventh at the end of the first lap, then was delayed further as he dropped to 10th by the fourth avoiding an accident in the Woodcote chicane at the end of lap three involving de Cesaris, Alan Jones and Gilles Villeneuve. But then he got his head down and charged. Nelson Piquet crashed his Brabham heavily; then Prost's car burned a valve. Suddenly, the McLaren was up to second place, albeit 25s adrift of Arnoux. And there it stayed for 30 laps. But on lap 50 the Renault's engine note changed; as Arnoux slowed, Watson went quicker and quicker and began scything down the gap, cheered on by an expectant crowd of his fellow countrymen. On lap 61 he swooped into the lead, and seven laps later was flagged off the winner of the British GP. It was McLaren's first Grand Prix victory since Fuji, four years earlier. And the first for a carbon fibre composite car.

Later, came the big shunt at Monza where Watson's MP4/1 was cut in half after he went off the road in the two fast Lesmo corners. But even as the engine and gearbox were torn off, the monocoque structure remained intact. Wattie had walked away from a 140mph crash, and while the car did not look very pretty afterwards it had not, as so many sceptics had expected, exploded into a cloud of black dust.

When it had first been shown to the media, Tyler Alexander held aloft the 70lb monocoque, which boasted a quite amazing torsional stiffness of 15,000lb per degree, well over twice what could reasonably have been expected of an aluminium chassis at that time. Now, after the remarkable demonstration of the inherent strength of its chassis in the Monza accident, the team was approached by Britain's Civil Aviation Authority. Still wrestling with the problem of how it could certify composite components as safe for aircraft construction, its technical officers wanted to share the data arising from the Lesmo crash. Later still, having of course borrowed much of this new technology from the aerospace industry, McLaren found itself a supplier to that very industry, even gaining a commendation from NASA itself.

It was a win-win situation. The McLaren MP4/1 not only radically improved McLaren's chances but genuinely reinvigorated the sport as well. No less significantly, as rival teams looked at ways of building carbon composite cars of their own, the construction methods introduced by Barnard's MP4/1 made possibly the largest single contribution to driver safety of any innovation in the sport's history. By feeding loads along the axis of the strands in the material, carbon composite cars were able to boast a much higher stiffness-to-weight ratio, making them not just lighter and faster but safer too.

For all its success, the MP4/1 was not the finished article, and with its tendency to porpoise there was certainly room for further aerodynamic development. Nor was it ever a particularly easy car to drive. The nickname earned by de Cesaris - 'de Crasheris' - gives some indication as to how well his season went, and also explains in part why after finishing with only a single point he was replaced by Niki Lauda for 1982.

Watson quickly discovered that there were some downsides to the new material, notably that it had no 'give'. "*If you banged your elbow in the cockpit, it really hurt.*" He had also been concerned about its crashworthiness and admitted that initially at least it had been hard to keep faith with Barnard's belief in it. The Monza accident finally convinced him, and others.

It changed many perceptions, inside and outside the sport. The McLaren MP4/1 had always been interesting because it had become a winner, but now the true advantages of its ground-breaking technology had been demonstrated worldwide. Potential applications for the new material were being identified almost weekly, and videos of Watson's crash were soon being used in the US to convince the military of the material's value as cladding for attack helicopters in need of underbody protection against fire from below. For this, and for the major leap forward that F1 safety took, the remarkable McLaren MP4/1 deserves all the credit it can get.

The 1981 Belgian Grand Prix at Zolder saw the team trying out a high mounted front wing first tried on the car at Imola. Watson ran as high as fourth before gear selection problems dropped him to seventh and out of the points.

After a third place in Spain and second in France, John Watson was to score an emotional first Grand Prix victory for the MP4/1 in front of his and the team's home crowd at the British GP.

Andrea de Cesaris scored points in two races and was often running in the top six but seemed to get involved in too many accidents. Here at a wet Montreal race he was running in fifth before a wheel-banging match with Piquet resulted in his demise.

As this was only testing for the 1981 British Grand Prix at Silverstone it meant that the MP4/1 was able to run in its full Marlboro livery.

By the time of the race the following weekend the cars carried what was officially called 'Strobe' livery. John Watson scored a memorable victory.

MP4/1 FORMULA 1
SPECIFICATION

MODEL	McLaren MP4/1
TYPE/FORMULA	Formula 1
YEAR OF PRODUCTION	1981
DESIGNER	John Barnard
EXAMPLES BUILT	4
ENGINE	Ford Cosworth DFV
CUBIC CAPACITY	2993cc
CARBURATION	Lucas fuel injection
POWER OUTPUT	470bhp

TRANSMISSION	McLaren/Hewland 5-speed
CHASSIS	Moulded carbon fibre/honeycomb monocoque
BODY	Carbon fibre composite panels
FRONT SUSPENSION	Upper rocker arm, operating inboard
	coil spring/damper, lower wishbone
REAR SUSPENSION	Upper wishbone/rocker arm operating
	inboard coil spring/damper, lower wishbone
BRAKES F/R	Outboard McLaren/Lockheed twin caliper
WHEELS DIAMETER x WIDTH F/R	13x11/13x16in

TYRES F/R	Michelin
LENGTH	170in - 4318mm
WIDTH	81in - 2057mm
HEIGHT	40in - 1016mm
WHEELBASE	104in - 2640mm
TRACK F/R	68/66in - 1730/1676mm
WEIGHT	1290lb - 585kg
PRINCIPAL DRIVERS	Watson, de Cesaris
IDENTIFYING COLOURS	Red/White

1982 FORMULA 1
McLAREN MP4/1B

After the seismic changes which had been necessary to enable the progression from M30 to MP4/1, the further evolution in 1982 to 'B' specification required what seemed like only relatively modest changes. Barnard attempted to make the innovative chassis even stiffer and to pare off a little more weight. Stiffer suspension was also offered together with a switch to Michelin tyres, and carbon brake discs made an appearance on the cars during the year.

Behind the scenes, however, the activity in and around McLaren International to make all this happen had been considerable. Mechanically the car was still quite conventional, still using rocker-arm suspension and relying on the trusty Ford Cosworth DFV, but Ron Dennis was already looking to the future and work at Porsche was well underway on a new turbocharged V6, the funding for which was coming from the Paris-based, Saudi-financed, Techniques D'Avant Garde (TAG). TAG boss Mansour Ojjeh became a very close friend of Ron and would go on to become a major shareholder in the McLaren Group.

The team's own moving-ground wind tunnel was meanwhile installed in the National Maritime Institute facility at Feltham in Middlesex, to simulate the most realistic environment possible in which to study the dynamic interface between a car body and the road surface. Further real-time aerodynamic work was carried out at Paul Ricard in southern France, and at Michelin's Ladoux test facility.

The switch to Michelin tyres was to be one of the most significant changes. Crossply tyres such as Goodyear's grew at speed because of the centrifugal force, thus compensating for the way in which aerodynamic downforce also increased at speed. By contrast, John Watson observed, the Michelins seemed to squash down under high centrifugal loading at high speed, thereby affecting the behaviour of the aerodynamic skirts beneath the chassis and occasionally even causing the car to bottom out over bumps. This required even more fine tuning in the chassis set-up to allow for this 'squidging' effect and for the car to settle under aerodynamic loading out on the circuit. As a consequence much time was spent adjusting spacers and bump rubbers to avoid taking up too much of the critical skirt travel.

Fortunately Michelin was keen to help the newly successful McLaren team, building bespoke 15 inch front tyres which showed better reactions than either of the conventional 13s. With all this help from Michelin McLaren soon discovered that the mechanical traction levels were so good that it could afford to run narrower rear tyres than its turbocharged rivals. As a result the MP4/1B benefited from another small but measurable aerodynamic gain via reduced drag, especially compared to the fast-improving Renaults.

Throughout the season the team experimented with various set-ups, varying both the track and wheelbase of the cars by as much as four inches in the latter case before settling on a two-inch extension. The carbon discs were similarly fitted for two races, in California and Brazil, although McLaren later admitted that in this case it simply didn't fully understand the technology it was acquiring from the aviation industry.

On the one hand carbon discs brought a valuable saving in weight, as Brabham's Gordon Murray had discovered nearly six years previously. They also held out the promise of a better coefficient of friction than conventional steel discs because they could run at very high temperatures, but unfortunately in 1982 it could take half a year simply to make a set and in a sport as fast-moving as F1 that just wasn't practical. Similarly, their extremely high operating temperature was fine when a car was running but posed all sorts of problems if it should pit, or if it was running in the wet.

The season started well, with Niki Lauda and Watson both in the points for the first race at Kyalami, in fourth and sixth places respectively. At Long Beach, however, the tables were turned. Following an early spin during testing, and despite losing pole to – of all people – de Cesaris who was now with Alfa Romeo, Lauda won the race and Watson came sixth after a variety of mechanical problems.

After just three races with McLaren, Lauda and the team were second in the World Championships behind Renault, with Watson lying third. Boycotting the San Marino race, as many leading British teams did, McLaren returned for the Belgian race which was overshadowed by the death of Ferrari's great star Gilles Villeneuve. Watson set fastest lap and eventually took his first victory in the MP4/1B, putting him just a point behind Prost's Renault, but Lauda was disqualified from third place when a post-race check revealed his car was 1.8kg under weight. McLaren had miscalculated the weight loss through tyre and brake wear. Wattie's car was legal, by a kilo.

Another superb win in the inaugural street race in Detroit round put Watson and McLaren ahead in their respective World Championships, the Ulsterman having called in for harder Michelins during a brief stop before charging back to victory. Watson lost his points lead after finishing third behind the Brabhams in Canada, whilst Lauda posted a fourth in Holland and won well at Brands Hatch before a wrist injury forced him to miss the German race. By this time the turbocharged Ferraris and Renaults were dominating, and although Lauda went on to pick up points in Austria and at Dijon for the Swiss Grand Prix, it wasn't enough. At Monza Watson scored his first points in three months, and went to the finale in Las Vegas still in contention for the title. But second place there to Michele Alboreto's Tyrrell was too little too late. Losing out respectively to Keke Rosberg and Ferrari, McLaren had to content itself with runner-up slots in both the Drivers' and Constructors' World Championships.

The 1982 season saw the return of Niki Lauda to the Grand Prix scene. At the British Grand Prix, held at Brands Hatch, he scored his second victory of the season in MP4/1-6.

In a season where no team dominated and there were 11 different winners of a Grand Prix, the MP4/1B won as many races as any other team and McLaren finished second in both the Drivers' (Watson) and Constructors' titles.

The 1982 MP4/1B was a logical development of the original MP4. Barnard's mission was to pare off some weight, improve stiffness and make minor improvements to the suspension, which involved changes to both the wheelbase and track.

MP4/1B FORMULA 1
SPECIFICATION

MODEL	McLaren MP4/1B
TYPE/FORMULA	Formula 1
YEAR OF PRODUCTION	1982
DESIGNER	John Barnard
EXAMPLES BUILT	5 (3 converted from MP4/1)
ENGINE	Ford Cosworth DFV
CUBIC CAPACITY	2993cc
CARBURATION	Lucas fuel injection
POWER OUTPUT	480bhp

TRANSMISSION	McLaren/Hewland 5-speed
CHASSIS	Moulded carbon fibre/honeycomb monocoque
BODY	Carbon fibre composite panels, sliding skirts
FRONT SUSPENSION	Upper rocker arm, operating inboard
	coil spring/damper, lower wishbone
REAR SUSPENSION	Upper wishbone/rocker arm operating
	inboard coil spring/damper, lower wishbone
BRAKES F/R	Outboard McLaren/Lockheed twin caliper
WHEELS DIAMETER x WIDTH F/R	13x11/13x16in

TYRES F/R	Michelin
LENGTH	175in - 4445mm
WIDTH	81in - 2057mm
HEIGHT	40in - 1016mm
WHEELBASE	105.6in - 2682mm
TRACK F/R	71.5/66in - 1816/1676mm
WEIGHT	1290lb - 585kg
PRINCIPAL DRIVERS	Watson, Lauda
IDENTIFYING COLOURS	Red/White

1983 FORMULA 1
McLAREN MP4/1C, MP4/1D & MP4/1E

With personnel changes, new regulations and a new engine on the horizon, this was to be a season of momentous changes at McLaren, and following negotiations with Ron Dennis and John Barnard those great stalwarts from Bruce's days, Teddy Mayer and Tyler Alexander, bowed out of the company.

The new season also brought new rules which outlawed ground-effect tunnel sections and required all cars to run flat-bottom chassis. While some management of the airflow beneath the car was still permitted, the intention was dramatically to reduce any associated benefits and thus to reduce downforce.

Some degree of ground effect could be restored by using an upswept diffuser at the rear and by smoothing the airflow around the rear wheels, but the overall effect of the rule changes was to disadvantage the less-powerful non-turbo cars quite significantly since they could no longer use their superior downforce to offset the greater horsepower of the turbocars. This remained the case even when Cosworth responded with a new short-stroke DFY version of its long-established V8, and with the 1499cc TAG Turbo V6 engine not yet up and running, this was to be a major cause for concern at McLaren International.

Any performance loss resulting from the abandonment of ground effect would have to be made up elsewhere, the most obvious answer being to compensate for the loss of undercar downforce by running larger front and rear wings. Unfortunately any gains would come at the expense of increased drag, which would again inevitably affect the less powerful V8-engined cars rather more than it would the turbocharged Renaults, Ferraris and Brabhams.

This left McLaren, in particular, in a dilemma. Clearly in the V8 camp at the start, the team needed to modify its cars in line with the new aerodynamics regulations. But the engineers and aerodynamicists fully expected mid-season to be joining the turbo brigade with their own new engine. As John Barnard put it, "*It might be counter-productive to go all the way with a new Cosworth car for what might be less than a full season.*"

Meanwhile other teams, including Brabham, Ferrari, Ligier, Tyrrell and Renault, quickly moved to slim down their designs in an attempt to take advantage of the changes. For Barnard, however, it was to be more a case of continuing along his chosen path so that by the time the 1983 season started the new MP4/1C, but for its flat underside and the absence of skirts, looked not unlike its predecessor. There were modest low-level aerodynamic trays immediately ahead of the rear wheels, a waisted platform behind the side radiator mountings and a slight coke-bottle effect, but the family resemblance was unmistakeable.

The arrangement of the Cosworth engine, rear suspension and transmission was exactly as before, but in order to accommodate the turbo engine when it came with its additional pipework, extra radiators, twin KKK turbochargers and intercoolers, no attempt was made to slim down the rear end too much. Barnard was convinced that he could compensate for this, believing: "*We still have one of the best lift/drag ratios amongst current cars.*"

Once again the car needed care when it came to setting it up, as there was sensitivity to ride height and suspension-rate changes. And the design of the front and rear wings was to be even more critical than before, now that they were providing 80 per cent of the total downforce.

Things started well, with Lauda third in Brazil, then Watson heading him home for an historic and totally unexpected back-to-front 1-2 in Long Beach after they struggled to get temperature into their qualifying tyres and started near the back of the grid. Watson was third in Detroit with fastest lap, third again in Holland, fifth in Germany and sixth in Canada, while Lauda added sixths in Britain and Austria. The nadir came at Monaco when the drivers struggled again to get sufficient temperature into Michelin's qualifying tyres and failed to qualify even though the French company had responded to McLaren's entreaties for improved rubber by sending new tyres to the Principality which arrived in time for practice and enabled them to shave an astonishing 1.8s off their dry lap times.

When the tyres worked, the MP4/1C could lead its Cosworth-brethren, but that was no longer sufficient to challenge the turbos. That made it doubly fortunate that by July, after a shakedown at Weissach, the new TAG Turbo TTE-PO1 V6 engine was installed in what was officially termed the MP4/1D for some serious testing at Silverstone ahead of the Dutch GP in August.

Perhaps irked that Lauda got the sole new car for that event, Watson drove outstandingly to take a podium finish and to upstage the debut of the new MP4/1E, which clearly still needed substantial sorting. With an estimated 700bhp at 11,700rpm Niki found that his new TAG-powered car was very fast in a straight line, but still lacked grip.

Subsequent races saw both drivers run the new cars, but they were still under development and did not show significant performance improvements relative to their opposition and were not reliable. But this development phase would be crucial in ironing out the faults ahead of 1984, when things would be very different.

The highlight of the 1983 season was an incredible 1-2 result at the Long Beach GP. Watson (above) and Lauda, who started 22nd and 23rd on the 24-car grid passed the entire field to score an historic victory. Watson's record still stands as the GP won from furthest back on the grid.

The regulations for 1983 outlawed groundeffects and made the management of airflow around the rear of the car a much more important factor. The exhaust was wrapped tight around the rear of the engine and exited above the rear suspension.

With the Cosworth-engined cars out of contention for the Championship, the team ran the new TAG-Turbo V6 engine in 1983 rather than wait until the start of the new season. It made its race debut at the 1983 Dutch Grand Prix where Lauda retired with brake trouble. By the opening race of 1984 the new MP4/2 was a fully competitive race winner.

MP4/1C FORMULA 1
SPECIFICATION

MODEL	McLaren MP4/1C
TYPE/FORMULA	Formula 1
YEAR OF PRODUCTION	1983
DESIGNER	John Barnard
EXAMPLES BUILT	1 (+3 converted from MP4/1B)
ENGINE	Ford Cosworth DFV/DFY
CUBIC CAPACITY	2993cc
CARBURATION	Lucas fuel injection
POWER OUTPUT	480-510bhp

TRANSMISSION	McLaren/Hewland 5-speed
CHASSIS	Moulded carbon fibre/honeycomb monocoque
BODY	Carbon fibre composite panels
FRONT SUSPENSION	Double wishbone, push-rod operating
	inboard coil spring/damper
REAR SUSPENSION	Upper wishbone/rocker arm operating
	inboard coil spring/damper, lower wishbone
BRAKES F/R	Outboard McLaren/AP Racing twin caliper
WHEELS DIAMETER x WIDTH F/R	13x11/13x16in

TYRES F/R	Michelin
LENGTH	167in - 4242mm
WIDTH	84in - 2133mm
HEIGHT	40in - 1016mm
WHEELBASE	105.8in - 2687mm
TRACK F/R	71.5/66in - 1816/1676mm
WEIGHT	1191lb - 540kg
PRINCIPAL DRIVERS	Watson, Lauda
IDENTIFYING COLOURS	Red/White

1984 FORMULA 1
McLAREN MP4/2

Having spent three seasons preparing to win on a regular basis, notwithstanding the six triumphs since 1981, McLaren at last had everything in place to sweep the board. It may have been slightly late joining the turbo generation, but the preparation for it had been typically thorough and from now on the team was ready to stamp an indelible mark on the 1980s.

By the start of 1984 everything that had been learned from the interim MP4/1E had been incorporated into the design of the new MP4/2, which John Barnard believed was far more integrated. The team had a much better understanding of the 80-degree one million Deutschmark TAG V6 and it was now producing an extra 50bhp compared to the previous season. Everything was neatly packaged, in one of the first truly homogenous F1 designs of the era, and after strenuous testing the MP4/2 was ready to catapult the team into the front rank.

The new car shared much in common with the outgoing MP4/1E, but the monocoque was redesigned to accommodate the shorter engine and the larger, 220-litre fuel cell that it required. The curve of the sidepods changed too, as the turbochargers were positioned as far forward as possible so that the pods could curve in at the rear to maximise the coke bottle and enclose the engine and gearbox in the most aerodynamically efficient way.

Remarkably, McLaren would dominate the season using just three cars: MP4/2-1 for Niki Lauda, MP4/2-2 for Alain Prost, and a T-car numbered MP4/3. Lauda, indeed, used just that one car throughout the entire 16-race season, the odd knock never severe enough to compromise the strength of the Hercules-built CFC monocoque.

Prost's return was a major coup, giving the team a tremendously strong driving partnership. The Frenchman was now a seasoned Grand Prix winner, and he had a point to prove after being fired by Renault when the French manufacturer's World Championship challenge collapsed in the South African denouement the previous year.

It quickly became apparent that in the MP4/2 Prost and Lauda had the tool to dominate the 1984 season from start to finish. With two World Championships under his belt, Lauda as the incumbent star insisted that he would do the majority of the testing and development of the car. However, as the season progressed there was no escaping the fact that the younger Prost was the faster driver. This was particularly so in qualifying, but over the course of the season 'The Professor' was also to win seven races to Lauda's five.

If the car had any weakness it was in the areas of braking and the gearbox. The team was still relying on a transmission unit designed for the less powerful Cosworth era. As for the brakes, it was still experimenting with CFC components whose performance under stress remained a major limiting factor. Different forms and shapes of cooling ducts were developed and tested, but as the season progressed all that really emerged was that on circuits demanding frequent heavy braking the time between one application and the next was insufficient to allow for cooling.

On the plus side, the performance of the new engine completely vindicated Ron Dennis's decision to commission Porsche. BMW had also been considered, but the need for bracing struts for its turbocharged four cylinder engine was incompatible with Barnard's intended rear-end design and he was similarly unhappy with the compromises which would have been required by the adoption of Renault's own V6. With the TAG engine he could dictate from the outset where key components were located, thus harmonising the installation in a manner not seen since Colin Chapman first worked with Cosworth to install the DFV in the Lotus 49.

McLaren's wind tunnel expertise was also key. Barnard told Motor Sport readers in 2005: "*I think we were well ahead of the other teams in terms of… the way we could anchor and move [our scale models]. So we had faith in our aero numbers. The combination of rear wing, winglets and diffuser worked tremendously on the MP4/2.*" By generating plenty of rear-end grip in this way, the car inspired great confidence in both drivers.

"*We knew from that first test that we had a strong car,*" Barnard said, but he admitted that he was frustrated with the new rule changes, calling the period of this highly successful car's gestation, "*One of my most annoying times in F1*". In particular he felt that the switch to flat-bottomed cars effectively robbed the team of up to 50 per cent of the engine's potential, nullifying much of the advantage it should have brought at a time when no other team had gone quite so far as to have a whole new engine built to suit the regulations then in force.

Even compromised in this way, however, the MP4/2 was to give McLaren those 12 wins from the 16 races, lead Lauda to his third Drivers' World Championship, and massacre the opposition in winning the Constructors' Cup by an incredible 86 points. True, a loose front wheel cost Prost the win at Dijon, Porsche still had some work to do on its engine, and the brake-cooling issue still needed to be resolved, while one can only imagine Prost's frustration at winning more races but losing out to Lauda by half a point. But in every other regard the MP4/2 provided McLaren with a near-perfect season, and everyone else on the grid with a warning shot that no-one could ignore.

During 1983 a development TAG engine was squeezed into a Porsche 911 Turbo roadcar and run on the test track in Germany. By the start of the 1984 season the engine was producing around 750bhp.

The previous season's engine development program paid dividends and meant that the 1984 season started off well. Alain Prost's first race back at McLaren resulted in a fine win in the Brazilian GP.

Although in many respects the MP4/2 looked similar to the previous year's car, it was a completely new design. The new rear-end body shape hugged the turbo engine more tightly and the rear wing sprouted two small extensions above the rear wheels.

SAIMA
8
UNIPART
HERCULES

SAIMA
8
Lauda
BOSS
TAG turbo
MICHELIN
MICHELIN
MICHELIN

The end of season Grand Prix finale in Portugal was a tense affair. Niki Lauda finished second 13 seconds behind race winner Prost (above) and took the Championship by just half a point from his teammate.

In the Dutch Grand Prix at Zandvoort Niki Lauda qualified sixth, fought his way through the traffic and finished second behind Prost.

Two weeks later at Monza Lauda qualified fourth but benefited from the misfortune of others and took an easy win, his fifth of the season.

MP4/2 FORMULA 1
SPECIFICATION

MODEL	McLaren MP4/2
TYPE/FORMULA	Formula 1
YEAR OF PRODUCTION	1984
DESIGNER	John Barnard
EXAMPLES BUILT	5
ENGINE	TAG Turbo TTE PO1 V6
CUBIC CAPACITY	1496cc
INDUCTION	Twin KKK turbochargers
POWER OUTPUT	750bhp

TRANSMISSION	McLaren/Hewland 5-speed
CHASSIS	Moulded carbon fibre/honeycomb monocoque
BODY	Carbon fibre single piece cockpit/engine cover & nose
FRONT SUSPENSION	Double wishbone, push-rod operating
	inboard coil spring/damper
REAR SUSPENSION	Upper wishbone/rocker arm operating
	inboard coil spring/damper, lower wishbone
BRAKES F/R	Outboard SEP carbon discs/McLaren twin caliper
WHEELS DIAMETER x WIDTH F/R	13x11/13x16in

TYRES F/R	Michelin
LENGTH	171in - 4343mm
WIDTH	84in - 2133mm
HEIGHT	39in - 991mm
WHEELBASE	109in - 2768mm
TRACK F/R	71.5/66in - 1816/1676mm
WEIGHT	1191lb - 540kg
PRINCIPAL DRIVERS	Prost, Lauda
IDENTIFYING COLOURS	Red/White

1985 FORMULA 1 McLAREN MP4/2B

Yet another McLaren driver crowned World Champion, and another Constructors' Championship win for the team itself, can leave the misleading impression that life at Woking in 1985 went on pretty much as it had the previous season – but that was far from the case.

McLaren was certainly still the team everyone had to watch, and the MP4/2B the car to catch. But while development work had continued apace with John Barnard and his colleagues beavering away to keep Alain Prost and Niki Lauda ahead of the pack, and KKK had devised a completely new pair of 'mirror image' blowers for the TAG V6, Michelin had withdrawn and obliged the team to revert to Goodyear. Later, a wrist injury forced Lauda to miss the European GP so John Watson returned in a stand-in role, and the Austrian's wretched final year in F1 ended with only 14 points. Prost, however, romped home with a title-winning 73 and five GP victories to Lauda's one.

The MP4/2B went from strength to strength, somewhat to the surprise of the opposition who had dared to hope that their own developments over the winter would have rendered the defending team slightly less competitive. The leading teams which were already using Goodyears certainly hoped so, having convinced themselves that after the less consistent performance of Goodyear's new radials during much of the previous season, Michelin's withdrawal would put McLaren on a more equal footing with them. Some observers also felt that the latest round of regulation changes – outlawing rear wing extensions in a bid to reduce downforce – would affect McLaren disproportionately.

Instead, Barnard's new turbocharger arrangement helped to keep the McLaren TAG firmly in play. He devised a typically innovative enhancement to alleviate problems experienced during the previous season. At that time the inlet for the KKK turbos was ahead of the rear wheel, in a high-pressure area which left the delicate impeller blades vulnerable to grit and debris. To resolve this he asked KKK to make right and left-handed turbos which could then be positioned closer to the engine, front-to-back, so that the inlet could be relocated behind the intercooler.

Externally, the new car looked at first glance much like its predecessor, most of the changes being detail ones beneath the skin, such as subtle aerodynamic detailing, and new suspension which incorporated pushrods for the first time, together with inboard auxiliary rockers and upper wishbones.

Any optimism in rival camps received something of a boost at the first race of the season in Brazil when it quickly became apparent that Ferrari, Williams and Lotus were usually going to qualify ahead of the MP4/2Bs. This was largely thanks to the more powerful engines supplied to those teams solely for qualifying, whilst the TAG-powered cars, unable to run at such high boost pressures, chose to rely on a better race package to (hopefully) win the day.

That confidence was borne out in Rio, the McLarens fronting the field during the warm-up and Prost dicing fiercely with Michele Alboreto's Ferrari before romping home in first place as an electrical failure took out Lauda. The Austrian was similarly unlucky at the next round in Portugal, his V6 refusing to function effectively above 10,000rpm, while Prost who had been lying second behind Ayrton Senna's Lotus Renault crashed out after aquaplaning on the straight.

Imola for the San Marino GP looked more promising, the MP4/2Bs playing their trump card in the shape of a trip computer set up to show how much fuel remained onboard. This was a crucially important weapon at a time of restricted fuel loads, and 'The Professor' used his to establish that he would run dry if he tried to keep pace, initially, with Senna. He sat back whilst both Senna and the Ferrari of Stefan Johansson ran out of fuel. It was a cunning, race-winning manoeuvre - until the scrutineers found his MP4/2B to be two kilogrammes underweight and disallowed the win. One of McLaren's key strengths had rebounded badly, costing nine points.

With his rigorously applied and highly professional driving skills more than making up for the turbo problems he was suffering for much of the race, Prost won at Monaco for the second year in succession. Canada and Detroit were markedly less successful, brake cooling proving a major headache thanks to the stop-start nature of the latter race, but despite problems with the CFC discs McLaren stuck with them, and when the circus returned to Paul Ricard the cars' inherently superior aerodynamics provided some ammunition against the more powerful Williams-Hondas. Lauda led Prost until he was removed by mechanical failure (possibly linked to running with too much boost) and Prost eventually finished third.

In Austria Lauda confirmed he was going to retire at the end of the season and failed to win in front of his home crowd, a turbo shaft fracturing on lap 40 after some magnificent driving. At Zandvoort he was finer still, beating Prost into second place although the latter was looking secure as the first-ever French World Champion. Lauda then missed the Belgian race due to a wrist injury, and failed to finish in both South Africa and Australia, winding up a disappointed 10th overall after a season of bitter ill-fortune. Prost though took the World Championship easily, and McLaren picked up another Constructors' trophy with a resounding 90 points.

Of the five MP4/2B chassis raced in 1985 only two were completely new cars. The other three were revised versions of the previous season's cars. A change of tyre manufacturer from Michelin to Goodyear meant changes to the suspension set-up.

In order to offer better crash protection to the driver, the 1985 technical regulations demanded that the nosebox design on Formula 1 cars be changed. However, this revision meant very little change in the overall appearance of the front end of the car.

At the rear of the car regulation changes meant a smaller wing, shorter sidepods and narrower bodywork. The oil cooler was tucked neatly ahead of the rear wing support.

Marlboro
SAIMA
2
GOODYEAR

SAIMA
Marlboro
2

SAIMA
2
Prost
BOSS
TAG turbo
Marlboro
Marlboro
GOODYEAR
EAGLE
GOODYEAR

1985 FORMULA 1 McLAREN MP4/2B

CONTINUED

Opposite.
The Monaco Grand Prix in May gave Alain Prost his second win of the 1985 season. He took the lead from Senna on lap 12 and fought off a strong challenge from Alboreto's Ferrari to win by five seconds.

MP4/2B FORMULA 1
SPECIFICATION

MODEL	McLaren MP4/2B
TYPE/FORMULA	Formula 1
YEAR OF PRODUCTION	1985
DESIGNER	John Barnard
EXAMPLES BUILT	5
ENGINE	TAG Turbo TTE PO1 V6
CUBIC CAPACITY	1496cc
INDUCTION	Twin KKK turbochargers
POWER OUTPUT	750bhp

TRANSMISSION	McLaren 5-speed
CHASSIS	Moulded carbon fibre/honeycomb monocoque
BODY	Carbon fibre single piece cockpit/engine cover & nose
FRONT SUSPENSION	Double wishbone, push-rod operating
	inboard coil spring/damper
REAR SUSPENSION	Upper wishbone/rocker arm operating
	inboard coil spring/damper, lower wishbone
BRAKES F/R	Outboard SEP carbon discs/McLaren twin caliper
WHEELS DIAMETER x WIDTH F/R	13x12/13x16.5in

TYRES F/R	Goodyear
LENGTH	172in - 4369mm
WIDTH	83in - 2108mm
HEIGHT	39in - 991mm
WHEELBASE	109in - 2768mm
TRACK F/R	71.5/66in - 1816/1676mm
WEIGHT	1191lb - 540kg
PRINCIPAL DRIVERS	Prost, Lauda
IDENTIFYING COLOURS	Red/White

1986 FORMULA 1
McLAREN MP4/2C

Finland's fast and aggressive ex-World Champion Keke Rosberg moved into Lauda's seat for 1986, but his and Alain Prost's new MP4/2Cs yet again looked pretty much like the previous year's cars.

Once again, however, the changes were under the skin. One of the most important was a smaller fuel tank, as new regulations limited cars to a maximum capacity of 195 litres instead of 220. This was to be John Barnard's last season with the team but until the end he continued to refine his pioneering design, instigating a new six-speed gearbox and a revised version of Bosch's superb Motronic engine management system. The car's overall dimensions remained unchanged, but maximum power was up to something approaching 800bhp at 12,000rpm.

Together with the arrival of Rosberg – allegedly 'the fastest man in Formula 1' – McLaren fans had plenty to look forward to. Many were keen to see whether Prost could buck the opinion of former champion Jackie Stewart, who long ago had mentioned how hard it was for both driver and team to remain hungry enough to win when they had already tasted success. Others wondered whether the flying Finn would manage to unseat Prost to become the de facto number one.

The answers to both questions took very little time to surface: a definite yes to the first – Prost was still ravenous – and an equally forthright no to the second, not least because of Barnard's refusal to change his car to reduce the understeer and better suit it to Rosberg's driving style.

As Barnard had designed it, the MP4/2C could not have been more perfect for Prost. It suited his smooth and scrupulously considered driving style, which always enabled him to find the speed when he needed it, without recourse to winding up the boost. Rosberg was inherently just as quick, but his speed came from his ebullient, press-on style, and that just did not work with the MP4/2.

Imola provided all the evidence anyone needed of the value of the new car, Prost romping home brilliantly despite a computer glitch which denied him an accurate reading of his fuel status. He crossed the line to the accompaniment of tyre and crowd noise only, having run out of fuel. Rosberg was less fortunate, however, and looked a tad foolish when he too ran dry two laps from the end. He later protested, "*I'm not a fool. I can read a fuel gauge!*" The same glitch was to blame.

Monaco was much better, however. Prost's third victory on the famous street circuit – he won by a spectacular 25s – was supported by a fantastic drive from Rosberg who fought his way up to second using some thrilling overtaking manoeuvres to charge through the traffic from his ninth-place start position.

And for Prost, at least, Belgium was eventful since a first-lap collision meant that instead of winning, which he certainly deserved, he came away with only a single Championship point. Canada was more fruitful, the Williams-Hondas of Mansell and Piquet taking first and third, with Prost and Rosberg managing to sandwich the Brazilian to take second and fourth. Detroit yielded a third place too, despite Prost's well-advertised dislike of the course and a shunt in practice.

France provided a repeat of the Canadian race, which meant points at least, but things went badly at Brands Hatch with Prost actually being lapped but taking third and Rosberg out with another gearbox failure. Hopes now rested on the German event, which in a sense was a semi-home fixture thanks to the immense contribution made by Porsche and Bosch, the latter even then busy making further revisions to the Motronic engine management set-up. Rosberg now had the set-up he had wanted and, having announced earlier in the week his decision to retire at the end of the season, he took his first pole of the season. He had a fine battle with Nelson Piquet, harrying the Williams-Honda driver again and again, before running out of fuel just a lap from the end. Prost too ran dry, and made his feelings clear by pushing his car towards the line even though he knew this was technically not allowed.

In Hungary both drivers qualified well for the inaugural event but then attempted to pit at the same time, with Rosberg being forced to go back out with a deflating tyre while the crew wrestled with an electrical fault in the T-car which Prost had been forced to use. Both eventually retired but in Austria things looked more promising with Rosberg charging hard against the apparently unstoppable Benetton-BMWs before having to pull out with a dead engine when second place looked secure. Once again Prost's experience shone through, however, and despite suffering similar problems he nursed his car along to a somewhat lucky victory.

In Italy he was less fortunate, his engine blowing up, whilst Rosberg took fourth for his last-ever GP points. Prost was out of sorts at Estoril but managed a second and in high-altitude Mexico he repeated that result, despite losing a cylinder. He then headed to Adelaide for the final showdown where a fantastic win - after Nigel Mansell blew a tyre and Piquet was called in for a precautionary stop - brought him a second consecutive Drivers' World Championship. McLaren finished second to Williams in the Constructors' title.

At the end of the season John Barnard decided to sell his shareholding in the team, and to head for pastures new.

Wearing the reigning Champion's number 1 on the nose of his car, Alain Prost won four Grand Prix races and finished on the podium on five other occasions in 1986. It was this consistency rather than outright race victories that won him the title for the second year in succession. He was the first driver to do so since Jack Brabham in 1960.

A six-speed gearbox was now standard equipment for the MP4 series of cars, although the carbon-fibre clutch the team tested for much of the season was never actually raced in 1986.

Prost
BOSS
Shell
Segafredo
ZANETTI
1
GOODYEAR
GOODYEAR
EAGLE
GOODYEAR
EAGLE

Prost
BOSS
Segafredo
ZANETTI
hell
1

After an absence of five years the Spanish Grand Prix returned to the calendar. The team scored its first points of the year with Prost third and Rosberg fourth.

Having challenged for the lead of the German Grand Prix both McLarens ran out of fuel on the penultimate lap. Rosberg was classified fifth and Prost sixth.

MP4/2C FORMULA 1
SPECIFICATION

MODEL	McLaren MP4/2C
TYPE/FORMULA	Formula 1
YEAR OF PRODUCTION	1986
DESIGNER	John Barnard
EXAMPLES BUILT	5
ENGINE	TAG Turbo TTE PO1 V6
CUBIC CAPACITY	1496cc
INDUCTION	Twin KKK turbochargers
POWER OUTPUT	750bhp

TRANSMISSION	McLaren 6-speed
CHASSIS	Moulded carbon fibre/honeycomb monocoque
BODY	Carbon fibre single piece cockpit/engine cover & nose
FRONT SUSPENSION	Double wishbone, push-rod operating
	inboard coil spring/damper
REAR SUSPENSION	Upper wishbone/rocker arm operating
	inboard coil spring/damper, lower wishbone
BRAKES F/R	Outboard SEP carbon discs/McLaren twin caliper
WHEELS DIAMETER x WIDTH F/R	13x11.5/13x16.25in

TYRES F/R	Goodyear
LENGTH	173in - 4394mm
WIDTH	83in - 2108mm
HEIGHT	39in - 991mm
WHEELBASE	110in - 2794mm
TRACK F/R	71.5/66in - 1816/1676mm
WEIGHT	1191lb - 540kg
PRINCIPAL DRIVERS	Prost, Rosberg
IDENTIFYING COLOURS	Red/White

1987 FORMULA 1 McLAREN MP4/3

With John Barnard gone, Steve Nichols, who had worked alongside Barnard since 1981, stepped in as McLaren's Formula 1 Project Leader. Stefan Johansson came on board to partner Alain Prost. The Swede had won the 1980 British Formula 3 Championship, driving a Project Four Racing Ralt.

Nichols laid the groundwork for a new design, hence the revised nomenclature. It was similar in concept to the MP4/2, but with a different monocoque. It was narrower at the back in order to improve airflow around the rear wheels and over the wing, and also had a different profile around the cockpit.

Otherwise there were, as Nichols was the first to admit, "*A lot of good things about the existing MP4/2,*" so with time short and most of the team responsible for the Barnard car still in place, it was agreed to establish just how much could be done in the time available, and how much of that actually needed to be done.

The push-rod suspension was left alone, since it was thought at the time that it would take considerable work on it to make even the most marginal gains. The previous car had performed very well in terms of its basic handling and being kind to its tyres. McLaren's own six-speed gearbox remained unchanged too, along with the basic rear wing design.

There was scope, however, to pare weight from the chassis, since this had only partly been modified when the smaller fuel cells had been introduced for 1986. Work in the wind tunnel also pointed towards some further development of the aerodynamics, and the introduction of new sidepods with side-exiting radiator outlets instead of top ones to optimise some changes to the cooling system.

The new tub still made use of the same processes and materials as before, but now had new bodywork and a lower engine cover which gave the completed car a noticeably sleeker appearance.

There was much work to do in the engine, the once-envied TAG-Porsche V6 now beginning at last to show its age. Throughout the winter Porsche worked hard on the engine management systems. In a bid to raise power, to 850bhp at 12,000rpm, and to improve overall economy and throttle response, Porsche increased the compression ratio three times but the law of diminishing returns made its presence felt and a misfire would sometimes set in. The engine's boost was also now controlled to accommodate a new requirement for pop-off valves to prevent boost pressure rising higher than 4.0bar.

While the V6 was still capable of turning in some truly outstanding performances – most obviously Prost and Johansson's first and second at Spa – the increase in power came at a cost of increased weight, which upset the balance of the engine slightly. This led to some problems with vibration, which together with the misfires was accompanied by a number of alternator drive-belt breakages.

In Brazil, after very little testing, Prost expressed himself mostly pleased with the car, especially its increased downforce, although his race engineer still had some work to do to cut the level of understeer. The engineer was Gordon Murray, who had joined from Brabham, and he was soon aided by the arrival of Neil Oatley from Haas-Lola, further strengthening the new McLaren line-up.

The season got off to a good start, with Prost winning in Rio and Johansson two places behind. At Imola, where both cars had a mixture problem, Prost retired on lap 15 with an alternator failure, and Johansson came fourth after losing a wing endplate in the wake of turbulence from one of the Brabhams. At Spa things flipped back the other way again, with Prost winning to equal Jackie Stewart's historic tally of 27 Grand Prix wins and Johansson the runner-up.

In Monaco, vibrations, computer glitches and belt breakages forced both drivers out and in the French round Johansson once again suffered belt failure although Prost at least managed third behind Nigel Mansell and Nelson Piquet's Williams-Hondas, even with his engine misfiring badly.

At Silverstone rumours began to surface that representatives of Honda had been spotted in Woking, and Prost confirmed he was remaining with the team for the next season. In Germany, Johansson came second despite losing a tyre, but Prost quit four laps from the end with yet another broken belt. The Frenchman won in Portugal, however, to set a new record with 28 Grand Prix wins, but overall the year belonged to Piquet and Williams.

Away from the circuit there was more to celebrate. At Monza it was confirmed that Honda would join McLaren at the end of 1987, and that Ayrton Senna would come onboard to partner 'The Professor'.

The fact remained that for the first time since 1983 a McLaren driver had not won the World Championship, but the team came second in the Constructors' Cup with a respectable 76 points.

At Hockenheim for the German Grand Prix, Stefan Johansson equalled his best-ever GP result with second place behind Piquet's Williams. It was a close call, though. Halfway round the last lap, a front tyre deflated and he crossed the line with a wheel hanging off.

New designer Steve Nichols felt that some of the chassis' mass could be removed and the monocoque of the MP4/3 was lower and slimmer both around and behind the cockpit area.

Although the front suspension and underbody area on the MP4/3 was slightly modified, the rear suspension set-up remained essentially the same as on the previous year's MP4/2B.

MP4/3 FORMULA 1

SPECIFICATION

MODEL	McLaren MP4/3
TYPE/FORMULA	Formula 1
YEAR OF PRODUCTION	1987
DESIGNER	Steve Nichols
EXAMPLES BUILT	6
ENGINE	TAG Turbo TTE PO1 V6
CUBIC CAPACITY	1496cc
INDUCTION	Twin KKK turbochargers
POWER OUTPUT	850bhp

TRANSMISSION	McLaren 6-speed
CHASSIS	Moulded carbon fibre/honeycomb monocoque
BODY	Carbon fibre single piece cockpit/engine cover & nose
FRONT SUSPENSION	Double wishbone, push-rod operating
	inboard coil spring/damper
REAR SUSPENSION	Upper wishbone/rocker arm operating
	inboard coil spring/damper, lower wishbone
BRAKES F/R	Outboard SEP carbon discs/McLaren twin caliper
WHEELS DIAMETER x WIDTH F/R	13x11.5/13x16.25in

TYRES F/R	Goodyear
LENGTH	172in - 4369mm
WIDTH	84in - 2134mm
HEIGHT	38in - 965mm
WHEELBASE	109in - 2768mm
TRACK F/R	71.5/66in - 1816/1676mm
WEIGHT	1191lb - 540kg
PRINCIPAL DRIVERS	Prost, Johansson
IDENTIFYING COLOURS	Red/White

1987 FORMULA 1 TEST CAR
McLAREN MP4/3B

Dimensionally the same as the MP4/3, and with identical suspension, the MP4/3B was created by taking Steve Nichols's 1987 car and converting it to run Honda's new RA 108E V6 engine in place of the TAG built Porsche V6.

For much of 1987 Honda had been the dominant engine supplier, and once fitted with its new V6 the McLaren MP4/3B ran as an engine test-bed during the 1987/88 off-season. With Alain Prost and then Ayrton Senna behind the wheel it fulfilled this crucial role right up until the first race of the new season, with some additional development work being carried out on the car at Honda's own circuit, Suzuka, in Japan.

Although it used a standard moulded carbon fibre/honeycomb composite-type MP4/3 chassis, the 3B was equipped with a special new casing for the McLaren six-speed gearbox and oil tank in order to accommodate the Honda engine. Oil and water-cooling arrangements remained as before, however, with special air-intercoolers installed, again to suit the Japanese engine.

The latter also called for a new engine cover and this had a slightly revised profile, although in every other respect the two cars built to this specification retained most of the existing MP4/3 bodywork and to most observers would have looked much the same. Underneath, however, the big change, the new engine, was to prove truly decisive for the team – as the astonishing results with the soon-to-be-revealed MP4/4 would show.

Nothing lasts for ever and much of McLaren's problems during the 1987 season were down to its choice of engines. While the continuing development of the once famously clean-sheet TAG Porsche design – for a good while (and understandably) much coveted by McLaren's rivals – had achieved a few miracles in its time, by this point it had all but reached it's the end of its development road.

The team at Porsche had worked long and hard to wring additional power from the unit, increasing its compression ratio in order to raise it to 850bhp at 12,000rpm whilst managing to improve both its throttle response and fuel consumption. In this form Prost claimed he was happy with the car, but there was no escaping its shortcomings, in particular the extra weight which came with the power hike and the loss of overall balance which resulted from this, and the lack of horsepower compared to rivals such as Honda, Ferrari and Renault.

Before long, vibrations, regular misfires and a number of alternator drive-belt breakages were sending a clear message that the package needed more than a simple overhaul. For McLaren, Honda's defection from the Williams camp (they stayed with Lotus for the 1988 season) could scarcely have come at a better time.

Designed for the new 1988 regulations which reduced fuel capacity to only 150 litres and introduced a new mandatory 2.8-bar turbo boost limit, the RA108E V6 underlined that Honda was in fighting form, determined to end the turbo era on a high. As a result the V6, whilst in a sense 'transitional' and 'interim' was to more than compensate for the changes which – with a total ban on turbo engines clearly imminent – would otherwise have heavily favoured McLaren's normally aspirated rivals.

As well as allowing for the new lower boost pressure, the engine's designers had brilliantly conceived a unit that could be located as low as possible in the chassis. That in turn enabled the drivers of what was to become the outstanding MP4/4 to lie even closer to the horizontal; Steve Nichols, Gordon Murray and Bob Bell were thus able to produce a car with an even shallower body profile than before as well as a much reduced frontal area.

Given what was to come, and despite the fact that it never raced itself, the MP4/3B was a significant machine in McLaren's history.

Over the winter of 1987/88 Ayrton Senna and Alain Prost took the hot seat and tested the Honda engined MP4/3B extensively. The cockpit was devoid of most of the electronics and adjustment controls used during races.

To most observers the MP4/3B looked identical to the regular MP4/3. Minor changes to the engine cover hid the major difference - the installation of the Honda RA108E V6 engine and a special gearbox/oil tank casing designed to suit the Honda engine.

Alain Prost felt the increased power of the Honda engine was offset by the extra weight and a subsequent loss of handling balance. Two cars were converted to this specification and over the course of the season one continued to be run as an engine development test car at Suzuka.

MP4/3B FORMULA 1 TEST CAR

MODEL	McLaren MP4/3B
TYPE/FORMULA	Formula 1 Test Car
YEAR OF PRODUCTION	1987
DESIGNER	Steve Nichols
EXAMPLES BUILT	2 converted from MP4/3
ENGINE	Honda RA108E Turbo V6
CUBIC CAPACITY	1496cc
INDUCTION	Twin IHI turbochargers
POWER OUTPUT	850bhp

TRANSMISSION	McLaren 6-speed
CHASSIS	Moulded carbon fibre/honeycomb monocoque
BODY	Carbon fibre single piece cockpit/engine cover & nose
FRONT SUSPENSION	Double wishbone, push-rod operating
	inboard coil spring/damper
REAR SUSPENSION	Upper wishbone/rocker arm operating
	inboard coil spring/damper, lower wishbone
BRAKES F/R	Outboard SEP carbon discs/McLaren twin caliper
WHEELS DIAMETER x WIDTH F/R	13x12/13x16.5in

TYRES F/R	Goodyear
LENGTH	173in - 4394mm
WIDTH	84.25in - 2140mm
HEIGHT	37in - 940mm
WHEELBASE	109in - 2768mm
TRACK F/R	71.5/66in - 1816/1676mm
WEIGHT	1191lb - 540kg
PRINCIPAL DRIVERS	Prost, Senna
IDENTIFYING COLOURS	Red/White

1988 FORMULA 1
McLAREN MP4/4

Having completed just a handful of laps in the new 1988 MP4/4, Alain Prost reportedly told Team Principal Ron Dennis that he knew the car would win the World Championship. Indeed, not long after that, Neil Trundle, McLaren's chief mechanic at the time and Dennis's former partner in Rondel Racing, admitted that many people in the team, "*Already felt we could even win all the races.*"

The high level of optimism at McLaren, following the arrival of its new Honda V6 engine and of Ayrton Senna as Prost's partner, was not diluted by rule changes for the 1988 season. These brought in a further reduction in fuel capacity to 150 litres and a mandatory 2.8-bar turbo boost limit, the benefit of both in theory going to McLaren's normally aspirated rivals in a move clearly made ahead of the imminent ban on turbo technology which would come into effect for 1989.

So swingeing was the fuel capacity rule that many expected 1988 to be a transitional year for the turbo teams rather than a winning one. But for McLaren at least it was to be nothing of the sort.

The new MP4/4 won 15 out of 16 races, losing only Monza which many felt was a self-inflicted defeat after Senna tripped over backmarker Jean-Louis Schlesser's Williams-Judd in the first chicane. The Brazilian started on pole no fewer than 13 times and won eight races to take the World Championship despite having been disqualified in the opener in Brazil. At the same time, winning a scarcely less remarkable seven rounds, Prost found himself just three points adrift of the top slot leaving McLaren's nearest rival, third placed Gerhard Berger, literally miles behind. By the end of the season McLaren had scored a phenomenal 199 points in the Constructors' Cup, almost three times the tally of runner-up Ferrari.

The car which enabled them to achieve all this, a design which Trundle still insists is, "*The perfect package, still the lowest and sleekest-looking car on display at the team HQ,*" was not only a highly effective development of the 1981 carbon composite concept but also one which was correct in its tiniest details. With light overall weight, outstanding downforce, highly efficient brakes and suspension, and a fabulous V6 in the form of Honda's RA168-E, Trundle is one of many who has no doubts that it was McLaren's best-ever car.

In the hands of two of the world's best drivers, the McLaren Honda MP4/4 was quickly to prove itself unbeatable. Honda's new engine was mounted so low in the chassis that it required a new six-speed, three-shaft gearbox, devised by David North in the UK and Pete Weisman in the US. With a shallower body profile, the drivers were also made to lie more prone – something which suited Senna's driving style but to which Prost objected until wind tunnel results rendered his arguments untenable.

Lowering everything in this way enabled Murray and aerodynamicist Bob Bell to reduce the car's frontal area by 10 per cent, which in turn helped improve the lift-to-drag ratio by six per cent because a simpler rear wing could be kept further away from the upper deck of the car. The wheelbase was four centimetres longer, and the car's longer nose housed a mandatory deformable structure.

Only when it came to the distance from the ground did Murray resist the temptation to go lower still, choosing instead "*To build with lots of wheel travel, sacrificing a little downforce by not running the car too close to the ground. That made it more comfortable and easier to set up.*"

Crucially his skill and famous attention to detail and determination to get it right were matched point-for-point by Ron Dennis, who told him: "*You have carte blanche – anything you don't like, change. Anything you want, you can have. I want to win World Championships." According to Murray, "He stuck to that absolutely, and that was key in the MP4/4's success.*"

This singular commitment brought new facilities to McLaren just when it needed them most. These included the team's first autoclave, but also new meeting rooms, new procedures to be rigorously applied, better record-keeping and above all much more detailed analysis of every performance, component and race (won or lost) to establish precisely what happened, when and why. Detail, detail, discipline and more detail – the hallmark of modern McLaren.

The results were quick in coming and speak for themselves. Reliability problems dropped off almost completely – Senna had gear linkage problems in Rio, and something similar at Imola and again at Ricard – and as the record books show the MP4/4 achieved such dominance over the course of a season that any minor failings are now more or less forgotten. Finishing the season with a points total just two shy of the combined total of every other team on the grid, it simply towered over its opposition even though it was the lowest car out there.

With his management using the buyout clause in his contract at Lotus, Ayrton Senna moved to McLaren for 1988. It proved a wise move as he won eight races and took the Drivers' title.

In its final year of development the 1.5-litre Honda RA168E V6 turbo engine was at times putting out in excess of 700bhp. The MP4/4 won all but one of the season's 16 Grand Prix races and scored three times the number of points as second place Ferrari in the Constructors' Championship.

The team produced a total of six MP4/4 chassis for the 1988 season, even though they would be obsolete by the end of the year when the new 3.5-litre normally aspirated engine rules came into force.

Shell
Shell
12

12
SHOWA
GOODYEAR
EAGLE
Senna
BOSS
POWERED by
HONDA
Shell
GOODYEAR
EAGLE
GOODYEAR

Alain Prost on the way to his 31st Grand Prix victory in Mexico 1988. This third win of the season meant he comfortably led the title race and would do so until the 11th round at Spa Francorchamps in August.

The Hungarian Grand Prix gave the McLaren duo their seventh 1-2 finish of the year. With three more before the end of the season they would set a record that will probably stand for all time.

In the dry qualifying session for the Belgian Grand Prix at Spa, Ayrton put MP4/4-5 on pole position for the ninth time that season. A typically wet race gave him his seventh win of 1988.

MP4/4 FORMULA 1
SPECIFICATION

MODEL	McLaren MP4/4
TYPE/FORMULA	Formula 1
YEAR OF PRODUCTION	1988
DESIGNER	Steve Nichols/Gordon Murray
EXAMPLES BUILT	6
ENGINE	Honda RA168E Turbo V6
CUBIC CAPACITY	1494cc
INDUCTION	Twin IHI turbochargers
POWER OUTPUT	900bhp

TRANSMISSION	McLaren 6-speed
CHASSIS	Moulded carbon fibre/honeycomb monocoque
BODY	Carbon fibre single piece cockpit/engine cover & nose
FRONT SUSPENSION	Double wishbone, push-rod/roller track system
	operating inboard coil spring/damper
REAR SUSPENSION	Upper wishbone/rocker arm operating
	inboard coil spring/damper, lower wishbone
BRAKES F/R	Outboard SEP carbon discs/McLaren twin caliper
WHEELS DIAMETER x WIDTH F/R	13x11.75/13x16.25in

TYRES F/R	Goodyear
LENGTH	173in - 4394mm
WIDTH	84in - 2134mm
HEIGHT	37in - 940mm
WHEELBASE	113.2in - 2875mm
TRACK F/R	71.8/65.8in - 1824/1670mm
WEIGHT	1191lb - 540kg
PRINCIPAL DRIVERS	Prost, Senna
IDENTIFYING COLOURS	Red/White

1988 FORMULA 1 TEST CAR
McLAREN MP4/4B

While meeting the challenge of new turbo regulations for the 1988 season with its V6, and with a new, much larger normally aspirated engine formula set for introduction the following year, winning once was clearly not going to be enough for Honda during its time with McLaren. Back home in Japan the company quickly established a second project team quite separate from the V6 engineers, to concentrate on the creation of a new 3.5-litre 'atmo' V10 for 1989.

On the track the close cooperation between the two organisations was to bring forth an immediate and outstanding harvest: In a thrilling season the MP4/4 rapidly established itself as the most successful single car in Formula 1 history with an unprecedented 199 points from a single season and no fewer than 15 wins and 10 superb 1-2 finishes. But in Honda's own workshops the progress was arguably just as impressive, with an all-new-for-1989 V10 quickly taking shape in the form of the 3.5-litre RA109A. Interestingly, only Renault and Honda opted for the 10-cylinder format initially, accepting it as the perfect compromise between outright power and torque, and external dimensions and ease of installation. Several key rivals, notably Ferrari who initially preferred a V12, were in due course obliged to follow suit.

To test the new engine the team at first considered using what has become known as the MP4/3C, a testbed created from a substantially revised MP4/3 chassis and running gear. This, however, was quickly abandoned in favour of MP4/4B shown here – as the name suggests a version of the 1988 race car – the change of vehicle choice being made in order to keep the project more up to date. Neil Oatley's MP4/4B thus became the principal development mule for the earliest iterations of the ground-breaking new Honda V10.

Once again the car used a carbon fibre composite monocoque chassis based on that of the turbo machines, but this was now fitted with a substantially larger fuel tank in line with the new regulations, as well as a completely new installation for the engine. A special gearbox casing was also designed to mate with the engine while the cooling system was heavily revised to suit a unit running more cylinders and no intercoolers.

Although from every angle the car looks familiar with its carbon fibre one-piece cockpit, engine cover and nose section assembly, it needed a change in the form of its overhead air intake which replaced the side intakes previously seen on the turbocar. It also gained revised bodywork to the rear of the sidepods, to accommodate the new engine installation. The wheelbase remained almost the same, however, at 114 inches, and the McLaren six-speed transmission, the McLaren SEP brakes, and the front and rear suspension were all carryovers.

Thus equipped, the MP4-4B first ran on European tracks in the mid-summer of 1988, and in the early part of 1989 it was flown to Suzuka where development continued under the Japanese. Over this period two MP4/4B chassis were built. These would be driven and comprehensively evaluated not just by the Alain Prost/Ayrton Senna 'dream team' but ahead of their individual input by Britain's Jonathan Palmer who was at that time McLaren's test driver.

The move from small-capacity turbo engine to larger-capacity, normally aspirated unit was a major shift both for McLaren and Honda. The transition from V6 to innovative V10 was also an exciting development for the sport. For these reasons alone, and even leaving aside McLaren's status as the title defenders, the MP4/4B found itself with quite a task on its hands and is thus an extremely important car in the team's long and illustrious history even if it remains relatively unknown. The work done with it enabled Honda to give the team an emphatic power advantage over its rivals.

The MP4/4B was built to help the team test and develop the new 3.5-litre Honda V10 engine. After being used extensively over the winter of 1988/89, as with the MP4/3B one of the two cars built was shipped to Honda in Japan for continued engine development.

From the middle of 1988 many thousands of miles were covered by the three contracted McLaren drivers, Senna, Prost and official test driver Jonathan Palmer. The V10 engine required a bespoke cooling system and the bodywork from sidepods rearward was revised to suit the engine installation.

MP4/4B FORMULA 1 TEST CAR

SPECIFICATION

MODEL	McLaren MP4/4B
TYPE/FORMULA	Formula 1 Test Car
YEAR OF PRODUCTION	1988
DESIGNER	Steve Nichols
EXAMPLES BUILT	3
ENGINE	Honda RA109E V10
CUBIC CAPACITY	3490cc
ELECTRONICS	Honda PGM injection/ignition
POWER OUTPUT	645bhp

TRANSMISSION	McLaren 6-speed
CHASSIS	Moulded carbon fibre/honeycomb monocoque
BODY	Carbon fibre single piece cockpit/engine cover & nose
FRONT SUSPENSION	Double wishbone, push-rod/roller track system
	operating inboard coil spring/damper
REAR SUSPENSION	Upper wishbone/rocker arm operating
	inboard coil spring/damper, lower wishbone
BRAKES F/R	Outboard SEP carbon discs/McLaren twin caliper
WHEELS DIAMETER x WIDTH F/R	13x11.75/13x16.25in

TYRES F/R	Goodyear
LENGTH	174in - 4420mm
WIDTH	83.5in - 2120mm
HEIGHT	37in - 940mm
WHEELBASE	114in - 2895mm
TRACK F/R	71.8/65.8in - 1824/1670mm
WEIGHT	1085lb - 492kg
PRINCIPAL DRIVERS	Prost, Senna, Palmer
IDENTIFYING COLOURS	Red/White

1989 FORMULA 1 McLAREN MP4/5

1989 meant all change for McLaren as the 3.5-litre normally aspirated Formula 1 came into force. The change had been flagged clearly many months in advance, and McLaren and Honda had been working on a car and engine package even as the MP4/4 was dominating the 1988 season. Even at Woking, however, few would have predicted that the first season of the non-turbo era would match the incredible results of the previous year, with McLaren walking away with further Drivers' and Constructors' World Championships.

Under Neil Oatley's guidance, the design team had created an all-new monocoque, new double wishbone suspension with pullrods up front and pushrods at the rear, and expected almost 700bhp from the 72 degree Honda RA109E V10. This drove through a longitudinal version of the David North/Pete Weismann three-shaft, six-speed gearbox, with a transverse unit arriving in mid-season. Honda's Osamu Goto made available eight new engines for the start of the year, though there was a slight delay to allow for a switch from belt- to gear-drive for the camshaft operation.

In the interests of aerodynamic flexibility Oatley's team stuck with the established practice of having a separate upper body, and though the monocoque looked similar to its forebears it incorporated a number of modifications as a result of a comprehensive review of the car's aerodynamic performance.

McLaren soon began to dominate the season, albeit not quite to the degree it had the previous year as the MP4/5 was not devoid of problems. There were some lubrication issues, which had reared their head during testing, and also some questions over the balance of the handling once Oatley's team had shaved off even more weight to meet the 505kg limit.

Even as the storm clouds were gathering over the relationship between Alain Prost and Ayrton Senna, it was clear that McLaren was once again the team to beat. Senna's collision in the first corner at Rio didn't alter the fact; neither did the clutch trouble which prevented Prost making an important pit stop, nor indeed complaints from both drivers about their respective throttle responses.

Much of this was resolved during some frenetic testing and development on the run-up to the San Marino GP. Upon arrival at Imola Prost promptly broke Nelson Piquet's three-year old lap record, while Senna won the race at an average speed of 125.479mph, making him more than three per cent faster than the previous year.

So far, so good – at least until Monaco where Prost publicly denounced Senna as a "*Man of no honour*". At Imola, he alleged, the latter had breached a no-passing agreement for which he, Senna, had apologised only belatedly and somewhat reluctantly. Thereafter the two spoke to each other only rarely, preferring to communicate with the other via Oatley, Steve Nichols or Jo Ramirez. The fact that they still won 10 races between them, enabling McLaren again to clinch the World Championship, speaks volumes for both the fundamental structure of the Honda-McLaren team and the quality of the MP4/5.

The new gearbox was still not ready for Monaco but new Brembo brakes were and these helped remove some more weight from the car. Once again Senna won, despite losing second gear, before more trouble flared up in Mexico where apparent disparities in the amount of fuel consumed by the two cars led Prost to question how fairly the team was dealing with the two drivers. It is more likely Senna simply drove further at high revs and that Prost's relatively lighter right foot (which had been such a benefit during the turbo era) worked slightly against him.

When the new transverse gearbox finally had its debut at Silverstone, a series of misfires and engine and gearbox failures followed. None of this prevented McLaren qualifying first and second, but in the race itself Senna ended up in a gravel trap. Indeed, despite all his complaints, it was to be Prost's season.

At Monza he announced that he was leaving again, this time for Ferrari. Senna, meanwhile, having won three races out of four, found his luck starting to unravel. Prost won in Italy, clinching for McLaren the Constructors' World Championship for the second year in a row and with four races still to be run, and by the season's end his 76-point total handed him yet another World Drivers' Championship. But not before the season had been sullied by the infamous coming-together of the two McLaren drivers in the Suzuka chicane, as they battled for the Japanese GP.

With Senna's car carrying the World Champion's number 1, Alain Prost in number 2 only won four races to Senna's six, but took his third Drivers' title by a 16-point margin.

The introduction of new engine regulations meant that the team now relied on the Honda V10 engine. In testing during 1988 Honda was quoting 600bhp, by the start of the 1989 season it was up to 650bhp and with continued development over the course of the season, by the end of the year it had reached 685bhp at 13,000rpm.

The most significant changes over the previous year's car were Neil Oatley's aerodynamic improvements which met the requirements of the RA109E V10 engine and its need for much greater cooling.

Shell
2
Shell

Prost
BOSS
POWERED by
HONDA
Shell
GOODYEAR
EAGLE
GOODYEAR
EAGLE
GOODYEAR
COURTAULDS
2
SHOWA

After Senna retired on the first lap with gearbox problems, polesitter Alain Prost won the French Grand Prix for the fourth time in his career.

Senna was desperate to win his home Grand Prix but a lengthy pitstop to replace the nose of his car on the first lap meant he could only finish 11th, two laps down.

At the next race, the San Marino Grand Prix at Imola, the team scored yet another 1-2 finish. On this occasion it was Senna ahead of Prost, both of them over a lap ahead of third-placed Nannini.

MP4/5 FORMULA 1
SPECIFICATION

MODEL	McLaren MP4/5
TYPE/FORMULA	Formula 1
YEAR OF PRODUCTION	1989
DESIGNER	Neil Oatley
EXAMPLES BUILT	8
ENGINE	Honda RA109E V10
CUBIC CAPACITY	3490cc
ELECTRONICS	Honda PGM injection/ignition
POWER OUTPUT	685bhp

TRANSMISSION	McLaren 6-speed/transverse 6-speed
CHASSIS	High modulus carbon fibre/honeycomb monocoque
BODY	Carbon fibre single piece cockpit/engine cover & nose
FRONT SUSPENSION	Double wishbone, pull-rod operating
	inboard coil spring/damper
REAR SUSPENSION	Double wishbone, push-rod operating
	inboard coil spring/damper
BRAKES F/R	Outboard SEP carbon discs/McLaren twin caliper
WHEELS DIAMETER x WIDTH F/R	13x11.75/13x16.25in

TYRES F/R	Goodyear
LENGTH	177in - 4496mm
WIDTH	84in - 2134 mm
HEIGHT	39in - 991mm
WHEELBASE	114in - 2895mm
TRACK F/R	71.8/65.75in - 1824/1669mm
WEIGHT	1102lb - 500kg
PRINCIPAL DRIVERS	Prost, Senna
IDENTIFYING COLOURS	Red/White

CHAPTER 04

MIKA HÄKKINEN

When I was with Lotus in 1991-92 McLaren was for me the Number One superteam: a really interesting outfit which always looked good, got fantastic results, and had a very high profile.

People think I took a gamble when I signed for McLaren because it already had two drivers signed up, but I didn't. Gambling is gambling and you never know if you are going to win, so I don't do it. However, I knew that I was good, I was the best, I was the fastest and Ron Dennis had to give me a try. I was very, very, confident and I took the risk that if Ayrton came back to race in 1994 maybe I wouldn't have a race seat and would only be testing.

I had quite a few offers from other teams that year, but McLaren was the Number One for me, Ron had promised me a race that year and so I wasn't concerned. He has always been the person who makes the decisions, so I knew I could rely on him.

My first Grand Prix drive came in Portugal in 1993 and I was confident. Of course Ayrton was my team-mate and being next to a great champion and seeing how hard I had to work to be on the same level was a real eye-opener. At that time we had the same Ford HB engine as Lotus had used, one which had never had any problems but was just not powerful enough. Everything else at McLaren was unbelievably fantastic though – gearbox, brakes, the materials it was using – so when Mercedes-Benz joined we had a really interesting time. They said we come here and we have to win and that kind of attitude gave me a lot more confidence.

Obviously it took some time to get it right – I had my first win only after seven years in Formula 1 – but it was worth the wait. Sometimes you look at the other side of the fence and think the grass is greener but, really, I had a great team behind me and to be honest I always thought we can do it, we can win and I can win the World Championship. I saw the development work that was going on in 1995, '96, and '97 and after that last year and I knew that we were going to do it. At McLaren everyone was so motivated, with so much energy. We had a good programme, good mechanics, good designers, and in 1998 a fantastic car, the ultimate machine in every respect, and I knew that it would happen.

Mika Häkkinen
World Drivers' Champion 1998 & 1999
McLaren MP4-13 & MP4-14

1990 FORMULA 1
McLAREN MP4/5B

With World Champion Alain Prost and Steve Nichols departing for Ferrari, thus cementing the Italian team's 1990 status as McLaren's strongest challenger, and Gordon Murray turning his attention to the McLaren F1 road car project, Neil Oatley and his design colleagues opted to refine the MP4/5 for Ayrton Senna and his incoming new team-mate Gerhard Berger rather than create an entirely new car.

The latter would probably have wished otherwise since he was too tall to fit into the car comfortably when he first tested it. It was otherwise clearly a winner, however, and while it was true that McLaren's principal challengers, Ferrari and Williams, were catching up, the opinion at Woking was that the existing car was a good basis on which to continue.

Honda produced a new derivative of its V10, the RA100E engine. The car's monocoque was broadly similar, however, but used a new high-modulus material from Hercules Corporation which promised even greater impact resistance. A new, slightly larger fuel cell was also installed, whilst the suspension geometry was altered at the front and the transverse gearbox substantially revised.

While the car still looked broadly similar, some evolutionary rather than radical revisions were also made to its aerodynamic profile with particular reference to the sidepods and radiator ducting. It also gained a new windscreen design and a distinctive multi-arched diffuser. That diffuser was superseded by mid-season, by which time Berger's seating position problems had finally been resolved by making his driving position slightly more upright than Senna's.

It was to be a busy time at McLaren. While one crew was designing and building MP4/5B race cars, work was starting in parallel on a MP4/5C test car to accommodate a new V12 Honda engine intended for the following season. The fact that the very first 'B' car then sustained some serious damage in Senna's hands didn't help matters, although the incident during pre-season shakedown trials at Silverstone provided some useful evidence to support the driver's assertion that the new chassis was rather more responsive than the MP4/5.

The season itself got off to a good start, however, with Senna quickly negating Berger's pole in the Phoenix opener and blasting his way to victory after a brief battle with the forceful Jean Alesi's Tyrrell. Thereafter he took pole position 10 times, but it was nevertheless obvious from the moment the new cars were completed that the team faced a greater challenge than it had in 1989. Not just from Prost at Ferrari (where he was partnered by Nigel Mansell), but also from Williams where Thierry Boutsen and Riccardo Patrese were making their presence felt with Renault V10 power in the FW13B.

None of this seemed to worry Senna, who led every race of the season except Hungary, where he was forced to chase Boutsen's Williams all the way to the finish, and Suzuka, where he cynically took out former team-mate Prost's Ferrari to claim a controversial second World Championship.

Over the course of the season the car improved significantly – helped in no small part by a new underbody which made it both easier to control and more comfortable to drive – with the factory burning the midnight oil to test and perfect all sorts of new aerodynamic components. The responsibility for this, and in particular for Senna's car, now fell to American Gordon Kimball, as Oatley moved on to design the V12-engined MP4/6 for 1991.

Honda too continued the development of its engine package, so that Senna's V10 was at times producing around 710bhp thanks to increased rev limits and new, lower density fuel which he used in qualifying. At Hockenheim Osamu Goto and his team unboxed a slightly lighter Version 4 power unit, with Version 5 coming along in time for Spa-Francorchamps and producing even better top-end results.

In the final analysis there is simply no arguing with any car which takes pole 12 times in a season. Nor with a car which handed its team yet another Drivers' World Championship and another Constructors' World Championship to sit alongside it. It was only for the second time in history that the latter had been won by the same team three times in succession, so the 1990 season says a lot about the quality of the McLaren operation. And given that the car the team relied on was evolutionary rather than an entirely new design, it says even more about the commitment both it and its engine supplier were willing to make in the face of greater challenges from increasingly strong competition.

The MP4/5 incorporated some significant aerodynamic changes over the previous year's car, including a multi-arch diffuser panel at the rear and slightly bulkier sidepods.

A new style of 'windscreen' was adopted part way through the season. In particular this helped with the more upright driving position of Gerhard Berger who joined the team to partner Ayrton Senna in 1990.

Shell
27

27

Senna
BOSS
POWERED by
HONDA
Shell
GOODYEAR
EAGLE F1
COURTAULDS
27

Even though Gerhard Berger had started from pole position and Senna (above) was only fifth on the grid, Ayrton still managed to win the 1990 United States Grand Prix in Phoenix, Arizona.

Ayrton Senna won six races in 1990 and took the Drivers' title by seven points from Alain Prost's Ferrari. McLaren also took the Constructors' title for the third year in a row.

After Senna crashed out of the final race of 1990 in Adelaide, it was left to Gerhard Berger to uphold McLaren honour with fourth place, this was his 11th points finish of the season.

MP4/5B FORMULA 1
SPECIFICATION

MODEL	McLaren MP4/5B
TYPE/FORMULA	Formula 1
YEAR OF PRODUCTION	1990
DESIGNER	Neil Oatley
EXAMPLES BUILT	7
ENGINE	Honda RA100E V10
CUBIC CAPACITY	3490cc
ELECTRONICS	Honda PGM injection/ignition
POWER OUTPUT	690bhp

TRANSMISSION	McLaren transverse 6-speed
CHASSIS	High modulus carbon fibre/honeycomb monocoque
BODY	Carbon fibre single piece cockpit/engine cover & nose
FRONT SUSPENSION	Double wishbone, pull-rod operating
	inboard coil spring/damper
REAR SUSPENSION	Double wishbone, push-rod operating
	inboard coil spring/damper
BRAKES F/R	Outboard Brembo/Carbone Industrie
WHEELS DIAMETER x WIDTH F/R	13x11.75/13x16.25in

TYRES F/R	Goodyear
LENGTH	176in - 4470mm
WIDTH	84in - 2133mm
HEIGHT	38in - 965mm
WHEELBASE	114in - 2895mm
TRACK F/R	71.8/65.75in - 1824/1669mm
WEIGHT	1102lb - 500kg
PRINCIPAL DRIVERS	Senna, Berger
IDENTIFYING COLOURS	Red/White

1990 FORMULA 1 TEST CAR McLAREN MP4/5C

A derivation of the 1990 MP4/5B race car, and once again designed by Neil Oatley, the MP4/5C on which design work had started in May of that year, was conceived as a mobile test bed for the first of a new generation of engines, Honda's RA121E V12.

It first ran in the late summer of 1990 alongside the familiar V10, having been built using essentially the same chassis as before but with revised engine mounts and all-new, elongated bodywork to accommodate the motor's extra length. The overall length of the car didn't actually increase a great deal, however, thanks to clever work shortening the length of the gearbox internals and thus the overall dimensions of the casing. As was by now established McLaren practise with test vehicles, its working life continued through the winter until MP4/6 was ready. After this one of the two chassis built was taken to Japan for additional development running by Honda, putting in many miles at Suzuka.

At its first shakedown test at Silverstone, the MP4/5C was driven by both Ayrton Senna and Gerhard Berger, as well as by two of the team's test drivers, Italian Emanuele Pirro and Scotsman Allan McNish, both of whom were later to make their names in sportscar racing. While the regular drivers were carrying out development work on the MP4/5B (including a Tyrrell-inspired 'high nose' variant) Jonathan Palmer also tested the MP4/5C for McLaren in a session at Monza in August 1990. He drove the car again at Chobham in southern England in October, at the same time trying out a 'semi-automatic' MP4/5B variant.

Later to join the team, David Coulthard also drove the development car fitted with the Honda V12 as part of his prize for winning the 1989 McLaren Autosport BRDC Young Driver of the Year Award. His first taste of Formula 1 power came in the hybrid MP4/5C on Silverstone's South Circuit on a cold, damp day in late November. Interviewed at the end of it, he said: *"It was nice to come here and see a McLaren with Coulthard on the side, and hopefully in a few years my name will be there again."*

Finally, in one last test of the V12 MP4/5C combination before the new car for 1991 was ready to be unveiled, Berger took part in the week-long session for all the teams at Estoril in mid-December. With one of the two chassis now hidden away in Japan, and the team not wanting to let the other teams get too good a view of the new V12, McLaren kept the car pretty much under wraps for the whole week. Despite this, Berger finished fifth fastest and less than one second off the pace of Prost's Ferrari.

There was debate whether the extra two cylinders of the V12 were really needed, and some parties in McLaren favoured further development of the V10. In particular, they would have liked it to lose weight. But Honda politics dictated a V12, and the V10s were eventually supplied to Tyrrell for 1991. The pro-V10 parties pointed out that, while it might be more powerful, the V12 was heavier and thirstier, which negated much of that advantage.

The 60° RA121E V12 gained not just additional cylinders but also a much larger piston area and, potentially, an even higher rev limit as well. In testing in the MP4/5C it showed itself to be thirstier than the V10, partly as a consequence of its greater weight. There were also greater losses from internal friction to deal with, but nevertheless the expectation was that with an output rumoured to be in the region of 720bhp any downsides would be compensated for. At the Monza test, however, there wasn't much to choose in terms of lap times between it and the V10-engined car as the benefits of the more powerful engine were offset by its additional weight.

Since it was not only heavier but longer, the new engine also necessitated a slightly stretched wheelbase, the final dimensions being some 3 inches longer than the V10-engined MP4-5B at 117 inches. At the same time substantial alterations were made to the cooling system radiators; special oil heat-exchangers were fitted to suit the new engine installation, and a new gearbox/oil tank casing assembly was introduced.

The suspension remained unchanged from the revised arrangement employed in the test car, however, but the monocoque was constructed using a new, even higher-modulus material from Hercules Aerospace in Utah. In the constant battle between overall strength, the weight of the complete monocoque, and torsional stiffness, this new formula for the grade of the carbon-fibre mix had been selected for its improved resistance to high-speed impact.

The MP4/5C used the new Honda V12 engine and was tested by more different drivers than any of the other test cars built. These included Senna, Berger, Pirro, McNish, Palmer and even David Coulthard.

With the much longer engine installed the MP4/5C had a stretched wheelbase and a revised cooling system that included specially built heat exchangers. There was also a new gearbox casing.

MP4/5C FORMULA 1 TEST CAR
SPECIFICATION

MODEL	McLaren MP4/5C
TYPE/FORMULA	Formula 1 Test Car
YEAR OF PRODUCTION	1990
DESIGNER	Neil Oatley
EXAMPLES BUILT	2
ENGINE	Honda RA121E V12
CUBIC CAPACITY	3493cc
ELECTRONICS	Honda PGM injection/ignition
POWER OUTPUT	700bhp

TRANSMISSION	McLaren transverse 6-speed
CHASSIS	High modulus carbon fibre/honeycomb monocoque
BODY	Carbon fibre single piece cockpit/engine cover & nose
FRONT SUSPENSION	Double wishbone, pull-rod operating
	inboard coil spring/damper
REAR SUSPENSION	Double wishbone, push-rod operating
	inboard coil spring/damper
BRAKES F/R	Outboard Brembo/Carbone Industrie
WHEELS DIAMETER x WIDTH F/R	13x11.75/13x16.3in

TYRES F/R	Goodyear
LENGTH	180in - 4572mm
WIDTH	83.5in - 2120mm
HEIGHT	39in - 990mm
WHEELBASE	117in - 2972mm
TRACK F/R	71.8/65.75in - 1824/1669mm
WEIGHT	1110lb - 503kg
PRINCIPAL DRIVERS	Senna, Berger, McNish, Pirro, Palmer
IDENTIFYING COLOURS	Red/White

1991 FORMULA 1 McLAREN MP4/6

While the V10 Honda RA100E had succeeded in holding off Renault's V10 and Ferrari's V12, the thinking within Honda was that it couldn't do for so much longer. For 1991, therefore, Ayrton Senna and Gerhard Berger found themselves seated ahead of yet another new engine, the RA121E Honda V12.

This was Honda's third engine configuration in just four seasons, and was an entirely new 60° unit with a greater piston area than the outgoing engine and a potentially higher rev limit. It was longer, heavier and thirstier than the V10, but it was hoped that an output reputed to be 720bhp would compensate for that. However, the engine installed in the MP4/5C test mule failed to convince Senna. Concerned that it simply wouldn't be sufficient to defeat Renault's new, improved V10, he was quick to tell the Japanese what he thought of it in his usual candid terms.

Though naturally concerned to hear this, the Japanese stuck to their guns, Akimasa Yasuoka arguing that, "*Honda traditionally detunes its engines for the first race of the season; we tend to go for reliability rather than power.*" In retrospect, it was perhaps right to do so for McLaren's season got off to the best possible start with no fewer than four wins in a row, the increased engine weight partly offset by the latest development of McLaren's six-speed gearbox.

The car itself, whilst looking similar to MP4/5B, was quite different in terms of its aerodynamic profile as designer Neil Oatley and his team had received some valuable input from Henri Durand who had joined from Ferrari in mid-1990.

Numerous changes had also to be made to the chassis, not least in order to accommodate the longer engine and the enlarged fuel cell needed to satisfy its greater thirst. Even with four centimetres added to its length the new tub was much stiffer in terms of torsional rigidity, and consisted of even fewer basic components than before. There were changes to the suspension too, an aspect of the car which had altered dramatically since the year before, with pushrod-activated coil-spring/dampers now mounted on top of the chassis ahead of the cockpit instead of being installed vertically either side of the footwell.

The changes called for some exterior alterations, so that the new suspension arrangement resulted in a slightly higher border round the cockpit while, with the larger water radiators now specified, the sidepods were also longer and taller. As the season progressed the aerodynamics were tweaked further, in part to offset the negative effects of increased weight and drag from the greater fuel load and revised cooling arrangements.

The increased fuel consumption posed challenges of its own, despite plenty of development on the engine management system, Senna twice ran out of fuel (at Silverstone and Hockenheim) but the Brazilian and his MP4/6 nevertheless remained unbeaten up to and including Monaco. Giving McLaren a comfortable lead in the Constructors' Cup, the margin thus gained was to prove crucially important as the team's performance began to slip and Williams-Renault began to gather pace with Nigel Mansell and Riccardo Patrese as its reliability improved.

In Montreal two things quickly became apparent. The first was that the Honda's extra power was simply insufficient to offset its greater weight relative to the V10s, particularly when its internal frictional losses continued to rise. The other was that the Williams FW14s, particularly Mansell's, were really getting into their stride.

Undeterred, Honda continued developing its V12. The Spec 1, which had triumphed at Phoenix, Interlagos and in the Principality, eventually gave way to a Spec 2 variant which was actually introduced ahead of Monaco, at Imola, and offered better mid-range punch thanks to its new induction system. The friction problems were also addressed with a Spec 3 version at Silverstone. New linked rocker arms were also employed in a bid to reduce roll, and a cockpit-adjustable ride-height mechanism was also added.

The fuel metering issues that made themselves so painfully felt during the British and German rounds were largely to do with Shell's experimentation with different fuel densities and viscosities. At Paul Ricard, another inaccurate readout forced Senna to drive conservatively, although following this Honda's research and development effort accelerated dramatically so that by the time he arrived in Hungary he had a car which could be safely revved to 14,800rpm, albeit only for short bursts.

In Budapest McLaren regained its form in the nick of time. With a lighter-than-ever chassis, and yet another heavily reworked engine with lighter cylinder heads, camshafts and connecting rods, Senna pulled something out of the bag and pushed the Williams duo back to second and third places. Despite suffering a gearbox failure, he managed it again at Spa for the Belgian Grand Prix, where he nursed his failing car home and saw his lead over Williams grow enormously following another retirement by Mansell. McLaren's rival was quickly restored to good fortune, however, commanding the field in both the Portuguese and Spanish races, the last of which saw Senna struggling on the wrong tyres.

At Suzuka the order flipped again, the correct tyres and yet more successful engine development leaving Senna in an unassailable position on 96 points. He returned to Brazil with a resounding third title, while Berger finished fourth with 43 points, having been handed victory by Senna in Suzuka. McLaren again took the Constructors' World Championship.

While Ayrton Senna easily won the 1991 Monaco Grand Prix, Gerhard Berger was involved in a first-lap incident, pitted to repair the damage and was out by lap 10.

With Shell supplying ever-changing fuel specifications, calibration of the onboard readout in the cockpit was proving difficult. More than once in 1991 the two drivers were needlessly forced to conserve their fuel.

The MP4/6 featured major changes to the suspension set-up, with the push-rod activated coil-spring dampers now mounted on top of the chassis rather than vertically in the footwell.

Senna
BOSS
POWERED by
HONDA
COURTAULDS
Shell
GOODYEAR
EAGLE F1
speedline
1

1991 FORMULA 1 McLAREN MP4/6

CONTINUED

The rain-shortened 1991 Australian Grand Prix in Adelaide saw Ayrton Senna hold off Nigel Mansell's Williams FW14 to score his seventh win of the season.

MP4/6 FORMULA 1
SPECIFICATION

MODEL	McLaren MP4/6
TYPE/FORMULA	Formula 1
YEAR OF PRODUCTION	1991
DESIGNER	Neil Oatley
EXAMPLES BUILT	11
ENGINE	Honda RA121E V12
CUBIC CAPACITY	3493cc
ELECTRONICS	Honda PGM injection/ignition
POWER OUTPUT	720bhp

TRANSMISSION	McLaren transverse 6-speed
CHASSIS	High modulus carbon fibre/honeycomb monocoque
BODY	Carbon fibre single piece cockpit/engine cover & nose
FRONT SUSPENSION	Double wishbone, push-rod operating
	longitudinal inboard coil spring/damper
REAR SUSPENSION	Double wishbone, push-rod operating
	vertical inboard coil spring/damper
BRAKES F/R	Outboard Brembo/Carbone Industrie
WHEELS DIAMETER x WIDTH F/R	13x12/13x16.3in

TYRES F/R	Goodyear
LENGTH	177in - 4496mm
WIDTH	83.5in - 2120mm
HEIGHT	38in - 965mm
WHEELBASE	117in - 2972mm
TRACK F/R	71.8/65.75in - 1824/1669mm
WEIGHT	1113lb - 505kg
PRINCIPAL DRIVERS	Senna, Berger
IDENTIFYING COLOURS	Red/White

1992 FORMULA 1 McLAREN MP4/7

In 1991 Ayrton Senna had been quick to accuse Honda of falling behind in its engine development. The following year there was no doubt that it had, and with the Williams team threatening to raise expectations yet again with its new, computer-controlled 'active' suspension FW14B, and with its drivers Nigel Mansell and Riccardo Patrese still in the ascendancy, it was soon apparent that the Woking team was in the now unfamiliar position of playing catch-up.

The previous year Honda had spent many hundreds of man-hours developing and improving the RA121E in order to stay ahead of Renault. One of the unfortunate consequences of this was that work on its replacement – the MP4/7's new 75° V10 RA122E/B – was substantially delayed. As a result it hadn't even been bench-tested until December and when it did finally make it into a chassis it was clear that, like its predecessor, it was thirsty. Despite an estimated 740bhp this would prove a major handicap as rival V10s increased in sophistication.

At the same time, rumours continued that Honda would withdraw at the end of the season.

Given the delays, and because the MP4/6 had in the end delivered the results needed the previous year, the decision was taken to stick with that car for the opening three races of the new season. The feeling was that the extra time could be spent in the wind tunnel, further refining the aerodynamics of the MP4/7; also perhaps that while the new engine wasn't quite up to scratch it was at least going to be paired with a chassis which was technically one of the best on the grid.

However, Ron Dennis soon reversed that decision, claiming to have had, "*A gut feeling that we would have to aim for a race debut in Brazil a month earlier*". A gut feeling, that is, which followed McLaren's observation of the Williams team in action. In testing it had become clear that with its increasingly fast and reliable Renault engine, and active suspension, the FW14B was a highly dangerous rival. As Dennis said: "*Williams clearly had a reliable package from the outset, so in order to stand a chance of winning the World Championship we just had to get the new car up and running as fast as possible.*"

Doing it this way, however, cut the remaining development time by as much as a third, something which inevitably piled on the pressure. Dennis himself later acknowledged what this meant, noting that, "*Nobody outside [F1] can understand what that meant in terms of engineering, administrative and financial resources. What we had to do was breathtaking.*"

No doubt, particularly as the new car was to represent a completely new concept for McLaren. The MP4/7's CFC monocoque was to be constructed within a 'female' mould rather than around a 'male' one, which had been the practice at McLaren since the company first pioneered composite materials with the ground-breaking MP4/1 more than 10 years earlier.

As well as overturning a decade's experience with carbon composites, the car introduced another new, transverse six-speed semi-automatic gearbox that not only featured McLaren's own electro-hydraulic activation (devised in partnership with TAG) but also so-called fly-by-wire controls. Taken almost for granted these days, this aerospace practise replaced a conventional throttle cable with a system of electronic sensors. By monitoring and responding directly to a driver's pedal inputs, fly-by-wire was able to control engine speeds automatically, thereby removing the need for the driver to take his foot off the throttle whilst shifting up or down.

Despite the many and varied pressures on the team, three cars were readied in time for Interlagos, although the precaution was taken of freighting out three MP4/6s just in case. Once racing got underway, however, it was clear that there was still work to do. Senna complained of unpredictable handling going into fast corners. It was also felt that the new engine, despite sporting pneumatic valve actuation to facilitate higher revs, actually offered little if anything more than the old one had. At the same time it was to take until Monaco to sort out a flexing underbody section and for Honda to produce the power which had been promised. Unfortunately, by that time Williams had run away with four wins to McLaren's zero, so the pressure was intense.

Fortunately, Senna's commitment was still absolutely 100 per cent, and likewise McLaren's own when it came to ensuring that pre-race preparation was as good as it could be. Thus its star driver was able to win in Monaco, Hungary and Italy. Berger, who was to leave at the end of his third season with McLaren and return to Ferrari, took wins in Canada and in Australia, in what was to be his final drive for the team. Together with Senna's second placing in Germany this was sufficient to leave McLaren in the runner-up position in the Constructors' World Championship with 99 points. Senna finished fourth overall in the Drivers' on 50, one ahead of Berger.

For a lesser team, that would have been a good year; for McLaren, however, after such an historically long run of spectacular victories, it was a bitter disappointment.

In December 1992, new team driver Michael Andretti tested the Honda-powered McLaren MP4/7 at Paul Ricard. It was the last time a McLaren would officially run with Honda power.

The MP4/7 featured McLaren's own hydraulically operated semi-automatic gearbox, controlled by activators on the steering wheel. It also featured fly-by-wire throttle control.

Whilst the previous year's MP4/6 soldiered on into 1992, the new MP4/7 spent extra hours in the wind tunnel and finally made its debut at the third round of the championship in Brazil. Attention to aerodynamic detail was evident in the complex multi-component rear wing.

Marlboro

COURTAULDS
1
Senna
BOSS
Marlboro
POWERED by
HONDA
Marlboro
COURTAULDS
Shell
GOODYEAR
EAGLE
GOODYEAR
EAGLE
GOODYEAR

Opposite
With second qualifying for the British Grand Prix at Silverstone in July being held in the wet, Gerhard Berger had no chance to improve on his fifth position from the previous day's session.

MP4/7 FORMULA 1
SPECIFICATION

MODEL	McLaren MP4/7
TYPE/FORMULA	Formula 1
YEAR OF PRODUCTION	1992
DESIGNER	Neil Oatley
EXAMPLES BUILT	10
ENGINE	Honda RA122E/B V12
CUBIC CAPACITY	3493cc
ELECTRONICS	Honda PGM injection/ignition
POWER OUTPUT	740bhp

TRANSMISSION	McLaren semi-auto transverse 6-speed
CHASSIS	High modulus carbon fibre/honeycomb monocoque
BODY	Carbon fibre single piece cockpit/engine cover & nose
FRONT SUSPENSION	Double wishbone, push-rod operating
	longitudinal inboard coil spring/damper
REAR SUSPENSION	Double wishbone, push-rod operating
	longitudinal inboard coil spring/damper
BRAKES F/R	Outboard Brembo/Carbone Industrie
WHEELS DIAMETER x WIDTH F/R	13x12/13x16.3in

TYRES F/R	Goodyear
LENGTH	177in - 4496mm
WIDTH	83.5in - 2120mm
HEIGHT	39in - 990mm
WHEELBASE	117in - 2972mm
TRACK F/R	71.8/65.75in - 1824/1669mm
WEIGHT	1115lb - 506kg
PRINCIPAL DRIVERS	Senna, Berger
IDENTIFYING COLOURS	Red/White

1993 FORMULA 1 McLAREN MP4/8

With Honda leaving F1, McLaren did not announce its new engine supplier until November 1992, and when the name was eventually revealed it was Ford. The return to Cosworth power, for the first time since 1983, it was disclosed, would be via a team-financed development of Ford's HB powerplant.

This was a light and economical 3.5-litre V8 and by no means a bad engine, but there was no escaping the fact that, whereas McLaren had previously been able to call upon bespoke power units from the likes of TAG Porsche and Honda, its new hi-tech MP4/8 would have to rely on a proprietary unit. One, moreover, which would be one specification behind that used by Benetton in its B193 because Ford already had a supply contract with them.

Ron Dennis had tried very hard to secure a deal with Renault, and even considered buying Ligier in order to obtain its Renault engines. McLaren would naturally have wanted to use Shell fuel and lubricants, and ultimately this proved a stumbling block with Renault's sponsor, Elf. There was thus no alternative but to invest an estimated £6 million in developing the HB.

Design work on the new MP4/8 thus started without a clear idea of which engine would be used, although McLaren's computer-aided design capabilities would at least enable the design team to make up for lost time.

Featuring a battery of advanced new technologies, the car was the company's most sophisticated design yet with new electronic engine management software, chassis control, data acquisition and telemetry systems. Designed and manufactured by McLaren Group subsidiary TAG Electronic Systems exclusively for McLaren, these systems were accompanied by a new, lightweight electronic control panel in the cockpit. Fitted into a new, improved chassis, the fuel-efficient Ford HB engine gave McLaren cause to be optimistic. It was hoped that whatever the car lacked in outright horsepower it would make up for with even better preparation and engineering, clever race strategies, a superb chassis and electronics from TAG. The new car was also to feature an even more advanced active suspension set-up and traction control.

And Ayrton Senna would drive it. Or would he? At times that seemed uncertain. For a while he appeared to be running on a race-by-race basis as he and Dennis negotiated over his financial demands with sponsors. Nevertheless, the season yielded five wins at a time when Williams Renault was the dominant force, compared to a singleton success for Benetton with the latest-spec engine. McLaren's tally in 1993 was all the more remarkable because, while Senna returned after a winter spent relaxing at home in Brazil, various rule changes meant that when Michael Andretti joined the team from the US he was effectively denied adequate time to familiarise himself with the circuits. As a consequence, having shown good speed when previously testing in the MP4/7 he failed to make his mark with the MP4/8 because of the lack of 'seat time' and was eventually replaced by one of the sport's coming-men, fresh from Lotus, Mika Häkkinen.

Senna really liked the MP4/8, particularly after testing at Silverstone where he ran his quickest laps there almost first time out. He proved his value to the team in the very first race at Kyalami by coming a close second to Prost's Williams despite suffering an active suspension problem. He quickly followed that with wins at home in Interlagos and in one of the greatest Grand Prix drives of all time in the wet at Donington Park. Andretti, meanwhile, crashed in all three events.

Despite a strong drive in France and a podium spot with third place at Monza, the American, the son of 1978 World Champion Mario Andretti, was unable to recapture the magic he showed in Indycar racing and after the Italian race Häkkinen stepped up from test driver to team driver.

Senna, meanwhile, continued to impress, taking a record sixth win at Monaco despite a massive shunt at Ste Devote corner during practice. Nobody who watched him in action doubted the Brazilian's commitment, even though the MP4/8 let him down in Imola, Montreal, Estoril and the Hungaroring. Worst of all was at Silverstone, when the team used Ford's new Series VIII engine for the first time, only for yet another fuel-reading glitch to leave him stranded on the very last lap for the third year in a row. Nevertheless, his season ended on an upswing.

At Suzuka, and then again at Adelaide, Senna succeeded in pulling off superb victories. The Australian success, it transpired, would be his last and at the time enabled McLaren to declare itself the most successful Grand Prix team of all time.

Senna trailed that year's champion, Alain Prost, by 23 points, but had humbled him on more than one occasion, most notably at Donington, in what was seen to be a less powerful car. Long before Adelaide, where emotions in the team ran high, he had announced that he would be leaving McLaren after six seasons and three World Championships, to join Williams. The team, meanwhile, went towards an uncertain future testing a Lamborghini V12-engined MP4/8B before inking a supply deal with Peugeot for the coming season.

The MP4/8 featured new electronic engine management software, chassis control and telemetry systems. All this could be monitored from the ultra lightweight cockpit mounted electronic control panel.

This squashed hedgehog appeared on the side of the MP4/8 was the McLaren team's response to the Sega hedgehog stickers that were put on the Williams cars to signify each Grand Prix victory by the Grove based team. McLaren added a sticker every time it beat Williams on track.

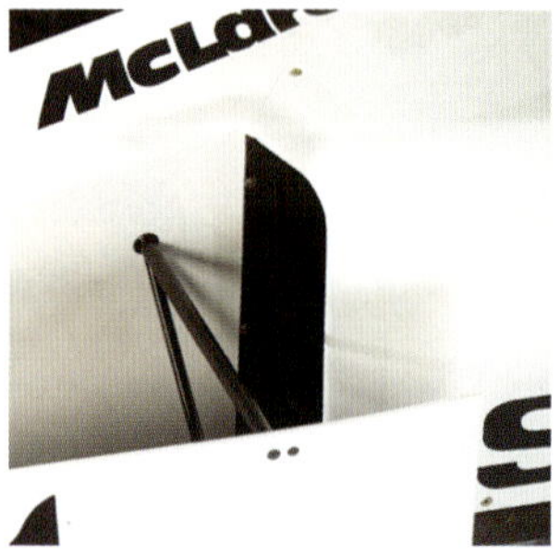

MP4/8 was the first McLaren chassis to use barge boards behind the front suspension. These helped manage the airflow around the sides of the monocoque and into the radiators.

McLaren
Shell
COURTAULDS
Power by Ford
BOSS
GOODYEAR
EAGLE
K mart
8

1993 FORMULA 1
McLAREN MP4/8

CONTINUED

In one of the most sensational opening laps in history Senna started the rain-soaked European GP at Donington Park fourth on the grid, dropped to fifth and then passed four cars to lead at the end of the lap. He lapped everyone up to second place and won the race by over 30 seconds.

At Donington Michael Andretti had another bad day. For the third race in a row he was eliminated after getting involved in an accident with another car, this time on the first lap.

By the Portuguese Grand Prix Mika Häkkinen had replaced Andretti. In his first GP for McLaren, Mika qualified an incredible third, ahead of Senna and ran in the top 4 until he crashed out on lap 33.

MP4/8 FORMULA 1

SPECIFICATION

MODEL	McLaren MP4/8
TYPE/FORMULA	Formula 1
YEAR OF PRODUCTION	1993
DESIGNER	Neil Oatley
EXAMPLES BUILT	8
ENGINE	Ford Cosworth HBE V8
CUBIC CAPACITY	3494cc
ELECTRONICS	TAG 2.12F ignition/injection
POWER OUTPUT	640bhp

TRANSMISSION	McLaren semi-auto transverse 6-speed
CHASSIS	High modulus carbon fibre/honeycomb monocoque
BODY	Carbon fibre single piece cockpit/engine cover & nose
FRONT SUSPENSION	Double wishbone, push-rod operating
	longitudinal inboard coil spring/damper
REAR SUSPENSION	Double wishbone, push-rod operating
	longitudinal inboard coil spring/damper
BRAKES F/R	Outboard Brembo/KH/Carbone Industrie
WHEELS DIAMETER x WIDTH F/R	13x11.5/13x13.8in

TYRES F/R	Goodyear
LENGTH	174in - 4420mm
WIDTH	78.8in - 2000mm
HEIGHT	39in - 990mm
WHEELBASE	114.25in - 2902mm
TRACK F/R	64/63.25in - 1626/1607mm
WEIGHT	1113lb - 505kg
PRINCIPAL DRIVERS	Senna, Andretti, Häkkinen
IDENTIFYING COLOURS	Red/White

1993 FORMULA 1 TEST CAR
McLAREN MP4/8B

Another test mule that was developed for a potential engine partner, the McLaren MP4/8B was adapted from the Ford HB V8-engined MP4/8 in order to assess the Chrysler-Lamborghini V12 in the autumn of 1993.

Once again the new engine, an 80° unit codenamed 3512, required both the wheelbase and bodywork of the original car to be stretched, the former by an additional 3.75 inches. The significantly longer engine also called for new mountings on the back of the monocoque and the front of the gearbox to be modified to mate with it. The latter was the standard transverse six-speeder with semi-automatic actuation, and the suspension was similarly unchanged from the regular season MP4/8 donor car with longitudinally mounted inboard spring/damper units operated by pushrods front and rear. Other changes included new McLaren Calsonic water and oil-cooling systems and a revised fuel cell. One familiar area was the Chrysler Lamborghini engine's TAG 2.12F injection system.

A top secret initial shakedown test of the car in this form was undertaken on the short South Circuit at far end of the Silverstone complex, on September 20th, after which the team travelled to South Wales for a couple more days of undercover testing at Pembrey, once again with Senna behind the wheel.

Immediately after the Portuguese Grand Prix the MP4/8B was shipped to the Estoril circuit in early October for a full week of F1 testing with all the other teams who had stayed on after the race. The car now had a modified engine with a power curve that had been revised at Senna's suggestion, and once again he drove. Mika Häkkinen also had a run. However, although Senna was very quick and set a best lap time of 1m 13.232s compared to Alain Prost's quickest time of the week for Ferrari of 1m 13.000s, and was reportedly 1.4s faster round Silverstone than he had been in the Ford HB-engined MP4/8, the MP4/8B project stalled.

The reason had everything to do with politics rather than with engineering. It was clear that the Ford deal offered little for the future, and there was disappointment that a proposed Ford V12 had been shelved. The Chrysler Lamborghini deal seemed promising, especially as Chrysler appeared keen to make a significant investment in it. But according to Technical Director Neil Oatley: "*We were only supplied with two Lamborghini engines for the initial development work, and since these came from its pool of engines that were also going to the Larrousse team, we really felt that Peugeot would be much more committed to working with us to develop a potential race-winning engine. To be honest, the Lamborghini engine was quite old technology, having been used by Lotus as far back as 1990, and we really couldn't see much of a future in working with them.*"

Chrysler had a completely different interpretation of the discussions and believed a deal had been agreed, and was livid when it fell apart as Ron Dennis inked supply terms instead with Peugeot. Lamborghini aspired to continue supplying the Larrousse team into 1994, but when the McLaren deal faltered, Chrysler withdrew from the sport and sold Lamborghini. Its brief sojourn as an F1 engine supplier was over.

The McLaren MP4/8B remains one of the sport's great what-might-have-been cars, and its story differs according to the teller. Fate, or perhaps Peugeot, intervened, and in the end only one chassis was ever built and tested. The car was never liveried in the familiar red and white Marlboro scheme, and remains in the McLaren collection in its virgin state. Its plain white bodywork carries nothing more than Goodyear logos on the front wing endpates and, complete with its V12 'Chrysler' engine, it provides an interesting insight into how a modern F1 car looks without the myriad sponsorship decals the world has become so used to since the late 1960s.

The MP4-8B was a special version of the 1993 race car built to accept the V12 Chrysler Lamborghini engine in place of the Ford V8 that the team used in 1993. With the engine mounting architecture modified to suit the longer motor the wheelbase was increased by 3.75 inches.

The bodywork was revised to suit the longer wheelbase. Bespoke water and oil cooling systems as well as a modified fuel cell were designed to suit engine. All the suspension, however, was standard MP4/8A specification.

MP4/8B FORMULA 1 TEST CAR

SPECIFICATION

MODEL	McLaren MP4/8B
TYPE/FORMULA	Formula 1 Test Car
YEAR OF PRODUCTION	1993
DESIGNER	Neil Oatley
EXAMPLES BUILT	1 (converted from MP4/8)
ENGINE	Chrysler Lamborghini V12
CUBIC CAPACITY	3498cc
ELECTRONICS	TAG 2.12F ignition/injection
POWER OUTPUT	670bhp

TRANSMISSION	McLaren semi-auto transverse 6-speed
CHASSIS	High modulus carbon fibre/honeycomb monocoque
BODY	Carbon fibre single piece cockpit/engine cover & nose
FRONT SUSPENSION	Double wishbone, push-rod operating longitudinal inboard coil spring/damper
REAR SUSPENSION	Double wishbone, push-rod operating longitudinal inboard coil spring/damper
BRAKES F/R	Outboard Brembo/KH/Carbone Industrie
WHEELS DIAMETER x WIDTH F/R	13x11.5/13x13.8in

TYRES F/R	Goodyear
LENGTH	177in - 4496mm
WIDTH	78.8in - 2000mm
HEIGHT	39in - 990mm
WHEELBASE	118in - 2997mm
TRACK F/R	66/63in - 1676/1600mm
WEIGHT	1113lb - 505kg
PRINCIPAL DRIVERS	Senna, Häkkinen
IDENTIFYING COLOURS	White

1993 ROADCAR McLAREN F1

On March 31st, 1998, at Germany's Ehra-Lessien Proving Ground, the McLaren F1 comprehensively beat the world speed record for production cars. Sportscar racer Andy Wallace drove a standard five-year-old factory car known as 'XP5' to an official, independently verified speed of 240.1mph on the 21-kilometre track. However, the story of the McLaren F1 had actually begun almost a decade before it went into the record books as the 'Fastest Production Car' in the world.

To trace its origins one must travel back to the 1988 Italian Grand Prix, a race now chiefly remembered as the only one all season which the McLaren MP4/4s of Ayrton Senna and Alain Prost failed to win.

Hours later, while waiting for a flight out of Linate, Ron Dennis and Gordon Murray were discussing the possibility of the company designing and building a no-holds-barred McLaren roadcar. At the time it seemed everyone was racing towards a street legal 200mph: Jaguar unveiled its XJ220; Yamaha wheeled out its quite extraordinary tandem-seat OX99-11; Bugatti surfaced again, this time in Italy, and then there was a legion of strangely named newcomers, such as the 16-cylinder Cizeta-Moroder and the MCA Centenaire.

The McLaren, however, was to outdo them all, not just in terms of its outright speed and highly polished performance, but also in the numbers produced, the time spent in production, the design concept, the quality of the engineering and above all its sheer élan. It was, as Motor Sport reminded its readers some months before that record-breaking run at Ehra-Lessien: "*A car created using the best brains and the greatest technological resources.*"

The simple truth, said the magazine, is that compared to every one of its rivals the McLaren F1, "*Is an immeasurably greater car… great not because of the undoubted extravagance of its design but because of its sheer sense.*" Even more than this, the editor noted, "*It is not simply the fastest mid-engined supercar ever built, but the most practical.*"

Murray was later to insist that its phenomenal speed was not the point of the car, "*just a consequence of the other things it does*". Even so, with such a blisteringly high top end, and with Autocar demonstrating in the F1's first full road test that it was quicker to 150mph than an ordinary sportscar was to 60, it was inevitable that the car would be noted first and foremost for its performance. After that came the price, a jaw-dropping £634,500 in the UK. The gold-lined engine bay and remote diagnostics also served occasionally to blind observers to the car's many other genuinely outstanding qualities.

Its trademark three-abreast seating layout, for example, was Murray's idea. Initially, Dennis had favoured an even more focused single-seater, but the South African had been thinking about his mid-seat supercar for many years, even doodling ideas for it as early as 1969. Murray also admitted to a number of supercar influences such as the Lamborghini Miura, and show cars such as the Bertone Caribou, as well as one of his all time favourites, the Lotus Elan. "*I like small cars and light cars,*" he told journalist Mick Walsh a decade after the car's launch. "*I like everything that Colin Chapman liked. [The Elan] was incredibly well packaged, and packaging is everything.*"

Perhaps, surprisingly, given that work on the F1 didn't finally get underway for another two decades, the car was drawn entirely by hand, with no computer-aided design whatsoever. Responsibility for the exterior and interior fell to the highly regarded ex-Lotus stylist Peter Stevens who worked from the inside out, waiting until the seating buck was made before starting, "*As I didn't want to create a style we'd fall in love with that would dictate the design.*"

It was, by any reckoning, a tight-lipped design team, and in the highly competitive world of supercars, where secrets are commonplace, details of this new road-going McLaren remained one of the very best of the best-kept secrets. For three years or more everyone with an interest knew something was going on; before getting the call Stevens recalls seeing a piece in Autosport prompting him to assume the team was already sewn up, but absolutely nobody outside the factory knew quite what to expect. The company would presumably be seeking to capitalise on its formidable Grand Prix record but hopes were high that McLaren wouldn't simply try to cash in on its stellar name with 'just another' supercar.

At the car's launch party in Monte Carlo in May 1993, Murray was at pains to underline that it hadn't done this. "*It's not just a case of going one step beyond,*" he said, speaking prior to the Grand Prix, "*this is an entirely new starting point for supercars.*" It certainly was. Not because it was very fast, although it had a higher top speed than the Formula 1 cars, but, rather, because from stem to stern the 1138kg car showcased numerous new and exciting technical innovations.

XP5 was the fifth and final prototype chassis built up by the development team before it started work on the first of the production cars. After a hard life of testing and promotional tours all over the world, XP5 now lives in semi-retirement on the Boulevard at MTC.

At the heart of the McLaren F1 is the made-to-order, 6.1-litre 48-valve BMW V12 engine. With an output in excess of 600bhp it produces one of the highest specific outputs for a large capacity naturally aspirated unit in production sportscar history.

K8 MCL

K8 MCL

XP5

1993 ROADCAR McLAREN F1

CONTINUED

Besides having the highest power-to-weight ratio of any previous production car, it was to be the first in the world to feature a complete carbon fibre composite monocoque and active aerodynamics to maintain a constant centre of pressure under hard braking. Taut-looking, tight and functional, it was also by supercar standards commendably light and small, and rather subtle in appearance. Murray's ground-breaking layout, with the seats staggered to give the centrally located driver elbow room, luggage in the flanks and fuel tank behind the driver, sounds and even looks quite simple, but has been recognised for what it is: a design of true genius.

Stevens later claimed that the car more or less designed itself around Murray's idea, and that only the details took time, but when one is seeking perfection it is precisely those small details which make the difference. There were no big wings or fins, nor ugly pop-up headlamps; the handbrake handle was wood to prevent it getting too hot; the accelerator pedal titanium.

In the deliberate absence of a radio, the 10-disc CD player was conceived by the Formula 1 team's sponsor Kenwood to be the smallest and lightest ever, while all essential cooling and ventilation ducts were neatly hidden or cleverly incorporated into the F1's singular but quietly dramatic shape. Customer cars were even fitted with modem sockets, each one neatly concealed behind caps bearing the F1 logo, so that the factory could download the engine diagnostics from a car anywhere in the world.

Similarly the BMW Motorsport engine was unsurpassingly state-of-the-art. With 6.1 litres, 48 valves, a quartet of catalytic converters and developing 627 horsepower at 7,000rpm and 443lb of torque, it was almost as powerful as the famed Can-Am McLarens of yore but infinitely more driveable, and continued to redefine the supercar. With a dozen individual coils providing direct ignition, chain-driven camshafts and constantly variable inlet valve timing, it proved to be superbly tractable, enabling a driver to rocket from 30mph to 225mph+ in the highest of its six gears.

It was little surprise that it wasn't just the press that was queuing up to praise the car: the experts loved it too. Le Mans winner Derek Bell admired its reserved appearance, particularly the fact, "*That it isn't covered in spoilers or other add-ons and there's nothing on it that shouldn't be there. It isn't a case of style for style's sake, which is refreshing.*" Bell also found the car outstanding to drive, "*something with straight honest power – no turbos or anything, it really is astounding. There's no hesitation on take-off, just instant and seemingly never-ending acceleration and the sound of the BMW V12 behind you is incredible.*" The brakes too were singled out for comment, the F1's Brembo four-pot monobloc calipers making their presence felt on huge ventilated discs.

Many of those who drove the car in the early days also commented on how usable it was, and how easy to drive compared to many of its more conventional, more hardcore rivals. While ferociously fast at the limit, and capable of delivering pulverising levels of power when asked to, around town the car still showed itself to be amazingly docile.

Inevitably it was hailed as a classic from the moment the covers came off in Monaco, something which more than justified another part of Murray's original brief, namely that "*If one of these cars were to be discovered in a barn in 60 years time it could be restored.*" Among other things that meant no irreplaceable injection plastic mouldings, hence a decision to fabricate the instrument panel (as it happens, Murray's favourite feature) with stainless steel dials, hand-painted with etched numbers, and with each needle individually machined. In a project with no compromise, nothing was left unconsidered or to chance.

The F1 remains even now a unique and truly remarkable machine. Stationary or moving it looks as good today as it did at its launch, its iconic style having never even begun to date. Prices now exceed the original cost of the car, which, if one can be forgiven for the vulgarity of mentioning the money, is perhaps the definitive measure of a car's worth in the connected worlds of driving passion and automotive art. Most importantly, though, the McLaren F1 has not been surpassed, not in its combination of performance, practicality and breadth of ability, and certainly not when one calibrates the absolute clarity of its conception and the overwhelming intelligence of its design and execution.

The official brochure produced for the launch of the F1 at the Monaco Sporting Club on the 28th May 1992 simply stated: "*The F1 will confirm McLaren Cars' entirely new standards of build quality and technological innovation for high-performance road cars.*"

Even the grip shape of the specially made Nardi F1 steering wheel involved many hours of research, design and development. A minimal Formula 1 style dash panel created in carbon composite carried specially made analogue instrumentation.

The intricately crafted right-hand manual gearchange was situated in the carbon chassis rail that runs alongside the driver. This panel also housed the ignition switch, starter button and air conditioning controls, as well as the electric window switch and right-hand mirror control.

F1 ROADCAR
SPECIFICATION

MODEL	McLaren F1
TYPE/FORMULA	Roadcar
YEAR OF PRODUCTION	1993-1998
DESIGNER	Gordon Murray/Peter Stevens
EXAMPLES BUILT	64
ENGINE	BMW V12
CUBIC CAPACITY	6064cc
INDUCTION	TAG 3.12 ignition/injection
POWER OUTPUT	627bhp

TRANSMISSION	Transverse 6-speed, limited slip differential
CHASSIS	Carbon fibre reinforced composite monocoque
BODY	Carbon fibre composite panels
FRONT SUSPENSION	Double wishbones, Ground Plane Shear centre sub-frame light alloy damper/co-axial coil spring, anti-roll bar
REAR SUSPENSION	Double wishbones, Inclined Axis Shear mounting, light alloy damper/co-axial coil spring, toe-in/toe-out control links
BRAKES F/R	Outboard 13/12in ventilated discs
WHEELS DIAMETER x WIDTH F/R	17x9/17x11.5in

TYRES F/R	Goodyear F1, Michelin SX-MXX3
LENGTH	169in - 4292mm
WIDTH	71.6in - 1820mm
HEIGHT	44.8in - 1140mm
WHEELBASE	107in - 2718mm
TRACK F/R	61.7/58in - 1568/1472mm
WEIGHT	2502lb - 1140kg
PRINCIPAL DRIVERS	n/a
IDENTIFYING COLOURS	n/a

1994 FORMULA 1 McLAREN MP4/9

The arrival of aggressive entrepreneur Bob Eaton at Lamborghini's US parent Chrysler might have made an Italian engine deal with McLaren look more likely: years earlier, when head of General Motors Europe, he had pushed hard to create an Opel F1 engine. In the end, though, Ron Dennis went with Peugeot, tying up the supply deal with remarkable speed given that the French company had only recently started work on its own 72° V10 Formula 1 powerplant with the help of ex-Renault engineer Jean-Pierre Boudy.

Dennis was under no illusions that McLaren and Peugeot faced a very difficult task. *"It will,"* he said, "*take time to equal or surpass the level of Renault performance, but I have a very positive view of the season. Aided by the superior performance we anticipate from Peugeot I am quite certain [the MP4/9] will be competitive and will win races in 1994.*"

The car was, nevertheless, insufficient to tempt Alain Prost out of retirement, although he did test it; so the team recruited Briton Martin Brundle to drive alongside Mika Häkkinen. Peugeot-connected Frenchmen Philippe Alliot and Yannick Dalmas handling the testing. The former did get a McLaren race drive that year, standing in for Häkkinen in Hungary when the latter was given a one-race suspension following an incident in Germany.

When the new McLaren-Peugeot was unveiled at Woking on January 20th 1994, it was clear that it had much in common with the Ford-engined MP4/8 although there were numerous subtle aerodynamic changes to the floor and sidepods to take account of the new five-valve Peugeot A4 engine. In truth, the final configuration was not readily determined, and not just because Peugeot switched to the four-valve A6 before the season started. Significantly, as neither engine had actually been run by the time Neil Oatley's MP4/9 was coming off the drawing board, much of the data the McLaren team used to design the cooling system had to be derived from its previous experience, and from Peugeot's with its 905 Le Mans sportscar.

Other modifications included a clutch activated by steering column paddle controls, the resulting two-pedal car being very much to Häkkinen's liking since it meant he could left-foot brake very late into corners without compromising the car's aerodynamic balance as one would during the momentary delay between coming off the throttle and applying the brakes in a conventional car.

At this time the McLaren six-speed gearbox also had a fully automatic downchange facility, although this was later outlawed by a regulation change. Power steering made its debut on the car too, and proved useful on some of the tighter circuits. McLaren's partner company TAG Electronics worked closely with Peugeot to refine its sophisticated onboard ignition/injection/data acquisition system. Providing a literally continuous flow of engine, chassis and performance data, this sort of telemetry was revolutionising the sport by giving race engineers in the pits continuous access to a mass of real-time data.

Peugeot Sport, under the management of former F1 racer and turbo pioneer Jean-Pierre Jabouille, was to show steady progress with its engineering, adding an extra 20bhp for the Imola race, and finding another 500rpm and thus another 15bhp by the time the Version 2 engine was ready for the French GP. Achieving this with revised camshafts, it then developed a somewhat confusingly named 'Version 2 Mark 2' with an additional 15bhp in time for Hungary, and a 'Version 2 Mark 3' for Jerez which gave the drivers another 10bhp.

Throughout this period changes were made to the car's cooling, particularly when at Barcelona the FIA changed the aerodynamic rules in the aftermath of the deaths of Roland Ratzenberger and Ayrton Senna at Imola. This helped a good deal as shorter diffusers produced less back pressure and significantly lowered the engine's operating temperatures. Much of the testing of the all-new engine had taken place in cooler weather and Peugeot's V10 had not really performed as everyone had hoped it would when it came to operating at higher temperatures.

Brundle in particular experienced many mechanical difficulties during the season, but the introduction of a new underbody profile and rear wing in mid-summer helped to improve the cars' handling in slow corners. Even so, no one expected 1994 to be a vintage year for McLaren, and in this they were not to be disappointed. Brundle found his strength to be in race lap times rather than qualifying, and his best result of the year was second at Monaco. Häkkinen proved quick in both qualifying and the races themselves, and certainly hit the spot with the boss. Dennis firmly believed in the Finn and declared: "*He has what it takes to become a World Champion.*"

Senna's departure had clearly weakened the team, and at times it seemed that little progress had been made in a transitional year. With two races still to be run it came as little surprise when an announcement was made that the two parties had decided to dissolve their partnership. Dennis had agreed a deal with Daimler that would create perhaps the most outstanding racing partnership of the modern era.

New team leader Mika Häkkinen had a string of podium finishes in 1994. His best result of the season was a second in the Belgian Grand Prix (top) at Spa. Two weeks later he was third (above) in the Italian Grand Prix at Monza.

For the 1994 season the team used the newly developed Peugeot V10 engine based on the one which the French manufacturer had used in its own sportscar during 1993. During the course of the 1994 season the engine ran in both 5-valve and pneumatic 4-valve configuration.

MP4/9 FORMULA 1
SPECIFICATION

MODEL	McLaren MP4/9
TYPE/FORMULA	Formula 1
YEAR OF PRODUCTION	1994
DESIGNER	Neil Oatley
EXAMPLES BUILT	8
ENGINE	Peugeot A4 F1, A6 F1 V10
CUBIC CAPACITY	3498cc
ELECTRONICS	TAG 2.12F ignition/injection
POWER OUTPUT	740bhp

TRANSMISSION	McLaren semi-auto transverse 6-speed
CHASSIS	High modulus carbon fibre/honeycomb monocoque
BODY	Carbon fibre single piece cockpit/engine cover & nose
FRONT SUSPENSION	Double wishbone, push-rod operating
	longitudinal inboard coil spring/damper
REAR SUSPENSION	Double wishbone, push-rod operating
	longitudinal inboard coil spring/damper
BRAKES F/R	Outboard Brembo/KH/Carbone Industrie
WHEELS DIAMETER x WIDTH F/R	13x11.75/13x13.7in

TYRES F/R	Goodyear
LENGTH	177in - 4496mm
WIDTH	77.5in - 1970mm
HEIGHT	39in - 990mm
WHEELBASE	117in - 2972mm
TRACK F/R	66.6/63in - 1692/1600mm
WEIGHT	1113lb - 505kg
PRINCIPAL DRIVERS	Häkkinen, Brundle, Alliot
IDENTIFYING COLOURS	Red/White

1995 RACECAR McLAREN F1 GTR

It was perhaps inevitable, given not just McLaren's whole raison d'etre but also Gordon Murray's professional background and expertise, that the F1 would eventually take to the race track, even though Ron Dennis had specifically denied such a possibility when the car was launched. Murray had no such plans either. He merely dreamed of building what was quickly and widely to become recognised as the 20th century's most exotic roadcar, and at the conclusion of a three-year design-and-build process he had achieved exactly that.

Before long, however, customers were asking for a racing version, and as the 1995 GT season drew nearer the number of requests began to climb. Leading them was racing driver Ray Bellm who, together with fellow F1 owner and German banker Dr Thomas Bscher, approached McLaren with an idea to race the cars in the BPR Karcher Global Endurance GT series. Initially McLaren was not taken with the idea, so Bellm went direct to Dennis, an old friend.

Thereafter an agreement was reached initially to develop a three-car customer racing programme, the third car being assigned to Lindsay Owen-Jones. The factory was not slow to respond; it couldn't afford to be with just a few months left before the start of the season.

The racing version of the F1 that went to Le Mans in June, the GTR, was only slightly modified from the standard roadgoing model. The regulations pegged its power below 600bhp, so the racecar was actually slightly less powerful. The GTRs also had to be fitted with steel rollcages, the steering rack ratios were quicker, and the rubber bushing in the suspension was removed. Development of downforce was limited to a single day in the wind tunnel under Murray's direction, whilst the OZ Racing wheels concealed even larger discs and calipers. Bellm loved the car. "*As a result of the changes it didn't load up in the same way [as the standard car] and you could really zip it around,*" he revealed.

The fact that the F1 GTR entered by Tokyo Ueno Clinic Team went on to win the famed endurance classic at the first attempt underlined the integrity of the original design. There was also a simple moral correctness to such a car being victorious at Le Mans: the F1 GTR was essentially a roadcar which is, after all, what Le Mans had originally been all about. Seven GTRs started, four others finishing third, fourth, fifth and 13th.

By any standards the 1995 race was an epic. The weather was appalling – it rained for 16 of the 24 hours – but the McLarens rose to the challenge, despite never having been raced before in the wet. A couple fell victim to that, one of them Bscher's Team Competition car that crashed out during the night. It had led earlier on, as had the other casualty, the Gulf-sponsored GTR driven by Owen-Jones and Pierre-Henri Raphanel.

Bellm recalled his worst moment: "*When the car got away from me through the Porsche curves and I slammed into the wall I thought, 'Oh Lord, this is it.'*" Instead he got back to the pits where repairs cost the team eight laps, enabling him to finish less than 30 minutes behind the winner. Once the car was fixed, he and co-drivers Maurizio Sandro Sala and Mark Blundell were able to make up an incredible 31 places to finish fourth.

Bellm expressed "*massive respect*" for the way eventual winner J.J. Lehto drove relentlessly all night through the weather. Even in the rain, in the Tokyo Ueno Clinic Team GTR he shared with Yannick Dalmas and Masanori Sekiya, the Finn was posting lap times up to 20 seconds faster than his rivals. After passing the lead car, the Harrods-liveried McLaren driven by Andy Wallace, Derek Bell and son Justin, Lehto was soon uncatchable and before long yet another McLaren-built machine had entered the racing record books.

Nor was it just that the La Sarthe classic that year was such a great race; it also represented several highly significant motorsport firsts. McLaren had won Le Mans at its first attempt. The F1 GTR had won the event in its first year of production, and not even Ferrari had managed that. It was also the first Le Mans win for a Finnish driver, and for a Japanese one, as well as being a first for BMW power.

As if that wasn't sufficient, the model also went on to win the 1995 Global GT Championship. The cars were not only fast, but consistent. The championship-winning car of Bscher and John Nielsen won only two races that year, but was nevertheless sufficiently reliable throughout the season to amass the necessary points.

The greatest supercar of its generation has been transformed into the most successful British sports racing car of modern times.

A Le Mans victory at its first attempt put the McLaren F1 into the record books. The Ueno Clinic car of Lehto, Dalmas and Sekiya (top) won the rain soaked race by a single-lap. Ray Bellm and Maurizio Sandro Sala (above) won the first two races of the 1995 BPR Karcher Global Endurance GT series but Nielsen/Bscher took the title.

Ray Bellm tries the first F1 GTR carbon-fibre chassis for size. The major sponsor of Bellm's GTC Motorsports team was Gulf Oil (Great Britain) and executives Danny Roden and Keith Oldham went to inspect progress on the project.

F1 GTR (1995) RACECAR

SPECIFICATION

MODEL	McLaren F1 GTR
TYPE/FORMULA	Racecar
YEAR OF PRODUCTION	1995
DESIGNER	Gordon Murray/Peter Stevens
EXAMPLES BUILT	9
ENGINE	BMW V12
CUBIC CAPACITY	6064cc
INDUCTION	TAG 3.12 ignition/injection
POWER OUTPUT	600bhp

TRANSMISSION	Aluminium case transverse 6-speed, lsd
CHASSIS	Carbon fibre reinforced composite monocoque
BODY	Carbon fibre composite panels
FRONT SUSPENSION	Double wishbones, light alloy damper/
	co-axial coil spring, anti-roll bar
REAR SUSPENSION	Double wishbones, light alloy
	damper/co-axial coil spring
BRAKES F/R	Outboard 15/14in ventilated carbon discs
WHEELS DIAMETER x WIDTH F/R	18x10.85/18x13in

TYRES F/R	Michelin
LENGTH	169in - 4292mm
WIDTH	71.6in - 1820mm
HEIGHT	44.8in - 1140mm
WHEELBASE	107in - 2718mm
TRACK F/R	61.3/58.6in - 1558/1488mm
WEIGHT	2315lb - 1050kg
PRINCIPAL DRIVERS	n/a
IDENTIFYING COLOURS	n/a

1995 FORMULA 1
McLAREN MP4/10

1995 marked another year of dramatic change at McLaren. Together with the introduction of the distinctive new MP4/10, the company was dealing with new drivers, a new engine supplier, in Mercedes-Benz, a key new technology sponsor in the Mobil Oil Corporation, a number of radical new ideas and more new regulations introduced by the sport's governing body.

The latter were an essential part of the FIA's safety drive and a desire to limit lap speeds following the tragic deaths the previous year of Roland Ratzenberger and Ayrton Senna at Imola. The package of measures included a return to the 3-litre formula which had held sway from 1966 until 1985. Only four-stroke engines were allowed, with no more than 12 cylinders, which effectively limited power to around 700bhp.

There were also strict limitations affecting other technologies, such as four-wheel drive and four-wheel steering, anti-lock brakes and electronic traction control mechanisms. Semi-automatic gearboxes were allowed, however, with a maximum of seven forward speeds. There were, inevitably, also restrictions on aerodynamics.

New regulations always kickstart engineers' creativity, so when McLaren unveiled its new car in the appropriate surroundings of London's Science Museum it was immediately obvious that it was quite unlike anything the company had produced before.

The most striking features of its unconventional design were a new high nose located well above the full-width front wing and a small 50cm wide winglet mounted directly over the engine cover. Conceived to develop even greater downforce, the latter relied on a loophole which McLaren had discovered in the rule book which permitted a car's body at this particular point to extend up to 25cm either side of the centre-line.

The high nose was designed to enhance airflow around the front of the car, enhancing the wing's efficiency and the effectiveness of the barge boards. Separating the nose from the front wing in this way also meant it could form a deformable structure that did not need to be freshly crash-tested each time a change was made to the wing itself.

Beneath the car too the aerodynamics had received special attention, as a new requirement for a longitudinal step in the underbody obliged teams to look at more ways to control the airflow from front to back.

Just as it had with Honda, McLaren worked very closely in a fully integrated programme with its new engine partner, Mercedes-Benz, which in turn was partnered with the small British company, Ilmor Engineering. This was based in Brixworth, Northamptonshire, and was run by its founders Mario Illien and Paul Morgan, two former Cosworth men. The new Mercedes-Benz FO 110D V10 was smaller than the outgoing Peugeot unit, and indeed some of the V8s, which greatly facilitated efficient packaging.

Mercedes-Benz and Ilmor conceived a completely new approach to engine architecture, in order to take advantage of the opportunities being offered by the new 50mm underbody step. It was clear that this arrangement would compromise the packaging of the engine, reducing the amount of space alongside it for ancillary equipment such as oil, water and hydraulic pumps. Ilmor thus proposed widening the vee angle to 75° so that the hydraulic pump could lie between the two banks of cylinders. Illien then created a new exhaust manifold which was essentially a tight spiral that left room beneath for the water and oil pumps.

Meanwhile, at McLaren, Neil Oatley really wanted to use a new longitudinal transmission, but lacking the time contented himself with another transverse six-speeder, a semi-automatic with a hand clutch mounted on the steering wheel paddles and bespoke electronic controls from TAG.

At this point pressure from sponsors brought in Nigel Mansell, at 41 clearly looking for a highly competitive car to mark his return to the sport, while Mika Häkkinen stayed with the team for the second full season of his initial three-year contract. Unfortunately, both drivers found the car too tight for comfort; indeed a completely new monocoque had to be built for the bulkier Mansell, requiring him to miss the first two races as Mark Blundell stood in while a wider version of the MP4/10B was created specifically for the 1992 World Champion.

The 1995 season saw the start of McLaren's relationship with Mercedes-Benz. The 3-litre Ilmor-built Mercedes-Benz FO 110D V10 engine was a smaller overall package than the previous year's engine and the MP4/10 chassis was smaller than ever.

McLaren

BOSS
McLaren
Mercedes-Be
TENCEL
Mobil
1
COURTAULDS
GOODYEAR
EAGLE
LOCTITE
ABAC
8

1995 FORMULA 1 McLAREN MP4/10

CONTINUED

Both Häkkinen and Blundell started reasonably well in Brazil and Argentina against strong opposition from Williams-Renault drivers Damon Hill and David Coulthard, and Benetton-Renault's Michael Schumacher. Nevertheless it was clear that the McLaren had a problem with front-end grip, and in Buenos Aires Häkkinen spun off with a puncture and Blundell succumbed to an oil leak from a cracked gearbox casing.

Thereafter, with Mansell back for the third race, in Imola, it became apparent that there were other problems too. Mansell complained about understeer in Barcelona, and although he qualified within half a second of his Finnish colleague, he was well off the pace by the time he slid off the road just before Schumacher threatened to lap him, and immediately parked the car in the McLaren garage. He had quit for good by Monaco, leaving his seat permanently to Blundell.

The younger Englishman was good for team morale, but the MP4/10B was still troubled. Things improved at Silverstone thanks to a new version of the Mercedes-Benz engine which had improved power, mid-range torque and driveability, and with this under his right foot Häkkinen set the fastest time during the race morning warm-up; at Hockenheim both drivers were running in the top six before their engines failed.

Much the same happened in Hungary, after which Mercedes-Benz worked hard to prepare fresh engines as McLaren went to work on its gearboxes and suspension readying the cars for a renewed assault at Spa. Unfortunately, Häkkinen spun there, but Blundell finished fifth before the team took second and fourth places at Monza following double retirements at Ferrari and Williams, and the early exit of Schumacher's Benetton.

The final iteration of the design, the MP4/10C, fared little better at Estoril, thanks to a series of minor problems with a new rear suspension arrangement, and at a very damp Nürburgring because of a decision to run slicks. Thereafter Häkkinen missed the Pacific GP following an appendix operation, but returned to finish a good second behind Schumacher at Suzuka. Unfortunately, Blundell crashed heavily there in the 130R corner during practice, but raced bravely to seventh place. Then in Adelaide came Häkkinen's narrow escape from death after a heavy crash in practice, caused by a puncture. He survived thanks to a trackside tracheotomy, and with renewed heart McLaren laid its plans for a stronger challenge in 1996.

Mika Häkkinen had a strong qualifying session for the second race of the season in Argentina and put his MP4/10 fifth on the grid. He retired on the first lap of the race when a heavy collision with Eddie Irvine's Jordan knocked off his left front wheel.

After Mansell had problems with the tight confines of the MP4/10 cockpit, in just 33 days the team designed and built a revised MP4/10B spec car with a wider cross-section around the dashboard area.

With major changes to the aerodynamic regulations for 1995 the team tried several rear end wing configurations. The high wing on top of the engine cover was used for the first four races of the season, but these side winglets were seen on the cars at most races.

In his first race for McLaren in Brazil, new recruit Mark Blundell scored a World Championship point for sixth place.

On lap 33 Mika Häkkinen retired from a strong third position in the German Grand Prix at Hockenheim with engine failure.

MP4/10 FORMULA 1
SPECIFICATION

MODEL	McLaren-Mercedes MP4/10
TYPE/FORMULA	Formula 1
YEAR OF PRODUCTION	1995
DESIGNER	Neil Oatley
EXAMPLES BUILT	5 + (6 MP4/10B)
ENGINE	Mercedes-Benz FO 110D V10
CUBIC CAPACITY	2997cc
ELECTRONICS	TAG 2.12F ignition/injection
POWER OUTPUT	680bhp

TRANSMISSION	McLaren semi-auto transverse 6-speed
CHASSIS	High modulus carbon fibre/honeycomb monocoque
BODY	Carbon fibre single piece cockpit/engine cover & nose
FRONT SUSPENSION	Double wishbone, push-rod & bellcrank
	operating longitudinal inboard coil spring/damper
REAR SUSPENSION	Double wishbone, push-rod & bellcrank
	operating longitudinal inboard coil spring/damper
BRAKES F/R	Outboard 11in AP Racing/Carbone Industrie
WHEELS DIAMETER x WIDTH F/R	13x11.7/13x13.75in

TYRES F/R	Goodyear
LENGTH	182in - 4625mm
WIDTH	78in - 1980mm
HEIGHT	39in - 990mm
WHEELBASE	115in - 2925mm
TRACK F/R	66.5/63.2in - 1690/1605mm
WEIGHT	1312lb - 595kg
PRINCIPAL DRIVERS	Häkkinen, Blundell, Mansell, Magnussen
IDENTIFYING COLOURS	Red/White

1996 ROADCAR
McLAREN F1 LM

The F1 GTR had secured its place in motorsport history by achieving a resounding victory on its Le Mans debut in what is still widely regarded as the world's greatest motor race. A week later the winning car was in action, still bearing the stains of its high-speed travel in France, at Lord March's Goodwood Festival of Speed. McLaren Cars took the decision to mark the historic occasion with a limited-edition commemorative model appropriately called the McLaren F1 LM.

'Limited Edition' really did mean precisely that, and despite the likely demand after the cars' stupendous performance at La Sarthe, just five production F1 LMs were made. There was one to commemorate each of the five McLaren finishers in the 1995 Grand Prix d'Endurance des 24 Heures du Mans, to give the race its full title. What's more, and in a warm and fitting salute to the company's late founder, three of the five were to be painted in McLaren papaya orange, the same, striking shade that had of course been used on many of Bruce McLaren's early Formula 1 and Can-Am race cars.

At the official launch of the car, Ron Dennis told the assembled press: "*It had been one of Bruce McLaren's dreams to produce the ultimate roadgoing sportscar. McLaren had achieved this initially with the standard production F1 model. Now in respect for Bruce's memory we finished the LMs – which really do provide a genuine racecar experience on the road – in the papaya orange colour which the team cars wore in Bruce's day. Our aim is always to produce excellence by design – the F1 LM simply underlines this commitment.*"

The concept of the F1 LM was to make as few changes as possible to a GTR racecar to enable its use on the public road. It was to run the most powerful engine of any F1 or F1-based derivative, roadcar or track star. All five were fitted with identical 1995 GTR-spec S 70/2 GTR LM engines and thanks to the absence of air restrictors – required on the track by FIA race regulations – this gave the LM a power output of 680bhp at 7,800rpm, and 703Nm of torque at just 4,500rpm. With a kerb weight of just 1,062kg the F1 LMs were also some 70kg lighter than the standard road-going cars, so they also boast the fastest in-gear acceleration of all the F1s; for example, 60 to 100mph in third gear took just three seconds, zero to 60mph could be reached in a fraction under three seconds and zero to 100mph inside a staggering seven seconds.

The car's racing heritage was much in evidence elsewhere too, for example, inside the cockpit where the driver was equipped with a carbon-fibre race seat while both passenger seats were moulded into the monocoque. The interior trim was kept to a minimum too, although all carbon materials in the cabin were painstakingly finished with several coats of high-gloss lacquer.

Outside, in addition to a full ground-effect underbody with diffuser, the cars featured special Le Mans front bodywork, 18in OZ magnesium alloy wheels – slightly wider than the standard car's nine and 11in rims at 10.85 and 13in respectively – and a distinctive carbon-fibre rear wing with a 'GTR-24 Heures du Mans Winners 1995' logo etched into the surface. Together with the bright orange finish and a discreet 'XP1 LM' logo on the sills, just ahead of the rear wheels, the completed cars were certainly unmistakable. As the rarest, most exclusive and most sought-after version of the McLaren F1 concept, they are almost certainly also the most valuable.

In the summer of 1999 at RAF Alconbury in Cambridgeshire, with McLaren's Ehra-Lessien driver Andy Wallace once more behind the wheel, the F1 LM set a new record for acceleration and braking. Travelling from zero to 100mph and back to zero in just 11.5seconds, the entire manoeuvre was completed in just 828ft of runway. Quite an achievement for a car which, as Gordon Murray himself was frequently at pains to point out, was never designed to break records.

Three of the five commemorative McLaren F1 LMs produced were painted papaya orange, the two others were black. All five featured GTR style body fittings and 18inch diameter road wheels compared to the production F1's 17inch wheels.

The distinctive carbon-fibre rear wing on the F1 LM carried a "GTR-24 Heures du Mans Winners 1995" logo, paying homage to the five cars that finished the 1995 Le Mans 24 hour race.

F1 LM ROADCAR
SPECIFICATION

MODEL	McLaren F1 LM
TYPE/FORMULA	Roadcar
YEAR OF PRODUCTION	1996
DESIGNER	Gordon Murray
EXAMPLES BUILT	5
ENGINE	BMW V12
CUBIC CAPACITY	6064cc
INDUCTION	TAG 3.12 ignition/injection
POWER OUTPUT	680bhp

TRANSMISSION	Transverse 6-speed racing unit, lsd
CHASSIS	Carbon fibre reinforced composite monocoque
BODY	Carbon fibre composite panels
FRONT SUSPENSION	Double wishbones, light alloy damper/
	co-axial coil spring, anti-roll bar
REAR SUSPENSION	Double wishbones, light alloy
	damper/co-axial coil spring
BRAKES F/R	Outboard 13/12in ventilated carbon discs
WHEELS DIAMETER x WIDTH F/R	18x10.85/18x13in

TYRES F/R	Michelin SX-MXX3
LENGTH	171.8in - 4365mm
WIDTH	71.6in - 1820mm
HEIGHT	44.1in - 1120mm
WHEELBASE	107in - 2718mm
TRACK F/R	61.8/57.6in - 1570/1464mm
WEIGHT	2341lb - 1062kg
PRINCIPAL DRIVERS	n/a
IDENTIFYING COLOURS	n/a

1996 FORMULA 1
McLAREN MP4/11A, MP4/11B & MP4/11C

After a year of reorganisation and change 1996 was to be a year of consolidation rather than victory, with McLaren substantially reworking its chassis and Mercedes-Benz doing likewise with the V10 engine. David Coulthard joined from the dominant Williams Renault team and, even with Mika Häkkinen clearly back on form after his Adelaide accident, it was a sobering thought that the third anniversary of McLaren's last win was imminent.

The work undertaken on the new car was considerable, the new MP4/11 sharing no more than 7.5 per cent of components with the MP4/10C and featuring a new Phase 3 Mercedes-Benz engine in which every single component had been renewed bar the oil pumps. This was part of Mercedes-Benz's stated aim to raise its power output by five per cent, with the compact 120kg unit now able to run up to 16,500rpm and offering much improved low-speed torque.

The engine completed its bench testing just seven days before the new car was up and running, but Häkkinen liked it immediately and despite slight concerns about the handling balance promptly posted his fastest-ever lap in testing at Estoril in 1m 19.65s.

Once more the car was produced under Neil Oatley's direction, with considerable input from Steve Nichols who had returned to the fold after a spell with Ferrari. He was involved closely with the design and function of the suspension geometry and configuration, and introduced carbon flexures in place of ball joints on the front suspension to reduce friction and to increase the car's overall stiffness.

While Henri Durand took care of the aerodynamics, Oatley concentrated more on the installation of the engine and transmission. The latter comprised the all-new McLaren-designed longitudinal six-speeder that he had wanted for the MP4/10. This featured semi-automatic changing courtesy of TAG Electronics, the same McLaren Group subsidiary having devised a more fully integrated engine and chassis control data acquisition package.

Initially neither driver was convinced by the MP4/11's handling, both Häkkinen and Coulthard expressing dissatisfaction with its behaviour on turn-in. With some input from quadruple World Champion Alain Prost, who had returned to work with McLaren as a technical consultant and development driver, work was soon underway to rectify this and improvements were made in time for the European GP at the Nürburgring, where Coulthard finished third.

Further refinements were introduced for the San Marino Grand Prix at Imola, and later still came some revisions to the front wing mounting points to correct a degree of flexing at the point where the wing attached to its hangers. The team also produced a special short-wheelbase car MP4/11B which made its debut in Monaco before being adopted as the new standard by Magny-Cours, as Mercedes-Benz continued work on the engine to improve its responsiveness.

For Belgium the car gained yet another refinement, this time a new front suspension. Rather more aerodynamic than before, this had been designed in line with another new interpretation of the technical regulations which had allowed Tyrrell to campaign streamlined wishbones.

The best result all year, however, was to be Coulthard's second place at Monaco, where Häkkinen wrote off MP4/11-5 after losing control during an acclimatisation run in teeming rain; prior to this he had been two seconds faster than the rest of the field.

Fortunately, the Finn bounced back and was soon overhauling his team-mate with no fewer than four third places in the British, Belgian, Italian and Japanese races. Coulthard had never really got to grips with the car, and admitted fighting "*to keep the rear end under control*".

As Coulthard discovered, the McLaren-Mercedes combination worked superbly on high-speed circuits such as Monza and Spa where less downforce was needed. Indeed, in Belgium he looked like he might win, before a spin on new tyres. Similarly at Monza the car had enabled a hard-driving Häkkinen to climb from 17th to third place after an unscheduled pit stop had left him way down the field.

Elsewhere, though, it performed less well, particularly on bumpy or uneven circuits where McLaren paid a price for placing what Ron Dennis called "*significant emphasis on reducing the car's pitch sensitivity.*" It succeeded on that point, but as a consequence the team "*experienced problems in the optimisation of the car at circuits which demand performance in a broad range of corners*". The upshot of all this was fourth place in the Constructors' World Championship, with 49 points.

For the upcoming 1997 season the F1 Technical Regulations were to be changed to considerably narrow the overall width of the car. As a development exercise for this, the team converted a pair of 1996 race cars to run with rather crude, metal, narrow track suspension, this car being known as the MP4/11C. During the autumn/winter of 1996 the car was tested by both Häkkinen and Coulthard.

A little bit of history came to an end as the season closed and Marlboro's sponsorship contract expired. Its relationship with McLaren spanned 23 years, at the time the longest such alliance in any sport.

By the Monaco Grand Prix in May the team was using the revised spec MP4/11B. While David Coulthard was on the podium in second place, Mika Häkkinen (above) could only manage sixth.

The small high rear wing, designed to fit into a loophole in the regulations, and which had first appeared on top of the engine cover in the early races of the 1995 season, made a reappearance on the MP4/11A.

The bargeboards first seen on MP4/8 were fitted tightly around the front suspension which featured new low-friction 'carbon-flexes' rather than the old style ball joints.

MP4/11A FORMULA 1

SPECIFICATION

MODEL	McLaren-Mercedes MP4/11A
TYPE/FORMULA	Formula 1
YEAR OF PRODUCTION	1996
DESIGNER	Neil Oatley
EXAMPLES BUILT	6
ENGINE	Mercedes-Benz FO 110E V10
CUBIC CAPACITY	2997cc
ELECTRONICS	TAG2000 ignition/injection
POWER OUTPUT	700bhp
TRANSMISSION	McLaren semi-auto longitudinal 6-speed
CHASSIS	High modulus carbon fibre/honeycomb monocoque
BODY	Carbon fibre single piece cockpit/engine cover & nose
FRONT SUSPENSION	Double wishbone, push-rod & bellcrank operating longitudinal inboard coil spring/damper
REAR SUSPENSION	Double wishbone, push-rod & bellcrank operating longitudinal inboard coil spring/damper
BRAKES F/R	Outboard 11in AP Racing/Carbone Industrie
WHEELS DIAMETER x WIDTH F/R	13x12/13x13.75in
TYRES F/R	Goodyear
LENGTH	179in - 4547mm
WIDTH	78.8in - 2000mm
HEIGHT	39in - 990mm
WHEELBASE	120in - 3050mm
TRACK F/R	66.7/63.5in - 1694/1612mm
WEIGHT	1320lb - 600kg
PRINCIPAL DRIVERS	Häkkinen, Coulthard
IDENTIFYING COLOURS	Red/White

Although it looked similar, the MP4/11 shared very little in the way of componentry with its predecessor. The new Phase 3 Mercedes-Benz FO 110E engine was a clean sheet approach.

MP4/11C FORMULA 1
SPECIFICATION

MODEL	McLaren-Mercedes MP4/11C
TYPE/FORMULA	Formula 1 Test Car
YEAR OF PRODUCTION	1996
DESIGNER	Neil Oatley
EXAMPLES BUILT	2 (from MP4/11A)
ENGINE	Mercedes-Benz FO 110E V10
CUBIC CAPACITY	2997cc
ELECTRONICS	TAG2000 ignition/injection
POWER OUTPUT	700bhp

TRANSMISSION	McLaren semi-auto longitudinal 6-speed
CHASSIS	High modulus carbon fibre/honeycomb monocoque
BODY	Carbon fibre single piece cockpit/engine cover & nose
FRONT SUSPENSION	Double wishbone, push-rod & bellcrank
	operating longitudinal inboard coil spring/damper
REAR SUSPENSION	Double wishbone, push-rod & bellcrank
	operating longitudinal inboard coil spring/damper
BRAKES F/R	Outboard 11in AP Racing/Carbone Industrie
WHEELS DIAMETER x WIDTH F/R	13x12/13x13.75in

TYRES F/R	Goodyear
LENGTH	179in - 4547mm
WIDTH	76in - 1930mm
HEIGHT	39in - 990mm
WHEELBASE	120in - 3050mm
TRACK F/R	64/60in - 1625/1524mm
WEIGHT	1320lb - 600kg
PRINCIPAL DRIVERS	Häkkinen, Coulthard
IDENTIFYING COLOURS	Red/White

1996 RACECAR McLAREN F1 GTR

In 1995 the factory had built just nine F1 GTRs, a figure it adhered to for the following season with two of the older cars (03R and 06R) being updated as the concept continued to develop to stay abreast of various new GT regulations. The car's first season in racing was in every sense going to be a hard one to beat. At the highest international level the genuine if undeniably exotic roadcar had succeeded in overhauling several purpose-built sportsracers.

McLaren nevertheless stepped up to the challenge, with a car which while clearly a very close relation of the previous GTR, was now slightly lower and had significantly improved aerodynamics which endowed it with superior levels of downforce. The cars nevertheless kept very close to the original Peter Stevens profile while shedding more weight, reaching 1012kg for the new 1000kg BPR GT Series regulations.

Ground clearance was reduced slightly, by 15 mm at the front. A more aggressive chin spoiler served to accentuate this nose-down attitude as well as increasing the length overall by 80mm. The modest aerodynamic revisions incorporated a smaller cooling duct cut into the front compartment lid while some of the body panels were modified slightly to make them more easily removable for pit work and other repairs.

The trusty 600bhp Type S70/3 GTR V12 remained largely unchanged but sat lower in the car and was now mated to an uprated gearbox housed in a new magnesium casing.

During 1996 the McLaren F1 GTRs notched up nine international BPR GT victories together with another five race wins in the prestigious All Japan Grand Touring Car Championship.

In the Far East Team Lark had purchased a brace of GTRs, planning to campaign them in the GT500 class of the All Japan GT Championship. The cars debuted at Suzuka, and scored another memorable McLaren 1-2 with Naoki Hattori and Ralf Schumacher at the wheel. Shortly afterwards, at Fuji, David Brabham and John Nielsen took another win.

At Sugo the Lark team badly damaged its own chassis, but was able to borrow another from GTC Competition for the final round. Eventually, with four outright wins to its credit, Team Lark went on to capture the GT500 Championship well ahead of the Toyota and Nissan works teams.

In Europe McLaren once again started the season well, with the GTC Competition team car chalking up the model's first BPR Championship win in the hands of Ray Bellm and James Weaver. McLarens won the first three races, and GTC Competition successfully took the Championship.

Le Mans was clearly the big one, its history and heritage more than making up for it not being an official part of any single race series. McLaren was naturally keen to defend its title, but the competition from the Le Mans Prototypes (LMP) class was far stiffer than it had been the previous year with Porsche's factory team very much in the ascendant. As a result, and despite fielding another seven F1 GTRs, McLaren was unable to repeat its win. However, the now legendary reliability meant that six of the seven GTRs finished the race, in fourth, fifth, sixth, eighth, ninth and 11th places.

After delivery was taken days before the first race of 1996 at Paul Ricard (top), there was simply no time to paint the Lindsay Owen-Jones/Raphanel F1 GTR. By the next race at Monza both the Gulf cars were in the familiar blue & orange colours. James Weaver (above) shared the car with Ray Bellm at every race that season.

As the Japanese GT500 Sportscar Championship progressed, the Team Lark cars were subjected to an ever-increasing weight penalty. By the end of the year the David Brabham/John Nielsen car (right) was forced to carry 40kg of ballast. Even so the team won four races that year and easily took the series.

F1 GTR (1996) RACECAR

SPECIFICATION

MODEL	McLaren F1 GTR
TYPE/FORMULA	Racecar
YEAR OF PRODUCTION	1996
DESIGNER	Gordon Murray
EXAMPLES BUILT	9
ENGINE	BMW V12
CUBIC CAPACITY	6064cc
INDUCTION	TAG 3.12 ignition/injection
POWER OUTPUT	600bhp

TRANSMISSION	Magnesium case transverse 6-speed, lsd
CHASSIS	Carbon fibre reinforced composite monocoque
BODY	Carbon fibre composite panels
FRONT SUSPENSION	Double wishbones, light alloy damper/
	co-axial coil spring, anti-roll bar
REAR SUSPENSION	Double wishbones, light alloy
	damper/co-axial coil spring
BRAKES F/R	Outboard 15/14in ventilated carbon discs
WHEELS DIAMETER x WIDTH F/R	18x10.85/18x13in

TYRES F/R	Michelin
LENGTH	172in - 4367mm
WIDTH	74.8in - 1900mm
HEIGHT	42.9in - 1090mm
WHEELBASE	107in - 2718mm
TRACK F/R	61.3/58.6in - 1558/1488mm
WEIGHT	2231lb - 1012kg
PRINCIPAL DRIVERS	n/a
IDENTIFYING COLOURS	n/a

1997 FORMULA 1 McLAREN MP4-12

A new era began for McLaren-Mercedes as the West tobacco brand came onboard as title sponsor in 1997, to replace Marlboro, and the other highly significant development later in the year was the arrival as Technical Director of Adrian Newey who joined from Williams-Renault at the start of August. A rather more subtle change was seen in the method of numbering the cars; whereas the generic nomenclature had previously been separated from the model number by a slash, now it was separated by a hyphen.

West's new race livery was initially kept under wraps, so that when the new MP4-12 made its debut at McLaren's Albert Drive factory in Woking on January 14th it was finished in McLaren's old trademark papaya orange, a neat touch. The new team colours of silver and black with red and white highlights were only shown later, at an official launch at London's Alexandra Palace complete with an all-star cast and live stage performances by the Spice Girls and Jamiroquai.

The fact that the first car was not completed until six o'clock on the morning of its launch – and was flown to Jerez for testing barely four hours after the event – gives some indication how comprehensively new this McLaren really was. It incorporated a number of technical innovations now required by new F1 regulations – including a rear crumple zone and collapsible steering column, reduced winglet area and suspension components of restricted depth-to-width ratio – and after every single component had been put under the microscope, 90 per cent of them were new or redesigned.

The MP4-12 was the result of many hours of research in the wind tunnel at the National Physical Laboratory in Teddington, Ron Dennis happily admitting to "*quantifiable gains*" here, although he was in little doubt that his rivals too would have made big advances in this area. But he felt that trying to evaluate such things was a waste of time: "*We just have to concentrate on developing the best car that we can.*"

This McLaren did, together with Mercedes-Benz which produced the FO 110E version of its V10 using an all-new, sand-cast aluminium alloy block whose design was determined by a range of different performance and installation parameters. Marginally heavier than before at 124kg, about the same as Ferrari's V10, it featured a new, lighter inlet system and a measurable hike in power. Significantly, though slightly wider than the old engine it was also 17mm lower, thereby reducing the car's centre of gravity. This in turn, with the reduced winglet area and rear crumple zone, required substantial aerodynamic work to be carried out on the rear end.

The car's preparation was immaculate, with Dennis declaring: "*Every component on the new car is better, and it is the sum of the total that will give us the performance we hope for. We have to play catch-up with Renault but we are closer than ever. If effort wins in motor racing, then we're going to win.*"

In pre-season testing his optimism seemed justified, and especially so when Coulthard won the first race of the season, in Australia, with Häkkinen finishing third. Though this was undoubtedly made slightly easier by the retirement of both Williams FW19s, the young Scot drove a cool race despite being under mounting pressure from Michael Schumacher's Ferrari. It was a fabulous result for the new West McLaren Mercedes team first time out.

Coulthard also won a superb race at Monza even though he was again concerned by the car's rear-end stability during much of the season. For his part Häkkinen, once again, seemed better able to adapt his driving style and was finally rewarded with a win at Jerez, his first in Formula 1, after Schumacher had controversially collided with the new World Champion, Jacques Villeneuve.

Elsewhere, McLaren's trademark resourcefulness demonstrated itself when it came to refuelling and pit strategies so that, at Buenos Aires, for example, where the car's harder compound tyres were not best suited, a one-stop strategy enabled Häkkinen to move from 17th to fifth place by the flag. Similar manoeuvring was on target to take the Finn to second place at Silverstone, where Coulthard was dogged by brake trouble, until his engine failed six laps from the end.

With a new F-spec version of the Mercedes-Benz engine, the cars were by this time enjoying a field-leading 740bhp at 16,000rpm, but even this proved insufficient to push McLaren's tally of wins for the season beyond three.

One of Adrian Newey's first moves when he joined as Technical Director in August was to introduce a revised front wing for the Austrian race to give the car improved front-end grip, as work continued on efforts to enhance its driveability with developments such as a sophisticated secondary braking system which (once ruled legal by the FIA) was mimicked in testing by some rival teams.

The results of these improvements were not overwhelming, but they were at least now making themselves felt even if nothing in 1997 could quite eclipse the latest Williams Renault. What mattered was that McLaren was once again establishing itself as a Grand Prix winner. With resources already being poured into the following year's effort, as the team directed much of its testing effort towards detailed preparation for the new era of narrow-track, grooved-tyre F1 cars, McLaren was very clearly back on track to become the pacesetter.

In the final race of the 1997 Formula 1 season, the European Grand Prix at Jerez, Mika Häkkinen took his maiden Grand Prix win and led David Coulthard home for a superb McLaren 1-2.

David Coulthard won two races in 1997. At the opening round of the season in Melbourne he scored McLaren's first win since Senna's victory in Adelaide at the end of 1993 and in September he drove chassis MP4-12-4, photographed here, to victory in the Italian GP at Monza.

The Ilmor-produced Mercedes-Benz FO 110E engine was wider and lower than the previous year's unit. Although it weighed slightly more, its lower centre of gravity and increased power helped the MP4-12 to three wins in 1997.

MP4-12 FORMULA 1

SPECIFICATION

MODEL	McLaren-Mercedes MP4-12
TYPE/FORMULA	Formula 1
YEAR OF PRODUCTION	1997
DESIGNER	Neil Oatley
EXAMPLES BUILT	7
ENGINE	Mercedes-Benz FO 110E, FO 110F V10
CUBIC CAPACITY	2997cc
ELECTRONICS	TAG2000 ignition/injection
POWER OUTPUT	720, 740bhp

TRANSMISSION	McLaren semi-auto longitudinal 6-speed
CHASSIS	McLaren moulded carbon fibre/honeycomb composite
BODY	Carbon fibre single piece cockpit/engine cover & nose
FRONT SUSPENSION	Double wishbone, push-rod operating
	longitudinal inboard coil spring/damper
REAR SUSPENSION	Double wishbone, push-rod operating
	longitudinal inboard coil spring/damper
BRAKES F/R	Outboard AP Racing/Hitco/Carbone Industrie
WHEELS DIAMETER x WIDTH F/R	13x11.75/13x13.7in

TYRES F/R	Goodyear
LENGTH	179in - 4546mm
WIDTH	78.8in - 2000mm
HEIGHT	38in - 965mm
WHEELBASE	118.7in - 3015mm
TRACK F/R	66.6/63.5in -1692/1612mm
WEIGHT	1320lb - 600kg
PRINCIPAL DRIVERS	Häkkinen, Coulthard
IDENTIFYING COLOURS	Silver/Anthracite/Black/Rocket Red

1997 ROADCAR
McLAREN F1 GT

After the sensationally quick F1 LM, McLaren had to build what was to be the final iteration of the F1 roadcar project. An even rarer car, this F1 GT was intended to be a genuine one-off roadcar, built solely to fulfil the new FIA homologation rules for the 1997 GTR racecar.

Given the go-ahead to develop the project in October of 1996, Gordon Murray and the team at McLaren had just three months before the deadline of January 1st 1997 which had been set for manufacturers to present their cars. Long hours in Woking resulted in the deadline being met, completion and road homologation of the GT road car within the allocated timeframe enabling the 1997 F1 GTR cars to compete in the first race.

Ironically, with several manufacturers not in a position to meet the deadline themselves, the regulation demanding homologation – a process which required a similar road-going version to be made and be available to paying customers prior to the start of the season – was suddenly postponed and set to take effect on the last day of the year instead. This effectively allowed rival manufacturers the luxury of building a no-holds-barred racecar and then turning that same chassis into a roadcar at the end of the year. It is interesting to wonder if McLaren would have built the same 97 GTR car if this regulation had been applied earlier.

However for McLaren the F1 GT roadcar, which became popularly known as the 'Longtail', turned into another success story. The original intention was only to build one, but two further cars were soon built to order, each of them for existing F1 customers. These two very special clients had seen the prototype in production at Unit 12 Woking Business Park and immediately placed an order. With typical attention to detail, these two customer cars acquired their own GT-specific parts and were handbuilt to the clients' requirements, being shipped to their new homes before the end of 1997.

It was the homologation of the GTR's bodyshape, the longer front and rear overhangs, the distinctive air intake and the large rear spoiler, which was to make the GT so striking. It also featured a much higher interior specification than even the F1 roadcar. The new interior design hinted at the classic era of Gran Turismo cars, and was hand-crafted in Connolly hide and Alcantara. Additional soundproofing and slightly higher gearing ensured relaxing and effortless high-speed cruising, which must surely be the raison d'etre for any GT car. In an official (and rare) McLaren Cars brochure for the F1 GT it was referred to as 'The Ultimate Grand Touring Car', a car with 'GT luxury with McLaren performance' and using 'an engine of total authority delivering instant performance, at any speed, in any gear.'

With the now-extended rear portions of the car cut with additional ventwork, NACA ducts set into the wings and its kick-up rear aerofoil, the car looked even more brutal than before. There was, nonetheless, no doubting the F1 GT's presence and entirely serious purpose.

All three F1 GTs were constructed around unmodified production monocoques and powered by the 627bhp version of the by-now familiar handbuilt McLaren-BMW S70/2 6.1-litre V12. Each was fitted with distinctive and GT-specific 18in diameter wheels, 10.85in wide at the front and 13 at the rear, which combined with the additional downforce meant the car carried special suspension settings. With nothing more than a simple GT badge on the rear left of the car to proclaim its identity, the modified bodywork of the F1 GT endowed the car with near-LM levels of downforce but less drag, thus making this F1 a fascinating vehicle in its own right.

'F1 GT, The Final Development' the brochure stated, and indeed it was. Thus ended what was for now, anyway, the final chapter in the history of one of the world's greatest-ever cars.

The interior of the F1 GT featured "*a new standard of luxury*" with hand-crafted Connolly hide and Alcantara panels to go with the extra sound-proofing. The rear panel simply carried a 'GT' badge.

The heavily revised bodywork of the F1 GT featured additional ventwork on top of the front wings, NACA ducts and a kick-up rear aerofoil.

F1 GT ROADCAR
SPECIFICATION

MODEL	McLaren F1 GT
TYPE/FORMULA	Roadcar
YEAR OF PRODUCTION	1997
DESIGNER	Gordon Murray
EXAMPLES BUILT	3
ENGINE	BMW V12
CUBIC CAPACITY	6064cc
INDUCTION	TAG 3.12 ignition/injection
POWER OUTPUT	627bhp

TRANSMISSION	Transverse 6-speed, lsd
CHASSIS	Carbon fibre reinforced composite monocoque
BODY	Carbon fibre composite panels
FRONT SUSPENSION	Double wishbones, Ground Plane Shear centre sub-frame light alloy damper/co-axial coil spring, anti-roll bar
REAR SUSPENSION	Double wishbones, Inclined Axis Shear mounting, light alloy damper/co-axial coil spring, toe-in/toe-out control links
BRAKES F/R	Outboard 13/12in ventilated discs
WHEELS DIAMETER x WIDTH F/R	18x10.85/18x13in

TYRES F/R	Michelin
LENGTH	194in - 4928mm
WIDTH	76.4in - 1940mm
HEIGHT	47.2in - 1200mm
WHEELBASE	107in - 2718mm
TRACK F/R	63.8/62.3in - 1620/1582mm
WEIGHT	2469lb - 1120kg
PRINCIPAL DRIVERS	n/a
IDENTIFYING COLOURS	n/a

1997 RACECAR McLAREN F1 GTR

According to Gordon Murray the change in emphasis in sportscar racing, and perhaps even more pointedly the people at Porsche, "*Forced us to build a racing car*." With more purpose-built machines taking to the track, and Le Mans once again in several manufacturers' sights as a most valuable tool when it came to boosting their overall image and marketing efforts, it was clear that McLaren would again have to raise its game.

The answer came in the form of the F1 GTR 97. The 1997 car was, according to a member of its development team, "*The only car in the championship built to the regulations. McLaren did it right; the car was based on a real roadcar.*" Most obviously a descendent of the two previous racecars, it still retained the basic production monocoque, but was a much larger car with longer front bodywork and a radical 'longtail' design, generating considerably more downforce but with less drag. To meet the regulations, McLaren built the F1 GT roadcar to homologate this body shape (See F1 GT on previous pages for the full story). Including the development car, 10 examples of the F1 GTR 97 were built.

Despite its larger size it was a much lighter car, weighing in at just 915 kg, an incredible achievement. Perhaps the most significant change, however, was mechanical. Whereas the earlier GTRs had retained the stock Paul Rosche production BMW engine, the capacity in the GTR 97 was dropped to 5990cc. Now designated the Type S70/3 GTR, and still producing 600bhp, the reduction was achieved by reducing the stroke by 1.1mm (from 87 to 85.9mm) although the bore stayed unchanged at 86mm. The result was significantly torque characteristics. At the same time a new sequential six-speed transmission was employed, along with new 20-spoke wheels and a host of detail improvements – no area of the car was left untouched from 1996.

With the BPR Championship having morphed into the FIA GT Championship, scratch-built racing cars were becoming the norm at the front of the grid. This meant the new GTR was preparing to duel with a variety of more obviously purpose-built machines, such as the powerful Mercedes-Benz CLK-GTR. For many this rule change threatened to ruin an otherwise appealing series, but it was good to see a number of McLaren privateers in 1995 and '96 specification cars keeping the spirit of the regulations alive. The major McLaren teams for 1997 were the BMW Motorsport-backed Schnitzer Motorsport and Team Davidoff.

At the start of the FIA Championship there was no denying the pace of the new Mercedes although it suffered mechanically during the first race of the season, dropping out before quarter distance. More significantly, however, by finishing 1-2-3-4, the new GTR 97 in the hands of the Schnitzer team demonstrated that McLaren had successfully closed in on Porsche's previous performance advantage and that it was back with a vengeance.

Mercedes fought back convincingly however, and in the next round at Silverstone Bernd Schneider and Alex Wurz finished less than a second behind the winning GTR of Peter Kox and Roberto Ravaglia. With J.J. Lehto and Steve Soper at the wheel, McLaren won again at Helsinki before Mercedes bounced back with its first win of the season, a resounding 1-2 on home ground at the Nürburgring. With a brief interlude to allow McLaren to slip in a win of its own in the Spa-Francorchamps 4 Hours, Mercedes followed up with three more 1-2 results.

Before another two end-of-season victories for Mercedes, a win at Mugello for Lehto and Soper gave the pair a total of four victories for the year and left the Schnitzer team, with a total of five race wins, second overall in the Championship, with Team Davidoff third. There is no doubt that the F1 GTRs' last season in frontline GT racing was hugely impressive.

At the non-championship Le Mans race, the 'longtail' GTRs finished in honourable second and third places overall, the Gulf/Davidoff car in the hands of Jean-Marc Gounon, Pierre-Henri Raphanel and Anders Olofsson, also winning its class.

Perhaps the best footnote to describe the philosophy of the 1997 GTR is to remember that, in 1998, Steve O'Rourke took his unmodified 1997 car back to Le Mans as a privateer and finished fourth overall against the might of the works teams.

The F1 GTR for 1997 featured the revisions that had been homologated following the construction of the F1 GT roadcar and was, according to Gordon Murray, *"the only car built to comply with the championship regulations."*

Ueno Clinic
Gulf
MICHELIN
MICHELIN
KENWOOD
KENWOOD

Gulf
Gulf
Gulf

MICHELIN
powered by BMW
24 HEURES DU MANS
ASA - ACO
41
L&C BMW
Tankfreight
KENWOOD
SEAFRANCE

The Gulf/Davidoff team finished the year third in the FIA GT championship. Here Pierre-Henri Raphanel passes the sister car of Bscher/Nielsen on his way to fifth at the A1-Ring.

At the official launch of the Gulf/Davidoff GTC team, Ray Bellm (left) poses with his team manager Michael Cane.

At the Spa round of the championship all three Davidoff cars were involved in a first-lap clash that put Anders Olofsson out of the race.

F1 GTR [1997] RACECAR
SPECIFICATION

MODEL	McLaren F1 GTR 'Longtail'
TYPE/FORMULA	Racecar
YEAR OF PRODUCTION	1997
DESIGNER	Gordon Murray
EXAMPLES BUILT	10
ENGINE	BMW V12
CUBIC CAPACITY	5990cc
INDUCTION	TAG 3.12 ignition/injection
POWER OUTPUT	600bhp

TRANSMISSION	Magnesium case transverse 6-speed
CHASSIS	Carbon fibre reinforced composite monocoque
BODY	Carbon fibre composite panels
FRONT SUSPENSION	Double wishbones, light alloy damper/
	co-axial coil spring, anti-roll bar
REAR SUSPENSION	Double wishbones, light alloy
	damper/co-axial coil spring
BRAKES F/R	Outboard 15/14in ventilated carbon discs
WHEELS DIAMETER x WIDTH F/R	18x10.85/18x13in

TYRES F/R	Michelin
LENGTH	194.2in - 4933mm
WIDTH	75.6in - 1920mm
HEIGHT	47.2in - 1200mm
WHEELBASE	107.2in - 2723mm
TRACK F/R	63.7/62.3in - 1617/1582mm
WEIGHT	2017lb - 915kg
PRINCIPAL DRIVERS	n/a
IDENTIFYING COLOURS	n/a

1998 TWO-SEATER FORMULA 1 CAR McLAREN MP4-98T

Conceived with McLaren's characteristic flair, and engineered and executed with its trademark attention to quality and fine detail, the two-seater MP4-98T was a superb attempt to acquaint lucky individuals with the thrill and sensation of an F1 car. The design philosophy behind this unique machine served in 1998 to underline the innovation and technical excellence with which the McLaren Group has come to be most closely associated.

In 1989 the newly formed McLaren Cars had introduced its ground-breaking one-plus-two seating configuration with its world record-shattering McLaren F1 roadcar which positioned the driver in the centreline. Now, with the similarly novel MP4-98T tandem-seater, came a one-plus-one configuration.

Designed as a promotional vehicle, the world's first two-seater Formula 1 car was created to provide a unique opportunity for individuals associated with the team: namely a high-speed circuit drive with the chance for a passenger to experience the power, acceleration, braking, cornering and exhilaration of a modern race car.

No less significantly, however, the new car was also engineered from the outset to incorporate a full set of fully compliant frontal, side impact and driver/passenger head protection panels built to 1997 FIA safety regulations. To this end an extensive analysis was carried out in order to assess the likely load factors and to include these in the fundamental criteria of the design and build process. As a result, rather than merely stretching a conventional F1 monocoque by inserting additional panels, an entirely new shape was created featuring integral sidepod structures together with enhanced torsional rigidity and additional driver and passenger protection. As such it was also to prove an ideal advertisement for McLaren's speciality of providing truly unique design and engineering solutions.

Powered by a 3-litre Mercedes-Benz V10 similar to that fitted to the team's race cars, and driving through the same six-speed semi-automatic gearbox, the car made its debut in Australia at the beginning of the 1998 season, appropriately liveried in the authentic West McLaren Mercedes team colours that were all too familiar to those fortunate enough to secure a ride.

From McLaren Cars Technical Director Gordon Murray's perspective, however, it was important that the finished machine did not simply follow the line of Grand Prix cars, "*All looking the same*". Rather, and as he had with the F1, Murray took the opportunity to design something completely new from scratch, observing that, "*It was a really interesting project, with just the kind of packaging issues I like.*"

The car definitely retained the McLaren-Mercedes family look, something which was always one of the project's core aims. To a great degree this was helped by the fact that it was only 150mm longer than the previous season's race-car. This had been achieved by reducing the car's fuel capacity by two-thirds and placing the passenger where ordinarily a 120-litre fuel cell would have been. The reduced range was hardly a problem, since the immense forces inherent in Formula 1 cars would almost certainly leave the average passenger feeling somewhat queasy after just three laps – an out lap, one flier and the in lap.

At the same time various packaging considerations required the passenger seat to be located well above the base of the monocoque, something which obviously raised the car's centre of gravity above the ideal for a genuine F1 racer but which on the plus side afforded the passenger much greater visibility during the ride.

Ironically at 6ft 4in Murray himself was too tall to experience the car himself, something he dismissed on the grounds that he makes a lousy passenger. But others can confirm that the experience was totally authentic, aided by the fact that the second seat was located right on the 98T's centre of gravity. Murray went on the record to say that he thought the car wouldn't be, "*Far off the lap times a 1998 Grand Prix car would do at the start of the race, with a full fuel load.*" An extraordinary achievement.

This was borne out by Martin Brundle's experience, the ex-Formula 1 driver – promptly nicknamed 'Parker' by the staff at the UK monthly magazine F1 Racing – having been appointed to the post of official 185mph McLaren team chauffeur. "*The car,*" he said, "*is little different from an F1 car in terms of feel. It's quick, very quick. We did a 1m 36s lap at Silverstone. Compare that with this year's pole position time, and you'll see what I mean. It's not slow.*"

At a West McLaren Mercedes promotion in Hamburg, in September 2000 David Coulthard gave rides to celebrity guests around the part cobbled streets of Hamburg.

At the Hockenheim round of the 2000 DTM Championship in October, 1984 World Champion Niki Lauda drove the MP4-98T two-seater car, chauffering several journalists round the circuit at high speed.

The MP4-98T wasn't just a modified Formula 1 car. It featured a new chassis with integrated sidepods and increased torsional rigidity. The passenger sat higher in the chassis than the driver and this protective headrest was placed between passenger and pilot to help the former cope with the huge g-forces.

With both past and present McLaren Formula 1 drivers taking the controls of the MP4-98T, any passenger lucky enough to secure a ride was sure to experience the ultimate adrenaline rush.

West

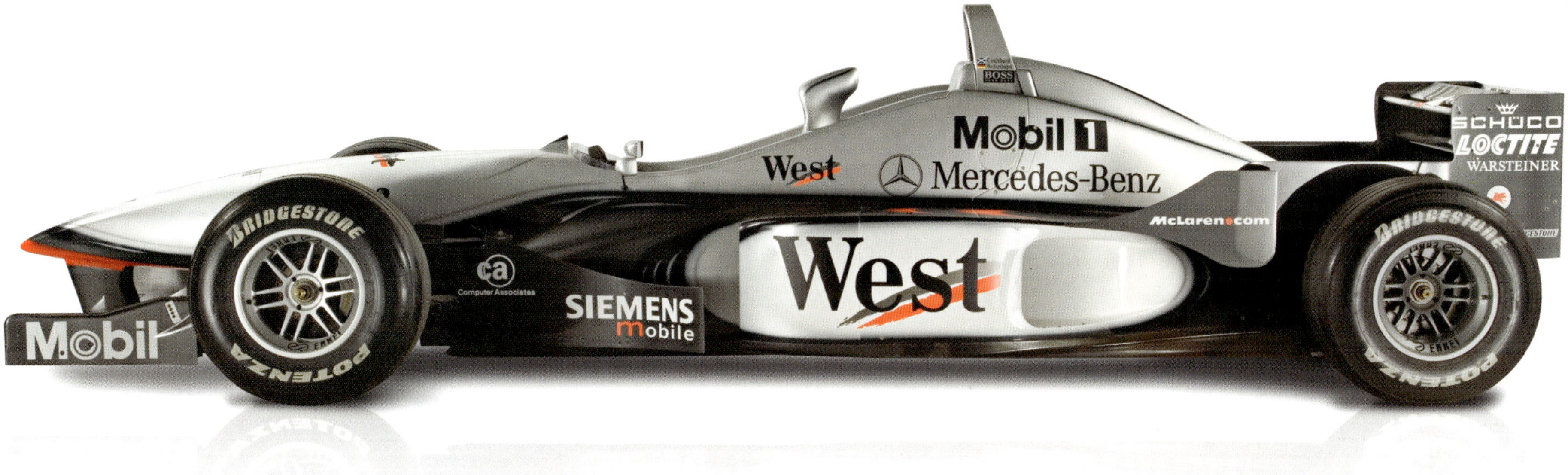
Mobil 1
West
Mercedes-Benz
McLaren.com
West
SIEMENS
mobile
Mobil
BRIDGESTONE
POTENZA
SCHÜCO
LOCTITE
WARSTEINER

1998 2 SEATER FORMULA 1 CAR McLAREN MP4-98T

CONTINUED

MP4-98T TWO-SEATER FORMULA 1 CAR

SPECIFICATION

MODEL	McLaren-Mercedes MP4-98T
TYPE/FORMULA	Two-seater Formula 1
YEAR OF PRODUCTION	1998
DESIGNER	Barry Lett/Gordon Murray
EXAMPLES BUILT	1
ENGINE	Mercedes-Benz FO 110G V10
CUBIC CAPACITY	2997cc
ELECTRONICS	TAG2000 ignition/injection
POWER OUTPUT	700bhp

TRANSMISSION	McLaren semi-auto longitudinal 6-speed
CHASSIS	McLaren moulded carbon fibre/honeycomb composite
BODY	Carbon fibre single piece cockpit/engine cover & nose
FRONT SUSPENSION	Double wishbone, push-rod operating
	longitudinal inboard coil spring/damper
REAR SUSPENSION	Double wishbone, push-rod operating
	longitudinal inboard coil spring/damper
BRAKES F/R	Outboard AP Racing/Hitco/Carbone Industrie
WHEELS DIAMETER x WIDTH F/R	13x11.75/13x13.7in

TYRES F/R	Bridgestone
LENGTH	185.5in - 4712mm
WIDTH	78.8in - 2000 mm
HEIGHT	43.5in - 1105mm
WHEELBASE	122.6in - 3115mm
TRACK F/R	64/63in - 1625/1600mm
WEIGHT	1322lb - 600kg
PRINCIPAL DRIVERS	Brundle, Häkkinen, Coulthard, Turner, Lauda
IDENTIFYING COLOURS	Silver/Anthracite/Black/Rocket Red

1998 FORMULA 1
McLAREN MP4-13

The creation of McLaren's unique two-seater did nothing to compromise the development of the 1998 team cars, and when these appeared it was evident that Adrian Newey had been working flat-out since joining the team from Williams in August the previous year.

Contractual restrictions meant he could not play an active role before that date, but clearly he still had plenty of time to consider the impact of the new regulations and to find the most beneficial way to comply with them. As Mercedes-Benz poured their expertise into the development of the new FO 110G V10, Newey and his team spent an incredible 12,000 man-hours finding new ways to recover the downforce which would otherwise have been sacrificed to the new rules.

This, together with a switch to Bridgestone tyres and a very real rekindling of team spirit once Mika Häkkinen discovered for himself the joys of winning at the highest level, quickly put McLaren back into a dominant position on the grid. From a base of three race wins in 1997, the team went on to win yet another Drivers' and Constructors' World Championship double, and its first with Mercedes-Benz and West.

Neil Oatley nevertheless recalled: "*We didn't really expect to be so competitive, at least until the car went to Barcelona, and literally the first run we did was quicker than anyone else had managed all week, so that gave us an inkling that we had a reasonably competitive car.*"

Oatley also wondered whether, "*because from a novelty point of view the MP4-13 was probably fairly uninteresting, maybe that was why it was so good.*" The design process, he said, was relatively late in starting – "*it was a fairly hurried car in that respect*" – but Newey brought a strong influence to bear on the monocoque shape and its aerodynamics. These were two factors which inevitably drove the whole programme, while other team members battled with the demands of the new narrower-track/grooved tyre regime.

The finished car was a neat and tidy package, relatively small and compact, and perhaps because there were no completely radical new features on it everything tended to work well from the very start. Still in place was the previous season's low-level nose design, but the front suspension was quite different with inboard vertical dampers and torsion bars in place of the previous car's horizontally mounted coil spring/damper units. The switch to Bridgestone cost the team some valuable time when it came to finalising the suspension geometry, but it proved worthwhile.

From the first race the team was, as Oatley observed, "*head and shoulders above everyone else*" with both Häkkinen and David Coulthard running "*like clockwork as well as being very quick.*" At Melbourne both drivers lapped the field, Coulthard leaving the way clear for Häkkinen to win the race.

Controversy followed in Brazil, with Ferrari querying the legality of McLaren's asymmetric braking system. Despite the FIA giving the okay during the winter, the stewards agreed with Ferrari. In the interest of the sport McLaren decided to withdraw the system rather than muddy the water in what it felt would be a Championship-winning year. This was a typically shrewd move, and even without the system the drivers managed another McLaren 1-2 leaving Ferrari's Michael Schumacher almost a lap behind.

At Buenos Aires, Schumacher fought back to win as Coulthard finished sixth. DC beat Häkkinen to win at Imola, and dominated again at Montreal until the throttle mechanism malfunctioned. "*Embarrassing,*" Ron Dennis called it, but the Finn soon reasserted his dominance after this and was never any lower than third on the grid, eventually posting nine poles, three second places and four thirds on the startline.

As the results show, Coulthard's throttle disaster was a rare failure, as was Häkkinen's retirement at Imola. Generally the cars performed exceptionally well although DC experienced a couple of bottom-end failures at Monza and Monaco while Häkkinen's handling went awry in Budapest when the front anti-roll bar worked loose, costing the team a race win.

The team took full advantage of the downtime between races to test and refine the car, and towards the end of the season Häkkinen was able to find that little bit extra. Despite winning six races with just two still up for grabs, he was tied neck-and-neck with Schumacher. At the Nürburgring, however, he left nothing to chance, storming ahead to a victory which left the German trailing by a significant, but hardly decisive, four points. As a result there was still everything to fight for at the last race in Japan. It was nail-biting stuff, a real down-to-the-wire situation.

Fortunately, the Mika magic held true. "*He drove an exceptional race at Suzuka.*" Oatley said. "*He was very quick all weekend, didn't make a single mistake, and the car was strong.*" By the end of the afternoon Häkkinen had delivered a great victory, and with exactly 100 points handed McLaren its first World Championship since Ayrton Senna's heyday. With one win of his own and six second-places Coulthard came third with 56 points, sufficient to give West McLaren Mercedes and the MP4-13 the Constructors' title as well.

"*I don't know how to start explaining my feelings,*" Häkkinen said. "*It was easier than some of the races have been this year. I have been in much more difficult situations than at this Grand Prix, but obviously I was aware this morning of the pressure that was falling on me. It was disturbing my performance a little bit, but then I seemed to calm down quite a lot. But there is always one problem when you are leading easily – and it happened to me with about 10 laps to go – which is the tendency for your mind to start thinking about other things. I almost started whistling inside the car...*"

The 1998 German Grand Prix at Hockenheim was a perfect weekend for the team. From first and second on the grid, Häkkinen led Coulthard (top) all the way to the chequered flag, to score a memorable 1-2. David Coulthard (above) splashes round Monza during wet practice for the Italian GP.

Driving superbly all year, Mika Häkkinen won eight races and clinched the Drivers' World Championship with a flawless flag-to-flag victory in the Japanese Grand Prix at Suzuka. With Coulthard third in the standings, the team also took the Constructors' title for the first time since 1991.

Mika

Mika

LOCTITE
WARSTEINER
BOSS
Mobil 1
Mercedes-Benz
Mika
Mika
COMPUTER ASSOCIATES
8
BRIDGESTONE
POTENZA
BRIDGESTONE
POTENZA
Mobil

The full McLaren-Mercedes driver line-up for 1998. Back row, left to right: Norman Simon, Nick Heidfeld, Mika Häkkinen, David Coulthard, Ricardo Zonta and Nicolas Minassian. Front left & right, Wesley Graves. Lewis Hamilton.

MP4-13 FORMULA 1
SPECIFICATION

MODEL	McLaren-Mercedes MP4-13
TYPE/FORMULA	Formula 1
YEAR OF PRODUCTION	1998
DESIGNER	Neil Oatley/Adrian Newey
EXAMPLES BUILT	7
ENGINE	Mercedes-Benz FO 110G V10
CUBIC CAPACITY	2997cc
ELECTRONICS	TAG2000 ignition/injection
POWER OUTPUT	760bhp

TRANSMISSION	McLaren semi-auto longitudinal 6-speed
CHASSIS	McLaren moulded carbon fibre/honeycomb composite
BODY	Carbon fibre single piece cockpit/engine cover & nose
FRONT SUSPENSION	Unequal length wishbone, push-rod & bell
	crank operating inboard torsion bar/damper
REAR SUSPENSION	Unequal length wishbone, push-rod & bell
	crank operating inboard torsion bar/damper
BRAKES F/R	Outboard AP Racing/Hitco carbon fibre
WHEELS DIAMETER x WIDTH F/R	13x12/13x13.7in

TYRES F/R	Bridgestone
LENGTH	179in - 4547mm
WIDTH	70.9in - 1800mm
HEIGHT	40in - 1016 mm
WHEELBASE	120.5in -3060 mm
TRACK F/R	55.5/55in - 1410/1397mm
WEIGHT	1322lb - 600kg
PRINCIPAL DRIVERS	Häkkinen, Coulthard
IDENTIFYING COLOURS	Silver/Anthracite/Black/Rocket Red

1999 FORMULA 1
McLAREN MP4-14

According to Neil Oatley, the success of the MP4-13 allowed West McLaren Mercedes *"to push the design of the MP4-14 more than we would have been comfortable with the previous year. We had more time with the next car, and could afford to be a little more adventurous in some of its mechanical aspects."*

None of this prevented yet another season's racing being run down to the wire, but what was evident from the word go was that McLaren's new car was one of its most ambitious designs ever. With a lighter, lower V10 from Mercedes-Benz, it also showcased a host of new innovations brought in by Adrian Newey.

Accordingly, at its launch Dennis explicitly rejected the word evolutionary, describing it instead as a new car which "*represents the biggest single step we felt we could take for 1999 with perhaps the smallest-ever percentage of carry-over components from last year's car.*"

The new FO 100H now developed around 785bhp at 16,700rpm, and Newey battled to make the most of this by recovering as much grip as possible which would otherwise have been lost to a mandated, footprint-reducing fourth groove in the front tyres. The car now sported a new mid-height nose with a pair of high-sided bargeboards mounted either side of the cockpit. To the rear, but ahead of the driven wheels, large deflector panels made the car instantly recognisable.

Newey also reordered the packaging to a great degree, something he would clearly have done a year earlier had the timeframe allowed. He relocated the oil tank and hydraulic system and fitted a new, shorter gearbox, and the reduced weight of the new car allowed for some more creative ballasting with various ancillaries stowed within the walls of the monocoque. New torsion-bar rear suspension was added to the mix, while the front remained fundamentally been on MP4-13.

The increased complexity and lower weight did not at first inspire complete confidence on the part of David Coulthard and Mika Häkkinen, when compared to the previous year's Championship winner. At the limit it was able to perform quite brilliantly, but as Managing Director Martin Whitmarsh observed, "*In terms of riding the bumps, stability on the straight and sheer chuckability, it gave away something to the MP4-13.*"

The reality was that, more or less as a natural consequence of its more complex design, the MP4-14 just took longer to get right so that for much of the year it was very much a case of one step forward, one step back. No one foresaw the reduction in rear grip which was to affect the latest Bridgestones early on. Similarly no one expected the year to start quite as badly as it did, with both cars stopping in the Australian opener. Later Häkkinen drove superbly to win in Brazil, where Coulthard was forced to retire with gearbox problems.

Thereafter Imola provided a glimmer of hope: Coulthard should have won, and might have but for difficulties with heavy traffic, and at Monaco Häkkinen finished third but was clearly unhappy with his car which was later stripped down and checked component-by-component. After that another reversal saw him win in Spain – actually it was a McLaren 1-2 – and again in Canada, before yet another change in fortunes left him qualifying in only 14th place at Magny-Cours. While Coulthard exited the French GP with electrical problems, the Finn was eventually able to recover and pull off second place. At Silverstone David Coulthard took a hugely popular win in front of his home crowd. Mika was forced to withdraw after shedding a wheel.

In Austria the two McLarens finished in the points immediately behind Eddie Irvine's Ferrari, but then at Hockenheim the Ulsterman was able to triumph again. In Hungary the old form reasserted itself, however, producing another McLaren 1-2 – the lead position Häkkinen's again – only for another reverse at Spa when the two cars touched wheels, leaving the Finn behind the Scot.

At Monza, the Nürburgring and Malaysia neither driver fared well so that by the time the circus reached Suzuka for the Japanese and final round, Häkkinen's two-point lead over Irvine, and McLaren's eight-point advantage over Ferrari, had turned instead to four-point deficits. Once again it was to be a truly nail-biting finish to the season, but Häkkinen duly delivered, driving a superb race to beat Schumacher and Irvine and clinch his second Drivers' World Championship. Another strong performance by Ferrari denied McLaren another double, however, as the 1999 Constructors' World Championship went to Maranello by four points.

"*This has been a very difficult year,*" the elated Mika said after becoming, at that time, only the seventh driver in F1 history to win back-to-back titles. "*To have won the Championship in the last Grand Prix is nerve-wracking. It's an experience which I can't recommend to anyone!*"

Seven wins out of 16 was good, but not good enough. West McLaren Mercedes was still the team to beat but while Mercedes-Benz had demonstrated outstanding levels of mechanical reliability, the car never quite measured up to it. The team had won through in the end, but despite a relentless programme of development which continued right through the series – as late as Suzuka Newey was still introducing refinements – there was no escaping the conclusion that the MP4-14 could have won the Championship by the end of the summer.

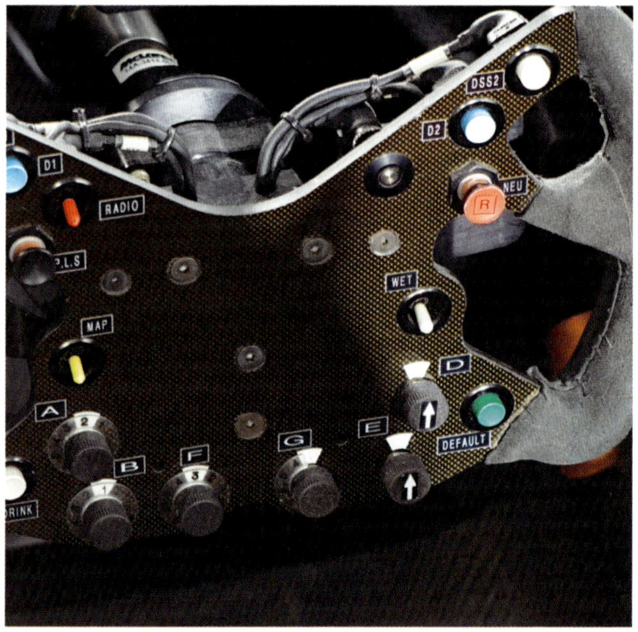

David Coulthard's attempts to back up his team-mate at the Japanese championship decider (top) were thwarted when he retired with gearbox problems on lap 39. Häkkinen didn't need his help though, and for the second year running took the title with a dominant victory in the last race of the season.

Outwardly the 1999 MP4-14 may have seemed very similar to the previous year's car but under the skin it was a huge step forward with a lighter, lower V10 engine from Mercedes-Benz and a host of new innovations from designer Adrian Newey and his team.

MP4-14 FORMULA 1

SPECIFICATION

MODEL	McLaren-Mercedes MP4-14
TYPE/FORMULA	Formula 1
YEAR OF PRODUCTION	1999
DESIGNER	Neil Oatley/Adrian Newey
EXAMPLES BUILT	8
ENGINE	Mercedes-Benz FO 110H V10
CUBIC CAPACITY	2997cc
ELECTRONICS	TAG2000 ignition/injection
POWER OUTPUT	785bhp

TRANSMISSION	McLaren semi-auto longitudinal 7-speed
CHASSIS	McLaren moulded carbon fibre/honeycomb composite
BODY	Carbon fibre single piece cockpit/engine cover & nose
FRONT SUSPENSION	Unequal length wishbone, push-rod & bell
	crank operating inboard torsion bar/damper
REAR SUSPENSION	Unequal length wishbone, push-rod & bell
	crank operating inboard torsion bar/damper
BRAKES F/R	Outboard AP Racing/Hitco carbon fibre
WHEELS DIAMETER x WIDTH F/R	13x12/13x13.7in

TYRES F/R	Bridgestone
LENGTH	179in - 4547mm
WIDTH	70.9in - 1800mm
HEIGHT	40in - 1016mm
WHEELBASE	119in - 3023mm
TRACK F/R	55/56in - 1397/1422mm
WEIGHT	1322lb - 600kg
PRINCIPAL DRIVERS	Häkkinen, Coulthard
IDENTIFYING COLOURS	Silver/Anthracite/Black/Rocket Red

vodafone
JOHNNIE WALKER
JOHNNIE WALKER
22
SAP
Mobil
vodafone

CHAPTER 05

LEWIS
HAMILTON

Although I've only driven for Vodafone McLaren Mercedes in Formula 1 for one full season, which was the exciting if stressful 2007 campaign, I don't really feel like a new boy at all. And that's because, although I arrived in Melbourne in March 2007 as a raw recruit to Grand Prix racing, I was already an old hand with the team.

Everyone knows the reason why, and it's this: when I was just 10 years old, having won a karting award at the prestigious black-tie dinner hosted annually by Autosport magazine in London, I took a deep breath and marched right up to Ron Dennis on the night itself.

"*One day I'm going to drive for McLaren,*" I told him – and within less than a dozen years it had happened.

I've worked hard, very hard, to get there, but it has all been worth the effort. I have been extremely fortunate to have had McLaren and Mercedes-Benz supporting me for the past 10 years and therefore feel a lot of gratitude: gratitude to Ron, of course, for the opportunity, belief and support, but also to Norbert Haug of Mercedes-Benz and to Martin Whitmarsh at McLaren and to many more people than I have space to name here. Most of all, though, I'm grateful to my dad, Anthony, who has sacrificed so much over so many years to push me to achieve my ambitions. And he's still pushing me.

In 2007 I finished second in the Drivers' World Championship. My car, the Vodafone McLaren Mercedes MP4-22, was a fantastic machine, and the unsung heroes behind me – the mechanics and engineers and everyone who works at Woking, Stuttgart and Brixworth – were just that: unsung heroes. Thanks, guys. As a team we got very close to taking the ultimate honours that year; but 'very close' isn't close enough, and we'll all be working as hard as we possibly can to go one better in 2008 and beyond.

If we succeed, we'll be adding to a glorious heritage – one that I'm enormously proud to be a part of. Many of the greatest names in the history of Grand Prix racing have driven for or been associated with McLaren; and, as well as being aware of the fantastic talent and resources that Vodafone McLaren Mercedes has at its disposal, I was very conscious of that heritage when earlier this year I re-signed for a further five seasons, taking my relationship with the team up to at least 2012.

I've been asked to write about this decade only – the 'Noughties', as it's sometimes called, and that's a great honour when you consider that I've only been a part of the Vodafone McLaren Mercedes race team for the very recent races.

The decade kicked off with those two McLaren stalwarts, Mika Häkkinen and David Coulthard, in the cockpits. In 2000 Mika was in contention for what would have been a historic third straight Drivers' World Championship – he'd triumphed for McLaren-Mercedes in both 1998 and 1999 – but in the end he was edged out by Michael Schumacher and Ferrari.

When Mika retired, he was replaced at McLaren-Mercedes by Kimi Räikkönen – who is now, as a Ferrari man himself, one of my fiercest rivals for World Championship glory. As a youngster watching Grands Prix in the early 'Noughties' on TV at home, I always rooted for Kimi – and, although he now drives for the opposition, I respect him still. He was a worthy World Champion in 2007, but you shouldn't forget that he and McLaren-Mercedes nearly took the honours in 2003 and 2005, too.

And through it all, leading and inspiring our team in equal measure, has been Ron: the man who has done more than any other individual to make McLaren what it is today. It has been, and remains, a privilege to work for him; and I know that the team that Bruce McLaren created more than 40 years ago, and which Ron has guided and nurtured so brilliantly since 1980, will continue to be a tribute to both of them for many years to come. I'll be aiming to do my bit to make sure it's a fitting tribute.

Lewis Hamilton
2nd Drivers' World Championship 2007
Vodafone McLaren Mercedes MP4-22

2000 FORMULA 1
McLAREN MP4-15

McLaren entered the new Millennium with the same engine partner, Mercedes-Benz, the same title sponsor, West, and for the fifth season in a row the same two drivers, Mika Häkkinen and David Coulthard. That made the pairing of the Finn and the Scot the longest-ever in the sport's history, and McLaren also became the first team ever to have three Grand Prix winners on board, as former Ligier and Prost racer Olivier Panis took over the duties as test driver.

His role was to be a key one. The new MP4-15 was more an evolution than a new car, but with continual changes to the aerodynamics and a new power-steering set-up coming on stream during the season, testing and development were to move even higher up the list of priorities. Coulthard was quick to acknowledge Panis's important place in the team, referring to the great benefit it was having, "*Somebody fulfilling this role whose judgement we could absolutely depend on and who was quick enough not to raise any doubts about the data he was inputting.*"

Adrian Newey's third car for McLaren incorporated a number of refinements which had been developed during the off-season during consultations with the FIA. Because of this Martin Whitmarsh maintained that, while some rivals might attempt to complain to the governing body, he had no worries about their legality even though some, such as the distinctive exhaust set-up with its central exit, and the hot-air radiator outlet 'chimneys' atop the sidepods, were novel.

Talk at the launch was not restricted to the car's technical aspects, however. Prior to the event, Daimler took the opportunity to confirm that it was exercising its right to buy 40 per cent of the TAG McLaren Group. At the same time Whitmarsh reflected on the considerable challenges facing the hitherto unfortunate Coulthard during the coming year. "*He is,*" he remarked, "*intelligent enough to realise that we considered other drivers for this season.*"

The team had no intention of repeating the poor start it had made in 1999, but this proved unavoidable. After taking the top two qualifying positions in Australia both cars retired when their new FO 110J Mercedes-Benz V10s suffered valve seal problems. Two weeks later Häkkinen's engine blew up again at Interlagos while he was leading, and having finished second on the road Coulthard was then disqualified for a wing-height infringement. But on the positive side the new cars were very fast and better at responding to changes and more comfortable on the limit than the MP4-14 had been.

At Imola Häkkinen held the lead for a long time, though once again Michael Schumacher's pace enabled him to win for Ferrari. It wasn't until Silverstone, courtesy of Coulthard, that the team had a victory to celebrate. Häkkinen made it a great day by finishing second, though he wasn't happy with his car's set-up even after small changes during his pit stop.

He finished second again at the Nürburgring, this time behind Schumacher, before winning in Barcelona after the German driver experienced tyre problems. Coulthard posted an impressive second, despite having stepped out unharmed after the Learjet in which he'd been travelling crash-landed four days earlier. At Monaco DC dominated as Häkkinen fell victim to a gearbox problem and Schumacher's suspension broke. The Scot won again at Magny-Cours with Häkkinen second and still complaining about his car. In Austria, however, a refreshed Häkkinen stormed through to win and to declare: "*We've solved our problems. I'm back to what I used to be and the Championship is not over yet.*"

With Schumacher failing to score both there and in Germany two weeks later, and with Häkkinen winning in Hungary as well as at Spa, he was not just back in contention but actually leading the Championship. Ferrari fought back with wins at Monza and Indianapolis, leaving Häkkinen trailing Schumacher by eight points with just two races left. He fought back hard at Suzuka but as the rain fell the advantage went to Schumacher. The German eventually won his first title with Ferrari, who also narrowly took the Constructors' World Championship, but the season had seen a classic battle between the two top teams.

The team had once again scored seven wins, and overall reliability had been much better with Häkkinen in the points for every race but three and Coulthard for all but four.

At Sepang for the Malaysian Grand Prix, the final race of the 2000 season, Mika Häkkinen came fourth and took the runner-up spot in the title race.

The MP4-15 was launched shortly after the announcement that Daimler would be buying 40% of the TAG McLaren Group. Over the course of the year the new car, powered by the 72 degree V10 Mercedes-Benz FO 110J engine won seven races.

MP4-15 FORMULA 1
SPECIFICATION

MODEL	McLaren-Mercedes MP4-15
TYPE/FORMULA	Formula 1
YEAR OF PRODUCTION	2000
DESIGNER	Adrian Newey/Neil Oatley
EXAMPLES BUILT	7
ENGINE	Mercedes-Benz FO 110J V10
CUBIC CAPACITY	2997cc
ELECTRONICS	STAR System (TAG-210)
POWER OUTPUT	795bhp

TRANSMISSION	McLaren semi-auto longitudinal 7-speed
CHASSIS	McLaren moulded carbon fibre/honeycomb composite
BODY	Carbon fibre single piece cockpit/engine cover & nose
FRONT SUSPENSION	Unequal length wishbone, push-rod & bell crank operating inboard torsion bar/damper
REAR SUSPENSION	Unequal length wishbone, push-rod & bell crank operating inboard torsion bar/damper
BRAKES F/R	Outboard carbon fibre discs
WHEELS DIAMETER x WIDTH F/R	13x12/13x13.7in

TYRES F/R	Bridgestone
LENGTH	178in - 4521mm
WIDTH	70.9in - 1800mm
HEIGHT	40in - 1016mm
WHEELBASE	120.5in - 3061mm
TRACK F/R	55/55.5in - 1397/1408mm
WEIGHT	1322lb - 600kg
PRINCIPAL DRIVERS	Häkkinen, Coulthard
IDENTIFYING COLOURS	Silver/Anthracite/Black/Rocket Red

2001 FORMULA 1
McLAREN MP4-16

The F1 regulations for 2001 effectively demanded a clean-sheet approach because, as Technical Director Adrian Newey acknowledged, while small they were highly significant.

The biggest was the requirement that the front wing be raised 50mm. *"That might seem modest,"* Newey said, *"but it has had quite a knock-on effect on the configuration of the remainder of the car. In addition we have a much smaller rear wing; the upper wing section is now limited in depth and to a total of three elements, whereas at places like Monaco and Hungary teams have run seven or even eight elements in the past. So there is a major reduction of downforce here."*

At the same time the design of the MP4-16 had to accommodate a number of new structural safety features, including stronger roll-hoops and greater padding to provide protection for the drivers' legs. The sides of the car also had to be capable of absorbing more energy in T-bone incidents, which called for longer sidepods since impact tests on the carbon fibre/aluminium composite chassis were carried out further forward along the cockpit.

Working closely as ever with Newey and the McLaren design team, Mercedes-Benz produced another new V10, the FO 110K, which delivered 800bhp through McLaren's longitudinal seven-speed semi-automatic gearbox. Unfortunately, Ferrari at this time almost certainly enjoyed a power advantage of around 20bhp. And the MP4-16 was not as reliable as it should have been, leading to problems in Australia, Spain, Monaco and Austria.

Mercedes-Benz's problems were made worse by the mid-season death of Ilmor co-founder Paul Morgan in a vintage aircraft accident, and by a ban on the use of beryllium as an engine material. Mario Illien had found it particularly useful as a hardening agent in alloys. Some of the team's problems also lay with the car itself, as Martin Whitmarsh admitted. In Melbourne the front suspension failed on Häkkinen's car, causing him to crash, while electronic faults in the traction and launch control affected Coulthard in Spain and Monaco, and Häkkinen in Austria. In addition there was an aerodynamic problem. *"When we first tried to run the car in Spain,"* Whitmarsh said, *"we were trying to analyse why we were having some different results when we ran on the circuit to what the wind tunnel had led us to expect."*

There was a problem with the front wing and it took time to identify what it was doing to the rest of the car, and to correct it. As a result, Whitmarsh later observed, *"By the time we got to the fifth race we were probably where we ought to have been at the start. From that point on we were into the normal race-to-race improvements with smaller aerodynamic increments."*

Despite these problems the MP4-16 gave David Coulthard his best season so far in Formula 1, with a win in Brazil just days after his 30th birthday, and another in Austria. A second place in San Marino, and two thirds, in the US and Japan, left him second overall in the Drivers' World Championship with 65 points. Unfortunately Häkkinen's performance was less impressive, and the Finn finished fifth overall with only 37 points. He had to wait until Silverstone in July before he won a race. Later, in Italy, he announced that having captured two World Championships, scored 19 race wins, set 26 pole positions and amassed a grand total of 420 points in his career, he would be taking a one-year sabbatical in 2002. Shortly afterwards, at Indianapolis, he added a 20th win to that tally, though at the time no one was to know it would actually be his last as he never did return to Formula 1 racing.

TAG Electronic Systems control units on the MP4-16 incorporated electronics for chassis, engine and data aquisition. It also supplied the electronic dashboard as well as the data analysis and telemetry systems.

The bodywork of the MP4-16 included a huge one-piece sidepod and engine cover, along with a separate floor section and structural nose with integral front wing.

Along with extra padding around the driver's legs, another of the new Formula 1 regulations for 2001 included the requirement that the driver's seat be removable without the need to cut or remove any of the seat belts.

West

Hakkinen
BOSS
Mobil 1
West
SCHÜCO
LOCTITE
WARSTEINER
3
McLaren.com
ca
Computer Associates
SIEMENS
mobile
West
BRIDGESTONE
POTENZA
Mobil

West
BRIDGESTONE
BRIDGESTONE
West
3
Mobil
1
SAP
SIEMENS
mobile
SIEMENS
mobile

The Austrian Grand Prix at the A1-Ring in May provided David Coulthard with his second Grand Prix win of the 2001 season.

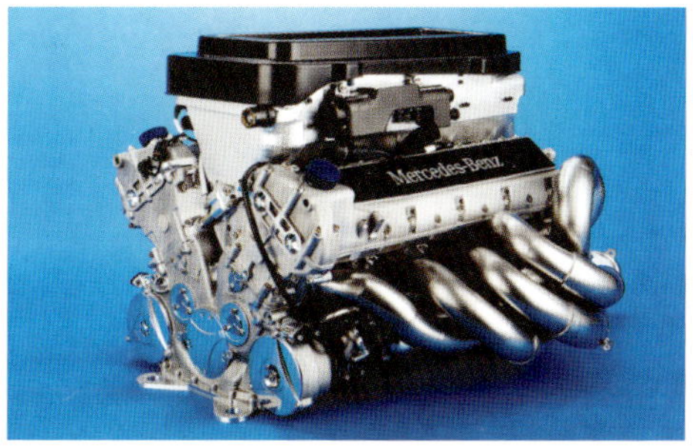

The 2997cc Mercedes-Benz FO 110K V10 engine had a cast aluminium alloy block with wet liners, a one-piece aluminium head and steel crankshaft.

MP4-16 FORMULA 1
SPECIFICATION

MODEL	McLaren-Mercedes MP4-16	TRANSMISSION	McLaren semi-auto sequential longitudinal 7-speed	TYRES F/R	Bridgestone
TYPE/FORMULA	Formula 1	CHASSIS	Moulded carbon fibre/aluminium honeycomb composite	LENGTH	181in - 4597mm
YEAR OF PRODUCTION	2001	BODY	Carbon fibre single piece cockpit/engine cover & nose	WIDTH	70.9in - 1800mm
DESIGNER	Adrian Newey/Neil Oatley	FRONT SUSPENSION	Unequal length wishbone, push-rod & bell	HEIGHT	40in - 1016mm
EXAMPLES BUILT	7		crank operating inboard torsion bar/damper	WHEELBASE	122in - 3099mm
ENGINE	Mercedes-Benz FO 110K V10	REAR SUSPENSION	Unequal length wishbone, push-rod & bell	TRACK F/R	56/55in -1422/1397mm
CUBIC CAPACITY	2997cc		crank operating inboard torsion bar/damper	WEIGHT	1322lb - 600kg
ELECTRONICS	STAR System (TAG-210)	BRAKES F/R	Outboard carbon fibre discs	PRINCIPAL DRIVERS	Häkkinen, Coulthard
POWER OUTPUT	810bhp	WHEELS DIAMETER x WIDTH F/R	13x12/13x13.7in	IDENTIFYING COLOURS	Silver/Anthracite/Black/Rocket Red

2002 FORMULA 1
McLAREN MP4-17A

One Finn replaced another, as Mika Häkkinen's place on the team was taken by Kimi Räikkönen, who had made a stupendous impression in his rookie season in 2001 with Sauber-Petronas. He and David Coulthard were joined by new test driver Alex Wurz, as Olivier Panis used his impressive test performances as a springboard to a new race driver with Toyota.

They had a new West McLaren Mercedes to drive, the MP4-17. The biggest changes to the MP4-16 concerned the aggressively sculptured aerodynamic lower front wishbone mountings. These now extended dihedrally from the base of the chassis, an idea which had been tested on the previous season's car. Significantly, the new car benefited from its development time in the new wind tunnel. This had come on stream at McLaren's new state-of-the-art headquarters, which was still under construction in Woking not far from the existing factory in Albert Drive.

"*The new wind tunnel has allowed us to do certain things that we couldn't in the previous facility,*" Adrian Newey revealed, without elaborating further.

A switch back to Michelin tyres was another reason why Newey had to redesign the suspension completely. "*Tyres can have a considerable effect on the weight of the steering, the aerodynamics and the whole balance of the car,*" he explained. "*Tyre characteristics are influenced by a great many variables... the condition of the asphalt on the track, the ambient temperature and the way the car is set up. As a result they will respond in a very non-linear manner.*"

There were difficulties in working with Michelin initially because the contract with Bridgestone did not expire until the end of 2001, but West McLaren Mercedes went into the new season full of optimism. Not all of it was justified, however. The car looked dramatic and its new, even smaller 90° V10 FO 110M Mercedes-Benz engine ran to more than 18,000rpm. But there was still a power deficit to Ferrari, and at the same time BMW-Williams had clearly raised its game, as had Honda and Cosworth. The FO 110M's reliability was at times poor, with Räikkönen suffering several engine failures and having to cut his revs dramatically at Suzuka in order to finish the race.

Not all of the problems were Mercedes-Benz's. Räikkönen's car broke a rear hub at Interlagos, and at Barcelona a broken exhaust and a manufacturing fault in the rear wing took him out of the race.

The season started well, however. On his debut for West McLaren Mercedes in Melbourne, Räikkönen finished on the podium after coming third. And development continued throughout the season with particular regard to cutting the overall weight and making a number of significant aerodynamic improvements. The rear end of the car was also altered considerably, with a new gearbox and suspension set-up mid-year. Here the team fell victim to poor timing, Newey admitting to over-optimism in the way the new equipment was readied just in time for the August test ban. As a result some of the changes were held over until the next year, and what would become the MP4-17D.

Over the course of the year both drivers turned in some memorable performances. There was just one victory, and that came courtesy of Coulthard at Monaco, his favourite circuit. But Räikkönen should have won in France, where he was heading Schumacher and had the Ferrari driver under control, until he was the first to encounter unflagged oil that had just been spilled by Allan McNish's broken Toyota. Räikkönen spun, handing the win to Schumacher. Coulthard was second in Canada, and took thirds in Brazil, France and the US, a couple of fifths, and a sixth. Räikkönen's highlight, meanwhile, was second in France after he recovered from his spin, thirds in Japan and the European Grand Prix at Nürburgring, and fourths in both Hungary and Canada.

A total of 65 points left the team third in the Constructors' World Championship behind Ferrari and BMW-Williams.

Over the course of the year development on the MP4-17 centered on aerodynamic tweaks and weight-saving measures. A heavily revised rear end including a new gearbox and suspension was ready by the middle of the summer.

The official launch of the MP4-17 was at Barcelona's Circuit de Catalunya. The car was driven by the team's third (test) driver, 27 year-old Austrian Alexander Wurz, who had joined the squad in 2001.

The 2002 Monaco Grand Prix would turn out to be the team's only win of the year. David Coulthard took the lead on the first lap and led all the way to the finish. Kimi Räikkönen (left) who joined at the start of the year dropped out on lap 44 after a coming together with Barrichello left him with severe handling problems.

MP4-17A FORMULA 1

SPECIFICATION

MODEL	McLaren-Mercedes MP4-17A
TYPE/FORMULA	Formula 1
YEAR OF PRODUCTION	2002
DESIGNER	Adrian Newey/Neil Oatley
EXAMPLES BUILT	9
ENGINE	Mercedes-Benz FO 110M V10
CUBIC CAPACITY	2997cc
ELECTRONICS	STAR System (TAG-210)
POWER OUTPUT	825bhp

TRANSMISSION	McLaren longitudinal sequential auto 7-speed
CHASSIS	Moulded carbon fibre/aluminium honeycomb composite
BODY	Carbon fibre single piece cockpit/engine cover & nose
FRONT SUSPENSION	Unequal length wishbone, push-rod & bell
	crank operating inboard torsion bar/damper
REAR SUSPENSION	Unequal length wishbone, push-rod & bell
	crank operating inboard torsion bar/damper
BRAKES F/R	Outboard carbon fibre discs
WHEELS DIAMETER x WIDTH F/R	13x12/13x13.7in

TYRES F/R	Michelin
LENGTH	183in - 4648 mm
WIDTH	70.9in - 1800mm
HEIGHT	40.5in - 1029mm
WHEELBASE	124in - 3150mm
TRACK F/R	55.5/55.5in - 1410/1410mm
WEIGHT	1322lb - 600kg
PRINCIPAL DRIVERS	Coulthard, Räikkönen
IDENTIFYING COLOURS	Silver/Anthracite/Black/Rocket Red

2002 SOAPBOX
McLAREN MP4-T5

One of the less well-known recent McLaren single seaters was the MP4-T5. Its origins lay in the annual Goodwood Festival of Speed, an event traditionally supported by McLaren which over the years has taken a number of contemporary and historic cars to the Sussex venue.

The MP4-T5's success owed a good deal to Mark Childs, who joined McLaren from university in 2001 and brought with him the experience of building a contender for the Goodwood Gravity Racing Club Soapbox Challenge the previous year.

Keen to repeat the experience once he had joined the Vehicle Development Department, where he was working on the Mercedes-Benz SLR McLaren, Childs admits to having pestered Gordon Murray for several months before the latter agreed to support an entry providing all the design and construction work was carried out in the evenings and at weekends.

The typically McLaren intention was to win the Soapbox Challenge, though Childs says that the project also functioned as an interesting team-building exercise within the company and encouraged good working relationships between employees in different departments. As with any other McLaren project the core team comprised a number of designers and technicians, but every employee was invited to join in; the Technical Graphics department, for example, created the distinctive livery.

The first task was to break down the engineering challenge to fundamental physics, identifying gravity as the only motive force, and aerodynamic drag and rolling resistance as the two key retarding forces. After minute study of the rules the team decided to enter the Streamliner rather than the Roadster class, the fully enclosed bodywork being then limited in terms of maximum length, width and mass, with a minimum driver eye-line height requirement. The budget was pegged by the rules at just £1000.

Thereafter the approach was typically McLaren: thorough and painstaking. The profile and corner radii of the Goodwood track were measured so that the data gathered could be used to build a mathematical model simulation to predict cornering forces and top speed. To minimise the frontal area the team also had to find a driver of suitably small stature and the necessary skills, such as reaction times and courage, to conduct a machine capable of speeds in excess of 60mph. McLaren test driver Chris Goodwin stepped up to the challenge, and the MP4-T5 was designed around his jockey-sized frame.

Initially using a template cut to show the basic profile, the vehicle's layout was worked on to arrive at the optimum weight distribution, minimal drag, and the best handling characteristics for Goodwood. This was then 3D modelled using computer-aided design (CAD), after which a wooden mock-up was constructed to assist the integration of all elements of the mechanical design. With insufficient time for any wind tunnel testing, the overall shape was derived using various neutral wing profiles and calculated estimations.

Patterns were then hand-made, then moulds, and finally the vehicle's carbon composite monocoque was completed, with front and rear bulkheads being manufactured from the damaged floor of an F1 GTR to give increased chassis stiffness and better driver protection. Other components, such as rod ends, carbon material, ballast, a four-point racing harness and a Formula 1 steering rack were similarly sourced from within the Group, while the steering wheel was based on the design from Mika Häkkinen's MP4-16 race car.

Some features were naturally custom-made, such as the lightweight, fared-in wheels, its vacuum-formed featherweight screen, and the twin front rim brakes. The vehicle had an exceptionally comprehensive specification, with the monocoque boasting a high strength to low weight ratio with a variety of different core sizes being used to increase chassis stiffness in all its high-stress areas. It also featured deformable front and rear crash structures, and front and rear roll-hoops, the latter being carbon items fully integrated into the monocoque.

For the first test day at Goodwood the team had no more to show than a few CAD drawings and some sketches, but by the second Childs and his colleagues had a fully operational machine. The day was spent setting it up adjusting various components to ensure it behaved as predicted, and fine-tuning the handling. The car then adopted its own unique McLaren branding, Ron Dennis giving the project his official blessing.

With stiff competition expected from BMW/Rolls-Royce, Lotus, Bugatti, Prodrive, Jaguar, Ford and Bentley, the team was quietly confident that it had the fastest car. In the end the results spoke for themselves. The McLaren MP4-T5 not only registering the fastest time of any car in all categories, but also setting a new course record of 65.1s.

Built from pieces of a damaged F1 GTR chassis, the carbon fibre composite monocoque of the MP4-T5 nears completion in the workshops of the Vehicle Development Department at Woking Business Park.

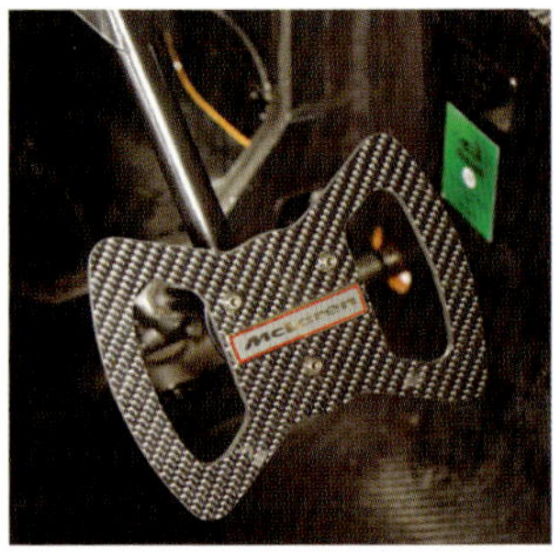

The steering wheel, such as it was, was based on the one fitted to the 2001 MP4-16 Formula 1 car driven by Häkkinen and Coulthard, albeit with fewer electronic controls, (see page 242).

With Chris Goodwin at the controls, the MP4-T5 took to the track for its first test run on the Goodwood hill. It wasn't until Ron Dennis had seen the vehicle pictured in Auto Express that he gave his full and official blessing to the project.

At the 2002 Goodwood Festival of Speed the MP4-T5 was the fastest 'Gravity Racer' of the weekend and set a new course record for the descent of Lord March's front driveway.

MP4-T5 SOAPBOX
SPECIFICATION

MODEL	McLaren MP4-T5
TYPE/FORMULA	Soapbox
YEAR OF PRODUCTION	2002
DESIGNER	Mark Childs
EXAMPLES BUILT	1
ENGINE	Gravity Powered
CUBIC CAPACITY	n/a
ELECTRONICS	n/a
POWER OUTPUT	n/a

TRANSMISSION	n/a
CHASSIS	Carbon fibre composite monocoque/driver safety cell
BODY	Integral to chassis, carbon fibre wheel
	covers and axle fairings
STEERING	Rack and pinion ex-McLaren Formula 1
FRONT SUSPENSION	Single axle, adjustable toe, castor and camber
REAR SUSPENSION	Single axle, adjustable toe and camber
BRAKES F/R	Twin front wheel rim brakes
WHEELS DIAMETER x WIDTH F/R	Custom 600x20mm

TYRES F/R	650 mm diameter road tyre (slicks)
LENGTH	76.8in - 1950mm
WIDTH	43.3in - 1100mm
HEIGHT - DRIVER EYELINE (regulation)	30.3in - 770mm
WHEELBASE (adjustable)	39.4in - 1000mm
TRACK F/R (adjustable)	51.2in - 1300mm
WEIGHT INC DRIVER MIN/MAX (regulation)	220/298lb - 100/135kg
PRINCIPAL DRIVERS	Chris Goodwin
IDENTIFYING COLOURS	Papaya

2003 FORMULA 1 McLAREN MP4-18A

The West McLaren Mercedes MP4-18 was so keenly anticipated and discussed by the media that some pundits were moved to describe it as *"the most anxiously awaited F1 car of the year,"* yet it never actually raced.

The MP4-17A had failed to win the World Championship in 2002 but it was a great piece of high-speed sculpture and provided Adrian Newey and his team with a good starting point for 2003 as work continued simultaneously on the MP4-18. For the latter, Ron Dennis was quick to accept that a quantum leap in performance was necessary. *"Nothing else will do,"* he insisted.

Accordingly, as work proceeded on MP4-18, Mercedes-Benz designed a radical new V10, the FO 110P, to make up what some observers calculated as a seven per cent power deficit to its main rivals. The team pioneered a new 'quick change' installation on the car, to speed up engine changes. The new powerplant was mated to a new lowline transmission.

The MP4-18 boasted a new carbon composite monocoque which was designed to be not just stiffer and lighter but also have a lower centre of gravity. Externally, the car's nose structure was shorter and lower, while the packaging of the rear end was aggressively tight and a small dorsal fin-shape to the engine cover added to its purposeful looks.

Simulation tests at McLaren using a range of powerful new diagnostic tools showed the car indeed to have taken a dramatic step forward from the baseline '17D' in terms of performance. Design work had concentrated on a number of developments intended to improve the overall aerodynamic efficiency while paying even closer attention to details and to new materials. It was also the first McLaren designed specifically to maximise the performance of the new Michelin tyres.

Significantly, and in part because continued development of the MP4-17 meant it retained a high degree of competitiveness into the 2003 season, the team adhered to its decision to conceive, design and engineer the MP4-18 for as long as it took to get it right rather than be bound by the starting date for the season, or the date of any particular race thereafter. It was assisted here by a period of rule stability, which meant that the car could evolve in a less frantic environment, although Newey disclosed that the basic design had been fixed by mid-February.

Dennis continued to insist, *"The car will only run when we can be satisfied that it is better than the '17D' and as reliable."* As a result it didn't make its first public appearance until May. By that time Kimi Räikkönen was making great use of the interim MP4-17D to fight for the lead in the Drivers' World Championship.

The new transmission used a carbon-fibre casing and boasted numerous innovations, and was one reason why the car was late. The design demanded some innovative manufacturing techniques that had given rise to more problems than had been anticipated.

Test pilot Alexander Wurz was hugely enthusiastic about the car, keenly expressing his "*excitement to be driving the MP4-18A for the first time*" and confirming that everything about it "*feels great*". Newey too expressed confidence that the car had what it took to take the battle to Ferrari, explaining that his design "*has probably had more research put into it than any other car I have worked on.*"

There was talk of the MP4-18 making its long awaited race debut, albeit with the old transmission, at the British GP at Silverstone in July, but that didn't happen; nor did it appear on Mercedes-Benz's home turf for the European Grand Prix at the Nürburgring, which had also been widely anticipated. Instead, amid revelations that the tight packaging of its rear bodywork led to underbonnet fires within five fast laps, the MP4-17D was kept in service to the end of the season and the new car was kept in abeyance. It eventually paved the way in terms of concept and new ideas for the cars that were to follow.

The team hoped that MP4-18A would be a huge leap forward in performance. In the end it never had the chance to race in a Grand Prix, but provided a solid stepping stone for the cars that followed in 2004 and 2005.

The monocoque on the radical MP4-18A was stiffer and lighter than the 2002 car's. With a lower centre of gravity, shorter nose and tighter rear end packaging it looked altogether more purposeful than its predecessor.

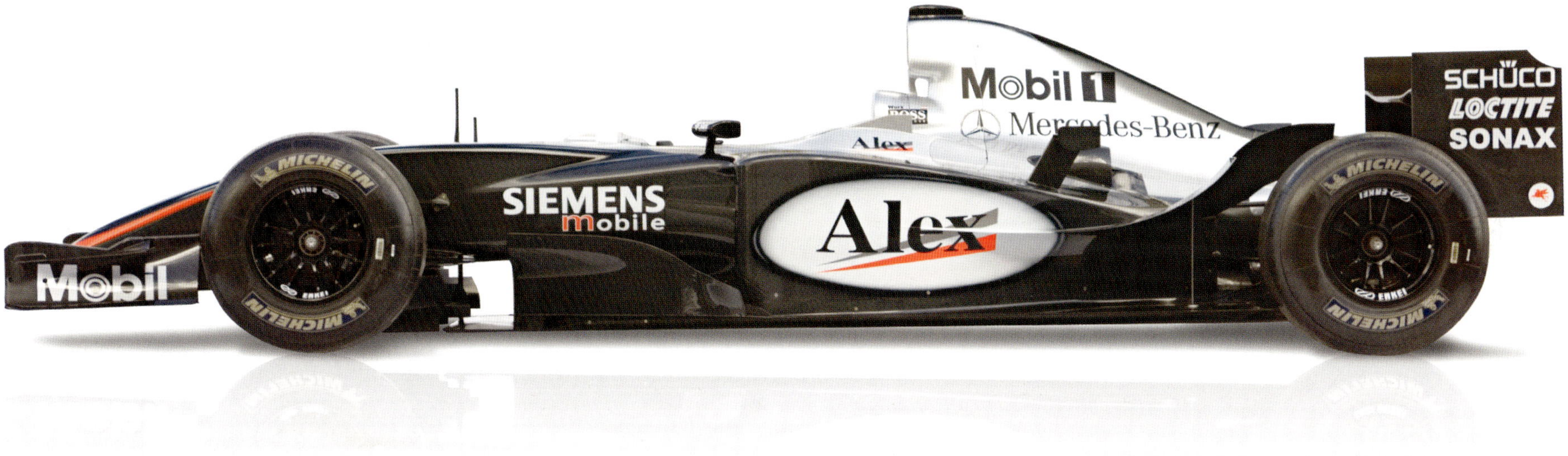

MP4-18A FORMULA 1
SPECIFICATION

MODEL	McLaren-Mercedes MP4-18A
TYPE/FORMULA	Formula 1
YEAR OF PRODUCTION	2003
DESIGNER	Adrian Newey
EXAMPLES BUILT	3 (+ 3 monocoques)
ENGINE	Mercedes-Benz FO 110P V10
CUBIC CAPACITY	2997cc
ELECTRONICS	STAR System (TAG-210)
POWER OUTPUT	860bhp

TRANSMISSION	McLaren semi-auto sequential longitudinal 7-speed
CHASSIS	Moulded carbon fibre/aluminium honeycomb composite
BODY	Carbon fibre single piece cockpit/engine cover & nose
FRONT SUSPENSION	Unequal length wishbone, push-rod & bell
	crank operating inboard torsion bar/damper
REAR SUSPENSION	Unequal length wishbone, push-rod & bell
	crank operating inboard torsion bar/damper
BRAKES F/R	Outboard carbon fibre discs
WHEELS DIAMETER x WIDTH F/R	13x12/13x13.7in

TYRES F/R	Michelin
LENGTH	182in - 4623mm
WIDTH	70.9in - 1800mm
HEIGHT	40in - 1016mm
WHEELBASE	122in - 3099mm
TRACK F/R	55/55in - 1397/1397mm
WEIGHT	1322lb - 600kg
PRINCIPAL DRIVERS	Coulthard, Räikkönen, Wurz
IDENTIFYING COLOURS	Silver/Anthracite/Black/Rocket Red

2003 FORMULA 1 McLAREN MP4-17D

It was an indication of how seriously McLaren was taking its programme with the MP4-18A that it elected to start the 2003 season with a heavily revised 'D' version of the MP4-17.

The latter design was powered by an updated version of the Mercedes-Benz FO 110M engine rather than the all-new FO 110P being prepared for use in the newer car. The MP4-17D was thus an interim model but featured significant changes which included a revised transmission, internal chassis modifications, and improvements to the aerodynamics and suspension. The development work was a big success. David Coulthard won the opening race in Australia, and was in contention in Malaysia too until suffering a spark box problem. Kimi Räikkönen, who had come third in Melbourne, scored his first Grand Prix triumph at Sepang to put himself at the head of the World Championship points table. He stayed there after just losing out to Giancarlo Fisichella's Jordan in a farcical wet Brazilian GP, and narrowly held on as Michael Schumacher finally put three consecutive wins together in his Ferrari.

Soon it became a three-way fight, as Ralf Schumacher and Juan Pablo Montoya pushed closer in their BMW-Williamses, but victory for Michael Schumacher in Canada finally put him at the top of the table. One of the turning points for Räikkönen, who was sixth in Montreal after a qualifying mistake obliged him to start from the pitlane, came at the GP of Europe at Nürburgring. He was romping away from the field when his engine broke.

Third place for the Finn at Silverstone narrowed the gap to Schumacher to seven points, with race victor Montoya a similar number behind Kimi. But when Montoya won at Hockenheim where Räikkönen was the victim of a first-corner accident, the Colombian moved ahead. Then second place in Hungary for Räikkönen, behind Alonso, left the scores as Schumacher 72, Montoya 71, Räikkönen 70.

Then came controversy at Monza, where a protest from Bridgestone (after Schumacher had finished a beaten and lapped eighth at the Hungaroring) led to the FIA reinterpreting its previous ruling on what constituted reasonable tyre wear. Michelin's front tyres, it decided, breached acceptable rates, obliging the French company at minimal notice to create new tyres for all of its teams, among them McLaren and Williams. Their momentum was seriously compromised as they acclimatised to the different characteristics of the new tyres, they lost valuable momentum. Schumacher, meanwhile, won in Italy and America, where Räikkönen was respectively fourth and second. The tide had turned. Going into the final round, Kimi was nine points behind Michael. Though the latter struggled to the eighth place he needed, second place for Räikkönen behind Schumacher's team-mate Rubens Barrichello left him second overall, two points shy.

Coulthard finished second in Germany, third in Japan, fourth in Brazil, fifth in San Marino, where Räikkönen had started from pole, and fifth again in Austria, France, Britain and Hungary. His 51 points put him seventh overall.

The MP4-17D may have been an interim car, but its tally of 142 points left it only two short of BMW-Williams and 16 off Ferrari's final score. And the introduction of various parts from the unraced MP4-18A, as the season developed, not only kept it in play but laid valuable groundwork for the MP4-19A which followed.

"*The reality,*" Martin Whitmarsh reflected, "*is that during the first third of the season we were distracted by concentrating on the new car, and by Canada it was clear that we needed to apply more energy into the MP4-17D project in order to maintain its Championship assault. All the work done to it wasn't actually designed to help us close on the leaders; it was intended to help us keep up and not drop back further down the grid.*"

Nevertheless, with only slightly better fortune the MP4-17D could have joined its illustrious forebears as a title winner.

The previous season's car was reworked into the MP4-17D for 2003 and proved highly competitive from the outset. Coulthard won the first race of the season in Australia, and Räikkönen, who triumphed at the next race in Malaysia, was unlucky not to win in Brazil when the race was red-flagged.

During the year the MP4-17D was further developed using ideas and data gained from running the MP4-18A. By Montreal the front suspension and brake cooling had been uprated and at Monza an engine upgrade and new aerodynamic package were incorporated.

SCHÜCO
LOCTITE
SONAX
Mobil 1
Kimi
SIEMENS
mobile
Mobil

2003 FORMULA 1
McLAREN MP4-17D

CONTINUED

Clever strategy from the team and an excellent performance from Coulthard in Australia gave him his 12th Grand Prix win in a McLaren, which would ultimately be his final victory for the team.

Two weeks later in Malaysia, Kimi Räikkönen took the first GP victory of his career and became the second-youngest winner in the sport's history. Still the youngest at that time: Bruce McLaren.

MP4-17D FORMULA 1
SPECIFICATION

MODEL	McLaren-Mercedes MP4-17D
TYPE/FORMULA	Formula 1
YEAR OF PRODUCTION	2003
DESIGNER	Adrian Newey/Neil Oatley
EXAMPLES BUILT	6
ENGINE	Mercedes-Benz FO 110M V10
CUBIC CAPACITY	2997cc
ELECTRONICS	STAR System (TAG-210)
POWER OUTPUT	885bhp

TRANSMISSION	McLaren semi-auto sequential longitudinal 7-speed
CHASSIS	Moulded carbon fibre/aluminium honeycomb composite
BODY	Carbon fibre single piece cockpit/engine cover & nose
FRONT SUSPENSION	Unequal length wishbone, push-rod & bell
	crank operating inboard torsion bar/damper
REAR SUSPENSION	Unequal length wishbone, push-rod & bell
	crank operating inboard torsion bar/damper
BRAKES F/R	Outboard carbon fibre discs
WHEELS DIAMETER x WIDTH F/R	13x12/13x13.7in

TYRES F/R	Michelin
LENGTH	183.5in - 4661mm
WIDTH	70.9in - 1800mm
HEIGHT	40.5in - 1029mm
WHEELBASE	124in - 3150mm
TRACK F/R	55/55.5in - 1397/1409mm
WEIGHT	1322lb - 600kg
PRINCIPAL DRIVERS	Coulthard, Räikkönen
IDENTIFYING COLOURS	Silver/Anthracite/Black/Rocket Red

2003 ROADCAR
MERCEDES-BENZ SLR McLAREN

There was never any doubt who Mercedes-Benz and McLaren had in their sights when they unveiled the new Mercedes-Benz SLR McLaren. You only had to consider the manner and location of its launch.

To start the ball rolling, Kimi Räikkönen and Alex Wurz drove the new car from Brescia's Piazza della Vittoria, the starting point for the legendary Mille Miglia in the very heartland of Italian motor racing. After painting the town not red but silver, Kimi and Alex arrived at the IAA Frankfurt Motorshow, driving onto the stage in the Mercedes-Benz exhibition hall for the official world premiere on September 9th, where they were joined on stage by David Coulthard.

The exotic new car's figures were staggering: just under 626bhp from a supercharged 5.5-litre V8, together with 780Nm of torque at only 3,250rpm; a top speed of 207mph; a 0-62mph time of just 3.8s and 0-125 in 10.6. As one reporter waxed lyrically, *"each of the triple barrels of the new sportscar's name resonates with top-drawer magic"*.

Two great marques of unmatched resources, history and depth of sporting know-how came together in a car worthy of their unique heritage: Mercedes-Benz, a pioneer of the automobile whose motor-racing jewels include the original 300 SLR that swept to victory over 1000 miles of Italian roads at never-to-be-broken record speed in the hands of Stirling Moss in the 1955 Mille Miglia; and McLaren, by far the most successful and innovative Grand Prix team in British motor-racing history.

With perfect timing and sense of occasion those three 'magic' elements were drawn together in a sportscar featuring everything you'd expect in a McLaren, particularly in the wake of the astounding F1 and its derivatives. Blend in the exceptional performance, values and cosseting road behaviour of Mercedes-Benz and you have an irresistible mix, featuring, among other things: two stage airbags; dual-zone automatic climate control; room in the boot for two sets of golf clubs. Mercedes-Benz's new roadcar certainly looked nothing like the F1, and as a car of the modern era it also featured technological advances such as carbon brakes and active aerodynamics.

The car first appeared as the 1999 SLR Vision concept at the Detroit Auto Show. It was one of the year's great showstoppers and one to which the £350,000 production car with its concealed starter button and side-exiting exhausts was to remain remarkably faithful. As a styling concept, based on a classic front-engine/rear-wheel-drive configuration, the engineering required a degree of compromise. As Gordon Murray stated at the time, *"Car design is a compromise, it's just where you draw the line that matters."*

Mercedes-Benz went so far as to describe the SLR as *"the world's first crossover supercar."* This was due to the unique collaboration between Mercedes-Benz and McLaren, including the way in which it drew on McLaren for its dynamics and aerodynamics, carbon composite shell, chassis, doors and bonnet, and Daimler's time-honed expertise in safety, quality and reliability.

There was no compromise, of course, in overall quality and performance, crashworthiness and durability, which naturally all met the same standards and careful calibration as any mainstream Mercedes-Benz model.

The car's engine was mounted up front as it was in the original SLR Vision, driving the rear wheels through AMG's Speedshift R five-speed gearbox. McLaren uniquely packaged the power unit a metre further back within the chassis to achieve near-perfect weight distribution with a 51 per cent rearward bias. The body construction was another unique innovation and all of it was deliciously racecar, including not just that basic carbon composite chassis and shell but also a carbon crash structure at the front, another first for a roadcar. With a 50 per cent weight advantage over steel, carbon composite also offered four to five times the energy absorption rate of conventional metals.

The aerodynamics drew heavily on McLaren's racing experience, with air ducts incorporated into the design to create a partial vacuum and thus generate negative lift. By converting this pressure directly into traction, the car was thus guaranteed impressive ride stability, while an airbrake boosted this effect by maintaining the centre of pressure under braking as well as enhancing the car's already hugely impressive performance in terms of active safety.

The optional 19inch, 9-spoke 'Turbine' alloy wheels fitted to the car photographed carry different width tyres at the front and rear. Each tyre valve carries a radio transmitting sensor which sends information on tyre pressure and temperature to an antenna in each wheel arch.

The SLR featured ground-breaking technology and outstanding innovations in the fields of performance, occupant protection, aerodynamics and comfort. These combined to produce a truly unique high-performance sportscar.

RX54 AEA
RX54 AEA

2003 ROADCAR MERCEDES-BENZ SLR McLAREN

CONTINUED

One of the first customers was one D. Coulthard, of Monaco. He put in an order for an early car and as a team driver was allowed the single concession of avoiding the normal requirement to pay a deposit. "*Typical super-fast roadcars struggle with the main thing that we all have on race cars, which is downforce,*" he observed, "*but the Mercedes-Benz SLR McLaren avoids such pitfalls.*" He was also impressed with the packaging. "*You sit in the SLR and it feels like it's been designed around the driver. You sit in some high-performance cars and think, 'Who on earth is that shape?'*"

Staggering high-speed stability, breathtaking ability to change direction, vivid acceleration and a chassis which was arguably a new roadcar best were the sort of attributes recorded in one road test. The British weekly Autocar took a showroom SLR across to Ehre-Lessien – scene of an earlier McLaren triumph, of course – and recorded a remarkable 36.9s time for the zero to 186mph dash.

One of the greatest qualities of the SLR, as noted by road testers, was how easy the car was to drive, thanks to its automatic transmission and the assurance the driver has from a standard specification which includes anti-lock brakes, Mercedes-Benz's Sensotronic Brake Control, and acceleration skid control. There again, there seems little doubt that most genuine enthusiasts, the sort of drivers who have actually ordered such a vehicle as an SLR and put it through its paces, would actually favour its hard edge. This emphasises the unique ability of the SLR to transform itself from a usable, docile, everyday car to one with proven race-track ability with incredible performance and handling.

The Mercedes-Benz SLR McLaren remains the perfect fusion of McLaren's racing expertise and Mercedes-Benz's engineering prowess. Thanks to the unique styling and performance, Mercedes-Benz has had no difficulty persuading people to try the figure-hugging driver's seat. By February 2006, they celebrated completion of the 1000th car to roll off the bespoke production line at the McLaren Technology Centre. For an ordinary roadgoing sports car that would have been a landmark; for the SLR it was a sensational achievement

The 5.5-litre Mercedes-AMG V8 powerplant, complete with a screw-type compressor, developed a peak output of 626bhp and delivered its maximum torque of 780Nm at just 3250rpm - a figure which remained constant across a broad engine speed range of up to 5000rpm.

The bodyshell of the SLR is made entirely from carbon fibre composite. A material which has an energy absorbtion four or five times higher than steel or aluminium.

The most distinctive feature of the SLR is the doors. Attached to the front roof pillars, they swing forwards and upwards at a 107-degree angle to allow easy access for both occupants.

MERCEDES-BENZ SLR McLAREN ROADCAR
SPECIFICATION

MODEL	Mercedes-Benz SLR McLaren
TYPE/FORMULA	Roadcar
YEAR OF PRODUCTION	2003
DESIGNER	Mercedes-Benz & McLaren
EXAMPLES BUILT	1213
ENGINE	Mercedes-AMG V8
CUBIC CAPACITY	5439cc
INDUCTION	Charge-air cooled screw-type compressor
POWER OUTPUT	626bhp

TRANSMISSION	Mercedes 5-speed automatic/3 stage manual shift
CHASSIS	Carbon fibre monocoque. longitudinal front crash cones
BODY	Carbon fibre composite panels
FRONT SUSPENSION	Aluminium double wishbone,
	coil spring/gas damper, anti-roll bar
REAR SUSPENSION	Aluminium double wishbone,
	coil spring/gas damper
BRAKES F/R	Outboard carbon fibre/ceramic discs
WHEELS DIAMETER x WIDTH F/R	18x9/18x11.5in, optional 19in

TYRES F/R	Michelin
LENGTH	183.3in - 4656mm
WIDTH	75.1in - 1908mm
HEIGHT	49.6in - 1261mm
WHEELBASE	106.3in - 2700mm
TRACK F/R	64.5/61.8in - 1638/1569mm
DIN WEIGHT	3732lb - 1693kg
PRINCIPAL DRIVERS	n/a
IDENTIFYING COLOURS	n/a

2004 FORMULA 1
McLAREN MP4-19A

The MP4-18A may never have felt the heat of competition but every lesson that McLaren learned in its design and construction went into its successor, the MP4-19A. The family resemblance was unmistakeable.

The new car was ready for testing weeks before Christmas thanks to the head start bequeathed by the MP4-18A. It displayed a similar approach to its overall packaging, which was much tighter at the rear end, and a similar overall outline. But the internal architecture of the two monocoques was substantially different. *"Appearances can be misleading,"* Martin Whitmarsh said. *"While the MP4-18A and MP4-19A chassis look very similar in profile, they are completely different in terms of their structures under the skin."*

Brake developments, the launch control systems, and a number of engine-based refinements were carry-overs from the MP4-18, but there was plenty that was new too and personnel were at pains to point out that it would be unwise to underestimate how much technology and experience had been applied to the new project.

MP4-19A was stiffer and stronger without any weight penalty, and boasted an even lower centre of gravity. It was powered by yet another new version of the Mercedes-Benz V10, designated FO 110Q, the focus of whose development had centred on a new FIA-mandated requirement that an engine had to last a whole Grand Prix weekend.

West McLaren Mercedes was bullish about the MP4-19A's chances. *"Our intention is to hit the ground running at the start of next season with a technical package that is capable of sustaining a consistent challenge for the World Championship from the very first race of the season,"* Ron Dennis said.

On the driving front there was further stability, with Kimi Räikkönen and David Coulthard paired again, and Alex Wurz now supported on the test side by Spanish former Arrows racer Pedro de la Rosa. There were changes in the sport itself, however, with two qualifying sessions being run back-to-back on each Saturday, and two new races, in Bahrain and China. Such was the schedule that the Monaco, European, Canadian, US, French and British Grands Prix were to be run within an eight-week period.

In Australia Räikkönen retired after a loss of coolant from the radiator resulted in engine failure, and Coulthard was only eighth. Work was needed to rectify handling problems and an ongoing power deficit. Dennis pointed to the difficulty of maintaining grip in the faster corners with the Michelin tyres, owing to problems caused by unseasonably low temperatures, but there was no disguising how disappointed the team was.

The lack of performance in Melbourne was baffling, for in virtually every test session prior to the start of the season the MP4-19A had been about a second quicker than the MP4-17D. In a desperate run, Räikkönen finished only fifth in Canada, sixth in America and eighth in Imola, and Coulthard sixth in Malaysia and Canada and seventh in America to go with that eighth in Australia, as the season neared its mid-point. A heavily revised version of the car, MP4-19B, could not come soon enough.

The opening race of the 2004 season wasn't a good one for the team. After qualifying 10th on the grid, Kimi Räikkönen (above) was out with engine failure by lap nine and David Coulthard who started 12th could only score a single point for eighth place, a lap down on the leader.

Like the 17D, the MP4-19A was conceived using lessons learnt from MP4-18A. Although their chassis' looked similar in profile they were quite different structures under the skin.

MP4-19A FORMULA 1

SPECIFICATION

MODEL	McLaren-Mercedes MP4-19A
TYPE/FORMULA	Formula 1
YEAR OF PRODUCTION	2004
DESIGNER	Adrian Newey
EXAMPLES BUILT	5
ENGINE	Mercedes-Benz FO 110Q V10
CUBIC CAPACITY	2997cc
ELECTRONICS	STAR2 System (TAG-310)
POWER OUTPUT	895bhp

TRANSMISSION	McLaren semi-auto sequential longitudinal 7-speed
CHASSIS	Moulded carbon fibre/aluminium honeycomb composite
BODY	Carbon fibre single piece cockpit/engine cover & nose
FRONT SUSPENSION	Unequal length wishbone, push-rod & bell crank operating inboard torsion bar/damper
REAR SUSPENSION	Unequal length wishbone, push-rod & bell crank operating inboard torsion bar/damper
BRAKES F/R	Outboard carbon fibre discs
WHEELS DIAMETER x WIDTH F/R	13x12/13x13.7in

TYRES F/R	Michelin
LENGTH	181in - 4597mm
WIDTH	70.9in - 1800mm
HEIGHT	40in - 1016mm
WHEELBASE	122in - 3099mm
TRACK F/R	55/56.5in - 1397/1435mm
WEIGHT	1322lb - 600kg
PRINCIPAL DRIVERS	Coulthard, Räikkönen
IDENTIFYING COLOURS	Silver/Anthracite/Black/Rocket Red

2004 FORMULA 1
McLAREN MP4-19B

Following the disappointing debut of the MP4-19A the team rushed through a new version, MP4-19B, in time for the French Grand Prix at Magny-Cours. Kimi Räikkönen, David Coulthard and testers Pedro de la Rosa and Alex Wurz had amassed 600 laps in it during a three-day test in Jerez de la Frontera in Spain, and there was optimism that it was a significant step forwards.

The car was based around a further modified Mercedes-Benz V10 with an uprated lubrication system, and a new monocoque with revised rear-end aerodynamics. Newly profiled sidepods and repositioned barge boards necessitated a repositioning of the radiators and, together with a new position for the hot-air sidepod exhausts, the winglets on top of the sidepods now featured two, rather than one, elements. The engine cover was also subtly redesigned and now ran more horizontally back from the roll-over hoop.

One of the primary aims was to improve the balance during cornering by addressing the differential between front and rear tyre temperatures that the rendered the MP4-19A difficult to set up.

Ron Dennis was optimistic: "*The hard work of the whole team is leading us in the right direction. Both our chassis and engine performance have taken a positive step forward.*"

The last eight Grands Prix of the 18-race season saw a steady improvement in performance for West McLaren Mercedes, brought on by both the chassis changes, and much improved engine performance and reliability. Räikkönen and Coulthard finished sixth and seventh respectively in the French Grand Prix, after the Scot had been an encouraging third fastest in qualifying. Trying a new style of brake discs which featured transverse grooves and in theory offered more response, Räikkönen then took pole position at Silverstone. He led the British GP until the first round of pit stops on lap 11, and finished a close second, two seconds adrift of Michael Schumacher's Ferrari.

Coulthard was seventh at Silverstone and fourth in Germany, where Räikkönen went out after 13 laps following an accident. In Hungary the Finn went the same distance before electrical problems in the injection system accounted for his MP4-19B; both drivers had relied on harder-compound Michelins for qualifying and been caught out by unusually low ambient and track temperatures which left them on the fifth and sixth rows of the grid. Coulthard struggled home ninth. Then came Spa, and redemption.

As Coulthard qualified a promising fourth Räikkönen started only 10th, but in a straight fight came through to beat the dominant Schumacher. There was drama at the start as the Finn's car was hit by Felipe Massa's Sauber-Petronas, but he was able to keep going and moved up steadily as three safety car periods dictated the pace. He passed Schumacher at the first restart, then Coulthard, to take third place behind the Renaults of Jarno Trulli and Fernando Alonso. He took the lead on the 12th lap, after Trulli made a pit stop and Alonso crashed, then maintained his advantage after his own two pit stops to lead Schumacher home by 3.1s in one of the greatest turnaround victories in history. It was his second win, McLaren's 138th, and a wonderful vindication for the new car. To rub it in, he also set the fastest lap. Coulthard sustained an early puncture, collided with Jaguar's Christian Klien after making up ground, and finished seventh after another recovery drive.

Monza brought sixth place for Coulthard and an engine failure for Räikkönen, and they were third and ninth in reversed order in the inaugural race in China. Sixth for the Finn and a collision with Rubens Barrichello for DC summarised Japan, but Räikkönen pushed Juan Pablo Montoya's winning BMW-Williams all the way in Brazil's finale to end a tough season on a bright note.

Räikkönen finished seventh in the Drivers' points table, Coulthard equal ninth with Ralf Schumacher. McLaren was fifth in the Constructors', its lowest position since 1981 and the first year of the MP4 dynasty. But the MP4-19B had shown the way forward.

An era ended as Coulthard left to join Red Bull for 2005 after nine seasons, 150 races, seven pole positions and a dozen wins for the Woking team, for whom he had first tested at Silverstone in November 1990. In his place came Montoya, who in Brazil had demonstrated his potential in the best possible way to his new employers.

In August Kimi Räikkönen took the only win of the year for the team. Having qualified 10th for the Belgian Grand Prix at Spa Francorchamps, he was up to fifth by the end of the first lap and in a straight fight, out-drove Michael Schumacher to claim his second GP victory.

With no significant weight penalty, the stronger and stiffer chassis of the MP4-19B was smaller than ever. The compact cockpit was a tight fit for the drivers, and test driver Alex Wurz had to have the extinguisher repositioned before he could get comfy behind the ever-more high-tech wheel.

MP4-19B FORMULA 1

SPECIFICATION

MODEL	McLaren-Mercedes MP4-19B
TYPE/FORMULA	Formula 1
YEAR OF PRODUCTION	2004
DESIGNER	Adrian Newey
EXAMPLES BUILT	4
ENGINE	Mercedes-Benz FO 110Q V10
CUBIC CAPACITY	2997cc
ELECTRONICS	STAR2 System (TAG-310)
POWER OUTPUT	910bhp

TRANSMISSION	McLaren semi-auto sequential longitudinal 7-speed
CHASSIS	Moulded carbon fibre/aluminium honeycomb composite
BODY	Carbon fibre single piece cockpit/engine cover & nose
FRONT SUSPENSION	Unequal length wishbone, push-rod & bell
	crank operating inboard torsion bar/damper
REAR SUSPENSION	Unequal length wishbone, push-rod & bell
	crank operating inboard torsion bar/damper
BRAKES F/R	Outboard carbon fibre discs
WHEELS DIAMETER x WIDTH F/R	13x12/13x13.7in

TYRES F/R	Michelin
LENGTH	182in - 4623mm
WIDTH	70.9in - 1800mm
HEIGHT	40in - 1016mm
WHEELBASE	122in - 3099mm
TRACK F/R	55/56.5in - 1397/1435mm
WEIGHT	1322lb - 600kg
PRINCIPAL DRIVERS	Coulthard, Räikkönen
IDENTIFYING COLOURS	Silver/Anthracite/Black/Rocket Red

2005 FORMULA 1 McLAREN MP4-20A

The new McLaren-Mercedes MP4-20A took a lot of its basic design from the unraced MP4-18A. "*We stuck to our guns,*" Neil Oatley said, "*because we had faith in it. We knew we had been too aggressive with the 18A, but that didn't make it a bad car. It made the choices wrong, but it didn't make the philosophy wrong.*"

This aggressive approach led to a car that was a genuine leap forward, but which was too light and, as a result, insufficiently rigid. "*We didn't really understand how to trade stiffness against performance against strength.*"

Now the latest car to bear the McLaren name incorporated all of the lessons that had been learned, from the MP4-18A and from the two iterations of the MP4-19. The MP4-20A looked quite different from its immediate predecessor, partly thanks to a change which was brought about by the new set of rules drawn up by the FIA for 2005. The front wing had to be raised another 50mm, the maximum height of the diffuser was restricted, and the rear wing had to be moved significantly forward, all in an attempt to reduce downforce. Changes were accordingly made in these areas, together with detail revisions to the deflectors and barge boards around and behind the front suspension. Technical Director Adrian Newey believed that downforce had been cut by as much as 28 per cent, according to wind tunnel data.

The suspension geometry was also revised, a large amount of work was carried out on the critical hydraulic systems, and there was a new version of the Mercedes-Benz V10, the FO 110R, which was required now to last for two GPs.

The early races were tough. Heavy rain during qualifying for the Australian opener left Räikkönen 10th and Montoya ninth on the grid and they worked up the field to finish eighth and sixth respectively. Montoya was fourth in Malaysia, but Räikkönen lost a possible victory. He was leading and had set fastest lap by the 24th tour, but a rear tyre deflation, due to a valve failure, forced him into a spin and then to crawl round for a replacement. He recovered to finish ninth.

Montoya injured himself prior to Bahrain and had to be replaced by Pedro de la Rosa - who finished fifth as Räikkönen made the podium with third place. Alex Wurz, standing in for Montoya, repeated that result in San Marino, where a driveshaft failure halted Räikkönen.

The big breakthrough came in Spain, where a dominant Räikkönen beat season pacesetter Fernando Alonso's Renault fair and square as a recovered Montoya bravely took seventh after a spin and problems with his refuelling rig. McLaren was back on track, as Räikkönen proved with another decisive win in Monte Carlo, where Montoya followed Alonso home with fifth place. The battle for the title was distilling into Alonso versus Räikkönen, with 49 and 27 points apiece.

A hat-trick was denied Kimi at Nürburgring when a calculated gamble to get to the finish with a flat-spotted and badly vibrating tyre backfired on the last lap, breaking the McLaren's right front suspension and forcing a non-finish as a grateful Alonso inherited victory. Montoya was seventh.

Räikkönen bounced back to win in Canada, then came the controversial US GP at Indianapolis where all the Michelin runners were forced to withdraw after the warm-up lap because of tyre problems. That was particularly galling for Kimi as he had qualified on the front row, and because a flypast win for Michael Schumacher brought him within three points of the Finn's 37. Alonso still led with 59. They finished in the order Alonso, Räikkönen, Schumacher in France, then Montoya won his first race for the team at Silverstone as Räikkönen completed the podium behind Alonso. Now the Spaniard had 77 points, the Finn 51. Alonso beat Montoya in Germany, with Räikkönen retiring after 35 laps with a hydraulic leak after leading from pole. With a 36-point advantage, Alonso looked safe until Kimi sliced away 10 by winning in Hungary, and another two by beating Alonso in the first Turkish GP. Now the gap was 24.

Montoya took a second victory to endorse the performance of the MP4-20A in Monza, where Alonso finished second and Räikkönen fourth after an engine failure in practice negated his pole position and obliged him to fight through from 11th place on the grid. At Spa he got his revenge, leading Alonso home as Montoya controversially crashed while lapping Antonio Pizzonia's Williams. Montoya then led a McLaren 1-2 in Brazil. It was the team's 40th. Third place there was sufficient for Alonso to put the title beyond Kimi's reach, however, with 117 points to 94. The Japanese and Chinese GPs remained. In the former Kimi drove the race of his life. Everything went wrong for the team in qualifying when both he and Montoya started from the back of the grid after sudden rain in qualifying rendered things a lottery. Kimi started 17th, Juan Pablo 18th. The consolation was that close rivals Michael Schumacher and Fernando Alonso were 14th and 16th. Montoya was eliminated in an accident on the first lap and Giancarlo Fisichella should have won for Renault, but Räikkönen drove a blistering race to catch and pass all of his rivals and deny the Italian literally at the beginning of the final lap.

Alonso bounced back to beat Räikkönen in China, with Montoya falling out after 24 laps. Thus a gripping season of redemption for McLaren ended with 10 victories, Räikkönen in second place in the Drivers' World Championship with 112 points to Alonso's 133 and Montoya fourth on 60, and McLaren-Mercedes second to Renault in the Constructors' with 182 points to 191.

Juan Pablo Montoya scored his third win of the season in Brazil (top) and finished fourth in the Championship. Despite taking seven wins in 2005, including the Japanese Grand Prix (above), Kimi Räikkönen had to be content with second in the title race.

The MP4-20A was generally considered to be the fastest car of the 2005 season, a fact no doubt helped by the reported 3,600 hours spent working on the car in the wind tunnel.

MP4-20A FORMULA 1

SPECIFICATION

MODEL	McLaren-Mercedes MP4-20A	TRANSMISSION	McLaren semi-auto sequential longitudinal 7-speed	TYRES F/R	Michelin
TYPE/FORMULA	Formula 1	CHASSIS	Moulded carbon fibre/aluminium honeycomb composite	LENGTH	182in - 4623mm
YEAR OF PRODUCTION	2005	BODY	Carbon fibre single piece cockpit/engine cover & nose	WIDTH	70.9in - 1800mm
DESIGNER	Adrian Newey	FRONT SUSPENSION	Unequal length wishbone, push-rod & bell	HEIGHT	41in - 1041mm
EXAMPLES BUILT	7		crank operating inboard torsion bar/damper	WHEELBASE	123in - 3124mm
ENGINE	Mercedes-Benz FO 110R V10	REAR SUSPENSION	Unequal length wishbone, push-rod & bell	TRACK F/R	55/56.5in - 1397/1435mm
CUBIC CAPACITY	2997cc		crank operating inboard torsion bar/damper	WEIGHT	1322lb - 600kg
ELECTRONICS	STAR2 System (TAG-310)	BRAKES F/R	Outboard carbon fibre discs	PRINCIPAL DRIVERS	Räikkönen, Montoya
POWER OUTPUT	920bhp	WHEELS DIAMETER x WIDTH F/R	13x12/13x13.7in	IDENTIFYING COLOURS	Silver/Anthracite/Black/Rocket Red

2006 FORMULA 1
McLAREN MP4-21A

Following its impressive recovery in 2005, McLaren-Mercedes headed into a new era in 2006 as the FIA introduced a new Formula 1 catering for 2.5-litre V8 engines.

Mercedes-Benz reacted with its all-new FO 108S V8 which weighed in at 95kg. During winter testing Räikkönen, Montoya and de la Rosa covered 8,692km in the new McLaren MP4-21 that was built to receive it, the equivalent of 28 Grands Prix. The lap times were competitive, and several times the V8 withstood the strain of two race weekends' worth of running and up to 50 per cent more, at Barcelona and Valencia and on the dynamometers.

The new car was an evolution of the MP4-20 with its carbon fibre and aluminium honeycomb composite monocoque, but was unusual inasmuch as it retained a separate dashboard. This was tiny, 120mm wide and weighing less than 100gm, with 15 light-emitting diodes across the top which let the drivers know when the optimum point had been reached to change gear. According to head of vehicle electronics, Charlie Hawkins, this was crucial: "*While the drivers have a tremendous feel for when to change gear, this gives them the all-important edge when it comes to precision.*"

While Fernando Alonso was again expected to be the primary opponent in his Renault, the news had broken the previous December that following discussions initiated by Ron Dennis immediately after the 2005 Brazilian GP, he had signed to join McLaren for 2007.

Optimism about the new car's capabilities seemed completely justified, but things went wrong for Räikkönen early in the season opener in Bahrain when a rear suspension failure during qualifying seriously damaged his car and left him at the back of the 22-car field. On race day, however, he fought through brilliantly to third place behind Alonso and Michael Schumacher, with Montoya in fifth.

In Malaysia Renault scored a 1-2, leaving Montoya to pick up fourth as Räikkönen was the victim of a first-lap accident. He bounced back with another second to Alonso in Melbourne, albeit some way behind him but able to match his pace in the final stages. Montoya suffered an hydraulic failure. The Colombian was third in San Marino, the Finn fifth, as Michael Schumacher headed Alonso home.

McLaren made its 600th Grand Prix start in the GP of Europe at Nürburgring, but Räikkönen could only finish fourth, and Montoya's engine broke. Spain was similarly disappointing, with another fifth and a retirement respectively. It was abundantly clear that a Championship challenge was going to be unlikely, as Renault led Ferrari and McLaren with 78 points to 59 and 42.

At Monaco things improved. Räikkönen ran second behind Alonso on the opening lap, was displaced by Mark Webber's Williams on the second until he refuelled on the 22nd, then led briefly on the 24th as Alonso refuelled. His own stop dropped him back to third until overheating following a safety car period saw the car set fire on the 49th lap. Montoya, however, was a smooth runner-up to the Spaniard, 14.5s adrift. "*We threw away Monaco,*" Martin Whitmarsh said trenchantly. "*We undeniably had the best package but the reality is that every element of our package needs to be better, so we're working hard to improve that situation.*"

The MP4-21, for example, shared its predecessor's admirable attribute of being able to preserve its rear tyres. But whereas such a quality had been invaluable in 2005, when a single set had to last the distance, the reintroduction of tyre changes in 2006 robbed the team of this important advantage. Now it was struggling to get enough heat into the rear tyres and hence decent traction, during qualifying. Alonso won again at Silverstone, where Schumacher finally got the better of Räikkönen after a great battle for second. Montoya was sixth.

Driver issues hit the headlines in Montreal, as speculation grew that Räikkönen was to leave the team. On the track the order of the top three was the same as at Silverstone, but Montoya was eliminated in an accident. The Colombian was under a lot of pressure by now, with four retirements in 10 races, and when he crashed into Räikkönen in the first corner of the US GP at Indianapolis the following week, his career with McLaren reached its conclusion. As he headed off to pastures new in America's NASCAR series, Pedro de la Rosa was drafted in as his interim replacement. The Spaniard finished seventh first time out in France, two places behind Kimi. The Finn was third in Germany as de la Rosa's fuel pump malfunctioned, then Kimi crashed spectacularly while leading in murky conditions in Hungary. He admitted that it was his fault as he lost concentration lapping Liuzzi's Toro Rosso. De la Rosa took up the cudgels and resisted Schumacher, to finish an excellent second to first-time winner, Jenson Button.

An accident claimed Räikkönen early in Turkey, where de la Rosa was fifth, then Kimi finished nine seconds behind Schumacher at Monza as F1's 'second Spaniard' suffered early engine failure. It was Kimi's turn to go out early in China, with throttle problems, and Pedro's to finish fifth.

When Brazil brought just another fifth for Räikkönen and eighth for de la Rosa, a disappointing season ended with McLaren third on 110 points in the Constructors' World Championship, to Renault's 206 and Ferrari's 201. Räikkönen was fifth in the Drivers' on 65, Montoya eighth on 26, and de la Rosa 11th on 19. It was time to regroup for what would go down in history as one of F1's most dramatic and controversial seasons.

After Kimi Räikkönen had chased Alonso's Renault for two-thirds of the Monaco Grand Prix, Juan Pablo Montoya (above) inherited second place when the Finn retired.

The hi-tech steering wheel of the MP4-21A is a work of technological art. The tiny LED dashboard above it shows the gear selected, the optimum change point and other vital information including lap times.

Emirates
Emirates
SAP
Mobil

Henkel
SCHÜCO
Windows + Solar
Hilton
Mobil 1
Mercedes-Benz
JOHNNIE
WALKER
SIEMENS
MICHELIN
MICHELIN
MICHELIN
MICHELIN
Mobil

2006 FORMULA 1
McLAREN MP4-21A

CONTINUED

After five seasons and nine Grand Prix wins for McLaren-Mercedes Kimi Räikkönen's last race for the team was in Brazil (above) where he finished sixth. His best result of 2006 was second in Australia. Early in the race Kimi follows Montoya (opposite), who retired with electrical problems.

MP4-21A FORMULA 1
SPECIFICATION

MODEL	McLaren-Mercedes MP4-21A
TYPE/FORMULA	Formula 1
YEAR OF PRODUCTION	2006
DESIGNER	McLaren Racing design team
EXAMPLES BUILT	7
ENGINE	Mercedes-Benz FO 108S V8
CUBIC CAPACITY	2400cc
ELECTRONICS	STAR2 System (TAG-310)
POWER OUTPUT	735bhp

TRANSMISSION	McLaren semi-auto sequential longitudinal 7-speed
CHASSIS	Moulded carbon fibre/aluminium honeycomb composite
BODY	Carbon fibre single piece cockpit/engine cover & nose
FRONT SUSPENSION	Unequal length wishbone, push-rod & bell
	crank operating inboard torsion bar/damper
REAR SUSPENSION	Unequal length wishbone, push-rod & bell
	crank operating inboard torsion bar/damper
BRAKES F/R	Outboard carbon fibre discs
WHEELS DIAMETER x WIDTH F/R	13x12/13x13.7in

TYRES F/R	Michelin
LENGTH	185in - 4706mm
WIDTH	70.6in - 1795mm
HEIGHT	43.3in - 1100mm
WHEELBASE	124.4in - 3160mm
TRACK F/R	57/55.9in - 1448/1419mm
WEIGHT	1322lb - 600kg
PRINCIPAL DRIVERS	Räikkönen, Montoya, de la Rosa
IDENTIFYING COLOURS	Chrome/Anthracite/Rocket Red

2006 ROADCAR
MERCEDES-BENZ SLR McLAREN 722 EDITION

While the original 2003 Mercedes-Benz SLR McLaren was acknowledged as an outstanding synthesis of both companies' core values, a car bred from both a passion for racing and the knowledge which can be gained from it at the highest level, its combination of performance and comfort, tradition and innovation, was capable of further development. And neither the factory nor McLaren's more enthusiastic SLR customers were blind to this.

Accordingly action at Woking focused on bringing further refinements to the project. The resulting machine took to the road midway through 2006 as the Mercedes-Benz SLR McLaren '722 Edition'.

Building on the original car's tradition in more ways than one, the new name paid homage to Britain's Sir Stirling Moss and his historic victory with journalist Denis 'Jenks' Jenkinson in the 1955 Mille Miglia. The two men, driving a Mercedes-Benz 300 SLR, set off at 7.22 in the morning (hence the racing number 722) before winning the event in a time and at an average speed which were never bettered.

Like the original SLR coupé the 722, of which just 150 were built, shared styling cues with Moss's vaunted machine. The most obvious were the distinctive 'gills' behind the front wheels and the array of side-exiting AMG sports exhausts. However, considerable additional work was done under the shell. The engine was still a hand-built 5.5-litre V8 from the AMG engine shop at Affalterbach, but was uprated to 650bhp with improved torque. As result the 0-62mph time was brought down to just 3.6s, and the 0-125 to an incredible 10.2. The top speed was also slightly raised, to 210.6mph, while the new 0-186mph time was 28s.

With its harsher bark and harder edge, the car was a direct response to existing customers' requests for a more focused car. Its handling characteristics were also a little closer to its track heritage than had been the original's, thanks to uprated suspension, aluminium dampers which were 15 per cent stiffer on bump, and a chassis which sat 10mm closer to the ground.

At the same time larger carbon-ceramic brake discs were fitted, with a diameter of 390mm, to give it even more impressive stopping power. The car also featured new 19inch light-alloy wheels with skeletal black spokes; forged rather than cast, these saved around 10lb of unsprung weight per corner.

Externally, the car remained largely as before, although there were a number of commendably discreet visual identifiers. Again conceived very much in line with customer wishes, and reflecting the transfer of cutting-edge technology from Formula 1, these included a modified front spoiler with a new air splitter, and a new diffuser. The former accounted for a 128 per cent increase in downforce over the front axle, while the adjustable rear spoiler was re-engineered to move through an additional five degrees. There were red '722' badges, and red brake calipers too.

There were changes inside as well, among them new bucket-type sports seats upholstered in leather and Alcantara for even greater lateral support. A grippier racing steering wheel with leather trim, new gearshift paddles, optional red dials and black carbon highlights provided some distinctive finishing touches.

America's respected Autoweek called the resulting confection "*a wolf in an Armani dinner suit*", and recognised that it was "*bestowed with more power, less weight, more capabilities and better handling than its potent progenitor. In this form the SLR needs - almost demands - a place to let loose and be free.*"

The '722 Edition' of the SLR featured a revised interior with new style seats, steering wheel, paddle shifters and the addition of Alcantara red leather accents to the cabin.

MERCEDES-BENZ SLR McLAREN 722 EDITION ROADCAR

SPECIFICATION

MODEL	Mercedes-Benz SLR McLaren 722 Edition
TYPE/FORMULA	Roadcar
YEAR OF PRODUCTION	2006
DESIGNER	Mercedes-Benz & McLaren
EXAMPLES BUILT	150
ENGINE	Mercedes-AMG V8
CUBIC CAPACITY	5439cc
INDUCTION	Charge-air cooled screw-type compressor
POWER OUTPUT	650bhp

TRANSMISSION	Mercedes 5-speed automatic/3 stage manual shift
CHASSIS	Carbon fibre monocoque, longitudinal front crash cones
BODY	Carbon fibre composite panels
FRONT SUSPENSION	Aluminium double wishbone,
	coil spring/gas damper, anti-roll bar
REAR SUSPENSION	Aluminium double wishbone,
	coil spring/gas damper
BRAKES F/R	Outboard carbon fibre/ceramic discs
WHEELS DIAMETER x WIDTH F/R	19x9/19x11.5in

TYRES F/R	Michelin
LENGTH	183.3in - 4656mm
WIDTH	75.1in - 1908mm
HEIGHT	49.3in - 1251mm
WHEELBASE	106.3in - 2700mm
TRACK F/R	64.5/61.8in - 1638/1569mm
DIN WEIGHT	3635lb - 1649kg
PRINCIPAL DRIVERS	n/a
IDENTIFYING COLOURS	n/a

2007 FORMULA 1
McLAREN MP4-22

The Vodafone McLaren Mercedes MP4-22 was first seen in action in Valencia, Spain, in January 2007, following a lavish launch that featured the team's cars running on the city's streets in front of crowds of over 250,000. The event celebrated the arrival of Vodafone as title sponsor.

It represented the result of a painstaking review of no fewer than 11,000 individual components, and work on the design had been initiated well over a year before with discussions about the clutch and gearbox as early as December 2005 and initial sketches for a number of aerodynamic concepts being made around the same time. March 2006 saw these early ideas further developed using CAD software, after which the first of many computational fluid dynamic simulations were run. Work in the wind tunnel at the McLaren Technology Centre did not commence until May, eventually reaching a peak in mid-2007 by which time the tunnel was operating 19 hours a day testing and retesting a succession of developments of the 60 per cent scale model.

Over many months the steady development of the new design involved the generation of more than 4,500 component drawings, and 3,500 tooling drawings as the team left nothing to chance in its attempt to get back on top.

It was clear that an immense amount of work had gone into the hunt for novel aerodynamic solutions. The resultant shrink-wrapped style of the bodywork covering the revised Mercedes-Benz FO 108T V8 was reminiscent of MP4-18A.

The team of aerodynamicists had narrowed the airbox as much as possible, and the distinctive dorsal fin was necessary in order to meet yet another new bodywork regulation. The lower-revving engine which resulted from further rule changes also allowed for the sidepods to be fitted with smaller chimneys with trim under-sculpted air intakes.

Another major innovation was the pylon-mounted rear wing, replacing a more conventional endplate-mounted item. The front wing was radically different too; it was another triple-tiered assembly which was now vane-mounted so that its main plane, hanging freely, jutted steeply forward. Due to new crash-protection regulations the car featured completely new rear crash structures which were wider and blunter. An additional 6mm thick panel also had to be bonded to the side of the driver cell, to offer enhanced protection against penetration by debris in an accident.

"Many cars' rear crash structures were becoming more pointed," explained Martin Whitmarsh, *"so they were becoming quite good penetration tools. If a car spun and went into another, it could have been quite perilous."* Frontal protection was also enhanced after the regulations raised the velocity of impact in the mandatory crash tests from 14 to 15 metres per second.

The FO 108T motor now ran to 19,000rpm following an FIA-mandated reduction in revs, and internal revisions had resulted in a fatter torque curve and better cooling, and were aimed to make the unit more driveable.

When the MP4-22 was first unveiled Whitmarsh made it clear that it was still far from finished aerodynamically. *"It is a snapshot taken some time ago,"* he revealed. *"We're finding new performance in the wind tunnel every day and will phase in a significant package of changes by week seven. You'll see the car sprouting a lot of new aero componentry."*

The other technical significant change, following Michelin's withdrawal at the end of 2006, was a switch back to Bridgestone rubber. Besides the interface of the vehicle with the road via the tyre contact patches, this also impacted on the aerodynamics as the front tyres affect the airflow over structures in their vicinity. Here CFD simulations relating to heat and fluid flow had allowed the car's designers and engineers to find the best way to accommodate the demands and benefits of the changes. The team was confident that the switch from Michelin would therefore not materially affect the suspension's operation and made the decision to stick with the previous year's keel arrangement.

By the second race of the year in Malaysia one of the team's two new drivers, Fernando Alonso (above) was already winning. Lewis Hamilton, who had finished third in the first race, went one better in Kuala Lumpur (left) and was second, close behind Alonso.

vodafone
vodafone

Santander

Mobil 1
Mercedes-Benz
Henkel
SCHÜCO
Windows + Solar
Hilton
aigo 爱国者
vodafone
JOHNNIE WALKER
BRIDGESTONE
POTENZA
BRIDGESTONE
POTENZA

2007 FORMULA 1 McLAREN MP4-22

CONTINUED

Besides the Vodafone sponsorship, there was big news for the racing and marketing departments in the new driver line-up. It was a major boost for the team to welcome aboard double World Champion Fernando Alonso, who brought valuable experience and focus and proven race-winning ability. And a media furore was ignited when it was finally confirmed that his partner would be 22-year-old rookie Lewis Hamilton, who had been a member of the McLaren and Mercedes-Benz squad since his karting days.

It was expected that Hamilton would help Alonso to gather points in the campaign for the Constructors' World Championship as he gained experience, but his career got off to a sensational start in Melbourne when he ran ahead of the Spaniard for many laps before finishing third as Kimi Räikkönen, now with Ferrari, led them home.

In Sepang for the Malaysian GP, Hamilton backed up Alonso all the way. The champion took his first win for the marque with Lewis also beating the Ferraris and setting fastest lap as he helped the team to score a dominant 1-2.

In Spain, Hamilton led Fernando home, second and fifth, as Ferrari's Felipe Massa won. Lewis was second again in Monaco, this time behind Alonso who scored McLaren's 150th victory.

No rookie in history had been the podium for his first five races, but Lewis was far from finished. In North America in June he won in both Montreal and Indianapolis to increase a sensational lead in the World Championship table, and with Alonso finishing seventh and second respectively, each time beaten by the rookie, the team led Ferrari in the Constructors' points, 106 to 71.

Hamilton was third in France and Britain as Ferrari hit back, Alonso taking seventh and second again before taking a timely victory in the GP of Europe at Nürburgring. That was where the Brit's amazing record run of podiums finally came to a halt as various adventures in a race run in changeable conditions, which followed a nasty qualifying shunt when a wheel broke, left him ninth, out of the points for the first time. Now he led Alonso by just two.

Lewis hit back with his third victory, in Hungary, after Fernando had been penalised grid places for blocking him in the pit lane as they disagreed over tactics in qualifying. This time Hamilton beat Räikkönen and Alonso had to be content with fourth, and now trailed his rookie team-mate by seven points.

Massa won again in Turkey, where Räikkönen followed him home, and Alonso was third after Hamilton, in contention for possible victory, was dropped to fifth when his right front tyre exploded. Vodafone McLaren Mercedes crushed Ferrari on its home ground at Monza, with Alonso heading Hamilton in another 1-2, then the Spaniard beat his team-mate again at Spa, where they finished third and fourth in the wake of the dominant red cars.

When Lewis took his fourth victory in torrential rain in Japan, as Alonso crashed, his points lead extended to 12 and he seemed almost home and dry. But then a tyre gamble did not come off in the penultimate race in China. Hamilton went off the wet road as he finally came into the pits for a wheel change on the 31st lap, and with Fernando finishing second between Räikkönen and Massa, the gap was back to four points. Räikkönen, meanwhile, was now only three points adrift of Alonso.

In the final race the Finn came through to snatch victory, and both World Championships for Ferrari. Alonso finished third, behind Massa, Hamilton seventh after losing crucial time with an electronic gearbox malfunction on the eighth lap. In the end he lost out by one agonising point to Räikkönen, having led the title race almost all the way through the season. Fernando also scored 109 points, but Lewis got the runner-up nod on results countback through his five second places.

Monaco 2007 saw the 150th Grand Prix win for the McLaren team. And what a way to do it. From pole position, Fernando Alonso (top) led home Lewis Hamilton (above) and both finished almost a lap ahead of the third place car.

MP4-22 FORMULA 1

SPECIFICATION

MODEL	McLaren-Mercedes MP4-22
TYPE/FORMULA	Formula 1
YEAR OF PRODUCTION	2007
DESIGNER	McLaren Racing design team
EXAMPLES BUILT	6
ENGINE	Mercedes-Benz FO 108T V8
CUBIC CAPACITY	2398cc
ELECTRONICS	STAR2 System (TAG-310)
POWER OUTPUT	765bhp

TRANSMISSION	McLaren semi-auto sequential longitudinal 7-speed
CHASSIS	Moulded carbon fibre/aluminium honeycomb composite
BODY	Carbon fibre single piece cockpit/engine cover & nose
FRONT SUSPENSION	Unequal length wishbone, push-rod & bell
	crank operating inboard torsion bar/damper
REAR SUSPENSION	Unequal length wishbone, push-rod & bell
	crank operating inboard torsion bar/damper
BRAKES F/R	Outboard carbon fibre discs
WHEELS DIAMETER x WIDTH F/R	13x12/13x13.7in

TYRES F/R	Bridgestone
LENGTH	187in - 4749mm
WIDTH	70.6in - 1795mm
HEIGHT	43.3in - 1100mm
WHEELBASE	124.4in - 3160mm
TRACK F/R	57.2/55.9in - 1454/1419mm
WEIGHT	1322lb - 600kg
PRINCIPAL DRIVERS	Alonso, Hamilton
IDENTIFYING COLOURS	Chrome/Rocket Red

2007 ROADCAR
MERCEDES-BENZ SLR McLAREN ROADSTER

Mercedes-Benz described the most obvious development of its SLR McLaren as "*an open-air adventure for all the senses,*" when it announced a convertible version in May 2007. As usual, the new model came off the production line at the McLaren Technology Centre in Woking.

An accurate glimpse of the model had been provided by the Vision SLR concept car in 1999, and a new super sportscar in the form of a convertible with a detachable top was a logical step forward given the huge success of its hardtop cousin.

Mechanically the cars were much the same, the maximum speed of the new convertible being an identical 207mph thanks to its reliance on the same supercharged AMG V8 engine which developed almost 626bhp and maximum torque of 780Nm delivered via AMG's Speedshift R five-speed automatic transmission. Just like the coupé, the roadster sprinted from zero to 62mph in just 3.8s.

It was also significant that although the new car, with its fully retractable top and wide-opening gullwing doors, had been designed expressly to offer owners the last word in undiluted, open-air driving enjoyment, every attempt was made to ensure that even with this much power and performance the roadster's driving comfort and suitability for everyday motoring in the real world would not be compromised.

The familiar, if complex, carbon composite chassis was substantially redeveloped to create a basic monocoque which was not only extremely lightweight but also offered similar torsional rigidity to the coupé.

Like the coupé, the convertible was designed from the outset to offer an exceptionally high degree of safety. This was ensured not just by the unique carbon composite crash structures, but via steel-reinforced A-pillars and two fixed roll-over hoops. The same comprehensive standard specification also featured the latest design of adaptive airbags, as well as knee and side airbags, seat belt pre-tensioners and a sophisticated radio transmitter based tyre-pressure monitoring system.

The two companies went to great lengths to ensure that the design of the new, fully retractable soft top blended harmoniously into the car's flowing lines. Available in a choice of three different colours, the fabric roof had also to display some quite remarkable additional qualities regardless of whether it was up or down. When up it had to remain fully weatherproof at speeds in excess of 200mph. When lowered, the design of the car had to be such that occupants could still have a reasonable conversation when travelling at speed.

Mercedes-Benz had made great advances in convertible roof design over the previous two decades, and the new roadster's roof could be opened or closed in less than 10 seconds. To be opened, it merely needed to be unlocked from the windscreen frame and nudged clear of it, after which it would fold away electrically. Thereafter an integrated aluminium cover elegantly sealed it out of sight when in the retracted position.

The finished car was also the product of many hours spent in the wind tunnel, the overall shape having been painstakingly optimised for high speeds but with careful regard to handling, aero-acoustics and aerodynamics. It also employed an important aerodynamic concept borrowed from the coupé version, the airbrake integrated into the boot lid along with a diffuser at the rear of the underside to provide increased downforce on the rear axle.

The standard specification was as opulent as the coupe's, with semi-aniline leather-upholstered carbon composite bucket seats; dual-zone automatic climate control; air-conditioning; an exceptionally high-quality BOSE premium sound system; a multi-function sport steering wheel with gear-change paddles; and a navigation system with integral radio and CD player.

The SLR coupé chassis was further developed to enhance torsional strength and passenger safety. In addition, the A-pillars were reinforced for the roadster with steel and two fixed roll-over bars were fitted behind the seats.

RK07 AVV

RK07 AVV

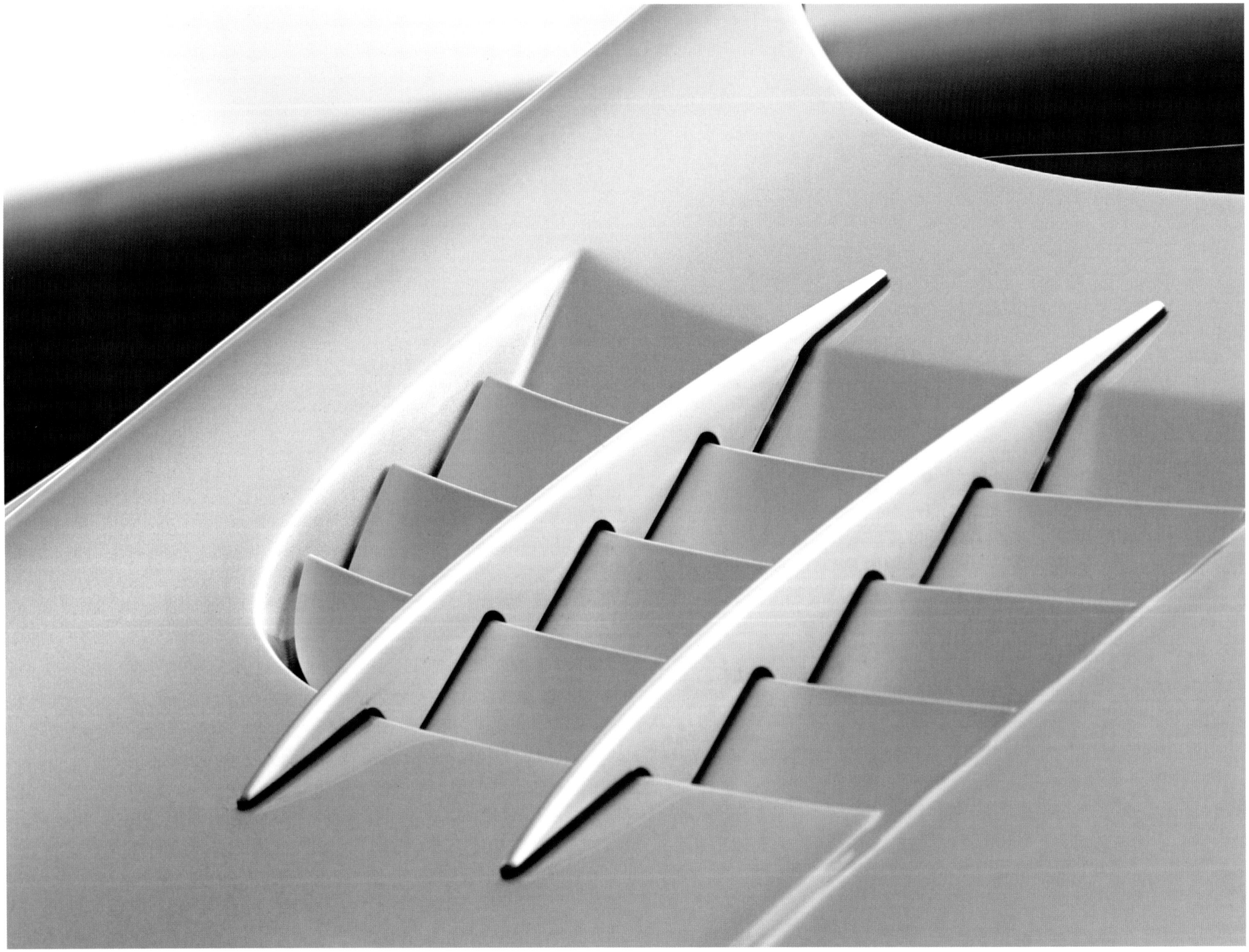

MERCEDES-BENZ SLR McLAREN ROADSTER ROADCAR

SPECIFICATION

MODEL	Mercedes-Benz SLR McLaren Roadster
TYPE/FORMULA	Roadcar
YEAR OF PRODUCTION	2007
DESIGNER	Mercedes-Benz & McLaren
EXAMPLES BUILT	236 as of February 2008
ENGINE	Mercedes-AMG V8
CUBIC CAPACITY	5439cc
INDUCTION	Charge-air cooled screw-type compressor
POWER OUTPUT	626bhp

TRANSMISSION	Mercedes 5-speed automatic/3 stage manual shift
CHASSIS	Carbon fibre monocoque, longitudinal front crash cones
BODY	Carbon fibre composite panels
FRONT SUSPENSION	Aluminium double wishbone,
	coil spring/gas damper, anti-roll bar
REAR SUSPENSION	Aluminium double wishbone,
	coil spring/gas damper
BRAKES F/R	Outboard carbon fibre/ceramic discs
WHEELS DIAMETER x WIDTH F/R	18x9/18x11.5in, optional 19in

TYRES F/R	Michelin
LENGTH	183.3in - 4656mm
WIDTH	75.1in - 1908mm
HEIGHT	50.4in - 1281mm
WHEELBASE	106.3in - 2700mm
TRACK F/R	64.5/61.8in - 1638/1569mm
DIN WEIGHT	3858lb - 1750kg
PRINCIPAL DRIVERS	n/a
IDENTIFYING COLOURS	n/a

2008 FORMULA 1 McLAREN MP4-23

The marque's most recent car, the MP4-23, was unveiled at the Mercedes-Benz Museum in Stuttgart-Untertürkheim on Monday, January 7th, Lewis Hamilton's 23rd birthday. The latest challenger from Woking was literally only completed the previous evening, and its debut coincided with the introduction of Finn Heikki Kovalainen as Fernando Alonso's replacement. He was joined on stage by Hamilton, Pedro de la Rosa and fellow test driver Gary Paffett, and 48 hours after the event the new car began a rigorous testing schedule at Spain's Circuito de Jerez de la Frontera.

Ron Dennis and Dr Dieter Zetsche, Chairman of the Board of Management of Daimler AG and Head of Mercedes-Benz Cars, were typically bullish about the new machine. Dennis confirmed the team's clear intention: *"We will fight for both the Drivers' and Constructors' World Championships. We are looking forward to another competitive season as we look to build on the momentum of last year. Every single member of the team has worked extremely hard since the end of the 2007 season to get the MP4-23 on track as soon as possible to ensure we have the maximum amount of testing time available before the cars leave for Australia."*

The MP4-23 had begun life 10 months previously, detailed simulation and analysis work forming an integral part of the development process. The latter was, as usual, an ongoing process that would continue right up until that first race just 68 days later, and beyond. There were 150 engineers assigned to the project from the outset when initial wind tunnel tests had taken place in late May 2007, and the first chassis was ready for the autoclave in mid-November. By the time the car was ready for its launch in Stuttgart some 14,000 engineering man-hours, and the same again in manufacturing time, had been invested in its gestation.

It represented a substantial evolution of the MP4-22, and though it was visually similar outwardly then, by the time it was flown Down Under upgrades to most of the aerodynamic surfaces, including wings, bodywork, barge boards and additional bodywork components, endowed it with its own clear identity.

The latest version of the 2.4-litre, eight-cylinder Mercedes-Benz FO 108V, a 90° unit conforming to the FIA-mandated 19,000rpm limit, and driving through McLaren's own seven-speed box, was installed in a chassis that represented a familiar mix of McLaren moulded carbon fibre/aluminium honeycomb composite technology incorporating the necessary crash structures and an integral safety fuel cell.

Testing at Jerez began first thing on the Wednesday after the launch and, with chassis number two being sent out directly from Woking, it was the first time the team had ever had two cars ready for the first day of testing. Heikki was delighted with his first day as an active Vodafone McLaren Mercedes driver, and expressed favourable early impressions: *"We have a comprehensive development schedule to work through over the next couple of months, but the performance today is definitely an encouraging starting point."*

The two cars completed 69 laps of the 4.4km circuit with the runs taking place in near perfect conditions - sunny in the morning, cloudy in the afternoon. Pedro de la Rosa posted the best lap time of 1m 19.655s, Kovalainen 1m 20.559s.

Lewis Hamilton had his first run in the new car the following day, when he ran 103 laps. He too was characteristically buoyant, describing the experience as "*fantastic*" and bettering de la Rosa's time. Having seen the completed car for the first time only days previously, at the Stuttgart launch, he also admitted to having been: *"Pretty impatient since then! As this is only the second day the car has been on track, I am pretty happy."*

Kovalainen faced a steeper learning curve in his new role, and despite finding the car different from the previous year's, improved his times and said that settling into his new team was proving very easy. Back at the circuit the following day, by which time the weather was providing slightly more trying conditions with some showers, and cooler track and ambient temperatures, Hamilton again posted the best lap time with 1m 19.691s, but Kovalainen was right behind him on 1m 19.752s.

The closeness of their two times - and of de la Rosa's performance earlier in the week - indicated that the team was achieving the consistency its new cars would need to deliver results. Significantly the three drivers had collectively covered nearly 2,000kms without any major issues coming to light, and had amassed a great deal of data which would be crucial for ongoing development.

It paid off handsomely, as Lewis got his 2008 title campaign off to the best possible start by winning the Australian Grand Prix with ease from pole position. Heikki was on course to back him strongly in second place, but ultimately finished fifth after falling victim to the third safety car intervention period.

As it made the transition to yet another fresh chapter in the ongoing story, McLaren had done so on a winning note and taken the lead in both the Drivers' and Constructors' World Championships.

Work on the MP4-23 began in May 2007 and the car spent over 3000 hours in the wind tunnel. Following its launch at the Mercedes-Benz Museum in Stuttgart, the car made its track debut at the Circuito de Jerez in southern Spain. Lewis Hamilton, Heikki Kovalainen (above) and Pedro de la Rosa were all present.

The MP4-23 was an evolution of the MP4-22 and as such there were little significant visual difference between the two. By the time the cars reached Australia for the first race of the season the team had made significant upgrades to the aerodynamic package. Lewis Hamilton dominated the race, winning from pole position.

MP4-23 FORMULA 1

SPECIFICATION

MODEL*	McLaren-Mercedes MP4-23
TYPE/FORMULA	Formula 1
YEAR OF PRODUCTION	2008
DESIGNER	McLaren Racing Design team
EXAMPLES BUILT	3 (May 2008)
ENGINE	Mercedes-Benz FO 108V V8
CUBIC CAPACITY	2398cc
ELECTRONICS	FIA Standard ECU (Microsoft MES)
POWER OUTPUT	765bhp

TRANSMISSION	McLaren semi-auto sequential longitudinal 7-speed
CHASSIS	Moulded carbon fibre/aluminium honeycomb composite
BODY	Carbon fibre single piece cockpit/engine cover & nose
FRONT SUSPENSION	Unequal length wishbone, push-rod & bell
	crank operating inboard torsion bar/damper
REAR SUSPENSION	Unequal length wishbone, push-rod & bell
	crank operating inboard torsion bar/damper
BRAKES F/R	Outboard carbon fibre discs, Akebono calipers
WHEELS DIAMETER x WIDTH F/R	13x12/13x13.7in

TYRES F/R	Bridgestone
LENGTH	188in - 4775mm
WIDTH	70.6in - 1795mm
HEIGHT	43.3in - 1100mm
WHEELBASE	125.5in - 3188mm
TRACK F/R	57.2/55.9in - 1454/1419mm
WEIGHT	1322lb - 600kg
PRINCIPAL DRIVERS	Hamilton, Kovalainen
IDENTIFYING COLOURS	Chrome/Rocket Red

POSTSCRIPT
MARTIN WHITMARSH

Inevitably, in Formula 1, you always have to look forward to what the next car is going to be. As this book is completed we are winning with MP4-23 but are already looking at MP4-24 and working on technologies that will be incorporated into MP4-25 and beyond.

But understanding our heritage is also important. I hope you have enjoyed reading about McLaren's cars. Before I joined the company, in 1989, it had already won quite a few Formula 1 World Championships, we had dominated the Can-Am Series and won the Indianapolis 500; during my time we have won a few more Formula 1 World Championships – not as many as I would have liked, obviously – and Le Mans.

No other marque in the world can lay claim to having triumphed in all those prestigious categories. And that is part of the strength of the McLaren brand.

While looking forward to making sure that we achieve success and develop our resources to maintain it, it is right to have spent time honouring the fact that McLaren would not be the enigmatic and magical brand that it is if Bruce McLaren hadn't started racing an Austin Ulster. If he hadn't decided to create his own team; if he and Denny hadn't gone over and dominated the Can-Am; if Emerson and James hadn't won the Formula 1 World Championship in the 1970s; if Niki and Alain and Ayrton and Mika hadn't won further titles in the 1980s and 1990s; if Mark Donohue and Johnny Rutherford hadn't won at Indianapolis; if we hadn't built the F1 and won at Le Mans.

It has been a pleasure to acknowledge here that over the past 42 years many thousands of people have given their energies, commitment and loyalty to develop the great cars which have created our heritage.

I am proud that a lot of the faces who were there long before I joined are still here today. For example, Ray 'Tex' Rowe's lineage goes all the way back to Bruce's Austin Ulster, while Tyler Alexander was there right alongside Bruce in the earliest days of the McLaren marque and still works in the race team.

They set the same sort of example of commitment and loyalty that Ron has in leading this company forward.

We achieve some incredible results because of the fantastic efforts of so many people who are highly motivated and have pride in a business whose past achievements richly deserve that pride.

This authoritative account and visual record of the fantastic achievements of those people who have dedicated themselves to the McLaren brand, stands as a tribute to the collective passion that has made McLaren the fantastic company that it is today. And a spur to motivate us to even greater achievements in the future.

Martin Whitmarsh
CEO Formula 1, Vodafone McLaren Mercedes
Chief Operating Officer, McLaren Group

vodafone
Mercedes-Benz
Mobil 1

APPENDIX 1

McLAREN – THE CARS 1964-2008

Model	Type/Formula	Year	Built	Engine	Type	Capacity	Designer(s)	Comments
McLaren M1A	Group 7 Sports	1964/65	2	Oldsmobile	V8	3900	McLaren	Automatic transmission used in 1965
McLaren-Elva M1A (MkI)	Group 7 Sports	1965	24	Oldsmobile/Ford	V8	3900-5000	McLaren	First Elva built customer McLaren
McLaren M1B	Group 7 Sports	1965/66	4*	Oldsmobile/Chevrolet	V8	4700-5400	Herd/McLaren	Body designed by Michael Turner
McLaren-Elva M1B (MkII)	Group 7/Can-Am	1966	28	Oldsmobile/Chevrolet/Ford	V8	4700-5400	Herd/McLaren	Elva built M1B
McLaren-Elva M1C (MkIII)	Can-Am	1967	25	Chevrolet/Ford/Oldsmobile	V8	4500-6000	Herd	Last car built by Elva
McLaren M2A	Prototype single seater	1965	1	Oldsmobile/Ford	V8	4500/6000	McLaren/Herd	First single seater McLaren
McLaren M2B	Formula 1	1966	2	Ford/Serenissima	V8	3000	McLaren/Herd	First McLaren Grand Prix car
McLaren M3A	Formula Libre/Hillclimb car	1966	3	Oldsmobile/Ford/Chevrolet	V8	4700-5400	McLaren/Herd	'Woosh-bonk' spaceframe car
McLaren M4A	Formula 2	1967	2	Ford Cosworth FVA	4cyl	1598	Herd	First McLaren Formula 2 car
McLaren-Trojan M4A/B	Formula 2/Formula B	1967	25	Ford Cosworth FVA	4cyl	1598	Herd	First Trojan built model
McLaren M4B	Formula 1	1967	1	BRM	V8	2070	Herd	Interim 1967 Formula 1 car, destroyed in fire
McLaren M5A	Formula 1	1967	1	BRM	V12	2998	Herd	Chassis M5A-1 ran first BRM V12 engine built
McLaren M6A	Can-Am	1967	3	Chevrolet	V8	5900	Herd/Coppuck	Can-Am Championship winning 1967 team cars
McLaren-Trojan M6B	Can-Am	1968	26	Chevrolet	V8	5900	Herd/Coppuck	Trojan built version of M6A
McLaren M6GT	Roadcar	1969	1	Chevrolet LT1	V8	5740	McLaren/Coppuck	Only M6GT built at McLaren, Bruce's roadcar
McLaren-Trojan M6GT	Roadcar	1969	3	Chevrolet LT1	V8	5740	McLaren/Coppuck	Trojan customer version of M6GT
McLaren M7A	Formula 1	1968/69	3	Ford Cosworth DFV	V8	2993	Herd/Coppuck	First Cosworth DFV engined McLaren
McLaren M7B	Formula 1	1969	1*	Ford Cosworth DFV	V8	2993	Coppuck	Pannier tank version of M7A
McLaren M7C	Formula 1	1969	1	Ford Cosworth DFV	V8	2993	Coppuck	One off with modified M7A monocoque
McLaren M7D	Formula 1	1970	1	Alfa Romeo T33	V8	2995	Coppuck	One off Alfa engined M7A
McLaren M8A	Can-Am	1968	3	Chevrolet	V8	6997	Coppuck/Marquart	1968 Can-Am Championship winner
McLaren M8B	Can-Am	1969	3*	Chevrolet	V8	6997	Coppuck/Marquart	Unbeaten 1969 Can-Am Championship winner
McLaren-Trojan M8C	Can-Am	1970	15	Chevrolet/Ford	V8	7000-7500	Coppuck/Marquart	Trojan built customer version of M8A
McLaren M8D	Can-Am	1970	4	Chevrolet	V8	7100-7600	Marquart	1970 Can-Am Championship winner - 'Batmobile'
McLaren-Trojan M8E	Can-Am	1971	15-18	Chevrolet	V8	7000-8095	Marquart	Trojan built customer version of M8D
McLaren M8F	Can-Am	1971	3*	Chevrolet	V8	7900-8400	Coppuck	Works car for 1971
McLaren-Trojan M8F/P	Can-Am	1972	10	Chevrolet	V8	8093	Coppuck	Trojan built customer version of M8F
McLaren M9A	Formula 1	1969	1	Ford Cosworth DFV	V8	2993	Marquart	Experimental four-wheel drive Formula 1 car
McLaren-Trojan M10A	Formula 5000/Formula A	1969	20	Chevrolet	V8	5000	Coppuck	First F5000 car from McLaren
McLaren-Trojan M10B	Formula 5000/Formula A	1970	21	Chevrolet	V8	5000	Coppuck	Revised M10A for 1970 season
M11	-	-	-	-	-	-	-	Number not used - possible confusion with M1B Mk.II
McLaren-Trojan M12	Can-Am/Group 7	1969	15	Chevrolet	V8	6997	Coppuck	1969 Trojan production Can-Am car on M6 tub
McLaren M12GT	Roadcar	1970	1?	Chevrolet	V8	7000	McLaren/Coppuck	Rumoured coupe built on M12 chassis
M13	-	-	-	-	-	-	-	Number not used - superstition
McLaren M14A	Formula 1	1970/71	3	Ford Cosworth DFV	V8	2993	Coppuck/Marquart	Last Formula 1 model driven by Bruce McLaren
McLaren M14D	Formula 1	1970	1	Alfa Romeo	V8	2995	Coppuck/Marquart	Alfa engined version of M14A
McLaren M15	Indianapolis/USAC	1970	3	Offenhauser (turbo)	4cyl	2600	Coppuck	McLaren's first 'Indy 500' USAC/Indianapolis car
McLaren M16	Indianapolis/USAC	1971	3	Offenhauser (turbo)	4cyl	2600	Coppuck	Classic wedge shaped Indy car
McLaren M16B	Indianapolis/USAC	1972	4	Offenhauser (turbo)	4cyl	2600	Coppuck	First 'Indy 500' winner for a McLaren (Donohue)
McLaren M16C	Indianapolis/USAC	1973	6	Offenhauser (turbo)	4cyl	2600	Coppuck	Heavily revised M16B
McLaren M16C/D	Indianapolis/USAC	1974	3*	Offenhauser (turbo)	4cyl	2600	Coppuck	1974 'Indy 500' winnner (Rutherford)
McLaren M16E	Indianapolis/USAC	1975	2	Offenhauser (turbo)	4cyl	2600	Barnard	John Barnard re-worked M16D
McLaren M16E	Indianapolis/USAC	1976	2*	Offenhauser (turbo)	4cyl	2600	Barnard	1976 'Indy 500' winnner (Rutherford)
M17	Sports Prototype	1971	-	Ford Cosworth DFV	V8	2993	Bellamy	Project cancelled
McLaren-Trojan M18	Formula 5000/Formula A	1971	8	Chevrolet	V8	5000	Bellamy	Production F5000 car for 1971
McLaren M19	Formula 1	1971/72	2	Ford Cosworth DFV	V8	2993	Bellamy	Bellamy's 'Coke bottle' shaped Formula 1 car
McLaren M19C	Formula 1	1972/73	2	Ford Cosworth DFV	V8	2993	Bellamy	Heavily revised car for 1972 & 1973
McLaren M20	Can-Am	1972	3	Chevrolet	V8	8095	Coppuck	Final Can-Am car from McLaren
McLaren M21	Formula 2	1972	1	Ford Cosworth BDA/BDF	4cyl	1899/1998	Bellamy	F2 car designed for proposed Trojan production
McLaren-Trojan M22	Formula 5000	1972	3	Chevrolet	V8	4950	Coppuck	Trojan production F5000 car for 1972
McLaren M23	Formula 1	1973	4	Ford Cosworth DFV	V8	2993	Coppuck	One of the most long-lived & successful Formula 1 cars
McLaren M23	Formula 1	1974	4	Ford Cosworth DFV	V8	2993	Coppuck	Double World Championship winner (Fittipaldi)
McLaren M23	Formula 1	1975	2	Ford Cosworth DFV	V8	2993	Coppuck	3 GP wins in 1975
McLaren M23	Formula 1	1976	4*	Ford Cosworth DFV	V8	2993	Coppuck	Drivers' Championship in 1976 (Hunt)
McLaren M23	Formula 1	1977	3	Ford Cosworth DFV	V8	2993	Coppuck	3 Grand Prix wins in fifth season
McLaren M24	Indianapolis/USAC	1977	6	Ford Cosworth DFX (turbo)	V8	2650	Coppuck	1977 Indycar based on M23
McLaren M24B	Indianapolis/USAC	1978	3	Ford Cosworth DFX (turbo)	V8	2650	Coppuck	Revised M24 for 1978 & 1979. Still running in 1982
McLaren M25	Formula 5000/Formula 1	1974-78	1	Chevrolet/Ford Cosworth DFV	V8	5000/2993	Barnard	One-off and final McLaren F5000 car
McLaren M26	Formula 1	1976-78	7	Ford Cosworth DFV	V8	2993	Coppuck	M23 replacement used from 1976 to 1978
McLaren M27	Formula 1	-	-	-	-	-	-	Project cancelled - superceeded by M28
McLaren M28	Formula 1	1979	3	Ford Cosworth DFV	V8	2993	Coppuck	McLaren's first 'ground-effects' car
McLaren M28C	Formula 1	1979	1*	Ford Cosworth DFV	V8	2993	Coppuck	Heavily revised M28
McLaren M29	Formula 1	1979-80	5	Ford Cosworth DFV	V8	2993	Coppuck	Hastily produced Williams copy 'ground-effects' car
McLaren M29C	Formula 1	1980-81	2*	Ford Cosworth DFV	V8	2993	Coppuck	Revised M29 for 1980
McLaren M30	Formula 1	1980	1	Ford Cosworth DFV	V8	2993	Coppuck	Further developed 'ground-effects' car
McLaren MP4/1	Formula 1	1981	4	Ford Cosworth DFV	V8	2993	Barnard	First carbon fibre chassis Formula 1 car
McLaren MP4/1B	Formula 1	1982	5*	Ford Cosworth DFV	V8	2993	Barnard	Updated MP4/1 for 1982
McLaren MP4/1C	Formula 1	1983	4*	Ford Cosworth DFV/DFY	V8	2993	Barnard	Updated MP4/1 for 1983
McLaren MP4/1D	Formula 1 Test Car	1983	1*	TAG Turbo (turbo)	V6	1496	Barnard	First TAG Turbo engined Formula 1 test car
McLaren MP4/1E	Formula 1	1983	3*	TAG Turbo (turbo)	V6	1496	Barnard	Late 1983 interim race car
McLaren MP4/2	Formula 1	1984	5	TAG Turbo (turbo)	V6	1496	Barnard	Double Championship winning car with revised engine
McLaren MP4/2B	Formula 1	1985	5*	TAG Turbo (turbo)	V6	1496	Barnard	Revised MP4/2 wins another Championship
McLaren MP4/2C	Formula 1	1986	5	TAG Turbo (turbo)	V6	1496	Barnard	Revised MP4/2B gives 3rd Drivers' title in a row
McLaren MP4/3	Formula 1	1987	6	TAG Turbo (turbo)	V6	1496	Nichols	First 'low-line' McLaren Formula 1 car
McLaren MP4/3B	Formula 1 Test Car	1987	2*	Honda RA108E (turbo)	V6	1496	Nichols	Test version of MP4/3 with new Honda V6 engine
McLaren MP4/3C	Formula 1 Test Car	1988	1	Honda RA109E	V10	3490	Nichols/Oatley	Honda V10 version of MP4/3 - never completed
McLaren MP4/4	Formula 1	1988	6	Honda RA168E (turbo)	V6	1494	Nichols/Murray	Record breaking first season with Honda engine
McLaren MP4/4B	Formula 1 Test Car	1988	3	Honda RA109E	V10	3490	Nichols	Late 1988 test car with Honda V10 engine
McLaren MP4/5	Formula 1	1989	8	Honda RA109E	V10	3490	Oatley	First season with normally aspirated engine

Driver A	Championship		Driver B	Championship		Driver C	Championship		Driver D	Championship		Driver E	Championship		Driver F	
	Position	Points		Position	Points		Position	Points		Position	Points		Position	Points		
Bruce McLaren	14=	3														
Bruce McLaren	-	-														
Bruce McLaren	14	3														
Bruce McLaren	-	-														
Bruce McLaren	5	22	Denny Hulme	3	33	Dan Gurney (AAR)	21=	3								
Denny Hulme	2 (inc above)		Jo Bonnier (EB)	21=	3											
Bruce McLaren	3	26	Denny Hulme	6	20	Vic Elford (AA)	13	3	Derek Bell	-	-	Basil van Royen (TL)	-	-		
Bruce McLaren	14	6	Denny Hulme	4	27	Peter Gethin	22=	1	Dan Gurney	22=	1	John Surtees (TS)	17	3	Jo Bonnier (EB)	-
Andrea de Adamich	-	-	Nanni Galli	-	-											
Denny Hulme	9=	9	Peter Gethin	9	9	Jackie Oliver			Mark Donohue (PW)	16	4	David Hobbs (PW)	-	-	Jo Bonnier (EB)	-
Denny Hulme	3	39	Peter Revson	5	23	Brian Redman	12	4	Jody Scheckter	-	-					
Denny Hulme	6	26	Peter Revson	5	38	Jody Scheckter			Jacky Ickx	9	12					
Emerson Fittipaldi	1st	55	Denny Hulme	7	20	Mike Hailwood (Y)	10	12	David Hobbs (Y)	-	-	Jochen Mass (Y)	-	-	Dave Charlton (LS)	-
Emerson Fittipaldi	2	45	Jochen Mass	7	20	Dave Charlton (LS)										
James Hunt	1st	69	Jochen Mass	9	19											
James Hunt	5	40	Jochen Mass	6	25	Gilles Villeneuve	-	-	Bruno Giacomelli	-	-	Brett Lunger (CR)	-	-	Emilio dVillota (IA)	-
James Hunt	13=	8	Patrick Tambay	13=	8	Bruno Giacomelli	-	-	Brett Lunger (BS)	-	-	Nelson Piquet (BS)	-	-	Tony Trimmer (MR)	-
John Watson	9	15	Patrick Tambay	-	-											
John Watson	10=	6	Alain Prost	15=	5											
John Watson	6	27	Andrea de Cesaris	18	1											
John Watson	2=	39	Niki Lauda	5	30											
John Watson	6=	22	Niki Lauda	10	12											
Alain Prost	2	71.5	Niki Lauda	1st	72											
Alain Prost	1st	73	Niki Lauda	10	14	John Watson	-	-								
Alain Prost	1st	72	Keke Rosberg	6	22											
Alain Prost	4	46	Stefan Johansson	6	30											
Alain Prost	2	87	Ayrton Senna	1st	90											
Alain Prost	1st	76	Ayrton Senna	2	60											
Ayrton Senna	1st	78	Gerhard Berger	4	43											
Ayrton Senna	1st	96	Gerhard Berger	4	43											
Ayrton Senna	4	50	Gerhard Berger	5	49											
Ayrton Senna	2	73	Michael Andretti	11=	7	Mika Häkkinen	15=	4								
Mika Häkkinen	4	26	Martin Brundle	7	16	Philippe Alliot	-	-								
Mika Häkkinen	7	17	Mark Blundell	10	13	Nigel Mansell	-	-	Jan Magnussen	-	-					
Mika Häkkinen	5	31	David Coulthard	7	18											
Mika Häkkinen	5=	27	David Coulthard	3=	36											
Mika Häkkinen	1st	100	David Coulthard	3	56											
Mika Häkkinen	1st	76	David Coulthard	4	48											
Mika Häkkinen	2	89	David Coulthard	3	73											
Mika Häkkinen	5	37	David Coulthard	2	65											
David Coulthard	5	41	Kimi Räikkönen	6	24											
David Coulthard	7	51	Kimi Räikkönen	2	91											
David Coulthard	9=	24	Kimi Räikkönen	7	45											
Kimi Räikkönen	2	112	JP Montoya	4	60	Pedro de la Rosa	19=	4	Alexander Wurz	17	6					
Kimi Räikkönen	5	65	JP Montoya	8	26	Pedro de la Rosa	11	19								
Fernando Alonso	2=	109	Lewis Hamilton	2=	109											
Lewis Hamilton			Heikki Kovalainen													

Key:

(AAR) – All American Racers
(EB) – Ecurie Bonnier
(AA) – Antique Automobiles
(TL) – Team Lawson
(TS) – Team Surtees
(PW) – Penske-White Racing
(Y) – Yardley McLaren (Works)
(LS) – Lucky Strike
(CR) – Chesterfield Racing
(IA) – Iberia Airlines
(BS) – BS Fabrications
(MR) – Melchester Racing

APPENDIX 3
McLAREN GRAND PRIX WINS

Win Number	Year	Date	Grand Prix	Circuit	Race Number	Driver	Model	Engine	Title Sponsor	Notes (on winning driver unless named)
1	1968	09.06.68	Belgian GP	Spa Francorchamps	5	Bruce McLaren	M7A	Cosworth DFV		
2		08.09.68	Italian GP	Monza	1	Denny Hulme	M7A	Cosworth DFV		
3		22.09.68	Canadian GP	Mont Tremblant	1	Denny Hulme	M7A	Cosworth DFV		1-2 Finish
4	1969	19.10.69	Mexican GP	Mexico City	5	Denny Hulme	M7A	Cosworth DFV		
5	1972	04.03.72	South African GP	Kyalami	12	Denny Hulme	M19A	Cosworth DFV	Yardley	
6	1973	17.06.73	Swedish GP	Anderstorp	7	Denny Hulme	M23	Cosworth DFV	Yardley	Fastest lap
7		14.07.73	British GP	Silverstone	8	Peter Revson	M23	Cosworth DFV	Yardley	Revson - First GP win
8		23.09.73	Canadian GP	Mosport Park	8	Peter Revson	M23	Cosworth DFV	Yardley	
9	1974	13.01.74	Argentine GP	Buenos Aires	6	Denny Hulme	M23	Cosworth DFV	Marlboro	
10		27.01.74	Brazilian GP	Interlagos	5	Emerson Fittipaldi	M23	Cosworth DFV	Marlboro	Pole Position
11		12.05.74	Belgian GP	Nivelles	5	Emerson Fittipaldi	M23	Cosworth DFV	Marlboro	Fastest lap (Hulme)
12		22.09.74	Canadian GP	Mosport Park	5	Emerson Fittipaldi	M23	Cosworth DFV	Marlboro	Pole Position
13	1975	12.01.75	Argentine GP	Buenos Aires	1	Emerson Fittipaldi	M23	Cosworth DFV	Marlboro	
14		27.04.75	Spanish GP	Barcelona	2	Jochen Mass	M23	Cosworth DFV	Marlboro	Race stopped after 29 laps (half points), Mass - First GP win
15		19.07.75	British GP	Silverstone	1	Emerson Fittipaldi	M23	Cosworth DFV	Marlboro	
16	1976	02.05.76	Spanish GP	Jarama	11	James Hunt	M23	Cosworth DFV	Marlboro	Pole Position, Fastest Lap (Mass)
17		04.07.76	French GP	Paul Ricard	11	James Hunt	M23	Cosworth DFV	Marlboro	Pole Position
18		01.08.76	German GP	Nürburgring	11	James Hunt	M23	Cosworth DFV	Marlboro	Pole Position
19		29.08.76	Dutch GP	Zandvoort	11	James Hunt	M23	Cosworth DFV	Marlboro	
20		03.10.76	Canadian GP	Mosport Park	11	James Hunt	M23	Cosworth DFV	Marlboro	Pole Position
21		10.10.76	US (East) GP	Watkins Glen	11	James Hunt	M23	Cosworth DFV	Marlboro	Pole Position, Fastest Lap
22	1977	16.07.77	British GP	Silverstone	1	James Hunt	M26	Cosworth DFV	Marlboro	Pole Position, Fastest Lap
23		02.10.77	USA (East) GP	Watkins Glen	1	James Hunt	M26	Cosworth DFV	Marlboro	Pole Position
24		23.10.77	Japanese GP	Mt. Fuji	1	James Hunt	M26	Cosworth DFV	Marlboro	
25	1981	18.07.81	British GP	Silverstone	7	John Watson	MP4/1	Cosworth DFV	Marlboro	
26	1982	04.04.82	USA (West) GP	Long Beach	8	Niki Lauda	MP4/1B	Cosworth DFV	Marlboro	Fastest Lap
27		09.05.82	Belgian GP	Zolder	7	John Watson	MP4/1B	Cosworth DFV	Marlboro	Fastest Lap
28		06.06.82	USA Detroit GP	Detroit	7	John Watson	MP4/1B	Cosworth DFV	Marlboro	
29		18.07.82	British GP	Brands Hatch	8	Niki Lauda	MP4/1B	Cosworth DFV	Marlboro	
30	1983	27.03.83	USA (West) GP	Long Beach	7	John Watson	MP4/1C	Cosworth DFV	Marlboro	Fastest Lap (Lauda),1-2 Finish
31	1984	25.03.84	Brazilian GP	Jacarepagua	7	Alain Prost	MP4/2	TAG Turbo	Marlboro	Fastest Lap
32		07.04.84	South African GP	Kyalami	8	Niki Lauda	MP4/2	TAG Turbo	Marlboro	1-2 Finish
33		06.05.84	San Marino GP	Imola	7	Alain Prost	MP4/2	TAG Turbo	Marlboro	
34		20.05.84	French GP	Dijon-Prenois	8	Niki Lauda	MP4/2	TAG Turbo	Marlboro	Fastest Lap (Prost)
35		03.06.84	Monaco GP	Monte Carlo	7	Alain Prost	MP4/2	TAG Turbo	Marlboro	Pole Position
36		22.07.84	British GP	Brands Hatch	8	Niki Lauda	MP4/2	TAG Turbo	Marlboro	Fastest Lap
37		05.08.84	German GP	Hockenheim	7	Alain Prost	MP4/2	TAG Turbo	Marlboro	Pole Position, Fastest Lap, 1-2 Finish
38		19.08.84	Austrian GP	Österreichring	8	Niki Lauda	MP4/2	TAG Turbo	Marlboro	Fastest Lap
39		26.08.84	Dutch GP	Zandvoort	7	Alain Prost	MP4/2	TAG Turbo	Marlboro	Pole Position, 1-2 Finish
40		09.09.84	Italian GP	Monza	8	Niki Lauda	MP4/2	TAG Turbo	Marlboro	Fastest La
41		07.10.84	European GP	Nürburgring	7	Alain Prost	MP4/2	TAG Turbo	Marlboro	
42		21.10.84	Portuguese GP	Estoril	7	Alain Prost	MP4/2	TAG Turbo	Marlboro	Fastest Lap (Lauda),1-2 Finish
43	1985	07.04.85	Brazilian GP	Jacarepagua	2	Alain Prost	MP4/2B	TAG Turbo	Marlboro	Fastest Lap
44		19.05.85	Monaco GP	Monte Carlo	2	Alain Prost	MP4/2B	TAG Turbo	Marlboro	
45		21.07.85	British GP	Silverstone	2	Alain Prost	MP4/2B	TAG Turbo	Marlboro	Fastest Lap
46		18.08.85	Austrian GP	Österreichring	2	Alain Prost	MP4/2B	TAG Turbo	Marlboro	Pole Position, Fastest Lap
47		25.08.85	Dutch GP	Zandvoort	1	Niki Lauda	MP4/2B	TAG Turbo	Marlboro	Fastest Lap (Prost),1-2 Finish
48		08.09.85	Italian GP	Monza	2	Alain Prost	MP4/2B	TAG Turbo	Marlboro	
49	1986	27.04.86	San Marino GP	Imola	1	Alain Prost	MP4/2C	TAG Turbo	Marlboro	
50		11.05.86	Monaco GP	Monte Carlo	1	Alain Prost	MP4/2C	TAG Turbo	Marlboro	Pole Position, Fastest Lap, 1-2 Finish
51		17.08.86	Austrian GP	Österreichring	1	Alain Prost	MP4/2C	TAG Turbo	Marlboro	
52		26.10.86	Australian GP	Adelaide	1	Alain Prost	MP4/2C	TAG Turbo	Marlboro	
53	1987	12.04.87	Brazilian GP	Jacarepagua	1	Alain Prost	MP4/3	TAG Turbo	Marlboro	
54		17.05.87	Belgian GP	Spa Francorchamps	1	Alain Prost	MP4/3	TAG Turbo	Marlboro	Fastest Lap,1-2 Finish
55		20.09.87	Portuguese GP	Estoril	1	Alain Prost	MP4/3	TAG Turbo	Marlboro	
56	1988	03.04.88	Brazilian GP	Jacarepagua	11	Alain Prost	MP4/4	Honda	Marlboro	Pole Position (Senna)
57		01.05.88	San Marino GP	Imola	12	Ayrton Senna	MP4/4	Honda	Marlboro	Pole Position, Fastest Lap (Prost), 1-2 Finish
58		15.05.88	Monaco GP	Monte Carlo	11	Alain Prost	MP4/4	Honda	Marlboro	Pole Position (Senna), Fastest Lap (Senna)
59		29.05.88	Mexican GP	Mexico City	11	Alain Prost	MP4/4	Honda	Marlboro	Pole Position (Senna), Fastest Lap, 1-2 Finish
60		12.06.88	Canadian GP	Montreal	12	Ayrton Senna	MP4/4	Honda	Marlboro	Pole Position, Fastest Lap, 1-2 Finish
61		19.06.88	USA (Detroit) GP	Detroit	12	Ayrton Senna	MP4/4	Honda	Marlboro	Pole Position, Fastest Lap (Prost), 1-2 Finish
62		03.07.88	French GP	Paul Ricard	11	Alain Prost	MP4/4	Honda	Marlboro	Pole Position, Fastest Lap, 1-2 Finish
63		10.07.88	British GP	Silverstone	12	Ayrton Senna	MP4/4	Honda	Marlboro	
64		24.07.88	German GP	Hockenheim	12	Ayrton Senna	MP4/4	Honda	Marlboro	Pole Position, 1-2 Finish
65		07.08.88	Hungarian GP	Budapest	12	Ayrton Senna	MP4/4	Honda	Marlboro	Pole Position, Fastest Lap (Prost), 1-2 Finish
66		28.08.88	Belgian GP	Spa Francorchamps	12	Ayrton Senna	MP4/4	Honda	Marlboro	Pole Position, 1-2 Finish
67		25.09.88	Portuguese GP	Estoril	11	Alain Prost	MP4/4	Honda	Marlboro	Pole Position
68		02.10.88	Spanish GP	Jerez	11	Alain Prost	MP4/4	Honda	Marlboro	Pole Position (Senna), Fastest Lap
69		30.10.88	Japanese GP	Suzuka	12	Ayrton Senna	MP4/4	Honda	Marlboro	Pole Position, Fastest Lap, 1-2 Finish
70		13.11.88	Australian GP	Adelaide	11	Alain Prost	MP4/4	Honda	Marlboro	Pole Position (Senna), Fastest Lap, 1-2 Finish
71	1989	23.04.89	San Marino GP	Imola	1	Ayrton Senna	MP4/5	Honda	Marlboro	Pole Position, Fastest Lap (Prost), 1-2 Finish
72		07.05.89	Monaco GP	Monte Carlo	1	Ayrton Senna	MP4/5	Honda	Marlboro	Pole Position, Fastest Lap (Prost), 1-2 Finish
73		28.05.89	Mexican GP	Mexico City	1	Ayrton Senna	MP4/5	Honda	Marlboro	Pole Position
74		04.06.89	USA (Phoenix) GP	Phoenix	2	Alain Prost	MP4/5	Honda	Marlboro	Pole Position (Senna), Fastest Lap (Senna)
75		09.07.89	French GP	Paul Ricard	2	Alain Prost	MP4/5	Honda	Marlboro	Pole Position
76		16.07.89	British GP	Silverstone	2	Alain Prost	MP4/5	Honda	Marlboro	Pole Position (Senna)
77		30.07.89	German GP	Hockenheim	1	Ayrton Senna	MP4/5	Honda	Marlboro	Pole Position, Fastest Lap, 1-2 Finish
78		27.08.89	Belgian GP	Spa Francorchamps	1	Ayrton Senna	MP4/5	Honda	Marlboro	Pole Position, Fastest Lap (Prost), 1-2 Finish
79		10.09.89	Italian GP	Monza	2	Alain Prost	MP4/5	Honda	Marlboro	Pole Position (Senna), Fastest Lap
80		01.10.89	Spanish GP	Jerez	1	Ayrton Senna	MP4/5	Honda	Marlboro	Pole Position, Fastest Lap

Win Number	Year	Date	Grand Prix	Circuit	Race Number	Driver	Model	Engine	Title Sponsor	Notes (on winning driver unless named)
81	1990	11.03.90	USA (Phoenix) GP	Phoenix	27	Ayrton Senna	MP4/5B	Honda	Marlboro	Pole Position, (Berger), Fastest Lap (Berger)
82		27.05.90	Monaco GP	Monte Carlo	27	Ayrton Senna	MP4/5B	Honda	Marlboro	Pole Position, Fastest Lap
83		10.06.90	Canadian GP	Montreal	27	Ayrton Senna	MP4/5B	Honda	Marlboro	Pole Position, Fastest Lap (Berger)
84		29.07.90	German GP	Hockenheim	27	Ayrton Senna	MP4/5B	Honda	Marlboro	Pole Position
85		26.08.90	Belgian GP	Spa Francorchamps	27	Ayrton Senna	MP4/5B	Honda	Marlboro	Pole Position
86		09.09.90	Italian GP	Monza	27	Ayrton Senna	MP4/5B	Honda	Marlboro	Pole Position, Fastest Lap
87	1991	10.03.91	USA (Phoenix) GP	Phoenix	1	Ayrton Senna	MP4/6	Honda	Marlboro	Pole Position
88		24.03.91	Brazilian GP	Interlagos	1	Ayrton Senna	MP4/6	Honda	Marlboro	Pole Position
89		28.04.91	San Marino GP	Imola	1	Ayrton Senna	MP4/6	Honda	Marlboro	Pole Position, Fastest Lap (Berger), 1-2 Finish
90		12.05.91	Monaco GP	Monte Carlo	1	Ayrton Senna	MP4/6	Honda	Marlboro	Pole Position
91		11.08.91	Hungarian GP	Hungaroring	1	Ayrton Senna	MP4/6	Honda	Marlboro	Pole Position
92		25.08.91	Belgian GP	Spa Francorchamps	1	Ayrton Senna	MP4/6	Honda	Marlboro	Pole Position, 1-2 Finish
93		20.10.91	Japanese GP	Suzuka	2	Gerhard Berger	MP4/6	Honda	Marlboro	Pole Position, Fastest Lap (Senna), 1-2 Finish
94		03.11.91	Australian GP	Adelaide	1	Ayrton Senna	MP4/6	Honda	Marlboro	Pole Position, Fastest Lap (Berger)
95	1992	31.05.92	Monaco GP	Monte Carlo	1	Ayrton Senna	MP4/7	Honda	Marlboro	
96		14.06.92	Canadian GP	Montreal	2	Gerhard Berger	MP4/7	Honda	Marlboro	Pole Position (Senna), Fastest Lap
97		16.08.92	Hungarian GP	Hungaroring	1	Ayrton Senna	MP4/7	Honda	Marlboro	
98		13.09.92	Italian GP	Monza	1	Ayrton Senna	MP4/7	Honda	Marlboro	
99		08.11.92	Australian GP	Adelaide	2	Gerhard Berger	MP4/7	Honda	Marlboro	
100	1993	29.03.93	Brazilian GP	Interlagos	8	Ayrton Senna	MP4/8	Ford HB	Marlboro	
101		11.04.93	European GP	Donington Park	8	Ayrton Senna	MP4/8	Ford HB	Marlboro	Fastest Lap
102		23.05.93	Monaco GP	Monte Carlo	8	Ayrton Senna	MP4/8	Ford HB	Marlboro	
103		24.10.93	Japanese GP	Suzuka	8	Ayrton Senna	MP4/8	Ford HB	Marlboro	
104		07.11.93	Australian GP	Adelaide	8	Ayrton Senna	MP4/8	Ford HB	Marlboro	Pole Position
105	1997	09.03.97	Australian GP	Melbourne	10	David Coulthard	MP4-12	Mercedes-Benz	West	
106		07.09.97	Italian GP	Monza	10	David Coulthard	MP4-12	Mercedes-Benz	West	Fastest Lap (Häkkinen)
107		26.10.97	European GP	Jerez	9	Mika Häkkinen	MP4-12	Mercedes-Benz	West	1-2 Finish, Häkkinen - First GP win
108	1998	08.03.98	Australian GP	Melbourne	8	Mika Häkkinen	MP4-13	Mercedes-Benz	West	Pole Position, Fastest Lap, 1-2 Finish
109		29.03.98	Brazilian GP	Interlagos	8	Mika Häkkinen	MP4-13	Mercedes-Benz	West	Pole Position, Fastest Lap, 1-2 Finish
110		26.04.98	San Marino GP	Imola	7	David Coulthard	MP4-13	Mercedes-Benz	West	Pole Position
111		10.05.98	Spanish GP	Barcelona	8	Mika Häkkinen	MP4-13	Mercedes-Benz	West	Pole Position, Fastest Lap, 1-2 Finish
112		24.05.98	Monaco GP	Monte Carlo	8	Mika Häkkinen	MP4-13	Mercedes-Benz	West	Pole Position, Fastest Lap
113		26.07.98	Austrian GP	A-1 Ring	8	Mika Häkkinen	MP4-13	Mercedes-Benz	West	Fastest Lap (Coulthard),1-2 Finish
114		02.08.98	German GP	Hockenheim	8	Mika Häkkinen	MP4-13	Mercedes-Benz	West	Pole Position, Fastest Lap (Coulthard), 1-2 Finish
115		27.09.98	European GP	Nürburgring	8	Mika Häkkinen	MP4-13	Mercedes-Benz	West	Fastest Lap
116		01.11.98	Japanese GP	Suzuka	8	Mika Häkkinen	MP4-13	Mercedes-Benz	West	
117	1999	11.04.99	Brazilian GP	Interlagos	1	Mika Häkkinen	MP4-14	Mercedes-Benz	West	Pole Position, Fastest Lap
118		30.05.99	Spanish GP	Barcelona	1	Mika Häkkinen	MP4-14	Mercedes-Benz	West	Pole Position, 1-2 Finish
119		13.06.99	Canadian GP	Montreal	1	Mika Häkkinen	MP4-14	Mercedes-Benz	West	
120		11.07.99	British GP	Silverstone	2	David Coulthard	MP4-14	Mercedes-Benz	West	Pole Position (Häkkinen), Fastest Lap (Häkkinen)
121		15.08.99	Hungarian GP	Hungaroring	1	Mika Häkkinen	MP4-14	Mercedes-Benz	West	Pole Position, Fastest Lap (Coulthard), 1-2 Finish
122		29.08.99	Belgian GP	Spa Francorchamps	2	David Coulthard	MP4-14	Mercedes-Benz	West	Pole Position & Fastest Lap (Häkkinen),1-2 Finish
123		31.10.99	Japanese GP	Suzuka	1	Mika Häkkinen	MP4-14	Mercedes-Benz	West	
124	2000	23.04.00	British GP	Silverstone	2	David Coulthard	MP4-15	Mercedes-Benz	West	Fastest Lap (Häkkinen), 1-2 Finish
125		07.05.00	Spanish GP	Barcelona	1	Mika Häkkinen	MP4-15	Mercedes-Benz	West	Fastest Lap,1-2 Finish
126		04.06.00	Monaco GP	Monte Carlo	2	David Coulthard	MP4-15	Mercedes-Benz	West	Fastest Lap (Häkkinen)
127		02.07.00	French GP	Magny Cours	2	David Coulthard	MP4-15	Mercedes-Benz	West	Fastest Lap,1-2 Finish
128		16.07.00	Austrian GP	A-1 Ring	1	Mika Häkkinen	MP4-15	Mercedes-Benz	West	Pole Position, Fastest Lap (Coulthard), 1-2 Finish
129		13.08.00	Hungarian GP	Hungaroring	1	Mika Häkkinen	MP4-15	Mercedes-Benz	West	Fastest Lap
130		27.08.00	Belgian GP	Spa Francorchamps	1	Mika Häkkinen	MP4-15	Mercedes-Benz	West	Pole Position
131	2001	01.04.01	Brazilian GP	Interlagos	4	David Coulthard	MP4-16	Mercedes-Benz	West	
132		13.05.01	Austrian GP	A-1 Ring	4	David Coulthard	MP4-16	Mercedes-Benz	West	Fastest Lap
133		15.07.01	British GP	Silverstone	3	Mika Häkkinen	MP4-16	Mercedes-Benz	West	Fastest Lap
134		30.09.01	USA GP	Indianapolis	3	Mika Häkkinen	MP4-16	Mercedes-Benz	West	
135	2002	26.05.02	Monaco GP	Monte Carlo	3	David Coulthard	MP4-17A	Mercedes-Benz	West	
136	2003	09.03.03	Australian GP	Melbourne	5	David Coulthard	MP4-17D	Mercedes-Benz	West	Fastest Lap (Räikkönen)
137		23.03.03	Malaysian GP	Sepang	6	Kimi Räikkönen	MP4-17D	Mercedes-Benz	West	Räikkonen - First GP win
138	2004	29.08.04	Belgian GP	Spa Francorchamps	6	Kimi Räikkönen	MP4-19B	Mercedes-Benz	West	Fastest Lap
139	2005	08.05.05	Spanish GP	Barcelona	9	Kimi Räikkönen	MP4-20A	Mercedes-Benz	West	Pole Position
140		22.05.05	Monaco GP	Monte Carlo	9	Kimi Räikkönen	MP4-20A	Mercedes-Benz	West	Pole Position
141		12.06.05	Canadian GP	Montreal	9	Kimi Räikkönen	MP4-20A	Mercedes-Benz	West	Fastest Lap
142		10.07.05	British GP	Silverstone	10	Juan Pablo Montoya	MP4-20A	Mercedes-Benz	West	Fastest Lap (Räikkönen)
143		31.07.05	Hungarian GP	Hungaroring	9	Kimi Räikkönen	MP4-20A	Mercedes-Benz	West	Fastest Lap
144		21.08.05	Turkish GP	Istanbul	9	Kimi Räikkönen	MP4-20A	Mercedes-Benz		Pole Position, Fastest Lap (Montoya)
145		04.09.05	Italian GP	Monza	10	Juan Pablo Montoya	MP4-20A	Mercedes-Benz		Pole Position, Fastest Lap (Räikkönen)
146		11.09.05	Belgian GP	Spa Francorchamps	9	Kimi Räikkönen	MP4-20A	Mercedes-Benz		Pole Position (Montoya)
147		25.09.05	Brazilian GP	Interlagos	10	Juan Pablo Montoya	MP4-20A	Mercedes-Benz		Fastest Lap (Räikkönen), 1-2 Finish
148		09.10.05	Japanese GP	Suzuka	9	Kimi Räikkönen	MP4-20A	Mercedes-Benz		Fastest Lap
149	2007	08.04.07	Malaysian GP	Sepang	1	Fernando Alonso	MP4-22A	Mercedes-Benz	Vodafone	Fastest Lap (Hamilton), 1-2 Finish
150		27.05.07	Monaco GP	Monte Carlo	1	Fernando Alonso	MP4-22A	Mercedes-Benz	Vodafone	Pole Position, Fastest Lap, 1-2 Finish
151		10.06.07	Canadian GP	Montreal	2	Lewis Hamilton	MP4-22A	Mercedes-Benz	Vodafone	Pole Position, Fastest Lap (Alonso), Hamilton - First GP win
152		17.06.07	USA GP	Indianapolis	2	Lewis Hamilton	MP4-22A	Mercedes-Benz	Vodafone	Pole Position, 1-2 Finish
153		22.07.07	European GP	Nürburgring	1	Fernando Alonso	MP4-22A	Mercedes-Benz	Vodafone	
154		05.08.07	Hungarian GP	Hungaroring	2	Lewis Hamilton	MP4-22A	Mercedes-Benz	Vodafone	Pole Position (Alonso)
155		09.09.07	Italian GP	Monza	1	Fernando Alonso	MP4-22A	Mercedes-Benz	Vodafone	Pole Position, Fastest Lap, 1-2 Finish
156		30.09.07	Japanese GP	Mt. Fuji	2	Lewis Hamilton	MP4-22A	Mercedes-Benz	Vodafone	Pole Position, Fastest Lap
157	2008	16.03.08	Australian GP	Melbourne	22	Lewis Hamilton	MP4-23A	Mercedes-Benz	Vodafone	Pole Position, Fastest Lap (Kovalainen)

Up to and including Australian Grand Prix 2008

APPENDIX 4
McLAREN FORMULA 1 RESULTS

Date	Event	Circuit	Race No.	Driver	Model	Qual.	Race Position	Reason/Notes
McLaren Formula 1 Works Team Results 1966-2008 - up to and including Australian Grand Prix 2008								
1966								
22.05.66	Monaco	Monte Carlo	2	B. McLaren	M2B	10	dnf	Oil leak
12.06.66	Belgian	Spa Francorchamps	24	B. McLaren	M2B	16	dns	Engine failure in practice
16.07.66	British	Brands Hatch	14	B. McLaren	M2B	13	6	First Championship points
24.07.66	Dutch	Zandvoort	20	B. McLaren	M2B	14	dns	Engine failure in practice
02.10.66	USA	Watkins Glen	17	B. McLaren	M2B	11	5	
23.10.66	Mexican	Mexico City	17	B. McLaren	M2B	15	dnf	Engine
1967								
07.05.67	Monaco	Monte Carlo	16	B. McLaren	M4B	9	4	
04.06.67	Dutch	Zandvoort	17	B. McLaren	M4B	14	dnf	Accident
27.08.67	Canadian	Mosport Park	19	B. McLaren	M5A	6	7	
10.09.67	Italian	Monza	4	B. McLaren	M5A	3	dnf	Engine
01.10.67	USA	Watkins Glen	14	B. McLaren	M5A	9	dnf	Overheating
22.10.67	Mexican	Mexico City	14	B. McLaren	M5A	8	dnf	Oil pressure
1968								
01.01.68	South African	Kyalami	1	D. Hulme	M5A	9	5	
12.05.68	Spanish	Jarama	1	D. Hulme	M7A	3	2	
12.05.68	Spanish	Jarama	2	B. McLaren	M7A	4	dnf	Oil leak
26.05.68	Monaco	Monte Carlo	12	D. Hulme	M7A	10	5	
26.05.68	Monaco	Monte Carlo	14	B. McLaren	M7A	9	dnf	Accident
26.05.68	Monaco	Monte Carlo	18	J. Bonnier	M5A	dnq	dns	
09.06.68	Belgian	Spa Francorchamps	6	D. Hulme	M7A	5	dnf	Transmission
09.06.68	Belgian	Spa Francorchamps	5	B. McLaren	M7A	6	1st	First GP win for a McLaren
09.06.68	Belgian	Spa Francorchamps	17	J. Bonnier	M5A	16	dnf	
23.06.68	Dutch	Zandvoort	1	D. Hulme	M7A	7	dnf	Engine
23.06.68	Dutch	Zandvoort	2	B. McLaren	M7A	8	dnf	Accident
23.06.68	Dutch	Zandvoort	19	J. Bonnier	M5A	19	8	
07.07.68	French	Rouen	8	D. Hulme	M7A	4	5	
07.07.68	French	Rouen	10	B. McLaren	M7A	6	8	
20.07.68	British	Brands Hatch	1	D. Hulme	M7A	11	4	
20.07.68	British	Brands Hatch	2	B. McLaren	M7A	10	7	
20.07.68	British	Brands Hatch	23	J. Bonnier	M5A	20	dnf	
04.08.68	German	Nürburgring	1	D. Hulme	M7A	11	7	
04.08.68	German	Nürburgring	2	B. McLaren	M7A	16	13	
08.09.68	Italian	Monza	1	D. Hulme	M7A	7	1st	
08.09.68	Italian	Monza	2	B. McLaren	M7A	2	dnf	Engine
08.09.68	Italian	Monza	3	J. Bonnier	M5A	21	6	
22.09.68	Canadian	St. Jovite	1	D. Hulme	M7A	6	1st	1-2 Finish
22.09.68	Canadian	St. Jovite	2	B. McLaren	M7A	8	2	
22.09.68	Canadian	St. Jovite	11	D. Gurney	M7A	4	dnf	Oil leak
22.09.68	Canadian	St. Jovite	22	J. Bonnier	M5A	18	dns	Engine wouldn't start
06.10.68	USA	Watkins Glen	1	D. Hulme	M7A	5	dnf	Accident
06.10.68	USA	Watkins Glen	2	B. McLaren	M7A	10	6	
06.10.68	USA	Watkins Glen	14	D. Gurney	M7A	7	4	
06.10.68	USA	Watkins Glen	17	J. Bonnier	M5A	18	dnf	Ignition
03.11.68	Mexican	Mexico City	1	D. Hulme	M7A	4	dnf	Accident
03.11.68	Mexican	Mexico City	2	B. McLaren	M7A	9	2	
03.11.68	Mexican	Mexico City	14	D. Gurney	M7A	5	dnf	
03.11.68	Mexican	Mexico City	17	J. Bonnier	M5A	dnq	dns	
1969								
01.03.69	South African	Kyalami	5	D. Hulme	M7A	3	3	
01.03.69	South African	Kyalami	6	B. McLaren	M7B	7	5	
01.03.69	South African	Kyalami	18	B. van Rooyen	M7A	9	dnf	
04.05.69	Spanish	Montjuich	5	D. Hulme	M7A	8	4	
04.05.69	Spanish	Montjuich	6	B. McLaren	M7C	13	2	
18.05.69	Monaco	Monte Carlo	3	D. Hulme	M7A	12	6	
18.05.69	Monaco	Monte Carlo	4	B. McLaren	M7C	11	5	
21.06.69	Dutch	Zandvoort	7	D. Hulme	M7A	7	4	
21.06.69	Dutch	Zandvoort	6	B. McLaren	M7C	6	dnf	Suspension
21.06.69	Dutch	Zandvoort	18	V. Elford	M7B	15	10	
06.07.69	French	Clermont Ferrand	4	D. Hulme	M7A	2	8	
06.07.69	French	Clermont Ferrand	5	B. McLaren	M7C	7	4	
06.07.69	French	Clermont Ferrand	10	V. Elford	M7B	10	5	
19.07.69	British	Silverstone	5	D. Hulme	M7A	3	dnf	Ignition
19.07.69	British	Silverstone	6	B. McLaren	M7C	7	3	
19.07.69	British	Silverstone	19	V. Elford	M7B	11	6	
19.07.69	British	Silverstone	20	D. Bell	M9A	15	dnf	Suspension
03.08.69	German	Nürburgring	9	D. Hulme	M7A	5	dnf	Gearbox
03.08.69	German	Nürburgring	10	B. McLaren	M7C	8	3	
03.08.69	German	Nürburgring	12	V. Elford	M7B	6	dnf	Accident, car destroyed
07.09.69	Italian	Monza	16	D. Hulme	M7A	2	7	
07.09.69	Italian	Monza	18	B. McLaren	M7C	5	4	
20.09.69	Canadian	Mosport Park	5	D. Hulme	M7A	5	dnf	Ignition
20.09.69	Canadian	Mosport Park	4	B. McLaren	M7C	8	5	
05.10.69	USA	Watkins Glen	5	D. Hulme	M7A	2	dnf	Gearbox
05.10.69	USA	Watkins Glen	6	B. McLaren	M7C	6	dns	Engine failure
19.10.69	Mexican	Mexico City	5	D. Hulme	M7A	4	1st	
19.10.69	Mexican	Mexico City	6	B. McLaren	M7C	7	dnf	Fuel system
1970								
07.03.70	South African	Kyalami	6	D. Hulme	M14A	6	2	
07.03.70	South African	Kyalami	5	B. McLaren	M14A	10	dnf	Engine
07.03.70	South African	Kyalami	7	J. Surtees	M7C	7	dnf	Fastest Lap
19.04.70	Spanish	Jarama	5	D. Hulme	M14A	2	dnf	Engine
19.04.70	Spanish	Jarama	11	B. McLaren	M14A	12	2	
19.04.70	Spanish	Jarama	20	A. de Adamich	M7D	dnq	dns	
19.04.70	Spanish	Jarama	8	J. Surtees	M7C	14	dnf	
10.05.70	Monaco	Monte Carlo	11	D. Hulme	M14A	3	4	
10.05.70	Monaco	Monte Carlo	12	B. McLaren	M14A	10	dnf	Suspension
10.05.70	Monaco	Monte Carlo	10	A. de Adamich	M7D	dnq	dns	
21.06.70	Dutch	Zandvoort	20	P. Gethin	M14A	11	dnf	Accident
21.06.70	Dutch	Zandvoort	32	D. Gurney	M14A	20	dnf	Gearbox
21.06.70	Dutch	Zandvoort	21	A. de Adamich	M14D	dnq	dns	
21.06.70	Dutch	Zandvoort	16	J. Surtees	M7C	14	6	
05.07.70	French	Clermont Ferrand	19	D. Hulme	M14A	7	4	Converted from M14D
05.07.70	French	Clermont Ferrand	17	D. Gurney	M14A	17	6	
05.07.70	French	Clermont Ferrand	16	A. de Adamich	M7D	15	n/c	
19.07.70	British	Brands Hatch	9	D. Hulme	M14A	4	3	Converted from M14D
19.07.70	British	Brands Hatch	10	D. Gurney	M7A	12	dnf	Oil pipe
19.07.70	British	Brands Hatch	11	A. de Adamich	M7D	19	dns	Fuel Leak
02.08.70	German	Hockenheim	4	D. Hulme	M14A	16	3	
02.08.70	German	Hockenheim	24	P. Gethin	M14A	17	dnf	Engine
02.08.70	German	Hockenheim	20	A. de Adamich	M14D	dnq	dns	
16.08.70	Austrian	Österreichring	21	D. Hulme	M14A	11	dnf	Engine
16.08.70	Austrian	Österreichring	23	P. Gethin	M14A	20	10	
16.08.70	Austrian	Österreichring	22	A. de Adamich	M14D	14	12	
06.09.70	Italian	Monza	30	D. Hulme	M14A	9	4	
06.09.70	Italian	Monza	32	P. Gethin	M14A	18	n/c	
06.09.70	Italian	Monza	34	A. de Adamich	M14D	13	8	
06.09.70	Italian	Monza	36	G. Galli	M7D	dnq	dns	
20.09.70	Canadian	St. Jovite	5	D. Hulme	M14A	15	dnf	Differential
20.09.70	Canadian	St. Jovite	6	P. Gethin	M14A	11	6	
20.09.70	Canadian	St. Jovite	8	A. de Adamich	M14D	12	dnf	Oil pipe
14.10.70	USA	Watkins Glen	8	D. Hulme	M14A	11	7	
14.10.70	USA	Watkins Glen	9	P. Gethin	M14A	21	14	
14.10.70	USA	Watkins Glen	10	A. de Adamich	M14D	dnq	dns	
14.10.70	USA	Watkins Glen	27	J. Bonnier	M7C	24	dnf	
25.10.70	Mexican	Mexico City	8	D. Hulme	M14A	14	3	
25.10.70	Mexican	Mexico City	9	P. Gethin	M14A	10	dnf	Engine
1971								
06.03.71	South African	Kyalami	11	D. Hulme	M19A	5	6	
06.03.71	South African	Kyalami	12	P. Gethin	M14A	11	dnf	Suspension
06.03.71	South African	Kyalami	23	J. Bonnier	M7C	23	dnf	
18.04.71	Spanish	Montjuich	9	D. Hulme	M19A	9	5	
18.04.71	Spanish	Montjuich	10	P. Gethin	M14A	7	8	
23.05.71	Monaco	Monte Carlo	9	D. Hulme	M19A	6	4	
23.05.71	Monaco	Monte Carlo	10	P.Gethin	M14A	14	dnf	Front suspension
10.06.71	Dutch	Zandvoort	26	D. Hulme	M19A	14	12	
10.06.71	Dutch	Zandvoort	28	P. Gethin	M19A	22	n/c	
04.07.71	French	Paul Ricard	9	D. Hulme	M19A	11	dnf	Ignition
04.07.71	French	Paul Ricard	10	P. Gethin	M19A	19	9	
17.07.71	British	Silverstone	9	D. Hulme	M19A	8	dnf	Engine
17.07.71	British	Silverstone	10	P. Gethin	M19A	14	dnf	Engine
17.07.71	British	Silverstone	11	J. Oliver	M14A	22	dnf	Accident
01.08.71	German	Nürburgring	18	D. Hulme	M19A	6	dnf	Fuel leak
01.08.71	German	Nürburgring	20	P. Gethin	M19A	19	dnf	Accident/Suspension
15.08.71	Austrian	Österreichring	9	D. Hulme	M19A	9	dnf	Engine
15.08.71	Austrian	Österreichring	10	J. Oliver	M19A	22	9	
15.08.71	Austrian	Österreichring	28	J. Bonnier	M7C	19	dns	
05.09.71	Italian	Monza	14	J. Oliver	M14A	13	7	
05.09.71	Italian	Monza	28	J. Bonnier	M7C	21	10	
19.09.71	Canadian	Mosport Park	9	D. Hulme	M19A	10	4	Fastest Lap
19.09.71	Canadian	Mosport Park	10	M. Donohue	M19A	7	3	
03.10.71	USA	Watkins Glen	7	D. Hulme	M19A	3	dnf	
03.10.71	USA	Watkins Glen	31	D. Hobbs	M19A	24	10	Replaced Donohue for race
03.10.71	USA	Watkins Glen	29	J. Bonnier	M7C	31	16	Out of fuel
1972								
23.01.72	Argentinian	Buenos Aires	17	D. Hulme	M19A	4	2	
23.01.72	Argentinian	Buenos Aires	18	P. Revson	M19A	3	dnf	Engine
04.03.72	South African	Kyalami	12	D. Hulme	M19A	5	1st	
04.03.72	South African	Kyalami	14	P. Revson	M19A	12	3	
01.05.72	Spanish	Jarama	11	D. Hulme	M19A	2	dnf	Gearbox
01.05.72	Spanish	Jarama	20	P. Revson	M19A	11	5	
14.05.72	Monaco	Monte Carlo	14	D. Hulme	M19C	7	15	
14.05.72	Monaco	Monte Carlo	15	B. Redman	M19A	10	5	
04.06.72	Belgian	Nivelles	9	D. Hulme	M19C	3	3	
04.06.72	Belgian	Nivelles	10	P. Revson	M19A	7	7	
02.07.72	French	Clermont Ferrand	2	D. Hulme	M19C	2	7	
02.07.72	French	Clermont Ferrand	11	B. Redman	M19A	15	9	
15.07.72	British	Brands Hatch	18	D. Hulme	M19C	11	5	
15.07.72	British	Brands Hatch	19	P. Revson	M19A	3	3	
30.07.72	German	Nürburgring	3	D. Hulme	M19C	10	dnf	Engine
30.07.72	German	Nürburgring	5	B. Redman	M19A	19	5	
13.08.72	Austrian	Österreichring	12	D. Hulme	M19C	7	2	Fastest Lap
13.08.72	Austrian	Österreichring	14	P. Revson	M19C	4	3	
10.09.72	Italian	Monza	14	D. Hulme	M19C	5	3	
10.09.72	Italian	Monza	15	P. Revson	M19C	8	4	
24.09.72	Canadian	Mosport Park	18	D. Hulme	M19C	2	3	
24.09.72	Canadian	Mosport Park	19	P. Revson	M19C	Pole	2	Pole Position
08.10.72	USA	Watkins Glen	19	D. Hulme	M19C	3	3	
08.10.72	USA	Watkins Glen	20	P. Revson	M19C	2	dnf/18	Ignition
08.10.72	USA	Watkins Glen	21	J. Scheckter	M19A	8	9	

Date	Event	Circuit	Race No.	Driver	Model	Qual. Position	Race Position	Reason/Notes
1973								
28.01.73	Argentinian	Buenos Aires	14	D. Hulme	M19C	8	5	
28.01.73	Argentinian	Buenos Aires	16	P. Revson	M19C	11	8	
11.02.73	Brazilian	Interlagos	7	D. Hulme	M19C	5	3	Fastest Lap=
11.02.73	Brazilian	Interlagos	8	P. Revson	M19C	12	dnf	Driveshaft
03.03.73	South African	Kyalami	5	D. Hulme	M23	Pole	5	Pole Position
03.03.73	South African	Kyalami	6	P. Revson	M19C	6	2	
03.03.73	South African	Kyalami	7	J. Scheckter	M19C	3	9	Engine
29.04.73	Spanish	Montjuich	5	D. Hulme	M23	2	6	
29.04.73	Spanish	Montjuich	6	P. Revson	M23	5	4	
20.05.73	Belgian	Zolder	7	D. Hulme	M23	2	7	
20.05.73	Belgian	Zolder	8	P. Revson	M23	10	dnf	Accident
03.06.73	Monaco	Monte Carlo	7	D. Hulme	M23	3	6	
03.06.73	Monaco	Monte Carlo	8	P. Revson	M23	15	5	
17.06.73	Swedish	Anderstorp	7	D. Hulme	M23	6	1st	Fastest Lap
17.06.73	Swedish	Anderstorp	8	P. Revson	M23	7	7	
01.07.73	French	Paul Ricard	7	D. Hulme	M23	6	8	Fastest Lap
01.07.73	French	Paul Ricard	8	J. Scheckter	M23	2	dnf	Accident
14.07.73	British	Silverstone	7	D. Hulme	M23	2	3	
14.07.73	British	Silverstone	8	P. Revson	M23	3	1st	
14.07.73	British	Silverstone	30	J. Scheckter	M23	6	dnf/dns	Accident/Race re-started
29.07.73	Dutch	Zandvoort	7	D. Hulme	M23	4	dnf	Engine
29.07.73	Dutch	Zandvoort	8	P. Revson	M23	6	4	
05.08.73	German	Nürburgring	7	D. Hulme	M23	8	12	
05.08.73	German	Nürburgring	8	P. Revson	M23	7	9	
05.08.73	German	Nürburgring	30	J. Ickx	M23	4	3	
19.08.73	Austrian	Österreichring	7	D. Hulme	M23	3	8	
19.08.73	Austrian	Österreichring	8	P. Revson	M23	4	dnf	Clutch
09.09.73	Italian	Monza	7	D. Hulme	M23	3	15	
09.09.73	Italian	Monza	8	P. Revson	M23	2	3	
23.09.73	Canadian	Mosport Park	7	D. Hulme	M23	7	13	
23.09.73	Canadian	Mosport Park	8	P. Revson	M23	2	1st	
23.09.73	Canadian	Mosport	0	J. Scheckter	M23	3	dnf	Accident
07.10.73	USA	Watkins Glen	7	D. Hulme	M23	8	4	
07.10.73	USA	Watkins Glen	8	P. Revson	M23	7	5	
07.10.73	USA	Watkins Glen	0	J. Scheckter	M23	10	dnf	Suspension
1974								
13.01.74	Argentinian	Buenos Aires	5	E. Fittipaldi	M23	3	10	
13.01.74	Argentinian	Buenos Aires	6	D. Hulme	M23	10	1st	
13.01.74	Argentinian	Buenos Aires	33	M. Hailwood	M23	9	4	
27.01.74	Brazilian	Interlagos	5	E. Fittipaldi	M23	Pole	1st	Pole Position
27.01.74	Brazilian	Interlagos	6	D. Hulme	M23	11	12	
27.01.74	Brazilian	Interlagos	33	M. Hailwood	M23	7	5	
30.03.74	South African	Kyalami	5	E. Fittipaldi	M23	5	7	
30.03.74	South African	Kyalami	6	D. Hulme	M23	9	9	
30.03.74	South African	Kyalami	33	M. Hailwood	M23	12	3	
30.03.74	South African	Kyalami	23	D. Charlton	M23	20	19	
28.04.74	Spanish	Jarama	5	E. Fittipaldi	M23	4	3	
28.04.74	Spanish	Jarama	56	D. Hulme	M23	8	6	
28.04.74	Spanish	Jarama	33	M. Hailwood	M23	17	9	
12.05.74	Belgian	Nivelles	5	E. Fittipaldi	M23	4	1st	
12.05.74	Belgian	Nivelles	6	D. Hulme	M23	12	6	Fastest Lap
12.05.74	Belgian	Nivelles	33	M. Hailwood	M23	13	7	
26.05.74	Monaco	Monte Carlo	5	E. Fittipaldi	M23	13	5	
26.05.74	Monaco	Monte Carlo	6	D. Hulme	M23	12	dnf	Accident
26.05.74	Monaco	Monte Carlo	33	M. Hailwood	M23	10	dnf	Accident
09.06.74	Swedish	Anderstorp	5	E. Fittipaldi	M23	9	4	
09.06.74	Swedish	Anderstorp	6	D. Hulme	M23	12	dnf	Rear suspension
09.06.74	Swedish	Anderstorp	33	M. Hailwood	M23	11	dnf	Fuel pump
23.06.74	Dutch	Zandvoort	5	E. Fittipaldi	M23	3	3	
23.06.74	Dutch	Zandvoort	6	D. Hulme	M23	9	dnf	Ignition
23.06.74	Dutch	Zandvoort	33	M. Hailwood	M23	4	4	
07.07.74	French	Dijon-Prenois	5	E. Fittipaldi	M23	5	dnf	Oil leak
07.07.74	French	Dijon-Prenois	6	D. Hulme	M23	11	6	
07.07.74	French	Dijon-Prenois	33	M. Hailwood	M23	6	7	
20.07.74	British	Brands Hatch	5	E. Fittipaldi	M23	8	2	
20.07.74	British	Brands Hatch	6	D. Hulme	M23	19	7	
20.07.74	British	Brands Hatch	33	M. Hailwood	M23	11	dnf	Accident
04.08.74	German	Nürburgring	5	E. Fittipaldi	M23	3	dnf	Suspension damage
04.08.74	German	Nürburgring	6	D. Hulme	M23	7	disq	Used spare car
04.08.74	German	Nürburgring	33	M. Hailwood	M23	12	dnf	Accident
18.08.74	Austrian	Österreichring	5	E. Fittipaldi	M23	3	dnf	Engine
18.08.74	Austrian	Österreichring	6	D. Hulme	M23	10	2	
18.08.74	Austrian	Österreichring	33	D. Hobbs	M23	17	7	
08.09.74	Italian	Monza	5	E. Fittipaldi	M23	6	2	
08.09.74	Italian	Monza	6	D. Hulme	M23	19	6	
08.09.74	Italian	Monza	33	D. Hobbs	M23	23	9	
22.09.74	Canadian	Mosport Park	5	E. Fittipaldi	M23	Pole	1st	Pole Position
22.09.74	Canadian	Mosport Park	6	D. Hulme	M23	14	6	
22.09.74	Canadian	Mosport Park	33	J. Mass	M23	12	16	
06.10.74	USA	Watkins Glen	5	E. Fittipaldi	M23	8	4	
06.10.74	USA	Watkins Glen	6	D. Hulme	M23	17	dnf	Engine
06.10.74	USA	Watkins Glen	33	J. Mass	M23	20	7	
1975								
12.01.75	Argentinian	Buenos Aires	1	E. Fittipaldi	M23	5	1	
12.01.75	Argentinian	Buenos Aires	2	J. Mass	M23	13	14	
26.01.75	Brazilian	Interlagos	1	E. Fittipaldi	M23	2	2	
26.01.75	Brazilian	Interlagos	2	J. Mass	M23	10	3	
01.03.75	South African	Kyalami	1	E. Fittipaldi	M23	11	n/c	
01.03.75	South African	Kyalami	2	J. Mass	M23	16	6	
01.03.75	South African	Kyalami	31	D. Charlton	M23	20	14	
27.04.75	Spanish	Montjuich	1	E. Fittipaldi	M23	26	dns	Withdrew
27.04.75	Spanish	Montjuich	2	J. Mass	M23	11	1st	Race stopped 29/75 laps
11.05.75	Monaco	Monte Carlo	1	E. Fittipaldi	M23	9	2	
11.05.75	Monaco	Monte Carlo	2	J. Mass	M23	15	6	
25.05.75	Belgian	Zolder	1	E. Fittipaldi	M23	8	7	
25.05.75	Belgian	Zolder	2	J. Mass	M23	15	dnf	Accident
08.06.75	Swedish	Anderstorp	1	E. Fittipaldi	M23	11	8	
08.06.75	Swedish	Anderstorp	2	J. Mass	M23	14	dnf	Water leak
22.06.75	Dutch	Zandvoort	1	E. Fittipaldi	M23	6	dnf	Engine
22.06.75	Dutch	Zandvoort	2	J. Mass	M23	8	dnf	Accident
06.07.75	French	Paul Ricard	1	E. Fittipaldi	M23	10	4	
06.07.75	French	Paul Ricard	2	J. Mass	M23	7	3	Fastest Lap
19.07.75	British	Silverstone	1	E. Fittipaldi	M23	7	1st	Race stopped due to rain
19.07.75	British	Silverstone	2	J. Mass	M23	10	7	Race stopped due to rain
03.08.75	German	Nürburgring	1	E. Fittipaldi	M23	8	dnf	Suspension
03.08.75	German	Nürburgring	2	J. Mass	M23	6	dnf	Tyre Failure
17.08.75	Austrian	Österreichring	1	E. Fittipaldi	M23	3	9	Race stopped due to rain
17.08.75	Austrian	Österreichring	2	J. Mass	M23	9	4	Race stopped due to rain
07.09.75	Italian	Monza	1	E. Fittipaldi	M23	3	2	
07.09.75	Italian	Monza	2	J. Mass	M23	5	dnf	Accident
05.10.75	USA	Watkins Glen	1	E. Fittipaldi	M23	2	2	Fastest Lap
05.10.75	USA	Watkins Glen	2	J. Mass	M23	9	3	
1976								
25.01.76	Brazilian	Interlagos	11	J. Hunt	M23	Pole	dnf	Pole Position, Accident
25.01.76	Brazilian	Interlagos	12	J. Mass	M23	6	6	
06.03.76	South African	Kyalami	11	J. Hunt	M23	Pole	2	Pole Position
06.03.76	South African	Kyalami	12	J. Mass	M23	4	3	
28.03.76	USA (West)	Long Beach	11	J. Hunt	M23	3	dnf	Accident
28.03.76	USA (West)	Long Beach	12	J. Mass	M23	14	5	
02.05.76	Spanish	Jarama	11	J. Hunt	M23	Pole	1st	Re-instated after appeal
02.05.76	Spanish	Jarama	12	J. Mass	M23	4	dnf	Fastest Lap, engine failure
16.05.76	Belgian	Zolder	11	J. Hunt	M23	3	dnf	Gearbox
16.05.76	Belgian	Zolder	12	J. Mass	M23	18	6	
30.05.76	Monaco	Monte Carlo	11	J. Hunt	M23	14	dnf	Engine
30.05.76	Monaco	Monte Carlo	12	J. Mass	M23	11	5	
13.06.76	Swedish	Anderstorp	11	J. Hunt	M23	8	5	
13.06.76	Swedish	Anderstorp	12	J. Mass	M23	13	11	
04.07.76	French	Paul Ricard	11	J. Hunt	M23	Pole	1st	Pole Position
04.07.76	French	Paul Ricard	12	J. Mass	M23	14	15	
18.07.76	British	Brands Hatch	11	J. Hunt	M23	2	disq	First on road
18.07.76	British	Brands Hatch	12	J. Mass	M23	12	dnf	Clutch
01.08.76	German	Nürburgring	11	J. Hunt	M23	Pole	1st	
01.08.76	German	Nürburgring	12	J. Mass	M23	9	3	
15.08.76	Austrian	Österreichring	11	J. Hunt	M23	Pole	4	Fastest Lap
15.08.76	Austrian	Österreichring	12	J. Mass	M23	12	7	
29.08.76	Dutch	Zandvoort	11	J. Hunt	M23	2	1st	
29.08.76	Dutch	Zandvoort	12	J. Mass	M26	15	9	
12.09.76	Italian	Monza	11	J. Hunt	M23	27	dnf	Accident
12.09.76	Italian	Monza	12	J. Mass	M23	28	dnf	Ignition
03.10.76	Canadian	Mosport	11	J. Hunt	M23	Pole	1st	
03.10.76	Canadian	Mosport	12	J. Mass	M23	11	5	
10.10.76	USA (East)	Watkins Glen	11	J. Hunt	M23	Pole	1st	Fastest Lap
10.10.76	USA (East)	Watkins Glen	12	J. Mass	M23	17	4	
24.10.76	Japanese	Mt.Fuji	11	J. Hunt	M23	2	3	
24.10.76	Japanese	Mt.Fuji	12	J. Mass	M23	12	dnf	Accident
1977								
09.01.77	Argentinian	Buenos Aires	1	J. Hunt	M23	Pole	dnf	Fastest Lap, Suspension
09.01.77	Argentinian	Buenos Aires	2	J. Mass	M23	5	dnf	
23.01.77	Brazilian	Interlagos	1	J. Hunt	M23	Pole	2	Fastest Lap
23.01.77	Brazilian	Interlagos	2	J. Mass	M23	4	dnf	Accident
05.03.77	South African	Kyalami	1	J. Hunt	M23	Pole	4	
05.03.77	South African	Kyalami	2	J. Mass	M23	13	5	
03.04.77	USA (West)	Long Beach	1	J. Hunt	M23	8	7	
03.04.77	USA (West)	Long Beach	2	J. Mass	M23	15	dnf	Vibration
08.05.77	Spanish	Jarama	1	J. Hunt	M26	7	dnf	Engine
08.05.77	Spanish	Jarama	2	J. Mass	M23	9	4	
08.05.77	Spanish	Jarama	36	E. de Villota	M23	23	13	
22.05.77	Monaco	Monte Carlo	1	J. Hunt	M23	7	7	
22.05.77	Monaco	Monte Carlo	2	J. Mass	M23	9	4	
05.06.77	Belgian	Zolder	1	J. Hunt	M26	9	7	
05.06.77	Belgian	Zolder	2	J. Mass	M23	6	dnf	Accident
05.06.77	Belgian	Zolder	36	E. de Villota	M23	dnq	dns	
19.06.77	Swedish	Anderstorp	1	J. Hunt	M26	3	12	
19.06.77	Swedish	Anderstorp	2	J. Mass	M23	9	2	
03.07.77	French	Dijon-Prenois	1	J. Hunt	M26	2	3	
03.07.77	French	Dijon-Prenois	2	J. Mass	M23	7	9	
16.07.77	British	Silverstone	1	J. Hunt	M26	Pole	1st	
16.07.77	British	Silverstone	2	J. Mass	M26	11	4	
16.07.77	British	Silverstone	40	G. Villeneuve	M23	9	11	
31.07.77	German	Hockenheim	1	J. Hunt	M26	4	dnf	Fuel Pump
31.07.77	German	Hockenheim	2	J. Mass	M26	13	dnf	Gearbox
14.08.77	Austrian	Österreichring	1	J. Hunt	M26	2	dnf	Engine
14.08.77	Austrian	Österreichring	2	J. Mass	M26	9	6	

APPENDIX 4
McLAREN FORMULA 1 RESULTS
CONTINUED

Date	Event	Circuit	Race No.	Driver	Model	Qual. Position	Race Position	Reason/Notes
28.08.77	Dutch	Zandvoort	1	J. Hunt	M26	3	dnf	Accident
28.08.77	Dutch	Zandvoort	2	J. Mass	M26	13	dnf	Accident
11.09.77	Italian	Monza	1	J. Hunt	M26	Pole	dnf	Accident
11.09.77	Italian	Monza	2	J. Mass	M26	9	4	
11.09.77	Italian	Monza	14	B. Giacomelli	M23	15	dnf	Accident
02.10.77	USA	Watkins Glen	1	J. Hunt	M26	Pole	1st	
02.10.77	USA	Watkins Glen	2	J. Mass	M26	15	dnf	Fuel Pump
09.10.77	Canadian	Mosport Park	1	J. Hunt	M26	2	dnf	Accident
09.10.77	Canadian	Mosport Park	2	J. Mass	M26	5	3	
23.10.77	Japanese	Mt.Fuji	1	J. Hunt	M26	2	1st	
23.10.77	Japanese	Mt.Fuji	2	J. Mass	M26	8	dnf	Engine
1978								
15.01.78	Argentinian	Buenos Aires	7	J. Hunt	M26	6	4	
15.01.78	Argentinian	Buenos Aires	8	P. Tambay	M26	9	6	
29.01.78	Brazilian	Interlagos	7	J. Hunt	M26	2	dnf	Accident
29.01.78	Brazilian	Interlagos	8	P. Tambay	M26	5	dnf	Accident
04.03.78	South African	Kyalami	7	J. Hunt	M26	3	dnf	Engine
04.03.78	South African	Kyalami	8	P. Tambay	M26	4	dnf	Accident
02.04.78	USA West	Long Beach	7	J. Hunt	M26	7	dnf	Accident
02.04.78	USA West	Long Beach	8	P. Tambay	M26	11	12 nrf	Accident
07.05.78	Monaco	Monte Carlo	7	J. Hunt	M26	6	dnf	Suspension
07.05.78	Monaco	Monte Carlo	8	P. Tambay	M26	11	7	
21.05.78	Belgian	Zolder	7	J. Hunt	M26	6	dnf	Accident
21.05.78	Belgian	Zolder	33	B. Giacomelli	M26	21	8	
04.06.78	Spanish	Jarama	7	J. Hunt	M26	4	6	
04.06.78	Spanish	Jarama	8	P. Tambay	M26	14	dnf	Accident
17.06.78	Swedish	Anderstorp	7	J. Hunt	M26	14	8	
17.06.78	Swedish	Anderstorp	8	P. Tambay	M26	15	4	
02.07.78	French	Paul Ricard	7	J. Hunt	M26	4	3	
02.07.78	French	Paul Ricard	8	P. Tambay	M26	6	9	
02.07.78	French	Paul Ricard	33	B. Giacomelli	M26	22	dnf	Engine
16.07.78	British	Brands Hatch	7	J. Hunt	M26	14	dnf	Accident
16.07.78	British	Brands Hatch	8	P. Tambay	M26	20	6	
16.07.78	British	Brands Hatch	33	B. Giacomelli	M26	16	7	
30.07.76	German	Hockenheim	7	J. Hunt	M26	8	dsq	Illegal short cut to pits
30.07.76	German	Hockenheim	8	P. Tambay	M26	11	dnf	Puncture/Accident
13.08.78	Austrian	Österreichring	7	J. Hunt	M26	8	7	
13.08.78	Austrian	Österreichring	8	P. Tambay	M26	14	16	
27.08.76	Dutch	Zandvoort	7	J. Hunt	M26	7	10 nrf	
27.08.76	Dutch	Zandvoort	8	P. Tambay	M26	14	9	
27.08.76	Dutch	Zandvoort	33	B. Giacomelli	M26	19	dnf	Accident
10.09.78	Italian	Monza	7	J. Hunt	M26	10	dnf	Distributor
10.09.78	Italian	Monza	8	P. Tambay	M26	19	5	
10.09.78	Italian	Monza	33	B. Giacomelli	M26	20	14	
01.10.78	USA	Watkins Glen	7	J. Hunt	M26	6	7	
01.10.78	USA	Watkins Glen	8	P. Tambay	M26	18	6	
08.10.78	Canadian	Montreal	7	J. Hunt	M26	19	dnf	Accident
08.10.78	Canadian	Montreal	8	P. Tambay	M26	17	8	
1979								
21.01.79	Argentinian	Buenos Aires	7	J. Watson	M28	6	3	
21.01.79	Argentinian	Buenos Aires	8	P. Tambay	M28	9	dnf	Accident, did not re-start
04.02.79	Brazilian	Interlagos	7	J. Watson	M28	14	8	
04.02.79	Brazilian	Interlagos	8	P. Tambay	M26	18	dnf	Accident
03.03.79	South African	Kyalami	7	J. Watson	M28	14	dnf	Ignition
03.03.79	South African	Kyalami	8	P. Tambay	M28	17	10	
08.04.79	USA West	Long Beach	7	J. Watson	M28	18	dnf	Fuel injection
08.04.79	USA West	Long Beach	8	P. Tambay	M28	19	dnf	Accident
29.04.79	Spanish	Jarama	7	J. Watson	M28	18	dnf	Engine
29.04.79	Spanish	Jarama	8	P. Tambay	M28	20	13	
13.05.79	Belgian	Zolder	7	J. Watson	M28	19	16	
13.05.79	Belgian	Zolder	8	P. Tambay	M26	dnq		
27.05.79	Monaco	Monte Carlo	7	J. Watson	M28	14	4	
27.05.79	Monaco	Monte Carlo	8	P. Tambay	M28	dnq		
01.07.79	French	Paul Ricard	7	J. Watson	M28	15	11	
01.07.79	French	Paul Ricard	8	P. Tambay	M28	20	10	
14.07.79	British	Silverstone	7	J. Watson	M29	7	4	
14.07.79	British	Silverstone	8	P. Tambay	M28	18	7	
29.07.79	German	Hockenheim	7	J. Watson	M29	12	5	
29.07.79	German	Hockenheim	8	P. Tambay	M29	15	dnf	Suspension
12.08.79	Austrian	Österreichring	7	J. Watson	M29	16	9	
12.08.79	Austrian	Österreichring	8	P. Tambay	M29	14	10	
26.08.79	Dutch	Zandvoort	7	J. Watson	M29	12	dnf	Engine
26.08.79	Dutch	Zandvoort	8	P. Tambay	M29	14	dnf	Engine
09.09.79	Italian	Monza	7	J. Watson	M29	19	dnf	Accident
09.09.79	Italian	Monza	8	P. Tambay	M29	14	dnf	Engine
30.09.79	Canadian	Montreal	7	J. Watson	M29	17	6	
30.09.79	Canadian	Montreal	8	P. Tambay	M29	20	dnf	Engine
07.10.79	USA	Watkins Glen	7	J. Watson	M29	13	6	
07.10.79	USA	Watkins Glen	8	P. Tambay	M29	22	dnf	Engine
1980								
13.01.80	Argentinian	Buenos Aires	7	J. Watson	M29	17	dnf	Accident/Oil Leak
13.01.80	Argentinian	Buenos Aires	8	A. Prost	M29	12	6	
27,01,80	Brazilian	Interlagos	7	J. Watson	M29	23	11	
27,01,80	Brazilian	Interlagos	8	A. Prost	M29	13	5	
01.03.80	South African	Kyalami	7	J. Watson	M29	21	11	
01.03.80	South African	Kyalami	8	A. Prost	M29	22	dns	Accident in Practice
30.03.80	USA West	Long Beach	7	J. Watson	M29	21	4	
30.03.80	USA West	Long Beach	8	S.South	M29	dnq	dns	
04.05.80	Belgian	Zolder	7	J. Watson	M29	20	nc	
04.05.80	Belgian	Zolder	8	A. Prost	M29	19	dnf	Transmission
18.05.80	Monaco	Monte Carlo	7	J. Watson	M29	dnq	dns	
18.05.80	Monaco	Monte Carlo	8	A. Prost	M29	10	dnf	Accident
01.06.80	Spanish	Jarama (non-ch)	7	J. Watson	M29	12	dnf	Accident
01.06.80	Spanish	Jarama (non-ch)	8	A. Prost	M29	6	dnf	Engine
29.06.80	French	Paul Ricard	7	J. Watson	M29	13	7	
29.06.80	French	Paul Ricard	8	A. Prost	M29	7	dnf	Transmission
13.07.80	British	Silverstone	7	J. Watson	M29	12	8	
13.07.80	British	Silverstone	8	A. Prost	M29	7	6	
10.08.80	German	Hockenheim	7	J. Watson	M29	20	dnf	Engine
10.08.80	German	Hockenheim	8	A. Prost	M29	14	11	
17.08.80	Austrian	Österreichring	7	J. Watson	M29	21	dnf	Engine
17.08.80	Austrian	Österreichring	8	A. Prost	M29	12	7	
31.08.80	Dutch	Zandvoort	7	J. Watson	M29	9	dnf	Engine
31.08.80	Dutch	Zandvoort	8	A. Prost	M30	18	6	
14.08.80	Italian	Imola	7	J. Watson	M29	14	dnf	Brakes/Wheel Bearing
14.08.80	Italian	Imola	8	A. Prost	M30	24	7	
29.09.80	Canadian	Montreal	7	J. Watson	M29	7	4	
29.09.80	Canadian	Montreal	8	A. Prost	M30	12	dnf	Accident/Suspension
05.10.80	USA	Watkins Glen	7	J. Watson	M29	9	12	
05.10.80	USA	Watkins Glen	8	A. Prost	M30	13	dns	Accident in Practice
1981								
07.02.81	South African	Kyalami (non-ch)	7	J. Watson	M29	15	5	
07.02.81	South African	Kyalami (non-ch)	8	A. de Cesaris	M29	9	dnf	Accident
15.03.81	USA West	Long Beach	7	J. Watson	M29	23	dnf	Engine
15.03.81	USA West	Long Beach	8	A. de Cesaris	M29	22	dnf	Accident
29.03.81	Brazilian	Jacarepagua	7	J. Watson	M29	15	8	
29.03.81	Brazilian	Jacarepagua	8	A. de Cesaris	M29	20	dnf	Fuel Pump/Electrics
12.04.81	Argentinian	Buenos Aires	7	J. Watson	MP4/1	11	dnf	Transmission
12.04.81	Argentinian	Buenos Aires	8	A. de Cesaris	M29	17	11	
03.05.81	San Marino	Imola	7	J. Watson	MP4/1	7	10	
03.05.81	San Marino	Imola	8	A. de Cesaris	M29	14	6	
17.05.81	Belgian	Zolder	7	J. Watson	MP4/1	5	7	
17.05.81	Belgian	Zolder	8	A. de Cesaris	M29	23	dnf	Gearbox
31.05.81	Monaco	Monte Carlo	7	J. Watson	MP4/1	10	dnf	Engine
31.05.81	Monaco	Monte Carlo	8	A. de Cesaris	MP4/1	11	dnf	Accident
21.06.81	Spanish	Jarama	7	J. Watson	MP4/1	4	3	
21.06.81	Spanish	Jarama	8	A. de Cesaris	MP4/1	14	dnf	Accident
05.07.81	French	Dijon-Prenois	7	J. Watson	MP4/1	2	2	
05.07.81	French	Dijon-Prenois	8	A. de Cesaris	MP4/1	5	14	
18.07.81	British	Silverstone	7	J. Watson	MP4/1	5	1st	
18.07.81	British	Silverstone	8	A. de Cesaris	MP4/1	6	dnf	Accident
02.08.81	German	Hockenheim	7	J. Watson	MP4/1	9	6	
02.08.81	German	Hockenheim	8	A. de Cesaris	MP4/1	10	dnf	Accident
16.08.81	Austrian	Zeltweg	7	J. Watson	MP4/1	12	6	
16.08.81	Austrian	Zeltweg	8	A. de Cesaris	MP4/1	18	8	
30.08.81	Dutch	Zandvoort	7	J. Watson	MP4/1	8	dnf	Electrics
30.08.81	Dutch	Zandvoort	8	A. de Cesaris	MP4/1	13	dns	Withdrawn
13.09.81	Italian	Monza	7	J. Watson	MP4/1	7	dnf	Accident
13.09.81	Italian	Monza	8	A. de Cesaris	MP4/1	16	7	
27.09.81	Canadian	Montreal	7	J. Watson	MP4/1	9	2	Fastest lap
27.09.81	Canadian	Montreal	8	A. de Cesaris	MP4/1	13	dnf	Accident
17.10.81	USA	Las Vegas	7	J. Watson	MP4/1	6	7	
17.10.81	USA	Las Vegas	8	A. de Cesaris	MP4/1	14	12	
1982								
21.01.82	South African	Kyalami	7	J. Watson	MP4/1B	9	6	
21.01.82	South African	Kyalami	8	N. Lauda	MP4/1B	13	4	
21.03.82	Brazilian	Jacarepagua	7	J. Watson	MP4/1B	12	2	
21.03.82	Brazilian	Jacarepagua	8	N. Lauda	MP4/1B	5	dnf	Accident/Suspension
04.04.82	USA West	Long Beach	7	J. Watson	MP4/1B	11	6	
04.04.82	USA West	Long Beach	8	N. Lauda	MP4/1B	2	1st	Fastest lap
09.05.82	Belgian	Zolder	7	J. Watson	MP4/1B	10	1st	Fastest lap
09.05.82	Belgian	Zolder	8	N. Lauda	MP4/1B	4	dsq	Car under weight
23.05.82	Monaco	Monte Carlo	7	J. Watson	MP4/1B	10	dnf	Oil Leak/Battery
23.05.82	Monaco	Monte Carlo	8	N. Lauda	MP4/1B	12	dnf	Engine
06.06.82	USA East	Detroit	7	J. Watson	MP4/1B	10	1st	
06.06.82	USA East	Detroit	8	N. Lauda	MP4/1B	17	dnf	Accident
13.06.82	Canadian	Montreal	7	J. Watson	MP4/1B	6	3	
13.06.82	Canadian	Montreal	8	N. Lauda	MP4/1B	11	dnf	Clutch
03.07.82	Dutch	Zandvoort	7	J. Watson	MP4/1B	11	9	
03.07.82	Dutch	Zandvoort	8	N. Lauda	MP4/1B	5	4	
18.07.82	British	Brands Hatch	7	J. Watson	MP4/1B	12	dnf	Accident
18.07.82	British	Brands Hatch	8	N. Lauda	MP4/1B	5	1st	
25.07.82	French	Paul Ricard	7	J. Watson	MP4/1B	12	dnf	Battery
25.07.82	French	Paul Ricard	8	N. Lauda	MP4/1B	9	8	
08.08.82	German	Hockenheim	7	J. Watson	MP4/1B	9	dnf	Suspension
08.08.82	German	Hockenheim	8	N. Lauda	MP4/1B	dnq	dns	Accident in Practice
15.08.82	Austrian	Zeltweg	7	J. Watson	MP4/1B	18	dnf	Engine/Overheating
15.08.82	Austrian	Zeltweg	8	N. Lauda	MP4/1B	10	5	
29.08.82	Swiss	Dijon-Prenois	7	J. Watson	MP4/1B	11	13	
29.08.82	Swiss	Dijon-Prenois	8	N. Lauda	MP4/1B	4	3	
12.09.82	Italian	Monza	7	J. Watson	MP4/1B	12	4	
12.09.82	Italian	Monza	8	N. Lauda	MP4/1B	10	dnf	Suspension/Brakes
25.09.82	USA	Las Vegas	7	J. Watson	MP4/1B	9	2	
25.09.82	USA	Las Vegas	8	N. Lauda	MP4/1B	13	dnf	Engine

Date	Event	Circuit	Race No.	Driver	Model	Qual.	Race Position	Reason/Notes
1983								
13.03.83	Brazilian	Jacarepagua	7	J. Watson	MP4/1C	16	dnf	Engine
13.03.83	Brazilian	Jacarepagua	8	N. Lauda	MP4/1C	9	3	
27.03.83	USA West	Long Beach	7	J. Watson	MP4/1C	22	1st	1-2 Finish
27.03.83	USA West	Long Beach	8	N. Lauda	MP4/1C	23	2	Fastest lap
17.04.83	French	Paul Ricard	7	J. Watson	MP4/1C	14	dnf	Throttle
17.04.83	French	Paul Ricard	8	N. Lauda	MP4/1C	12	dnf	Wheel Bearing
01.05.83	San Marino	Imola	7	J. Watson	MP4/1C	24	5	
01.05.83	San Marino	Imola	8	N. Lauda	MP4/1C	18	dnf	Accident
15.05.83	Monaco	Monte Carlo	7	J. Watson	MP4/1C	dnq	dns	
15.05.83	Monaco	Monte Carlo	8	N. Lauda	MP4/1C	dnq	dns	
22.05.83	Belgian	Spa Francorchamps	7	J. Watson	MP4/1C	20	dnf	Accident
22.05.83	Belgian	Spa Francorchamps	8	N. Lauda	MP4/1C	15	dnf	Engine
05.06.83	USA East	Detroit	7	J. Watson	MP4/1C	21	3	Fastest lap
05.06.83	USA East	Detroit	8	N. Lauda	MP4/1C	18	dnf	Suspension
12.06.83	Canadian	Montreal	7	J. Watson	MP4/1C	20	6	
12.06.83	Canadian	Montreal	8	N. Lauda	MP4/1C	19	dnf	Accident
16.07.83	British	Silverstone	7	J. Watson	MP4/1C	24	9	
16.07.83	British	Silverstone	8	N. Lauda	MP4/1C	15	6	
06.08.83	German	Hockenheim	7	J. Watson	MP4/1C	23	5	
06.08.83	German	Hockenheim	8	N. Lauda	MP4/1C	18	dsq	Reversed in Pit Lane
14.08.83	Austrian	Zeltweg	7	J. Watson	MP4/1C	17	9	
14.08.83	Austrian	Zeltweg	8	N. Lauda	MP4/1C	14	6	
28.08.83	Dutch	Zandvoort	7	J. Watson	MP4/1C	15	3	
28.08.83	Dutch	Zandvoort	8	N. Lauda	MP4/1E	19	dnf	Brakes
11.09.83	Italian	Monza	7	J. Watson	MP4/1E	15	dnf	Engine
11.09.83	Italian	Monza	8	N. Lauda	MP4/1E	13	dnf	Electrics
25.09.83	European	Brands Hatch	7	J. Watson	MP4/1E	10	dnf	Accident
25.09.83	European	Brands Hatch	8	N. Lauda	MP4/1E	13	dnf	Engine
15.10.83	South African	Kyalami	7	J. Watson	MP4/1E	15	dsq	Starting Infringement
15.10.83	South African	Kyalami	8	N. Lauda	MP4/1E	12	11	
1984								
25.03.84	Brazilian	Jacarepagua	7	A. Prost	MP4/2	4	1st	Fastest Lap
25.03.84	Brazilian	Jacarepagua	8	N. Lauda	MP4/2	6	dnf	Electrics
07.04.84	South African	Kyalami	7	A. Prost	MP4/2	5	2	
07.04.84	South African	Kyalami	8	N. Lauda	MP4/2	8	1st	1-2 Finish
29.04.84	Belgian	Zolder	7	A. Prost	MP4/2	8	dnf	Distributor
29.04.84	Belgian	Zolder	8	N. Lauda	MP4/2	14	dnf	Water Pump
06.05.84	San Marino	Imola	7	A. Prost	MP4/2	2	1st	
06.05.84	San Marino	Imola	8	N. Lauda	MP4/2	5	dnf	Engine
20.05.84	French	Dijon-Prenois	7	A. Prost	MP4/2	5	7	Fastest Lap
20.05.84	French	Dijon-Prenois	8	N. Lauda	MP4/2	9	1st	
03.06.84	Monaco	Monte Carlo	7	A. Prost	MP4/2	Pole	1st	
03.06.84	Monaco	Monte Carlo	8	N. Lauda	MP4/2	8	dnf	Accident
17.06.84	Canadian	Montreal	7	A. Prost	MP4/2	2	3	
17.06.84	Canadian	Montreal	8	N. Lauda	MP4/2	8	2	
24.06.84	USA East	Detroit	7	A. Prost	MP4/2	2	4 (5)	Tyrrell disqualified
24.06.84	USA East	Detroit	8	N. Lauda	MP4/2	10	dnf	Electrics
07.07.84	USA	Dallas	7	A. Prost	MP4/2	7	dnf	Accident
07.07.84	USA	Dallas	8	N. Lauda	MP4/2	5	dnf	Accident, Fastest lap
22.07.84	British	Brands Hatch	7	A. Prost	MP4/2	2	dnf	Gearbox
22.07.84	British	Brands Hatch	8	N. Lauda	MP4/2	3	1st	Fastest lap
05.08.84	German	Hockenheim	7	A. Prost	MP4/2	Pole	1st	1-2 Finish, fastest lap
05.08.84	German	Hockenheim	8	N. Lauda	MP4/2	7	2	
19.08.84	Austrian	Österreichring	7	A. Prost	MP4/2	2	dnf	Accident
19.08.84	Austrian	Österreichring	8	N. Lauda	MP4/2	4	1st	Fastest lap
26.08.84	Dutch	Zandvoort	7	A. Prost	MP4/2	Pole	1st	1-2 Finish
26.08.84	Dutch	Zandvoort	8	N. Lauda	MP4/2	6	2	
09.09.84	Italian	Monza	7	A. Prost	MP4/2	2	dnf	Engine
09.09.84	Italian	Monza	8	N. Lauda	MP4/2	4	1st	Fastest lap
07.10.84	European	Nürburgring	7	A. Prost	MP4/2	2	1st	
07.10.84	European	Nürburgring	8	N. Lauda	MP4/2	15	4	
21.10.84	Portuguese	Estoril	7	A. Prost	MP4/2	2	1st	1-2 Finish
21.10.84	Portuguese	Estoril	8	N. Lauda	MP4/2	11	2	Fastest lap
1985								
07.04.85	Brazilian	Jacarepagua	1	N. Lauda	MP4/2B	9	dnf	Fuel Meetering Unit
07.04.85	Brazilian	Jacarepagua	2	A. Prost	MP4/2B	6	1st	Fastest lap
21.04.85	Portuguese	Estoril	1	N. Lauda	MP4/2B	7	dnf	Engine
21.04.85	Portuguese	Estoril	2	A. Prost	MP4/2B	2	dnf	Accident
05.05.85	San Marino	Imola	1	N. Lauda	MP4/2B	8	4	
05.05.85	San Marino	Imola	2	A. Prost	MP4/2B	6	dsq	Car underweight
19.05.85	Monaco	Monte Carlo	1	N. Lauda	MP4/2B	14	dnf	Accident
19.05.85	Monaco	Monte Carlo	2	A. Prost	MP4/2B	5	1st	
16.06.85	Canadian	Montreal	1	N. Lauda	MP4/2B	17	dnf	Engine
16.06.85	Canadian	Montreal	2	A. Prost	MP4/2B	5	3	
23.06.85	USA East	Detroit	1	N. Lauda	MP4/2B	12	dnf	Brakes
23.06.85	USA East	Detroit	2	A. Prost	MP4/2B	4	dnf	Accident/Brakes
07.07.85	French	Paul Ricard	1	N. Lauda	MP4/2B	6	dnf	Gearbox
07.07.85	French	Paul Ricard	2	A. Prost	MP4/2B	4	3	
21.07.85	British	Silverstone	1	N. Lauda	MP4/2B	10	dnf	Electrics
21.07.85	British	Silverstone	2	A. Prost	MP4/2B	3	1st	Fastest lap
04.08.85	German	Hockenheim	1	N. Lauda	MP4/2B	12	5	Fastest lap
04.08.85	German	Hockenheim	2	A. Prost	MP4/2B	3	2	
18.08.85	Austrian	Österreichring	1	N. Lauda	MP4/2B	3	dnf	Engine
18.08.85	Austrian	Österreichring	2	A. Prost	MP4/2B	Pole	1st	Fastest lap
25.08.85	Dutch	Zandvoort	1	N. Lauda	MP4/2B	10	1st	1-2 Finish
25.08.85	Dutch	Zandvoort	2	A. Prost	MP4/2B	3	2	Fastest lap
08.09.85	Italian	Monza	1	N. Lauda	MP4/2B	16	dnf	Transmission
08.09.85	Italian	Monza	2	A. Prost	MP4/2B	5	1st	
15.09.85	Belgian	Spa Francorchamps	1	N. Lauda	MP4/2B	dnq	dns	Accident in Practice
15.09.85	Belgian	Spa Francorchamps	2	A. Prost	MP4/2B	Pole	3	Fastest lap
06.10.85	European	Brands Hatch	1	N. Lauda	MP4/2B	21	7	
06.10.85	European	Brands Hatch	2	A. Prost	MP4/2B	6	4	
19.10.85	South African	Kyalami	1	N. Lauda	MP4/2B	8	dnf	Turbo
19.10.85	South African	Kyalami	2	A. Prost	MP4/2B	9	3	
03.11.85	Australian	Adelaide	1	N. Lauda	MP4/2B	16	dnf	Brakes/Accident
03.11.85	Australian	Adelaide	2	A. Prost	MP4/2B	4	dnf	Engine
1986								
23.03.86	Brazilian	Jacarepagua	1	A. Prost	MP4/2C	9	dnf	Engine
23.03.86	Brazilian	Jacarepagua	2	K. Rosberg	MP4/2C	7	dnf	Engine
13.04.86	Spanish	Jerez	1	A. Prost	MP4/2C	4	3	
13.04.86	Spanish	Jerez	2	K. Rosberg	MP4/2C	5	4	
27.04.86	San Marino	Imola	1	A. Prost	MP4/2C	4	1st	
27.04.86	San Marino	Imola	2	K. Rosberg	MP4/2C	6	5	
11.05.86	Monaco	Monte Carlo	1	A. Prost	MP4/2C	Pole	1st	1-2 Finish, Fastest lap
11.05.86	Monaco	Monte Carlo	2	K. Rosberg	MP4/2C	9	2	
25.05.86	Belgian	Spa Francorchamps	1	A. Prost	MP4/2C	3	6	Fastest lap
25.05.86	Belgian	Spa Francorchamps	2	K. Rosberg	MP4/2C	8	dnf	Engine
15.06.86	Canadian	Montreal	1	A. Prost	MP4/2C	4	2	
15.06.86	Canadian	Montreal	2	K. Rosberg	MP4/2C	6	4	
22.06.86	USA East	Detroit	1	A. Prost	MP4/2C	7	3	Transmission
22.06.86	USA East	Detroit	2	K. Rosberg	MP4/2C	9	dnf	
06.07.86	French	Paul Ricard	1	A. Prost	MP4/2C	5	2	
06.07.86	French	Paul Ricard	2	K. Rosberg	MP4/2C	7	4	
13.07.86	British	Silverstone	1	A. Prost	MP4/2C	6	3	
13.07.86	British	Silverstone	2	K. Rosberg	MP4/2C	5	dnf	Gearbox
27.07.86	German	Hockenheim	1	A. Prost	MP4/2C	2	6	
27.07.86	German	Hockenheim	2	K. Rosberg	MP4/2C	Pole	5	
10.08.86	Hungarian	Hungaroring	1	A. Prost	MP4/2C	3	dnf	Accident
10.08.86	Hungarian	Hungaroring	2	K. Rosberg	MP4/2C	5	dnf	Suspension
17.08.86	Austrian	Österreichring	1	A. Prost	MP4/2C	5	1st	
17.08.86	Austrian	Österreichring	2	K. Rosberg	MP4/2C	3	9	
07.09.86	Italian	Monza	1	A. Prost	MP4/2C	2	dsq	Starting Infringement
07.09.86	Italian	Monza	2	K. Rosberg	MP4/2C	8	4	
21.09.86	Portuguese	Estoril	1	A. Prost	MP4/2C	3	2	
21.09.86	Portuguese	Estoril	2	K. Rosberg	MP4/2C	7	dnf	Engine
12.10.86	Mexican	Mexico City	1	A. Prost	MP4/2C	6	2	
12.10.86	Mexican	Mexico City	2	K. Rosberg	MP4/2C	11	dnf	Puncture
26.10.86	Australian	Adelaide	1	A. Prost	MP4/2C	4	1st	
26.10.86	Australian	Adelaide	2	K. Rosberg	MP4/2C	7	dnf	Tyre delamination
1987								
12.04.87	Brazilian	Jacarepagua	1	A. Prost	MP4/3	5	1st	
12.04.87	Brazilian	Jacarepagua	2	S. Johansson	MP4/3	10	3	
03.05.87	San Marino	Imola	1	A. Prost	MP4/3	3	dnf	Altenator
03.05.87	San Marino	Imola	2	S. Johansson	MP4/3	8	4	
17.05.87	Belgian	Spa Francorchamps	1	A. Prost	MP4/3	6	1st	1-2 Finish, Fastest lap
17.05.87	Belgian	Spa Francorchamps	2	S. Johansson	MP4/3	10	2	
31.05.87	Monaco	Monte Carlo	1	A. Prost	MP4/3	4	9	
31.05.87	Monaco	Monte Carlo	2	S. Johansson	MP4/3	7	dnf	Engine
21.06.87	USA East	Detroit	1	A. Prost	MP4/3	5	3	
21.06.87	USA East	Detroit	2	S. Johansson	MP4/3	11	7	
05.07.87	French	Paul Ricard	1	A. Prost	MP4/3	2	3	
05.07.87	French	Paul Ricard	2	S. Johansson	MP4/3	9	8	
12.07.87	British	Silverstone	1	A. Prost	MP4/3	4	dnf	Clutch
12.07.87	British	Silverstone	2	S. Johansson	MP4/3	10	dnf	Engine
26.07.87	German	Hockenheim	1	A. Prost	MP4/3	3	7 nrf	
26.07.87	German	Hockenheim	2	S. Johansson	MP4/3	8	2	
09.08.87	Hungarian	Hungaroring	1	A. Prost	MP4/3	4	3	
09.08.87	Hungarian	Hungaroring	2	S. Johansson	MP4/3	8	dnf	Transmission
16.08.87	Austrian	Österreichring	1	A. Prost	MP4/3	9	6	
16.08.87	Austrian	Österreichring	2	S. Johansson	MP4/3	14	7	
08.09.87	Italian	Monza	1	A. Prost	MP4/3	5	15	
08.09.87	Italian	Monza	2	S. Johansson	MP4/3	11	6	
20.09.87	Portuguese	Estoril	1	A. Prost	MP4/3	3	1st	
20.09.87	Portuguese	Estoril	2	S. Johansson	MP4/3	8	5	
27.09.87	Spanish	Jerez	1	A. Prost	MP4/3	7	2	
27.09.87	Spanish	Jerez	2	S. Johansson	MP4/3	11	3	
18.10.87	Mexican	Mexico City	1	A. Prost	MP4/3	5	dnf	Accident
18.10.87	Mexican	Mexico City	2	S. Johansson	MP4/3	15	dnf	Accident
01.11.87	Japanese	Suzuka	1	A. Prost	MP4/3	2	7	Fastest lap
01.11.87	Japanese	Suzuka	2	S. Johansson	MP4/3	9	3	
15.11.87	Australian	Adelaide	1	A. Prost	MP4/3	2	dnf	Brakes/Accident
15.11.87	Australian	Adelaide	2	S. Johansson	MP4/3	8	dnf	Brakes
1988								
03.04.88	Brazilian	Jacarepagua	11	A. Prost	MP4/4	3	1st	
03.04.88	Brazilian	Jacarepagua	12	A. Senna	MP4/4	Pole	dsq	Starting Infringement
01.05.88	San Marino	Imola	11	A. Prost	MP4/4	2	2	Fastest lap
01.05.88	San Marino	Imola	12	A. Senna	MP4/4	Pole	1st	1-2 Finish
15.05.88	Monaco	Monte Carlo	11	A. Prost	MP4/4	2	1st	
15.05.88	Monaco	Monte Carlo	12	A. Senna	MP4/4	Pole	dnf	Accident, Fastest lap
29.05.88	Mexican	Mexico City	11	A. Prost	MP4/4	2	1st	1-2 Finish, fastest lap
29.05.88	Mexican	Mexico City	12	A. Senna	MP4/4	Pole	2	
12.06.88	Canadian	Montreal	11	A. Prost	MP4/4	2	2	
12.06.88	Canadian	Montreal	12	A. Senna	MP4/4	Pole	1st	1-2 Finish, fastest lap

APPENDIX 4
McLAREN FORMULA 1 RESULTS
CONTINUED

Date	Event	Circuit	Race No.	Driver	Model	Qual.	Race Position	Reason/Notes
19.06.88	USA East	Detroit	11	A. Prost	MP4/4	4	2	Fastest lap
19.06.88	US East	Detroit	12	A. Senna	MP4/4	Pole	1st	1-2 Finish
03.07.88	French	Paul Ricard	11	A. Prost	MP4/4	Pole	1st	1-2 Finish, fastest lap
03.07.88	French	Paul Ricard	12	A. Senna	MP4/4	2	2	
10.07.88	British	Silverstone	11	A. Prost	MP4/4	4	dnf	Handling
10.07.88	British	Silverstone	12	A. Senna	MP4/4	3	1st	
24.07.88	German	Hockenheim	11	A. Prost	MP4/4	2	2	
24.07.88	German	Hockenheim	12	A. Senna	MP4/4	Pole	1st	1-2 Finish
07.08.88	Hungarian	Hungaroring	11	A. Prost	MP4/4	7	2	Fastest lap
07.08.88	Hungarian	Hungaroring	12	A. Senna	MP4/4	Pole	1st	1-2 Finish
28.08.88	Belgian	Spa Francorchamps	11	A. Prost	MP4/4	2	2	
28.08.88	Belgian	Spa Francorchamps	12	A. Senna	MP4/4	Pole	1st	1-2 Finish
11.09.88	Italian	Monza	11	A. Prost	MP4/4	2	dnf	Engine
11.09.88	Italian	Monza	12	A. Senna	MP4/4	Pole	10	
25.09.88	Portuguese	Estoril	11	A. Prost	MP4/4	Pole	1st	
25.09.88	Portuguese	Estoril	12	A. Senna	MP4/4	2	6	
02.10.88	Spanish	Jerez	11	A. Prost	MP4/4	2	1st	Fastest lap
02.10.88	Spanish	Jerez	12	A. Senna	MP4/4	Pole	4	
30.10.88	Japanese	Suzuka	11	A. Prost	MP4/4	2	2	
30.10.88	Japanese	Suzuka	12	A. Senna	MP4/4	Pole	1st	1-2 Finish, fastest lap
13.11.88	Australian	Adelaide	11	A. Prost	MP4/4	2	1st	1-2 Finish, fastest lap
13.11.88	Australian	Adelaide	12	A. Senna	MP4/4	Pole	2	
1989								
26.03.89	Brazilian	Jacarepagua	1	A. Senna	MP4/5	Pole	9	
26.03.89	Brazilian	Jacarepagua	2	A. Prost	MP4/5	5	2	
23.04.89	San Marino	Imola	1	A. Senna	MP4/5	Pole	1st	1-2 Finish
23.04.89	San Marino	Imola	2	A. Prost	MP4/5	2	2	Fastest lap
07.05.89	Monaco	Monte Carlo	1	A. Senna	MP4/5	Pole	1st	1-2 Finish
07.05.89	Monaco	Monte Carlo	2	A. Prost	MP4/5	2	2	Fastest lap
28.05.89	Mexican	Mexico City	1	A. Senna	MP4/5	Pole	1st	
28.05.89	Mexican	Mexico City	2	A. Prost	MP4/5	2	5	
04.06.89	USA West	Phoenix	1	A. Senna	MP4/5	Pole	dnf	Electrics
04.06.89	USA West	Phoenix	2	A. Prost	MP4/5	2	1st	
18.06.89	Canadian	Montreal	1	A. Senna	MP4/5	2	dnf	Engine
18.06.89	Canadian	Montreal	2	A. Prost	MP4/5	Pole	dnf	Suspension
09.07.89	French	Paul Ricard	1	A. Senna	MP4/5	2	dnf	Transmission
09.07.89	French	Paul Ricard	2	A. Prost	MP4/5	Pole	1st	
16.07.89	British	Silverstone	1	A. Senna	MP4/5	Pole	dnf	Gearbox/Accident
16.07.89	British	Silverstone	2	A. Prost	MP4/5	2	1st	
30.07.89	German	Hockenheim	1	A. Senna	MP4/5	Pole	1st	1-2 Finish, Fastest lap
30.07.89	German	Hockenheim	2	A. Prost	MP4/5	2	2	
13.08.89	Hungarian	Hungaroring	1	A. Senna	MP4/5	2	2	
13.08.89	Hungarian	Hungaroring	2	A. Prost	MP4/5	5	4	
27.08.89	Belgian	Spa Francorchamps	1	A. Senna	MP4/5	Pole	1st	1-2 Finish
27.08.89	Belgian	Spa Francorchamps	2	A. Prost	MP4/5	2	2	Fastest lap
10.09.89	Italian	Monza	1	A. Senna	MP4/5	Pole	dnf	Engine
10.09.89	Italian	Monza	2	A. Prost	MP4/5	4	1st	Fastest lap
24.09.89	Portuguese	Estoril	1	A. Senna	MP4/5	Pole	dnf	Accident
24.09.89	Portuguese	Estoril	2	A. Prost	MP4/5	4	2	
01.10.89	Spanish	Jerez	1	A. Senna	MP4/5	Pole	1st	Fastest lap
01.10.89	Spanish	Jerez	2	A. Prost	MP4/5	3	3	
22.10.89	Japanese	Suzuka	1	A. Senna	MP4/5	Pole	dsq	Outside Assistant
22.10.89	Japanese	Suzuka	2	A. Prost	MP4/5	2	dnf	Accident
05.11.89	Australian	Adelaide	1	A. Senna	MP4/5	Pole	dnf	Accident
05.11.89	Australian	Adelaide	2	A. Prost	MP4/5	2	dns	Safety Concerns
1990								
11.03.90	USA	Phoenix	27	A. Senna	MP4/5B	5	1st	
11.03.90	USA	Phoenix	28	G. Berger	MP4/5B	Pole	dnf	Fastest Lap, Clutch
25.03.90	Brazilian	Jacarepagua	27	A. Senna	MP4/5B	Pole	3	
25.03.90	Brazilian	Jacarepagua	28	G. Berger	MP4/5B	2	2	Fastest Lap
13.05.90	San Marino	Imola	27	A. Senna	MP4/5B	Pole	dnf	Wheel
13.05.90	San Marino	Imola	28	G. Berger	MP4/5B	2	2	
27.05.90	Monaco	Monte Carlo	27	A. Senna	MP4/5B	Pole	1st	Fastest Lap
27.05.90	Monaco	Monte Carlo	28	G. Berger	MP4/5B	5	3	
10.06.90	Canadian	Montreal	27	A. Senna	MP4/5B	Pole	1st	
10.06.90	Canadian	Montreal	28	G. Berger	MP4/5B	2	4	1min Penalty, Fastest Lap
24.06.90	Mexican	Mexico City	27	A. Senna	MP4/5B	3	dnf	Puncture
24.06.90	Mexican	Mexico City	28	G. Berger	MP4/5B	Pole	3	
08.07.90	French	Magny Cours	27	A. Senna	MP4/5B	3	3	
08.07.90	French	Magny Cours	28	G. Berger	MP4/5B	2	5	
15.07.90	British	Silverstone	27	A. Senna	MP4/5B	2	3	
15.07.90	British	Silverstone	28	G. Berger	MP4/5B	3	dnf	Throttle
29.07.90	German	Hockenheim	27	A. Senna	MP4/5B	Pole	1st	
29.07.90	German	Hockenheim	28	G. Berger	MP4/5B	2	3	
12.08.90	Hungarian	Hungaroring	27	A. Senna	MP4/5B	4	2	
12.08.90	Hungarian	Hungaroring	28	G. Berger	MP4/5B	3	16 nrf	Accident
26.08.90	Belgian	Spa Francorchamps	27	A. Senna	MP4/5B	Pole	1st	
26.08.90	Belgian	Spa Francorchamps	28	G. Berger	MP4/5B	2	3	
09.09.90	Italian	Monza	27	A. Senna	MP4/5B	Pole	1st	Fastest Lap
09.09.90	Italian	Monza	28	G. Berger	MP4/5B	3	3	
23.09.90	Portuguese	Estoril	27	A. Senna	MP4/5B	3	2	
23.09.90	Portuguese	Estoril	28	G. Berger	MP4/5B	4	4	
30.09.90	Spanish	Jerez	27	A. Senna	MP4/5B	Pole	dnf	Radiator
30.09.90	Spanish	Jerez	28	G. Berger	MP4/5B	5	dnf	Accident
21.10.90	Japanese	Suzuka	27	A. Senna	MP4/5B	Pole	dnf	Accident
21.10.90	Japanese	Suzuka	28	G. Berger	MP4/5B	4	dnf	Accident
04.11.90	Australian	Adelaide	27	A. Senna	MP4/5B	Pole	dnf	Accident
04.11.90	Australian	Adelaide	28	G. Berger	MP4/5B	2	4	
1991								
10.03.91	USA	Phoenix	1	A. Senna	MP4/6	Pole	1st	
10.03.91	USA	Phoenix	2	G. Berger	MP4/6	7	dnf	Fuel Pump
24.03.91	Brazilian	Interlagos	1	A. Senna	MP4/6	Pole	1st	
24.03.91	Brazilian	Interlagos	2	G. Berger	MP4/6	4	3	
28.04.91	San Marino	Imola	1	A. Senna	MP4/6	Pole	1st	1-2 Finish
28.04.91	San Marino	Imola	2	G. Berger	MP4/6	5	2	Fastest Lap
12.05.91	Monaco	Monte Carlo	1	A. Senna	MP4/6	Pole	1st	
12.05.91	Monaco	Monte Carlo	2	G. Berger	MP4/6	6	dnf	Accident
02.06.91	Canadian	Montreal	1	A. Senna	MP4/6	3	dnf	Alternator
02.06.91	Canadian	Montreal	2	G. Berger	MP4/6	6	dnf	Electrics
16.06.91	Mexican	Mexico City	1	A. Senna	MP4/6	3	3	
16.06.91	Mexican	Mexico City	2	G. Berger	MP4/6	5	dnf	Engine
07.07.91	French	Magny Cours	1	A. Senna	MP4/6	3	3	
07.07.91	French	Magny Cours	2	G. Berger	MP4/6	5	dnf	Engine
14.07.91	British	Silverstone	1	A. Senna	MP4/6	2	4 nrf	Out of Fuel
14.07.91	British	Silverstone	2	G. Berger	MP4/6	4	2	
28.07.91	German	Hockenheim	1	A. Senna	MP4/6	2	7 nrf	Out of Fuel
28.07.91	German	Hockenheim	2	G. Berger	MP4/6	3	4	
11.08.91	Hungarian	Hungaroring	1	A. Senna	MP4/6	Pole	1st	
11.08.91	Hungarian	Hungaroring	2	G. Berger	MP4/6	5	4	
25.08.91	Belgian	Spa Francorchamps	1	A. Senna	MP4/6	Pole	1st	1-2 Finish
25.08.91	Belgian	Spa Francorchamps	2	G. Berger	MP4/6	4	2	
08.09.91	Italian	Monza	1	A. Senna	MP4/6	Pole	2	Fastest Lap
08.09.91	Italian	Monza	2	G. Berger	MP4/6	3	4	
22.09.91	Portuguese	Estoril	1	A. Senna	MP4/6	3	2	
22.09.91	Portuguese	Estoril	2	G. Berger	MP4/6	2	dnf	Engine
29.09.91	Spanish	Barcelona	1	A. Senna	MP4/6	3	5	
29.09.91	Spanish	Barcelona	2	G. Berger	MP4/6	Pole	dnf	Engine
20.10.91	Japanese	Suzuka	1	A. Senna	MP4/6	2	2	Fastest Lap
20.10.91	Japanese	Suzuka	2	G. Berger	MP4/6	Pole	1st	1-2 Finish
03.11.91	Australian	Adelaide	1	A. Senna	MP4/6	Pole	1st	
03.11.91	Australian	Adelaide	2	G. Berger	MP4/6	2	3	Fastest Lap
1992								
01.03.92	South African	Kyalami	1	A. Senna	MP4/6B	2	3	
01.03.92	South African	Kyalami	2	G. Berger	MP4/6B	3	5	
22.03.92	Mexican	Mexico City	1	A. Senna	MP4/6B	6	dnf	Transmission
22.03.92	Mexican	Mexico City	2	G. Berger	MP4/6B	5	4	Fastest Lap
05.04.92	Brazilian	Interlagos	1	A. Senna	MP4/7	3	dnf	Electrics
05.04.92	Brazilian	Interlagos	2	G. Berger	MP4/7	4	dnf	Overheating
03.05.92	Spanish	Barcelona	1	A. Senna	MP4/7	2	9 nrf	Accident
03.05.92	Spanish	Barcelona	2	G. Berger	MP4/7	7	4	
17.05.92	San Marino	Imola	1	A. Senna	MP4/7	3	3	
17.05.92	San Marino	Imola	2	G. Berger	MP4/7	4	dnf	Accident
31.05.92	Monaco	Monte Carlo	1	A. Senna	MP4/7	3	1st	
31.05.92	Monaco	Monte Carlo	2	G. Berger	MP4/7	5	dnf	Gearbox
14.06.92	Canadian	Montreal	1	A. Senna	MP4/7	Pole	dnf	Electrics
14.06.92	Canadian	Montreal	2	G. Berger	MP4/7	4	1st	Fastest Lap
05.07.92	French	Magny Cours	1	A. Senna	MP4/7	3	dnf	Accident
05.07.92	French	Magny Cours	2	G. Berger	MP4/7	4	dnf	Engine
12.07.92	British	Silverstone	1	A. Senna	MP4/7	3	dnf	Gearbox
12.07.92	British	Silverstone	2	G. Berger	MP4/7	5	5	
26.07.92	German	Hockenheim	1	A. Senna	MP4/7	3	2	
26.07.92	German	Hockenheim	2	G. Berger	MP4/7	4	dnf	Misfire
16.08.92	Hungarian	Hungaroring	1	A. Senna	MP4/7	3	1st	
16.08.92	Hungarian	Hungaroring	2	G. Berger	MP4/7	5	3	
30.08.92	Belgian	Spa Francorchamps	1	A. Senna	MP4/7	2	5	
30.08.92	Belgian	Spa Francorchamps	2	G. Berger	MP4/7	6	dnf	Transmission
13.09.92	Italian	Monza	1	A. Senna	MP4/7	2	1st	
13.09.92	Italian	Monza	2	G. Berger	MP4/7	5	4	
27.09.92	Portuguese	Estoril	1	A. Senna	MP4/7	3	3	Fastest Lap
27.09.92	Portuguese	Estoril	2	G. Berger	MP4/7	4	2	
25.10.92	Japanese	Suzuka	1	A. Senna	MP4/7	3	dnf	Engine
25.10.92	Japanese	Suzuka	2	G. Berger	MP4/7	4	2	
08.11.92	Australian	Adelaide	1	A. Senna	MP4/7	2	dnf	Accident
08.11.92	Australian	Adelaide	2	G. Berger	MP4/7	4	1st	
1993								
14.03.93	South African	Kyalami	7	M. Andretti	MP4/8	9	dnf	Accident
14.03.93	South African	Kyalami	8	A. Senna	MP4/8	2	2	
28.03.93	Brazilian	Interlagos	7	M. Andretti	MP4/8	5	dnf	Accident
28.03.93	Brazilian	Interlagos	8	A. Senna	MP4/8	3	1st	
11.04.93	European	Donington Park	7	M. Andretti	MP4/8	6	dnf	Accident
11.04.93	European	Donington Park	8	A. Senna	MP4/8	4	1st	Fastest Lap (through pits)
25.05.93	San Marino	Imola	7	M. Andretti	MP4/8	6	dnf	Accident
25.05.93	San Marino	Imola	8	A. Senna	MP4/8	4	dnf	Hydraulics
09.05.93	Spanish	Barcelona	7	M. Andretti	MP4/8	7	5	
09.05.93	Spanish	Barcelona	8	A. Senna	MP4/8	3	2	
23.05.93	Monaco	Monte Carlo	7	M. Andretti	MP4/8	9	8	
23.05.93	Monaco	Monte Carlo	8	A. Senna	MP4/8	3	1st	
13.06.93	Canadian	Montreal	7	M. Andretti	MP4/8	12	14	
13.06.93	Canadian	Montreal	8	A. Senna	MP4/8	8	18 nrf	Alternator
04.07.93	French	Magny Cours	7	M. Andretti	MP4/8	16	6	
04.07.93	French	Magny Cours	8	A. Senna	MP4/8	5	4	
11.07.93	British	Silverstone	7	M. Andretti	MP4/8	11	dnf	Accident
11.07.93	British	Silverstone	8	A. Senna	MP4/8	4	5 nrf	Out of Fuel
25.07.93	German	Hockenheim	7	M. Andretti	MP4/8	12	dnf	Accident

APPENDIX 4
FORMULA 1 RESULTS

Date	Event	Circuit	Race No.	Driver	Model	Qual.	Race Position	Reason/Notes
25.07.93	German	Hockenheim	8	A. Senna	MP4/8	4	4	
15.08.93	Hungarian	Hungaroring	7	M. Andretti	MP4/8	11	dnf	Throttle
15.08.93	Hungarian	Hungaroring	8	A. Senna	MP4/8	4	dnf	Throttle
29.08.93	Belgian	Spa Francorchamps	7	M. Andretti	MP4/8	14	8	
29.08.93	Belgian	Spa Francorchamps	8	A. Senna	MP4/8	5	4	
12.09.93	Italian	Monza	7	M. Andretti	MP4/8	9	3	
12.09.93	Italian	Monza	8	A. Senna	MP4/8	4	dnf	Accident
26.09.93	Portuguese	Estoril	7	M. Häkkinen	MP4/8	3	dnf	Accident
26.09.93	Portuguese	Estoril	8	A. Senna	MP4/8	4	dnf	Engine
24.10.93	Japanese	Suzuka	7	M. Häkkinen	MP4/8	3	3	
24.10.93	Japanese	Suzuka	8	A. Senna	MP4/8	2	1st	
07.11.93	Australian	Adelaide	7	M. Häkkinen	MP4/8	5	dnf	Brakes
07.11.93	Australian	Adelaide	8	A. Senna	MP4/8	Pole	1st	
1994								
27.03.94	Brazilian	Interlagos	7	M. Häkkinen	MP4/9	8	dnf	Engine
27.03.94	Brazilian	Interlagos	8	M. Brundle	MP4/9	18	dnf	Accident
17.04.94	Pacific	TI Aida	7	M. Häkkinen	MP4/9	4	dnf	Hydraulics
17.04.94	Pacific	TI Aida	8	M. Brundle	MP4/9	6	dnf	Overheating
01.05.94	San Marino	Imola	7	M. Häkkinen	MP4/9	8	3	
01.05.94	San Marino	Imola	8	M. Brundle	MP4/9	13	8	
15.05.94	Monaco	Monte Carlo	7	M. Häkkinen	MP4/9	2	dnf	Accident
15.05.94	Monaco	Monte Carlo	8	M. Brundle	MP4/9	8	2	
29.05.94	Spanish	Barcelona	7	M. Häkkinen	MP4/9	3	dnf	Engine
29.05.94	Spanish	Barcelona	8	M. Brundle	MP4/9	8	dnf	Transmission
12.06.94	Canadian	Montreal	7	M. Häkkinen	MP4/9	7	dnf	Engine
12.06.94	Canadian	Montreal	8	M. Brundle	MP4/9	12	dnf	Electrics
03.07.94	French	Magny Cours	7	M. Häkkinen	MP4/9	9	dnf	Engine
03.07.94	French	Magny Cours	8	M. Brundle	MP4/9	12	dnf	Engine
10.07.94	British	Silverstone	7	M. Häkkinen	MP4/9	5	3	
10.07.94	British	Silverstone	8	M. Brundle	MP4/9	9	dnf	Engine
31.07.94	German	Hockenheim	7	M. Häkkinen	MP4/9	8	dnf	Accident
31.07.94	German	Hockenheim	8	M. Brundle	MP4/9	13	dnf	Engine
14.08.94	Hungarian	Hungaroring	7	P. Alliot	MP4/9	14	dnf	Water Leak
14.08.94	Hungarian	Hungaroring	8	M. Brundle	MP4/9	6	4, nrf	Alternator
28.08.94	Belgian	Spa Francorchamps	7	M. Häkkinen	MP4/9	8	2	
28.08.94	Belgian	Spa Francorchamps	8	M. Brundle	MP4/9	13	dnf	Accident
11.09.94	Italian	Monza	7	M. Häkkinen	MP4/9	7	3	
11.09.94	Italian	Monza	8	M. Brundle	MP4/9	15	5	
25.09.94	Portuguese	Estoril	7	M. Häkkinen	MP4/9	4	3	
25.09.94	Portuguese	Estoril	8	M. Brundle	MP4/9	7	6	
16.10.94	European	Jerez	7	M. Häkkinen	MP4/9	9	3	
16.10.94	European	Jerez	8	M. Brundle	MP4/9	15	dnf	Engine
06.11.94	Japanese	Suzuka	7	M. Häkkinen	MP4/9	8	7	
06.11.94	Japanese	Suzuka	8	M. Brundle	MP4/9	9	dnf	Accident
13.11.94	Australian	Adelaide	7	M. Häkkinen	MP4/9	4	dnf	Accident
13.11.94	Australian	Adelaide	8	M. Brundle	MP4/9	9	3	
1995								
26.03.95	Brazilian	Interlagos	7	M. Blundell	MP4/10A	9	6	
26.03.95	Brazilian	Interlagos	8	M. Häkkinen	MP4/10A	7	4	
09.04.95	Argentinian	Buenos Aires	7	M. Blundell	MP4/10A	17	dnf	Gearbox
09.04.95	Argentinian	Buenos Aires	8	M. Häkkinen	MP4/10A	5	dnf	Accident
30.04.95	San Marino	Imola	7	N. Mansell	MP4/10B	9	10	
30.04.95	San Marino	Imola	8	M. Häkkinen	MP4/10A	6	5	
14.05.95	Spanish	Barcelona	7	N. Mansell	MP4/10B	10	dnf	Handling
14.05.95	Spanish	Barcelona	8	M. Häkkinen	MP4/10A	9	dnf	Fuel Pressure
28.05.95	Monaco	Monte Carlo	7	M. Blundell	MP4/10B	10	5	
28.05.95	Monaco	Monte Carlo	8	M. Häkkinen	MP4/10B	6	dnf	Engine
11.06.95	Canadian	Montreal	7	M. Blundell	MP4/10B	10	dnf	Engine
11.06.95	Canadian	Montreal	8	M. Häkkinen	MP4/10B	7	dnf	Accident
02.07.95	French	Magny Cours	7	M. Blundell	MP4/10B	13	11	
02.07.95	French	Magny Cours	8	M. Häkkinen	MP4/10B	8	7	
16.07.95	British	Silverstone	7	M. Blundell	MP4/10B	10	5	
16.07.95	British	Silverstone	8	M. Häkkinen	MP4/10B	8	dnf	Gearbox
30.07.95	German	Hockenheim	7	M. Blundell	MP4/10B	8	dnf	Engine
30.07.95	German	Hockenheim	8	M. Häkkinen	MP4/10B	7	dnf	Engine
13.08.95	Hungarian	Hungaroring	7	M. Blundell	MP4/10B	13	dnf	Engine
13.08.95	Hungarian	Hungaroring	8	M. Häkkinen	MP4/10B	5	dnf	Engine
27.08.95	Belgian	Spa Francorchamps	7	M. Blundell	MP4/10B	6	5	
27.08.95	Belgian	Spa Francorchamps	8	M. Häkkinen	MP4/10B	3	dnf	Accident
10.09.95	Italian	Monza	7	M. Blundell	MP4/10B	9	4	
10.09.95	Italian	Monza	8	M. Häkkinen	MP4/10B	7	2	
24.09.95	Portuguese	Estoril	7	M. Blundell	MP4/10B/C	12	9	
24.09.95	Portuguese	Estoril	8	M. Häkkinen	MP4/10B	13	dnf	Engine
01.10.95	European	Nürburgring	7	M. Blundell	MP4/10B/C	10	dnf	Accident
01.10.95	European	Nürburgring	8	M. Häkkinen	MP4/10B/C	9	8	
22.10.95	Pacific	TI Aida	7	M. Blundell	MP4/10C	10	9	
22.10.95	Pacific	TI Aida	8	J. Magnussen	MP4/10B/C	12	10	
29.10.95	Japanese	Suzuka	7	M. Blundell	MP4/10C	24	7	
29.10.95	Japanese	Suzuka	8	M. Häkkinen	MP4/10B/C	3	2	
12.11.95	Australian	Adelaide	7	M. Blundell	MP4/10C	10	4	
12.11.95	Australian	Adelaide	8	M. Häkkinen	MP4/10B	dnq	dns	Accident in Practice
1996								
10.03.96	Australian	Melbourne	7	M. Häkkinen	MP4/11	5	5	
10.03.96	Australian	Melbourne	8	D. Coulthard	MP4/11	13	dnf	Throttle
31.03.96	Brazilian	Interlagos	7	M. Häkkinen	MP4/11	7	4	
31.03.96	Brazilian	Interlagos	8	D. Coulthard	MP4/11	14	dnf	Accident
07.04.96	Argentinian	Buenos Aires	7	M. Häkkinen	MP4/11	8	dnf	Throttle
07.04.96	Argentinian	Buenos Aires	8	D. Coulthard	MP4/11	9	7	
28.04.96	European	Nürburgring	7	M. Häkkinen	MP4/11	9	8	
28.04.96	European	Nürburgring	8	D. Coulthard	MP4/11	6	3	
05.05.96	San Marino	Imola	7	M. Häkkinen	MP4/11	11	dnf	Engine
05.05.96	San Marino	Imola	8	D. Coulthard	MP4/11	4	dnf	Gearbox
19.05.96	Monaco	Monte Carlo	7	M. Häkkinen	MP4/11B	8	6 nrf	Accident
19.05.96	Monaco	Monte Carlo	8	D. Coulthard	MP4/11B	5	2	
02.06.96	Spanish	Barcelona	7	M. Häkkinen	MP4/11B	10	5	
02.06.96	Spanish	Barcelona	8	D. Coulthard	MP4/11B	14	dnf	Accident
16.06.96	Canadian	Montreal	7	M. Häkkinen	MP4/11B	6	5	
16.06.96	Canadian	Montreal	8	D. Coulthard	MP4/11B	10	4	
30.06.96	French	Magny Cours	7	M. Häkkinen	MP4/11B	5	5	
30.06.96	French	Magny Cours	8	D. Coulthard	MP4/11B	7	6	
14.07.96	British	Silverstone	7	M. Häkkinen	MP4/11B	4	3	
14.07.96	British	Silverstone	8	D. Coulthard	MP4/11B	9	5	
28.07.96	German	Hockenheim	7	M. Häkkinen	MP4/11B	4	dnf	Gearbox
28.07.96	German	Hockenheim	8	D. Coulthard	MP4/11B	7	5	
11.08.96	Hungarian	Hungaroring	7	M. Häkkinen	MP4/11B	7	4	
11.08.96	Hungarian	Hungaroring	8	D. Coulthard	MP4/11B	9	dnf	Engine
25.08.96	Belgian	Spa Francorchamps	7	M. Häkkinen	MP4/11B	6	3	
25.08.96	Belgian	Spa Francorchamps	8	D. Coulthard	MP4/11B	4	dnf	Accident
08.09.96	Italian	Monza	7	M. Häkkinen	MP4/11B	4	3	
08.09.96	Italian	Monza	8	D. Coulthard	MP4/11B	5	dnf	Accident
22.09.96	Portuguese	Estoril	7	M. Häkkinen	MP4/11B	7	dnf	Accident
22.09.96	Portuguese	Estoril	8	D. Coulthard	MP4/11B	8	13	
13.10.96	Japanese	Suzuka	7	M. Häkkinen	MP4/11B	5	3	
13.10.96	Japanese	Suzuka	8	D. Coulthard	MP4/11B	8	8	
1997								
09.03.97	Australian	Melbourne	9	M. Häkkinen	MP4-12	6	3	
09.03.97	Australian	Melbourne	10	D. Coulthard	MP4-12	4	1st	
30.03.97	Brazilian	Interlagos	9	M. Häkkinen	MP4-12	4	4	
30.03.97	Brazilian	Interlagos	10	D. Coulthard	MP4-12	12	10	
13.04.97	Argentinian	Buenos Aires	9	M. Häkkinen	MP4-12	17	5	
13.04.97	Argentinian	Buenos Aires	10	D. Coulthard	MP4-12	10	dnf	Accident
27.04.97	San Marino	Imola	9	M. Häkkinen	MP4-12	8	6	
27.04.97	San Marino	Imola	10	D. Coulthard	MP4-12	10	dnf	Engine
11.05.97	Monaco	Monte Carlo	9	M. Häkkinen	MP4-12	8	dnf	Accident
11.05.97	Monaco	Monte Carlo	10	D. Coulthard	MP4-12	5	dnf	Accident
25.05.97	Spanish	Barcelona	9	M. Häkkinen	MP4-12	5	7	
25.05.97	Spanish	Barcelona	10	D. Coulthard	MP4-12	3	6	
15.06.97	Canadian	Montreal	9	M. Häkkinen	MP4-12	9	dnf	Accident
15.06.97	Canadian	Montreal	10	D. Coulthard	MP4-12	5	7	Fastest Lap
29.06.97	French	Magny Cours	9	M. Häkkinen	MP4-12	10	dnf	Engine
29.06.97	French	Magny Cours	10	D. Coulthard	MP4-12	9	7 nrf	Accident
13.07.97	British	Silverstone	9	M. Häkkinen	MP4-12	3	dnf	Engine
13.07.97	British	Silverstone	10	D. Coulthard	MP4-12	6	4	
27.07.97	German	Hockenheim	9	M. Häkkinen	MP4-12	3	3	
27.07.97	German	Hockenheim	10	D. Coulthard	MP4-12	8	dnf	Transmission
10.08.97	Hungarian	Hungaroring	9	M. Häkkinen	MP4-12	4	dnf	Hydraulics
10.08.97	Hungarian	Hungaroring	10	D. Coulthard	MP4-12	8	dnf	Alternator
24.08.97	Belgian	Spa Francorchamps	9	M. Häkkinen	MP4-12	5	dsq	Fuel Irregularities
24.08.97	Belgian	Spa Francorchamps	10	D. Coulthard	MP4-12	10	dnf	Accident
07.09.97	Italian	Monza	9	M. Häkkinen	MP4-12	5	9	Fastest Lap
07.09.97	Italian	Monza	10	D. Coulthard	MP4-12	6	1st	
21.09.97	Austrian	A1-Ring	9	M. Häkkinen	MP4-12	2	dnf	Engine
21.09.97	Austrian	A1-Ring	10	D. Coulthard	MP4-12	10	2	
28.09.97	Luxembourg	Nürburgring	9	M. Häkkinen	MP4-12	Pole	dnf	Engine
28.09.97	Luxembourg	Nürburgring	10	D. Coulthard	MP4-12	6	dnf	Engine
12.10.97	Japanese	Suzuka	9	M. Häkkinen	MP4-12	4	4	
12.10.97	Japanese	Suzuka	10	D. Coulthard	MP4-12	6	dnf	Engine
26.10.97	European	Jerez	9	M. Häkkinen	MP4-12	5	1st	1-2 Finish
26.10.97	European	Jerez	10	D. Coulthard	MP4-12	6	2	
1998								
08.03.98	Australian	Melbourne	7	D. Coulthard	MP4-13	2	2	
08.03.98	Australian	Melbourne	8	M. Häkkinen	MP4-13	Pole	1st	Fastest Lap, 1-2 Finish
29.03.98	Brazilian	Interlagos	7	D. Coulthard	MP4-13	2	2	
29.03.98	Brazilian	Interlagos	8	M. Häkkinen	MP4-13	Pole	1st	Fastest Lap, 1-2 Finish
12.04.98	Argentinian	Buenos Aires	7	D. Coulthard	MP4-13	Pole	6	
12.04.98	Argentinian	Buenos Aires	8	M. Häkkinen	MP4-13	3	2	
26.04.98	San Marino	Imola	7	D. Coulthard	MP4-13	Pole	1st	
26.04.98	San Marino	Imola	8	M. Häkkinen	MP4-13	2	dnf	Gearbox
10.05.98	Spanish	Barcelona	7	D. Coulthard	MP4-13	2	2	
10.05.98	Spanish	Barcelona	8	M. Häkkinen	MP4-13	Pole	1st	Fastest Lap, 1-2 Finish
24.05.98	Monaco	Monte Carlo	7	D. Coulthard	MP4-13	2	dnf	Engine
24.05.98	Monaco	Monte Carlo	8	M. Häkkinen	MP4-13	Pole	1st	Fastest Lap
07.06.98	Canadian	Montreal	7	D. Coulthard	MP4-13	Pole	dnf	Throttle
07.06.98	Canadian	Montreal	8	M. Häkkinen	MP4-13	2	dnf	Gearbox
28.06.98	French	Magny Cours	7	D. Coulthard	MP4-13	3	6	Fastest Lap
28.06.98	French	Magny Cours	8	M. Häkkinen	MP4-13	Pole	3	
12.07.98	British	Silverstone	7	D. Coulthard	MP4-13	4	dnf	Accident
12.07.98	British	Silverstone	8	M. Häkkinen	MP4-13	Pole	2	
26.07.98	Austrian	A1-Ring	7	D. Coulthard	MP4-13	14	2	Fastest Lap
26.07.98	Austrian	A1-Ring	8	M. Häkkinen	MP4-13	3	1st	1-2 Finish
02.08.98	German	Hockenheim	7	D. Coulthard	MP4-13	2	2	Fastest Lap
02.08.98	German	Hockenheim	8	M. Häkkinen	MP4-13	Pole	1st	1-2 Finish
16.08.98	Hungarian	Hungaroring	7	D. Coulthard	MP4-13	2	2	
16.08.98	Hungarian	Hungaroring	8	M. Häkkinen	MP4-13	Pole	6	

APPENDIX 4
McLAREN FORMULA 1 RESULTS
CONTINUED

Date	Event	Circuit	Race No.	Driver	Model	Qual.	Race Position	Reason/Notes
30.08.98	Belgian	Spa Francorchamps	7	D. Coulthard	MP4-13	2	7 nrf	Accident
30.08.98	Belgian	Spa Francorchamps	8	M. Häkkinen	MP4-13	Pole	dnf	Accident
13.09.98	Italian	Monza	7	D. Coulthard	MP4-13	4	dnf	Engine
13.09.98	Italian	Monza	8	M. Häkkinen	MP4-13	3	4	Fastest Lap
27.09.98	Luxembourg	Nürburgring	7	D. Coulthard	MP4-13	5	3	
27.09.98	Luxembourg	Nürburgring	8	M. Häkkinen	MP4-13	3	1st	Fastest Lap
01.11.98	Japanese	Suzuka	7	D. Coulthard	MP4-13	3	3	
01.11.98	Japanese	Suzuka	8	M. Häkkinen	MP4-13	2	1st	
1999								
07.03.99	Australian	Melbourne	1	M. Häkkinen	MP4-14	Pole	dnf	Throttle
07.03.99	Australian	Melbourne	2	D. Coulthard	MP4-14	2	dnf	Hydraulics
11.04.99	Brazilian	Interlagos	1	M. Häkkinen	MP4-14	Pole	1st	Fastest Lap
11.04.99	Brazilian	Interlagos	2	D. Coulthard	MP4-14	2	dnf	Gearbox
02.05.99	San Marino	Imola	1	M. Häkkinen	MP4-14	Pole	dnf	Accident
02.05.99	San Marino	Imola	2	D. Coulthard	MP4-14	2	2	
16.05.99	Monaco	Monte Carlo	1	M. Häkkinen	MP4-14	Pole	3	Fastest Lap
16.05.99	Monaco	Monte Carlo	2	D. Coulthard	MP4-14	3	dnf	Oil Leak
30.05.99	Spanish	Barcelona	1	M. Häkkinen	MP4-14	Pole	1st	1-2 Finish
30.05.99	Spanish	Barcelona	2	D. Coulthard	MP4-14	3	2	
13.06.99	Canadian	Montreal	1	M. Häkkinen	MP4-14	2	1st	
13.06.99	Canadian	Montreal	2	D. Coulthard	MP4-14	4	7	
27.06.99	French	Magny Cours	1	M. Häkkinen	MP4-14	14	2	
27.06.99	French	Magny Cours	2	D. Coulthard	MP4-14	4	dnf	Fastest Lap
11.07.99	British	Silverstone	1	M. Häkkinen	MP4-14	Pole	dnf	Fastest Lap, Lost Wheel
11.07.99	British	Silverstone	2	D. Coulthard	MP4-14	3	1st	
25.07.99	Austrian	A1-Ring	1	M. Häkkinen	MP4-14	Pole	3	Fastest Lap
25.07.99	Austrian	A1-Ring	2	D. Coulthard	MP4-14	2	2	
01.08.99	German	Hockenheim	1	M. Häkkinen	MP4-14	Pole	dnf	Tyre failure
01.08.99	German	Hockenheim	2	D. Coulthard	MP4-14	3	5	Fastest Lap
15.08.99	Hungarian	Hungaroring	1	M. Häkkinen	MP4-14	Pole	1st	1-2 Finish
15.08.99	Hungarian	Hungaroring	2	D. Coulthard	MP4-14	3	2	Fastest Lap
29.08.99	Belgian	Spa Francorchamps	1	M. Häkkinen	MP4-14	Pole	2	Fastest Lap
29.08.99	Belgian	Spa Francorchamps	2	D. Coulthard	MP4-14	2	1st	1-2 Finish
12.09.99	Italian	Monza	1	M. Häkkinen	MP4-14	Pole	dnf	Accident
12.09.99	Italian	Monza	2	D. Coulthard	MP4-14	3	5	
26.09.99	European	Nürburgring	1	M. Häkkinen	MP4-14	3	5	Fastest Lap
26.09.99	European	Nürburgring	2	D. Coulthard	MP4-14	2	dnf	Accident
17.10.99	Malaysian	Sepang	1	M. Häkkinen	MP4-14	4	3	
17.10.99	Malaysian	Sepang	2	D. Coulthard	MP4-14	3	dnf	Fuel Pressure
31.10.99	Japanese	Suzuka	1	M. Häkkinen	MP4-14	2	1st	
31.10.99	Japanese	Suzuka	2	D. Coulthard	MP4-14	3	dnf	Gearbox
2000								
12.03.00	Australian	Melbourne	1	M. Häkkinen	MP4-15	Pole	dnf	Engine
12.03.00	Australian	Melbourne	2	D. Coulthard	MP4-15	2	dnf	Engine
26.03.00	Brazilian	Interlagos	1	M. Häkkinen	MP4-15	Pole	dnf	Engine
26.03.00	Brazilian	Interlagos	2	D. Coulthard	MP4-15	2	dsq	Front Wing Irregularities
09.04.00	San Marino	Imola	1	M. Häkkinen	MP4-15	Pole	2	Fastest Lap
09.04.00	San Marino	Imola	2	D. Coulthard	MP4-15	3	3	
23.04.00	British	Silverstone	1	M. Häkkinen	MP4-15	3	2	Fastest Lap
23.04.00	British	Silverstone	2	D. Coulthard	MP4-15	4	1st	1-2 Finish
07.05.00	Spanish	Barcelona	1	M. Häkkinen	MP4-15	2	1st	Fastest Lap, 1-2 Finish
07.05.00	Spanish	Barcelona	2	D. Coulthard	MP4-15	4	2	
21.05.00	European	Nürburgring	1	M. Häkkinen	MP4-15	3	2	
21.05.00	European	Nürburgring	2	D. Coulthard	MP4-15	Pole	3	
04.06.00	Monaco	Monte Carlo	1	M. Häkkinen	MP4-15	5	6	Fastest Lap
04.06.00	Monaco	Monte Carlo	2	D. Coulthard	MP4-15	3	1st	
18.06.00	Canadian	Montreal	1	M. Häkkinen	MP4-15	4	4	Fastest Lap
18.06.00	Canadian	Montreal	2	D. Coulthard	MP4-15	2	7	
02.07.00	French	Magny Cours	1	M. Häkkinen	MP4-15	4	2	
02.07.00	French	Magny Cours	2	D. Coulthard	MP4-15	2	1st	Fastest Lap, 1-2 Finish
16.07.00	Austrian	A1-Ring	1	M. Häkkinen	MP4-15	Pole	1st	1-2 Finish
16.07.00	Austrian	A1-Ring	2	D. Coulthard	MP4-15	2	2	Fastest Lap
30.07.00	German	Hockenheim	1	M. Häkkinen	MP4-15	4	2	
30.07.00	German	Hockenheim	2	D. Coulthard	MP4-15	Pole	3	
13.08.00	Hungarian	Hungaroring	1	M. Häkkinen	MP4-15	3	1st	Fastest Lap
13.08.00	Hungarian	Hungaroring	2	D. Coulthard	MP4-15	2	3	
27.08.00	Belgian	Spa Francorchamps	1	M. Häkkinen	MP4-15	Pole	1st	
27.08.00	Belgian	Spa Francorchamps	2	D. Coulthard	MP4-15	5	4	
10.09.00	Italian	Monza	1	M. Häkkinen	MP4-15	3	2	Fastest Lap
10.09.00	Italian	Monza	2	D. Coulthard	MP4-15	5	dnf	Accident
24.09.00	US	Indianapolis	1	M. Häkkinen	MP4-15	3	dnf	Engine
24.09.00	US	Indianapolis	2	D. Coulthard	MP4-15	2	5	Fastest Lap
08.10.00	Japanese	Suzuka	1	M. Häkkinen	MP4-15	2	2	Fastest Lap
08.10.00	Japanese	Suzuka	2	D. Coulthard	MP4-15	3	3	
22.10.00	Malaysian	Sepang	1	M. Häkkinen	MP4-15	2	4	Fastest Lap
22.10.00	Malaysian	Sepang	2	D. Coulthard	MP4-15	3	2	
2001								
04.03.01	Australian	Melbourne	3	M. Häkkinen	MP4-16	3	dnf	Suspension
04.03.01	Australian	Melbourne	4	D. Coulthard	MP4-16	6	2	
18.03.01	Malaysian	Sepang	3	M. Häkkinen	MP4-16	4	6	Fastest Lap
18.03.01	Malaysian	Sepang	4	D. Coulthard	MP4-16	8	3	
01.04.01	Brazilian	Interlagos	3	M. Häkkinen	MP4-16	3	dnf	Electronics
01.04.01	Brazilian	Interlagos	4	D. Coulthard	MP4-16	5	1st	
15.04.01	San Marino	Imola	3	M. Häkkinen	MP4-16	2	4	
15.04.01	San Marino	Imola	4	D. Coulthard	MP4-16	Pole	2	
29.04.01	Spanish	Barcelona	3	M. Häkkinen	MP4-16	2	9 nrf	Clutch
29.04.01	Spanish	Barcelona	4	D. Coulthard	MP4-16	3	5	
13.05.01	Austrian	A1-Ring	3	M. Häkkinen	MP4-16	8	dnf	Electronics
13.05.01	Austrian	A1-Ring	4	D. Coulthard	MP4-16	7	1st	Fastest Lap
27.05.01	Monaco	Monte Carlo	3	M. Häkkinen	MP4-16	3	dnf	Handling
27.05.01	Monaco	Monte Carlo	4	D. Coulthard	MP4-16	Pole	5	Fastest Lap
10.06.01	Canadian	Montreal	3	M. Häkkinen	MP4-16	8	3	
10.06.01	Canadian	Montreal	4	D. Coulthard	MP4-16	3	dnf	Engine
24.06.01	European	Nürburgring	3	M. Häkkinen	MP4-16	6	6	
24.06.01	European	Nürburgring	4	D. Coulthard	MP4-16	5	3	
01.07.01	French	Magny Cours	3	M. Häkkinen	MP4-16	4	dns	Gearbox/Formation Lap
01.07.01	French	Magny Cours	4	D. Coulthard	MP4-16	3	4	Fastest Lap
15.07.01	British	Silverstone	3	M. Häkkinen	MP4-16	2	1st	Fastest Lap
15.07.01	British	Silverstone	4	D. Coulthard	MP4-16	3	dnf	Accident
29.07.01	German	Hockenheim	3	M. Häkkinen	MP4-16	3	dnf	Engine
29.07.01	German	Hockenheim	4	D. Coulthard	MP4-16	5	dnf	Engine
19.08.01	Hungarian	Hungaroring	3	M. Häkkinen	MP4-16	6	5	Fastest Lap
19.08.01	Hungarian	Hungaroring	4	D. Coulthard	MP4-16	2	3	
02.09.01	Belgian	Spa Francorchamps	3	M. Häkkinen	MP4-16	7	4	
02.09.01	Belgian	Spa Francorchamps	4	D. Coulthard	MP4-16	9	2	
16.09.01	Italian	Monza	3	M. Häkkinen	MP4-16	7	dnf	Transmission
16.09.01	Italian	Monza	4	D. Coulthard	MP4-16	6	dnf	Engine
30.09.01	USA	Indianapolis	3	M. Häkkinen	MP4-16	4	1st	
30.09.01	USA	Indianapolis	4	D. Coulthard	MP4-16	7	3	
14.10.01	Japanese	Suzuka	3	M. Häkkinen	MP4-16	5	4	
14.10.01	Japanese	Suzuka	4	D. Coulthard	MP4-16	7	3	
2002								
03.03.02	Australian	Melbourne	3	D. Coulthard	MP4-17A	4	dnf	Gearbox
03.03.02	Australian	Melbourne	4	K. Räikkönen	MP4-17A	5	3	Fastest Lap
17.03.02	Malaysian	Sepang	3	D. Coulthard	MP4-17A	6	dnf	Engine
17.03.02	Malaysian	Sepang	4	K. Räikkönen	MP4-17A	5	dnf	Engine
31.03.02	Brazilian	Interlagos	3	D. Coulthard	MP4-17A	4	3	
31.03.02	Brazilian	Interlagos	4	K. Räikkönen	MP4-17A	5	12 nrf	Rear Hub
14.04.02	San Marino	Imola	3	D. Coulthard	MP4-17A	6	6	
14.04.02	San Marino	Imola	4	K. Räikkönen	MP4-17A	5	dnf	Exhaust
28.04.02	Spanish	Barcelona	3	D. Coulthard	MP4-17A	7	3	
28.04.02	Spanish	Barcelona	4	K. Räikkönen	MP4-17A	5	dnf	Rear Wing
12.05.02	Austrian	A1-Ring	3	D. Coulthard	MP4-17A	8	6	
12.05.02	Austrian	A1-Ring	4	K. Räikkönen	MP4-17A	6	dnf	Engine
26.05.02	Monaco	Monte Carlo	3	D. Coulthard	MP4-17A	2	1st	
26.05.02	Monaco	Monte Carlo	4	K. Räikkönen	MP4-17A	6	dnf	Accident
09.06.02	Canadian	Montreal	3	D. Coulthard	MP4-17A	8	2	
09.06.02	Canadian	Montreal	4	K. Räikkönen	MP4-17A	5	4	
23.06.02	European	Nürburgring	3	D. Coulthard	MP4-17A	5	dnf	Accident
23.06.02	European	Nürburgring	4	K. Räikkönen	MP4-17A	6	3	
07.07.02	British	Silverstone	3	D. Coulthard	MP4-17A	6	10	
07.07.02	British	Silverstone	4	K. Räikkönen	MP4-17A	5	dnf	Engine
21.07.02	French	Magny Cours	3	D. Coulthard	MP4-17A	6	3	Fastest Lap
21.07.02	French	Magny Cours	4	K. Räikkönen	MP4-17A	4	2	
28.07.02	German	Hockenheim	3	D. Coulthard	MP4-17A	9	5	
28.07.02	German	Hockenheim	4	K. Räikkönen	MP4-17A	5	dnf	Puncture
18.08.02	Hungarian	Hungaroring	3	D. Coulthard	MP4-17A	10	5	
18.08.02	Hungarian	Hungaroring	4	K. Räikkönen	MP4-17A	11	4	
01.09.02	Belgian	Spa Francorchamps	3	D. Coulthard	MP4-17A	6	4	
01.09.02	Belgian	Spa Francorchamps	4	K. Räikkönen	MP4-17A	2	dnf	Engine
15.09.02	Italian	Monza	3	D. Coulthard	MP4-17A	7	7	
15.09.02	Italian	Monza	4	K. Räikkönen	MP4-17A	6	dnf	Engine
29.09.02	USA	Indianapolis	3	D. Coulthard	MP4-17A	3	3	
29.09.02	USA	Indianapolis	4	K. Räikkönen	MP4-17A	6	dnf	Engine
13.10.02	Japanese	Suzuka	3	D. Coulthard	MP4-17A	3	dnf	Throttle
13.10.02	Japanese	Suzuka	4	K. Räikkönen	MP4-17A	4	3	
2003								
09.03.03	Australian	Melbourne	5	D. Coulthard	MP4-17D	11	1st	
09.03.03	Australian	Melbourne	6	K. Räikkönen	MP4-17D	15	3	Fastest Lap
23.03.03	Malaysian	Sepang	5	D. Coulthard	MP4-17D	4	dnf	Electrics
23.03.03	Malaysian	Sepang	6	K. Räikkönen	MP4-17D	7	1st	
06.04.03	Brazilian	Interlagos	5	D. Coulthard	MP4-17D	2	4	
06.04.03	Brazilian	Interlagos	6	K. Räikkönen	MP4-17D	4	2	
20.04.03	San Marino	Imola	5	D. Coulthard	MP4-17D	12	5	
20.04.03	San Marino	Imola	6	K. Räikkönen	MP4-17D	6	2	
04.05.03	Spanish	Barcelona	5	D. Coulthard	MP4-17D	8	dnf	Accident
04.05.03	Spanish	Barcelona	6	K. Räikkönen	MP4-17D	20	dnf	Accident
18.05.03	Austrian	A1-Ring	5	D. Coulthard	MP4-17D	14	5	
18.05.03	Austrian	A1-Ring	6	K. Räikkönen	MP4-17D	2	2	
01.06.03	Monaco	Monte Carlo	5	D. Coulthard	MP4-17D	6	7	
01.06.03	Monaco	Monte Carlo	6	K. Räikkönen	MP4-17D	2	2	Fastest Lap
15.06.03	Canadian	Montreal	5	D. Coulthard	MP4-17D	11	dnf	Gearbox
15.06.03	Canadian	Montreal	6	K. Räikkönen	MP4-17D	20	6	
29.06.03	European	Nürburgring	5	D. Coulthard	MP4-17D	Pole	dnf	Accident
29.06.03	European	Nürburgring	6	K. Räikkönen	MP4-17D	9	dnf	Engine
06.07.03	French	Magny Cours	5	D. Coulthard	MP4-17D	5	5	
06.07.03	French	Magny Cours	6	K. Räikkönen	MP4-17D	4	4	
20.07.03	British	Silverstone	5	D. Coulthard	MP4-17D	12	5	
20.07.03	British	Silverstone	6	K. Räikkönen	MP4-17D	3	3	
03.08.03	German	Hockenheim	5	D. Coulthard	MP4-17D	10	2	
03.08.03	German	Hockenheim	6	K. Räikkönen	MP4-17D	5	dnf	Accident
24.08.03	Hungarian	Hungaroring	5	D. Coulthard	MP4-17D	9	5	
24.08.03	Hungarian	Hungaroring	6	K. Räikkönen	MP4-17D	7	2	
14.09.03	Italian	Monza	5	D. Coulthard	MP4-17D	8	dnf	Fuel Pressure

Date	Event	Circuit	Race No.	Driver	Model	Qual.	Race Position	Reason/Notes
14.09.03	Italian	Monza	6	K. Räikkönen	MP4-17D	4	4	
28.09.03	USA	Indianapolis	5	D. Coulthard	MP4-17D	8	dnf	Gearbox
28.09.03	USA	Indianapolis	6	K. Räikkönen	MP4-17D	Pole	2	
12.10.03	Japanese	Suzuka	5	D. Coulthard	MP4-17D	7	3	
12.10.03	Japanese	Suzuka	6	K. Räikkönen	MP4-17D	8	2	
2004								
07.03.04	Australian	Melbourne	5	D. Coulthard	MP4-19A	12	8	
07.03.04	Australian	Melbourne	6	K. Räikkönen	MP4-19A	10	dnf	Engine
21.03.04	Malaysian	Sepang	5	D. Coulthard	MP4-19A	9	6	
21.03.04	Malaysian	Sepang	6	K. Räikkönen	MP4-19A	5	dnf	Engine
04.04.04	Bahrain	Sakhir	5	D. Coulthard	MP4-19A	10	dnf	Hydraulics
04.04.04	Bahrain	Sakhir	6	K. Räikkönen	MP4-19A	20	dnf	Engine
25.04.04	San Marino	Imola	5	D. Coulthard	MP4-19A	11	12	
25.04.04	San Marino	Imola	6	K. Räikkönen	MP4-19A	20	8	
09.05.04	Spanish	Barcelona	5	D. Coulthard	MP4-19A	10	10	
09.05.04	Spanish	Barcelona	6	K. Räikkönen	MP4-19A	13	11	
23.05.04	Monaco	Monte Carlo	5	D. Coulthard	MP4-19A	8	dnf	Accident
23.05.04	Monaco	Monte Carlo	6	K. Räikkönen	MP4-19A	5	dnf	Engine
30.05.04	European	Nürburgring	5	D. Coulthard	MP4-19A	18	dnf	Engine
30.05.04	European	Nürburgring	6	K. Räikkönen	MP4-19A	4	dnf	Engine
13.06.04	Canadian	Montreal	5	D. Coulthard	MP4-19A	9	6	
13.06.04	Canadian	Montreal	6	K. Räikkönen	MP4-19A	8	5	
20.06.04	USA	Indianapolis	5	D. Coulthard	MP4-19A	12	7	
20.06.04	USA	Indianapolis	6	K. Räikkönen	MP4-19A	7	6	
04.07.04	French	Magny Cours	5	D. Coulthard	MP4-19B	3	6	
04.07.04	French	Magny Cours	6	K. Räikkönen	MP4-19B	9	7	
11.07.04	British	Silverstone	5	D. Coulthard	MP4-19B	6	7	
11.07.04	British	Silverstone	6	K. Räikkönen	MP4-19B	Pole	2	
25.07.04	German	Hockenheim	5	D. Coulthard	MP4-19B	4	4	
25.07.04	German	Hockenheim	6	K. Räikkönen	MP4-19B	3	dnf	Fastest Lap, Rear Wing
15.08.04	Hungarian	Hungaroring	5	D. Coulthard	MP4-19B	12	9	
15.08.04	Hungarian	Hungaroring	6	K. Räikkönen	MP4-19B	10	dnf	Fuel System
29.08.04	Belgian	Spa Francorchamps	5	D. Coulthard	MP4-19B	4	7	
29.08.04	Belgian	Spa Francorchamps	6	K. Räikkönen	MP4-19B	10	1	Fastest Lap
12.09.04	Italian	Monza	5	D. Coulthard	MP4-19B	10	6	
12.09.04	Italian	Monza	6	K. Räikkönen	MP4-19B	7	dnf	Engine
26.09.04	Chinese	Shanghai	5	D. Coulthard	MP4-19B	10	9	
26.09.04	Chinese	Shanghai	6	K. Räikkönen	MP4-19B	2	3	
10.10.04	Japanese	Suzuka	5	D. Coulthard	MP4-19B	8	dnf	Accident
10.10.04	Japanese	Suzuka	6	K. Räikkönen	MP4-19B	12	6	
24.10.04	Brazilian	Interlagos	5	D. Coulthard	MP4-19B	12	11	
24.10.04	Brazilian	Interlagos	6	K. Räikkönen	MP4-19B	3	2	
2005								
06.03.05	Australian	Melbourne	9	K. Räikkönen	MP4-20A	10	8	
06.03.05	Australian	Melbourne	10	JP Montoya	MP4-20A	9	6	
20.03.05	Malaysian	Sepang	9	K. Räikkönen	MP4-20A	6	9	Fastest Lap
20.03.05	Malaysian	Sepang	10	JP Montoya	MP4-20A	11	4	
03.04.05	Bahrain	Sakhir	9	K. Räikkönen	MP4-20A	9	3	
03.04.05	Bahrain	Sakhir	10	P. de la Rosa	MP4-20A	8	5	Fastest Lap
24.04.05	San Marino	Imola	9	K. Räikkönen	MP4-20A	Pole	dnf	Driveshaft
24.04.05	San Marino	Imola	10	A. Wurz	MP4-20A	7	3	
08.05.05	Spanish	Barcelona	9	K. Räikkönen	MP4-20A	Pole	1st	
08.05.05	Spanish	Barcelona	10	JP Montoya	MP4-20A	7	7	
22.05.05	Monaco	Monte Carlo	9	K. Räikkönen	MP4-20A	Pole	1st	
22.05.05	Monaco	Monte Carlo	10	JP Montoya	MP4-20A	17	5	
29.05.05	European	Nürburgring	9	K. Räikkönen	MP4-20A	2	11 nrf	Suspension
29.05.05	European	Nürburgring	10	JP Montoya	MP4-20A	5	7	
12.06.05	Canadian	Montreal	9	K. Räikkönen	MP4-20A	7	1st	Fastest lap
12.06.05	Canadian	Montreal	10	JP Montoya	MP4-20A	5	dsq	Illegal Pit Exit
19.06.05	USA	Indianapolis	9	K. Räikkönen	MP4-20A	2	dnf	Withdrew
19.06.05	USA	Indianapolis	10	JP Montoya	MP4-20A	11	dnf	Withdrew
03.07.05	French	Magny Cours	9	K. Räikkönen	MP4-20A	13	2	Fastest Lap
03.07.05	French	Magny Cours	10	JP Montoya	MP4-20A	8	dnf	Hydraulics
10.07.05	British	Silverstone	9	K. Räikkönen	MP4-20A	12	3	Fastest Lap
10.07.05	British	Silverstone	10	JP Montoya	MP4-20A	3	1st	
24.07.05	German	Hockenheim	9	K. Räikkönen	MP4-20A	Pole	dnf	Fastest Lap, Hydraulics
24.07.05	German	Hockenheim	10	JP Montoya	MP4-20A	19	2	
31.07.05	Hungarian	Hungaroring	9	K. Räikkönen	MP4-20A	4	1st	Fastest Lap
31.07.05	Hungarian	Hungaroring	10	JP Montoya	MP4-20A	2	dnf	Driveshaft
21.08.05	Turkish	Istanbul	9	K. Räikkönen	MP4-20A	Pole	1st	
21.08.05	Turkish	Istanbul	10	JP Montoya	MP4-20A	4	3	Fastest Lap
04.09.05	Italian	Monza	9	K. Räikkönen	MP4-20A	Pole	4	Fastest Lap
04.09.05	Italian	Monza	10	JP Montoya	MP4-20A	2	1st	
11.09.05	Belgian	Spa Francorchamps	9	K. Räikkönen	MP4-20A	2	1st	
11.09.05	Belgian	Spa Francorchamps	10	JP Montoya	MP4-20A	Pole	14th	
25.09.05	Brazilian	Interlagos	9	K. Räikkönen	MP4-20A	5	2	Fastest Lap
25.09.05	Brazilian	Interlagos	10	JP Montoya	MP4-20A	2	1st	1-2 Finish
09.10.05	Japanese	Suzuka	9	K. Räikkönen	MP4-20A	17	1st	Fastest Lap
09.10.05	Japanese	Suzuka	10	JP Montoya	MP4-20A	18	dnf	Accident
16.10.05	Chinese	Shanghai	9	K. Räikkönen	MP4-20A	3	2	Fastest Lap
16.10.05	Chinese	Shanghai	10	JP Montoya	MP4-20A	5	dnf	Engine
2006								
12.03.06	Bahrain	Sakhir	3	K. Räikkönen	MP4-21A	22	3	
12.03.06	Bahrain	Sakhir	4	JP Montoya	MP4-21A	5	5	
19.03.06	Malaysian	Sepang	3	K. Räikkönen	MP4-21A	7	dnf	Accident
19.03.06	Malaysian	Sepang	4	JP Montoya	MP4-21A	6	4	
02.04.06	Australian	Melbourne	3	K. Räikkönen	MP4-21A	4	2	Fastest Lap
02.04.06	Australian	Melbourne	4	JP Montoya	MP4-21A	5	dnf	Accident
23.04.06	San Marino	Imola	3	K. Räikkönen	MP4-21A	8	5	
23.04.06	San Marino	Imola	4	JP Montoya	MP4-21A	7	3	
07.05.06	European	Nürburgring	3	K. Räikkönen	MP4-21A	5	4	
07.05.06	European	Nürburgring	4	JP Montoya	MP4-21A	9	dnf	Engine
14.05.06	Spanish	Barcelona	3	K. Räikkönen	MP4-21A	9	5	
14.05.06	Spanish	Barcelona	4	JP Montoya	MP4-21A	12	dnf	Accident
28.05.06	Monaco	Monte Carlo	3	K. Räikkönen	MP4-21A	3	dnf	Fire
28.05.06	Monaco	Monte Carlo	4	JP Montoya	MP4-21A	4	2	
11.06.06	British	Silverstone	3	K. Räikkönen	MP4-21A	2	3	
11.06.06	British	Silverstone	4	JP Montoya	MP4-21A	8	6	
25.06.06	Canadian	Montreal	3	K. Räikkönen	MP4-21A	3	3	Fastest lap
25.06.06	Canadian	Montreal	4	JP Montoya	MP4-21A	7	dnf	Accident
02.07.06	USA	Indianapolis	3	K. Räikkönen	MP4-21A	9	dnf	Accident
02.07.06	USA	Indianapolis	4	JP Montoya	MP4-21A	11	dnf	Accident
16.07.06	French	Magny Cours	3	K. Räikkönen	MP4-21A	6	5	
16.07.06	French	Magny Cours	4	P. de la Rosa	MP4-21A	8	7	
30.07.06	German	Hockenheim	3	K. Räikkönen	MP4-21A	Pole	3	
30.07.06	German	Hockenheim	4	P. de la Rosa	MP4-21A	9	dnf	Fuel Pump
06.08.06	Hungarian	Hungaroring	3	K. Räikkönen	MP4-21A	Pole	dnf	Accident
06.08.06	Hungarian	Hungaroring	4	P. de la Rosa	MP4-21A	5	2	
27.08.06	Turkish	Istanbul	3	K. Räikkönen	MP4-21A	8	dnf	Accident
27.08.06	Turkish	Istanbul	4	P. de la Rosa	MP4-21A	12	5	
10.09.06	Italian	Monza	3	K. Räikkönen	MP4-21A	Pole	2	Fastest Lap
10.09.06	Italian	Monza	4	P. de la Rosa	MP4-21A	7	dnf	Engine
01.10.06	Chinese	Shanghai	3	K. Räikkönen	MP4-21A	5	dnf	Throttle
01.10.06	Chinese	Shanghai	4	P. de la Rosa	MP4-21A	7	5	
08.10.06	Japanese	Suzuka	3	K. Räikkönen	MP4-21A	11	5	
08.10.06	Japanese	Suzuka	4	P. de la Rosa	MP4-21A	13	11	
22.10.06	Brazilian	Interlagos	3	K. Räikkönen	MP4-21A	2	5	
22.10.06	Brazilian	Interlagos	4	P. de la Rosa	MP4-21A	12	8	
2007								
18.03.07	Australian	Melbourne	1	F. Alonso	MP4-22	2	2	
18.03.07	Australian	Melbourne	2	L. Hamilton	MP4-22	4	3	
08.04.07	Malaysian	Sepang	1	F. Alonso	MP4-22	2	1st	1-2 Finish
08.04.07	Malaysian	Sepang	2	L. Hamilton	MP4-22	4	2	Fastest Lap
15.04.07	Bahrain	Sakhir	1	F. Alonso	MP4-22	4	5	
15.04.07	Bahrain	Sakhir	2	L. Hamilton	MP4-22	2	2	
13.05.07	Spanish	Barcelona	1	F. Alonso	MP4-22	2	3	
13.05.07	Spanish	Barcelona	2	L. Hamilton	MP4-22	4	2	
27.05.07	Monaco	Monte Carlo	1	F. Alonso	MP4-22	Pole	1st	Fastest Lap, 1-2 Finish
27.05.07	Monaco	Monte Carlo	2	L. Hamilton	MP4-22	2	2	
10.06.07	Canadian	Montreal	1	F. Alonso	MP4-22	2	7	Fastest Lap
10.06.07	Canadian	Montreal	2	L. Hamilton	MP4-22	Pole	1st	First win Hamilton
17.06.07	USA	Indianapolis	1	F. Alonso	MP4-22	2	2	
17.06.07	USA	Indianapolis	2	L. Hamilton	MP4-22	Pole	1st	1-2 Finish
01.07.07	French	Magny Cours	1	F. Alonso	MP4-22	10	7	
01.07.07	French	Magny Cours	2	L. Hamilton	MP4-22	2	3	
08.07.07	British	Silverstone	1	F. Alonso	MP4-22	3	2	
08.07.07	British	Silverstone	2	L. Hamilton	MP4-22	Pole	3	
22.07.07	European	Nürburgring	1	F. Alonso	MP4-22	2	1st	
22.07.07	European	Nürburgring	2	L. Hamilton	MP4-22	10	9	
05.08.07	Hungarian	Hungaroring	1	F. Alonso	MP4-22	Pole	4	
05.08.07	Hungarian	Hungaroring	2	L. Hamilton	MP4-22	2	1st	
26.08.07	Turkish	Istanbul	1	F. Alonso	MP4-22	4	3	
26.08.07	Turkish	Istanbul	2	L. Hamilton	MP4-22	2	5	
09.09.07	Italian	Monza	1	F. Alonso	MP4-22	Pole	1st	Fastest Lap, 1-2 Finish
09.09.07	Italian	Monza	2	L. Hamilton	MP4-22	2	2	
16.09.07	Belgian	Spa Francorchamps	1	F. Alonso	MP4-22	3	3	
16.09.07	Belgian	Spa Francorchamps	2	L. Hamilton	MP4-22	4	4	
30.09.07	Japanese	Suzuka	1	F. Alonso	MP4-22	2	dnf	Accident
30.09.07	Japanese	Suzuka	2	L. Hamilton	MP4-22	Pole	1st	Fastest Lap
07.10.07	Chinese	Shanghai	1	F. Alonso	MP4-22	4	2	
07.10.07	Chinese	Shanghai	2	L. Hamilton	MP4-22	Pole	dnf	Stuck in Grvel trap
21.10.07	Brazilian	Interlagos	1	F. Alonso	MP4-22	4	3	
21.10.07	Brazilian	Interlagos	2	L. Hamilton	MP4-22	2	7	
2008								
16.03.08	Australian	Melbourne	22	L. Hamilton	MP4-23	Pole	1st	
16.03.08	Australian	Melbourne	23	H. Kovalainen	MP4-23	3	5	Fastest Lap

APPENDIX 5
McLAREN INDIANAPOLIS RESULTS

Year	Date	Driver	Model	Chassis Number	Race Number	Engine	Sponsor/Entrant	Colour(s)	Qualifying Position	Qualifying Speed	Race Position	Race Speed	Laps Completed	Laps Led	Prize $
1970	30.05.70	Carl Williams	M15	M15-3	75	Offenhauser	Bruce McLaren Motor Racing	Orange/Blue	19	166.590	9		197		22,352
	30.05.70	Peter Revson	M15	M15-2	73	Offenhauser	Bruce McLaren Motor Racing	Orange/Blue	16	167.942	22		87		16,627
1971	29.05.71	Peter Revson	M16	16-2	86	Offenhauser	McLaren Cars	Orange	Pole	178.696	2	157.419	200		103,198
	29.05.71	Denny Hulme	M16	16-3	85	Offenhauser	McLaren Cars	Orange	4	174.910	17		137		17,887
	29.05.71	Mark Donohue	M16	16-1	66	Offenhauser	Sunoco/US Racing	Blue	2	177.087	25		66	52	26,697
	29.05.71	Gordon Johncock	M15	M15-3	7	Offenhauser	Norris Industries/Vollstedt Enterprises	Orange	12	171.388	29		11		13,458
1972	27.05.72	Mark Donohue	M16B	16B-1	66	Offenhauser	Sunoco McLaren/Penske	Blue	3	191.408	1st	162.962	200	13	218,763
	27.05.72	Gary Bettenhausen	M16B	16B-4	7	Offenhauser	Sunoco McLaren/Penske	Blue	4	188.877	14		182	138	41,284
	27.05.72	Gordon Johncock	M16B	16B-3	24	Offenhauser	Gulf McLaren	Orange	26	188.511	20		113		17,823
	27.05.72	Peter Revson	M16B	16B-2	12	Offenhauser	Gulf McLaren	Orange	2	192.885	31		23		15,924
	27.05.72	John Mahler	M15	M15-1	31	Offenhauser	Harbor Fuel Oil/Vanguard Racing	Orange	29	179.497	22		99		16,013
	27.05.72	Denny Zimmerman	M15	M15-3	17	Offenhauser	Bryant Heat & Cool/Vollstedt Enterprises	Orange	28	180.027	19		116		17,320
1973	28/30.05.73	Johnny Rutherford	M16C	16D-5	7	Offenhauser	Gulf McLaren/McLaren Cars	Orange/Blue	Pole	198.413	9		124/133		29,904
	28/30.05.73	Peter Revson	M16C	16C-2	15	Offenhauser	Gulf McLaren/McLaren Cars	Orange	10	192.606	31		3		13,779
	28/30.05.73	Roger McCluskey	M16	16-2	3	Offenhauser	Lindsey Hopkins Buick	Blue/White	14	191.928	3		131		60,753
	28/30.05.73	Gary Bettenhausen	M16C	16C-3	5	Offenhauser	Sunoco DX/Roger Penske	Blue/Red	5	195.599	5		130		37,966
	28/30.05.73	John Martin	M16B	16B-2	89	Offenhauser	Automotive Technology	Red	24	194.384	8		124		25,377
	28/30.05.73	Bobby Allison	M16C	16C-1	12	Offenhauser	Sunoco DX/Roger Penske	Blue/Red	12	192.308	32		1		13,722
	28/30.05.73	Salt Walther	M16	16-3	77	Offenhauser	Dayton-Walther/Walmotor	White/Blue	17	190.739	33		0		13,963
	28/30.05.73	Al Loquasto	M16B	16B-4	86	Offenhauser	Sunoco DX/Roger Penske	Blue/Red	dnq						
1974	26.05.74	Johnny Rutherford	M16C/D	16C-5	3	Offenhauser	McLaren Cars	Orange	25	190.446	1st	158.589	200	122	245,032
	26.05.74	David Hobbs	M16C/D	16C/D-6	73	Offenhauser	Carling Black Label/McLaren Cars	Blue/Red	9	184.833	5		196		32,074
	26.05.74	John Martin	M16B/C	16B-2	89	Offenhauser	Sea Snack/Automotive Technology	Red	22	180.406	11		169		21,393
	26.05.74	Mike Hiss	M16C/D	16C-1	68	Offenhauser	Norton Spirit/Penske Racing	Blue/Yellow	3	187.490	14		158		21,697
	26.05.74	Salt Walther	M16C	16C-2	77	Offenhauser	Dayton-Walther/Walmotor	White/Blue/Red	14	183.927	17		141		18,197
	26.05.74	Jim Hurtubise	M16B	16B-1	56	Offenhauser	Miller High Life/Gohr	White	28	180.288	25		31		15,324
	26.05.74	Gary Bettenhausen	M16C/D	16C-3	8	Offenhauser	Score/Penske Racing	Red/Blue	11	184.492	32		2		14,230
	26.05.74	John Mahler	M16	16-4	74	Offenhauser	Woods	Black	dnq						
	26.05.74	Al Loquasto	M16B	16B-4	86	Offenhauser	Martin Guitars/Al Loquasto Sr.	Yellow/White	dnq						
1975	25.05.75	Johnny Rutherford	M16E	16E-1	2	Offenhauser	Gatorade/McLaren Cars	White/Green	7	185.998	2	148.308	174/174	5	97,886
	25.05.75	Harkey/Walther	M16C	16C-2	33	Offenhauser	Dayton-Walther/Walmotor	Blue/Red	23	183.786	10		162		22,899
	25.05.75	Tom Sneva	M16C/D	16C-3	68	Offenhauser	Norton Spirit/Penske Racing	Blue/Yellow	4	190.094	22		125		17,829
	25.05.75	Bobby Allison	M16C/D	16C-1	16	Offenhauser	CAM2 Motor Oil/Penske Racing	Red	13	184.398	25		112	1	14,827
	25.05.75	John Martin	M16B	16B-2	89	Offenhauser	Automotive Technology	Red	16	183.655	27		61		14,551
	25.05.75	Lloyd Ruby	M16E	16E-2	7	Offenhauser	Allied Polymer/McLaren Cars	White	6	186.984	32		7		15,583
	25.05.75	Salt Walther	M16C/D	16C/D-6	77	Offenhauser	Dayton-Walther/Walmotor	Blue	9	185.701	33		2		14,954
	25.05.75	Graham McRae	M16	16-2	75	Offenhauser	Silver Floss Sauerkraut	Silver/Black	dnq						
1976	30.05.76	Johnny Rutherford	M16E	16E-2	2	Offenhauser	Hy-Gain/Team McLaren	Orange	Pole	188.957	1st	148.725	102/102	48	255,321
	30.05.76	Tom Sneva	M16C/D	16C-4	68	Offenhauser	Norton Spirit/Penske Racing	Blue/Red/White	3	186.355	6		101	1	30,960
	30.05.76	Mario Andretti	M16C/D	16C-1	6	Offenhauser	CAM2 Motor Oil/Penske Racing	Red	19	189.404	8		101		28,331
	30.05.76	Salt Walther	M16C/D	16C/D-6	77	Offenhauser	Dayton-Walther/Walmotor	Blue/Red/White	22	182.797	9		100		23,728
	30.05.76	Al Loquasto	M16B	16B-4	86	Offenhauser	Frostie Root Beer/Al Loquasto Sr.	White/Yellow	24	182.002	25		95		15,420
	30.05.76	David Hobbs	M16C	16C-2	33	Offenhauser	Dayton-Walther/Walmotor	Blue/Red	31	183.580	29		10		15,281
	30.05.76	Spike Gehlhausen	M16	16-2	19	Offenhauser	Spirit of Indiana/Carl Gehlhausen	Yellow/Blue/White	25	181.717	33		0		14,197
1977	29.05.77	Tom Sneva	M24	24-004	8	Cosworth DFX	Norton Spirit/Penske Racing	Blue/White	Pole	198.884	2	160.918	200	3	109,947
	29.05.77	Jerry Sneva	M16	16-1	36	Offenhauser	21st Amendment/J.C.Bidwell	White/Red	16	186.616	10		187		26,617
	29.05.77	Cliff Hucul	M16E	16E-2	29	Offenhauser	Team Canada/Hucul, Hunter & Arndt	White/Red	27	187.198	22		72		17,747
	29.05.77	Mario Andretti	M24	24-002	9	Cosworth DFX	CAM2 Motor Oil/Penske Racing	Red/White	6	193.351	26		47		17,468
	29.05.77	Al Loquasto	M16B	16B-4	86	Offenhauser	Frostie Root Beer/Al Loquasto Sr.	White/Yellow	15	187.647	28		28		17,448
	29.05.77	Clay Regazzoni	M16C	16C-4	38	Offenhauser	Theodore Racing/EJ Simpson	Red/Yellow	29	186.047	30		25		15,643
	29.05.77	Johnny Rutherford	M24	24-001	2	Cosworth DFX	First National City/Team McLaren	White/Blue/Red	17	197.325	33		12		19,472
	29.05.77	Spike Gehlhausen	M16	16-2	19	Offenhauser	PV Corp	Blue	dnq						
	29.05.77	Clay Regazzoni	M16C	16C-1	39	Offenhauser	Theodore Racing/EJ Simpson	Red	dnq						
	29.05.77	Larry Dickson	M16E	16E-1	80	Offenhauser	WKYG Radio/Polak	Blue	dnq						
	29.05.77	Larry McCoy			63	Offenhauser	Spirit of America	Red/White	dnq						
	29.05.77	Bob Harkey	M16B	16B-2	30	Offenhauser	Bill Freeman Caesars	Red/Whit/Blue	dnq						
	29.05.77	Salt Walther	M16C/D	16C/D-6	77	Offenhauser	Dayton-Walther	Blue/Red/White	dnq						
1978	28.05.78	Wally Dallenbach	M24	24-005	6	Cosworth DFX	Sugaripe Prune/Jerry O'Connell	Yellow/Red	7	195.228	5		195		35,632
	28.05.78	Johnny Rutherford	M24B	24B-001	4	Cosworth DFX	First National City/Team McLaren	White/Blue/Red	4	197.098	13		180		31,805
	28.05.78	Jerry Karl	M16C	16C/D-6	88	Offenhauser	Machinists Union/Frank Fiore	Blue/Red/White	28	187.549	14		176		20,930
	28.05.78	Larry Dickson	M24		80	Cosworth DFX	Stay-On Car Glaze/Russel Polak	Blue/White	9	193.434	22		104		22,659
	28.05.78	Salt Walther	M24	24-004	77	Cosworth DFX	Dayton-Walther/Walmotor	Blue/White	22	193.226	28		24		16,560
	28.05.78	Jerry Sneva	M16B	16B-3	30	Offenhauser	Smock Material Handling/Bill Freeman	Blue/Red/White	32	187.226	31		18		18,120
	28.05.78	Cliff Hucul	M16E	16E-2	29	Offenhauser	Wendys Hamburgers/Cliff Hucul	Yellow/Red	27	187.803	33		4		15,534
	28.05.78	Graham McRae	M16C	16C-2	33	Offenhauser	Dayton-Walther	Blue/Red/White	dnq						
	28.05.78	Al Loquasto	M16B	16B-4	86	Offenhauser	Frostie Root Beer/Al Loquasto Sr.	White/Yellow	dnq						
1979	27.05.79	Roger McCluskey	M24		72	Cosworth DFX	National Engineering Co.	White/Blue/Red	25	183.908	13		191		26,392
	27.05.79	Tom Sneva	M24B	24-005	1	Cosworth DFX	Sugaripe Prune/Jerry O'Connell	Yellow/Red	2	192.998	15		188		30,578
	27.05.79	Larry Dickson	M24		80	Cosworth DFX	Russ Polak	Blue/Yellow/Red	24	184.181	24		86		19,149
	27.05.79	Johnny Rutherford	M24B		4	Cosworth DFX	Budweiser/Team McLaren	White/Red	8	188.137	18		168		30,729
	27.05.79	Cliff Hucul	M16C/D	16E-2	29	Offenhauser	Hucul Racing/Huncul, Hunter & Arndt	White/Red	18	186.200	29		22		21,605
1980	25.05.80	Tom Sneva	M24B	24-005	9	Cosworth DFX	Bon Jour Action Jeans/Jerry O'Connell	Yellow	33	185.290	2	142.524	200	16	128,945
	25.05.80	Dana Carter	M16E	16E-1					dnq						
	25.05.80	Tom Frantz	M16	16-1					dnq						
	25.05.80	Bill Engelhart	M24		29	Cosworth DFX	Master Lock/Beaudoin Racing	Yellow/Blue	22	184.237	11		193		32,303
	25.05.80	Jerry Karl	M16C	16C-2	38	Chevrolet	Tonco Trailer Co./Willie Compton	White	28	183.011	21		64		26,747
1981	24.05.81	Vern Schuppan	M24B	24-005	33	Cosworth DFX	Red Roof Inns/Theodore Racing	White/Blue/Red	18	186.548	3		199		87,974
	24.05.81	Tony Bettenhausen	M24		16	Cosworth DFX	Provimi Veal/H&R Racing	Blue	16	187.013	7		195		44,064
	24.05.81	Jerry Karl	M16C	16C-2	38	Chevrolet	Tonco Trailer Co./Jerry Karl	Red	31	186.008	15		189		35,480
1982	30.05.82	Phil Krueger	M24B	24-005	89	Cosworth DFX	Joe Hunt		dnq						

APPENDIX 6
McLAREN LE MANS RESULTS

Year	Driver	Model	Chassis Number	Race Number	Engine	Entrant/Sponsor	Colour(s)	Qualifying Position	Qualifying Time	Race Position	Race Laps	Notes/Reason
1995												
17th-18th June												
	JJ. Lehto	F1 GTR	01R	59	BMW V12	Kokusai Kaihatsu Racing/Ueno Clinic	Black	9	3.57.18	1st	298	
	Y. Dalmas	F1 GTR	01R	59	BMW V12	Kokusai Kaihatsu Racing/Ueno Clinic	Black	9	4.04.91	1st	298	
	M. Sekiya	F1 GTR	01R	59	BMW V12	Kokusai Kaihatsu Racing/Ueno Clinic	Black	9	4.06.62	1st	298	
	A. Wallace	F1 GTR	06R	51	BMW V12	Mach One Racing DPR/Harrods	Yellow & Green	13	3.58.80	3	296	
	D. Bell	F1 GTR	06R	51	BMW V12	Mach One Racing DPR/Harrods	Yellow & Green	13	4.02.25	3	296	
	J. Bell	F1 GTR	06R	51	BMW V12	Mach One Racing DPR/Harrods	Yellow & Green	13	4.03.35	3	296	
	R. Bellm	F1 GTR	02R	24	BMW V12	Gulf Racing GTC/Gulf Oil	Blue & Orange	11	4.02.81	4	291	
	M. Sala	F1 GTR	02R	24	BMW V12	Gulf Racing GTC/Gulf Oil	Blue & Orange	11	4.02.56	4	291	
	M. Blundell	F1 GTR	02R	24	BMW V12	Gulf Racing GTC/Gulf Oil	Blue & Orange	11	3.58.47	4	291	
	F. Giroix	F1 GTR	07R	50	BMW V12	Giroix Racing Team/Jacardi	Blue	15	4.04.47	5	290	
	O. Grouillard	F1 GTR	07R	50	BMW V12	Giroix Racing Team/Jacardi	Blue	15	3.59.66	5	290	
	J-D. Delatraz	F1 GTR	07R	50	BMW V12	Giroix Racing Team/Jacardi	Blue	15	4.05.11	5	290	
	J-L. Maury-Laribiere	F1 GTR	05R	42	BMW V12	BBA Competition/Tuiles TBF	Silver	20	4.17.56	13	266	
	M. Sourd	F1 GTR	05R	42	BMW V12	BBA Competition/Tuiles TBF	Silver	20	4.04.52	13	266	
	H. Poulain	F1 GTR	05R	42	BMW V12	BBA Competition/Tuiles TBF	Silver	20	4.27.15	13	266	
	J. Mass	F1 GTR	03R	49	BMW V12	West Competition DPR/West FM	White & Red	12	4.06.66	dnf	131	Accident
	J. Nielsen	F1 GTR	03R	49	BMW V12	West Competition DPR/West FM	White & Red	12	3.58.56	dnf	131	Accident
	T. Bscher	F1 GTR	03R	49	BMW V12	West Competition DPR/West FM	White & Red	12	4.10.48	dnf	131	Accident
	L. Owen-Jones	F1 GTR	08R	25	BMW V12	Gulf Racing GTC/Gulf Oil	Blue & Orange	14	4.08.53	dnf	77	Accident
	P-H. Raphanel	F1 GTR	08R	25	BMW V12	Gulf Racing GTC/Gulf Oil	Blue & Orange	14	3.59.05	dnf	77	Accident
	P. Alliot	F1 GTR	08R	25	BMW V12	Gulf Racing GTC/Gulf Oil	Blue & Orange	14	4.03.73	dnf	77	Accident
1996												
15th-16th June												
	T. Bscher	F1 GTR 'LM'	03R	30	BMW V12	West Competition DPR/(West)	White & Red	22	4.09.239	4	338	
	J. Nielsen	F1 GTR 'LM'	03R	30	BMW V12	West Competition DPR/(West)	White & Red	22	3.55.924	4	338	
	P. Kox	F1 GTR 'LM'	03R	30	BMW V12	West Competition DPR/(West)	White & Red	22	3.55.992	4	338	
	L. Owen-Jones	F1 GTR 'LM'	15R	34	BMW V12	Gulf Racing GTC/Gulf Oil	Blue & Orange	10	4.00.781	5	335	
	P-H. Raphanel	F1 GTR 'LM'	15R	34	BMW V12	Gulf Racing GTC/Gulf Oil	Blue & Orange	10	3.51.292	5	335	
	D. Brabham	F1 GTR 'LM'	15R	34	BMW V12	Gulf Racing GTC/Gulf Oil	Blue & Orange	10	3.58.197	5	335	
	A. Wallace	F1 GTR 'LM'	06R	29	BMW V12	Mach One Racing DPR/Harrods	Yellow & Green	24	3.56.021	6	328	
	O. Grouillard	F1 GTR 'LM'	06R	29	BMW V12	Mach One Racing DPR/Harrods	Yellow & Green	24	3.59.809	6	328	
	D. Bell	F1 GTR 'LM'	06R	29	BMW V12	Mach One Racing DPR/Harrods	Yellow & Green	24	4.05.543	6	328	
	J. Cecotto	F1 GTR 'LM'	17R	39	BMW V12	Team Bigazzi SRL/Fina	White	12	3.51.547	8	324	
	N. Piquet	F1 GTR 'LM'	17R	39	BMW V12	Team Bigazzi SRL/Fina	White	12	3.58.404	8	324	
	D. Sullivan	F1 GTR 'LM'	17R	39	BMW V12	Team Bigazzi SRL/Fina	White	12	3.59.571	8	324	
	R. Bellm	F1 GTR 'LM'	12R	33	BMW V12	Gulf Racing GTC/Gulf Oil	Blue & Orange	8	3.57.880	9	323	
	JJ. Lehto	F1 GTR 'LM'	12R	33	BMW V12	Gulf Racing GTC/Gulf Oil	Blue & Orange	8	3.49.951	9	323	
	J. Weaver	F1 GTR 'LM'	12R	33	BMW V12	Gulf Racing GTC/Gulf Oil	Blue & Orange	8	3.53.304	9	323	
	S. Soper	F1 GTR 'LM'	16R	38	BMW V12	Team Bigazzi SRL/Fina	White & Blue	6	3.48.534	11	318	
	J. Laffite	F1 GTR 'LM'	16R	38	BMW V12	Team Bigazzi SRL/Fina	White & Blue	6	4.01.195	11	318	
	M. Duez	F1 GTR 'LM'	16R	38	BMW V12	Team Bigazzi SRL/Fina	White & Blue	6	3.59.026	11	318	
	F. Giroix	F1 GTR 'LM'	11R	53	BMW V12	Kokusai Kaihatsu Racing/Franck Muller	Orange	16	3.54.026	dnf	146	Engine/Gearbox
	J-D. Deletraz	F1 GTR 'LM'	11R	53	BMW V12	Kokusai Kaihatsu Racing/Franck Muller	Orange	16	3.59.783	dnf	146	Engine/Gearbox
	M. Sala	F1 GTR 'LM'	11R	53	BMW V12	Kokusai Kaihatsu Racing/Franck Muller	Orange	16	3.56.170	dnf	146	Engine/Gearbox
1997												
14th-15th June												
	J-M. Gounon	F1 GTR 'Longtail'	20R	41	BMW V12	Gulf Team Davidoff GTC/Davidoff	Blue, Orange & Black	25	3.53.598	2	360	
	P-H. Raphanel	F1 GTR 'Longtail'	20R	41	BMW V12	Gulf Team Davidoff GTC/Davidoff	Blue, Orange & Black	25	3.48.369	2	360	
	A. Olofsson	F1 GTR 'Longtail'	20R	41	BMW V12	Gulf Team Davidoff GTC/Davidoff	Blue, Orange & Black	25	4.00.734	2	360	
	P. Kox	F1 GTR 'Longtail'	26R	43	BMW V12	Team BMW Motorsport/Fina	White & Blue	22	3.50.704	3	358	
	R. Ravaglia	F1 GTR 'Longtail'	26R	43	BMW V12	Team BMW Motorsport/Fina	White & Blue	22	3.57.542	3	358	
	E. Helary	F1 GTR 'Longtail'	26R	43	BMW V12	Team BMW Motorsport/Fina	White & Blue	22	3.48.057	3	358	
	R. Bellm	F1 GTR 'Longtail'	25R	39	BMW V12	Gulf Team Davidoff GTC/Davidoff	Blue, Orange & Black	27	3.55.517	dnf	326	Engine fire
	A. Gilbert-Scott	F1 GTR 'Longtail'	25R	39	BMW V12	Gulf Team Davidoff GTC/Davidoff	Blue, Orange & Black	27	3.48.665	dnf	326	Engine fire
	M. Sekiya	F1 GTR 'Longtail'	25R	39	BMW V12	Gulf Team Davidoff GTC/Davidoff	Blue, Orange & Black	27	3.56.682	dnf	326	Engine fire
	JJ. Lehto	F1 GTR 'Longtail'	24R	42	BMW V12	Team BMW Motorsport/Fina	White & Blue	6	3.45.402	dnf	238	Accident
	S. Soper	F1 GTR 'Longtail'	24R	42	BMW V12	Team BMW Motorsport/Fina	White & Blue	6	3.50.516	dnf	238	Accident
	N. Piquet	F1 GTR 'Longtail'	24R	42	BMW V12	Team BMW Motorsport/Fina	White & Blue	6	3.55.260	dnf	238	Accident
	K. Tsuchiya	F1 GTR 'Longtail'	27R	44	BMW V12	Team Lark McLaren/Lark	Red & Black	16	3.47.108	dnf	81	Accident
	A. Nakaya	F1 GTR 'Longtail'	27R	44	BMW V12	Team Lark McLaren/Lark	Red & Black	16	4.02.333	dnf	81	Accident
	G. Ayles	F1 GTR 'Longtail'	27R	44	BMW V12	Team Lark McLaren/Lark	Red & Black	16	3.57.708	dnf	81	Accident
1998												
6th-7th June												
	S. O'Rourke	F1 GTR 'Longtail'	24R	40	BMW V12	EMKA Racing/EMI	Red, White & Yellow	24	4.03.809	4	343	
	T. Sugden	F1 GTR 'Longtail'	24R	40	BMW V12	EMKA Racing/EMI	Red, White & Yellow	24	3.50.863	4	343	
	B. Auberlen	F1 GTR 'Longtail'	24R	40	BMW V12	EMKA Racing/EMI	Red, White & Yellow	24	3.53.792	4	344	
	T. Bscher	F1 GTR 'Longtail'	22R	41	BMW V12	Thomas Bscher/Loctite	Black	23	3.55.158	dnf	228	Accident
	R. Capello	F1 GTR 'Longtail'	22R	41	BMW V12	Thomas Bscher/Loctite	Black	23	3.50.566	dnf	228	Accident
	E. Pirro	F1 GTR 'Longtail'	22R	41	BMW V12	Thomas Bscher/Loctite	Black	23	3.54.223	dnf	228	Accident

APPENDIX 7
McLAREN CAN-AM RESULTS

Year	Date	Circuit	Race Number	Driver	Model	Engine	Qualifying		Race		Laps Completed	Notes/Reason
							Position	Time	Position	Time		
1966	McLaren Can-Am Works Team Results 1966-1972											
	11.09.66	St. Jovite	4	Bruce McLaren	M1B	Chevrolet	2	1m38.50s	2	2h 06m 56.50s	75	
	11.09.66	St. Jovite	5	Chris Amon	M1B	Chevrolet	3	1m38.80s	3		74	Fastest lap
	18.09.66	Bridgehampton	5	Chris Amon	M1B	Chevrolet	4	1m33.40s	2	1h 53m 22.90s	70	
	18.09.66	Bridgehampton	4	Bruce McLaren	M1B	Chevrolet	3	1m33.40s	3		70	
	25.09.66	Mosport Park	5	Chris Amon	M1B	Chevrolet	2	1m53.00s	dnf		66	Collision
	25.09.66	Mosport Park	4	Bruce McLaren	M1B	Chevrolet	3	1m53.50s	dnf		41	Collision
	16.10.66	Laguna Seca	4	Bruce McLaren	M1B	Chevrolet	3	1m05.48s	3	1h 05m 48.00s	106	
	16.10.66	Laguna Seca	5	Chris Amon	M1B	Chevrolet	5	1m06.11s	dnf		36	Engine
	30.10.66	Riverside	5	Chris Amon	M1B	Chevrolet	7	1m46.90s	dnf		57	Battery
	30.10.66	Riverside	4	Bruce McLaren	M1B	Chevrolet	Pole	1m44.70s	dnf		29	Ignition
	13.11.66	Las Vegas	4	Bruce McLaren	M1B	Chevrolet	6	1m36.50s	2	1h 56m 26.50s	70	
	13.11.66	Las Vegas	5	Chris Amon	M1B	Chevrolet	3	1m35.50s	dnf		21	Suspension
1967												
	03.09.67	Road America	5	Denny Hulme	M6A	Chevrolet	2	2m12.70s	1st	1h 54m 53.00s	50	Fastest lap
	03.09.67	Road America	4	Bruce McLaren	M6A	Chevrolet	Pole	2m12.60s	dnf		6	Oil leak
	17.09.67	Bridgehampton	5	Denny Hulme	M6A	Chevrolet	Pole	1m29.85s	1st	1h 50m 07.60s	70	Fastest lap, 1-2 Finish
	17.09.67	Bridgehampton	4	Bruce McLaren	M6A	Chevrolet	2	1m30.17s	2	1h 50m 55.30s	70	
	23.09.67	Mosport Park	5	Denny Hulme	M6A	Chevrolet	Pole	1m20.80s	1st	1h 51m 25.70s	80	Fastest lap, 1-2 Finish
	23.09.67	Mosport Park	4	Bruce McLaren	M6A	Chevrolet	2	1m21.10s	2	1h 52m 01.00s	80	
	15.10.67	Laguna Seca	4	Bruce McLaren	M6A	Chevrolet	Pole	1m02.69s	1st	1h 58m 55.83s	106	Fastest lap
	15.10.67	Laguna Seca	5	Denny Hulme	M6A	Chevrolet	3	1m03.20s	dnf		80	Blown engine
	29.10.67	Riverside	4	Bruce McLaren	M6A	Chevrolet	2	1m39.60s	1st	1h 46m 28.70s	62	Fastest lap
	29.10.67	Riverside	5	Denny Hulme	M6A	Chevrolet	3	1m40.60s	dnf		2	Accident
	12.11.67	Las Vegas	5	Denny Hulme	M6A	Chevrolet	5	1m31.40s	dnf		51	Fastest lap, blown engine
	12.11.67	Las Vegas	4	Bruce McLaren	M6A	Chevrolet	Pole	1m30.80s	dnf		7	Blown Engine
1968												
	01.09.68	Road America	5	Denny Hulme	M8A	Chevrolet	2	2m09.90s	1st	2h 06m 55.80s	50	1-2 Finish
	01.09.68	Road America	4	Bruce McLaren	M8A	Chevrolet	Pole	2m09.80s	2	2h 07m 30.70s	50	
	15.09.68	Bridgehampton	4	Bruce McLaren	M8A	Chevrolet	2	1m27.77s	dnf		62	Fastest Lap, main bearing
	15.09.68	Bridgehampton	5	Denny Hulme	M8A	Chevrolet	Pole	1m27.69s	dnf		53	Broken rod
	29.09.68	Edmonton	5	Denny Hulme	M8A	Chevrolet	Pole	1m26.00s	1st	1h 57m 36.70s	80	1-2 Finish
	29.09.68	Edmonton	4	Bruce McLaren	M8A	Chevrolet	2	1m26.00s	2	1h 57m 44.70s	80	Fastest lap =
	13.10.68	Laguna Seca	5	Denny Hulme	M8A	Chevrolet	3	1m01.98s	2		79	
	13.10.68	Laguna Seca	4	Bruce McLaren	M8A	Chevrolet	Pole	1m01.44s	5		79	
	27.10.68	Riverside	4	Bruce McLaren	M8A	Chevrolet	Pole	1m38.51s	1st	1h 46m 36.10s	62	
	27.10.68	Riverside	5	Denny Hulme	M8A	Chevrolet	2	1m38.72s	5		59	
	10.11.68	Las Vegas	5	Denny Hulme	M8A	Chevrolet	2	1m29.98s	1st	1h 52m 15.38s	70	
	10.11.68	Las Vegas	4	Bruce McLaren	M8A	Chevrolet	Pole	1m29.63s	6		69	Fastest lap
1969												
	01.06.69	Mosport Park	4	Bruce McLaren	M8B	Chevrolet	Pole	1m18.20s	1st	1h 51m 27.30s	80	Fastest lap, 1-2 Finish
	01.06.69	Mosport Park	5	Denny Hulme	M8B	Chevrolet	2	1m18.80s	2	1h 51m 28.20s	80	
	15.06.69	St. Jovite	5	Denny Hulme	M8B	Chevrolet	2	1m32.20s	1st	1h 37m 52.00s	60	Fastest lap, 1-2 Finish
	15.06.69	St. Jovite	4	Bruce McLaren	M8B	Chevrolet	Pole	1m31.70s	2	1h 39m 05.60s	60	Fastest lap =
	13.07.69	Watkins Glen	4	Bruce McLaren	M8B	Chevrolet	Pole	1m02.21s	1st	1h 35m 17.60s	87	1-2 Finish
	13.07.69	Watkins Glen	5	Denny Hulme	M8B	Chevrolet	2	1m02.54s	2	1h 36m 18.40s	87	Fastest lap
	27.07.69	Edmonton	5	Denny Hulme	M8B	Chevrolet	Pole	1m22.90s	1st	1h 56m 34.80s	80	Fastest lap
	27.07.69	Edmonton	4	Bruce McLaren	M8B	Chevrolet	2	1m22.90s	dnf		36	Broken piston
	17.08.69	Mid-Ohio	5	Denny Hulme	M8B	Chevrolet	Pole	1m25.90s	1st	2h 02m 16.60s	80	
	17.08.69	Mid-Ohio	4	Bruce McLaren	M8B	Chevrolet	2	1m26.20s	2	2h 03m 07.00s	80	
	31.08.69	Road America	4	Bruce McLaren	M8B	Chevrolet	2	2m07.40s	1st	1h 51m 39.00s	50	1-2 Finish
	31.08.69	Road America	5	Denny Hulme	M8B	Chevrolet	Pole	2m06.30s	2	1h 51m 39.10s	50	Fastest lap
	14.09.69	Bridgehampton	5	Denny Hulme	M8B	Chevrolet	2	1m24.94s	1st	1h 45m 40.58s	70	Fastest lap, 1-2 Finish
	14.09.69	Bridgehampton	4	Bruce McLaren	M8B	Chevrolet	Pole	1m24.62s	2	1h 45m 41.00s	70	
	28.09.69	Michigan	4	Bruce McLaren	M8B	Chevrolet	2	1m32.90s	1st	1h 48m 14.09s	65	1-2-3 Finish
	28.09.69	Michigan	5	Denny Hulme	M8B	Chevrolet	Pole	1m32.50s	2	1h 48m 14.10s	65	Fastest lap
	28.09.69	Michigan	1	Dan Gurney	M8B	Chevrolet	27	No time	3	1h 48m 14.15s	65	
	12.10.69	Laguna Seca	4	Bruce McLaren	M8B	Chevrolet	Pole	59.53s	1st	1h 27m 29.77s	80	
	12.10.69	Laguna Seca	5	Denny Hulme	M8B	Chevrolet	2	59.75s	2	1h 27m 30.29s	80	Fastest lap
	12.10.69	Laguna Seca	3	Chris Amon	M8B	Chevrolet	30	No time	dnf		71	Differential
	26.10.69	Riverside	5	Denny Hulme	M8B	Chevrolet	Pole	1m34.03s	1st	1h 40m 05.00s	61	Fastest lap
	26.10.69	Riverside	4	Bruce McLaren	M8B	Chevrolet	2	1m34.43s	dnf		34	Accident
	09.11.69	Texas Speedway	4	Bruce McLaren	M8B	Chevrolet	3	1m34.30s	1st	1h 54m 42.40s	70	
	09.11.69	Texas Speedway	5	Denny Hulme	M8B	Chevrolet	Pole	1m31.60s	dnf		59	Fastest lap, engine
1970												
	14.06.70	Mosport Park	48	Dan Gurney	M8D	Chevrolet	Pole	1m16.80s	1st	1h 47m 05.60s	80	Fastest lap
	14.06.70	Mosport Park	5	Denny Hulme	M8D	Chevrolet	2	1m17.60s	3		78	
	28.06.70	St. Jovite	48	Dan Gurney	M8D	Chevrolet	Pole	1m33.00s	1st	2h 01m 47.50s	75	
	28.06.70	St. Jovite	5	Denny Hulme	M8D	Chevrolet	2	1m33.30s	dnf		50	Fastest lap, engine
	12.07.70	Watkins Glen	48	Dan Gurney	M8D	Chevrolet	2	1m03.22s	9		81	
	12.07.70	Watkins Glen	5	Denny Hulme	M8D	Chevrolet	Pole	1m02.76s	1st	1h 41m 16.00s	87	
	26.07.70	Edmonton	5	Denny Hulme	M8D	Chevrolet	Pole	1m23.60s	1st	1h 54m 05.50s	80	Fastest lap, 1-2 Finish
	26.07.70	Edmonton	48	Peter Gethin	M8D	Chevrolet	2	1m24.00s	2	1h 54m 39.00s	80	
	23.08.70	Mid-Ohio	5	Denny Hulme	M8D	Chevrolet	Pole	1m26.60s	1st	2h 01m 03.30s	80	Fastest lap
	23.08.70	Mid-Ohio	7	Peter Gethin	M8D	Chevrolet	4	1m29.70s	9		71	Camshaft
	30.08.70	Road America	7	Peter Gethin	M8D	Chevrolet	6	2m17.90s	1st	1h 54m 16.10s	50	
	30.08.70	Road America	5	Denny Hulme	M8D	Chevrolet	Pole	2m10.60s	disq		37	Fastest lap, outside assistance
	13.09.70	Road Atlanta	7	Peter Gethin	M8D	Chevrolet	3	1m19.67s	7		68	Fastest lap=, gearbox
	13.09.70	Road Atlanta	5	Denny Hulme	M8D	Chevrolet	2	1m18.68s	dnf		10	Accident damage
	27.09.70	Donnybrooke	5	Denny Hulme	M8D	Chevrolet	2	1m30.90s	1st	1h 47m 10.20s	70	Fastest lap

Year	Date	Circuit	Race Number	Driver	Model	Engine	Qualifying Position	Qualifying Time	Race Position	Race Time	Laps Completed	Notes/Reason
1970	27.09.70	Donnybrooke	7	Peter Gethin	M8D	Chevrolet	4	1m31.70s	2	1h 48m 09.60s	70	
	18.10.70	Laguna Seca	5	Denny Hulme	M8D	Chevrolet	Pole	1m00.60s	1st	1h 25m 58.80s	80	
	18.10.70	Laguna Seca	7	Peter Gethin	M8D	Chevrolet	2	1m00.60s	dnf		37	Battery
	01.11.70	Riverside	5	Denny Hulme	M8D	Chevrolet	2	1m34.69s	1st	1h 40m 27.40s	61	
	01.11.70	Riverside	7	Peter Gethin	M8D	Chevrolet	6	1m36.28s	dnf		21	Blown engine
1971												
	13.06.71	Mosport Park	5	Denny Hulme	M8F	Chevrolet	2	1m18.00s	1st	1h 48m 15.20s	80	Fastest lap, 1-2 Finish
	13.06.71	Mosport Park	7	Peter Revson	M8F	Chevrolet	3	1m18.10s	2	1h 48m 16.10s	80	
	27.06.71	St. Jovite	5	Denny Hulme	M8F	Chevrolet	Pole	1m32.90s	2	2h 00m 35.90s	75	Fastest lap
	27.06.71	St. Jovite	7	Peter Revson	M8F	Chevrolet	3	1m35.00s	3		74	
	11.07.71	Road Atlanta	7	Peter Revson	M8F	Chevrolet	2	1m18.00s	1st	1h 42m 09.00s	75	
	11.07.71	Road Atlanta	5	Denny Hulme	M8F	Chevrolet	Pole	1m17.70s	2	1h 42m 29.00s	75	
	25.07.71	Watkins Glen	7	Peter Revson	M8F	Chevrolet	2	1m05.23s	1st	1h 32m 54.14s	82	
	25.07.71	Watkins Glen	5	Denny Hulme	M8F	Chevrolet	3	1m05.47s	2	1h 33m 41.23s	82	Fastest Lap
	22.08.71	Mid-Ohio	7	Peter Revson	M8F	Chevrolet	2	1m26.57s	7		73	Fastest Lap, driveshaft
	22.08.71	Mid-Ohio	5	Denny Hulme	M8F	Chevrolet	Pole	1m26.09s	dnf		0	Driveshaft
	29.08.71	Road America	7	Peter Revson	M8F	Chevrolet	23	No time	1st	1h 50m 04.76s	50	
	29.08.71	Road America	5	Denny Hulme	M8F	Chevrolet	Pole	2m06.66s	dnf		17	Fastest lap, crankshaft
	12.09.71	Donnybrooke	7	Peter Revson	M8F	Chevrolet	Pole	1m26.51s	1st	1h 45m 46.64s	70	1-2 Finish
	12.09.71	Donnybrooke	5	Denny Hulme	M8F	Chevrolet	2	1m26.95s	2	1h 46m 35.02s	70	Fastest lap
	26.09.71	Edmonton	5	Denny Hulme	M8F	Chevrolet	2	1m21.40s	1st	2h 07m 47.10s	80	Fastest lap
	26.09.71	Edmonton	7	Peter Revson	M8F	Chevrolet	Pole	1m20.30s	12		67	
	17.10.71	Laguna Seca	7	Peter Revson	M8F	Chevrolet	Pole	58.78s	1st	1h 33m 56.86s	90	Fastest Lap
	17.10.71	Laguna Seca	5	Denny Hulme	M8F	Chevrolet	2	58.82s	3	1h 34m 30.85s	90	
	31.10.71	Riverside	5	Denny Hulme	M8F	Chevrolet	Pole	1m31.96s	1st	1h 37m 36.00s	61	Fastest lap, 1-2 Finish
	31.10.71	Riverside	7	Peter Revson	M8F	Chevrolet	2	1m32.95s	2	1h 38m 22.62s	61	
1972												
	11.06.72	Mosport Park	5	Denny Hulme	M20	Chevrolet	3	1m15.20s	1st	1h 46m 40.00s	80	
	11.06.72	Mosport Park	4	Peter Revson	M20	Chevrolet	2	1m15.00s	3		78	Fastest lap, crankshaft
	09.07.72	Road Atlanta	4	Peter Revson	M20	Chevrolet	3	1m14.46s	dnf		13	Rotor arm
	09.07.72	Road Atlanta	5	Denny Hulme	M20	Chevrolet	Pole	1m14.13s	dnf		4	Accident
	23.07.72	Watkins Glen	5	Denny Hulme	M20	Chevrolet	2	1m40.47s	1st	1h 46m 14.04s	60	1-2 Finish
	23.07.72	Watkins Glen	4	Peter Revson	M20	Chevrolet	Pole	1m39.18s	2		60	Fastest lap
	06.08.72	Mid-Ohio	5	Denny Hulme	M20	Chevrolet	2	1m24.11s	4		76	Fastest lap
	06.08.72	Mid-Ohio	4	Peter Revson	M20	Chevrolet	3	1m24.58s	dnf		31	Transmission
	27.08.72	Road America	4	Peter Revson	M20	Chevrolet	25	2m31.04s	dnf		21	Clutch
	27.08.72	Road America	5	Denny Hulme	M20	Chevrolet	Pole	2m04.56s	dnf		11	Magneto
	17.09.72	Donnybrooke	4	Peter Revson	M20	Chevrolet	4	1m26.86s	dnf		24	Engine
	17.09.72	Donnybrooke	5	Denny Hulme	M20	Chevrolet	3	1m25.78s	dnf		12	Cracked block
	01.10.72	Edmonton	5	Denny Hulme	M20	Chevrolet	3	1m20.55s	2	1h 51m 12.00s	80	
	01.10.72	Edmonton	4	Peter Revson	M20	Chevrolet	4	1m20.66s	6		77	
	15.10.72	Laguna Seca	4	Peter Revson	M20	Chevrolet	3	59.40s	19		52	Gearbox
	15.10.72	Laguna Seca	5	Denny Hulme	M20	Chevrolet	5	1m00.57s	dnf		16	Timing chain
	29.10.72	Riverside	4	Peter Revson	M20	Chevrolet	4	1m32.41s	2	1h 39m 17.18	61	
	29.10.72	Riverside	5	Denny Hulme	M20	Chevrolet	2	1m32.00s	19		45	Cam follower

Can-Am Challenge Cup Wins By Driver 1966-1972

Driver	Wins	Cars
Denny Hulme	22	McLaren M6A, McLaren M8A, McLaren M8B, McLaren M8D, McLaren M8F, McLaren M20
Bruce McLaren	9	McLaren M6A, McLaren M8A, McLaren M8B
Peter Revson	5	McLaren M8F
George Follmer	5	Porsche 917/10 TC
John Surtees	4	Lola T70
Dan Gurney	3	Lola T70, McLaren M8D
Mark Donohue	3	Lola T70, McLaren M6B, Porsche 917/10 TC
Jackie Stewart	2	Lola T260
Phil Hill	1	Chaparral 2E
John Cannon	1	McLaren M1B
Peter Gethin	1	McLaren M8D
Tony Dean	1	Porsche 908
François Cevert	1	McLaren M8

Can-Am Challenge Cup Wins By Constructor 1966-1972

Make	Wins
McLaren	42
Lola	8
Porsche	7
Chaparral	1

APPENDIX 8
CAN-AM CHAMPIONSHIP RESULTS 1966-1972

Year	Pos.	Driver	Car	Points
1966				
	1st	John Surtees	Lola T70	27
	2	Mark Donohue	Lola T70	21
	3	Bruce McLaren	McLaren M1B	20
	4	Phil Hill	Chaparral 2E	18
	5	Jim Hall	Chaparral 2E	12
	6	Chris Amon	McLaren M1B	10
	7	Dan Gurney	Lola T70	9
	8	Chuck Parsons	McLaren M1B	6
	9=	John Cannon	McLaren M1B	4
	9=	George Follmer	Lola T70	4
	9=	Peter Revson	McLaren M1B	4
	9=	Graham Hill	Lola T70	4
	13	Earl Jones	McLaren M1B	3
	14	Masten Gregory	McLaren M1B	2
	14=	Paul Hawkins	Lola T70	2
	14=	Lothar Motschenbacher	McLaren M1B	2
1967				
	1st	Bruce McLaren	McLaren M6A	30
	2	Denny Hulme	McLaren M6A	27
	3=	John Surtees	Lola T70	16
	3=	Mark Donohue	Lola T70	16
	5	Jim Hall	Chaparral 2G	15
	6=	George Follmer	Lola T70	10
	6=	Mike Spence	McLaren M1B	10
	8	Bud Morley	McLaren M1B, Lola T70	5
	9=	Peter Revson	Lola T70	3
	9=	Parnelli Jones	Lola T70	3
	9=	Charlie Hayes	McKee	3
	12=	Skip Scott	McLaren M1C	2
	12=	Roger McCluskey	Lola T70	2
	12=	Lothar Motschenbacher	Lola T70	2
	12=	Chris Amon	Ferrari P4	2
1968				
	1st	Denny Hulme	McLaren M8A	35
	2	Bruce McLaren	McLaren M8A	24
	3	Mark Donohue	McLaren M6B	23
	4	Jim Hall	Chaparral 2G	12
	5	Lothar Motschenbacher	McLaren M6B	11
	6	John Cannon	McLaren M1B	10
	7	George Follmer	Lola T70	6
	8=	Jerry Titus	McLaren M6B	5
	8=	Sam Posey	Caldwell D7C, Lola T160	5
	8=	Chuck Parsons	Lola T160	5
	11	George Eaton	McLaren M1C	4
	12=	Peter Revson	McLaren M6B	3
	12=	Swede Savage	Lola T160, McLaren M6B	3
	14	Dick Brown	McLaren M6B	2
	15=	Dan Gurney	M6B 'McLeagle', Lola T160	1
	15=	Charlie Hayes	McKee	1
1969				
	1st	Bruce McLaren	McLaren M8B	165
	2	Denny Hulme	McLaren M8B	160
	3	Chuck Parsons	Lola T163	81
	4	Jo Siffert	Porsche 908 & 917PA	56
	5	George Eaton	McLaren M12	50
	6	Chris Amon	Ferrari 612P & 712P, McLaren M8B	39
	7	Lothar Motschenbacher	McLaren M12	35
	8	Tony Dean	Porsche 908	31
	9	John Surtees	McLaren M12, Chaparral 2H	30
	10	John Cordts	McLaren M1C, McLaren M6B	24
	11=	Peter Revson	Lola T163	22
	11=	Dan Gurney	M6B 'McLeagle'	22
	11=	Mario Andretti	McLaren M6B	22
	14	Dick Brown	McLaren M6B	13
	15	Jack Brabham	Ford G7A	12

Year	Pos.	Driver	Car	Points
1970				
	1st	Denny Hulme	McLaren M8D	132
	2	Lothar Motschenbacher	McLaren M8B, M12 & M8C	65
	3	Peter Gethin	McLaren M8D	56
	4	Dave Causey	Lola T163	47
	5	Jackie Oliver	Autocoast Ti22	45
	6	Tony Dean	Porsche 908	44
	7	Dan Gurney	McLaren M8D	42
	8	Peter Revson	Lola T220	39
	9	Bob Brown	M6B 'McLeagle'	35
	10	Roger McCaig	McLaren M8C	34
	11	Chris Amon	March 707	28
	12	Gary Wilson	Lola T163	27
	13	Pedro Rodriguez	Ferrari 512S, BRM P154	26
	14	Chuck Parsons	Lola T160/3	19
	15=	Vic Elford	Porsche 917, AVS Shadow, Lola T70, McLaren M6B, Chaparral 2J	16
	15=	Oscar Koveleski	McLaren M8B	16
1971				
	1st	Peter Revson	McLaren M8F	142
	2	Denny Hulme	McLaren M8F	132
	3	Jackie Stewart	Lola T260	76
	4	Jo Siffert	Porsche 917/10	68
	5	Lothar Motschenbacher	McLaren M8D	52
	6	Milt Minter	Porsche 917PA	37
	7	Tony Adamowicz	McLaren M8B	34
	8	Chuck Parsons	McLaren M8E/D	30
	9	Vic Elford	McLaren M8E & M8D	25
	10	Hiroshi Kazato	Lola T222	19
	11	Sam Posey	Ferrari 512M, McLaren M8E	16
	12=	Dave Causey	Lola T222	14
	12=	John Cordts	McLaren M8C , Lola T160	14
	14=	Tom Dutton	McLaren M6B	12
	14=	Gregg Young	McLaren M8E/D	12
	14=	Howden Ganley	BRM P167	12
	14=	Jackie Oliver	Shadow Mk2	12
1972				
	1st	George Follmer	Porsche 917/10 TC	130
	2=	Denny Hulme	McLaren M20	65
	2=	Milt Minter	Porsche 917/10 & TC	65
	4	Mark Donohue	Porsche 917/10 TC	62
	5	François Cevert	McLaren M8F	59
	6	Peter Revson	McLaren M20	48
	7	David Hobbs	Lola T310	39
	8	Jackie Oliver	Shadow Mk3	37
	9	Peter Gregg	Porsche 917/10 TC	34
	10	Charlie Kemp	Lola T222	27
	11	Lothar Motschenbacher	McLaren M8D	26
	12	Gregg Young	McLaren M8F	23
	13=	Jean-Pierre Jarier	Ferrari 712M	11
	13=	Bob Nagel	Lola T222	11
	15	Carlos Pace	Shadow Mk3	10

APPENDIX 9
McLAREN CARS PHOTOGRAPHED – CREDITS

Model	Country	With Thanks To
McLaren M1A	-	n/a
McLaren-Elva M1A	USA	Harry Mathews
McLaren M1B	USA	Thomas Antonelli
McLaren-Elva M1B MkII	USA	Bruce McCaw
McLaren-Elva M1C MkIII	USA	Harry Mathews
McLaren M2A	-	n/a
McLaren M2B	UK	Tom Wheatcroft
McLaren M3A	UK	Ron Smith
McLaren M4A	UK	McLaren Group
McLaren-Trojan M4A/B	USA	Harry Mathews
McLaren M4B	-	n/a
McLaren M5A	USA	Bruce McCaw
McLaren M6A	USA	Harry Mathews
McLaren-Trojan M6B	USA	Bob Lee
McLaren-Trojan M6B 'McLeagle'	USA	Andy Boone
McLaren M6GT	USA	Harry Mathews
McLaren M7A	UK	Tom Wheatcroft
McLaren M7B	-	n/a
McLaren M7C	UK	McLaren Group
McLaren M7D	-	n/a
McLaren M8A	NZ	The Bruce McLaren Trust
McLaren M8B	USA	Tom Frederick/Chuck Haines
McLaren-Trojan M8C	USA	Ray Cohen
McLaren M8D	USA	Harry Mathews
McLaren M8D	UK	McLaren Group
McLaren-Trojan M8E	USA	Harry Mathews
McLaren M8F	USA	Harry Mathews
McLaren-Trojan M8F/P	USA	Wade Carter
McLaren M9A	UK	Tom Wheatcroft
McLaren-Trojan M10A	-	n/a
McLaren-Trojan M10B	UK	Barry Davison
McLaren-Trojan M12	USA	Jerry Winston
McLaren M14	USA	Harry Mathews
McLaren M14	UK	McLaren Group
McLaren M15	UK	McLaren Group
McLaren M16	-	n/a
McLaren M16B	USA	Indianapolis Motor Speedway
McLaren M16C	USA	Patrick Ryan
McLaren M16D	-	n/a
McLaren M16E	UK	McLaren Group
McLaren-Trojan M18	UK	Frank & Judy Lyons
McLaren M19A	-	n/a
McLaren M19C	USA	Harry Mathews
McLaren M20	USA	Harry Mathews
McLaren M21	UK	McLaren Group
McLaren-Trojan M22	USA	Harry Mathews
McLaren M23	UK	Jody Scheckter
McLaren M23	UK	McLaren Group
McLaren M23	USA	Greg Galdi
McLaren M23	IT	Andrea Burani
McLaren M24	-	n/a
McLaren M24B	UK	McLaren Group
McLaren M25	BRA	Abba Kogan
McLaren M26	UK	McLaren Group
McLaren M26	UK	Frank & Judy Lyons

Model	Country	With Thanks To
McLaren M28	UK	McLaren Group
McLaren M28C	-	n/a
McLaren M29	UK	McLaren Group
McLaren M29C	IT	Mauro Pane
McLaren M30	USA	Sean Allen
McLaren MP4/1	UK	McLaren Group
McLaren MP4/1B	UK	McLaren Group
McLaren MP4/1C	UK	McLaren Group
McLaren MP4/1D	-	n/a
McLaren MP4/1E	-	n/a
McLaren MP4/2	UK	McLaren Group
McLaren MP4/2B	UK	McLaren Group
McLaren MP4/2C	UK	McLaren Group
McLaren MP4/3	UK	McLaren Group
McLaren MP4/3B	UK	McLaren Group
McLaren MP4/4	UK	McLaren Group
McLaren MP4/4B	UK	McLaren Group
McLaren MP4/5	UK	McLaren Group
McLaren MP4/5B	UK	McLaren Group
McLaren MP4/5C	UK	McLaren Group
McLaren MP4/6	UK	McLaren Group
McLaren MP4/7	UK	McLaren Group
McLaren MP4/8	UK	McLaren Group
McLaren MP4/8B	UK	McLaren Group
McLaren F1	UK	McLaren Group
McLaren MP4/9	UK	McLaren Group
McLaren F1 GTR 1995	UK	McLaren Group
McLaren MP4/10	UK	McLaren Group
McLaren MP4/10B	-	n/a
McLaren F1 LM	UK	McLaren Group
McLaren MP4/11	UK	McLaren Group
McLaren MP4/11B	-	n/a
McLaren MP4/11C	UK	McLaren Group
McLaren F1 GTR 1996	UK	McLaren Group
McLaren MP4-12	UK	McLaren Group
McLaren F1 GT	UK	McLaren Group
McLaren F1 GTR 1997	UK	McLaren Group
McLaren MP4-98T	UK	McLaren Group
McLaren MP4-13	UK	McLaren Group
McLaren MP4-14	UK	McLaren Group
McLaren MP4-15	UK	McLaren Group
McLaren MP4-16	UK	McLaren Group
McLaren MP4-17A	UK	McLaren Group
McLaren MP4-17D	UK	McLaren Group
McLaren MP4-T5	UK	McLaren Group
McLaren MP4-18	UK	McLaren Group
McLaren MP4-19A	UK	McLaren Group
McLaren MP4-19B	UK	McLaren Group
Mercedes-Benz SLR McLaren	UK	McLaren Group
McLaren MP4-20A	UK	McLaren Group
McLaren MP4-21A	UK	McLaren Group
Mercedes-Benz SLR McLaren 722	UK	McLaren Group
McLaren MP4-22	UK	McLaren Group
Mercedes-Benz SLR McLaren Roadster	UK	McLaren Group
McLaren MP4-23	UK	McLaren Group